Chevrolet & GMC Light Truck

OWNER'S BIBLE™

By Moses Ludel

A Hands-on Guide to Getting the Most From Your Chevrolet or GMC

BentleyPublishers.com

Chevrolet & GMC Light Truck

OWNER'S BIBLE

Chevrolet/GMC history, see Chapter 1

Operator's tips, see Chapter 3

Servicing your truck, see Chapter 4

Engine tuning, see Chapter 8

TABLE OF CONTENTS

Brake and bearing servicing, see Chapter 12

Winches and accessories, see Chapter 15

Engine upgrades, see Chapter 16

Transmission upgrades, see Chapter 17

Suspension lift kits, see Chapter 18

BENTLEY PUBLISHERS® | Automotive Reference™

Bentley Publishers, a division of Robert Bentley, Inc.
1734 Massachusetts Avenue
Cambridge, MA 02138 USA
800-423-4595 / 617-547-4170

Information that makes the difference®

BentleyPublishers®.com

Technical contact information

We welcome your feedback. Please submit corrections and additions to us at:

http://www.BentleyPublishers.com

Errata information

We will evaluate submissions and post appropriate editorial changes online as text errata or tech discussion. Appropriate errata will be incorporated with the book text in future printings. Read errata information for this book before beginning work on your vehicle. See the following web address for additional information:

http://www.BentleyPublishers.com/errata/

WARNING—Important Safety Notice

In this book we have attempted to describe repairs, modifications and accessories which may be used with Chevrolet and GMC vehicles, using examples and instructions which we believe to be accurate. However, the examples, instructions, and other information are intended solely as illustrations and should be used in any particular application only by personnel who are experienced in the repair and modification of Chevrolet and GMC vehicles and who have independently evaluated the repair, modification or accessory. Implementation of a modification or attachment of an accessory described in this book may render the vehicle, attachment, or accessory unsafe for use in certain circumstances. REPAIR AND MODIFICATION OF AUTOMOBILES ARE DANGEROUS UNDERTAKINGS UNLESS UNDERTAKEN WITH FULL KNOWLEDGE OF THE CONSEQUENCES.

Do not use this book unless you are familiar with basic automotive repair procedures and safe workshop practices. This book illustrates procedures required for some service and modification work; it is not a substitute for full and up-to-date information from the vehicle manufacturer or aftermarket supplier, or for proper training as an automotive technician. Note that it is not possible for us to anticipate all of the ways or conditions under which vehicles may be serviced or modified or to provide cautions as to all of the possible hazards that may result.

The vehicle manufacturer and aftermarket suppliers will continue to issue service information updates and parts retrofits after the editorial closing of this book. Some of these updates and retrofits will apply to procedures and specifications in this book. We regret that we cannot supply updates to purchasers of this book.

We have endeavored to ensure the accuracy of the information in this book. Please note, however, that considering the vast quantity and the complexity of the information involved, we cannot warrant the accuracy or completeness of the information contained in this book.

FOR THESE REASONS, NEITHER THE PUBLISHER NOR THE AUTHOR MAKES ANY WARRANTIES, EXPRESS OR IMPLIED, THAT THE EXAMPLES, INSTRUCTIONS OR OTHER INFORMATION IN THIS BOOK ARE FREE OF ERRORS OR OMISSIONS, ARE CONSISTENT WITH INDUSTRY STANDARDS, OR THAT THEY WILL MEET THE REQUIREMENTS FOR A PARTICULAR APPLICATION, AND WE EXPRESSLY DISCLAIM THE IMPLIED WARRANTIES OF MERCHANTABILITY AND OF FITNESS FOR A PARTICULAR PURPOSE, EVEN IF THE PUBLISHER OR AUTHOR HAVE BEEN ADVISED OF A PARTICULAR PURPOSE, AND EVEN IF A PARTICULAR PURPOSE IS INDICATED IN THE BOOK. THE PUBLISHER AND AUTHOR ALSO DISCLAIM ALL LIABILITY FOR DIRECT, INDIRECT, INCIDENTAL OR CONSEQUENTIAL DAMAGES THAT RESULT FROM ANY USE OF THE EXAMPLES, INSTRUCTIONS OR OTHER INFORMATION IN THIS BOOK. IN NO EVENT SHALL OUR LIABILITY WHETHER IN TORT, CONTRACT OR OTHERWISE EXCEED THE COST OF THIS BOOK.

Your common sense and good judgment are crucial to safe and successful automotive work. Read procedures through before starting them. Think about how alert you are feeling, and whether the condition of your vehicle, your level of mechanical skill or your level of reading comprehension might result in or contribute in some way to an occurrence which might cause you injury, damage your vehicle, or result in an unsafe repair or modification. If you have doubts for these or other reasons about your ability to perform safe work on your vehicle, have the work done at an authorized Chevrolet or GMC dealer or other qualified shop.

Part numbers listed in this book are for identification purposes only, not for ordering. Always check with your authorized Ford delaer to verify part numbers and availability before beginning service work that may require new parts.

Before attempting any work on your Chevrolet or GMC truck, read the Warnings and Cautions in the rear of the book and any warning or caution that accompanies a procedure or description in the book. Review the Warnings and Cautions each time you prepare to work on your Chevrolet or GMC truck.

Special tools required to perform certain service operations are identified in the book and are recommended for use. Use of tools other than those recommended in this service book may be detrimental to the car's safe operation as well as the safety of the person servicing the car.

This book is prepared, published and distributed by Bentley Publishers, 1734 Massachusetts Avenue, Cambridge, Massachusetts 02138 USA. Chevrolet and GMC have not reviewed and do not warrant the accuracy or completeness of the technical specifications and information described in this book.

ISBN: 978-0-8376-0157-1
Job Code: GOWC-08

Library of Congress Cataloging-in-Publication Data

Ludel, Moses.
Chevrolet & GMC light truck owner's bible / by Moses Ludel.
p. cm.
Includes index.
ISBN 0-8376-0157-6
1. Chevrolet trucks. 2. GMC trucks. I. Title.
TL230.5.C45L83 1995
629.233--dc20 95-15303 CIP

The paper used in this publication is acid free and meets the requirements of the National Standard for Information Sciences-Permanence of Paper for Printed Library Materials. ∞

Manufactured in the United States of America

Preface

I've never known anyone who appreciated Chevrolet and GMC trucks more than Frank Fraser. Frank grew up near Stockton, California, at a time when prosperous farmers drove shiny new Buicks, and Steinbeck's Dust Bowl refugees rattled along in dilapidated cars and trucks.

Frank traded at the Gardnerville Hancock Station where I, as a fourteen-year-old with a Nevada scooter license and a weary 1955 Allstate-Cushman to support, pumped gas and cleaned bug remains from sun baked windshields. A hitch in the U.S. Marine Corps had rounded out Frank's language skills and profoundly affected his world view. I listened to his every word.

In 1963, Frank operated a busy janitorial service, moonlighting with an egg route between a large poultry ranch at Stockton and the Lake Tahoe/Gardnerville Area. Among his rolling stock was a battered orange-and-black 1950 GMC 1/2-ton pickup. The odometer read somewhere past 60,000 miles, but the speedometer never worked from the day Frank bought the truck. The real mileage was more like 260,000.

My folks believed that hard work was an essential part of growing up. As a consequence, they let me ride with Frank on his midnight runs to Stockton, California, where, in the wee morning hours, we loaded wire crates filled with cartons of fresh "Cackle Berry" eggs.

As we drove, I rolled down the metal edged window glass to exchange Frank's Camel cigarette smoke for the crisp aroma of Ponderosa pines. When Frank accelerated the engine, twenty-cent a quart "reclaimed" bulk oil pumped past the piston rings to burn in the upper cylinders. The acrid odor filtered through gaps in the firewall and floorboards, obscuring the scent of manzanita and tall, shadowy evergreen trees that lined the moonlit highway.

For hours I listened to the steady drone of that inline six-cylinder engine, the whine of the four-speed gearbox and the clanks within the torque tube rear axle. When Frank worked the floorshift lever, the clutch pedal arm slapped against the sagging sheet metal beneath the floorboard; the cab shuddered as the grimy clutch engaged.

Occasionally, the worn brakes pulled to one side or the other, but they never failed us. When the GMC traversed a set of railroad tracks, the worn kingpins set off a front wheel shimmy. On more than one trip, a fatigued exhaust system clamp snapped, requiring emergency repairs with strategically placed mechanic's wire.

We returned on old U.S. 40, as the first egg delivery was at Crystal Bay, Lake Tahoe. Those were the final years of construction on the high altitude sections of Interstate

Preface

80, and lines of traffic snaked down the treacherous old Donner Summit road. Frank held the GMC in compound low and second gear to keep the cab-height cargo in place.

I credit Frank Fraser with my first knowledge of the differences between a Chevrolet truck and GMC or "Jimmy." As I share in this book, those differences were once significant. When Frank compared the full-pressure oiling system of his GMC 248 engine to the archaic dip-and-splash oilers in a wrecking yard 216 Chevy, I realized the superiority of those early GMC sixes.

Helping Frank remove a torque tube rear axle assembly, aided only by a fistful of tools and a pair of rusty hydraulic jacks, was a useful ground school. When we bled the brakes, the last roadside step after replacing a fatigued U-joint, Frank's confidence prevailed. The simplicity and rugged utility of that classic truck kept us rolling.

Frank Fraser's enthusiasm for these trucks was infectious. Years later, as a fleet truck mechanic, I had the gratification of professionally overhauling the powertrains and chassis of several 1949–62 General Motors trucks. Working in a modern, fully equipped shop, with journeyman's tools and a library lined with factory-level service guidebooks, offered a much broader perspective, and I developed an even greater appreciation for Chevrolet and GMC light and medium duty trucks.

As a consumer, I have owned a string of General Motors light trucks. My two-wheel drive models included a 1958 3600-Series 3/4-ton Chevrolet pickup, a 1962 Chevrolet C-10 1/2-ton with the 235 inline six and a 1960 GMC short wheelbase Stepside bed 1/2-ton with the massive 305 cubic inch medium duty truck V-6—GMC's standard offering that year. My General Motors four-wheel drive ownership began with two Chevrolet K-10 4x4 pickup models and a K2500 4WD truck. Currently, my family relies on a 1986 K2500 GMC nine-passenger Suburban, the most versatile vehicle of the bunch.

My first Chevy and GMC 4x4s, a 1970 and 1968 model, respectively, offered traditional General Motors stamina with the convenience of a modern powertrain and power options. Later, as a married student at the University of Oregon with a growing family, I purchased a nice short wheelbase 1973 K-10 4x4 pickup with over 90,000 miles on the odometer. This highly evolved chassis served our family for years, requiring only routine maintenance.

As an automotive journalist and columnist, my assignments regularly include on- and off-road tests of all Chevrolet and GMC full-size light trucks. A more memorable report was the 1986 GMC/Starcraft camouflage-colored "Ducks Unlimited Edition" 4x4 Suburban, with captain's chair seating and television set. In addition to locking gun cabinets for hunting rifles and shotguns, the specialized vehicle sported a jon-boat on its roof rack!

For rugged trailer pullers, the latest C/K3500 4WD Sierra Crew Cab chassis and C/K2500 4WD Suburban have ranked among my top test experiences. Test models with the 7.4L TBI V-8 engine and 4L80E transmission stand out. The stunning looks and versatility of a Sierra chassis Yukon or Blazer/Tahoe 4WD, equipped with the optional turbocharged 6.5L diesel V-8 and a wisely matched 4L80E automatic transmission, also received high marks. Most recently, my test chores included a new 4WD K2500 Suburban with this rugged 6.5L turbo-diesel and a full complement of trailering options. Through this book, you will gain an appreciation for the value and rugged service that any full-size Chevrolet or GMC truck model offers.

My years of knuckle busting began as a truck fleet mechanic and culminated as a GMC Truck dealership line mechanic. In fleet truck service, the emphasis is preventive maintenance, a philosophy that I promote throughout this book. Routine preventive maintenance can reduce the demand for major repair work. Such "downtime prevention" strategies contribute to greater powertrain reliability, a safer chassis and vehicle longevity. Within this book I explain in detail why *all* of my General Motors trucks have provided long and comparatively trouble-free service.

In the performance chapters of this book, you will discover the close relationship between proven engineering and useful performance modifications. Often, truck needs differ dramatically from those of passenger cars. The performance chapters focus solely on Chevrolet and GMC light truck requirements.

Ease of maintenance means that GM trucks offer a rewarding place to sharpen your mechanical skills. Equipped with this book and a Genuine Chevrolet or GMC Truck factory service manual for your model, you can perform many repairs on your own—or even tackle the full mechanical restoration of a high mileage truck.

Even the owner who prefers not to work on his or her vehicle will find the repair and troubleshooting sections of real value. By understanding your truck's service needs, you can effectively interact with GM dealership personnel or an independent shop. Increased awareness contributes to proper diagnosis and quality repairs.

The life of my mentor and friend Frank Fraser has now passed. Notably, Frank maintained his commitment to General Motors trucks throughout his hard working days, which ended with a well-drilling business near Gardnerville, Nevada. Of no surprise, Frank's drilling rig rested on a military surplus GMC 6x6 chassis, powered by a tenacious 302 Jimmy inline six.

Like Frank Fraser, today's Chevrolet and GMC truck owners value safety, utility, reliability and performance—the four precepts that inspired this book.

Chapter 1

Evolution of Chevrolet and GMC Light Trucks

MORE THAN ANY OTHER EVENT, the birth of General Motors Corporation validated the strength of the motor vehicle industry. Merging several automobile lines and establishing a lasting economic base for building cars, trucks and military vehicles, General Motors provided the energy and resources for rapid technological advancements.

The need for commercial vehicles in an expanding economy encouraged General Motors to produce Chevrolet light trucks as World War I ended. Between the two World Wars, Chevrolet truck sales increased dramatically, and at the peak of the Great Depression, General Motors held the largest share of the truck market in the United States.

Such rapid growth, amidst strong competition from Ford Motor Company and Dodge, is a tribute to far more than the marketing strength and economic clout of General Motors. The massive success of General Motors trucks rests with products that met the demands of American buyers, trucks that served best in the broadest range of application.

The design and styling of Chevrolet and GMC trucks has created more marques than all other truck manufacturers combined. Good looks alone, however, do not build such recognition. Beyond their winning appearance, General Motors trucks have consistently relied upon functional, work-oriented powertrains and rugged chassis engineering.

American truck buyers have always placed a priority on utility, and here General Motors' engineering delivered. Trucks must work hard yet prove economical to operate. Chassis and powertrain reliability remains a primary expectation of truck owners and fleet operators.

In the pre-World War II period, General Motors' large number of car lines each had their own powertrain and

0014000

Fig. 1-1. *Chevrolet and GMC Trucks were each well known as separate lines by 1939. Similar sheet metal, chassis and geartrain components left buyers with a choice between two in-line six-cylinder engines of proven quality. Shown is a 1940 Chevrolet Pickup.*

chassis divisions. This led General Motors to develop more technological breakthroughs and successful advances than any other vehicle manufacturer in the world.

For Chevrolet light trucks, this meant easier access to new technology, more refinement of mechanical features and greater flexibility for meeting consumer needs. Similarly, GMC Trucks, which emerged as a separate line in the mid-1920s to serve a growing commercial vehicle market, would venture into the light truck market of the late 1930s with an established reputation for high quality and rugged utility.

Two Truck Lines for the American Road

By the Great Depression Era, General Motors trucks held a considerable market edge. Today's truck restorers might rightfully insist that Chevrolet's popularity resulted from exceptional body styling and good looks. In fact, Chevrolet trucks offered far more powertrain and chassis innovation than the competition, which made these light truck models more versatile, serviceable and affordable to keep.

The most significant difference in powertrain design was the use of an overhead valve (valve-in-head or OHV) type inline six-cylinder engine. While all other light truck builders relied upon L-head (valve-in-block) powerplants, Chevrolet had proven the OHV design with both four- and six-cylinder engines.

For the truck user, whether a rancher in Montana or delivery service in rural Minnesota, easy service of an inline six was an important consideration. Although Ford's 1932 introduction of a V-8 in its commercial cars (which included light trucks) was a successful market move, Chevrolet's OHV six could easily compete with the L-head Ford engines—and in many ways offered easier service.

By 1937, Chevrolet introduced the new 216.5 (216) cubic inch six. This engine, less than ten cubic inches larger than the previous design, introduced several significant engineering advances. The 3.50-inch bore and 3.75-inch stroke was closer to "square" (equal bore and stroke dimensions) than the previous 206.8 cubic inch engine, which had a 3-5/16-inch bore and 4-inch stroke.

At a 6.25:1 compression ratio, capable of running on any kind of gasoline available, the engine produced 85 horsepower at 3200 rpm and 170 lb/ft of peak torque at 900 rpm. The low speed torque peak, in particular, endeared owners to this engine. Such a torque rise is only found in today's heavy duty diesel engines.

The 216 six is one of the legendary "Stovebolt" designs, named for General Motors' use of slotted head screws to attach the pushrod cover and other engine tinware. These engines, and the first generation (1941–53) 235.5 (235) cubic inch engines offered in bigger heavy duty trucks, afforded easy in-the-chassis service and overhaul prospects. From changing ignition points to performing a

0014001

Fig. 1-2. *Chevrolet introduced the 216 in 1937, an inline valve-in-head six with a 3.50-inch bore and 3.75-inch stroke. The 6.25:1 compression ratio engine produced 85 horsepower at 3200 rpm and 170 lb/ft of peak torque at a remarkably low 900 rpm.*

0014002

Fig. 1-3. The 216 six engine was used from 1937 through 1953 through one-ton capacity. By 1953, the 216 produced 92 horsepower at 3400 rpm. Torque was 176 lb/ft at 1500 rpm, enough for Chevrolet to maintain top share in the truck market.

valve grind, Stovebolts were simple compared to Ford flathead V-8s and other L-head engines of that era.

> NOTE —
> The first generation 235.5 cubic inch Chevrolet sixes, built from 1941–53, differ from the 1954–62 version. For the sake of service and parts identification, I will refer to the 235.5 light truck six as either "early 235" (1941–53) or "later 235" (1954–up) design.

The early version of the 235 six is much like the 216 engine and has spun-in and precision machined babbitt rod bearings, "dip-and-splash" connecting rod oiling and a relatively low pressure lubrication system. The oil pan supports a series of oiling troughs for the rod dippers plus nozzles aimed at each dipper for pressure oiling at higher engine speeds.

Chevrolet engineering worked hard at perfecting the bearing materials, then matched this to a rigid and specially hardened crankshaft to enhance the service life of these early engines. The proven popularity of high pressure oiling and insert-type replacement connecting rod bearings, however, caused Chevrolet Division to abandon the elaborate dip-and-splash design and spun-in rod bearings after 1953.

All 1937–53 Chevrolet light trucks (through one-ton capacity) use the 216 engine. The early version of the 235 engine was available in larger trucks from 1941–53. The similarity between the old version of the 235 six and 216 cubic inch engine encouraged the swapping of these larger engines into the lighter truck chassis.

In its final 1953 form, the 216 six produced 92 horsepower at 3400 rpm. The torque rating of 176 lb/ft at 1500 rpm was still sufficient enough to outsell all other light truck models, although Ford's new F-100 and F-250 market share was formidable. Chevrolet took notice.

GMC Brings Its Cache of Quality Engines

When GMC revealed its light truck line in 1939, it had behind it all of the reputation and engineering advancements of the Truck & Coach Division. Notably, GMC had made several advances in crankshaft, cylinder head and lubrication design. Severe service in larger over-the-road commercial trucks had produced a series of unbreakable GMC inline sixes.

The first GMC light trucks borrowed Chevrolet sheet metal and basic chassis features, a pattern that repeats itself throughout GMC's light truck marketing history. Although GMC market share lagged well behind Chevrolet, Ford, Dodge and even I-H in 1939–40, GMC light truck sales exceeded Dodge and I-H by the onset of World War II.

From the postwar model years forward, GMC sales have ranged from brisk to a lull. In no way does this indicate that GMC trucks lacked the integrity of the ever popular Chevrolet trucks. The opposite was true, as GMC established an early image of exceptional quality. Upscale mechanical and accessory features distinguished the GMC model line from Chevrolet's status as an economical, mass produced utility truck.

GMC also had no trouble living up to its "big truck" image. One engine that evolved from this experience was GMC's 228 cubic inch OHV inline six, a proven puller that by 1939 rated 80 horsepower at 3000 rpm with 178 lb/ft of peak torque at a remarkable 1000 rpm. Like Chevrolet's 216 six, the rapid torque rise attracted light truck buyers. Although the horsepower and torque ratings were only marginally higher than the Chevrolet 216 engine, the 228 was the most rugged and practical American light truck engine design of the era. It quickly established itself as a powerful, long lasting engine.

Like International-Harvester, GMC dealerships were able to share the image of a large commercial truck line with light truck buyers. Owners of late 1930s to 1959 GMC light truck models were fortunate indeed. The inline OHV

0014003

Fig. 1-4. For 1939, GMC's 228 cubic inch OHV inline six rated 80 horsepower at 3000 rpm with 178 lb/ft of peak torque at a remarkable 1000 rpm. Like Chevrolet's 216, the quick torque rise attracted buyers. The basic engine design would change displacement several times and serve GMC light trucks through 1959.

0014004

Fig. 1-5. Chevrolet's 216 Stovebolt six uses dip-and-splash trough oiling. Normal oil pressure for a 216 is only 12 to 15 PSI at highway cruise speed.

six-cylinder engines of this period (GMC's 228, 236, 248, 256, 270 and 302) were all derivative of the proven 228 design. The most popular offerings included the 248.5 (248) and 269.5 (270) cubic inch versions.

All were incredibly rugged, and featured a full-pressure oiling system and modern insert-type connecting rod and main bearings.

Compare this to Chevrolet's 1937 216, with its dip-and-splash trough oiling. While Chevrolet engines relied upon older oiling technology, mid-1930s GMC Truck engineering advanced the 228 into the modern era. Normal oil pressure for a 216 Chevy Stovebolt six is 12 to 15 PSI at cruising speed, while late-1930s to 1959 GMC light truck sixes feed 35 to 40 PSI pressure to the bearings.

Additionally, the GMC sixes take eight quarts of oil to fill their crankcase, compared to five quarts for the critical needs of a trough-oiled Chevy 216 or early dip-and-splash 235 engine. The deep oil pan of GMC engines is attributable to large truck technology.

These lubrication system differences extend even to the oil pressure gauges. The Chevrolet's oil pressure gauge spans a much lower range than the GMC instrument. When Chevrolet truck owners install a later 1954–62 235 six in place of a 216 or early (1941–53) 235 engine, it is common for the oil pressure gauge to "peg" and become damaged. With such installations, use of a retrofit aftermarket oil gauge is common.

Both the 216/235 and 228-302 sixes have only four crankshaft main support bearings. However, the rod and main bearing journal diameters are substantial. While many features of the Chevrolet and GMC sixes have a similar appearance, parts interchangeability is limited. As complete assemblies, these engines can fit either chassis if such a swap includes use of the correct motor mounts, bellhousing, cooling system components and accessories.

Unsurpassed Styling and Chassis Engineering

By the late 1930s, as GMC pressed forward under its own light truck badge, the design of General Motors trucks was both distinctive and attractive to buyers. The sleek body lines of Fisher Body Works, so dramatically presented in General Motors' passenger car lines, also reflected in Chevrolet and GMC trucks.

0014005

Fig. 1-6. General Motors' pre-WWII trucks were distinctive and attractive to buyers. Chevrolet held top place in the U.S. light truck market, and styling like this lightly customized 1939 half-ton helped attain that position.

0014006 / 0014445

Fig. 1-7. The rugged chassis design of 1947–54 Advance-Design trucks was far ahead of other domestic truck producers. While Ford clearly broke styling ground with its 1948–56 F-Series trucks, the chassis integrity and overall quality of General Motors' 1947–59 model light trucks were unbeatable.

A pattern of good looking trucks would contribute to the marketing dominance of General Motors trucks. While Ford's 1932–40 V-8 cars have a huge and loyal following among American hot rodders, the Chevrolet and GMC light trucks from the late 1930s onward rank toe-to-toe with respective models of Ford light trucks.

In fact, the supreme quality and rugged chassis design of General Motors' 1947–54 Advance-Design trucks came well ahead of other domestic truck producers. Ford, notably, broke styling ground with its 1948–56 F-Series trucks, but the chassis engineering and overall construction of light Ford F-trucks was never better than General Motors' 1947–59 light truck models.

As some examples of those chassis differences, General Motors light trucks were the first in the industry (1941) to use recirculating ball manual steering gears. A design introduced in General Motors' 1940 luxury passenger cars, Saginaw Division's recirculating ball-and-nut steering gears contribute to superior handling and ease of operation.

Additionally, this patented gear design can serve for years beyond the lifespan of worm-and-roller, cam-and-lever and worm-and-sector steering gears common to competitor's trucks built until well into the 1960s. General Motors' willingness to introduce such a quality steering gear, without any market pressure to do so, is just one indication of its desire to build better trucks.

Similarly, while all light trucks of the 1940s offered three-speed transmissions (with synchromesh on 2nd

0014007

Fig. 1-8. Heavy duty Muncie SM420 four-speed (shown) with synchromesh on 2nd through 4th gears, as well as steering gears with recirculating ball-and-nut, brought exceptional stamina, versatility and driveability into the lighter 3100 (1/2-ton) to 3800 (one-ton) series Advance-Design light trucks.

and 3rd gears), Chevrolet and GMC surpassed Ford with the first option of a synchromesh four-speed (with synchromesh on 2nd through 4th gears). Owing to the magnitude of General Motors' sub-assembly divisions, the heavy duty Muncie SM420 four-speed brought 2-ton capacity truck stamina into the lighter 3100 (1/2-ton) to 3800 (one-ton) series option list in late 1947.

Offering the SM420 in General Motors' lightest duty truck provided a gear ratio of lower than 7:1 in the non-synchromesh compound low (1st gear). (All forward speed gears are helically cut except compound low, which relies upon a straight cut first-and-reverse sliding gear.) The 7.05:1 ratio is among the lowest gear reduction ratios ever offered in an American light truck synchromesh transmission. Compound low enhances pulling power, provides vehicle control at crawl speeds and offers exceptional compression braking and tractability on grades.

The ultra-long life expectancy of an SM420 transmission is legend. Easy downshifting to a synchromesh 2nd gear, which can essentially act as 1st gear for taking off with a light load, is possible without the need to stop or double-clutch. With a second gear ratio lower than first gear in most three-speed transmissions, the SM420 was a popular General Motors light truck option from 1948–67.

By comparison, Ford light truck owners, even buyers of the "all new" 1948 F-Series light trucks, suffered along with a straight-cut (spur gear) non-synchromesh four-speed transmission until 1952. That year, Warner's T-98 four-speed became an option on the last F-1 to F-3 models.

General Motors' 1940 and up standard three-speed transmissions also have helically cut gears with a unique cone-type synchronizer design. These SM318 and SM319 three-speed truck transmissions (built from 1940 until 1968) provide for quiet overall operation and smooth downshifting between third and second gears. This basic gearbox design served in trucks from 1/2-ton to 1-ton capacity and with engines ranging from the 90 horsepower 216 six to the light truck version of Chevrolet's 283 and 327 V-8s.

0014008

Fig. 1-9. The frame-up restoration of Jim Homer's 1955 First Series Chevrolet pickup is awesome. An added feature of the 3/4-ton 3600-Series show truck is its NAPCO 4WD conversion. NAPCO equipped Advance-Design era trucks are scarce, and Jim's truck won first place when the paint was barely dry. Seven years of effort went into this project.

1955 First Series: Models in Transition

The Advance-Design models carried the Chevrolet and GMC truck lines from the era of low horsepower six-cylinder engines to the eve of the modern V-8 era. As the release date ran late for the all-new 1955 trucks, General Motors continued to market a facsimile of the 1954 Advance-Design model well into the spring of 1955.

The 1954 and First Series 1955 (1954 design) General Motors trucks were well poised for the transition. Styling, which included a one-piece windshield and a single crossbar in the grille, offered a hint of the 1955 Second Series truck profile. Although the chassis was distinctly of 1947 variety, changes in the powertrains were portentous.

Chevrolet's all-new 235 Thriftmaster six-cylinder in-line engine would capably meet user needs into the early 1960s. Although the new six had the common 235.5 cubic inch displacement of the earlier 235 engine, the boost in compression ratio to 7.5:1 and a 112 horsepower rating was just in time for the light-truck horsepower wars.

This later 235 engine was actually the same design that Chevrolet introduced in 1953 Powerglide-equipped (automatic transmission) passenger cars and the new Corvette. The engine featured a long-overdue full-pressure lubrication system and precision-insert connecting rod bearings. Easily serviceable, highly reliable and developing enough power to satisfy most light haulers, the new 235 was a welcome change.

Fo 1954, GMC continued to offer its quality 7.5:1 compression ratio 248 six in the light trucks, with 100 horsepower at 3100 rpm and 202 lb/ft torque at a remarkable 1000 rpm level. The torque of the 235 Chevy six is nearly that high at 200 lb/ft, however, Chevy's Thriftmaster six requires 2000 rpm to achieve this figure.

By 1955, GMC's last 248 GMC D-series engine delivered 130 horsepower at 3600 rpm and 214 lb/ft peak torque at a faster 1550 rpm. The era of massive low speed lugging power was ending. High octane Tetra-Ethyl leaded fuels permitted higher compression ratios, which suited General Motors' Kettering-type V-8 engines well.

Making torque at a higher rpm was common for the over-square (larger bore than stroke dimension) Kettering V-8s. Pioneered with the 1949 Cadillac and Oldsmobile

The Jobmaster 261 Six

The new 1954 235 truck engine had a counterpart, the 261 cubic inch design. Using the same stroke (3-15/16 inches) as the 235 and a 3/16-inch larger bore (3-3/4 inches), the 1954–55 261 truck engine had 7.17:1 compression ratio and delivered 135 horsepower and 200 lb/ft peak torque.

In 1956 Jobmaster form, a boost in compression ratio to 7.8:1 and other refinements raised the 261's horsepower figure to 148 at 4000 rpm, while torque rose to 232 lb/ft at 2000 rpm.

The 261 makes a relatively easy retrofit for 1937–62 Chevrolet light trucks. Among its several performance features, versions of the 261 use the same high torque camshaft found in the Blue Flame Corvette six.

0014009

Fig. 1-10. For 1954, GMC's 248 six produced 100 horsepower at 3100 rpm and 202 lb/ft peak torque at 1000 rpm. The last 248 D-series GMC six, built for some 1955 trucks, has 130 horsepower at 3600 rpm and 214 lb/ft peak torque at a faster 1550 rpm. The era of ultra-low-speed inline six-cylinder lugging power ended here.

OHV V-8s, Charles F. Kettering's highly successful engineering concept served as a foundation for two new engines offered in 1955 Second Series Chevrolet and GMC trucks.

In 1954, both Chevrolet and GMC light trucks were available with a rugged Hydra-Matic Drive automatic transmission option. The popularity of automatic transmissions was evident in the passenger car market, and General Motors believed that light trucks were also candidates.

This transmission was the very best. Hydra-Matics of the dual-range, band-type offered unusually high stamina. Four forward speeds began with a 3.82:1 ratio on the 1/2-ton truck applications and a 4.71:1 ratio on 3/4-ton

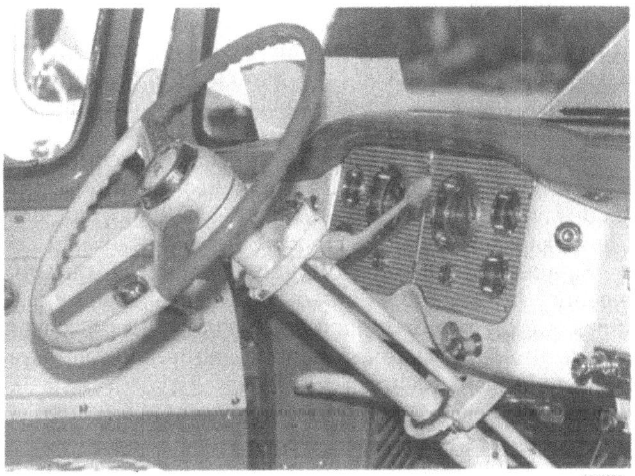

0014058

Fig. 1-11. The dual range band-type Hydra-Matic Drive with column shift was a highly durable four-speed automatic transmission. First introduced in 1954 Chevrolet and GMC light trucks, the unit was similar to proven Cadillac, Oldsmobile and Pontiac car versions. B&M Automotive immortalized this exceptional design with a racing build-up called the "B&M Hydro-Stick."

and one-ton models. The drive torus-type coupler permitted curb idle speeds as low as 400 rpm with no vehicle creep at an idle.

The four-speed Hydra-Matic would see greater use in the V-8 era, but buyers of Hydra-Matic equipped 1954 models were not disappointed. A very low first gear ratio, relatively close spacing of the first/second and third/fourth gear ratios, and the extremely rugged construction of an iron cased Hydra-Matic gave these trucks ample power, utility and a long service life—unlike the automatic transmissions offered by other domestic truck builders during that era

Minor revision of the rear engine and transmission mounting crossmember was necessary on the 1954 chassis to accommodate the very heavy Hydra-Matic transmission option and to stiffen the frame to handle the improved torque of Chevrolet's new 235 inline six.

Nineteen fifty-four and First Series 1955 General Motors 1/2-ton trucks were the last to use the closed torque-tube driveline. Half-ton rated trucks had used this design for decades, while the 3/4-ton and larger trucks with full-floating rear axles had benefitted from the easier serviceability of an open driveshaft.

0014011

Fig. 1-12. Torque-tube driveline was last used in 1954 and First Series 1955 General Motors 1/2-ton trucks. Open driveshafts (shown) made service easier on 3/4-ton and larger models.

For removal of the transmission or replacement of a driveline universal joint, the torque-tube rear axle is a nemesis. Although the rear axle, driveline and torque-tube bushings seldom give trouble, a routine clutch replacement or transmission overhaul can become a service fiasco. The 1955 Second Series to mid-1960s half-tons offer very simple access to the rear driveline, transmission and clutch.

Nineteen fifty-four and First Series 1955 models were also the last trucks with six-volt electrics. While several General Motors car lines had switched to 12-volt electrics by 1954, light trucks would retain six-volt systems through the First Series 1955 models. The Second Series 1955 models would benefit from 12-volt starting and charging systems, a practical need with the new V-8 engine option.

0014012

Fig. 1-13. Second Series 1955 models have 12-volt starting and charging systems. The new V-8 option and increasing compression ratios made six-volt electrics obsolete.

The sweeping changes planned for 1955 Second Series trucks required a heavier chassis and more geartrain stamina. At odds with this overall upgrading was the continued use of ball-type front wheel bearings on General Motors' light trucks and passenger cars. Chevrolet and GMC trucks would wait until 1963 to gain the long service life and improved stamina of tapered roller front wheel bearings.

1955 Second Series Brings on the V-8 Era

Utility and economical service have been the backbone of American light truck technology. That General Motors' 1954–55 First-Series light trucks remained highly competitive, with only an inline six-cylinder engine, attests to this fact.

Chevrolet sold a huge volume of light trucks to utility and construction companies, mining and agricultural users and the United States Government. These buyers valued the inline six's low speed torque, fuel savings and durability. Despite Ford's persistent use of V-8 engines, which Chevrolet and GMC matched handily in the late 1955 models, the six-cylinder engine continued to dominate overall sales figures until the late 1960s.

Still, despite the success of General Motors' light truck six-cylinder engines, the 1950s unfolded as a time when fuel was inexpensive and octane ran high. A V-8 horsepower race waged throughout the U.S. automobile market, and 1955 became a landmark year for Chevrolet passenger cars and the Corvette as the new 265 V-8 swept into the realm of racing.

The 265 design minimized excess mass and simplified the valvetrain to such a degree that its rpm potential surpassed that of all other domestic V-8 engines. Chevrolet light trucks would also benefit from this streamlined small-block V-8 engine.

While the stamped tinware of the valve covers, timing cover and oil pan appeared far less substantial than the larger Buick, Oldsmobile, Pontiac and Çadillac V-8s, these measures translated to an engine that barely outweighed the inline sixes. Compact and light, the 265 occupied a minimal amount of space in the engine bay.

Corvette's four-barrel version of this engine used an 8:1 compression ratio, delivered 195 horsepower at 5000

0014013

Fig. 1-14. V-8 engine option, a new body style, and updated frame make Second Series trucks stand out. The lightweight 265 small-block V-8 truck engine features an economical two-barrel intake system, high torque mechanical lifter camshaft and mild 7.5:1 compression ratio. Horsepower peak for 1955 light truck engines is 145 at 4000 rpm while torque reaches 238 lb/ft at a useful 2000 rpm.

rpm and pounded out 260 lb/ft torque at 3000 rpm. For the utilitarian Task Force light trucks, an economical two-barrel intake system, high torque mechanical lifter camshaft and 7.5:1 compression dropped the horsepower to 145 at 4000 rpm. The torque peak reached 238 lb/ft, delivered at a more useful 2000 rpm.

In truck form, the small-block Chevy V-8 looked more like the spartan 235 six than a Corvette performance engine. For owners who wanted oil filtration, the option was a by-pass filter unit, much like the sixes, that mounted atop the intake manifold. A full-flow oil filtration system would not adorn the 265 engine until 1957, during the pioneer V-8's last year of production.

When the compression went up on the 235 six in 1956, horsepower jumped to 140 at 4200 rpm and torque reached 210 lb/ft at 2000 rpm. Especially in the 3100-series half-ton and new 3200 (long bed half-ton) models, the 235 six found the ample response that it deserved.

Performance fever and the introduction of exciting new truck models like Chevrolet's Cameo bed pickup encouraged many buyers to consider the 265 V-8 and, in 1957, Chevrolet's new and even larger 283 V-8 engine option.

Small-block V-8s proved highly adaptable, admirably meeting the needs of a broad base of users. This mid-1950s market included the first wave of RV users, primarily in pursuit of camper shells, travel trailers, pleasure boats and the new cabover campers.

GMC Turns to Pontiac Power

Second Series 1955 GMC models came with 12-volt electrics and a different V-8 engine approach than Chevrolet. Rather than utilize Chevrolet's new 265 small-block V-8, GMC light trucks began the V-8 era with Pontiac's all new 287.2 cubic inch design (which GMC labeled the 288). This was not a superficial choice and followed the early GMC pattern of engines that produced brute torque.

0014014

Fig. 1-15. Pontiac's 287 V-8 shared several design features with the new Chevrolet V-8 engine, including innovative stamped rocker arms that lightened the valvetrain mass. Pontiac/GMC 288, 316, 336-A and 347 V-8s served light trucks during the 1955 Second Series through 1959 period.

A few years ago, I discussed this decision with some current members of GMC Truck's engineering and marketing staff. One member speculated that GMC probably chose the Pontiac 287 V-8 because Chevrolet's V-8 engine supply was limited, and the "Pontiac engine was available." I disagree, preferring to believe that such a move reflected GMC's upscale image and traditional "truck-based" engineering goals.

Pontiac's 287 (GMC 288), 317 (GMC 316) and 347 V-8s shared several design features with the Chevrolet V-8 engine. Both were Kettering over-square type engines with the well proven successes of Oldsmobile, Cadillac and Buick behind their development. Unlike these three predecessors, however, the Chevrolet and Pontiac V-8s featured stamped rocker arms, which lightened the valvetrain mass considerably and helped these engines evolve into high performance marques during the 1960s. Chevrolet's tiny 265 powerplant would first metamorphose into the 283, 327 and early Z-28 302, which later evolved into the larger main bearing (big journal) engines of 302, 307, 327, 350 and 400 cubic inches. The smog-era 262 Chevy V-8 is also derived from this design.

Similarly, Pontiac would begin with its original 287 V-8,then increase size to 317, 347, 370, 389 and 421 cubic inches. Later, the 350, 400, 428 and 455 variations also took advantage of the original 287 design. Pontiac engineers were very cautious, and with each increase in displacement, the bearing/journal sizes, coolant circulation and lubrication needs would undergo evaluation and necessary upgrades.

I am intimately familiar with Pontiac/GMC V-8 engines of that era. Somewhat lighter in weight than other General Motors mid-luxury or luxury car engines, these Pontiac V-8s offer versatility, high torque and the kind of stamina that a truck builder with GMC's standards wanted.

The original GMC 288 light truck engine had a 7.4:1 compression ratio. While Chevrolet's 265 featured a 3.75-inch bore and 3-inch stroke, the Pontiac engine offered the same cylinder bore diameter with a 3.25-inch stroke. This quarter-inch longer stroke helped produce 246 lb/ft peak torque at a relatively low 2400 rpm. The horsepower peak of 155 was at a comparatively low 3600 rpm.

Such differences soon separated Chevrolet V-8s from the GMC/Pontiac engines. By 1957, a GMC version of the 347 had 7.8:1 compression and produced a massive 354 lb/ft peak torque at 2400 rpm. 206 horsepower at 3600 rpm proved plenty for a light truck's needs.

> **NOTE —**
> An oddly configured 336 cubic inch GMC V-8, which used Pontiac's 317 engine bore with a 347's crankshaft stroke, was a GMC Truck offering during 1958 and 1959. These were the last two years that GMC light trucks offered Pontiac-designed V-8s.

With its deep iron timing cover and high volume coolant circulation system within the block and cylinder heads, the Pontiac/GMC V-8 engine was surely a more expensive engine to produce than the small-block Chevy V-8. Suggesting that GMC bought these engines simply because they "were available" in 1955 would overlook the fact that GMC trucks continued to use Pontiac V-8s from the Second Series models through 1959.

Even when Chevrolet's ill-fated 348 cubic inch V-8 reliably served in the medium duty Chevrolet truck line, GMC continued to offer Pontiac's 347 V-8 and its own indestructible 248 and 270 inline sixes. I believe this was a deliberate choice, an effort to attain the quality, integrity and high torque output expected of GMC trucks.

The balance of my theory is that Pontiac automobile engines were available with a band type Dual Range Hydra-Matic Drive in 1955 and 1956. As GMC anticipated the sale of automatic transmission-equipped trucks, Pontiac V-8s would make a much easier installation than, say, Buick car engines that offered the peculiar Dynaflow automatic transmission.

Of interest, the Buick 322 V-8 did show up as Chevrolet's Loadmaster engine in the larger medium duty trucks of the 1957–59 era, and GMC used Oldsmobile 324 V-8s in some 1955–56 medium duty trucks—plus the Olds 371 V-8 in these same models from 1957 through 1959. For light truck use, however, the Pontiac V-8s worked best.

Beginning in 1955 and lingering as late as 1972, GMC Truck Division made other component purchases outside of Chevrolet's parts bins. One example is the use of Spicer's model 45 rear axle, a variation of the popular 44 unit, which GMC utilized until the late 1960s in 1/2-ton models.

Likewise, larger capacity 3/4-ton trucks opted for the full-floating type Spicer 60 axle unit, while some heavy-duty 1/2-ton models use the very rare Spicer 60 semi-floater. If this was due to a supply shortage of General Motors' own Corporate and Saginaw type axles, GMC Truck opted for some of the highest quality, most proven products available.

Strong Trucks with a Nice Face

Unquestionably, the Second Series 1955–59 Chevrolet and GMC Trucks have earned more styling accolades than any other models. In addition to stunning body lines, these trucks offer an easy to service and rugged chassis, relative-

0014015

Fig. 1-16. Beginning with Second Series 1955 models, GMC Truck Division made several geartrain purchases outside Chevrolet's parts bins. Spicer's Model 45 rear axle, a variation of the popular 44 unit, was a GMC 1/2-ton offering through the mid-1960s.

ly light overall weight, broad engine bays, open drivelines, stout powertrains and durable axle assemblies.

For restorers, collectors and builders of "street trucks," the Second Series 1955–59 model General Motors trucks have high appeal. Of very special interest is the Chevrolet Cameo and GMC suburban pickup models.

In 1953, Corvette had introduced the use of fiberglass to mass produced auto bodies, and the all-steel Chevrolet Nomad and Pontiac Safari station wagons proved that any model could offer a stylish sport version.

Chevrolet applied this technology and philosophy to the highly stylized outer bed walls and tailgate of the prized 1955–58 Cameo short wheelbase 1/2-ton pickup models. Here was the perfect complement for a 3100 truck's flowing cab lines, its graceful hood and eyebrowed headlight assemblies that reflected the high styling of Chevrolet cars.

GMC also offered Cameo-type bed options like the Town & Country and Suburban packages, which today make prized collectibles. These 100-Series models look much like their Chevrolet 3100-Series Cameo counterpart. Obvious styling differences between Chevrolet and GMC trucks were in the grille/hood areas and instrumentation.

Many buyers purchased the Cameo or suburban pickup strictly for its straight walled, side loading bed. In the late 1960s, a once white and red-trimmed Cameo pickup gassed up regularly at the local service station where I traded. The one-owner truck never carried less than fifteen buckets of house paint and four ladders in its palette-colored and crumbling bed.

Unlike the luxurious Nomad or Safari wagons, Cameos often fell into the hands of utility buyers who abused the fiberglass unmercifully. The 1958 introduction of an all steel Fleetside bed made the Cameo option obsolete—or at least saved these special models from a horrible fate. Today, the remaining 1955–58 Cameo and Suburban models fetch a premium price.

0014016

Fig. 1-17. Unlike the conventional Stepside models, the stylized Chevy Cameo and GMC Suburban bed featured straight walls that permitted side loading. Some buyers mistook the Cameo and Suburban for an easier-to-load work truck and quickly damaged the truck's light fiberglass sides and tailgate cover. Today, the rare Cameo or Suburban short wheelbase half-ton pickup makes a worthy collectible item.

The rear cab quarter windows that characterized the DeLuxe Cab option of the Advance-Design era evolved into the wrap-around full width rear window option found in many 1955–59 cabs. Dramatic on Cameo and suburban bed models, these full-view windows also upgraded the cabs of other Chevrolet and GMC trucks.

Aside from their stunning mid-1950s style, these 1955–59 models mix classical beauty with modern perfor mance. The 1960–66 Chevrolet and GMC trucks would advance chassis and powertrain technology much further, but none of these models surpassed the styling of the Second Series 1955–59 General Motors trucks.

1960: Bigger Trucks, Big Changes

While the ladder frame, solid-beam front axle and leaf springs had served General Motors trucks from the start, 1959 would be the last year for such technology in the two-wheel drive light trucks. In a bold gesture, 1960 Chevrolet and GMC light truck engineering advanced to fully independent front suspension.

The 1960 truck models required an all new frame to accommodate upper and lower front control arms. Unlike General Motors' automobiles, the front suspension employed torsion bars rather than coil springs. This engineering was the first application of torsion bars with A-arm suspension on a U.S.-built truck.

For the rear suspension of 1/2-ton (C-10/1000), heavy-duty 1/2-ton GMC-1500 and the 3/4-ton (C-20/2500) models, two link-arms support the axle. A coil spring rides at each arm. One-ton (C-30/3000) and heavier chassis models, with full-floating rear axles and dual wheels, still rely upon conventional rear leaf springs. For the lighter models, a heavy duty rear leaf spring option provided conventional leaf springs in place of the link-arms and coil springs.

Steering linkage now took on a passenger car profile, with a centerlink, idler arm and two shorter tie-rods. Linkage type (add-on) power steering, by then an option of several years, was again available on the new 1960 chassis.

0014017

Fig. 1-18. Nineteen sixty truck models required an all new frame to accommodate upper and lower front control arms and unique torsion bar suspension. 1960 was the first application of torsion bars with A-arm suspension on a U.S.-built truck.

0014018

Fig. 1-19. Also in 1960, GM light trucks introduced rear link-arm support for the axle. A coil spring rides at each link arm. One-ton and heavier chassis with full-floating rear axles and dual wheels came with conventional leaf springs.

0014019

Fig. 1-20. While steering linkage, ball-joints and A-arms resemble designs found in passenger cars, the 1960–up General Motors 2WD light truck chassis is a workhorse. Independent front suspension (IFS) provides improved ride quality without sacrificing durability. 1960-62 models have torsion bars, while 1963-up 2WD trucks (shown) feature coil springs.

Despite a radical departure from the earlier body style and an obvious increase in cab width, the new half-ton rated trucks were only one-inch longer in wheelbase than their counterpart 1959 3100 models. Ride quality excelled while load capacity remained ample.

Although many looked at the shift to front ball-joints and A-arm suspension as a departure from traditional truck engineering, these extremely well-built suspension systems were way beyond passenger car quality. Every component was a match for the severe loads and rugged service demanded of a truck. Other than the added procedures for wheel alignment, which now required caster, camber and toe-in checks, service needs were easily understood and implemented.

These 1960 models were also the first General Motors light trucks to have suspended brake and clutch pedals, and both Chevrolet and GMC featured hydraulic clutch linkage for manual transmission models. Uniquely, the clutch release fork was at the right side of the bellhousing on these hydraulic clutch applications.

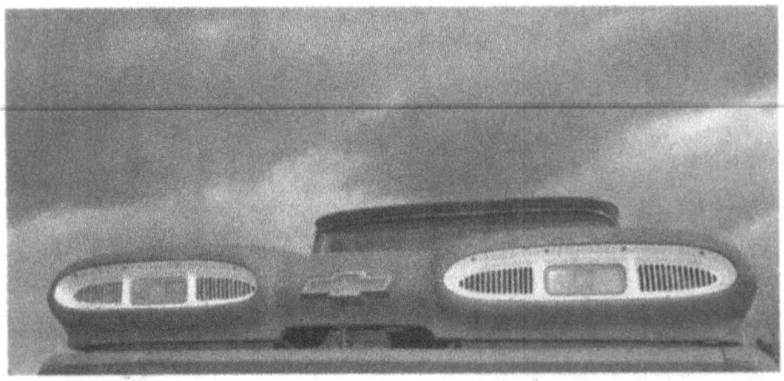

0014020

Fig. 1-21. Styling for 1960–61 shared cues from 1959–60 Chevrolet passenger cars. Despite huge sales success of 1960 and 1961 model Chevrolet and GMC light trucks, designers toned down body lines for 1962 models. Shown here is highly stylized 1960–61 hood contour.

In step with the latest styling changes at Ford and Dodge Truck, General Motors widened the cab, lowered the roof line and added distinctive body cues. For 1960, an apparent desire to achieve symmetry in the body design led to huge cat-like eyebrows in the hood plus a right side hump in the dashboard that matched the shape of the driver's side instrument panel. The styling shared cues from the 1959 and 1960 Chevrolet passenger cars, however, the exaggerated effect on the truck cab and hood fell short. Despite the huge sales success of 1960 and 1961 model Chevrolet light trucks, the stylists would tone down the body lines by 1962.

Again the Fleetside and classic Stepside bed models were available, in several wheelbase configurations and chassis ratings to meet broad user demands. The RV/camper era was in full swing by now, and light truck buyers ordered from a massive list of optional equipment.

Chevrolet's 8.5:1 compression ratio, two-barrel carbureted 283 V-8 was now a respectable 160 horsepower at 4200 rpm and produced 275 lb/ft peak torque at 2400 rpm. This gave Chevrolet light trucks the kind of power needed for hauling a recreational trailer or a pleasure boat and camper.

GMC Opts for V-6 Power

In a move that still puzzles many of us GMC Truck buffs, the 1960 models were without a V-8 engine option. GMC's all-new 305A-Series V-6 was the only engine available in the light trucks.

The earliest version of this engine had a one-barrel carburetor and a camshaft profile with a huge appetite for gasoline. Later 305D and 305E versions with two-barrel carburetors and an improved camshaft design could deliver 142 horsepower at 3800 rpm plus a highly impressive 260 lb/ft peak torque at a remarkably low 1600 rpm.

This was the kind of lugging power that had characterized the 270 and 302 cubic inch inline sixes. Better yet, the compression ratio of the big 305 V-6 was 7.75:1, capable of tolerating all grades of fuel.

Durability of the 305 V-6 is, undisputedly, top rate. The basic 305 and 351 GMC V-6 engineering served the medium duty truck applications, and the use of these engines in a light truck was virtually overkill.

Consideration for cooling was so extensive on the 305 V-6, with its enormous block and cylinder head ports and

0014307

Fig. 1-22. Unlike Chevrolet, 1960 GMC light truck models were without a V-8. GMC's all-new 305A-Series V-6 was the only engine available. While fuel economy suffered on early 305 V-6s, the later two-barrel carbureted design shown here delivered 142 horsepower at 3800 rpm and an impressive 260 lb/ft peak torque at a very low 1600 rpm.

a massive water pump circulation rate, that even the lightest half-ton Model 1000 truck application requires 33 to 34 quarts of coolant for a full fill. By contrast, a 1960 Chevrolet C-10 half-ton with a 235 inline six, or even the 283 V-8, takes less than 18 quarts to fill.

GMC sold to those who respected "real trucks." Riding on a reputation that included high torque power, the choice of Hydra-Matic Drive or durable heavy duty manual transmissions and a long roster of practical accessories, the GMC Trucks began the 1960s with their autonomy intact. They would leave this decade on another note.

The Hydra-Matic Drive was still available in 1960 GMC Trucks, and Chevrolet offered the unit as one option, with the two-speed Powerglide as another offering. Any truck owner who ordered the Hydra-Matic was well ahead of the game, as this was the more versatile and ruggedly built four-speed transmission.

By 1962, Chevrolet buyers opting for the only automatic transmission option found themselves with a two-speed Powerglide. GMC, meanwhile, still used the dual-range Hydra-Matic and Spicer rear axles (both front and rear on K-models). Unfortunately, GMC Truck component autonomy began to falter with the 1964 models.

The radical chassis advances of 1960 were altered slightly by 1963. Costly to produce and vulnerable to impact damage, the torsion bars of the independent front suspension system were dropped in favor of more conventional coil springs on the 1963 models.

Also missing from the 1963 light truck models was the hydraulic clutch linkage system. The clutch release arm returned to the left side of the bellhousing, and mechanical linkage would prevail until well into the 1980s.

1964–70: Division Lines Begin to Dissolve

After three decades of independent powerplant production, the GMC light trucks began using Chevrolet engines. The change resulted from the introduction of Chevrolet's new seven-main-bearing 230 and 292 cubic inch inline sixes in 1963.

NAPCO Conversions and the First Factory 4x4 Models

A great deal of confusion exists around which year Chevrolet and GMC introduced four-wheel drive as a factory option. NAPCO (Northwestern Auto Parts Company), a very well known aftermarket producer of four-wheel drive conversion kits since the late 1940s, had provided General Motors truck dealerships with an easy-to-install aftermarket kit, the Powr-Pak, to fit a conventional leaf spring and open driveshaft chassis.

0014022

Through the Advance-Design era, NAPCO kits fit 3/4-ton and larger models with a full-floating rear axle and longer wheelbase. The kit consisted of a Rockwell two-speed transfer case/power divider, a live front axle assembly that replaced the solid-beam 2WD front axle, and all levers, mounting hardware, the front driveshaft and attachments to complete the installation at a local General Motors truck dealership. Powr-Pak kits with twin-levers have Rockwell transfer units, while later single-lever kits use a lighter weight Spicer transfer box.

Due to the simplicity of all pre-1960 2WD General Motors truck chassis, with front and rear leaf springs and an accessible undercarriage, the NAPCO dealership-level conversion takes on the appearance of a factory installed kit.

In NAPCO's literature, ease of installation suggests that fleet users can use the kit on one truck, remove it, and then install the package on another vehicle. "No cutting of the Chevrolet/GMC frame....NAPCO drills only four holes in the frame."

Originally an offshoot of WWII General Motors surplus military hardware, later refined versions of the kit relied upon a NAPCO-built live front axle assembly with a common drop-in center section from a General Motors differential. This and other familiar hardware allowed NAPCO to boast, "Parts and service available at 7,522 Chevrolet dealers throughout the United States."

Chevrolet and GMC began promoting the NAPCO-type installation as an option in 1957 and 1958, and I have seen promotional advertising films depicting these NAPCO 4WD conversion trucks as new Chevrolet models. They show every resemblance to the dealer kits available prior to these years. GMC Truck advertised its "new" 4x4 models as the Blue Chip trucks, and they were available in 1957

0014023

Jim Homer's immaculately restored 1955 First Series Chevrolet 3600 truck is among the best NAPCO examples around. Such thorough engineering made it very easy to call this original equipment (OEM) four-wheel drive.

on chassis as light as the 1/2-ton 100-Series. Likewise, kits were available for Chevrolet's 1/2-ton 1955 Second Series and newer models through 1959.

Until 1960, these kits brought a new realm of versatility and maximum tractability to Chevrolet and GMC trucks. The all-new 1960 2WD independent front suspension chassis, however, signaled the end of simple 4WD conversions. For the first time, General Motors offered an all-new, specially designated factory 4x4 frame. The K-models featured a full length ladder frame, leaf springs front and rear, a Spicer 44 closed knuckle live front axle and a two-speed transfer case.

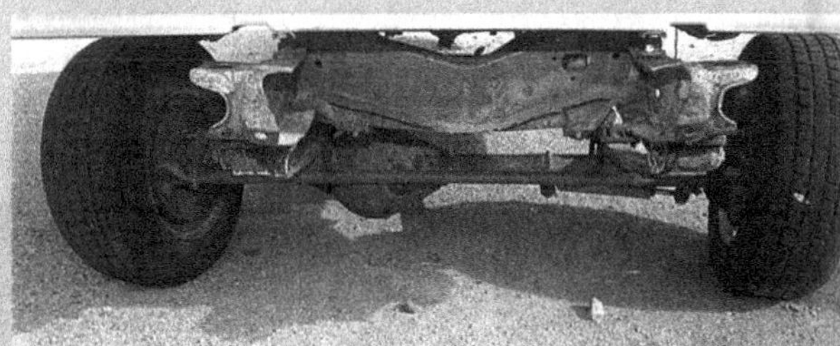
0014024

General Motors' 1960 K-models were the first real "factory" 4x4s. The new K-truck OEM frames accepted leaf springs front and rear, a Spicer 44 closed knuckle live front axle and a two-speed transfer case.

Nineteen sixty stands as a milestone year in the light truck market, the year that General Motors became a full competitor with Ford's F-Series 4x4s, the Dodge Power Wagon and the I-H All-Wheel Drive trucks. By the end of the decade, General Motors would offer the most innovative and popular line of 4x4 light trucks in the industry, including the K-10 (GMC's K-1500) through K-20 (GMC's K-2500), the K-5 Blazer/Jimmy plus the K-10/1500 and K-20/2500 Suburban 4WDs.

0014025

Fig. 1-23. *Chevrolet's seven-main-bearing 230 and 292 cubic inch inline sixes came on line in 1963. These engines share considerable engineering with the reliable 283 V-8, including a common cylinder bore diameter and the first six-cylinder use of Chevrolet's V-8 bellhousing pattern. Shown here is the later 250 cubic inch version of this engine.*

These new engines drew upon engineering and even some components from the simple and reliable 283 small-block V-8. The light truck sixes now shared a common cylinder bore diameter with the Chevrolet 283 V-8 and, for the first time, used the common Chevrolet V-8 bellhousing pattern.

Despite its remarkable durability, the GMC 305 V-6's massive fuel consumption was now a widely known problem, and GMC needed to restore its image as an affordable and economical truck to operate. The new Chevrolet six was an obvious solution. Without fanfare, GMC introduced the 230 as a 1964 engine option.

By 1966, the similar seven-main bearing 250 six came on line, and GMC again took the cue and added this engine to its option list. Standardization of parts could prove beneficial now, as fiscal accountability would become the hallmark of good business practice by the late 1960s. Gone were the days of a burgeoning market that allowed highly diverse research and looser production methods.

Alas, the 283 Chevy V-8 was put at GMC's disposal in 1967, followed by the 307 and 327 V-8s in 1968 and the 350 in 1969. It was now clear to 1955–59 GMC buffs that holding out for a Pontiac/GMC V-8 connection was futile. As the new body style emerged in 1967, further melding of Chevrolet and GMC truck product took place.

Arguably, the period 1969–71 could be considered the final amalgamation of GMC and Chevrolet light truck product. During this time, the 305E V-6 was dropped from the GMC light truck option list, the rear axle choices narrowed, and the same axles now appeared in parallel models of Chevrolet and GMC trucks.

Technology had advanced rapidly, as power options, disc front brakes on 4x4s (1971), and broad layers of trim and accessory packages further complicated the possibility of GMC remaining autonomous. With the advent of computer build orders and the merger of GMC and Chev-

0014026

Fig. 1-24. *1969–71 represents the final merging of GMC and Chevrolet light truck product. Gone is GMC's 305E V-6, and the same axles now serve parallel Chevrolet and GMC models. Disc front brakes were major advance for 1971 K-trucks.*

rolet truck assembly lines, fewer differences meant easier quality control, proper pricing and marketing gains. Judging by the products, GMC light trucks lost the balance of their independence by 1971. The trim levels, power options, powertrain/geartrain features and available equipment for Chevrolet and GMC Trucks became one.

From this point forward, each Chevrolet trim and accessory package would have its GMC counterpart, albeit under a different marketing name, for example Chevrolet's Silverado versus GMC's Sierra Classic. Even factory order number codes were common between the lines. With a few keystrokes on a computer build sheet, the distinctions between a Chevrolet and GMC truck ended.

Many suggest that GMC should simply have merged with Chevrolet in 1971, but there were many good reasons why two light truck marketing lines worked well. The upscale image established by GMC over the years had created a unique dealership base for these trucks, often allied with Pontiac, Oldsmobile and Cadillac automobile lines. These higher end car dealerships found the GMC Truck line both attractive and supportive of image.

Reciprocally, loyal Chevrolet buyers preferred the one-stop shopping convenience of buying both their cars and light trucks at the same dealership. Besides, the integration of the two products also meant that GMC Truck quality was available at the local Chevy store. Image went both ways.

Largely for marketing reasons and to support its franchised dealerships, General Motors today continues to market GMC Trucks under a separate badge. In the midst of wide consumer interest in both light trucks and upscale models like the 4WD Sierra-chassis Suburban, dealers proudly display either badge of high quality General Motors trucks.

Successful Sport Utility Vehicles

Chevrolet and GMC light trucks of the 1967–72 period enjoyed tremendous sales. The recreational use of pickup trucks and an emerging class of sport utility vehicles (SUVs) played perfectly into General Motors' light truck design and planning.

While the 1961 I-H Scout was patterned after the CJ Jeeps, and Ford's slightly larger 1966 Bronco entry offered a very similar approach, General Motors waited until 1969 to unleash its SUV challenge. The all-new Chevrolet Blazer and the following season's GMC Jimmy became an instant success story.

The new Blazer/Jimmy struck a perfect balance between the Jeepster, Bronco or Scout size vehicles and the popular full-size Jeep Wagoneer and I-H Travelall. Better yet, the Blazer/Jimmy models boasted a shortened K-10/K-1500 chassis featuring every advantage of a full-size truck.

0014027

Fig. 1-25. New K-5 4x4 Blazer/Jimmy easily outclassed the Jeepster, Bronco and I-H Scouts. The K-5 matched chassis stamina and powertrain offerings of full-size trucks like the Jeep Wagoneer and I-H Travelall. Blazer/Jimmy models utilized a shortened K-10/K-1500 chassis with every advantage of General Motors' full-size truck components. (Photo courtesy of Warn Industries)

From a production standpoint, this made perfect sense. The same options, assembly techniques, powertrain features and basic chassis meant that buyers received the benefit of proven real truck technology. This also proved wise from a marketing angle, as consumers who looked at the smaller SUV 4x4s were appalled at their poor ride quality and lack of performance.

By contrast, the new Blazer and Jimmy featured the advanced technology pioneered in General Motors' 1967 K-truck chassis. This frame and suspension lowered the ride height of the 4x4 models and also provided the advantage of a revolutionary reverse arch, tapered leaf (progressively rated) front spring design. Ride quality improved dramatically without sacrificing load capacity.

Saginaw's integral power steering gear, the best in the world, came into the 4x4 truck option list in 1969, just in time for the introduction of the new K-5 Blazer. Options like vacuum assisted brakes and integral power steering enhanced the driving appeal of light trucks.

The two-wheel drive light truck models abandoned linkage type power steering in favor of integral power gears during the 1968 model year, while 4x4s continued to use an add-on type linkage power assist through 1968.

Between 1969 and 1972, Chevrolet and GMC light trucks phased out the use of the two-speed Powerglide automatic transmission option (called Pow-R-Flo in truck versions). The new options were the more versatile and durable Turbo-Hydramatics, the TH350 and the heavy duty TH400 three-speeds. Beginning in 1969, all 4x4 K-models optioned a version of the TH350.

The Turbo (THM) 400 would serve as the archetypal standard for heavy hauling, severe duty and use behind engines like the 454 big-block V-8. In 1976, as General Motors expanded the K-models to include the new K-30/3500 one-ton capacity trucks, the Turbo 400 became available for the first time in a light 4x4 model.

For the manual transmission buff, Muncie Division's SM465 heavy duty four-speed truck gearbox became available in the 1968 C- and K-models. This option came into the K-5 Blazer/Jimmy line as well. The SM465 is among the most durable four-speed truck transmissions ever built, well suited to two-ton models. That K-5s and light trucks were available with this unit attests to General Motors' attempt to build a rugged utility vehicle.

NOTE —
Prior to 1979, some General Motors light trucks used the New Process 435 four-speeds. This is also a very rugged design. Likewise, while most late 1960s and early 1970s 4x4 K-models use the very stout NP205 transfer case, some came equipped with the durable Spicer 20 unit.

Beginning with the Second Series 1955 models, Chevrolet relied upon General Motors' corporate transmission offerings. GMC also offered these General Motors units plus several stronger gearboxes from Borg-Warner. In some applications, Chevrolet light trucks would offer the Warner transmissions as a heavy duty option. By the mid-1960s, some three-speed manual transmissions had synchromesh on all forward gears.

0014453

Fig. 1-26. 1967–72 General Motors light trucks bridged classical styling with modern and rugged engineering. These model years introduced refinements that would keep General Motors in the forefront of light truck sales.

Another important advance came in 1971, when the GMC and Chevrolet 4x4 full-size trucks became the first in the industry to offer disc front brakes as standard equipment. This move, coupled with the use of an open-knuckle Dana 44 front axle, propelled General Motors trucks to a new level of handling ease.

The General Motors trucks continued to meet utility and workhorse demands while treating buyers to the best ride quality, handling, braking and safety engineering of any light truck in the marketplace. All General Motors two- and four-wheel drive light truck models, including K-5s and Suburbans, were built around bonafide full-size truck chassis with superior stamina and advanced technology.

During 1971, the combined sales of Chevrolet and GMC trucks soared beyond the closest competitor. The pattern repeated itself in 1972, as the tremendous demand for light trucks pressed General Motors to maximum production capacity.

The 1967 body style change had now evolved through a variety of trim package offerings, and 1971–72 General Motors light trucks were a milestone. These two model years have become highly prized by restorers, 4WD enthusiasts, street truck builders, collectors and those who appreciate the traditional quality, fine styling and rugged engineering of Chevrolet and GMC trucks.

Best Trucks Ever Built

Powertrain stamina and chassis integrity reached an all-time high with General Motors' truck models built between 1971 and 1979. All effort focused on the use of durable components.

For delivering maximum utility and longevity, these trucks provide a substantial ladder frame with exceptional crossmember integrity, disc front brakes, well tuned tapered front leaf spring suspension (4x4 models), rugged A-arms and steering arm/spindles (2WD trucks) plus durable rear axle assemblies.

The Saginaw recirculating ball manual and integral power steering systems, cross-flow radiator cooling, vacuum booster assisted disc front brakes, and high output electrical charging systems enhanced these models. Handling is superior to all earlier trucks, enhanced further by the use of stabilizer/sway bars.

0014029

Fig. 1-27. The 292 six consumes a good quantity of fuel at highway speeds but has ideal lugging ability. For severe duty and low speed pulling, in environments like ranching, farming and mining, the 292 inline six excels.

Cab comfort, popular trim packages with various upholstery upgrades, two-tone paint options, accessories like power door locks and windows, air conditioning and many other luxury appointments filled the massive option list. Popular automatic transmission options ease driveability, making these General Motors trucks handle much like a well-built passenger car, without giving up traditional truck value, reliability, structural integrity or utility.

The emergence of the light truck as a multi-purpose SUV picked up momentum during the 1970s. Trailering packages, a wide range of powertrain options and several tiers of trim and appointments gave the 1971–79 General Motors light trucks the widest possible buyer appeal. Base trucks remained highly durable and packed with value. Standard engine offerings were the rugged inline sixes like the 250 (light duty models) and ultra-high-torque 292 (heavier chassis models). Optional V-8s ranged from the 307, ever-popular 350, 400 big-block (402) and 400 small-block to the 305 small-block and the 454 big-block.

The 250 and 292 sixes, offered from 1963 until the mid-1980s, were very reliable, reasonably economical and ideal for agricultural and commercial users. Arguably, the 292 consumed considerable fuel, but the engine's lugging ability was ideal for severe duty, low-speed pulling.

The 307 was essentially a big main-bearing journal replacement for the earlier 283, offering an economical two-barrel carburetor and strong torque output. This design served well through 1973.

For overall versatility, the Quadrajet four-barrel 350, mostly in four-bolt main bearing cap variety for truck use, appealed to a huge number of buyers during the 1970s. Highly flexible, the 350's ability to produce strong torque and great horsepower enabled it to tolerate emission constraints far better than most other engines.

The 396 big-block V-8 played a short but impressive role as the highest performance (1968–69) engine option in Chevrolet light truck history. From 1970 through 1972, the de-tuned 400 big-block (actually a 0.030-inch overbored 396 engine of 402 cubic inch displacement) provided 2WD trucks with a lower compression, high torque engine for towing and warmer performance.

0014030

Fig. 1-28. In 1973, General Motors replaced the 400 big-block with the more muscular 454 V-8. Today equipped with advanced TBI induction and electronic spark control, the 454 big-block enjoys a large following among heavy haulers and trailer pullers. (Photo courtesy of Chevrolet Motor Division)

Emission constraints continued to drive horsepower and torque figures down. In 1973, General Motors replaced the 400 big-block with the more muscular 454 big-block V-8.

The 454 was well known in passenger car circles. In its LS-6 and LS-7 Corvette and high performance passenger car form, the engine easily achieved its advertised 450 and 460 horsepower ratings through the use of ultra-high compression ratios and radical camshaft grinds. The 1973 truck 454 would be a substantially de-tuned version, however, with a mild four-barrel carburetor and only 8.25:1 compression.

Net horsepower figures, now an industry standard, rated the 1973 454 with 245 horsepower at 4000 rpm and 375 lb/ft torque at 2800 rpm. With massive torque, these engines were only available in 2WD models and were coupled with either the four-speed SM465 manual gearbox or the hefty TH400 design automatic. To this day, the heavy duty 454 powertrain package serves Camper Special and heavy towing needs.

In 1976, the passenger car 400 small-block engine became a four-barrel option alongside the 350 and 454 V-8s. The 400 small-block, constrained by a heavy dose of emission controls and high operating temperature requirements, produced good power but succumbed to design weaknesses.

The bore centers of this 400 small-block engine were like the 350, but the extra 0.125-inch of bore diameter required siamesed middle cylinder jackets. Without coolant circulation around the middle cylinders, local heat could cause overheating problems and related casting damage. The 400 small-block soon faded from the option list, its last offering in 1980 truck models.

In step with EPA emission requirements and the Energy Crisis era, the 305 small-block V-8 emerged. This was a small-bore (3.74-inch), long stroke (3.48-inch) engine that delivered improved torque and appealed to buyers who wanted decent fuel economy and reasonable performance. The 305 came on line in 1977 and survives as the standard powerplant in full-size light trucks.

The 305 has nearly the same cylinder bore dimension as the original 1955 265 Chevrolet V-8, yet the stroke is a full 0.48-inch longer. The result is a fuel efficient engine that develops excellent low end torque, behaving much like a larger V-8. High torque enables use of taller (numerically lower) axle gear ratios, which contribute to better fuel economy and less tailpipe pollution per mile. Unfortunately, there is a limit to what fewer cubic inches can do. The 305 V-8 is severely overworked in the higher curb weight truck applications and often succumbs to such stress.

The 350 small-block V-8, with its 4.00-inch bore and 3.48-inch stroke, has provided the best overall service of any Chevrolet-design light truck engine. The rugged 350 offers the balance of power and reasonable economy that truck owners want, and the 1987 introduction of modern throttle body fuel injection (TBI/EFI) helps carry forward a tradition that began with the 1969 trucks.

Of significance from 1971 through 1979, the four-wheel drive models benefit from highly durable transfer cases and axles. The New Process 205 gear-drive transfer case has proven stronger than any other light truck unit. In 1973, automatic transmission models began using the New Process 203 chain-drive transfer case, a rugged unit by any standard, that served as a key component in the full-time 4x4 systems.

Through 1979, these two transfer cases provided exceptional service on all light truck applications. Even the one-ton rated K-30 model, introduced in 1976, was well within the capacity of these transfer cases. The K-30 became the first K-model to use the beefier TH400 transmission, which complemented a massive GM Corporate 14-bolt rear axle.

Heavy duty Chevrolet and GMC Suburban 4WD K-20/2500 models also benefitted from the TH400 automatic beginning in 1980. The TH400 transmission has served heavy duty two-wheel drive models like the high performance SS 454 special edition pickup, in trucks equipped for heavy hauling, or when a big-block V-8 requires more stamina.

The rugged New Process 205 gear drive transfer case survives through the conventional (non-Sierra) one-ton capacity K-30/K-3500 4WD models. The last use of the NP205 transfer case was in the 1991 Crew Cab K-30/3500 one-ton 4x4 chassis.

1975–87: Years of Adjustment

The 1970s brought far more than a growing interest in light trucks. By mid-decade, the oil/energy crisis launched a new epoch in geo-politics. Increased government involvement in natural resource issues and air quality had a drastic effect on automobile and light truck design. The double-nickel speed limit, stringent emission control requirements and radically rising fuel costs each affected light truck engineering and marketing strategies.

0014031

Fig. 1-29. By the mid-1980s, while heavier duty applications continued to use the rugged TH400 three-speed automatic, (pictured here in my 1986 GMC Suburban K2500 4x4), Hydra-Matic Division's 700R-4 overdrive automatic became a mainstay for lighter GVWR models.

General Motors and other vehicle manufacturers responded first with detuned engines and taller (numerically lower) axle gearing. By the mid-1970s, the economy truck axle ratios of the 1960s were being regarded as optional trailer pulling gearsets, while he standard axle ratios found in light trucks were essentially those found in a 1960s economy car.

Engine performance also dropped. Declining horsepower resulted from heavier emission requirements, the catalytic converters required on light duty models from 1975 forward, and the tuning necessary to survive on new low-octane unleaded fuels.

Most Federal (49-State) emissions trucks over 8500 pound GVWR (Gross Vehicle Weight Rating) were exempt from catalytic converter and unleaded fuel requirements until 1987. This gave heavier haulers like the C/K-20/2500 or C/K-30/3500 models some advantage, although the low octane fuels still restricted compression ratios. Even 49-State vehicles required clean tailpipes, and many non-catalyst trucks had dual air injection pumps and a heavy complement of other smog controls.

To further reduce engine rpm at cruise speed, egineers employed overdrive and lower (numerically higher) axle gearing. In 1982, the new 700R-4 four-speed automatic transmission became an option on light truck models. For California's even more demanding tailpipe emission requirements, this transmission would be the sole offering in several models.

The concept was fine. Use of an overdriving automatic meant that lower axle gearing could raise the performance and hauling capacity of light trucks. Overdrive would provide an extra gear to reduce engine rpm at highway cruising speeds. Unfortunately, the durability of the early 700R-4 transmission fell short of the TH350 and TH400 Turbo-Hydramatics.

A planetary-type automatic overdrive subjected to severe loads is always at risk. The load in overdrive was excessive in 700R-4 applications that pulled heavy loads, and General Motors refrained from offering the overdrive automatic in heavy duty applications. This meant that the

TH400 would be available when necessary, and even the TH350 remained in limited use.

By 1985, General Motors' Hydra-Matic Division had addressed the majority of the 700R-4 unit's weaknesses, and the overdrive automatic became a mainstay for lighter GVWR models. The C/K-20/C/K-2500 Suburbans and C/K-30/C/K3500 one-ton models continued to use the rugged TH400 three-speed automatic.

Improved Powertrains Fit the Times

The 250 inline six left the engine lineup in 1985, replaced by the new 262 (4.3L) Vortec V-6. The four-barrel carbureted Vortec engine, essentially a 350 V-8 minus two cylinders, offered good torque, reasonable fuel economy, and a more modular design that could carry General Motors light trucks forward with more common components.

The formidable carbureted 292 inline six would survive through 1986 with somewhat poorer economy than the 4.3L. With the all-new Sierra truck chassis only a year away, the 1987 engines underwent the most significant and useful change in recent history: electronic Throttle Body Injection (TBI).

Electronic fuel injection and spark management was long overdue in light trucks. Ford had paved the way in 1986 with its use of Multi-Point Injection on 302 truck V-8s. Now Chevrolet and GMC light truck V-6 and V-8 engines would have the many advantages of fuel injection with a comparatively simple, lower fuel pressure TBI system.

The two-barrel throttle body assembly looks much like a carburetor and functions through a common intake plenum/manifold. Easy to troubleshoot and less complex than high-pressure multi-point injection, TBI proved a wise way to introduce new technology.

Horsepower and torque figures immediately climbed. Tailpipe emissions dropped abruptly, without the heavy use of emission controls. All TBI engines looked neater, were easier to service and had simpler emission plumb-

Light Truck Diesel Alternative

Faced with rising fuel costs and emission requirements, General Motors brought diesel power to the automobile and light truck lines in the late 1970s. Despite a wealth of experience with the Detroit two-stroke diesels, engineers opted for an existing Oldsmobile gasoline V-8 as the foundation for the original 350 diesel V-8 powerplant.

The 1977 Cadillac Seville and 1978 Chevrolet/GMC light trucks piloted one of General Motors' worst technological nightmares. In its first form, the 350 diesel caused a flurry of warranty problems and customer complaints. Largely due to the stresses of a 22.5:1 compression ratio, the 350 diesel engine suffered from head gasket sealing troubles, block failures and cylinder head casting cracks. The later DX series block and other improvements lowered the parts failure rate dramatically, and General Motors successfully used the DX 350 diesel in luxury cars through 1985.

Despite its ultimate acceptance, the 350 diesel lacked the power that former gasoline V-8 customers demanded. Pressed to perform like a gasoline passenger car engine, the 350 diesel used a good deal of fuel and still lacked the passing acceleration of even a 305 Chevrolet gas V-8. After 1981, General Motors dropped the 350 diesel from the light truck option list.

Having suffered humiliation with a marginal entry into the diesel engine realm, General Motors applied its truck engineering skills. The outcome was an all-new 379 cubic inch (6.2L) diesel V-8. In 1982, this naturally aspirated diesel engine became an option in all Chevrolet and GMC light truck models, including the K-5 Blazer/Jimmy.

By design, the 6.2L is a medium duty diesel truck engine. Unlike the heavy duty class Detroit engines, it operates within a broader rpm range. This makes the 6.2L diesel perform more like the familiar gasoline engines.

While lacking in both gross horsepower and torque when compared to a 454 gasoline engine, the 6.2L diesel has achieved success and a substantial following with its dependability and miserly fuel consumption. With only modest changes, the 6.2L diesel serves well into the 1990s, a fuel efficient workhorse with a ready market.

0014034

Turbocharged 6.5L V-8 diesel is ideal for trailer pulling, overall fuel economy gains and strong performance. Latest L65 engine is capable of 190 horsepower at 3400 rpm and a massive 385 lb/ft peak torque at 1700 rpm. Beefier block bulkheads, re-engineered coolant passages and oil gallery re-sizing meet the added needs of turbocharging. (Photo courtesy of Chevrolet Motor Division)

The 6.2L V-8 diesel became the foundation for the later naturally aspirated and Borg-Warner turbocharged 6.5L V-8 diesel engines. The 6.5L design offers several improvements in the areas of block webbing reinforcement, oil sealing and reduction of cold start noise.

The turbocharged 6.5L diesel is an ideal engine for trailer pulling, overall fuel economy gains and strong performance. Filling the horsepower gap and answering to consumer concerns, the 6.5L diesel now squarely challenges the highly competitive Navistar 7.3L V-8 and Cummins 5.9L inline six-cylinder turbocharged diesels that power Ford and Dodge light trucks.

0014032

Fig. 1-30. General Motors' light truck V-6 and V-8 engines gained substantially from 1987 introduction of throttle body injection (TBI). Two-barrel throttle body assembly looks much like a carburetor. Easy to troubleshoot and less complex than high pressure multi-port injection, TBI is a major advance beyond carburetion.

ing. Even the 454 big-block realized noticeable fuel economy gains. Former hour-and-a-half spark plug changes now took less than thirty minutes.

EFI and electronic spark management revolutionized the automotive industry. Despite the limitations of low octane fuels, real performance was once again possible. Fuel consumption dropped significantly, and EFI could easily adjust for altitude changes and various load demands.

General Motors took technology a step further with the introduction of roller hydraulic valve lifters. New camshaft lobe profiles could manipulate valve opening and closing to meet performance, emissions and economy demands.

The newest technology also allowed higher compression ratios and provided for instant spark retard in response to detonation (ping). As a result, engines now run at maximum tolerable spark advance during all phases of operation—without the fear of harmful spark knock.

Use of the lowest octane fuels simply means that further spark retard is necessary. Likewise, a tank full of higher octane fuel will enable more spark advance and better performance output.

So significant is the contribution of EFI and the newest generation of 4L60E and 4L80E automatic overdrive transmissions that a fully loaded C/K3500 Sierra Crew Cab 4WD truck can tow a trailer at maximum Gross Combination Weight (GCW) and still deliver 10.5 miles to the gallon of fuel.

I drew this statistic when testing such a truck over a 500 mile mountain and desert route. The one-ton 4WD Crew Cab test vehicle had the rugged 4L80E four-speed automatic overdrive transmission and the 7.4L (454 cubic inch) EFI/TBI V-8 rated 230 net horsepower at 3600 rpm.

0014033

Fig. 1-31. My tests have found that a 454 V-8 with EFI/TBI and the 4L80E automatic overdrive transmission will allow a fully loaded C/K3500 Sierra Crew Cab 4WD truck to tow a car-pulling trailer at maximum Gross Combination Weight (GCW) and still deliver 10.5 miles to the gallon of fuel.

The Ever-popular Suburbans and Carryalls

Willys asserted that its 1946 light duty Station Wagon model was the first all-steel wagon in America. While this did hold true for automobile-based station wagons, it surely was not the whole story.

A full decade earlier, General Motors had launched the all-steel Suburban-type truck models in response to the growing need for a quality multi-passenger cargo hauler. At that time, station wagons were custom built of wood, cloth and steel, and most bodies rode on passenger car frames. General Motors altered that approach significantly.

0014035

Like many light truck builders in the mid-1930s, General Motors offered a variety of panel delivery trucks. Wisely selecting a panel truck for its new Suburban model, instead of a passenger car-based sedan delivery, General Motors created a highly versatile mass production vehicle.

While Jeep's full-size Wagoneer, the I-H Travelall and Dodge's short-term Town Wagon venture of the late 1950s have all succumbed, the General Motors Suburban, still in its basic panel truck-with-windows form, continues to capture a loyal following. Today's Chevrolet and GMC Suburban models can account for sales in excess of 95,000 annual units. Production is expected to double.

Beginning with the 1936 model year, Suburban/Carryall models have featured the chassis, powertrain and front bumper to B-pillar sheet metal of current Chevrolet or GMC light trucks. Popular in both 1/2-ton and 3/4-ton versions, Suburbans target users who want plenty of passenger seating plus the option of removing seats for loading cargo. When cargo hauling, the Suburban serves much like the Panel Delivery models that once shared their sheet metal with the Suburban/Carryall.

Offering the styling and chassis innovations of each light truck model year, the Suburban continues to benefit from the popularity of Chevrolet and GMC Truck engineering. With its longer, more stable wheelbase, the Suburban has secured a sure place in the light truck market.

By 1969, the 4WD version of the Suburban began to attract interest from beyond the logging and mining companies. New light truck advances like Saginaw power steering and introduction of the Turbo 350 transmission option made the Suburban and other General Motors light trucks much easier to drive.

Since 1969, the Suburban has grown beyond its small niche segment and merged with the burgeoning SUV market. By the mid-1970s, with only AMC's Jeep Wagoneer as competition, new Suburban 2WD and 4WD models lined row after row of America's travel trailer parks. The Suburban's trailer toting status continues to hold sway over pickups and other SUVs, including the full-size Blazer/Tahoe and Jimmy/ Yukon. Unless a couple wants to pull a fifth-wheel behind their pickup, or a family can justify the lengthy 168.5-inch wheelbase of a Crew Cab, only a properly equipped C/K2500 Suburban can haul nine people, two dogs, a roof rack full of bicycles and a 30-foot travel trailer—all at the same time!

0014037

Like the earliest Suburban/Carryall, today's stunning C/K2500 Turbo-Diesel powered 4WD model (left) reflects all of the chassis and powertrain features of other light truck models. Sheet metal from the front bumper to B-pillar (behind the front doors) is a match for all other C/K Sierra light trucks. My 1986 GMC (right) has solid front axle, while C/K2500 features IFS 4x4.

Remarkably, the Suburban offers the same stamina and rugged utility as other full-size General Motors truck chassis without sacrificing ride quality. Our family's current 1986 GMC K2500 Suburban 4x4 is packed with options yet can tow a massive travel trailer. Thanks to General Motors' careful suspension tuning, the vehicle drives so easily that we often forget it's a real truck.

Even more impressive, with the third seat removed and the second seats folded forward, a stack of eight-foot long folding tables can fit inside the cargo doors. Other notable feats include hauling half of our son's baseball team; taking two Golden Retriever dogs and eight people on a picnic; reaching our winter cross-country skiing haunts with a full load of passengers; and, certainly of significance, being on ready call for Search & Rescue work in mountainous snow country.

Now that's a 3/4-ton Suburban 4x4. Naturally, the only replacement vehicle we have considered is the new Sierra C/K2500 4WD Suburban with its wide array of options—including the new L65 Turbo-Diesel V-8. Our current 1986 350 gasoline V-8 model runs great at over 100,000 miles, but the newer IFS 4WD chassis, electronically controlled diesel power and the 4L80E overdrive just keep calling.

0014038

Fig. 1-32. Highly acclaimed 2WD and 4WD IFS Sierra chassis offer superior handling, braking and load sensing suspension. Chassis refinements and advances in computer matching of shock absorbers, stabilizers and spring rates have achieved their highest level with these models.

0014039

Fig. 1-33. Advanced styling and sweeping interior/cab design of Sierra trucks steal attention from dramatic chassis improvements. One-piece door window glass, functional slope of front sheet metal, a streamlined bed and subtle ground effects make an immediate impression.

Without the loaded car trailer and a bed full of camping equipment, this ample powertrain delivered 13.5 mpg at highway cruise speeds. By comparison, the carbureted 454 engine in a 1986 K-30/K-3500 one-ton Crew Cab would deliver 6 to 8 mpg loaded and 10 to 11 mpg running empty.

C/K Sierra Truck Chassis Breakthroughs

While 1960 stands as a milestone year for 2WD chassis advancements on Chevrolet and GMC trucks, the 1988 model year holds that distinction for the popular 4WD models. An all-new light truck chassis and body design, designated *Sierra* for both the GMC and Chevrolet model lines, delivered the first fully independent A-arm type front suspension (IFS) system on a full-size domestic 4x4 truck.

Arguably, this technology shares many features with the compact S/T-truck 4x4s, which pioneered General Motors' use of 4WD IFS in 1983. Serving trucks to one-ton load capacity, however, requires considerable upgrading and concern for high stress demands.

The most obvious difference on both 2WD and 4WD IFS Sierra trucks is their superior handling, braking and load sensing suspension. The chassis refinements and advances in computer matching of shock absorbers, stabilizers and spring rates have achieved their highest level with this 1988 and newer chassis.

Testing these Sierra chassis trucks, including pickups, Suburbans, Yukon and full-size Blazer/Tahoe has provided me with a deep appreciation for the wide array of engineering advancements found in these models. From steering ease and better handling to improved ride quality, performance and fuel economy, the Sierra Trucks stand at the forefront of technology.

The advanced IFS front end and drive system in the 4WD K-models represents the first fully independent design available in a full-size truck. Ford F-Series trucks with Twin-Traction Beam suspension and the Dodge Truck's more traditional solid axle cannot match the range of wheel movement, broad tire arcs or caster and camber changes possible with the 4WD Sierra's suspension and steering.

Since 1980, the lighter duty 4WD models have relied upon aluminum housed, chain drive transfer cases, and the C/K Sierra Truck models continue this trend. The latest systems offer durable Shift-on-the-Fly gear changing mechanisms and other driveability enhancements.

General Motors' joint effort with New Process in the production of advanced New Venture gearbox and transfer case drive systems provides the assurance of ongoing quality. Such a partnership can go far toward matching geartrain and engine demands.

Five-speed overdrive manual transmissions, which also came on line with the Sierra chassis, have undergone several evolutionary changes. The newest versions offer greater stamina and smoother operation. In effect, the Sierra chassis, powertrain, styling and accessories have improved with each successive model year.

The newest and most refined Sierra truck models offer the utility and durability that traditional General Motors light truck buyers expect. In an era when first time light truck buyers continue to flood Chevrolet and GMC Truck dealerships, the Sierra models make an impression.

Chevy and GMC Trucks, like apple pie, say a lot about America and its people. Nearly eighty years into production, General Motors trucks still stand for a hard day's work, maximum dependability and lots of value—with enough left over for some good fishin' and fun!

Chapter 2

Buying a Light Truck

POST-WORLD WAR II AMERICA was a society on the move. Years of rationed vehicle sales had created a huge need for light trucks, with buyers ranging from construction companies, farmers, mining operations and ranchers to utility companies, delivery services and suburban users.

The 1939, 1940 and 1941–42 General Motors truck chassis sold very well and built a satisfied owner base. Switching from war-time production to a civilian market was easier for General Motors than other manufacturers, as the familiar and worthy 1942 light trucks were once again in full production before the end of 1945. Exceptional sales kept these trucks rolling out of numerous GM plants until the all-new 1947 Advance-Design models were ready to market.

Although the 1939–46 Chevrolet and GMC Trucks offer classical body styling and a very durable chassis, truck sales during the 1947–54 Advance-Design period outstripped the total for all previous years in General Motors' truck history. Beyond their alluring body style and rugged engineering, Advance-Design trucks reflected the economic prosperity of American society during the postwar era.

Technological advances and a dedication to quality helped build the success of these trucks. I would characterize the engineering of Advance-Design models as a wholehearted effort to produce the best trucks possible. The 1947–54 Advance-Design vehicles carry a substantial load; they steer and stop well; and their powertrains provide exceptional service. Simply put, these remarkably durable trucks came ready for the long haul.

The resale value of Chevrolet and GMC trucks is legend. While Second Series 1955–59 3100 models hold collectible status for their classic body style and V-8 era engineering, a properly restored 1971–87 K-10/1500 or K-20/2500 4x4 can look great, haul massive loads and deliver a dozen or more years of rugged service. Boasting an advanced chassis design and host of convenience options, these later trucks also hold a premium value.

0014040

Fig. 2-1. *While 1967–72 C/K trucks have gained a following among "street truck" builders, the restoration of 1939–59 era Chevrolet and GMC light trucks still holds an edge. The classic 114-inch short wheelbase 1957 3100-Series Chevrolet Cameo or 100-series GMC Suburban bed pickup, powered by a Turbo-Fire 265 or 283 V-8 or a Pontiac/GMC 347 V-8 fetches a top price and makes an excellent investment.*

The styling of General Motors trucks never grows old, and the overwhelming number of Chevrolet and GMC units sold from the post-WWII period to the present provides buyers with a wide range of quality two- and four-wheel drive used truck models.

For the new truck buyer, the C/K Sierra-design chassis offers a broad range of platforms and powertrain options. New Chevrolet and GMC trucks provide commercial and private users with an exceptional work truck, multi-purpose vehicle or foundation for recreation.

A growing number of buyers have discovered the value and structural integrity of light trucks. General Motors Sierra models now serve an even wider range of daily transportation and family demands. Crew cab trucks, once the beast of burden "crummies" that hauled loggers and back breaking cargos over miles of gravel Forest Service roads, now comfortably carry families of six to their favorite hiking trails, fishing holes and ski slopes.

While the interior and luxury appointments of Sierra trucks rival upscale passenger cars, the chassis and powertrain maintain traditional stamina and a rugged work capacity. The Sierra chassis' marketing success results from an ability to give buyers traditional truck value in a stylish and easy to drive package.

0014043

Fig. 2-2. From the Advance-Design years forward, various models carry distinct designations. For 1947–59 models, you can easily spot the Chevrolet 3100 (1/2-ton), 3600 (3/4-ton) and 3800 (one-ton) trucks. Counterpart GMC Truck models were the Models 100, 150 and 250. Beginning with Second Series' 1955, a new 3200 (GMC 102) long bed 1/2-ton model met many users' needs.

1. SELECTING THE RIGHT TRUCK

A successful truck buy begins with understanding your needs, then finding a truck with the right equipment and stamina to match your goals. Even a restored Advance-Design model could deliver quality service if you select the chassis and powertrain that meet your hauling plans.

Aside from a vehicle flawed with mechanical defects, the primary source of dissatisfaction among new and used truck buyers is selection of incorrect equipment. Whether your truck provides multi-purpose transportation or must haul a massive cargo over rough roads, the Gross Vehicle Weight Rating (GVWR)/chassis, powertrain and options will determine its worth.

0014044

Fig. 2-3. Model identification plates play an important role when ordering parts or determining load carrying capacity. Check the model code and GVWR rating when shopping for your used GMC or Chevrolet truck.

Chevrolet and GMC trucks can provide value, but you must select the right chassis capacity for your needs. Choosing the correct chassis and GVWR is easy with General Motors light trucks, as each model series has its corresponding chassis and powertrain stamina based upon the GVWR.

Even the earliest Advance-Design chassis are distinctly different. In 1947, Chevrolet began labeling 1/2-ton rated models as 3100-Series, the 3/4-ton models were 3600-Series and the one-ton load capacity trucks earned a 3800-Series status. Although that era offered few distinctions between engines and transmissions, the frame, springs, rear axle and gear ratios were dramatically different in each of the three truck series.

0014501

Fig. 2-4. The popularity of four-wheel drive gives new and used GM light truck buyers a wide variety of choices. For light hauling chores, the C/K-1500 Sierra 4x4 chassis has offered independent front suspension and exceptional value since 1988. (Truck courtesy of Giles Chevrolet)

Fig. 2-5. 1988 was a change year with the introduction of the Sierra truck chassis. However, the 1973 chassis design and body style continue through 1991 in K-5 Blazer/Jimmy models, the Suburban models and the C/K-30/3500 Crew Cab chassis.

Significant change years for chassis re-engineering or major body restyling of General Motors light trucks are easily identified: 1947 (Advance-Design), 1955 (Second Series), 1960, 1967, 1971 (essentially the 1967 platform with addition of disc front brakes), 1973 (major body change) and 1988 (introduction of the Sierra models).

Anatomy of a Half-ton Truck

In cargo capacity and fundamental design, even the 1939 General Motors light trucks hold some similarities to the latest C/K Sierra chassis models. While load ratings remain a significant concern, American full-size 1/2-ton trucks have traditionally offered far more product than import and compact models with similar GVWR ratings.

At the most basic level, 1939 to present General Motors full-size trucks all feature ladder frames. (In automotive manufacturing parlance, these are also "driveable chassis" designs.) From 1955 (Second Series) forward, all GM trucks offer hypoid-style open driveline rear axles. With the exception of lighter duty 1960–72 2WD models, all models have offered semi-elliptic rear leaf springs, and 2WD trucks have provided independent front suspension since 1960.

Until 1955, all Chevrolet and GMC trucks featured valve-in-head (OHV) inline six-cylinder engines. Second Series 1955 trucks introduced the new Chevrolet and Pontiac/GMC OHV V-8 engines. (See Chapter 1 for information on the design, evolution and application of General Motors light truck engines.) From Second Series 1955 forward, all Chevrolet trucks offer both six-cylinder and V-8 engines. (Since Second Series 1955, GMC has offered sixes and V-8s in all years except 1960–66, when only six-cylinder engines were available.)

In assessing the chassis of 1939 and newer GMC and Chevrolet light trucks, all have hydraulically actuated

Weighing the GVWR Issue

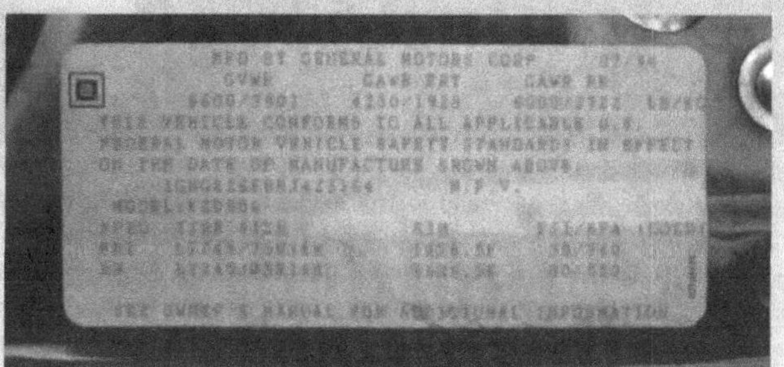

Each of us has heard tales of trucks that carried loads way beyond their rated capacity. When Frank Fraser and I hauled "Cackle Berry" eggs over old Donner Summit in 1963, Frank's well-worn 1950 GMC was at least 700 pounds overloaded on every trip. Our excuse was that I was fourteen years old and ignorant, and Frank had a unique sense of humor, nerves of steel, a low transportation budget and a busy egg route.

Rated load capacity goes far beyond how much weight a set of springs can carry. If heavier springs alone could make a one-ton C/K3500 Sierra truck, the cost of heavy duty haulers would drop dramatically. While the wheelbase and body panels often match, a 1/2-ton rated truck offers substantially less chassis and powertrain stamina than a one-ton GVWR model.

If you can identify your hauling needs and cargo carrying demands, selecting a truck becomes easier. The most significant differences in load capacity (GVWR or GCW) ratings involve the frame, chassis and geartrain strength.

0014047

Fig. 2-6. All General Motors light trucks through 1959 have leaf front and rear springs. 4x4 K-models offer leaf front and rear springs through the 1987 pickups and the 1991 Suburbans, K-5 Blazer/Jimmy models and K-30/3500 Crew Cab models. 1988–up Sierra 4WD trucks feature torsion bar independent front suspension. Torsion bar IFS is also used on 1960–62 2WD light trucks.

wheel brakes. (General Motors vehicles switched to hydraulic brakes several years ahead of Ford. The first Ford light trucks to use hydraulic brakes were 1939 models.) All General Motors trucks offer four-wheel drum brakes through 1970, while 1971 and newer Chevrolet and GMC light trucks gain the substantial advantage of disc front brakes.

Integral power steering, dual braking systems with anti-lock, high tech EFI, added safety features and unimaginably comfortable interiors characterize the newer Sierra trucks, yet like the 1939 GM light trucks, a new 1/2-ton C/K1500 model pickup is still a formidable hauler by any standard.

Three-quarter-ton Virtues

The 1947 (Advance-Design) 3/4-ton 3600-Series Chevrolet and GMC Model 150 chassis established some long-term rules for 3/4-ton light trucks. Greater cargo capacity translated as a heavier frame, stronger axles and hefty springs.

Engineering tradition places the 3/4-ton models well beyond the lighter duty 1/2-ton, yet lower in curb weight and load capacity than a one-ton rated truck. For Advance-Design models, I would characterize the Chevrolet 3600 and GMC 150 as more akin to a one-ton capacity Chevrolet 3800 or GMC 250 than the 3100 or 100 chassis.

I make this call because the 3/4-ton's full-floating rear axle, larger front kingpins and big braking system more closely resemble the design of a one-ton model. This precedent carries through until the 1980s, when Chevrolet and GMC 3/4-ton trucks gradually shifted to semi-floating rear axle designs. In many Sierra trucks, a standard 3/4-ton C/K2500 model with lighter GVWR equipment will more closely resemble a long wheelbase 1/2-ton C/K1500 than the beefier one-ton rated C/K3500 chassis.

In the 1930s, large trucks popularized full-floating axles. This design provides for a separate rear wheel hub assembly and axle shaft. The design is described more fully in Chapter 10, but the bottom line is that this design is well-suited to trucks that carry severe loads, and has always meant increased service life. Chevrolet and GMC 3/4-ton and one-ton light trucks have used the full-floating axle for this reason. A full-floater is easy to identify, and until the mid-1980s, you could readily spot a C- or K-20/2500 and C- or K-30/3500 model truck.

Some C/K2500 3/4-ton and C/K3500 Sierra one-ton trucks have semi-floating rear axles, although the ring gear size, axle shaft diameters and axle bearings of a one-ton truck are substantially larger than the lighter duty C/K models. Although many late-model Chevrolet and GMC 3/4-ton trucks have semi-floating rear axles, the 3/4-ton pre-Sierra models continued to use traditional eight-lug wheels. Today's C/K2500 Sierra trucks, however, use six-lug wheels like the K1500 4WD 1/2-ton model.

A long-bed K-10/1500 1/2-ton, K-20/2500 3/4-ton and K-30/3500 one-ton may share beds and sheet metal, but similarities end here. Beginning in 1976, the K-30/3500 trucks use a larger modular section in the frame. Axle upgrades on the 1976 K-30/3500 include a solid

0014048

Fig. 2-7. Engines must match the load. The 454 V-8, here in late EFI/TBI form, serves well with the C/K3500's GVWR capacity. When the load increases, fuel economy drops, yet the added horsepower means less engine stress and wear.

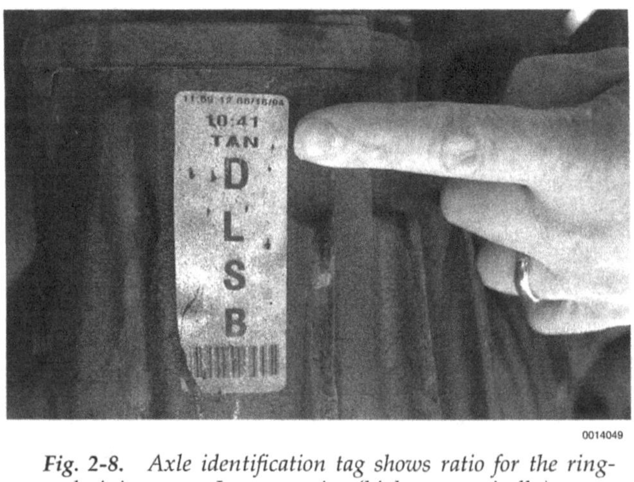

0014049

Fig. 2-8. Axle identification tag shows ratio for the ring-and-pinion gears. Lower gearing (higher numerically) means better pulling power and crawling ability. For a C/K2500 or C/K3500, lower gearing means a 4.10 or 4.56:1 ratio. Tall gearing, for economy and primarily light load use, would be the 3.42 to 3.73:1 range.

0014050

Fig. 2-9. When the beefy General Motors Corporate 14-Bolt rear axle went from full- to semi-floating design, another change was the ring gear size. Our 1986 4WD K2500 Suburban's rear axle was a semi-floating type with a ring gear diameter of 9.5 inches—a full inch smaller than the 1984 Suburban full-floating Corporate 14-bolt design. Jeff Sugg's MIT shop in El Cajon, California retrofitted a complete 1984 axle assembly into our 1986 model, enabling us to gain the stamina and towing capability we want. (For details, see chapter on geartrain performance modifications.)

Dana 60 front unit in place of the Dana 44 or Corporate 10-bolt axle offered on K-20/2500 models.

The 1976 K-30/3500 models also introduced the TH400 automatic transmission and 454 V-8 options to 4x4 trucks, just as today's Sierra C/K3500 trucks and Suburbans over 8500 pounds GVWR offer the 4L80E option coupled to the 454 EFI/TBI V-8. A larger frame supports the load, while the heavy duty powertrain assures owner satisfaction over the long haul.

Whether trailer pulling or lugging a camper, the 3/4-ton and one-ton models provide substantially more stamina than a 1/2-ton. This can translate as a better cooling system, much larger brakes, power options, axle gear ratios aimed at a higher GVWR and tires that can withstand the added weight. If heavy trailering is your goal, pass up the long- or short-bed 1/2-ton.

Many buyers opt for a larger truck to provide for adequate load capacity. The only downside is fuel economy, the higher cost of tires and shorter engine life if the axle gearing is much lower (numerically higher). Beyond these concerns, anyone seeking a long-bed pickup would be wise to choose a 3/4-ton model.

One-ton Only If You Mean Business

The irony of common body panels is that a C/K3500 can be purchased with the same cab and bed as a long wheelbase C/K1500. In 1955, General Motors began offering the 3200 (GMC 102) 1/2-ton models with an eight-foot bed length. Prior to 1955, a quick glance could distinguish a short-bed 3100 1/2-ton from the longer bed 3600 3/4-ton or 3800 one-ton models.

An optional long-wheelbase 1/2-ton model confuses buyers who assume that the longer bed means a massive

0014051

Fig. 2-10. Truck type synchromesh four-speed transmissions have been popular in General Motors trucks. From 1947–67, the SM420 was a rugged offering. Its successor, the SM465 (shown), is even more massive and serves through 1991 in non-Sierra models. Either of these iron-case gearboxes or the New Process 435 will deliver a maximum payload and longevity.

load capacity as it once did. Chassis capacity and bed size are separate issues. While stake beds surely give the illusion of a heavy hauling capacity, such accessory beds were often found on older 1/2-ton cab-and-chassis trucks sold for use in agricultural work.

One-ton stake and pickup bed trucks were popular in the 1939 to 1959 work truck market. As more suburban buyers bought trucks for recreational use and lighter hauling, the popularity of one-ton pickups waned in the 1960s. A Chevrolet C-30 or GMC equivalent one-ton model served mostly as a dual rear wheeled carrier for stake beds, cargo boxes, tow hoists and other special equipment. Even the new Camper Special models were based around the lighter 3/4-ton chassis.

As campers and recreational vehicle use increased in size and popularity, Chevrolet and GMC recognized the need for a massive one-ton Camper Special. The C- and K-30/3500 chassis of the 1973–87 era provided the original Doolie models that could carry a house-sized camper.

In 1976, the one-ton Doolie was available with a four-wheel drive option for the first time. This package far outstripped the features of Ford's popular Super Camper Special models. For the Doolie 4x4, a 454 V-8 option and rugged geartrain choices assured stamina. So equipped, these models can easily carry a massive camper with a mini-yacht in tow.

Today, when the load calls for maximum strength, the C/K3500 two- and four-wheel drive models provide the caliber of chassis and axle stamina that get the job done. Available in a variety of wheel bases, ranging from the ever popular 131.5-inch length common to lighter duty C/K pickups to the 168.5-inch wheelbase of the Crew Cab, the C/K3500 (single drive rear wheel or Doolie version) tops General Motors' light truck list.

If you need maximum stamina and durability coupled with the highest GVWR and GCW ratings available in General Motors light trucks, look closely at the Sierra C/K3500 models. Ride quality is outstanding, and the L65 turbo-diesel option offers maximum pulling power on a reasonable fuel budget.

0014052

Fig. 2-11. *Latest C/K3500 Sierra Doolie remains the premier hauler for a multitude of uses. For toting a massive camper or a horse trailer, here's the package. Available options blend convenience and rugged stamina. Since 1976, heavy haulers and recreationalists have taken advantage of the Doolie's superior strength and exceptionally high GVWR/GCW ratings.*

0014067

Fig. 2-12. *Once a logging contractor's favorite "crummie," the Crew Cab chassis has evolved into a multi-purpose vehicle. The latest 168.5-inch wheelbase Sierra Crew Cab comes in single or dual rear wheels and either two- or four-wheel drive. Many families find this a great way to carry a camper or drive comfortably to the ski slopes.*

The latest TBI 454 V-8 gasoline engine and 4L80E automatic transmission option delivers better fuel economy than any previous 454 light truck powertrain—but expect higher fuel costs with a gasoline hauler. If you plan to keep the truck a long time, consider the new clean-air 6.5L diesels, as fuel savings will amortize the option cost over time. Besides, you'll feel more like a "big trucker" with turbo-diesel power, especially with a trailer in tow.

2. Shopping for the Right Components

In the magazine and newspaper column questions that I field, my recommendation is always "buy the heaviest components available." While a new truck buyer can actually build a C/K Sierra truck to suit, buyers of used vehicles must understand the various packages and options available during past model years.

Shock absorber condition may not be relevant on a used vehicle purchase, as they usually need replacing. However, the presence of upgraded shocks often indicates other improvements, like a bigger sway bar diameter or heavier springs.

Likewise, a heavy duty truck four-speed transmission may also include a large diameter clutch. These kinds of options extend the lifespan of a vehicle, and a used truck buyer needs this kind of advantage. The only heavy duty option that I would avoid is a set of snow plow front springs on a 4x4—unless I planned to mount a very heavy winch or snow plow out front.

Fuel economy is a valid concern, but you need components that match your usage needs. As one example, if you want reasonable economy but plan to pull a 29-foot travel trailer up and down steep mountain passes, then an economy axle ratio, which might help when driving without a load, is both a nuisance and a hazard for towing the hefty trailer.

While towing, your truck needs maximum power and good compression braking. An economy axle will not provide either. Late model trucks with an overdrive option can deliver reasonable fuel economy in overdrive (seldom used when pulling a heavy load) while tolerating a towing or numerically lower axle ratio. If fuel economy is an issue, this kind of compromise enhances the versatility of your newer truck.

Likewise, certain components can serve better and last much longer. In the 1960s, when General Motors experienced brisk sales of pickups intended for carrying campers, a column shifted three-speed transmission was still standard on light trucks. While this transmission and a heavy duty three-speed option were reasonably durable for lighter loads, the SM420 and SM465 four-speed options afforded much higher stamina plus the added versatility of a compound low gear.

Passenger car transmission designs have haunted the truck market forever, and these include the early drum-and-cone type synchronizer three-speed gearboxes found from 1940 to the late 1960s. When I was a truck fleet mechanic, I regularly overhauled these SM318 and 319 units, which wasn't a difficult task at all. However, gear parts are very expensive now, and a truck four-speed like the SM420 in a 1/2-ton truck could outlast one of these three-speed units by three or four times. I heartily recommend an iron case SM420, SM465 or New Process NP435 gearbox. These provide a better margin of stamina than the lighter aluminum transmissions introduced in the late 1980s. The four-speed truck transmission usually comes with a heavy duty or larger diameter clutch assembly.

If a five-speed overdrive is essential, the latest heavy duty units can match the service of earlier truck four-speeds. As a rule, if a particular transmission is available with larger engines, like the 454 gas V-8 or 6.5L V-8 turbo-diesel, assume that this same transmission will hold up well behind a smaller engine.

I look for the highest torque rating available in the five-speed manual overdrive units. General Motors' very latest Heavy-Duty D-Spec (NV4500) unit is standard on C/K pickups over 8500 pounds GVWR and Crew Cabs. This unit is the first five-speed with the kind of reliability that owners of earlier trucks gained from the SM465

0014055 / 0014444

Fig. 2-13. *Five-speed overdrive transmissions of the Sierra Truck era have evolved considerably. The very latest NV4500 units that General Motors offers in high GVWR trucks are rugged all-synchromesh manual gearboxes with stamina like the earlier iron case truck four-speed transmissions.*

units. The Heavy Duty D-Spec features *two* power take-off outlets.

For automatic transmissions, the TH400 aluminum cased three-speed unit is General Motors' best design and offers rugged service. From the late 1960s onward, these units find their way into heavy duty chassis applications and trucks with an optional high output engine, like the 454 V-8. In the early 1990s, the heavy duty 4L80E over-

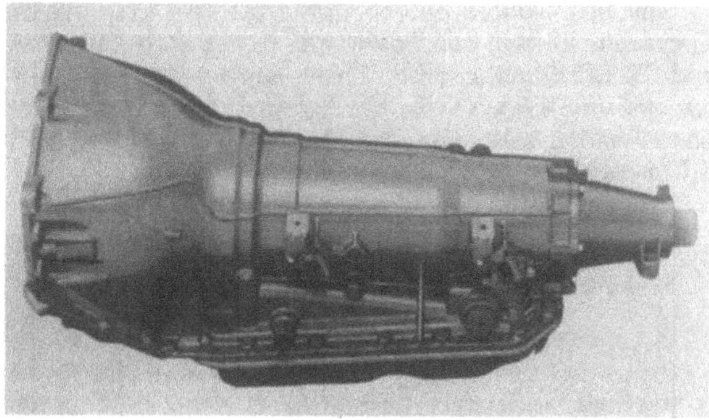

0014056

Fig. 2-14. *General Motors' TH400 (Turbo 400) aluminum cased automatic is among the most rugged light truck transmissions available. Used successfully behind 454 gas V-8s, diesel engines and in the heavy GVWR/GCW chassis, this proven design offers low maintenance and long service. The 4L80E automatic overdrive unit shown has now succeeded the TH400 for heavy-duty use. (Courtesy of General Motors)*

drive automatic came on line, a good match for TH400 reliability and stamina.

TH350 automatic transmissions were a reliable unit for 1/2-ton rated trucks and models using low horsepower output engines. The TH350 was offered extensively in 1969 to early 1980s K-10/1500 and K-20/2500 4WD models, a testimony to the unit's reliability. The Turbo 400 remains the better choice, however, for severe pulling or hauling heavy loads.

The 700R-4 automatic overdrive unit, with its evolved 4L60E design, came on line in the 1982 models and took until 1985 to reach the level of reliability that a truck deserves. This transmission has evolved into the much improved 4L60E electronically shifted unit and today enjoys wide application in lighter GVWR trucks.

> **NOTE —**
> In the chapters that address operating a truck and geartrain performance modifications, I discuss the 700R-4 at length. Some special rebuilding procedures can raise the reliability level of an early 700R-4 unit and keep it together. (See other chapters for details.)

The only time that a heavy duty chassis becomes a liability is when a unit repair or overhaul is necessary. Larger engines, transmissions and axles cost more to service than light duty units. Here the trade-off is that the heavy duty components may outlast lighter equipment by as much as 100,000 miles. Again, if a well maintained 1/2-ton and a one-ton truck carry exactly the same loads for an identical distance, the one-ton should go much further before major service is necessary.

Unless you have no need for a larger truck, find such models cumbersome to operate, or prefer the ride of a light duty GVWR, take the big truck or a model with heavy duty options. These components may cost more at the point of purchase, but they also enhance the truck's value when the time comes to sell or trade the vehicle.

The best General Motors light truck rear axles are the Corporate 14-bolt full-floater and heavy duty Spicer 60 and 70 full-floating units. These larger axles meet 3/4-ton and one-ton GVWRs. For lighter 1/2-ton trucks with semi-floating rear axles, the 12-bolt cover GM unit with 8-7/8-inch ring gear works well.

Some rare Spicer 60-35 semi-floating axles were used during the 1960s and as late as the early 1970s, primarily on GMC heavy duty 1/2-ton trucks, and these also make for good stamina and rugged service. The Spicer 44 is a rugged unit primarily used in 1955–70 GMC 1/2-ton 2WDs and both Chevrolet and GMC 4x4s.

Best Picks in Used Chevrolet and GMC Trucks

In my view, 1939 to present General Motors trucks fit into ten groups. Some divide easily by styling or chassis distinctions, while others tie more loosely into categories that consider engineering advances (or setbacks) and powertrain changes. Since several of these categories overlap, I would encourage a close look at all groups. This may help you decide which equipment will work best for your model choice.

1. 1939–46 (built into early 1947 model year) 1/2-ton (115-inch) wheelbase: Who wouldn't want one of these classic beauties? Although the technology of the 1947 Advance-Design models is far ahead of these earlier trucks, the period styling makes for a wonderful restoration project, a show stopper and Sunday driver.

2. 1947 to First Series 1955 Chevrolet 3100 (GMC 100) through 3800 (GMC 250) Advance-Design: Utility blends with aesthetic appeal in packages like the DeLuxe. I like all GMC light models for their rugged OHV inline sixes. Chevrolet comes of age with 1954 235 and 261 sixes. Stick with four-speed SM420 transmissions and choose a series/chassis that matches your GVWR needs. For serviceability, I prefer open driveline 3/4-ton models like the Chevrolet 3600 or GMC 150. Restorers and stylists generally pick the shorter wheelbase Chevrolet 3100 or GMC 100 series.

3. 1955 Second Series to 1959 Chevrolet and GMC: There isn't a bad one in the bunch! From the Chevrolet 3100/GMC 100 to Chevrolet's 3800/GMC 250 series, these may be the best pre-modern trucks built. The most popular restoration projects are the 1/2-ton 114-inch (short) wheelbase models. I like the V-8 engines for throttle response and versatility, while the inline sixes make a rugged and more economical powertrain. The field of equipment is of such quality with these model years that the issue comes down to looks and load capacity (GVWR). I've owned a brutish 1958 3600 3/4-ton capacity work truck with 4.57 gears, a 235 inline six and 6900 pounds GVWR, but for sheer aesthetic appeal or a frame-up restoration, I would pick a 1957 GMC short-wheelbase Stepside or Cameo-type Suburban Pick-Up bed model with the 347 Pontiac/GMC V-8, either a four-speed SM420 gearbox or Hydra-Matic Drive and the wraparound rear window. Toss in a NAPCO 4x4 system and I'd be even happier. Or, I would settle for Chevrolet's equivalent 3100-series Stepside or Cameo with the Turbo-Fire 283 V-8.

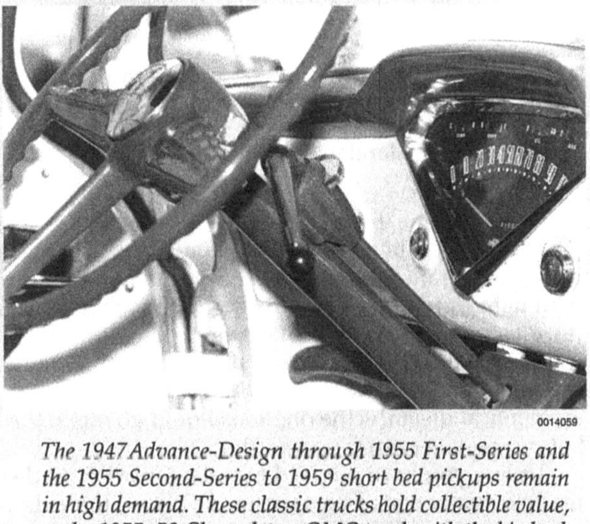

0014059

The 1947 Advance-Design through 1955 First-Series and the 1955 Second-Series to 1959 short bed pickups remain in high demand. These classic trucks hold collectible value, and a 1955–58 Chevrolet or GMC truck with the big back window and Cameo/Suburban Pick-Up type bed ranks among the most desirable.

4. 1960–66 2WD and 4WD: For rugged models, you could hardly beat these years. I bought a used one-owner 1960 GMC short-wheelbase Stepside 1000 series truck in 1971. At 90,000 miles, the 305 V-6 ran like new and produced massive torque. The 2WD independent front suspension was a marvel and in top shape. For fuel economy, however, I would opt for the Chevrolet 230 or 250 inline six or even the 283 V-8. Factory 4x4 K-models built a solid reputation for rugged service. If you want a serious day's work, avoid the two-speed Powerglide and light duty three-speed transmissions. Go for the 283 V-8 and an SM420 four-speed if possible.

5. 1967–72: The style and modest chassis changes of 1967 were less impressive than the way these models evolved. The new 4WD low chassis profile (tapered front leaf springs with a reverse arch) was a major advance. However, the closed knuckle live front end, manual or linkage-power steering and drum front brakes surely detracts from the 1967–70 models. In 1968, the 307, 327 and even the big-block 396 V-8s came on line, followed by the 350 V-8 in 1969 as a replacement for the 327. All this set the stage for the 1971 and 1972 models, which were the best of the bunch. For 4WD K-models, 1971–72 offers the best technology around: Saginaw integral power steering, an open-knuckle disc brake front axle, the SM465 four-speed or Turbo 350 automatic, vacuum assist brakes and a host of other options. The transfer case and other geartrain pieces were some of the best ever built.

6. 1973–79 C- and K-models: These years make an excellent choice in 2WD or 4x4s. Although models equipped with full-time 4x4 detract from an otherwise perfect 4x4 powertrain, even the NP203 chain drive full-time system is as rugged as any design offered today. When the K-30 4x4 Doolie came on line in 1976, the NP203 chain-drive and NP205 gear-drive cases served well. For a one-ton, my pick is the K-30/3500 from 1976–87, plus Crew Cabs

continued

The Spicer/Dana 44 is a popular solid front axle for 1/2-ton and 3/4-ton 4x4s. Ball joint pivot/open knuckle versions of the Dana 44, used from 1971 onward in General Motors light trucks with disc front brakes, offer advantages over the earlier closed knuckle units. GM 10-bolt live front axles also provide decent service in these lighter models. For one-ton K-30/3500 purposes, however, the Dana 60 front axle is the unit of choice, the heaviest duty front axle available for a light truck. Note the GVWR *per axle* and GCW rating of any truck that you might buy. Axle ratings also determine brake sizing.

through 1991. For C- and K-10/1500 1/2-ton and C- and K-20/2500 3/4-ton models, 1973–79 is a top era. 1/2-ton rear axles get lighter duty at the end of this era, so I would look for a model like the 1973 K-10 4x4, equipped with the part-time NP205 transfer case and SM465 truck four-speed. Similarly, the 1974–78 K-10/1500s make good picks, with the superior HEI electronic ignition introduced in 1975. For a tow vehicle, the C- or K-20 and C- or K-30 of this era would make top choices. Look for sway bars and integral Saginaw power steering.

7. 1980–84 Suburban K-20/2500 and K-20/2500 pickups: Those 3/4-ton 4x4 chassis with a full-floating Corporate 14-bolt rear axle make a top choice, and look for the TH400 automatic transmission, an available option for the first time in higher GVWR 3/4-ton 4x4 models built from 1981–84. Watch for the switch here, to a semi-floating rear axle beginning in 1981 3/4-ton models with lower GVWR ratings. Our 1986 Suburban K2500 4x4 had the semi-floating 14-bolt rear axle, and we retrofitted an earlier full-floater. Properly equipped with a full-floating rear axle and TH400 or SM465 transmission, a 1980–84 3/4-ton C- or K-20 model works very well.

8. 1985–87 C- and K-models: This is the end of the heavy emission era, and 1985–86 trucks suffer from pre-EFI smog controls. Our 1986 K2500 Suburban, the last carbureted 350 V-8, has 49-State emissions status and 8600 pounds GVWR. Therefore, the chassis does not require a catalytic converter. The engine has *two* air pumps and a host of other smog equipment, however, that turns a simple spark plug change into a morning project. Despite this, the truck is well built and offers wonderful towing capability plus reasonable fuel economy for its weight. If mileage is a concern, avoid the last 292 six, 4.3L V-6 and 305 V-8 with carburetion. The 350 V-8 will do better. Also, service access and fuel economy of the last carbureted 454 V-8 is poor, so hold out for a 1987 EFI model. The 6.2L diesel V-8 makes a lot of sense for these years, but only when coupled to a TH400 three-speed automatic or SM465 four-speed truck gearbox. (The 700R-4 overdrive automatic has never been my choice for anything beyond light hauling.)

9. 1988–91 C/K models: This is a mixed group, as the Sierra chassis comes on line in 1988, yet the Suburban and Blazer/Jimmy continue on the earlier chassis. Likewise, the Crew Cab C- and K-30 remain a carryover from 1987. The Sierra trucks get better each year, with geartrain stamina and upgrades in the chassis. If you want a traditional model Blazer/Jimmy or Suburban 4WD with a solid front axle, here's your last chance. EFI/TBI is a welcome addition to the entire engine lineup, as torque and horsepower begin to climb here. Go for the high GVWR chassis in any model choice. If you plan serious towing with a Suburban two- or four-wheel drive model, always buy a C- or K-2500 3/4-ton chassis.

10. 1992–up Sierra C/K chassis: IFS 4WD is here to stay. 1992 is a milestone year, with the introduction of the new C/K3500 Crew Cab, the line of Sierra based Blazer/Yukon and Suburban models, and a total commitment to the late chassis. I really like the gains in fuel efficiency and performance of the 1992 454 gas V-8 and 6.5L turbo-diesel engines. The 4L80E automatic transmission is worth the step to 8501-plus pounds GVWR. If your budget won't allow for a new truck, consider a 1992 or later C/K2500 2WD or 4WD pickup or Suburban. Any of the C/K1500 models of this era work fine if they meet your GVWR requirements. For a one-ton truck that rides like a well-balanced lighter truck and hauls a massive load without complaint, the C/K3500 Sierra chassis ranks high.

0014060

Electronic fuel and spark management has revolutionized the automotive industry. 1987 is the milestone year for General Motors' introduction of EFI in light trucks. This is the key to better fuel economy, improved performance and clean air.

0014057

Fig. 2-15. Heavy duty options cost a good deal when new. At resale, add-ons like heavy duty suspension or cooling return this value. Four-wheel drive is one option that holds high resale value over the entire life of the truck. Consider four-wheel drive an excellent investment.

For real hauling, the best new or used buys include heavy duty suspension, heavy duty factory cooling add-ons, larger brakes, a heavy duty transmission and drive axle(s), a factory chassis mounted towing package (including mirrors) and a high factory GVWR/GCW rating. Keep in mind, though, that a towing package suggests severe use, so make sure you know the history of a used truck prospect.

3. INSPECTING A USED TRUCK

As a used truck buyer, the fear of waking to a pile of scrap iron in your driveway is real. Gloomy repair expenses create anxiety about buying any used vehicle. Insight, however, can demystify the process. Add to this the promise that no matter how much you want a truck, desire won't override good judgement. This may be tough, as the search for a quality used truck often leads to junk. When you finally find a presentable piece of iron, the impulse is to buy it. That's when you must be wary.

0014061

Fig. 2-16. As a used truck buyer, you can look for hard to spot options on the build sheet of modern era trucks. These codes and descriptions can help you decide whether the truck will meet your needs. This also suggests the expectations that the original owner had for the truck.

The Chassis

The condition of the frame is the most important aspect of a used truck. You can recondition cosmetic areas and mechanical assemblies, but a twisted, broken or fatigued frame means severe trouble. Several symptoms suggest that a truck's frame has sustained damage, and I always begin looking at a used truck by crawling under it and checking for obvious signs of wear and abuse.

Damage is easy to spot: bent springs, spring hangers or frame crossmembers; torn cables or hoses; a twisted skid plate on a 4x4 or damaged frame horns at the bumper attachment points. Axle misalignment presents itself as worn tires. If you have suspicions about a truck's frame condition, suggest that the seller accompany you to a reputable frame and alignment shop. Have the frame checked for straightness on a four-wheel alignment rack.

Taking critical measurements between points on the frame will indicate whether the truck has sustained damage or suffers from fatigue and cracks. The frame specialist can also check for wear at the steering linkage, the steering gearbox, spring hangers, bushings and steering joints.

0014062

Fig. 2-17. Frame damage is a serious problem, sometimes impossible to repair safely. If in doubt about the condition of a used truck prospect, take the vehicle to a reputable frame and alignment shop for closer inspection.

Drivelines and Axles

Jack and support the truck safely off the ground, and depending upon the design of the front end, check the steering ball-joints or kingpins (called knuckle/kingpin bearings or ball-joints on a 4x4 model). Grab each front wheel at six and twelve o'clock and rock the wheel in and out. Play shows inboard of the wheels at the kingpins or ball-joints of 2WD models and the kingpin bearings or ball-joints on 4x4s.

> **NOTE —**
> Checking for IFS steering knuckle ball joint play requires unloading the coil spring or torsion bar. Place a floor jack safely beneath the lower control arm and raise the arm until both ball joints are relieved of pre-load.

On a 4x4 truck, note whether the knuckle seals, CV-joint boots (Sierra IFS type) or axle tubes leak grease or gear lube. With all trucks, check for wheel bearing looseness and any signs of damage at the wheel bearings, front and rear axles or universal joints. For 4x4 models, leaking seals and water are the primary destroyers of wheel assembly parts, steering knuckle pieces and axle components.

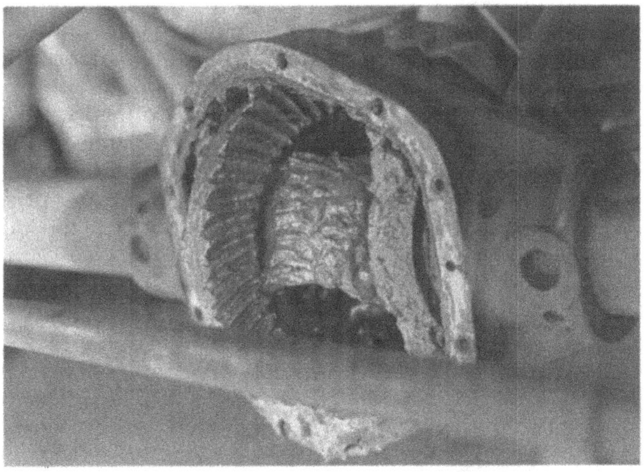

0012050

***Fig. 2-18.** Front wheel driving axle trouble can mean expensive repairs. Check for wear at steering knuckle bearings, wheel bearings and axle joints. (See service chapter for details.) Water in an axle housing can ruin expensive gears and bearings.*

Any indication of water in an axle housing, transfer case or transmission assembly should raise concern. These components make up the high cost repair areas of the geartrain.

Check for excess play at the ring and pinion gears by rotating each driveshaft back and forth. Distinguish U-joint looseness from gear problems. While driveshafts cost plenty, axle assembly overhauls are even more expensive.

When you test drive the truck, listen for whining, clunks or growling. Axle noises telegraph during acceleration, coasting and deceleration. U-joint or driveshaft play sounds like a metallic clicking or snapping noise when you change speed or jerk the throttle open and shut, especially at a steady road speed in a higher gear.

Clutch and Transmission

The clutch can be difficult to access, especially on 4x4 models. Owners often sell their truck rather than replace a worn clutch. Official flat-rate labor to replace a clutch can run in excess of five hours on some 4x4s. Add clutch parts and flywheel machining, and the job can cost as much, or more, than a good used engine.

Check the clutch by moving the transmission shifter to high gear at 20 mph. With the clutch pedal depressed, bring the engine speed to 2000 rpm, hold the throttle steady, then quickly let the clutch pedal go. Listen carefully.

If the engine speed drops immediately to a near idle, the clutch cover (pressure plate) assembly and disc are likely okay. A gradual decrease in speed usually indicates that the clutch is slipping or needs adjustment. Also make certain the clutch does not shudder during engagement.

Often the clutch needs minor adjustment, but when clutch mis-adjustment is bad enough to allow slippage, major damage is well underway. Slippage generates heat and friction, which translates as parts wear and fatigue.

Transmission woes telegraph unique noises. While test driving, listen for crunch and gear clash. In each gear, pull gently on the shifter while accelerating lightly. If the synchronizers and shifter detents are okay, you'll feel resistance in the lever. When the transmission immediately slides out of gear, suspect a weak synchronizer assembly.

Synchronizer wear also shows up on a downgrade, as deceleration causes the transmission to jump out of gear. Bearing or gear tooth wear will also cause the transmission to slip out of gear.

Automatic Transmission

An automatic transmission may slip or chatter on take-off. Harsh shifts are another sign of trouble. A shuddering sensation, much like a bad manual clutch or weak motor mounts, also means real problems. Acrid and burnt fluid, leaks or erratic shifts suggest that an automatic transmission is in bad shape.

Repairs generally involve a major overhaul. Again, tough access to some truck transmissions, especially on 4x4s, raises repair costs considerably. If you suspect automatic transmission troubles, get a transmission overhaul estimate before making an offer on the truck.

Labor to remove, overhaul and install an automatic transmission in a 4x4 truck runs upward of 10 hours. Add to this the expensive parts involved, and your used truck buy has a whole new price perspective.

CHAPTER 2

Engine

A common misconception about used vehicles is that the engine is most important. Especially on larger trucks and 4x4s, an axle, transmission or major brake system rebuild can exceed the cost of an engine overhaul. Installing a complete engine is often easier and quicker than removing and overhauling the transmission or an axle.

Before buying a used truck, you'll still want to make sure the engine is sound. An engine's basic requirements include: 1) normal and even compression, 2) accurate valve timing, 3) correct valve lift at each valve, and 4) normal bearing clearances and oil pressure. If you can borrow the truck or encourage the owner to comply, have the engine oscilloscope analyzed or tested on a chassis dynamometer.

On a scope, a quick check of dynamic compression can compare cylinder spark loads and help determine approximate compression. Check the weakest cylinder with a compression gauge or, better yet, a cylinder leakdown tester. (You will find a complete explanation of engine troubleshooting in the service chapters.)

If you find signs of overheat, look further. Excess rust or chronic boilover can indicate aeration caused by cylinder gases leaking into the cooling system from a cracked block or head casting, a blown head gasket or a defective water pump. Run a cooling system pressure test, and also check for normal coolant circulation. (See the cooling system chapter for troubleshooting details.)

0012051

Fig. 2-19. *An engine oscilloscope and leakdown tester are quick means for determining engine condition. Find weakest cylinder with scope analysis, then run a leakdown test to determine source of compression loss. (See service chapter for troubleshooting details.)*

Engine Oiling System

Engine bearing and lubrication problems are tricky to diagnose. On trucks with an oil pressure gauge, it's far easier to observe oil pressure under load. Check the consistency of the engine oil to make sure that heavy additives do not alter the oil pressure.

After the engine has set for some time, listen for knocks at cold start-up. Warm the engine completely, watching the oil pressure during this period. Drive the truck under load, up hills and such, and constantly moni-

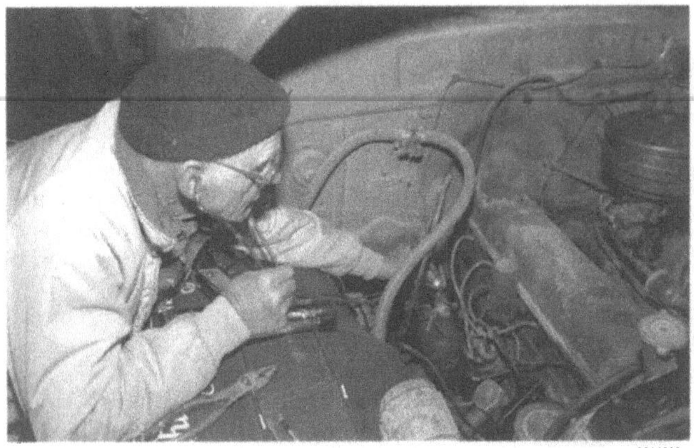

0014063

Fig. 2-20. *A stethoscope can pinpoint engine noises. If oil pressure is low or oil looks stiff, listen carefully for knocks and rattles. Thick oil or a heavy dose of additives can sometimes mask severe engine wear or damage. Here, Joe Menesini listens to his GMC 228.*

tor the oil pressure. Pressure should stay within the normal operating range over the entire test drive.

An automotive stethoscope or even a long hollow tube makes an excellent diagnostic tool for finding internal engine noises. Get used to the amplified sound, though, or the engine will resonate like a metallic thrashing machine. Learn to isolate various noises, such as the normal clicking of a mechanical fuel pump.

Isolate loose piston pin noise or a cracked piston by shorting or disconnecting each spark plug wire and seeing whether the knock is still there. Rod and main bearing noises will also decrease by eliminating spark.

If you lack the equipment or skill to do the job, consider paying a professional mechanic to check the engine, geartrain or cooling system. If you find that the truck is not in good shape, you can either negotiate a better price or consider your money well spent in that you did not buy a worn-out truck.

Body and Accessories

Sheet metal, body mounts and rubber body seals also take abuse. The effects of sun, rain, snow and salted roads beat trucks mercilessly. Rubber rots, hinges twist and windows rattle in worn channels. The degree of wear can be a measurement of the overall abuse the truck has suffered.

Radio, heater and air conditioning systems are costly and time-consuming to repair. Don't accept suggestions that the air conditioner simply needs a recharge. Ask the seller to have the system charged before you agree to buy the truck.

Belts, hoses, wiring, the battery, filters and routinely serviced items speak for the truck's maintenance. Look thoroughly under the hood, and assess the kind of replacement parts that the owner has used. Ultra-cheap parts mean a neglected truck.

Other signs of trouble are a broken speedometer and vague records of mileage. This isn't really important on a 1948 model, but it sure should color your thinking about a late 1980s truck. A lack of lube stickers, missing pedal pads, bald tires and a poor paint finish are ominous signs. You want a well-kept truck, one that received regular maintenance.

0012052

Fig. 2-21. Body rust is the most expensive and difficult of repairs. Inspect sheet metal with a magnet if you suspect that plastic filler has concealed large areas of rust or collision damage. Routing out rust and a restoration paint job can cost more than any other repair on the truck.

Pollution Controls and Vehicle Registration

Since 1971, pollution controls on light truck engines have proliferated. The emission control era started in the early 1960s with a PCV valve and closed crankcase. Then the smog pump emerged, followed by the exhaust gas recirculation (EGR) valve and evaporative systems for fumes. The mid–1970s brought on catalytic converters and unleaded fuel, and more recently, electronic fuel injection and spark management have become part of the emission program.

Smog laws, enforced by individual states and the federal government, mean that your used truck purchase must have a functional and complete OEM emission control system. If equipment is missing, non-operative or malfunctioning, you will have a problem registering the truck. Mandatory inspection programs have become common, with California serving as a model for the entire United States.

0014064

Fig. 2-22. In most states, emission control restoration is necessary for registration of a used vehicle. To pass visual inspection, all pollution control hardware must be in place, including the OEM air cleaner, correct carburetion (EFI on later engines) and approved manifolds. If you doubt the legality of a system, consult an inspection facility before buying the truck. Tune-up decal describes OEM emission hardware.

0014042

Fig. 2-23. Chevrolet and GMC Truck dealerships have access to an extensive line of truck parts, while the aftermarket and NOS sources provide both maintenance and rarer restoration pieces. Chevrolet has expanded its line of restoration parts for Genuine Chevrolet buffs who strive for authenticity.

A truck engine stripped by the previous owner of its emission hardware, or an engine transplant unauthorized by your state's smog program, means real trouble. Replacing items like original equipment intake and exhaust manifolds, smog pump, electrical and vacuum controls, catalytic converter, EGR valve and a host of other pieces can run way beyond the cost of a good used engine.

> **NOTE —**
> A modified engine with non-approved aftermarket headers, intake manifold, carburetor or EFI, air cleaner, ignition and other components is a prime candidate for failing the visual portion of an emission control test. (See emission control section for further details.)

To meet legal demands, make the seller responsible for the restoration of the smog system. Otherwise, reduce the vehicle's price to cover the equipment necessary for compliance. If you have questions about necessary equipment or its cost, get an estimate from a licensed smog shop, authorized dealership or your state motor vehicle pollution control agency before you buy the truck.

4. BUYING A NEW LIGHT TRUCK

Light trucks, once regarded strictly as utility or work vehicles, have metamorphosed from beasts of burden into modern multi-purpose transportation. Over the years, buyers and sales personnel have also changed. Years ago, truck and farm equipment sales often took place at the same outlet. Today, more car buyers find themselves first-time truck buyers at a truck dealership.

Whether or not you are new to light truck ownership, four-wheeling or recreational vehicles, you can still take charge of selecting and ordering your new truck. Buyer's remorse, due mainly to winding up with the wrong options and equipment, is too common. Everyone wants to get a good deal, yet many buyers shop for a vehicle solely on the basis of price, with only a vague sense for what equipment to buy.

Dealer showroom literature often does not explain the full range of options available, and further research is likely necessary. Truck dealers have detailed specification

0014498

Fig. 2-24. New C/K Sierra trucks have refinements and fresh styling. A GM truck can provide years of quality service and an excellent investment. Identify your needs, then tailor your new truck's equipment to meet the demand. If necessary, make a special order purchase. (Truck courtesy of John L. Sullivan Chevrolet)

and equipment ordering books, and the fleet sales manager has expertise at how to spec out a new truck.

Such order books describe far more items than you will find in glossy point-of-sale materials. A complete, factory-tailored new truck always makes better sense than hastily selecting that random "nice color" truck on the lot. For a special order, see the dealership's sales manager or fleet manager.

Selecting the Right Chassis

Veteran truck buyers learned equipment needs from pounding over highways and dirt roads with a full cargo. Four-wheelers find places where studio lamps and advertising props can't reach. Begin your truck selection by determining whether a standard chassis has enough stamina for your needs. If not, the order and pricing books describe heavy duty options that will better meet your requirements.

By reviewing the equipment listed in the dealer's order book, you can buy factory engineered and installed components that serve your needs. Understand truck chassis and suspension ratings. Even if a light duty frame and springs can support a weight of 1000-plus pounds, an axle gear ratio or transmission designed for passenger car-type fuel economy will not meet continuous hauling demands. It's not just load capacity but also the life-span of powertrain and chassis pieces that distinguish a truck's toughness.

Factory Upgrades

Boost your truck's load carrying capacity with a heavy duty spring option, heavy duty shock absorbers, a better wheel and tire combination and a trailer towing package. The cost of heavy duty OE springs is a fraction of what aftermarket springs will cost later. Remember that the manufacturer credits back the cost of standard parts when you order heavy duty factory installed upgrades.

When ordering springs, many buyers assume that if heavier is good, the heaviest available springs must be better. This is not always true, especially with full size trucks. The order catalog, for example, has traditionally listed "snow plow" front springs as an option for 4x4s. Without the massive weight of a snow plow, these stiff springs can jar your bones.

Unless you run snow plow equipment or have an overhanging load that bears heavily on the front axle, stick with the regular heavy duty suspension package. Always opt for the heaviest gear and axle components available. For full-size trucks built years ago, ordering a four-speed manual transmission was the difference between a passenger car type three-speed and a 2-ton capacity truck gearbox.

When available, a heavier front or rear axle assembly is equally valuable, and so is a heavy duty clutch or brake upgrade. When ordering these components, despite the initial added cost, you may buy years of extra service for your truck.

Heavy duty factory shocks are a must. Often, you will end up replacing worn-out standard duty shocks in 12,000 to 15,000 miles of normal on- and off-pavement

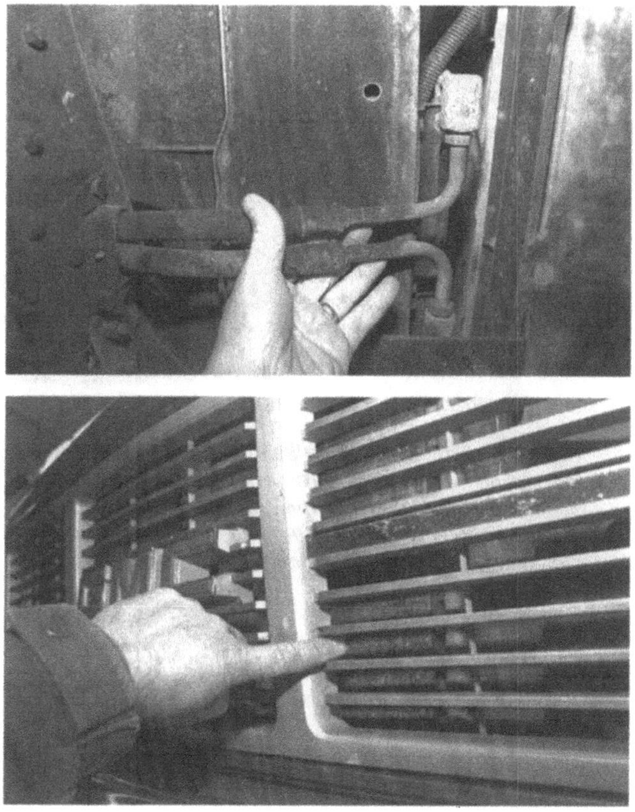

0014066 / 0014447

Fig. 2-25. Factory upgrades, like this auxiliary engine oil cooler, can enhance engine life and improve performance. Cost of such factory options is competitive with aftermarket devices. General Motors has carefully engineered these parts and their installation.

use. Another important item is an optional heavy duty anti-sway bar (front and rear if available). This will enhance cornering and stability of your truck. Often, the anti-sway bar(s), heavy shocks, heavy duty charging and upgrade cooling system come as part of the trailer towing or Camper Special package.

Engine and Transmission Choices

One of the worst fates in the aftermath of a new truck purchase is the discovery that the vehicle does not meet your towing or cargo load needs. This often occurs when you pick the wrong engine, transmission and axle ratio combination or when the pursuit of fuel economy overrides all other considerations.

Many of today's trailer towing gear ratios were considered economy ratios twenty years ago. These axles may work fine for breezing down the highway unloaded, but with a heavy camping trailer in tow, the strain is just too much. You snail crawl up grades, while serious engine or transmission damage develops. A trailer of 2500 or more pounds, if towed often, requires a larger V-8 option and heavy duty cooling for the engine and transmission.

As a rule, a lighter 1/2-ton truck chassis cannot hold up under constant trailering loads. In addition to frame and suspension shortcomings, the engine cooling capacity, braking ability, and smaller tires compromise your safety. For heavy hauling, economy must yield to a larger chassis. Turn your attention toward a 3/4-ton or larger truck with a heavy duty frame and a healthy V-8 powerplant. Opt for a C/K2500 or C/K3500 chassis. The frame, springs, brakes, axle stamina and powertrain will match your towing needs.

Check GVWR and GCW ratings carefully, and know your cargo and trailer weights before selecting a chassis package or powertrain. General Motors offers gross load guidelines for determining the right truck and necessary options.

Transmission Options

Automatic transmissions have become increasingly more popular. They sometimes meet special physical needs of drivers but most often satisfy those with no desire to work a manual transmission and clutch. During the 1980s, three-speed automatics with an overdriving fourth gear came into the truck market. The demand for fuel savings and improved gear ratios have increased the popularity of late model electronically shifted overdrive automatics.

> **NOTE —**
> Although automatics can offer good control in sand, a manual transmission and low axle ratios remain the wisest approach for downgrades and pulling massive loads.

For full-sized light trucks, the most durable manual transmissions have been iron-cased, heavy duty truck four-speed units with a compound low gear. The last General Motors light trucks to offer such gearboxes were 1991 K-5 Blazer/Jimmy and Crew Cab trucks. Today's iron-case D-Spec Heavy Duty (NV4500) overdriving five-speed can match the stamina of earlier truck type four-speed transmissions.

American trucks now offer five-speed overdrive gearboxes to maximize fuel economy. The trend has produced transmissions that serve both hauling and economy needs with a low first gear ratio, synchromesh on all forward speeds and an overdriving fifth gear for fuel savings.

Accessories for Survival

Look for factory extras that will increase your truck's life expectancy. For example, air conditioning or a heavy duty trailering electrical system may include items like a heavy duty alternator, a larger battery and harnesses for trailer wiring. Factory-installed air conditioning usually includes a heavy duty radiator and engine cooling upgrade. Again, the factory provides heavy duty options for merely the cost difference between standard pieces and these heavier components.

You can often order upgrade brakes. A heavy duty brake system may come as a stand alone option or with a towing package. Heavy duty brakes might include a heavier master cylinder, bigger vacuum booster, and even larger brake shoes, disc pads, drums or rotors.

Factory equipment must meet high quality standards. Always consider factory-installed tow hooks, tow hitch

0014499

Fig. 2-26. For 1995, the full-size Blazer gained a new badge, the "Tahoe." Available for the first time in a 4-door version, Tahoe reflects the C/K chassis and profile. The 4-door version shares the 117.5" wheelbase with the C/K pickup. GMC offers a parallel "Yukon" version.

0014500

Fig. 2-27. Although shorter than the C/K Suburban, Tahoe and Yukon 4-door models offer easy rear seat entry plus the popular rear cargo door option familiar to the Suburban. Tahoe and Yukon 4-door offers the exceptional quality and stamina expected from General Motors trucks.

assemblies and wiring harnesses. Consider tire options. A few dollars extra can provide a major gain here. Look over the factory tire options and compare them in the marketplace. Avoid getting stuck with short-lived, under-capacity standard tires. Match your new truck's tires to your turf.

Consider Special Ordering Your New Truck

Your factory authorized dealer may have just the truck you want in stock. Check the dealer's inventory first. You might get lucky and drive home immediately with a new vehicle. If, however, the stocked vehicles fall short of your needs, avoid buying someone else's truck. Ask your local dealer to trade with another dealer or special order your truck. Although it's fun to get something new while you're in a buying mood, waiting for the right truck assures years of satisfaction and pleasure. The trade-off is worth the wait.

Chapter 3

Operating Your Truck

MY APPRECIATION FOR LIGHT TRUCKS began in 1963, when our family moved to Carson Valley, Nevada. Here, surrounded by the majestic Sierras and a lesser range of desert juniper and pinion pine, sprawled fifty square miles of alfalfa fields and cattle grazing land. Criss-crossing the Valley, a host of paved and gravel roads linked the sagebrush covered foothills, broad pastures and willow-lined irrigation ditches.

Southern California, which quickly became a memory, had offered an entirely different climate and culture. By the early 1960s, a high octane freeway lifestyle flaunted factory muscle cars, vintage hot rods and surfers' woody station wagons. At Carson Valley, the principal rolling stock was trucks, and "high horsepower" meant a good cutting horse that stood fifteen hands or taller.

0014069

Fig. 3-2. As a trailer puller, hauler or recreational vehicle, your properly equipped General Motors truck has plenty of personality. Make a place in your family photo album for this rig. The C/K Sierra Suburban makes an ideal trailer puller.

1. LIVIN' IN TRUCK COUNTRY

Carson Valley was surely truck country, the kind of terrain and inclement weather that sharpens wits and compels good driving skills. During the 1960s, when harsh winters froze the ground hard and mean Sierra storms threatened livestock, pickup and stake bodied trucks lugged implements and hauled bales of cattle fodder.

By early summer, when the first hay cuts came, the ranchers and their trucks labored even harder. The scorching heat of August had a rancher up before dawn, often weary by mid-morning, and headed for Minden to get a friendly cup of coffee at the pharmacy next to the Post Office. Here their pickups lined up, cattle racks looped with twine ropes, the tube-type traction tires caked with mud. Two- and four-wheel drives, these iron workhorses helped raise productivity, ferried bulky goods and battled the seasonal challenges of high altitude cattle country.

0014068

Fig. 3-1. Sunrise Pass, old abandoned minesites and wild horses characterize the Pine Nut Range, where I first four-wheeled. In the mid-1960s, Chevrolet and GMC 4x4s rode high on leaf springs and solid driving axles. Here is our 1973 K-10 4x4 on a re-visit to the wild horse haunts in 1980.

Behind the Wheel

I started high school during the heyday of the 1960s Muscle Car Era. Although I took my first driving test in our family's CJ-5 Jeep, my first car was a 1955 Chevrolet Model 150 two-door coupe. The Jeep satisfied my growing outdoor recreational interests, while the Chevy held the promise of an honorable place in the school parking lot.

Many Douglas High School kids, especially those whose families owned big cattle ranches, drove high performance cars. The mid-1960s was an era of ultra-high octane and Nevada's "basic speed law," which we tested thoroughly with the likes of 409, 396 and 427 big-block Chevys and Ford 406 and 427 powered cars. Even in a rural ranching community, cars were fashionable while trucks were best left for ranch work, hunting and exploring back country.

I knew trucks well and serviced plenty of them in my after school and summer service station job. At the time, however, I preferred tuning the warm small-block 265 V-8 transplant in my Chevy coupe to cleaning an oil bath air cleaner or greasing kingpins in a 216 six powered Stovebolt Chevy truck.

As a light and medium duty truck fleet mechanic a few years later, the muscle car mania of the early and mid-1960s served as a great ground school for my craft. The intensity of interest in cars during that era heightened my appreciation for quality technology. Chevrolet

Fig. 3-3. Cattle country at Western Nevada's high valleys offers majestic views, bitter winters and hot, dry summers. General Motors light trucks serve ranching community life well. Rugged 4x4s remain the most popular models.

and GMC trucks were also drawn along by the Muscle Car Era. Performance took on a broad meaning for both car and truck owners by 1969. Ultimately, my experience at high performance automotive work served well in the preventive care and overhaul of trucks. Around trucks, I felt my rural roots.

More Modern Truckin'

I have owned, worked on or tested an enormous number of trucks. As a recreationalist, truck fleet mechanic, heavy equipment operator and automotive journalist, I've driven full-size trucks built by Jeep, International Harvester, Chevrolet, GMC, Ford, Dodge and even Studebaker.

As a mechanic, I worked on a fleet that included several General Motors trucks. A number of 3100-Series 1955–59 models, a 1960 10-Series and a 1949 GMC stake bed 450 with a 270 OHV inline six were notable. These trucks had ultra-reliable chassis and powertrains, and even with high mileage, they revealed why General Motors trucks were so popular. No mechanic had a better training ground than these models, as they were fundamental, simple to work on and responded readily to preventive service procedures.

By the mid-1970s, my personal truck was a 1970 short-wheelbase Chevrolet K-10 4x4 with a Turbo 350 automatic and 350 V-8. Power steering and brakes were a real step forward from my 1960 GMC 1000-Series short Stepside bed model that preceded this truck. While I will never forget the GMC 305 V-6's massive torque (nor the 34-quart cooling system!), the K-10 was my first feel for the many benefits of newer truck technology.

I would, however, consider our later 1973 K-10 4x4 as my first modern truck. A modest Custom trim level, the short-wheelbase Fleetside bed pickup had the 350 V-8, power steering and power assisted disc front brakes, the SM465 truck four-speed manual transmission and the gear drive NP205 transfer case.

Fig. 3-4. The later 235 Chevy truck six, built from 1954–62, was a popular and rugged engine. My 1958 3600-Series work truck had well over 180,000 miles on the odometer before oil blew past the rings. A teardown revealed 0.017-inch taper on the worst cylinder, yet the engine had just managed a 1700 mile trip from Nevada to Colorado and back.

Ironically, the 1973 K-10 had 90,000 miles on the odometer when we bought it. That truck was with us for four years, eventually accumulating a total of 142,000 miles, and *nothing* failed. I am a staunch advocate of preventive maintenance, tuning the engine regularly, and at 120,000 miles, I became nervous about the clutch. We had pulled maximum GCW loads on several household

Fig. 3-5. In my estimation, the chassis, powertrain and geartrain of our 1973 Chevrolet K-10 rank to this day as the most rugged of any half-ton capacity 4x4 ever built. The basic platform/design survived to 1991 in K-5 Jimmys and Blazers and the Suburban K-models.

moves, but to my surprise, the clutch disc still had plenty of service life left.

We'd still be pining over our decision to sell that truck, however, our present 1986 Suburban K2500 4WD with nine-passenger seating, front and rear air conditioning and the plush Sierra Classic package has surely been a pleasure to own and highly reliable.

Keeping your General Motors truck alive and operating well depends upon regular service. The service chapters of this book share many of the techniques that I acquired while maintaining General Motors light trucks. That experience fostered an appreciation for original equipment quality replacement parts and regular, preventive-type maintenance. Such an approach will help your truck's powertrain and chassis deliver maximum service and value.

Equally important, the ways in which you use and operate your truck will determine the degree and quality of service possible. I believe that true "lemons" are virtually non-existent among General Motors truck models, although any production vehicle can require warranty repairs—or even a recall for a potential safety hazard or mechanical shortcoming.

Fig. 3-6. Again, I found a pristine pre-owned truck with relatively high mileage (74,000) on the odometer. With an 8600-pound GVWR rating, our 1986 GMC Suburban's original 350 V-8, TH400 automatic transmission and 3/4-ton 4x4 chassis still work wonderfully at over 100,000 miles.

Fig. 3-7. Use of OEM quality replacement parts is one assurance that your General Motors truck will deliver maximum performance over a long service life.

A General Motors Truck and Your Lifestyle

Beyond their notable work skills, two- and four-wheel drive trucks complement an active lifestyle. Individually suited for family recreation, foul weather security and off-pavement chores, General Motors light truck models have many talents. Operated within their broad design limits, the powertrain and chassis can deliver many years of dependable service.

In our family, the children have grown up with various pickup trucks and sport utility vehicles. 4x4s have been the family's access to hunting, fishing, hiking, firewood and some of North America's most rugged and picturesque back country. As a Search-and-Rescue volunteer, my 4x4 vehicles also serve the local community.

Trucks hold a special place in our household. As a source of recreation and cornerstone for wholesome family fun and community involvement, four-wheel-drive trucks have served us particularly well. A General Motors truck, whether new or a good used model, can provide you and your family with a rich outdoor life and year around motoring.

2. LEARNING TO DRIVE YOUR GENERAL MOTORS TRUCK

Although technology has changed both the appearance and comfort level of light trucks, operating techniques remain much the same. Especially with 4x4 models, irregular road surfaces have always posed a challenge. Although knowing your truck's equipment and controls proves important, understanding its handling characteristics is of even greater concern.

Light trucks, designed to carry a cargo, generally suffer from poor weight distribution. Running empty, the back end of your truck may feel loose and unpredictable on icy, wet or muddy roads. Fortunately for General Motors trucks, the overall curb weight is substantial, which offsets these liabilities to a degree.

If your truck handles strangely, first rule out any chassis-mechanical or tire related problems. (See the service chapters of the book for details.) You may find the root of your concern by running the vehicle over a set of truck

0014076

Fig. 3-8. A higher center-of-gravity and stiff spring rates characterize most light trucks. With the bed empty, weight bias shifts toward the front, leaving a lightened rear end susceptible to spinout on icy, off-camber highways. Under such road conditions, the rear axle can slip sideways and start the spin. Without a cargo, a positive traction rear differential can exaggerate these side-slip tendencies.

scales to determine the weight on each axle. Figure the weight distribution.

Since light weight at the back of a truck can become trouble, many owners install a shell (cap or canopy) or permanently store useful items in the bed. A tool box is another method for adding ballast to better distribute weight.

During winter months, some owners carry an extra load in the bed, items like snow chains or even sacks of aggregate rock laid above or rearward of the axle. A heavy step rear bumper also helps. Late model General Motors C/K trucks have anti-lock brakes, which dramatically reduce the risk of spinout and dangerous loss of directional stability when braking hard with a light load. Beyond this, you need to familiarize yourself with the handling characteristics of the truck.

Not a Camaro Z-28

Driving a full-size GM truck can be fun, however, truck and car handling differs dramatically in the areas of center-of-gravity, weight distribution and suspension responsiveness. As a result, your truck cannot respond or handle like a well tuned car suspension.

The need to carry a substantial cargo over rough roads, which requires a relatively long wheelbase, means that truck bodies ride higher than a car. With the body mounted above a driveable chassis (ladder frame), the cab and bed ride considerably taller than a car. For ground clearance and wheel travel, the light truck's ladder frame rides higher than a car's frame or unibody.

Larger diameter tires, a higher frame and body height, and a powertrain that rides further above the ground mean that a General Motors truck, like any other vehicle in this class, has a higher center-of-gravity. In simple terms, this translates as more vulnerability to roll over, although the GM full-size trucks' relatively wide wheel track width helps offset risk to a degree.

Coupled with the higher center-of-gravity is a spring package designed for a cargo hauler. The high load capacity means that the truck's springs are stiffer than a car's, especially when the truck has no cargo. As a consequence, trucks respond much differently on corners. Simply put, the cornering ability, resistance to roll over, likelihood of spinout, ability to drift, lateral force reaction or any other automotive handling yardstick will find that trucks handle differently than cars.

Moreover, a given truck will even handle differently when loaded or unloaded. Be aware of these factors when orienting yourself to a light truck. When you can predict the handling of your truck under a wide variety of driving circumstances, loads and tire types, you will find comfort in the fact that a GM truck can be as stable as any other light truck in its class.

0014078

Fig. 3-9. Compared to a Camaro or Firebird/Trans Am, a C/K pickup has a robust chassis and much stouter components. In a tight corner, however, the Z-28 or Trans Am squats low and hugs the road. Higher center-of-gravity, stiffer springs and tall chassis height give the truck an unfair disadvantage. Most 4x4 models ride even higher than their 2WD truck counterparts.

Two- Versus Four-wheel Drive

Two- and four-wheel drive trucks also handle differently. Most 4x4 GM trucks ride higher than comparable 2WD models, with a higher center-of-gravity and even more awkward weight distribution. The front wheel drive system places additional weight forward of the truck's midline, while the need for ground clearance demands a taller ride height.

Pre-1967 K-model 4x4s have very high ride heights, and these trucks, naturally, are more susceptible to handling quirks and roll over. 4x4 light trucks of that era epitomize the high center-of-gravity issue. For these models, an increase in track width can, to a degree, offset the obvious safety risk of a high center-of-gravity. (See chapters on suspension modifications and tire/wheel changes.)

Another concern is the use of a tall cabover-type camper. Camper Special and trailering packages use increased spring rates, add axle capacity and even provide necessary stabilizer bars for handling the extra load. Cabover campers radically alter the roll center and center-of-gravity of a truck. Added safety equipment is a must.

0014079

Fig. 3-10. 1960–66 General Motors K-model 4x4s represent the classic trucks of the "high-boy" era. Note tall frame height and low hanging transfer case.

If you decide that a cabover camper is a necessity, use caution when driving with a full load. Allow adequate stopping distances, take corners at reasonable speeds and observe road conditions. Avoid crisis situations that demand fast moves—such maneuvers could end in a roll over. (See suspension and accessories chapters for tips on trailering or hauling a heavy cargo or camper.)

Whether your GM light truck has two- or four-wheel drive, the driving techniques for four-wheeling can help any truck operator. For this reason, I have devoted the balance of the current chapter to 4x4 and off-pavement driving concerns. Owners of two-wheel drive trucks will find much of this information relevant.

4x4 and Off-pavement Driving

The main difference between a 4x4 truck and a rear drive two-wheel drive truck or automobile is the live front axle and transfer case. In addition to the customary brake, accelerator and clutch controls, a 4x4 truck's transmission and transfer case have separate shift levers.

Although shifters for four and five-speed manual transmissions come through the floorboard, trucks equipped with an automatic or light duty three-speed transmission usually have column shift controls. The 4x4 transfer case requires a control, which usually provides modes for high range, low range and two- or four-wheel drive.

Since 1960, manually shifted GM K-model 4x4s have utilized a single lever for the transfer case. Every K-model built from 1960 to the present has featured a two-speed transfer case/power divider. The low range mode in four-wheel drive adds versatility and exceptional pulling power.

The single stick transfer case control modes include 2WD high, 4WD high, neutral and 4WD low ranges. Neutral mode on earlier units can operate a Power Take Off (PTO) component of the transfer case. Those 1973–79 K-models equipped with the NP203 full-time 4x4 system offer 4WD high, 4WD low, 4-high-lock and 4-low-lock modes to serve various driving conditions.

Operating a 4x4 K-model Truck

Two-wheel drive high range is much like driving a comparable two-wheel drive GM truck. Power flows only to the rear axle, and the transfer case operates at a 1:1 ratio. The rear driveshaft spins at the same speed as the transmission output shaft.

In 4WD high or high-lock range, both the front and rear driveshafts spin at the same speed as the transmission output shaft. High range 2WD is useful for hard surface highways and most civilized driving conditions. In high range, the front or rear drive axle gear ratio, multiplied by the first (or compound low) gear ratio, will determine the overall reduction ratio.

0014448

Fig. 3-11. In 1967, General Motors lowered the 4x4 K-models with a modified chassis design and use of reverse arch, progressively rated (tapered) front leaf springs—an industry first.

0014080

Fig. 3-12. For safety's sake and powertrain survival, consult your GM truck owner's handbook or the 4WD instruction decal located in the cab for directions on operating the four-wheel drive system. This is a complex gear mechanism with very expensive components. General Motors knows what your truck's geartrain will tolerate.

NOTE —
To appreciate the lowest gear ratio available with a two-speed transfer case, multiply the transfer case low range ratio by the lowest gear (first or compound low) ratio in the transmission. Now multiply this number by the front or rear axle ratio. This is the overall reduction ratio in low range.

When in four-wheel drive high or low range, your truck offers substantially better traction, with the front axle pulling while the rear axle pushes the truck. 4x4 powertrains, however, with the exception of full-time 4x4 systems in non-lock mode, cannot tolerate four-wheel drive use on hard surfaced roads. Here, front axle pull and rear axle push will not take place in full synchronization, and the result is gear bind. This condition, characterized by a frozen transfer case lever or free-wheeling hubs, can damage the powertrain. (On 1973–79 NP203 full-time 4x4 units, a differential system within the transfer case can prevent gear bind, and you get the benefit of four-wheel drive use on all surfaces.)

Front axle engagement on hard surfaced roads also affects steering. The axle shafts transmit torque, which jacks the steering assemblies as the front wheels strive for traction. On a loose surface road, these problems are

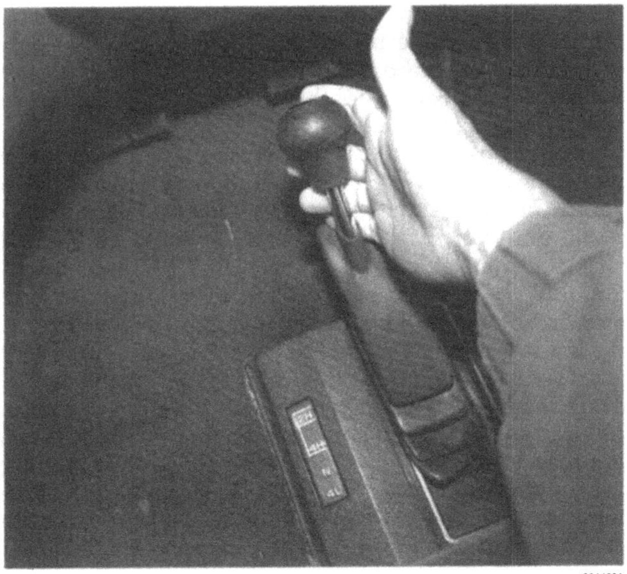

0014081

Fig. 3-13. Traditional part-time 4x4 transfer case shift positions include 2-High, 4-High, Neutral, 4-Low. (Shift patterns may vary on your late truck.) Become familiar with these modes and their locations. For safety's sake, know how to shift into any position without looking at the floorboard or knob.

seldom noticeable. Dirt, snow, mud or ice provide the necessary margin of slip for four-wheel drive operation.

All GM K-model trucks with part-time 4x4 have a two-wheel drive mode for running on hard surfaces. Preserving your powertrain means using four-wheel drive only when the road surface will allow some degree of slip. This also limits use of 4WD low range to ice, snow, mud and off-pavement surfaces.

On short, steep pavement pulls like a boat ramp, I use 4x4 mode as a means of moving the trailer. Since the pull is straight, risk of gear bind is minimal. At the top of the ramp, on flat ground, I relieve bind by rocking the truck gently forward and back as I shift the transmission from reverse to drive (forward gear) and then neutral. With the transmission in neutral, I move the transfer case shifter to 2WD mode, then turn hubs to FREE.

If your truck has an automatic transmission and you use 4WD low range on a boat ramp, first rock the truck, then stop completely and place the transmission shifter in PARK mode. You can now move the transfer case shifter from 4WD Low to 2WD High range. By contrast, if you place an automatic transmission in neutral after rocking the truck, the transmission output shaft will begin to spin when you move the transfer case shifter through its neutral range. Spinning gears will cause severe gear clash as you move the transfer case shifter to a driving range.

Free-wheeling Front Hubs

Most 4x4 trucks spend the majority of their service life on the highway or well graded gravel roads. The front axle assembly on a part-time 4x4 system seldom sees use. Here, free-wheeling hubs can reduce wear at the front axle shafts, U-joints and the differential assembly.

The first K-model 4x4s came without free-wheeling hubs, and unless the dealer or an owner installed aftermarket hubs, the front axle shafts, differential and front driveshaft spun and created fuel robbing drag for the life of the truck.

Now a common component on 4x4s, free-wheeling hubs reduce parts wear and increase fuel economy. If your truck has manual free-wheeling hubs, use the FREE mode while in two-wheel drive for sustained periods.

In the early 1980s, many truck models introduced the use of automatic locking hubs that engage when you shift to 4WD mode, either high or low range. As the torque flows to each front wheel, the hub assembly has an internal clutch mechanism that automatically locks the hub. In this mode, the hub functions much like a conventional (manual) hub in LOCK position. An exception are those automatic hub designs that fail to provide compression braking and simply free wheel on downgrades.

Although automatic locking hubs eliminate the need for manual operation, they do require backing up the truck to disengage the lock mechanisms. When road conditions once again permit use of 2WD mode, you must stop the truck, make sure the transfer case is in 2WD mode, then back the truck up (usually fifteen feet) to disengage the automatic hubs.

Shifting a 4WD Transfer Case

During intermittent icy highway conditions, you can leave your manual or automatic locking hubs in lock mode. During stretches of hard-surfaced road, simply shift out of front axle drive mode (4WD) with the transfer case lever. When the mountain pass or snow zone is past,

0014082

Fig. 3-14. During foul weather, leaving hubs in LOCK mode with the transfer case in 2WD will permit easy engagement of 4WD high range as road conditions worsen. On occasion, engaging the free-wheeling hubs for a few miles is actually valuable. This will lubricate parts, keep seals from becoming brittle and reduce the risk of condensation buildup in the axle housing.

stop the truck, make certain the transfer case is in 2WD mode, and either manually unlock your front hubs or, if equipped with automatic locking hubs, safely back your truck up.

Later model transfer cases have shift-on-the-fly. These gear units allow you to move from 2WD high to 4WD high without effort. *Under no circumstance, however, can you shift any transfer case to low range without stopping the vehicle.* Although some transfer cases will tolerate engagement of low range gears at a very low vehicle speed, the best way to engage low range is at a complete stop.

> *WARNING —*
> *Slow down first before downshifting between transmission gears in low range. The low range gear reduction will exaggerate the speed drop between gears. The result is like slamming on the brakes.*

For engaging the front axle drive at any speed, you will find that unloading torque from the gears helps ease the shift. If your truck has a manual transmission, you can leave the transmission in gear and momentarily depress the clutch pedal. Move the transfer case lever from 2WD high to 4WD high as if you were shifting gears in the transmission. For automatic transmission models, leave the transmission in drive range, but release the throttle as you pull the transfer case lever from 2WD to 4WD high range.

Consult your GM truck owner's handbook or the instructional decals before engaging low range 4WD. An automatic transmission will require placing the transmission in neutral or park range before you move the transfer case lever to 4WD Low Range. Otherwise, the transmission will spin the gears at speed as the transfer case shift lever passes through its Neutral mode. Severely abusive gear clash will result if you attempt to engage the low range gears while the transfer case input shaft spins.

When to Use Four-wheel Drive

Faced with the perils of sleet and dropping temperatures, owners appreciate their 4x4 trucks. When the highway surface is wet, temperatures continue to drop, and it's still a few degrees above treacherous black ice, the time is right to lock your manual hubs.

Early readiness is your best hedge against trouble. Lock your hubs before visibility decreases and traffic begins to stagger. Leaving the pavement when the visibility worsens could cause a wreck. The driver of the next vehicle might see your brake lamps, misinterpret your motive for leaving the road and overreact by making a dangerous move.

If the weather clearly calls for ice and snow, lock your manual hubs before you leave home. You can drive for many miles with the hubs locked and the transfer case in 2WD high range without damaging the front axle system.

When I was a heavy equipment operator, I once drove from Carson City, Nevada to Jackson, California over Carson Pass in my 1970 Chevy K-10. Reports called for a severe late winter storm, more likely a blizzard. I engaged the truck's manual hubs at the eastern base of the Sierras and left them in LOCK until the 2,000 foot level on the west side, some ninety miles later. Snow was four inches deep on the pavement at Hope Valley and over twelve inches deep across the road at the summit. There was no parking turnout in sight.

With hubs locked, you can engage 4WD high range while moving. As highway conditions worsen, or if a stretch of ice lies ahead, engage 4WD and stay in this mode until you pass the hazard. At that point, simply shift the transfer case lever back to 2WD high mode. You'll likely repeat this procedure several times on long stretches of intermittent ice, snow and dry pavement.

If a dry, straight section of pavement lasts for a very short spell (1/8th mile or less), I leave the transfer case in 4WD mode, stay very light on the throttle to reduce torque application and work the steering carefully. When the road is straight, geartrain stress and risk of binding are minimal. I believe that under these conditions, shifting the transfer case in and out of 4WD places far more strain on components and creates unnecessary demands for the driver.

3. Off-pavement Four-wheel Drive

When the pavement ends and the dirt begins, consider your truck's traction needs. Since a softer roadway allows some slip and eliminates the risk of gear bind, it's wise to engage your hubs, whether you're using 4WD mode or not. Spinning the front axle system places a light load on the powertrain, while the benefit of locking the hubs is that four-wheel drive is available at the flip of the transfer case lever.

Commonly, before entering a gravel trail, four-wheelers will lock the hubs and drop tire pressures for increased traction and to lessen chassis bounce on irregular road surfaces. Lowered tire pressures can also reduce risk of tread and sidewall damage from rocks.

Many four-wheelers, however, get carried away with airing down tires. Each tire design and vehicle load has a minimum safe inflation pressure. Lower pressures also increase the risk of unseating the bead. Unseating a bead or driving with severe sidewall flexing can ruin your expensive tires or cause tire failure and loss of control.

My rough guideline for airing down is that a tire with a 32 to 35 psi maximum load pressure will tolerate no lower than 22 to 24 psi pressure, and this for only short distances at slow speeds. As pressure drops, so does a tire's load capacity. You trade greater traction for higher heat buildup and more risk of tire fatigue and failure. (See tire details in other chapters.)

Concentrate on good driving habits and minimize your wheelspin. Wheelspin loses traction, places tires at risk and can cause environmental damage. Good driving techniques will take your truck much further than excessively low tire pressures.

The number one cause of environmental damage, and the clearest sign of an inexperienced four-wheeler, is unnecessary tire spin. Your best traction is a tire tread surface that makes full contact with the road. You can minimize wheelspin by reducing throttle pressure or shifting to a higher gear in the transmission. This will apply less torque to the wheels and lessen the likelihood of tire spin.

0014083

Fig. 3-15. "Airing down" is common vernacular for off-pavement trail runners. While ride and traction improve, airing down reduces load carrying capacity. Dropping pressures to run in sand makes sense, however, always air back up to normal when you've passed the hazards. Re-check pressures when tires are cold. (See Chapter 18, Suspension, Wheel, and Tire Upgrades.)

WARNING —
A spinning tire is dangerous. General Tire suggests, "AVOID excessive tire spinning when your vehicle is stuck in snow, mud or sand. Never exceed 35 mph indicated on the speedometer. The centrifugal forces generated by a free spinning tire/wheel assembly may cause a sudden tire explosion resulting in vehicle damage and/or serious personal injury. Use a gentle backward and forward rocking motion to free your vehicle for continued driving. Never stand near or behind a tire spinning at high speed while attempting to push a vehicle that is stuck."

The Terrain

Terrain dictates when to use four-wheel drive. Experience teaches that it's always better to engage 4WD before entering a hazard than once you commit your truck. Negotiating mud and snow requires steady pulling traction, and stopping in the middle of a muddy trail courts disaster. Trying to regain traction can result in spinning tires and damage to a fragile environment. Wherever possible, keep moving while minimizing tire spin and chassis bounce.

The Steepest Hills

If the trail gets rocky or steep and your truck begins bouncing, it's time for low range. Low range will reduce throttle effort and drastically lower the vehicle's speed. The gear reduction in low range will allow your vehicle to idle through rocky or rough stretches.

In 4WD high range, your truck might idle at 3 to 5 mph in first gear. Placing the transfer case in low range would drop speed to nearly one mile per hour. This allows far more control of the truck and reduces risk of damage. Low range stopping and starting is also simpler, especially on inclines. Use of lighter throttle pressure and less braking action reduce risk of wheelspin or dangerous skidding.

When top speed on a rough trail is 10 to 20 miles per hour, I place the transfer case in low range 4WD and leave it there. This allows use of all forward transmission gears to keep up with the crowd and also provides crawl speeds and excellent compression braking for moving slowly through rocky obstacles. This is the key to a long service life for your truck.

NOTE —
When you downshift between transmission gears in low range, slow down first. The low range gear reduction will exaggerate the speed drop between gears, and the result is like slamming on the brakes.

Low range is a valuable braking mechanism. When facing a very steep decline, select the transmission gear that will control your truck's speed. Always minimize the use of wheel brakes on slick or poor traction surfaces. If a

0014084

Fig. 3-16. Shift to 4WD and low range before driving up steep hills. At slow speeds, low range will provide more control and be able to reduce speed to a crawl pace on descents. Low range will drastically reduce use of brakes.

wheel(s) lock up with application of the brakes (which they do readily on ice or sand covered granite boulders), skidding will result. Approach deep sand like you would ice: if you need to slow down, apply the brakes lightly, with a gentle pumping action. Do not lock the wheels.

The best traction is a tire that continues to rotate. At the slowest imaginable speeds, in low range first gear, your 4x4 truck's tires can still provide traction over the entire area of the tread surface. If possible, avoid skidding. Keep your tires rotating under engine compression braking to provide the highest percentage of traction.

The reduction ratio of low range also provides exceptional pulling power. Assuming that your truck can get traction, 4WD low range will permit even the most modestly powered six-cylinder 4x4 K-model, which by itself weighs over 4,000 pounds, to move a stalled 8,000 lb. flatbed truck. Pulls like freeing a vehicle from a ditch can easily be performed if your 4x4 can get traction.

If you need to move a heavy vehicle for more than a few feet, avoid using 4WD lock mode on a hard surfaced road. Never hook the chain or strap to a trailer ball, driveshaft, spring hanger, steering components or an axle housing that has brake pipes or hoses running along its surface.

There are many situations where four-wheeling is unsafe or will cause damage to the environment. When your 4x4 truck totters on the edge of disaster, winching is far more practical than driving. A properly angled winch cable can function as both the motive force and an anchor for your delicately balanced truck. If losing traction means poor vehicle control, use a winch. (See winching instructions in the accessories chapter.)

Uphill and Downhill

Negotiating steep hills causes more adrenaline flow than any other four-wheel drive maneuver. Angles, especially downslopes, appear distorted and ominous. This is just as well, as the real threat of losing control on a descent deserves all of your attention. When going uphill in four wheel drive, the front wheels claw for traction and tend to pull your truck into line. Downward, these same wheels want to skid, slip sideways and search awkwardly for traction.

On ascents, minimize wheelspin. When descending, use the correct gear to minimize skidding and the need to apply your truck's brakes. Moderation has never had a better mentor than four-wheeling.

In rough and angled terrain, excess movement courts disaster. Oversteering and understeering can cross the vehicle up at just the wrong moment. On both ascents and descents, if your truck loses directional stability, the risk of roll over increases.

WARNING —

- *Never drive sideways across a hill. If side tilt overcomes your truck's roll center and center-of-gravity, the vehicle is likely to turn over.*

- *If your 4x4 turns completely sideways on a steep sideslope, prepare to roll over. Always wear a seatbelt/harness and install a full roll cage if you intend to climb risky slopes. If you must get out of the vehicle, do so only on the uphill side.*

0014086

Fig. 3-17. *When approaching an uphill section or downslope, line the truck up squarely and avoid driving sideways across the hill. Driving sideways on a slope is a rollover about to happen. Stay straight and move steadily.*

If you find your truck beginning to turn sideways on a loose traction downslope, keep your foot off the brake pedal. Steer into the skid, as if the vehicle were on ice or snow. If timely, accelerate very gently to pull the vehicle straight. Either of these techniques requires nerves of steel, acute sensitivity and your conviction that the truck cannot straighten out any other way.

Hair-raising Hill Climb Techniques

During the 1960s, four-wheeling competitive events became popular. Organized hill climbs attracted large crowds, and the winning formula was traction, torque and solid driving skill. Typically, a 4x4 needed enough muscle to claw its way up a rocky shale slope. Exotic traction tires and axle locking devices increased the chances of a win. Here, many of us learned the finer points of high-horsepower traction.

Most hill climb courses were remarkably steep. In some of my archival photos from that era, course judges stand with one leg a foot and a half higher than the other, leaning into the hillside to stay upright. Walking these hills was nearly impossible. Most slopes were simply crude cuts made by a D-8 Caterpillar tractor at its maximum slope angle. Some courses were even more primitive.

Modified short wheelbase Jeeps, Scouts, early Broncos and an occasional Blazer/Jimmy or 4x4 pickup screamed at redline as they charged the hill. The winner was, simply, the truck in each class (four-cylinder, six-cylinder or V-8) that reached the highest point on the hill.

Axles, clawing through paddle tires and spinning mercilessly, grabbed what meager traction the rocky hillside could furnish. Judges leaped out of the path of airborne 4x4s that left the ground under full power, landing forty feet off the course with their nose ends still aimed uphill. Often, with the engine throttled wide open as the tires bit, the frame jerked into line, gaining the truck an even greater height on the hill.

The risk of getting sideways was extreme. Of all the driving techniques I gleaned from these hill climbs, the most significant was how to maintain control of a 4x4 that loses traction while climbing a steep slope. The trick is a rapid shift to reverse gear before backing down, then descending under compression braking while avoiding the use of hydraulic wheel brakes.

This is a critical maneuver that demands quick hands and feet. As soon as the truck reaches its furthest point on

0014090

Fig. 3-18. Competitive hill climbs and sand drags demand nerves of steel and lightning reflexes. High horsepower drag racing in loose sand requires four-wheel drive. At Sand Lake, Oregon, this vintage General Motors 4x4 pickup takes on a major competitor.

the hill and traction becomes futile, you must depress the clutch pedal quickly, simultaneously shift the transmission to reverse and release the clutch pedal before the truck starts to roll backward.

Timing is all important. If you miss reverse and the transmission is in neutral, you will roll backward out of control. (The non-synchromesh reverse gear in a manual transmission will not permit a shift to reverse with the truck moving.) Stuck in neutral, the only option is to use the brakes. Applied on a steep and loose slope, the brakes want to lock the wheels, which usually throws the truck into a skid. This can swing the vehicle sideways into a roll over.

The important steps are to: 1) shift your manual transmission to reverse just as the truck peaks its forward momentum, 2) release the clutch pedal immediately and steer straight backward with the engine idling, and 3) rely on engine compression braking with minimal, if any, application of the wheel brakes. These steps must take place in rapid succession, and if your coordination and the engine tune is right, the truck's engine should keep the tires creeping in reverse.

WARNING —
Competitive 4x4 hill climbing is a hazardous sport. Damage to your vehicle and personal injury are real possibilities. Like other forms of competition, rules and safety regulations apply. Never attempt these competitive maneuvers without the benefit of a full roll cage, approved safety equipment, emergency medical personnel, close supervision and full acceptance of the risks involved.

Pitfalls of an Automatic Transmission

Four-by-four hill climbs place trucks with automatic transmissions at a disadvantage. Although a torque converter helps multiply torque for successful hill and sand assaults, backing down slopes with an automatic in reverse can prove hazardous. With the engine idling or stalled, the torque converter slips, acting much like neutral. This encourages use of the brakes as vehicle speed increases, and that's when trouble begins. Application of the brakes can lock the wheels, and when the tires skid, the truck may turn sideways and roll over.

An automatic transmission has many advantages, including good throttle control and torque application in sand, predictable pulling in mud and tremendous torque for going up reasonable hills that don't require backing down. If, however, your plans include negotiating serious downslopes under compression or backing down steep hills in reverse, consider the superior control of a manual transmission and clutch.

Low Environmental Impact

The popularity of four-wheeling has an effect on the environment. TREAD LIGHTLY, Inc. and other organizations encourage low impact four-wheeling and respectful use of public lands. Although the concept is new to some recreationalists, many of us have been treading lightly for decades.

In the summer of 1964, I attended Nevada Range Camp, a 4-H/USDA Extension Service project for high school students. Fifteen miles south of U.S. Highway 50 near Austin, Nevada, our base was the Reese River Valley at Big Creek. We studied erosion and other soil conserva-

0012068

Fig. 3-19. In a semi-arid high desert environment, we must vitally protect the land from soil erosion and loss of topsoil. Three decades ago, Nevada ranchers and Indians dealt severely with "city slick" recreationalists who made tire ruts in precious soil, tore up sagebrush, meandered from designated roads, chased cattle and knocked down stream banks.

0014091

Fig. 3-20. Should you cross? Not if there's a bridge nearby. Aware four-wheelers always take the easiest route, one that leaves the least impact on the land. There's plenty of opportunity for high adventure along primitive trails. Save your 4x4 truck for those places.

0012074

Fig. 3-21. Restore soil when you've been stuck. Treading lightly requires back filling holes to leave the path intact for future four-wheelers and other users.

tion matters, witnessed the planting of wild wheat over a vast semi-arid mountain range and learned about the fragile nature of desert environments.

If only the whole four-wheeling crowd could experience such a school. At the Reese River Reservation we learned firsthand how indigenous people apply their knowledge of the land to cattle ranching. At dusk near our camp, we teased untamed fourteen-inch trout from a yardstick wide stream that feeds melted spring snow into the Reese River.

For my strong belief in low impact four-wheeling, I am indebted to Nevada ranchers, the Bureau of Land Management, the USDA/U.S. Forest Service and American Indians. Neither I nor any of my four-wheeling friends have torn up sagebrush, damaged stream eco-sys-

Tread Lightly Four Wheeling

Through the efforts of Clifford G. Blake, a U.S. Forest Service manager and advocate of multiple-use policy, TREAD LIGHTLY, Inc. became the first joint public/private sector venture aimed at wise recreational use of public lands.

As National Coordinator of the U.S. Forest Service Tread Lightly program, Cliff's vision encouraged the major manufacturers of motor vehicles and outdoor recreational equipment to take a direct role in serving consumers by promoting environmentally sound use of public lands.

Charter members of TREAD LIGHTLY, Inc., a non-profit organization, include domestic and import vehicle manufacturers, OHV and power sport equipment manufacturers, aftermarket component builders, the outdoor and four-wheel drive media, tire producers and a number of concerned groups, including the Izaak Walton League.

Chevrolet Division of General Motors is a member of TREAD LIGHTLY, Inc., and has become a major contributor of funds. Chevrolet Division's public relations staff provide valuable time and resources. The national TREAD LIGHTLY office also works closely with the U.S. Forest Service, the BLM and other agencies at promoting sensible multiple use of public lands. It is the aim of members to use, and not abuse, the environment.

As an OHV writer and recreationalist, I have joined with other concerned four-wheel drive enthusiasts in supporting TREAD LIGHTLY, Inc. As a charter member and advocate, I have co-instructed TREAD LIGHTLY 4WD clinics (funded by a Chevrolet grant) throughout the U.S. Through education and low impact land use advocacy, TREAD LIGHTLY, Inc., helps preserve our access to trails that generations of four-wheeling families have enjoyed. I encourage public land users to join TREAD LIGHTLY, Inc., and make a difference. For membership information, phone 1-800-966-9900.

The Tread Lightly Creed

T–ravel only where motorized vehicles are permitted. Never blaze your own trail.

R–espect the rights of hikers, skiers, campers, and others to enjoy their activities undisturbed.

E–ducate yourself by obtaining travel maps and regulations from public agencies, complying with signs and barriers and asking owner's permission to cross private property.

A–void streams, lakeshores, meadows, muddy roads and trails, steep hillsides, wildlife and livestock.

D–rive responsibly to protect the environment and preserve opportunities to enjoy your vehicle on wild lands.

When it comes to trail etiquette, remember hikers and horses. Your truck kicks up dust, makes noise and raises terror in the eyes of unsuspecting people and horses. If you sense that hikers or horseback riders might be nearby, slow down. Show courtesy, pass with caution and be considerate. The only way we'll all maintain access to North America's grand and scenic outdoors is through sharing and cooperation. There's plenty of fun and land for everyone—and you know, sometimes it's fine to walk or hike.

tems, left livestock gates open or blazed our own trails across a fragile landscape.

Beyond the few bad apples who consciously destroy the environment, many 4x4 truck owners simply have no knowledge of how to four-wheel. Unaware of either the natural environment or the dynamics of their four-wheel drive trucks, naive recreationalists can abuse both their expensive equipment and our land.

4. Special Uses for Your 4WD Truck

Your General Motors 4WD truck can perform a multitude of useful chores. One of the most gratifying aspects of four-wheel drive trucks is their utility value and ability to serve the community. When hazardous weather strands motorists and emergency vehicles are the only stock still rolling, 4x4 trucks lead the way. You will greatly enrichen your four-wheeling experience by helping other motorists. A 4x4 truck owner is duty bound to serve, much like a Canadian Royal Mounted Police officer.

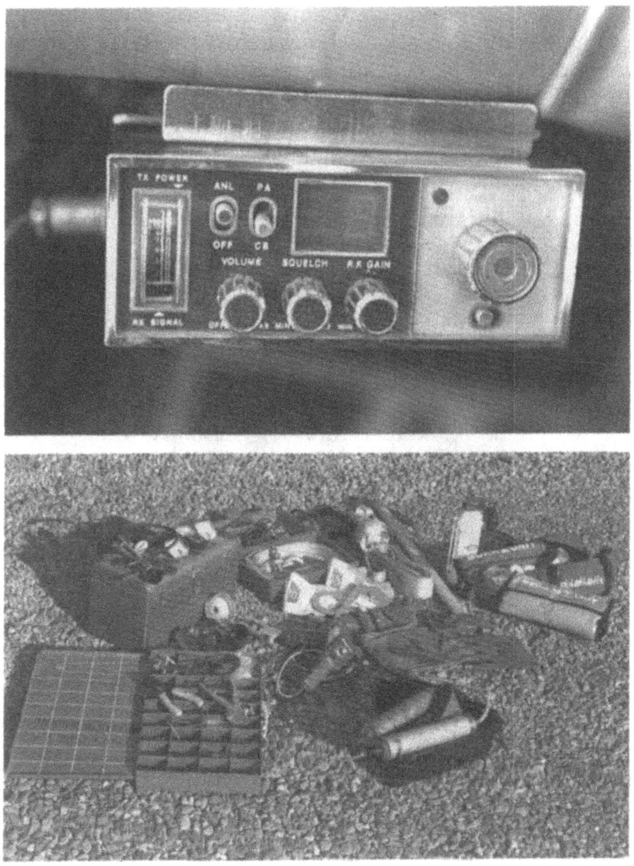

0012070 / 0012071

Fig. 3-22. 4WD trucks can be valuable emergency vehicles. Equipped with a C.B. radio, a winch, winch accessories, a Hi-Lift jack and a Max tool kit, your General Motors K-truck can assist stranded motorists. If you enjoy community service and own a 4WD truck, consider joining a local Search-and-Rescue unit.

Many 4x4 owners carry this responsibility further, joining local Search-and-Rescue (SAR) organizations. Likewise, most volunteer firefighters who live at rough climate zones own 4x4 trucks. When responsibilities demand readiness, regardless of weather conditions, a 4x4 truck serves best.

SAR Volunteerism

When we lived on the west slope of Oregon's Cascade Range. I was a Search-and-Rescue (SAR) volunteer through the local 4WD club and Lane County Sheriff's Department. In hazardous weather and during the summer months when campers flow into the high country for recreation, my telephone rang at the wee hours. A number of us would roll out of sound sleep and into our gassed and ready 4x4 trucks.

For SAR, a 4x4 truck serves best. On one occasion, we pulled a 4x4 pickup, with a fifth wheel trailer in tow, from a closed roadway covered by 18 inches of snow. The paved road, plowed to a point, had suddenly turned into a snow field. The driver continued, winding up 150 yards out in the slushy snow. Equipped with ham and CB radios, he called for help. We responded.

On another occasion, we searched for two 10-year-old boys who had ridden their bicycles into the Waldo Wilderness and couldn't find their way out. By two in the morning, both youngsters were safe in their families' campsites.

Typically, your local sheriff's department heads up SAR activities. If you have an interest in learning survival skills and acquiring the many tools necessary to effectively find and assist lost hikers, hunters, recreationalists and travelers, consider volunteering for SAR. The work is highly rewarding.

Snow Plowing and Other Utility Uses

Commercial users have always appreciated General Motors 4x4 trucks. A front-mounted snowplow is a common accessory for parking lot owners, ski lodges and even pri-

0014092

Fig. 3-23. A snow plow converts your 4x4 K-model truck into a versatile utility machine. Make certain your truck's chassis has necessary modifications and equipment to handle the added weight of a snow plow.

vate residences where steep driveways become a hazard during the winter months.

General Motors K-model 4x4s are frequently seen on construction and mine sites, and their role at enhancing the productivity of American farms and ranches is legend. In many of these environments, a 4x4 truck has become the standard vehicle, capable of moving heavy materials along remote and hazardous roads. For modern society, the 4x4 truck has effectively replaced mules, burros, llamas and teams of oxen as our beast of burden.

Some of the more popular accessories that have developed for industrial and agricultural uses of 4x4 trucks are PTO and electrically operated winches, posthole diggers, boom hoists, plows, harrow discs and auxiliary lighting. On-board welders can provide the field mechanic with a complete repair shop at the most remote station.

0014087

Fig. 3-24. *Lock your manual hubs and flip the transfer case lever into four-wheel drive before entering a water crossing. If in doubt about loose, slippery or muddy terrain, always use four-wheel drive. Low range serves in rocky or dangerously steep terrain. Low range 4WD provides compression braking and far more control of the truck. Here's a typical place for 4WD low range and use of the lower transmission gears.*

Advanced Trail Running

Faced with temptation, a hill that rises into the pastel sky or a washed out trail that accesses a favorite fishing hole, my friend Al Herndon simply shrugs his shoulders and says, "You use two-wheel drive until you get stuck... Then you lock your hubs, shift into four-wheel drive, and back out!"

Sage advice, Al. Four-wheelers, however, often scorn such practicality. Sometimes Nature provides her very own surprises. Sand that appears hard packed suddenly swallows your 4WD truck to its frame. Your frozen tracks through a bog at dawn give no hint of the underlying mud soup that will churn like homemade butter by mid-morning. Last year's solid road, now ripped by torrential flooding and muddy rock slides, lies ahead—you still need to get through safely, with your cargo intact.

Wise four-wheelers all agree, the best route through an area is the easiest one. Long before trails had fashionable difficulty classifications, experienced four-wheelers would scan hillsides, washes, streams, and rock piles, sizing up the terrain. A dozen mountaintops and desolate valleys from home, the challenge is to not get stuck. Here, a CB radio, winch, tree saver strap and a low impact anchoring device make essential traveling companions.

Driving Through Sand Traps

Imagine a road, not just your ordinary fire road or graded gravel road, but a trail that winds through rugged high desert country. Ahead looms a sandy wash, likely a dry riverbed of deep, loose sand. In flood season, a race of water tears through the steeply walled canyon, swirling around tall rocks that now bake under a summer sun....

Since the ancients first rotated stone wheels, the number one obstacle to travel has been sand. Granular, loose and deceptive, sand operates by its own rules. When monsoons or summer rains saturate the ground, sand can be hard, packed, and tractable. In dry weather, however, the same material defies even the best floatation tires.

For traveling loose sand, your best bet is steady forward momentum, while keeping wheelspin at a minimum. The slightest amount of traction loss and sand wins. Once wheels lose their grip, especially at both axles, disaster lurks.

Traveling in sand begins with basics. Lock your front hubs before entering the wash. Engage your four-wheel drive system, and if the load feels heavy, use low range. High floatation tires also make a difference in sand. (See chapter on tires and wheels.)

Moving forward, you can feel the traction and load by listening to the engine. When I was an apprentice heavy equipment operator, the older hands taught us that the cutting depth of a dozer or grader blade translated to various levels of tension at the seat of our pants. Maintain steady progress, and concentrate on constant throttle pressure and a firm control of the steering wheel.

If your engine coughs as you bump a smooth rock and the truck momentarily bogs, watch out! As the clutch engages or you bump the throttle, the truck is highly susceptible to tire spin. Too much throttle pressure now and your 4x4 will quickly become buried to the frame at the rear wheels and down to the springs at the front.

What now? If you're alone without a winch, the tool of choice is the multi-purpose Handyman or Hi-Lift type jack. (Also see accessory chapter for winch details and information on a portable anchor to use with a winch.) These tall, industrial strength jacks can be used for a variety of chores: pushing, pulling or lifting. In combination with a chain or cable, a multi-purpose jack can also serve as a come-along.

A hefty board is usually necessary for a firm jack foot. Jack up each wheel and back fill the holes with sand or rocks. Place pieces of brush beneath and in front of the tires. When you attempt to move the truck, avoid spinning the tires and apply power smoothly.

0014093

Fig. 3-25. Plan ahead. What was solid frozen ground in the morning may be impassable mud by the time you return in the afternoon.

Plan your trip in advance. Read road and trail conditions on a map or call the local Forest Service or BLM office for road reports. Aside from getting stuck, the number one fear of all four-wheelers, and justifiably so, is a roll over. Twisty, off-camber hillsides and slippery mountain trails have totalled many 4x4s. The best means for avoiding a roll over at some remote place is careful consideration of terrain.

Three conditions characterize most roll-overs: 1) the vehicle faces too much side angle, which overcomes the center-of-gravity and equilibrium; 2) a shift of weight upsets equilibrium on an otherwise negotiable sideslope; or 3) exaggerated speed, in any situation, compromises stability. This last point relates to off-camber side slopes, speeding around curves, or flirting with danger on casual 4x4 terrain by adding the element of excess speed.

Unfortunately, many four-wheelers, especially newcomers to the art of off-pavement driving, confuse sport with speed. These two terms are not synonymous. Safe recreational trail driving is a far cry from desert racing.

0014089

Fig. 3-26. A winch can take over where four-wheel traction cannot do the job. Wherever wheelspin jeopardizes the environment, use a winch. As the TREAD LIGHTLY philosophy spreads, expect wider use of winches and protective tree saver straps. Encourage fellow four-wheelers to stay on established trails and avoid damaging fragile eco-systems.

My friends Ivan "Ironman" Stewart and Rod Hall have each mastered fast desert travel on four wheels. Like other professional racers, however, they quickly discourage fast driving in sensitive and uncertain environments, especially in a production type truck.

For most recreationalists, safe and methodical trail driving proves challenging enough. This includes driving over rocky, slippery, sandy, snow-covered or mountainous terrain. The winning objective is to get your family, friends and 4x4s through tough trails in one piece.

5. 4WD CLUBS

As bats darted through the treetops, silhouetted by trailing twilight, our youngest son slept soundly in his bedroll. A pair of coyotes howled as my wife stared warily across the campfire. "Moses," she asked, "why do we persist in traveling alone? Isn't there some way to have four-wheel drive fun without mimicking a Paleolithic vision quest?"

Why Go It Alone?

Group travel can provide more resources and the safety of numbers. Traveling as a group adds several other benefits: social activities, fun sporting activities and a place to build life-long friendships with those who share your appreciation for outdoor recreation. Additionally, the local, state, and national 4x4 groups serve as lobbyists for our continued access to public recreational lands.

My wife, Donna, is a prolific reader who often shoves clippings and news briefs under my nose. "Look at this copy of *IN GEAR* that you grabbed at the SCORE Show. Every off-road thing that we're interested in doing is covered here," she exclaimed, rifling through California Association of 4WD Clubs' monthly publication. "The calendar of events lists several of the runs and family outings that we've talked about."

CA4WDC's *IN GEAR* and publications like *United's Voice*, printed quarterly by United Four-Wheel Drive Associations (UFWDA), brim with calendar events and newsworthy reports of 4x4 club activities throughout the United States and Canada. These and other four-wheel drive publications can broaden your 4WD contacts.

Regional publications include activities suited to entire families, off-road survival tips, equipment ads, vehicle classifieds, accounts of trail rides, poker runs, 4x4 breakfast runs and group barbecues. A calendar of fund-raising benefits, public interest projects, social functions and future runs can help members organize their free time.

How to Find a 4WD Club

For newcomers to four-wheeling, clubs are an ideal way to learn safe driving skills and how to tread lightly on the land. Regional sanctioning associations promote family recreation, publish newsletters and encourage clubs to protect trails and sponsor local activities.

If four-wheeling with a group of outdoor enthusiasts sounds like your kind of good time, contact the nearest state or regional association of 4x4 clubs. The better organized local clubs usually belong to regional and national sanctioning bodies.

The umbrella over all regional, state and locally sanctioned clubs is United Four-Wheel Drive Associations (UFWDA), 4505 W. 700 South, Shelbyville, IN 46176 or phone 1-800-44-UFWDA. UFWDA can provide guidelines for forming your own four-wheel drive group or provide referrals to regional associations and local clubs.

There are liabilities that accompany any vehicle owners' association. If you plan to form a local club, charters and by-laws should follow established guidelines. State and regional associations or UFWDA can furnish advice.

Anatomy of a Club Run

Sponsored by the Central District of CA4WDC, the Molina Ghost Run near Coalinga, California draws folks from as far away as Nevada and Oregon. Local legends and mining lore encourage a "Fright Night" headlamp run on opening night each year.

Most four-wheelers enter the dry camp (situated just below New Idria and halfway between Hernandez Reservoir and Coalinga) by way of Los Gatos Road. Some drive from the Highway 101 side of the mountains, winding down from Hollister, California.

Those arriving early enough on Friday can join the Fright Night trek through the surrounding hills. Hundreds of participants arrive late Friday, setting up their camps after registering. Motorhomes and camper pickups serve as tow vehicles for shorter wheelbase Jeep, Landcruiser, Bronco, Jimmy/Blazer and Scout 4x4s. For tight and twisty trail running, these shorter models hold an edge. 4x4 pickups do well on the poker run and other daylight trails.

Friday night, as the dry camp fills, a live band plays. Most avoid partying, though, preferring to prepare for the post-dawn run on Saturday morning. Sleep will be elusive, as a steady flow of late arrivals rumble noisily into camp until the wee hours.

Saturday morning, staff lines the registered vehicles up for the day run. A poker game ensues en route. Each checkpoint provides a playing card, and drivers build a poker hand as the run proceeds. A huge procession of vehicles eventually snakes the hills, while everyone shares in a spectacular view and the excitement of the trail.

As scenes from higher peaks reveal a breathtaking California spring, participants unwind. The Molina Run's main attraction is the Saturday tour through the hills west of the San Joaquin Valley. These same hills inspired the early California settlers and, in the Twentieth Century, the pioneering prose of John Steinbeck. Tall grass and brush sweep the region from February through April. Traditionally, the Molina Run takes place in mid-March.

0012075

Fig. 3-27. How do you feed 600 hungry four-wheelers? In style! CA4WDC/Central District clubs serve steak, corn on the cob, chili, beverages and—What? Haagen Daz ice cream in a dry camp? Now that's roughin' it.

As the sky darkens, the last vehicles return to camp, their occupants ready for the best tasting dinner a herd of trail beaten and hungry four-wheelers can imagine. Steak, beans, corn-on-the-cob, rolls, Haagen Daz ice cream and hot or cold beverages put smiles on everyone's face.

CA4WDC's Central District chefs and staff spend the whole day preparing this meal, and it shows. The hoard of altitude-teased appetites appreciate the effort. CA4WDC volunteers work hard to assure the success of the Molina event. Certainly, anyone who's eaten a Molina Run barbecue dinner, or the hot eggs and sausage on Sunday morning, has gone home happy.

Saturday night is sheer fun and relaxation. After a long trip to reach Molina and pounding the hills all day, four-wheelers are ready for the live band. With liquor sanctions lifted for the evening, many adults imbibe the spirits, yet everyone follows the rules faithfully: *No Drinking And Driving Allowed!* Most dance and enjoy the music, then meander back to their campsites, where campfire tales provide the late night entertainment.

Sunday breakfast precedes a vehicle show and the 4x4 Trials Competition. The trials event is new to West Coast four-wheelers and has begun to attract a following through the efforts of the Molina Run staff. (See appendix for more information on 4x4 trials.) Central District folks see that everyone remembers these contests, presenting the winners with impressive trophies.

The Molina Run takes all ages into consideration. Each participant, including the smaller children, has plenty of fun. New friendships develop, campfire camaraderie runs high and next year's event becomes the main topic of discussion before the weekend winds to an end.

Chapter 4

Working on Your Truck

YOU WILL FIND YOUR GENERAL MOTORS TRUCK easy to service. Quick access to components and sub-assemblies helps simplify routine maintenance, while a light truck's utilitarian design makes field fixes possible. Many owners learn the basics of automotive repair by working on their truck.

All General Motors light truck models feature a relatively uncomplicated chassis, a conventional powertrain layout and familiar accessory sub-assemblies. Although 1969–up trucks have more engine emission controls and power options, the chassis and powertrain components remain easy to identify.

Over the last decade, the introduction of automatic and manual overdrive transmissions, plus changes in the automotive industry's methods of complying with EPA and CAFE standards, have altered engine and geartrain distinctions.

Light truck emission control requirements have always fit particular GVWR categories. Tiers include trucks up to 6,000 pounds GVWR (light duty emissions), 6,001 to 8,500 pounds GVWR, trucks between 8,501 and 10,000 pounds GVWR (heavy duty emissions) and trucks over 10,000 pounds. Over the years, the 6,001 to 8,500 pound GVWR category has bounced between light and heavy duty emission control requirements.

As these categories and regulations change continually, your main concern is requirements for your particular year and model engine and chassis. When ordering replacement parts, you'll need to know the GVWR, vehicle identification number and the information on the underhood emission decal.

The decal notes the engine type, family and whether 49-State (Federal) or 50-State (California) requirements apply. California engines, although typically demanding more emission controls than federal engines, must also comply with EPA/Federal emission standards. Emission equipment is summarized on the decal.

Fig. 4-1. A conventional ladder-type frame assures General Motors light truck stamina. Often described as a driveable chassis design, a ladder frame supports the suspension, body and powertrain. Shown here is a 1941 Chevrolet pickup chassis.

CHAPTER 4

1. THE GENERAL MOTORS TRUCK CHASSIS

The General Motors light truck ladder frame chassis and powertrains covered within this book fit into six categories:

1. 1939–54 2WD solid-beam front axle models with leaf springs
2. 1955–59 2WD solid-beam front axle models with leaf front springs and the NAPCO/factory endorsed 4WD models
3. 1960–66 early independent front suspension (IFS) 2WD and the leaf front spring factory 4x4 K-models
4. 1967–72 IFS 2WD and the newer tapered front leaf spring 4x4 K-trucks
5. 1973–87 conventional C- and K-models plus 1988–91 full-size K-5 Blazer, Jimmy, Suburbans and C/K-30 Crew Cab models
6. 1988–up Sierra C (2WD/IFS) and K (4WD/IFS) chassis trucks

To date, most General Motors trucks have featured semi-elliptic leaf rear springs. The exceptions are those 1960–72 1/2- and 3/4-ton 2WD models equipped with link suspension and rear coil springs. The front spring design changes from traditional semi-elliptic leaf type to IFS/torsion bars in 1960 2WD models. These early IFS 2WD trucks change to coil front springs in 1963.

Four-by-four models offer semi-elliptic springs at the front and rear axles from the first NAPCO conversions and 1960 factory K-models until the 1967 introduction of reverse arch tapered/progressive rate leaf front springs. (Semi-elliptic leaf rear springs remain to the latest Sierra 4x4 chassis.) Tapered leaf front springs survive as late as 1991 on the K-5 Blazer/Jimmy, K-10/1500 and K-20/2500 Suburbans, and K-30 Crew Cabs.

Commonly described as a driveable chassis, the General Motors light truck ladder frame has several advantages. As with other full-size American trucks, these strong chassis help offset the effects of body rust and fatigue. A restorer will often replace the entire cab of a rusted 1939 or newer light truck yet find the vintage frame intact and fully functional.

From a service standpoint, the ladder frame requires little maintenance. Support members, such as spring and shock absorber anchor mounts, attach solidly to the frame. Although early truck spring shackles require periodic lubrication, the frame rails and crossmembers are maintenance-free. Aside from periodic power washing and brushing away surface scale and debris, an undamaged frame seldom needs more than occasional paint and undercoating.

Leaf springs anchor at one end with a pivot bolt and bushings. During suspension travel, a swinging shackle at the opposite end of the main leaf permits fore and aft spring movement. All 1959 and earlier GM truck spring shackles and anchor bolts feature grease fittings and re-

0014095

Fig. 4-2. 1939–59 General Motors light trucks provide plenty of grease fittings. Use of bronze spring-shackle bushings requires periodic service with chassis lubricant. 1960–up 2WD and 1967–up 4WD models have rubber bushings and require less maintenance.

placeable bronze bushings. K-models continue use of greaseable suspension components through 1966. Later trucks equipped with leaf springs and rubber-type spring bushings require less periodic maintenance.

Solid-beam and IFS Front Axles

While the Standard model Chevrolet passenger cars still offered leaf front springs and a solid-beam axle in 1939, other Chevrolet car models offered independent front suspension. All Chevrolet and GMC trucks through the 1959 models have semi-elliptic leaf front springs and a solid-beam front axle.

This conventional and proven layout was a standard with most truck builders. (Ford provided the passenger car transverse leaf spring/wishbone suspension through 1941 in 1/2-ton truck models.) Semi-elliptic front springs continue through 1966 on solid axle 4x4 K-models. With the exception of the change to tapered progressive rate front leaf springs in 1967, all solid front axle K-models continue to use this basic chassis layout until the introduction of the late Sierra chassis with its IFS design.

The 2WD solid front axle, commonly called an I-beam or mono-beam type, attaches to the springs with U-bolts and offers a high degree of stamina. Steering knuckles pivot on kingpins, and the steering linkage is a simple and efficient design. Kingpins, recognized for their high degree of stability and durability, remain a mainstay with 2WD GM light trucks through 1959 models.

In 1960, General Motors introduced independent front suspension (IFS) on both Chevrolet and GMC 2WD light truck models. Unlike Ford's limited range of motion with Twin I-Beam suspension, the 1960 GM light truck IFS is a bonafide fully independent system that allows a full range of wheel travel and angles.

With pivoting double A-arms and a steering knuckle/spindle with ball-joints, the IFS front end resembles passenger-car designs. The similarity ends with looks, however, as the heft of the light truck's ball-joints and other components make this a rugged suspension system. Allowing for finer adjustment, these IFS systems hold wheel alignment well and offer long service.

0014496

Fig. 4-3. In good condition, the 1960–62 torsion bar suspension system provides exceptional ride quality and durability. The 2WD model switch to coil springs in 1963 simplifies the chassis layout, as the long torsion bars no longer stretch rearward from the lower control arms. Either suspension system is worthy, and General Motors trucks through the C-40 series use this basic design.

0014097

Fig. 4-4. Full-floating axle design provides wheel support in the event of an axle shaft failure. All General Motors 3/4-ton and one-ton models into the early 1980s boast full-floating rear axles. One-ton Doolie and similar heavy duty, high GVWR models continue the full-floating axle tradition with the newest Sierra truck chassis.

Live Front and Rear Driving Axles

Four-by-four K-models have three distinct front axle systems: 1) NAPCO through 1970 closed-knuckle solid front axles with full-floating type wheel hubs, leaf springs and drum brakes; 2) 1971–up conventional chassis K-models with an open-knuckle solid front axle, disc brakes and leaf springs; and 3) 1988–up Sierra chassis IFS 4x4 with semi-floating front axles and torsion bars.

Rear axles for various models are either full- or semi-floating type. Half-ton models use semi-floating rear axles (torque-tube type through 1955 First Series), while 3/4-ton and one-ton trucks into the 1980s use full-floating axles. Beginning with early 1980s 3/4-ton models, use of semi-floating axles has increased on both 3/4-ton and even one-ton models. Today, only the heaviest duty models and C/K Doolies retain the time-honored full-floating rear axle.

Beginning with some 1981 20-Series (3/4-ton) pickups, General Motors introduced the first semi-floating 8-lug wheel rear axles. Heavy duty 3/4-ton models, including the C/K-20/2500 Suburban, retained the full-floating rear axle design until the mid-1980s. All one-ton (C/K-30/3500) models use the full-floating rear axle design through 1987. At the mid 1990s, full-floating rear axles have made a comeback on some 3/4-ton C/K models.

The last uses of a solid live front axle with full-floating wheel hubs were the 1991 K-5 Blazer/Jimmy, K-model Suburbans and the K-30/3500 Crew Cab. I will refer to these and all pre-Sierra 4WD models as having *conventional 4x4* as opposed to the Sierra chassis' 4WD semi-floating IFS system.

Early solid live front axle models with closed-knuckle steering joints have sealed, ball-shaped castings that extend from the axle tubes. These provide a cavity for oiling the enclosed axle shafts and steering knuckle joints.

Later solid (conventional) axle models feature open-knuckle live axles, with ball-stud steering knuckle pivots. Here, the axle shaft, visible between the end of the axle tube and the steering knuckle, features a cross-type U-joint to permit steering.

The open-knuckle joint requires less maintenance, provides less trouble, and affords tighter turning angles than a closed knuckle axle. Earlier closed-knuckle axles often develop seal leaks and weep grease. Also, the shimmed kingpin bearings on early axles require a precise pre-load adjustment, making service more complex. (See service section for details.)

Chevrolet and GMC engineering aims for long service life and parts integrity. General Motors K-model live front axles with full-floating hubs serve as one example of superior strength in design. Although the Sierra truck 4WD chassis has shifted to CV-joints with half-shafts and a semi-floating wheel hub arrangement, these models also represent high quality and durable engineering.

The Sierra chassis IFS has revolutionized full-size truck 4WD. Introduced in 1988, this live front axle system features a frame mounted differential, two pivoting half-shafts, and four CV-joints, much like the front wheel drive system of domestic General Motors luxury cars.

For truck use, the Sierra 4WD system boasts heavy duty components including long, rugged torsion bars. This assures the smooth ride quality and load capacity that today's light truck owners want. The rugged double A-arm suspension also delivers durability. In many respects, this suspension breakthrough rides on the proven front suspension design of 1960–62 2WD General Motors light trucks.

Since 1955 Second Series models, all General Motors light trucks feature open propeller/driveshafts. (Half-ton models from 1939 through 1955 First Series have enclosed torque tube drivelines.) Open drivelines permit quicker service and easier removal of the transmission or rear axle and center-section assemblies.

0014124 / 0014454

Fig. 4-5. General Motors K-model 4x4s from 1960–70 have closed-knuckle Spicer 44 front axles (top). By 1971, open-knuckle style Dana 44 axles (bottom) serve K-10/1500 and K-20/2500 models. (Corporate 10-bolt axles have also served well here.) K-30/3500 one-ton 4x4s, introduced in 1976, feature the massive heavy duty open-knuckle Dana 60 axle.

Rear axles require little periodic maintenance beyond oil level checks and oil changes. Axle shaft bearings or full-floating hub bearings offer a long service life, and the overall stamina of General Motors light truck axles is excellent. Chevrolet and GMC have used torque-tube, drop-in carrier type and integral type axle assemblies in various light truck models.

2. STEERING GEAR AND LINKAGE

In 1940, General Motors luxury cars began using the corporation's highly innovative recirculating ball-and-nut manual steering gears. Undisputedly superior to all other designs, General Motors' recirculating ball-and-nut gears soon replaced the light trucks' worm-and-roller and worm-and-sector gears.

During the 1941 model year, GMC and Chevrolet light trucks adopted General Motors (Saginaw) recirculating ball-and-nut steering gears. Several decades later, other domestic truck makes purchased either Saginaw's recirculating ball-and-nut gear assemblies or found reasonable copies. Mimicry is a high compliment, and GM/Saginaw recirculating ball-and-nut steering has its likenesses throughout the world.

On General Motors solid-beam (2WD and 4WD) front axle steering systems, the steering gear's pitman arm pivots fore and aft. A drag-link connects the pitman arm with a steering arm at the left steering knuckle (on the domestic left hand drive models).

For these solid axle models, a single tie-rod connects the left and right steering knuckle arms. Moving the drag-link will simultaneously turn the steering knuckles

0014098 / 0014132

Fig. 4-6. Saginaw Division's recirculating ball-and-nut integral power steering (top) has a reputation for superior service and durability. Beginning in 1968, many General Motors light trucks benefit from these gears. Linkage type power steering (bottom), offered as a limited option from 1955–68, is more complex and vulnerable to damage.

Fig. 4-7. General Motors' Saginaw-type recirculating ball-and-nut manual steering is superior to all other designs. Precisely machined worm shaft groove acts as an inner half of the ball bearing race, while the nut provides the matching groove. Reduced friction means easier steering and longer service life. General Motors was decades ahead of other truck manufacturers in the switch to recirculating ball-and-nut type manual steering gears.

and wheel spindles. This fundamental layout is common to all solid front axle 2WD and conventional 4WD (non-IFS) models.

Beginning with the 1960 IFS 2WD front ends, the steering linkage and location of the steering gear change. The linkage looks much like a passenger car system designed for double A-arm suspension. The steering pitman arm moves left to right, and a centerlink connects the pitman arm to an idler arm that mounts opposite the pitman arm at the right frame rail (on left hand drive models).

Short tie-rods attach the centerlink to each front steering knuckle/spindle. This three-piece tie-rod assembly is similar to GM passenger car types, although the truck components are much sturdier and designed for a tough day's work. Ball-stud joints in the linkage allow the necessary movement as the IFS A-arms travel up and down with the road surface changes.

During the mid-1950s, the demand for power steering encouraged GM to offer add-on linkage power assist. With linkage power assist, the control valve mounts on the draglink or centerlink at the pitman arm attachment point. The control valve directs pressurized hydraulic fluid into a power ram. This ram attaches between the truck's frame and either the one-piece tie-rod on a solid axle model or the centerlink on IFS 2WD models.

The linkage assist power steering option continued through 1967 on IFS two-wheel drive models and into 1968 on 4x4s. Much improved Saginaw integral power steering of recirculating ball-and-rack design first came on line as an option in some 1968 2WD trucks. In 1969, integral power steering gears became available as an option on 4x4 models. Integral type recirculating ball-and-nut power steering offers major gains in stamina and efficiency.

Recirculating ball steering gears are precise mechanisms that often go their entire service life without adjustment. Other than very minor sector-shaft mesh adjustment at high mileage, any indication of excess play at the steering pitman arm, sector shaft or wormshaft bearings is an indication of internal damage. In this case, the gear needs a teardown for inspection and overhaul. Make all adjustments in the manner described within the factory shop manual for your model. (See other service chapters for additional details.)

3. DRUM AND DISC BRAKE SYSTEMS

Late 1930s and newer General Motors truck braking systems consist of a hydraulic master cylinder that feeds brake fluid through pipes and high strength brake hose to each wheel cylinder or disc caliper. Pedal pressure actuates the master cylinder piston (dual pistons on 1967–up tandem master cylinders), causing brake fluid to flow.

Typical General Motors drum brake systems have one hydraulic cylinder per wheel. These cylinders have twin, opposing pistons that move outward as fluid enters the cylinder. Depending upon the model and brake type, General Motors drum brakes apply pressure via several methods, each design described generically as self-energizing.

Overall, earlier four-wheel drum brake systems are inferior to disc front/drum rear designs. Although General Motors engineered drum brake sizes to match chassis and advertised load capacities, drum type brakes simply cannot offer the braking efficiency, resistance to fade and overall performance of disc brakes.

All General Motors light trucks use drum front and rear brakes through 1970. Both 2WD and 4WD models introduce disc front brakes in 1971, and this is a noteworthy milestone. Disc brakes generally provide superior stopping force, quicker recovery from exposure to water, straighter stops, and ease of overhaul.

General Motors truck braking has always been adequate, however, significant improvements began in 1967 with the dual braking systems. Disc front/drum rear brakes were a huge improvement in 1971, and by 1988, C/K-Sierra trucks began employing anti-lock rear braking systems. Since 1992, four-wheel anti-lock braking has been available.

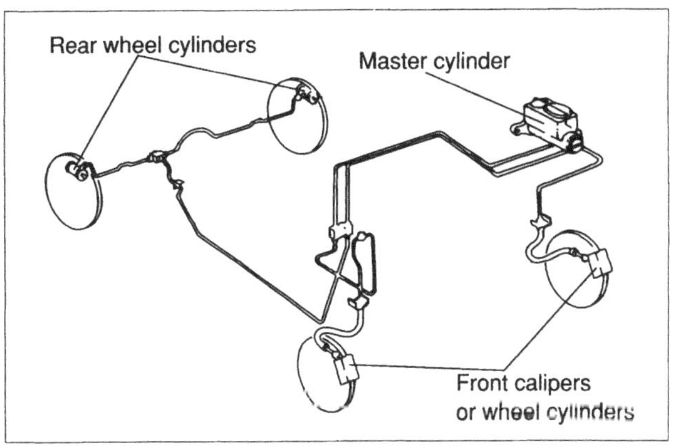

Fig. 4-8. The General Motors light truck braking system is similar to most other American truck designs. A pedal actuated master cylinder forces fluid into each of the hydraulic wheel cylinders or disc brake calipers. Friction brake shoes or pads act against metal drums or rotors.

0012464

Fig. 4-9. Self-energizing brakes, with both shoes sharing a common anchor bolt or pin, utilize the rotational force of the drum to force the brake shoes more firmly against the braking surface of the drum. Added force enhances braking without need for additional hydraulic pressure. The first General Motors light trucks to use this Duo-Servo-type brake system were 1951 1/2-ton models.

0014099

Fig. 4-10. Later General Motors trucks feature rear-wheel and even four-wheel anti-lock braking systems. Here, a four-wheel anti-lock system (ABS) assures less skidding when the load is light, on slick pavement or during hard application of the brakes.

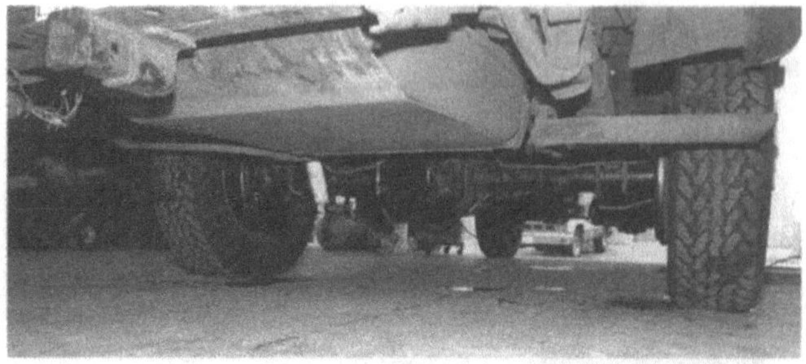

0014100

Fig. 4-11. Emergency/parking brakes are at the rear wheels on General Motors light trucks through one-ton capacity. When brake lining is wet, muddy, oil soaked or glazed, the cable actuated emergency/parking brakes offer marginal service at best.

Emergency/Parking Brake

For 1939 and newer General Motors light trucks, the parking brake mechanism is basic. Mechanical cable linkage activates the rear wheel brake shoes when the driver applies the hand brake or emergency/parking brake foot lever.

On models with self-energizing Duo-Servo-type brakes (beginning with GM 1/2-ton models in 1951 and later light truck models with the single anchor bolt toward the top of the brake backing plate), the parking brake is most effective with the vehicle on flat ground or parked facing downhill. This is because of the self-energizing design. Remember this when you park with the truck facing uphill. Make sure your automatic transmission is in Park or that a manual transmission is in its lowest gear.

Road debris and oil contamination from leaky axle seals can lower the efficiency of the emergency/parking brakes. Also, if you have a very heavy load and need to park on a steep hill, consider using chock blocks behind the front and rear wheels as a backup.

4. ORIENTATION TO TRUCK ENGINES

> **NOTE —**
> Chapter 1 and Chapter 2 describe the design characteristics and performance attributes of Chevrolet and GMC light truck engines. This section's comments apply more to the general maintenance requirements and serviceability of these engines. For troubleshooting, tune-up procedures and light service, see the service chapters.

For Chevrolet light trucks, the 1937–53 inline OHV 216 six was a mainstay. Similarly, between 1939 and 1959, GMC trucks offered the proven 228, 248, 270 and similar OHV inline sixes. The 216 and its counterpart early version of the 235 offer ease of service, and these engines maintain tune for long periods of time. The 1954–62 late 235 and 261 cubic inch sixes also offer easy maintenance.

For these four main bearing earlier inline GMC and Chevrolet sixes, the Delco-Remy breaker point distributor is readily accessible. Spark plugs lie within easy reach, and the various one-barrel carburetors (including Carter,

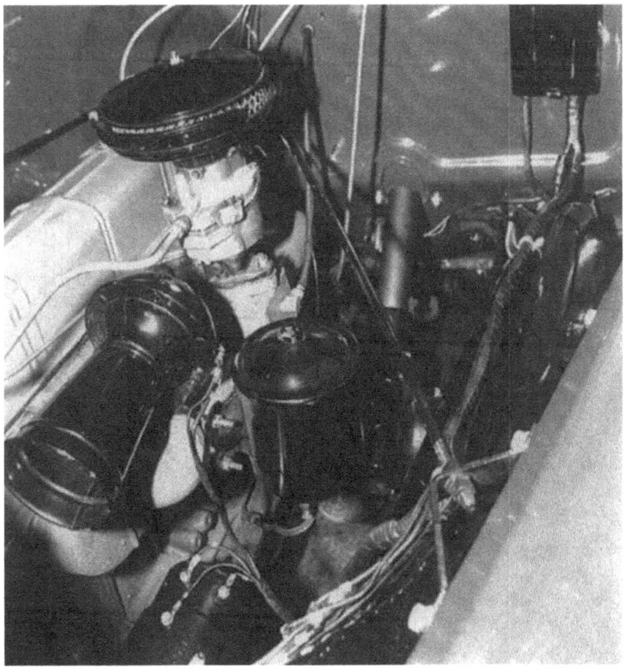

0014101

Fig. 4-12. The early GMC (1939–59) and Chevrolet (1937–62) light truck OHV inline sixes have four main bearings. Oil filtration is through a by-pass type filter. The filter assembly mounts at the intake manifold. If your engine does not have a by-pass filter, find one and install it with new oil lines.

GM/Rochester and Zenith) on these engines can be adjusted or even field serviced with ease.

With the exception of some mid-1950s Blue Flame varieties of the 235 engine, all of these four main bearing Chevrolet and GMC inline six-cylinder engines have mechanical lifters that require periodic valve adjustment. This is an oily job, but once mastered, provides satisfying results and a sense of accomplishment.

Oil filtration on these engines is the by-pass type. This means that the engine has no provision for a full-flow oil filter like that found on more modern engines. These engines definitely need the by-pass filter assembly (mounted to the intake manifold) for a reasonable amount of oil cleansing. If your engine does not have a by-pass filter, find one and install it with new oil lines.

The earliest 1955 and 1956 Chevrolet 265 V-8s in manual transmission passenger cars and some trucks had mechanical lifters that also require valve adjustment. (Most 265 V-8 light truck engines use hydraulic lifters from 1955 onward.) These hydraulic lifters are adjustable on Chevrolet V-8 engines. Set properly when the engine is new or freshly rebuilt, however, they will usually go the entire engine service life without a need for readjustment.

Pontiac/GMC V-8s also use hydraulic valve lifters. These engines should never require valve adjustment during their service life, as the adjuster nut is actually a *lock nut* that bottoms against a shoulder on the rocker arm stud. Pontiac V-8 rocker stud heights determine valve clearance, and these stud heights are set at the factory or whenever a machine shop performs cylinder head surfacing work.

0014102

Fig. 4-13. The 1955 and 1956 265 V-8 OHV small-block Chevrolet engine (shown) has no provision for a full-flow oil filter on the block. Many of these engines have by-pass filters mounted on the intake manifold; however, this OE version has no filter at all. This modern V-8 with an oil filtration system that dates to the earliest Stovebolt sixes is an anomaly. By 1957, the 265 and new 283 V-8s use a cartridge type full-flow filter assembly bolted to a casting pad on the engine block where the road draft exits on this 1955 engine.

0014103

Fig. 4-14. GMC's 1955 Pontiac 287 V-8 came complete with a full-flow type cartridge oil filter assembly mounted on the block. Derived from an upscale car line, this GMC 288 V-8 offered more features than Chevrolet's new 265 V-8 design.

The Chevrolet and Pontiac/GMC V-8s have somewhat inconvenient tune-up access, as the distributor mounts at the rear of these engines. In 1955 and 1956, these distributors require removal of the cap to set the points.

Beginning in 1957, GM light truck V-8s feature the famous window cap distributor that revolutionized ignition point service. You can insert an allen head wrench through the distributor cap window (taking care not to shock your-

0014104

Fig. 4-15. Anyone who has ever adjusted the valves on a running small-block Chevy V-8 can appreciate the value of these oil stopper clips. I still keep this set of clips in my toolbox as a reminder: Oil will squirt everywhere if you do not use these devices.

self with a high-voltage snap from the condenser) and set the points' dwell angle with the engine running.

The next best thing to a window cap distributor is the switch to HEI electronic ignitions on all General Motors light trucks in 1975. HEI requires only an occasional rotor and distributor cap change (or module replacement when defective) and a periodic check of the base spark timing.

In 1963, Chevrolet revamped its six-cylinder inline engine. The new 230 light truck powerplant featured a seven main bearing block with a valve train very similar to the small-block V-8. In fact, I liken this 194/230/250/292 series of engines to the 283 small-block V-8.

The 230, 250 and 292 truck engines are very easy to service, and with hydraulic valve lifters, tune-up involves fewer steps than with earlier sixes. This rugged engine design survives to the mid-1980s as the 250/4.1L and 292/4.8L. Before the onset of heavy emission controls, the 230/250/292 light truck engine was the easiest engine of all to tune or service.

GMC dropped the Pontiac V-8 by 1960 and introduced its own 305 V-6 gas engine. This huge mass of iron is likely the most ruggedly constructed light truck engine ever offered by any manufacturer. Actually a medium duty truck design, the 305 V-6 has mechanical lifters and requires valve adjustment as part of the tune-up routine. Simple carburetors and easy access to spark plugs make this a very easy engine to service, although the distributor mounts at the rear as with Chevrolet and GMC V-8s.

The small-block and big-block Chevrolet V-8s have been ideally suited for truck applications. Simplicity of design is a hallmark, and the similarities between the big- and small-block designs make tuning similar. Both engine types rely on hydraulic lifters, and although their overall size differs, the layout of components is, remarkably, the same.

Tuning and routine service of the carbureted and TBI/EFI small-block and big-block V-8s, and even the 4.3L V-6, are very similar. Common carburetor designs and similar TBI units, interchangeability of parts and oth-

0014105

Fig. 4-16. The GMC 305/351 V-6 design suits medium duty trucks. In-frame overhauling my 1960 GMC 1/2-ton with the 305-A V-6, I discovered the tremendous durability built into these engines. The cylinder heads weigh as much as big-block Chevy V-8 types, and the 305 offers the best engineering and construction found in any V-6 truck engine. You will find these V-6s in GMC light trucks as late as 1969.

0014125

Fig. 4-17. Big-block light truck V-8 engines came on line in the late 1960s, along with the rugged TH400 Turbo-Hydramatic three speed automatic. The 396 V-8 soon had its counterpart in the 400 big-block, which was actually a 0.030-inch overbore of the 396 for a displacement of 402 cubic inches. Biggest of the offerings was the 454, introduced in 1973 light trucks and continuing to this day as the 7.4L trailer puller and hauler.

0014106

Fig. 4-18. The small-block Chevrolet truck V-8s evolve from the basic 1955 265 design. Smaller main bearing journal 283 and 327 V-8s and the "big journal" 327, 307, 350 and 305 engines have each delivered tremendous service and reliability. Since 1969 the 350 V-8, particularly the four-bolt main bearing version, has established itself as the premiere light truck engine for overall economy, performance and durability.

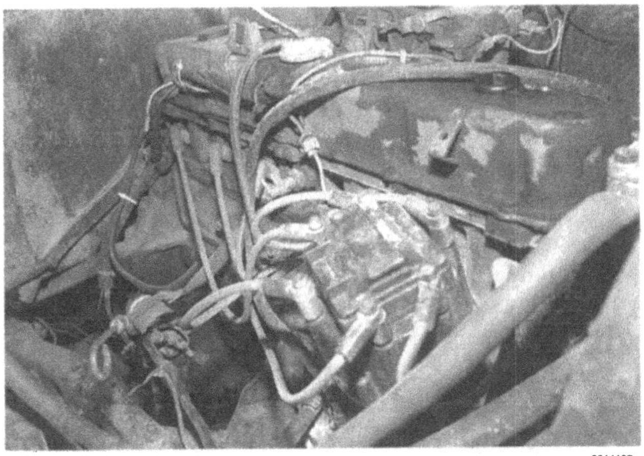

0014107

Fig. 4-19. The 230 and 292 inline OHV six-cylinder engines introduced in 1963 survived as the 4.1L (250 cid) and 4.8L (292 cid) sixes into the mid-1980s. 230 and the larger 250 engines deliver strong torque and good economy. The 292 is better noted for massive torque than its marginal economy. Each of these engines is very rugged and durable. The 250 and 292 could easily have survived into the 1990s with EFI/TBI, but the 262/4.3L Vortec V-6 made them obsolete.

er useful likenesses make the routine service of all Chevrolet-design V-engines straightforward.

You will like the 1987 introduction of EFI in the form of Throttle Body Injection (TBI). Easy parts identification and even the prospect of troubleshooting this system by yourself will quickly explain why General Motors chose this type of induction over tuned-port or multi-point injection. Later TBI engines are more accessible, require less

0014109

Fig. 4-20. 6.2L V-8 diesels came on line as a 1982 light truck option. In the aftermath of the ill-fated 350 V-8 diesel, the 6.2L proved its worth and then some. Family friends with a 6.2L diesel powered 1986 K2500 Suburban still enjoy their truck at 170,000 miles—and they've never experienced major engine trouble. Durable and fuel efficient, the 6.2L diesel has a loyal following.

0014110

Fig. 4-21. The latest 6.5L L65 V-8 Turbo-Diesel promises a long service life and real stump pulling torque. This is the diesel that performs like a big-block gas V-8, yet the fuel bill remains small. Engineered for today's light truck user, the L65 option was my choice for a new 1994 Suburban K2500 4WD intended for trailer pulling. If you want torque and performance plus the virtues of diesel economy, this clean burning, electronically injected diesel delivers.

emission plumbing and deliver satisfying performance. Easy maintenance remains a theme with these engines, and you will find that the TBI system requires very little attention beyond fuel and air filter changes. Extra underhood room is a welcome change.

The 6.2L and newer 6.5L diesels continue this theme, with fuel, air and oil filter changes the primary service needs. Much to General Motors' credit, the later engines require less attention yet deliver maximum service and durable performance. From my experience, adding a high grade synthetic engine oil can provide trouble-free service and deliver heavy payloads for a couple hundred thousand miles.

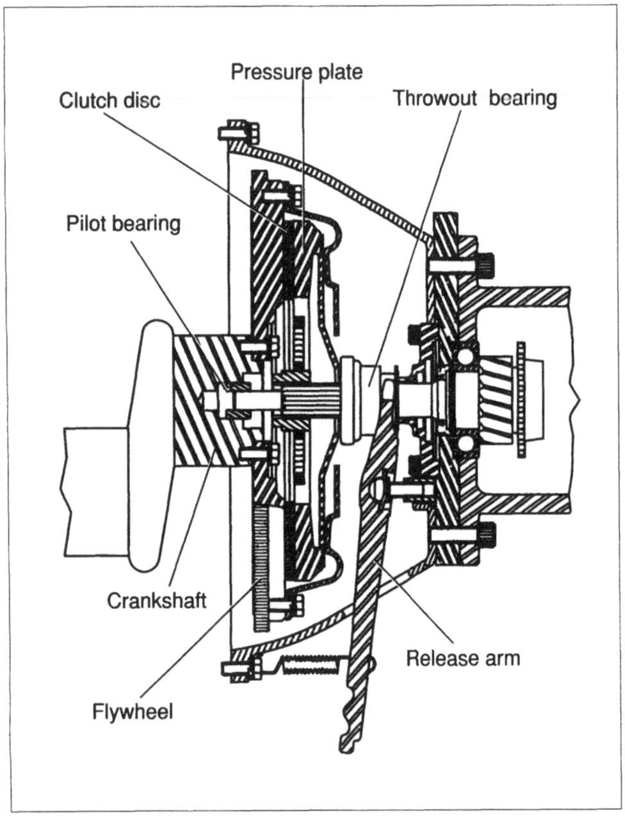

0012096

Fig. 4-22. Chevrolet and GMC trucks have used a conventional clutch and release mechanism. The throwout bearing rides on the transmission front bearing retainer and presses against the clutch release fingers during disengagement. A crankshaft pilot bearing centers and supports the input shaft.

5. TRANSMISSIONS AND TRANSFER CASES

A wide range of manual and automatic transmissions have been coupled to General Motors light truck engines. For four-wheel drive, the geartrain requires an additional component, the transfer case, which delivers power to each driving axle.

The standard GM clutch assembly is common to other trucks and automobiles. Spring-type clutch covers of several designs have been used in General Motors light trucks. Each clutch provides the clamping force necessary to press the clutch disc between an engine-driven steel flywheel and the clutch cover's face or pressure plate.

A pilot bearing at the rear of the engine crankshaft supports the nose end of the manual transmission input shaft/gear, while the clutch release or throwout bearing rides on the front bearing retainer of the transmission.

Clutch Linkage

General Motors trucks use a variety of clutch linkage types. 1939–59 models have through-the-floor pedal assemblies attached to the frame, and the clutch linkage operates from below the cab floor. This is a good arrangement, as the frame, linkage and engine move along the same plane. A pair of side motor mounts at the bellhousing help provide smooth mechanical linkage operation.

0014449

Fig. 4-23. General Motors truck clutch linkage design has varied. Below-the-floor pedal and rod system was a mainstay from the 1930s through 1959. Hydraulic clutch linkage (shown) was a big change for 1960, then ends after 1962. Mechanical linkage carries from 1963 to the later General Motors trucks, which return to hydraulic linkage.

Since 1960, the two linkage designs have been hydraulic (a master cylinder, hose and slave cylinder) and mechanical linkage (a cross-shaft and series of link rods). These designs vary in reliability.

Poor linkage design is a weakness on some GM truck models, especially where cross-shafts move with the engine and cause vibration and rough clutch engagement. When working properly, the smoothest clutch linkage is a hydraulic design. This type of linkage is not affected by chassis twist or engine torque flexing.

Clutch linkage requires close periodic inspection. Worn parts usually fail when your truck is under load or off-pavement. For this reason, clutch linkage is a vital part of preventive care. (See the service section for preventive maintenance of your truck's clutch linkage.)

Rugged Automatic Transmissions

General Motors realized early that automatic transmissions suited many light truck owners. In 1954, the light Chevrolet and GMC trucks introduced the option of a four-speed Hydra-Matic Drive transmission. GM's selection was wise, as the now legendary early dual range (band type) Hydra-Matic had already proven its worth in luxury cars.

The Hydra-Matic is a durable transmission with a fluid coupler and planetary gearsets that deliver a very low first-gear ratio. This provides good breakaway performance. Some truck buyers, already familiar with the Hydra-Matic drive in Cadillac, Oldsmobile and Pontiac passenger cars, were willing to try this new technology. Unfortunately, coupled to a smaller displacement OHV six, the massive Hydra-Matic could hardly prove its worth.

Word soon circulated that these transmissions were expensive to service and offered sluggish performance. I once had the opportunity to drive a 1954 GMC pickup with the Hydra-Matic Drive. Frankly, despite the great

0014112

Fig. 4-24. The original iron-case four-speed Hydra-Matic Drive transmissions are very rugged and practical for a V-8 powered truck. From 1954–62, various six-cylinder and V-8 Chevrolet and GMC trucks benefitted from the Hydra-Matic. Chevrolet began switching to the lighter duty two-speed Powerglide (called Pow-R-Flo in trucks) as early as 1961 and kept this option available through some 1971 models. The Powerglide choice still has many of us puzzled. Four-speed (direct 1:1 ratio high gear) Hydra-Matic Drive was last offered in 1962 GMC and Chevrolet light truck models.

torque of the 248 six, the truck only felt strong at breakaway and low speeds. The excessive spread between the second- and third-gear ratios meant sluggish performance. Unlike a 185-horsepower 1954 Oldsmobile 324 V-8, the humble 248 inline six made a poor showing.

Poor fuel economy was another complaint with the early light truck automatics. However, particular successes in passenger cars, mostly with large displacement engines, encouraged GM to offer the Hydra-Matic Drive with the new Chevrolet 265 V-8 and 287 Pontiac/GMC V-8s in 1955. This proved successful, and sales of trucks with the Hydra-Matic option increased dramatically.

About the point that Hydra-Matic Drive had proven itself, General Motors made a very strange decision. The four-speed iron-case automatic had been out of the car lines since 1957, leaving the trucks as sole users of the original Hydra-Matic unit. In 1961, light trucks began using the two-speed Powerglide transmission from Chevrolet Division.

The Powerglide is a durable but obviously limited design. These transmissions have rugged components and actually hold up well. (Highly modified Powerglides serve in today's Pro-Stock drag racing cars.) However, only two forward gear ratios place severe restrictions on performance and towing capability.

For several years, the Powerglide was the sole automatic transmission option and only available in the 2WD

0014113

Fig. 4-25. Pre-Sierra conventional chassis Suburban 2WD and 4x4 3/4-ton models have made good use of the TH400 automatic. 2WD models used the TH400 extensively, and in the late 1970s, the TH400 began serving heavy duty Suburban 4x4 applications. Shown here is my 8,600-pound GVWR 1986 K2500 with its TH400 transmission and attached transfer case. 1992 and newer Sierra chassis 4WD Suburbans rated over 8,500-pounds GVW use the 4L80E electronically shifted automatic overdrive.

trucks. Fortunately, by the mid-1960s General Motors' Hydra-Matic Division had developed the all-new Turbo-Hydramatic 350 and 400 series transmissions, which ultimately led to widespread use of these automatic transmissions in light trucks.

As early as 1966, some 2WD light trucks benefit from the TH400 three-speed automatic. This very rugged transmission, used in larger cars, high horsepower muscle cars and light trucks, has proven superior to all other General Motors passenger car and light truck designs. (In the high performance realm, General Motors' Turbo 400 matches Ford's C-6 and Chrysler's 727 Torqueflite transmissions, each known for their durable service, ability to handle massive loads, and longevity.)

The earliest (1969) K-model 4WD pickups to offer an automatic transmission option use the lighter duty TH350 three-speed. Much stronger TH400 units remained popular in 2WD heavy duty applications.

Unfortunately, the far more rugged (Turbo) TH400 did not enter 4WD service until the 1976 K-30/3500 one-ton heavy duty models. Even after 1976, the TH350 continues in K-10/1500 and K-20/2500 4WD pickups. This pattern of using the Turbo 400 in high performance or heavy duty usage applications continues through the 1991 K-30/3500 4x4 conventional chassis (solid front axle) Crew Cab.

I am very partial to the TH400 and late 4L80E four-speed overdrive type automatics. The 4L80E, which has subtly improved since its 1992 debut, derives stamina from the TH400's basic design.

By contrast, the 700R-4 automatic and its later 4L60E electronically shifted counterpart have roots in the lighter TH350 models. The 700R-4 four-speed overdrive automatic, introduced to light trucks in 1982, was initially expected to fulfill every emission, fuel economy and performance need. Perhaps the 700R-4 would have done so, but several weaknesses in the original design led to trouble.

NOTE —
See the geartrain performance chapter for details on how to upgrade 1982 to mid-1980s 700R-4 transmissions.

By 1985, General Motors eliminated the more blatant weaknesses of the 700R-4, and this transmission has increased in both popularity and reliability ever since. By the late 1980s, a 700R-4 overdrive automatic could perform as well as a TH350, which if used properly will deliver very long and admirable service.

Manual Transmission Overview

The various manual transmissions used in Chevrolet and GMC light trucks have offered good to excellent service. Early GM/Muncie SM318 and 319 type three-speeds were standard equipment on most 1/2-ton and 3/4-ton models (even some one-tons) of their era. These units have synchromesh on second and third gear only. Later GM/Saginaw three-speeds have synchromesh on all three forward speeds.

With the switch to an open driveline on 1955 Second Series 1/2-ton models, an overdrive transmission could be easily fitted to the light truck chassis. Just in time for the economic slump of the mid-1950s, these overdrives were a useful option. The three-speed transmission with overdrive was available in General Motors trucks through 1968.

In addition to the GM three-speeds, several Warner heavy-duty three-speeds served various trucks over the years. These units, often found as standard equipment in a heavy-duty 1/2-ton package or even a 3/4-ton model, differ in gear strength, synchromesh design and overhaul methods.

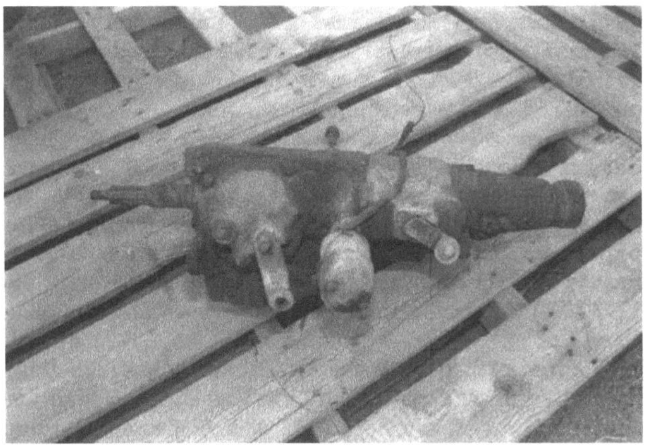

0014114

Fig. 4-26. *The SM318 or 319 transmission was standard equipment on most GM light duty trucks built from 1940–68. Offered for both torque-tube and open driveshaft-style rear axle models, these three-speeds are easy to service and overhaul. Durable when used properly, the design features a unique cone-and-drum synchronizer assembly that all Chevrolet and GMC mechanics recognize. This is a fun unit to rebuild if you use a factory level shop manual. Shown here is a rare overdrive version, available from 1955 on.*

If you own a Second Series 1955 or newer General Motors truck with the three-speed manual transmission, identify the unit before service. During the earlier Advance Design era, nearly all three-speed transmission offerings were GM Corporate designs. (Some heavy duty 1954 and First Series 1955 three-speed transmissions are Warner T-89 types. The Warner T-85 and other units emerge after 1955.)

Although I enjoy the ease of overhaul of the SM318/319 and other three-speeds, I am really not a fan of three-speed light truck transmissions. All of these designs have passenger car roots. (The basic SM318/319 gearbox survived in early Corvette V-8 models.) A truck requires greater gear and bearing strength for the constant stresses of heavy payloads and towing.

My favorite General Motors manual transmissions include the Muncie SM420 and SM/CH465 truck-type four-speeds with compound low gear. General Motors has also used the New Process 435 four-speed truck gearbox, which certainly rivals the SM420 and 465 units for stamina. These three models provide two-ton truck torque capacities and offer many extra years of trouble-free service.

I have always advocated use of four-speed truck type transmissions for heavy duty applications or any kind of serious pulling. For the 1988–up Sierra chassis models with five-speed overdrive offerings, I am most attracted to the latest New Venture 4500-series gearbox.

This D-Spec transmission is a massive unit, the first real heavy duty five-speed manual overdrive transmission. You will find the 4500-series five-speed in the latest Sierra trucks with GVWR ratings over 8,500 pounds and engines like the L65 Turbo-Diesel V-8.

NOTE —
See the performance geartrain chapter for details on retrofitting the NV-4500 D-Spec five-speed manual transmission to earlier General Motors light trucks.

Transfer Cases

Nineteen-fifties NAPCO 4x4 conversions and General Motors 1960–66 K-model transfer cases mount separately (divorced) from the transmission. On these divorced transfer case models, a short driveline connects the transmission and transfer case.

Beginning in 1967, the transfer case attaches directly to the rear of the transmission via an adapter casting. Both of these two-speed transfer case designs serve as a power divider (directing power flow to the front axle), and as a means for achieving exceptionally low gearing through low range mode in 4WD.

Gear-driven part-time 4x4 systems, like the original NAPCO and GM factory transfer case designs, offer a distinct two-wheel drive mode. In this mode, power flows from the engine through the transmission to the transfer case, then rearward to the rear axle. Here, the front propeller shaft receives no power from the transfer unit.

In 4-Wheel High or 4-Wheel Low, power flows through the front and rear driveshafts to both axles. Low range provides a reduction gearset, with a ratio factor between 2:1 and nearly 3:1 (depending upon the year and

0014115

Fig. 4-27. Original two-speed transfer case in NAPCO conversions and early factory K-models mounts separately from the transmission. A short driveshaft connects the transmission to the transfer case. This divorced style ends after 1966 K-models.

transfer case model application). The transfer case is a crucial part of the light truck four-wheel drive system.

General Motors K-trucks have offered several transfer case designs, including gear and chain drive types. Chain drive emerged in the 1970s, when full-time 4x4 popularity peaked. Part-time 4x4 transfer cases, with aluminum housings and chain drive, are currently popular. Aluminum-housed transfer cases are lighter and more energy efficient. For some applications, however, the earlier gear drive units serve better.

The earliest GM K-model transfer cases were two-speed Rockwell and Spicer types, used on 1/2-ton and 3/4-ton rated trucks. By the late 1960s, General Motors began using the modern New Process 205 gear drive units, the wisest move possible. Spicer's Model 20 transfer case units continued to serve some K-trucks for several years.

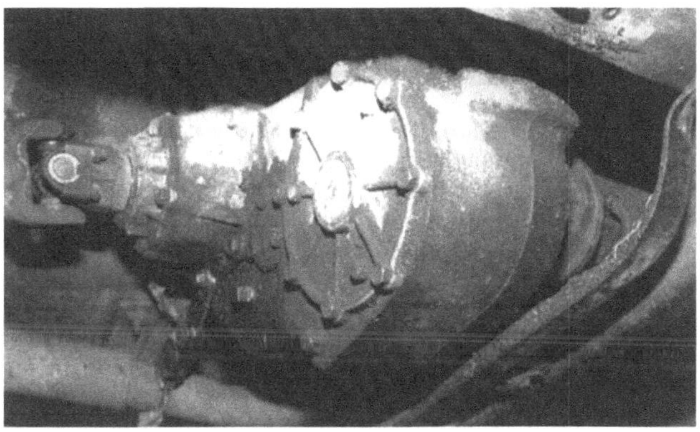

0014116

Fig. 4-28. New Process NP205 gear drive transfer case is the most durable unit ever offered in light American trucks. General Motors uses this part-time transfer unit as late as the 1991 K-30/3500 conventional (solid) front axle Crew Cab. When maximum durability counts, the NP205 prevails.

Both of these transfer units are high quality two-speed varieties with far more flexibility than the single-speed Dana Model 21 power divider that compromised the 1965–76 Ford F100 1/2-ton 4x4 trucks equipped with manual transmissions. This single factor won large sales for General Motors K-10/1500 4x4 pickups. The Turbo-Hydramatic option in 1969 added one more attraction to General Motors four-wheel drive light trucks.

In 1973, General Motors followed other truck manufacturers and began offering full-time 4x4 systems with the chain drive New Process 203 transfer case. The NP203 is a very durable design, however, emphasis on fuel economy and concerns about excess drivetrain wear soon diminished consumer interest in these easy to operate full-time systems. Fortunately, this unit was only offered on automatic transmission K-models and some 1974 manual transmission equipped trucks. The last use of the NP203 on an automatic transmission equipped K-truck was 1979. Used truck buyers should be alert for front driveline and axle steering joint wear. (Many owners convert their NP203 units to part-time operation with the installation of an aftermarket transfer case conversion kit and free-wheeling front hubs.)

The iron-cased NP205 unit, in my opinion, is the best transfer case ever offered in a light duty truck. General Motors and Dodge continued using these units with one-ton truck applications into the 1990s, also installing the NP205 unit behind the Dodge/Cummins turbocharged diesels.

In 1980, American truck manufacturers, insisting that they needed lighter transfer case units with lower (numerically higher) gearing in low range, began using a variety of aluminum housed two-speed transfer cases. General Motors and others experimented with the New

0014117

Fig. 4-29. Since 1980, General Motors has used several New Process and, currently, the New Venture part-time chain drive transfer cases. The NP208 underwent improvements since 1980, and the New Process chain-drive unit in my 1986 Suburban K2500 has gone over 100,000 miles without trouble.

Process NP208 unit, which features a planetary gear reduction system and a chain drive to the output shaft that serves the front axle.

These NP208 transfer cases perform well but lack the long and trouble-free lives offered by NP205 part-time 4x4 units. All NP208 and subsequent chain drive transfer case units have light aluminum cases and an increased number of wear points. On the bright side, the reduction ratios for low range are very low (numerically high), which offers a great crawl pace, heavy lugging ability in low range and less overall load on the powertrain during 4WD low range operation.

If your General Motors 4WD truck has an NP203, NP208 or any of the later New Process or New Venture transfer cases, routine service is crucial. Most of these transfer cases use automatic transmission fluid (ATF) or light oil as a lubricant. (See the owner's handbook for your truck to determine correct specifications.) Watch for seal leaks and seepage at case halves, where anaerobic sealers sometimes fail. Change fluid at recommended intervals, and pay close attention to the color of oil or ATF.

Driveshafts

Power flow between the transfer case and axles on a General Motors four-wheel drive truck model is through conventional propeller shafts. Two-wheel drive trucks use a similar rear driveline. Most often, General Motors truck driveshafts have Spicer cross-type U-joints with a single tube and slide coupler or a two-piece (splined) driveshaft.

Larger trucks or models with longer wheelbases often employ a mid-shaft or carrier support bearing, which serves a two-piece driveline. Slide couplers and splined sections compensate for axle movement by lengthening or shortening the overall driveshaft length as the axle moves with suspension travel.

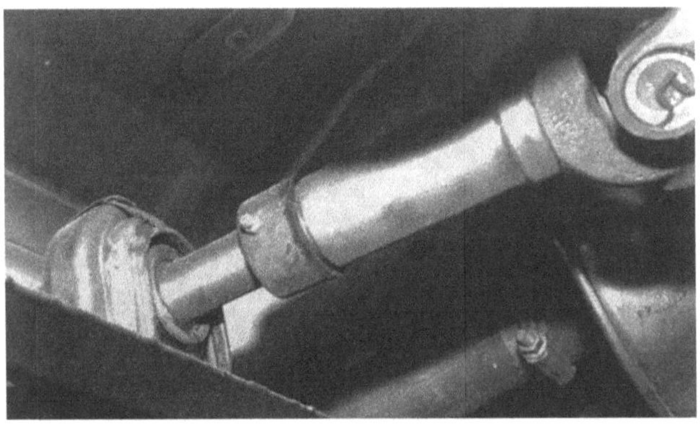

0014118

Fig. 4-30. Mid-shaft/carrier bearing is common on long wheelbase trucks. Many General Motors light trucks use such a setup. Bearing and two-section driveline reduce vibration and the need for one excessively long driveshaft tube.

Driveline service usually consists of required routine lubrication and inspection of the U-joints and spline sections. At high mileage and when damage occurs, the driveline will need repairs or overhaul. (For details, see service chapters.)

6. Repairs on Your GM Truck

Your truck's serviceable components fit into several subgroups. The common chassis and powertrain layout provides an easy orientation. Once familiar with your truck's design, you can readily make repairs.

Unless you must remove the crankshaft, engine work is possible in the chassis. The engine bays of GM trucks are broad and designed to facilitate service. An exception to this rule is a large V-8-powered truck with a full complement of power accessories.

Powertrain Orientation

You can quickly become familiar with your truck's features. Servicing driveshafts, cables, the brakes, shock absorbers (airplane type removable units) and wheels is fast and straightforward. On 4x4 models, the transfer case is either divorced or detaches from the transmission, making it easier to remove each of these units. Reducing the weight of the transmission/transfer case assembly permits easier handling of parts and reduces risk of damage.

Axle service, generally performed in the truck, follows standard guidelines for Spicer-type or Saginaw integral designs and GM/Corporate and Eaton carrier type housings. Spicer/Dana axles have been widely used on American trucks. They have an excellent reputation for reliability.

0014119

Fig. 4-31. Factory General Motors truck shop manual is your assurance of a job that meets OEM standards. If you plan to keep your truck and do your own service work, invest in a service book(s) for your particular truck model and year. (See appendix for sources of older factory guidebooks.)

Like trained Chevrolet or GMC truck mechanics, you'll find the factory service manual very valuable. By following factory recommended procedures for disassembly and installation of parts, you can perform professional level work. Your General Motors truck deserves the highest work standards and competency.

The Workplace

When servicing your truck, a clean and well-prepared workspace is essential. Geartrain and chassis parts are expensive. Losing parts can create lengthy delays, as many components have special order status.

By establishing neat work habits at the beginning of a repair or restoration project, you will speed up the work process and assure success. Each part has its place. Before starting a repair, lay out labelled coffee cans or similar non-breakable containers to hold the nuts and bolts.

Parts illustrations, either from this book or the detailed unit repair section of your factory General Motors shop manual, should accompany the job. Especially on an older pre-owned Chevrolet or GMC truck, which could have suffered years of mediocre repairs, you should account for each part illustrated in the guidebook.

Use Correct Tools

Before starting any repair, review the tools required. General Motors trucks sometimes need specialty wrenches or other devices to complete a diagnosis or repair. You will find references to such tools in this book or your factory shop/overhaul manual. Avoid the loss of time and knuckle tissue by using proper tools.

Some safety basics apply when working on your truck. Repairs to the undercarriage and wheel service frequently require chassis hoisting. The use of floor jacks and jackstands is a must. The ideal jackstands for light truck work have four-cornered platforms and a minimum of five-ton rating per stand. Stay away from light duty tube-type stands. They provide far less stability when you wrestle with a transmission or transfer case.

Jacks and Lifting

Quality hydraulic floor jacks are another safety requirement. Minimally, your floor jack must be of 1-1/2 ton or greater capacity. Whenever possible, avoid lifting the entire front or rear of the truck with a single jack. Never rely upon a hydraulic jack to support the truck while you work beneath the body or chassis. Insert jack stands immediately to avoid overloading your jack. When lifting the truck for wheel and tire removal, take extra time and use jackstands. Safety is primary.

0014121

Fig. 4-33. As a rule, you can position floor jacks beneath the solid front axle beam(s) or an axle housing. Allow room to place jackstands at the frame rails or other locations. Leave work room and space to remove stands.

0014120

Fig. 4-32. Assure a margin of safety when working on your truck. A 1-1/2-ton rated floor jack and 5-ton (per stand) rated jackstands offer features found in professional equipment. Invest in quality. Your safety is at stake.

To position your jackstands, note the design of the chassis. Your Chevrolet/GMC owner's handbook or a factory shop manual outlines the points for lifting and positioning stands. Common support points on General Motors trucks are the frame rails and beneath the axle housing tubes or solid axle beam. Space jacks evenly, as near to the spring mounting points as possible. These are locations engineered to support the truck.

Avoid placing a jackstand in any area of the chassis where rocking might result. Never place a floor jack or jackstand under steering linkage, brake pipes/hoses, exhaust system parts or body sheet metal. Note the reinforced chassis sections and axle points recommended for positioning a jack. If you are uncertain about the lift points for your chassis, consult your local Chevrolet or GMC Truck dealership service representative or refer to a factory shop manual covering your model.

WARNING —
Never work under a lifted vehicle unless it is solidly supported on stands designed for the purpose. Keep the jackstands well spaced and secure. Allow ample and unobstructed space to work. Do not work under a vehicle supported solely by a jack.

Hoisting Equipment

Powertrain and axle unit repairs involve very heavy sub-assemblies. If your service goals involve the removal and replacement of the axles, engine, transmission or transfer case, be prepared to handle these heavy units. Consider renting the correct hoisting tool(s) or a portable engine hoist from your local rental yard. Rental firms often have transmission/transfer case jacks as well. When performing heavy work, always ask a robust friend for assistance.

Hoists and specialty tools help prevent damage to your truck. Personal injuries are also less likely when hydraulic force takes the place of brute strength. The manhandling of parts, such as attempts to install a weighty transmission by hand, can lead to broken components and severe bodily injury.

Failure to detach all of the hardware before hoisting can result in major damage. Take time to envision the sub-assembly standing alone. Check the step-by-step service procedures and parts diagrams to make sure that you have disconnected all necessary hardware and linkages. Ask an assistant to watch progress from a different vantage point.

0012106

Fig. 4-34. *Inline sixes are long and require care during removal. A "cherry picker" hoist provides the angle and control to lift an engine. Use a tilt cable, and avoid swinging the engine or damaging parts.*

In the case of engine removal, always secure the engine with suitable chain or cables. Find balance points to assure the stability of the engine as you raise it, and also pay attention to the angle of pull. Use strong, high grade attachment hardware and, if available, an engine tilt cable that allows angle adjustments as you hoist.

Special Safety Considerations

For work around coil suspension springs, like those found on 1963–up 2WD General Motors light trucks, be extra careful. Also use extreme care when servicing models with front torsion bars, like the 1960–62 2WD trucks and the late Sierra chassis 4WDs.

Before changing springs, either allow the spring to safely extend and fully unload its force or constrain the spring with a special coil spring compressor. Consult your factory-level shop manual for the recommended method for your model.

WARNING —
Compressed coil force exceeds a ton, and an unrestrained spring can come loose and cause severe bodily injury or damage to the truck.

Always account for the size of the transmission or transfer case assembly when placing the chassis on stands. If you intend to slide the transmission from beneath the truck, be certain that there is sufficient room. A disconnected transmission or axle, laying trapped beneath the truck, is like the story of the man who built a boat in his basement.

7. THE TRUCK OWNER'S TOOLBOX

On- and off-pavement driving environments are full of hazards and mechanical threats. The prepared truck owner carries an on-board complement of hand tools and simple diagnostic equipment.

At home, for the General Motors truck owner who performs maintenance and repairs on his or her vehicle, a variety of tools support the workshop. If you plan to work on your own truck, your tool selection must meet a wide range of service needs, including tools for periodic maintenance and light repair work, troubleshooting, and diagnosis.

Reference Books: The Literary Tools

This book serves as your orientation and reference guide for preventive care, tune-up and diagnosis of mechanical troubles. If your skill level and ambitions include sub-assembly repairs and overhaul, I highly recommend a Chevrolet or GMC Truck factory shop manual.

Stick with a bonafide General Motors supported publication like the *Chevrolet Truck Shop Manual* or *GMC Truck Shop Manual* for your particular model. Such a book is available through your local Chevrolet or GMC Truck dealership's parts department or a new/used book source in the case of older models. These publications provide the most information, greatest detail and best illustrations.

In your model's factory-level shop manual and the owner's glovebox handbook, you will find concise information on tune-up specifications, fitup tolerances and fluid capacities. For overhaul of the engine, chassis, geartrain and electrical sub-assemblies, a factory-level shop manual provides the necessary details and those specifications considered essential by General Motors truck engineers.

For over twenty-five years, my truck repair work has benefitted from the use of OEM/factory-level shop manuals and professional trade manuals like MOTOR'S *Truck* and the *Mitchell Service Manual*. These books are available to the mechanical trade and consumers.

Filling Your Toolbox

Your light truck garage requires a full assortment of U.S. size wrenches and tools to cover the later metric hardware. Since the late 1970s, General Motors cars and light truck components adhere to both domestic and metric tooling and sizes.

Hand tools should include open and box ended wrenches plus sockets in 1/4", 3/8" and 1/2" square-drive sets. You will also need specialty sockets for spark plugs, wheel lugs and the front wheel bearing adjuster and lock nuts on 4x4s.

The wheel bearing nut wrench is a necessity. Many pre-owned 4x4 domestic trucks show signs of severely abused front wheel bearing nuts. Instead of using the correct socket, unequipped mechanics apply a hammer and chisel to the corners of the hex or round (slotted) type locking nuts. This not only ruins the nuts but also eliminates any chance of accurately measuring the torque setting on either the bearing adjusting nut or the lock nut.

4x4 front axle spindle nut wrenches are available in most retail auto parts stores. OTC, Snap-On and others produce flat-walled, 1/2" square-drive hex sockets for precisely this purpose. The large nut size and small space between the nut and inner face of the hub makes use of a conventional socket or wrench impossible.

Many General Motors 4x4 models use wheel bearing nuts that require a special four-lug socket. The steering knuckle upper ball-joint stud seat on Dana open-knuckle axles adjusts with a similar tool. A special socket is available for accurately positioning these ball-joint stud seats and setting correct ball-joint preload.

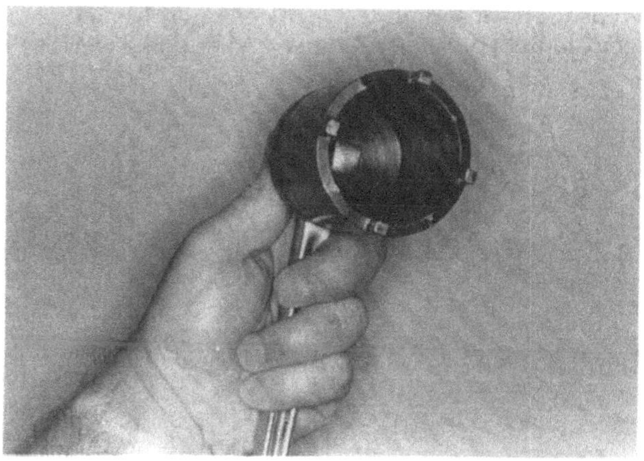

0012107

Fig. 4-35. *Front wheel bearing spindle nut wrenches are a must. This specialty socket, available through NAPA and other auto supply retailers, is for later model 4x4s. Such sockets are also available for earlier hex nuts. Never use a hammer and punch to remove or tighten spindle nuts.*

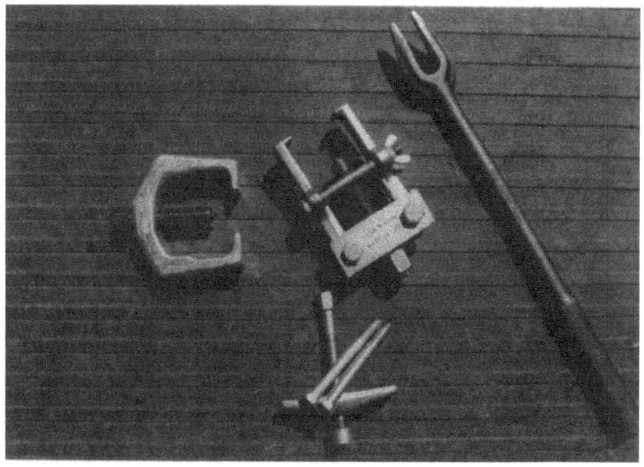

0012108

Fig. 4-36. *Specialty pullers will ease steering linkage disassembly. Use of the right tool prevents damage to expensive safety components.*

0012109

Fig. 4-37. *Many jobs require use of a hydraulic press. If a press is beyond your budget, take your heavy bearing, gear or bushing work to an automotive machine shop. Attempts to improvise with a hammer are wasteful and dangerous.*

Additional Chassis and Powertrain Tools

Your other chassis service tools should include tie-rod and Pitman/steering arm pullers, a pickle fork and those tools commonly used for working on any other domestic truck. For earlier General Motors truck owners, both the 4x4 kingpin bearings and the steering gear adjustments require an accurate pull-type spring scale.

0012110

Fig. 4-38. A dial indicator and magnetic stand are very useful. For adjusting wheel bearing end play and runout on shafts, use a dial indicator. You can also detect camshaft lobe wear with a dial indicator.

Cross-type U-joint service, a frequent truck repair procedure, may be performed successfully with a bench vise and some sockets, although more elaborate specialty tools are available. Some types of driveshaft work and other service operations may demand access to a hydraulic press, bearing/gear pullers and fixtures.

You can take such tasks to an automotive machine shop or rent equipment at a local rental yard. The cost of equipment and frequency of use will dictate whether you should buy a hydraulic press.

For transmission and clutch alignment work, a dummy input shaft for alignment is always practical, as transmissions and attached transfer cases are a major weight obstacle—especially with four- or five-speed iron-case truck transmissions.

You can fabricate transmission locating dowels by removing the heads from long bolts. Thread the bolts into the bellhousing's upper transmission mounting holes. These simple guide pin dowels can prevent clutch disc damage during transmission installation.

Spicer/Dana and GM/Saginaw integral axle work calls for use of a spreader to relieve tension on the carrier bearing cups during removal of the differential carrier. (Although axle overhaul is often left to a professional, you can perform this kind of work with the right tools and proper service data.) Removing axle shafts, wheel hubs or brake parts may require use of special pullers and handtools.

Precise Measurements

Competent truck repairs require precise adjustments and measurements. Shimming bearings, checking shaft end float, adjusting backlash of gears, setting wheel bearing endplay and other chores require use of a dial indicator and magnetic stand or a gooseneck holding fixture to help with awkward measurements. You will also need a precision micrometer(s) for measuring shaft diameters and checking the thickness of shims, rotors and bearings.

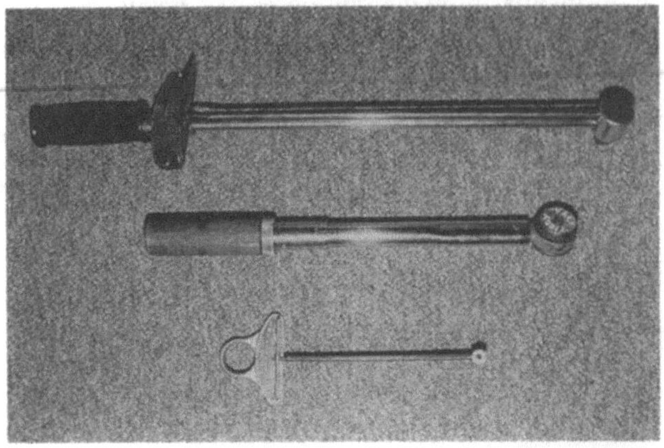

0012111

Fig. 4-39. Torque wrenches come in a variety of sizes. This assortment serves every need from companion flange nuts to ultra-sensitive automatic transmission band adjustments.

General Motors truck service and overhaul work demand a wide range of torque wrenches: 1/4" drive inch-pound, 3/8" drive inch/foot-pound, 1/2" square-drive foot-pound and even a 3/4" square-drive heavy duty type. If cost is prohibitive, rent or borrow a quality torque wrench. Make sure the calibration is correct.

Nitty Gritty Tools

Your basic hand tools should include a hacksaw, a variety of chisels, punches and drifts (both hard steel and malleable brass), Allen hex wrenches, and in the case of later model trucks, Torx-type drivers. General Motors trucks have also used various clutch head and exotic cross head screw patterns.

Seal and bearing cup driver sets are optional, as careful improvisation often works satisfactorily. Always wear safety goggles whenever you work with air impact tools, sharp cutting tools, hammers, chisels or punches.

Fuel Line and Brake Work Tools

For brake tubing nuts and fuel pipe fittings, a flare nut wrench set is mandatory. (Open end wrenches will damage compression and flare nuts.) Other brake work tools

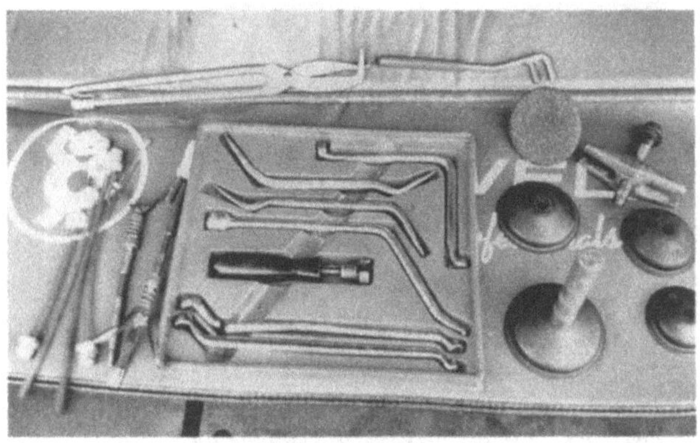

0012112

Fig. 4-40. The right tools assure a quality job. Both disc and drum brake systems require specialty tools. If you intend to perform brake work, invest in quality brake tools.

include adjuster spoon wrenches, spring pliers, retainer/hold down tools, wheel cylinder piston clamps and bleeder hose.

Disc brake work requires a pad/caliper piston spreader and a micrometer for checking disc thickness/variance. There are special hones for wheel cylinder, master cylinder and disc caliper rebuilding.

Air Tools: Speed and Efficiency

Air wrenches are a major timesaver. A wide range of pneumatic tools quickly tame difficult repair jobs. In addition to time savings, air impact wrenches can enhance the quality of high torque, heavy duty repairs.

This is especially true with older sub-assemblies suffering from seized hardware and rust accumulation. (Specially hardened, impact quality sockets should always be used with air wrenches.) Also, hardware like transmission output yoke nuts and U-joint/pinion flange nuts require high torque settings. Air tools for the removal and installation of these large nuts can eliminate the awkward use of a breaker bar and special holding fixtures.

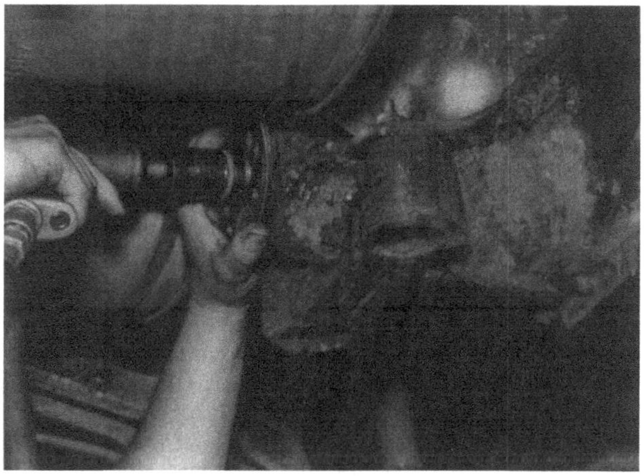

0012113

Fig. 4-41. *Air wrenches and other pneumatic tools save time and ease truck repair work, especially the removal and installation of shaft nuts on the transmission, transfer case or axles.*

When using air tools, avoid overtightening. Always check final torque with a torque wrench. Avoid using a pneumatic impact gun to fully tighten or torque precision fasteners.

Tools for Engine Overhaul

In-the-chassis engine overhaul requires common tools like a valve spring compressor, cylinder ridge reamer, hone, and ring compressor. For a major out-of-chassis rebuild, you will sublet re-boring the block, grinding the crankshaft and valves, fitting piston pins, installing cam bearings and other machine shop procedures.

Before taking on a major engine overhaul, consider the cost of tools and how often you will perform this kind of task. Professional mechanics invest constantly in specialty tools necessary to properly perform automotive work. If you want to perform professional level work, the tools needed could prove costly.

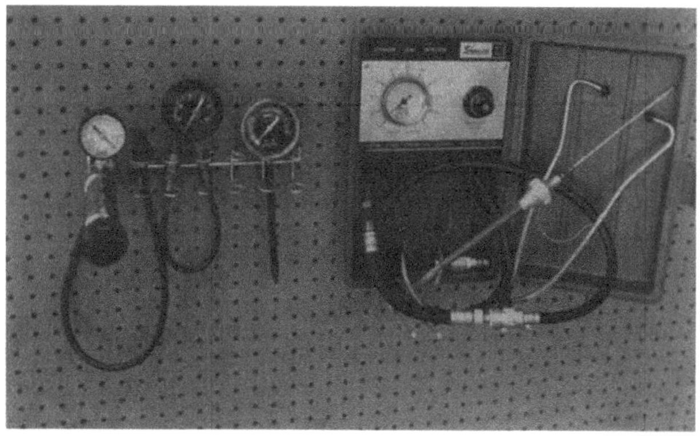

0012114

Fig. 4-42. *A vacuum pump or gauge tests ignition, carburetor and emission devices. A compression gauge and cylinder leakdown tester can diagnose internal engine troubles.*

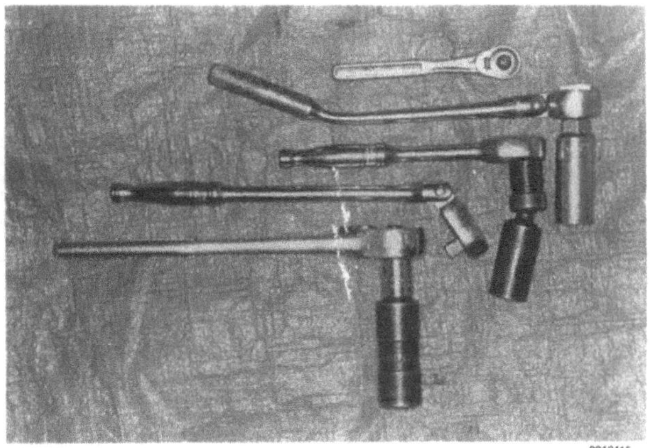

0012115

Fig. 4-43. *A variety of handtools ease your truck work. These ratchets and sockets serve specific needs, including spark plug changes and removal of wheel lug nuts.*

Tune-up and Engine Diagnostic Equipment

The tune-up needs of your General Motors truck engine depend upon the model and engine type. Various fuel, spark and ignition systems have different tool requirements.

Early trucks provide the arguable simplicity of a breaker point primary ignition, supported by a remote ignition coil and high tension spark cables. A common misunderstanding is that breaker points are easier to service. The more contemporary HEI electronic distributor is equally easy to troubleshoot and repair. (See tune-up, repair and troubleshooting procedures in service chapters.)

Servicing your earlier GM truck's breaker point distributor requires traditional tune-up tools. A point feeler gauge set helps adjust the point gap. (Tappet feeler gauges are for engine valve stem clearance adjustments.) For accurate, parallel spark plug gaps, use a gapping pliers. Simpler wire-type feeler gauges work fine on used plugs and fit easily in your on-board tool kit.

A dwell meter provides precise breaker point adjustment, while a timing light verifies timing after you have

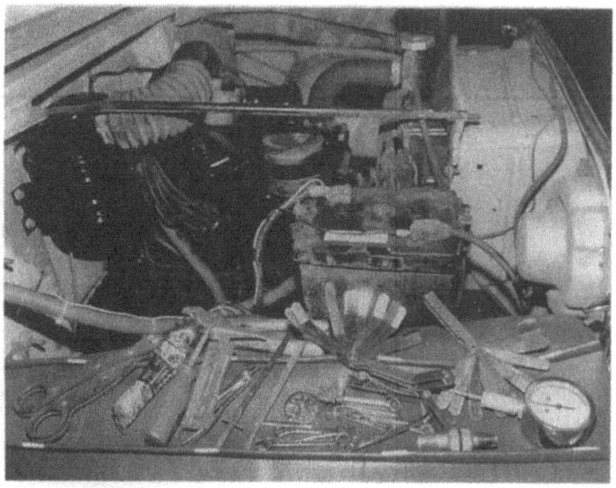

0012116

Fig. 4-44. Ignition tune-up tools should match your truck's requirements. Some of my automotive tools date back thirty years. Ignition wrenches, point files, breaker cam lubricant and feeler gauges were common to the breaker point ignition era.

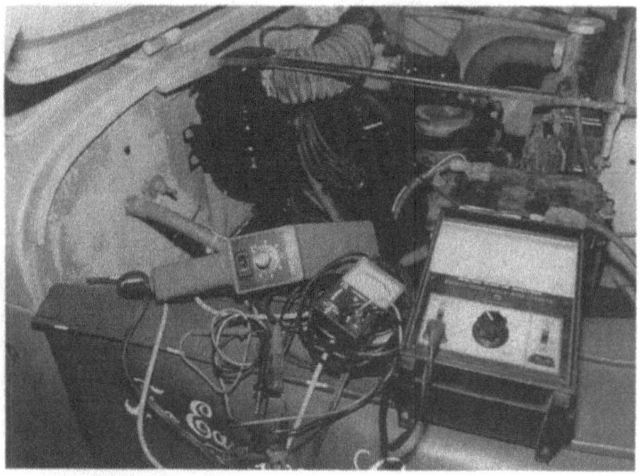

0012117

Fig. 4-45. A dwell meter, timing light and volt-ohmmeter help with tuning and troubleshooting. Volt-ohmmeter has become an important electronic/electrical troubleshooting tool.

set the point dwell angle. The volt/ohmmeter is an ideal companion for your electrical troubleshooting and tune-up work, offering quick, concise diagnosis of everything from shorts and open circuits to testing alternator or generator current and battery voltage.

For precise performance, setting the breaker point spring tension assures accurate spark at all engine speeds while extending point life. Today, this is rarely necessary. Modern, high quality replacement points have pre-set tension.

Carburetor tuning requires a float height gauge and needle/seat removal tool. A complete assortment of quality screwdrivers (clutch head, straight slot, Phillips and Torx) is necessary for repairs and tuning chores.

Ignition wrenches are versatile for breaker point replacement and other electrical system repairs. A continuity tester is helpful, although the volt/ohmmeter surpasses

0012118

Fig. 4-46. Round out your tune-up tools with a fuel pump tester, vacuum gauge, float height gauge, needle/seat driver, assorted screw drivers, Allen wrenches, Torx sockets and a distributor terminal brush. During the heyday of Stovebolt and Jimmy inline OHV sixes, breaker point spring gauge served as a precision tuning tool.

the effectiveness of any test lamp. Although pinpoint tester probes allow testing through wire insulation, I avoid use of these testers. They can damage insulation, weaken your wiring and make the circuit susceptible to shorts.

Electrical System Tools

When working alone, I find a remote starter switch handy. This permits cranking the engine from beneath the hood. A remote starter tool is helpful for compression testing. With all spark plugs removed and the high tension spark current safely isolated or eliminated (check your factory shop manual for procedure), you can hold the throttle open, crank the engine and watch the compression gauge—all from beneath the hood.

0012119

Fig. 4-47. Traditional General Motors starter solenoids allow reasonably easy use of remote starter switch. For quickly aligning timing marks or checking compression, the remote switch is an asset. Use extreme caution near hot exhaust manifolds.

0012120

Fig. 4-48. Induction meters provide a quick view of starter current draw or generator/alternator output. Held over the starter cable or charge wire, meter reads magnetic field and displays this as a quantity of current.

Regular battery maintenance, a critical need for all trucks, requires tools for cleaning the cable terminals and posts. A battery hydrometer test is useful when you suspect a dead cell, while simpler voltmeter tests answer most battery questions.

Another quick diagnostic tool for starter and charging systems is the induction meter. These meters sense magnetic current flow through the starter or charge circuit cable, showing the approximate output in amperes. In seconds, you can roughly determine current flow rate or draw.

Engine Compression and Cylinder Leakdown Tests

Although the compression gauge registers cranking compression (a quick reference to overall engine condition), a more reliable test is cylinder leakdown percentages. The leakdown tester pressurizes a cylinder through the spark plug hole, with the piston at top-dead-center (TDC) of its compression stroke. If the valves, rings, head gasket or castings fail to seal normally, the tester indicates the volume or percentage of the leak.

The advantage of the leakdown test is two-fold. First, the piston rests at the point of greatest cylinder wear (maximum taper). With parts immobile, leakage and piston ring blowby show up readily. It is not uncommon for an engine to display normal cranking compression yet have 30% or higher leakdown due to poor ring seal. Eight to ten percent leakage means an engine is in top shape.

Second, the leakdown tester immediately indicates the area of the leak. If an intake valve leaks, air will blow back through the carburetor or EFI throttle body. A leaking exhaust valve sends an audible signal out the tailpipe. Piston ring wear telegraphs through the dipstick tube, oil filler hole or crankcase vent.

If a professional quality leakdown tester is unavailable or more costly than your budget allows, the traditional substitute is an air-hold fitting designed for changing valve springs. Screw the fitting into a spark plug hole. With the piston at TDC on its compression cycle, adjust air line pressure to a point between 60 and 80 psi. Attach the air hose coupler to the fitting. Listen for high volume leaks and pinpoint where leakage occurs.

0014122

Fig. 4-49. A leakdown tester exceeds all other methods of evaluating engine seal. Gauge is capable of pinpointing worn valves, defective piston rings, a blown head gasket or casting cracks.

Electronic Ignition Tools

Since 1975, General Motors truck engines feature High Energy Ignitions (HEI) with an electronic module that eliminates the need for breaker points. Earlier HEI still relies on vacuum and centrifugal spark advance mechanisms.

Later GM truck models have computer driven electronic spark and fuel management. Beginning in 1987, GM switched its gasoline fueled light truck engines from carburetion to Throttle Body Injection (TBI/EFI).

0014123

Fig. 4-50. Electronic ignitions have reduced service requirements. This 1986 GM HEI distributor on a Federal (49-State) emissions K2500 Suburban is accessible and serviceable. For these ignitions, the primary troubleshooting tool is a volt-ohmmeter.

From a service standpoint, the electronic distributor has actually reduced truck maintenance. Electronic ignitions eliminate the need to gap points and set dwell. Instead, troubleshooting now consists of ohmmeter and voltage tests. Here, a precision digital-type volt/ohmmeter proves invaluable, a must tool.

Timing Light

The timing light has remained an important element of ignition tuning, as normal wear to the camshaft timing chain and distributor drive mechanism still requires periodic tests of spark timing. The ideal timing light has a built-in advance, which allows testing the vacuum advance function and the mechanical (centrifugal) advance if so equipped. Better timing lights are inductive variety. This means that you may hook the connector to the insulation of number-one cylinder's spark cable without disconnecting the cable from the spark plug.

Distributor machines, once popular for testing a distributor unit off the engine, have nearly become obsolete. I still prefer this method for programming distributor spark advance mechanisms. Unfortunately, few shops can provide such services any more.

Timing lights with built-in advance now use the engine as a test stand for spinning the distributor to 1000 to 1250 rpm (2000 to 2500 crankshaft rpm). The timing light's advance mechanism allows zeroing the timing to the factory TDC mark or any other degree setting within the timing light's range. This allows an accurate readout of the distributor's total spark advance.

Stay clear of the fan when using the engine to increase distributor rpm, as fan separation or water pump shaft failure could cause severe bodily injury, even death. Limit rpm as much as possible. If you can perform tests with a cool engine, consider temporarily removing the fan belt(s) and other belts while testing the distributor on the engine. Carefully watch engine temperature, and only perform these tests while the engine remains cool.

Many of the General Motors truck engines have distributor vacuum and centrifugal advance mechanisms. (The late engines with EFI use the computer to adjust all timing functions.) The use of a hand held vacuum pump aids in testing the vacuum type ignition spark advance mechanism.

Tools for Checking Emission Controls

A vacuum pump/pressure tester also serves as a tune-up tool for emission control devices. You can test the exhaust gas recirculation valve (EGR), found on many GM truck engines built since the early 1970s, with a vacuum pump. Additionally, applying vacuum to various emission control parts, like the thermal vacuum switch and bi-metallic air cleaner switch, helps locate leaks and troubles.

As many emission switches rely on coolant temperature, an accurate temperature gauge is necessary. To test the opening point for a thermal vacuum switch, for example, requires both a thermometer and vacuum test tool. Emission control troubleshooting proves far more productive when these tools are available.

On a pre-owned GM truck, emission control devices and hoses may be missing. For restoring the system, I strongly recommend Mitchell's *Emission Control Manual*

0012122

Fig. 4-51. *A quality hand vacuum pump/pressure gauge is valuable. Emission control devices like this EGR valve can be tested easily with a vacuum pump.*

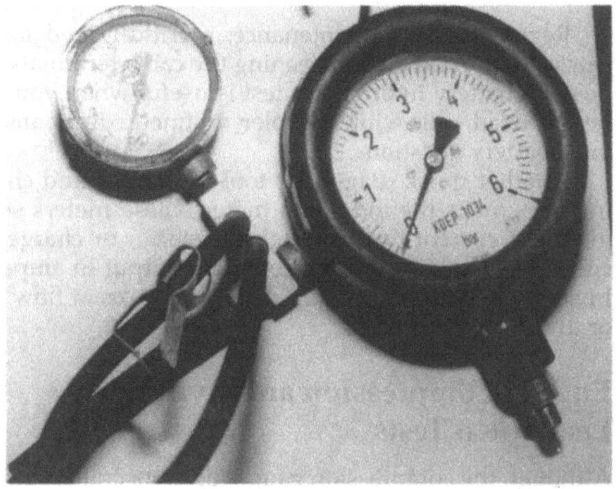

0012123

Fig. 4-52. *Fuel pump pressure affects carburetor needle and seat action. Electronic fuel injection systems require higher, precisely regulated fuel pressure. These gauges pinpoint trouble.*

or your Chevrolet/GMC Truck factory shop manual. Either will provide diagrams and illustrations of the original equipment components. Your Chevrolet or GMC Truck dealership's parts department is the best source for emission legal replacement parts.

Cooling System Tools

General Motors truck engines depend on their cooling systems for survival. Radiator cleanliness, the correct thermostat, the right coolant mixtures and a properly working fan provide the backbone of engine cooling efficiency. For both radiator cap and cooling system tests, a hand pump tester provides quick results. Locating head gasket seepage or a cracked engine casting is also within the scope of a cooling system pressure tester.

For anti-freeze and coolant protection tests, inexpensive radiator hydrometers are available. The reliability of your truck's radiator cap and the concentration of coolant/anti-freeze play a vital role in boil-over protection.

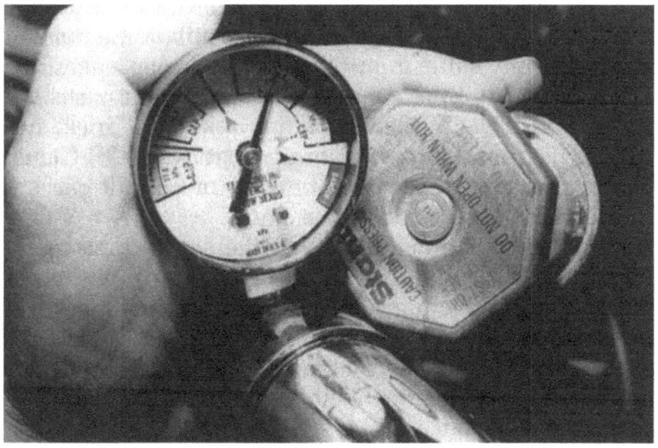

0012124

Fig. 4-53. STANT pressure tester can verify cooling system pressure, find leaks and determine overall condition of the cooling system. This gauge has served for fifteen years, saving a considerable amount of diagnostic time and effort.

Radiator cap pressure also raises the boiling point of the coolant mix.

It is therefore essential to maintain correct pressure in your truck's cooling system. STANT and other companies provide pressure testers for both radiator cap and radiator/cooling system diagnosis. (See the service chapter.)

Soft Tools

Conventional composition gaskets leak from the effects of heat (embrittlement), shrinkage or their inability to fill minute gaps and voids. The gap need not be very large, like a valve cover with a few thousandths of an inch of gasket gap. Such a leak, however, could easily spill an entire crankcase of oil along a remote back country trail. Aging, fatigue and oxidation can affect neoprene, rubber, cork, and even steel gaskets.

0012125

Fig. 4-54. General Motors and aftermarket suppliers offer sealants and chemical soft tools that meet OEM guidelines for your truck. Specialized items, such as rubber bonder, mirror adhesive, thread locking liquids and gasket forming materials, meet rigid standards and assure a quality repair.

Chemical products and sealants, known in the automotive trade as "soft tools," make the ideal companion for your truck's traveling toolbox.

RTV silicone sealants are unlike conventional gaskets. Rather than deteriorate when exposed to corrosive oils, products like Permatex/Loctite's Ultra Blue actually become more flexible, pliant and oil resistant. During engine assembly, you should use silicone products at the oil pan gasket corners, especially between cork and neoprene junctions, such as those found with intake manifold gaskets. Along the trail or in an emergency, Ultra Blue can create a thermostat housing gasket, valve cover gasket, oil pan gasket or timing cover gasket. Ultra Blue and Ultra Copper make smart companions for off-pavement travel.

When selecting an RTV high temperature silicone for exhaust system joints and flanges, make sure the volatility level of the sealant is correct. For applications involving emission control oxygen sensors, use low-volatility sealant. Higher volatility sealants can seriously damage the sensor. Most factory warranties on emission hardware will not cover the replacement of an oxygen sensor damaged by the use of high-volatility RTV sealant.

Never use a non-automotive silicone sealant, like bathtub caulk, on your engine or geartrain parts. On manual gearboxes and axle housings, the correct RTV silicone sealant provides a sturdy, permanent fitup of parts. For some parts assemblies, GM now uses anaerobic sealers that cure in the absence of air. Mechanisms like gasketless transfer cases and alloy transmission housings often require anaerobic type sealants.

> *WARNING —*
> *While many mechanics use silicone sealants to replace conventional gaskets, there are some geartrain parts that use a pre-cut gasket as a selective fit spacer. Unless otherwise specified in your factory shop manual, avoid the use of RTV sealant with selective fit gaskets.*

For axle differential covers and all oil exposed seals, automotive RTV silicone can help eliminate seepage. GM trucks, especially 4x4s, can flex and distort paper gaskets, and older transmission and transfer case cut gaskets are notorious for leaking. Many late powertrain components no longer use cut gaskets, substituting the more flexible silicone products.

RTV sealant allows a more direct fitup of parts, which reduces flexing, keeps hardware from loosening and helps prevent parts misalignment. Although neoprene-lipped seals still serve on many shaft surfaces, the outer jacket of these seals should also be lightly coated with automotive RTV silicone before driving the seal into place. This includes timing cover seals, transmission front shaft and output shaft seals and axle shaft seals. Although coating the jacket of a seal will not prevent the lip portion from failing, you can reduce the likelihood of housing bore-to-seal seepage.

Once you become familiar with the properties and proper uses of these sealants and adhesives, they prove as handy as your screwdrivers and wrenches. Often, soft tools provide faster, more permanent repairs than con-

Fig. 4-55. For front wheel alignment at home, consider an inexpensive toe-set bar. Toe-in is easy to calculate and adjust on a solid front axle truck.

ventional gaskets—especially when your makeshift garage is in remote back country.

Miscellaneous Chores

There are other tasks that you may want to perform on your Chevrolet or GMC light truck. In particular, front end alignment is a relatively easy job on a 2WD solid beam or 4WD solid hypoid front driving axle. Adjusting toe-in may be within the scope of your service work. The setting of caster and camber, however, involves more skill, special tools and sometimes special parts. A solid front axle with springs in good shape seldom requires caster or camber adjustment.

Toe-in changes caused by normal wear of steering linkage take place over time. Inexpensive toe-set alignment bars, available through Eastwood Company and other outlets, serve the home mechanic. These toe bars can easily be used on 2WD solid beam and solid axle 4x4 trucks. Performing your truck's toe-set provides savings in both service costs and longer tire life.

A variety of miscellaneous tools serve your truck's needs. Body work and paint, detailing chores and repair of upholstery are often part of a complete restoration. With proper maintenance or restoration, your General Motors truck will deliver years of rugged service.

8. SOURCING CHEVROLET/GMC TRUCK PARTS

For many models, your local GM truck dealer remains the most reliable parts source. Chevrolet has recently expanded its line of Genuine Chevrolet restoration parts for earlier models, a boon to restorers.

Genuine General Motors, Delco-Remy and Rochester parts provide a high quality standard and your assurance of proper fitup. When restoring your truck to OEM standards, your local Chevrolet or GMC Truck dealership can often assist.

The indomitable nature of General Motors trucks, the massive numbers of older GM trucks still on the road and the collectible value of particular models has encouraged aftermarket suppliers to provide replacement parts. Popularity of 1939–59 pickups alone assures a brisk niche market for remaining new original stock (NOS) General Motors parts and accurate replica or rebuilt parts for models built over five decades ago.

Chassis components are available through quality lines like MOOG and TRW, even for many of the early trucks. For truck engines, many with passenger car counterparts, repair pieces remain readily accessible. The sheer numbers of Chevrolet and GMC (plus Pontiac V-8) engines built assure the likelihood of parts availability for many years. Even the Stovebolt 216 OHV sixes remain popular enough for vendors to market new, reproduction or rebuilt parts.

Automotive parts outlets and machine shops throughout North and South America are very familiar with all General Motors light truck engines. "Perishable" and fast moving items like shock absorbers, ignition parts, filters, belts and hoses are available through local parts outlets, especially national retailers like NAPA. Whether a new or vintage model, your GM truck will always be among the most popular and roadworthy vehicles in its class.

Aftermarket Geartrain Sources

Axle, transmission, driveshaft and transfer case pieces are available from a number of sources. Many geartrain pieces have industry-wide use. Dana, Spicer, Borg-Warner (Warner Gear Division), New Process, Eaton and other manufacturers have produced a variety of gear components for General Motors and other American-built trucks.

In some instances, interchangeability of parts between makes is possible. Often, though, the GM truck version of a gear or powertrain component is unique, which will make parts sourcing more complicated. For older models, aftermarket parts sources often have easier access to parts than the modern GM dealership, including items for engine rebuilding, re-wiring sources, fuel system repair parts, chassis/suspension and steering components, brake parts, and even some new or replica body panels.

Mail-Order Aftermarket

The brisk aftermarket of 4WD and off-highway vehicle parts also serves General Motors light trucks. Businesses like Dick Cepek and Four-Wheel Parts (Wholesalers) do a huge mail-order and retail business. Product lines range from tires and off-road accessory items to winches and utility products for 4x4 trucks. Geartrain and traction devices are also available.

J.C. Whitney and other mail-order retailers have kept suburban and rural GM truck owners in parts for many years. Whitney and Eastwood Company serve restorers of vintage trucks, and Whitney now caters to the burgeoning recreational truck market. For details on a variety of parts sources, see the appendix. In the accessories and performance chapters, I describe many of the available aftermarket enhancements.

Local Parts Outlets

The local auto parts store can help with tune-up and routine service parts. Choose the best available tune-up components for your truck. Bargain hunting for replacement parts is unwise. When genuine Delco-Remy parts are not available, I have four aftermarket preferences (starting with my top choice): NAPA/Echlin, Autolite, Bendix and Standard-Blue Streak.

Water crossings and foul-weather driving conditions require a much higher standard of performance from your GM truck. Especially with 4x4 models, water-proofing is a practical goal for your ignition distributor, coil and secondary spark cables. (See tune-up and performance chapters for details on ignition service and upgrades.)

Quality Filtration

For consistent performance, use genuine AC-Delco replacement air and fuel filters. High performance filtration systems are available from aftermarket sources including K&N Engineering and AMSOIL. (See performance chapter for details.)

Any General Motors truck exposed to poor quality fuels or water contamination, especially diesel engines, needs an add-on fuel filtration system. This includes diesel water trap filters and similar devices for gasoline engines that operate in regions where fuel has a high water content.

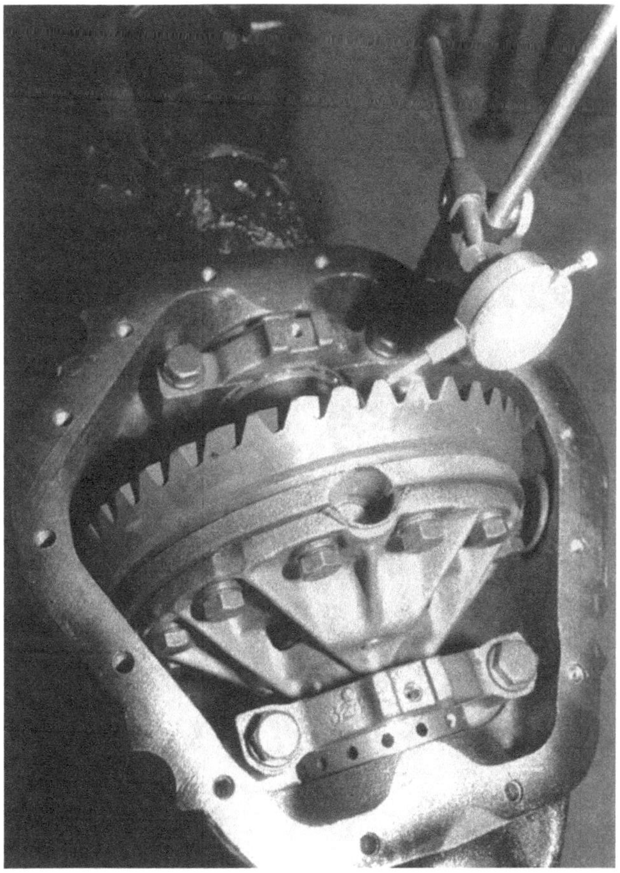

0014126

Fig. 4-56. An axle assembly or automatic transmission overhaul requires special tools and skills. Unless you are building a career around light truck mechanics, consider sending these types of jobs to a specialist.

9. ASSIGNING WORK TO A SHOP

For many consumers, nurturing a second career as an automotive/truck mechanic is impractical. You may find that performing hands-on mechanical work has no appeal. Perhaps your lifestyle or work space is too busy for servicing your own vehicle. Sometimes, the cost of special tools or the sheer scope of a repair job ranges beyond your capacity. Chasing parts and tying up your vehicle for unreasonable periods can be costly and stressful.

Assigning such jobs to a specialist can save considerable time and assure quality workmanship. You'll save in the long run by setting your ego or the challenge aside and simply recognizing that you would be better off assigning the work elsewhere.

Assess the Job

Whether you enjoy servicing your vehicle or saving the cost of labor on repairs, each task has its challenges. My approach to mechanics always begins with a thorough review of the job, starting at the factory service guidebook for my vehicle. The factory manuals assist at troubleshooting problems and give step-by-step instructions for performing mechanical tasks. Each repair includes a list of specialty tools required.

The factory shop manual can even serve truck owners who plan to assign repairs. If you can pinpoint the actual problem, or at least narrow the field of possibilities, you have a distinct advantage when approaching a shop or dealership service facility.

The Well-informed Customer

If you assign work to an independent shop or dealership's service department, your sense for the repairs needed can help the staff. When your diagnosis is accurate, the mechanic can focus on the actual trouble and save time—and your money—by not having to troubleshoot the job. If you suspect that extra service is being sold, your own shop manual can verify whether such service id warranted for the kind of troubles and repairs in question.

Having written and worked from repair orders within a truck dealership environment, I suggest that you approach the service department with diplomacy. Surveys often reveal that American consumers mistrust auto repair facilities. Surely, there are unscrupulous shops or service operations that set profit above all other consid-

0014128

Fig. 4-57. Since the mid-1980s, vehicle manufacturers have placed far more emphasis on customer satisfaction. Ethical transactions at the service department are encouraged, often through incentives for achieving a high Customer Satisfaction Index (CSI) when customers are polled about service quality and ethics. OBD (On-board Diagnostic) equipment raises customer satisfaction.

erations, but the current trend has been toward improved customer relations.

Your best safeguard is information. Become a well-informed consumer who has a sense for the task at hand and reasonable costs. In fairness, remember that the shop staff has more experience at troubleshooting and repairs. If you insist that a certain repair be done, you will pay whether that was the problem or not. When there is a gray area, you are wiser to pay for further diagnostic work and an opinion from the professional mechanic.

Flat-rate Cost Estimating

In some cases, you will find that shopping around (phoning different shops, asking friends where they do business, etc.) is an effective way to determine a fair cost for repairs. When you know the exact work needed and are certain that the truck will perform properly once a competent shop does these tasks, then you can do your own cost estimation work.

The standard practice for billing automotive service in the United States and Canada is by "flat rate." This provides a basis for estimating repair costs and paying the mechanic. Flat-rate work differs substantially from clock or hourly labor billing, the latter varying greatly on a given job due to different mechanics' skill levels, obstacles in a given job, or tools available in the shop.

As a former fleet and dealership truck mechanic, my personal library includes flat-rate labor and parts estimating guidebooks offered by Chilton, Motor and Mitchell. These books are the professional trade variety found in independent repair shops and dealerships. Automotive/truck dealerships also use new vehicle warranty labor time schedules.

The flat-rate guidebook lists specific labor operations and the recognized fair time to perform tasks. You can acquire such books, new or used, and actually do your own labor estimating before shopping for repairs. It is also reasonable to ask the service writer/salesperson to provide a labor time guidebook.

Become familiar with the guide's format and how to read an estimate. For example, many procedures overlap. The overhaul of an engine will say whether the overhaul includes removal-and-replacement (R & R) of the engine from its chassis. If so indicated in the guidebook, the shop should not charge for R & R of the engine plus the overhaul. Tune-up procedures may include diagnosis. If so indicated, you should not pay for diagnosis as a separate procedure.

I also find the parts estimating section of my books valuable, although in fairness, parts pricing changes frequently.

Ethics and the Flat-rate System

Flat-rate pays minimal (if any) time for diagnostic work. Most vehicles brought into the shop for repair focus only on a current trouble symptom. Flat-rate time does not include preventive maintenance or inspection. If you want thorough service and inspection of your truck, that is a separate labor procedure, which bears an additional cost.

The flat-rate mechanic must make quick and accurate assessment of a problem and propose a repair procedure. When the paid repair fails to make a difference, a credibility gap develops. The shop likely contends that you should pay for the first repair, especially if an observable improvement occurred. You, on the other hand, may feel that the shop failed to cure the symptoms yet took your hard earned money.

If no change in the original symptom took place, the flat-rate system (when ethically applied) says that your mechanic has earned a "come back." This means the mechanic absorbs the labor cost of the first repair, and sometimes the shop absorbs the parts cost. This punishment of the mechanic supposedly serves as an incentive to prevent hasty or inaccurate diagnosis.

The largest complaint that consumers have about the flat-rate system is its emphasis on parts replacement. Unfortunately, since a hard hourly flat-rate program can only apply to repairs entailing R & R of parts, the system does encourage outright parts replacement.

The flat-rate system implies that automotive troubleshooting and repair estimating are an exact science. In fact, jobs like troubleshooting a late model electronic fuel and spark management system can become ensnared in the mysteries of systems overlap—or mired in the complexities and idiosyncratic nature of computer programming. Such engineering issues often reach beyond the control of a service technician.

In my view, many automotive labor procedures can fall within consistent time frames—R & R operations like a transmission overhaul, differential rebuild, engine overhaul, alternator replacement or brake system overhaul. However, I also believe that mechanics deserve more time for diagnostic work. This would encourage more thorough repairs and increase the likelihood of long term, preventive remedies.

Knowledge Is Your Best Bet

In the automotive flat-rate system, here is how the R & R incentive works: You approach the service shop with a complaint that your truck's engine has a misfire. The ethical mechanic in a well-equipped shop will put the engine on an oscilloscope and analyze the exhaust content and ignition performance.

Let's say your six-cylinder engine shows that #2 cylinder's spark firing line is weak. As a fleet mechanic, I would check resistance of the plug wire at #2 cylinder

0014129

Fig. 4-58. Most repair personnel commonly replace, rather than overhaul, a sub-assembly. The argument is often cost effectiveness, even with the extreme of replacing entire assemblies. Cheaper goods and cost competitive rebuilt parts have denigrated the role of field service technicians and mechanics who once took responsibility for actually fixing a worn or defective product or sub-assembly.

0014130

Fig. 4-59. Diagnostic equipment can save time and provide detailed insight into problems. If a shop has high quality diagnostic equipment, you can expect more reasonable and accurate estimates. Such shops should expect to pay for equipment with satisfied customers and repeat business.

and compare this reading with other wires. The air filter and other parts would deserve a quick look, but once the ignition system was isolated as a problem, I'd focus on restoring the plug firing line for #2 cylinder. If I found that other wires, the distributor components or spark plugs looked marginal, some of those parts would also be replaced.

A flat-rate mechanic, wanting to avoid a costly comeback and recognizing that the parts department likes additional sales, decides to cover all possibilities. The parts list soon includes a fuel filter, air cleaner, six new platinum spark plugs, a distributor rotor, a full set of spark plug wires and the PCV valve.

The service estimator/writer/salesperson usually calls the customer and gains approval for installation of these parts. Here is how the dialog might go: "Ms. Jones, your engine's misfire is ignition related, but the mechanic feels that the engine shows other wear points, and he would like to perform a complete tune-up. When was the engine tuned last?"

To the salesperson, this question is critical. If you had such work done recently, there would be no basis for buying all these parts and service. The mechanic would simply replace the one spark plug wire and bill accordingly.

As a consumer, you need to make decisions based upon your knowledge of the vehicle's service history and the factory recommended service guidelines. Your factory-level shop manual describes the normal intervals between tune-ups and other routine maintenance. Keeping a trail of maintenance work orders helps you prevent an overly zealous service writer from re-selling work recently done.

Ask, nicely, how the mechanic arrived at the conclusion that all of these parts need replacement. Since the diagnosis involves ignition or fuel problems, ask what diagnostic equipment aided the conclusions. Did the equipment suggest that all of these parts needed replacement to end the symptoms and restore reliable and economical operation of the engine?

Unless a problem is obvious, request thorough diagnostic procedures. General Motors' latest interactive computer diagnostic equipment, a highly advanced tool, can interrogate the latest fuel and spark management and electronically controlled transmission programming. If a service facility like your local dealership has such equipment, you can radically reduce the risk of engine or powertrain mis-diagnosis and unnecessary repair work. Money spent here is spent wisely.

Remember that the adage "too much knowledge is dangerous" applies. Don't flaunt your wisdom and insight. You will find that an ethical mechanic or service writer will happily share information and engage in dialog. Such an exchange is valuable, as there are many diagnostic gaps that only a mechanic's experience can overcome.

Chapter 5

Lubrication and Maintenance

REGULAR MAINTENANCE is the most important way to attain maximum service from your General Motors light truck. Preventive care proves cost effective and assures reliable performance when your truck needs it.

Preventive maintenance can reduce the risk of hazardous and costly breakdowns. As a truck fleet mechanic and heavy equipment operator, I trained at visualizing potential weaknesses in a chassis, engine and geartrain. The best place for making these observations was during routine lubrication and service.

Although much of a truck's maintenance is routine, such care has a direct effect on your safety. For 4x4 trucks that travel to remote and nearly inaccessible places, regular maintenance could prevent a serious breakdown or equipment related accident. Even simple fluid or filter changes will help ensure good engine performance and fuel efficiency when the going gets tough.

1. Do Your Own "Full-service" Maintenance

Most modern gasoline stations fail to meet motorists' needs. Drivers at many Full Service pumps pay up to two-fifths more per gallon for fuel, expecting genuine vehicle care. Perhaps their windshield receives attention or the attendant will ask if the oil needs checking. After several minutes beneath the hood, some attendants return to inquire, "Where's the oil dipstick?"

When I was a high school student in the mid-1960s, there was Bud Berrum's Chevron, across the highway from the C.O.D. Garage at Minden, Nevada. I worked after school and summers for Bud, and he ran a real service station. As attendants, we catered to customers' needs, and that meant thorough service.

If you drove into Bud's Chevron while I was on shift, your cares were over. I'd pump 94 to 110 octane gas into your tank, check your oil, drive belts, hoses, automatic transmission fluid, brake fluid, battery and windshield washer fluid.

Without leaving a streak, I'd whisk away the summer bugs or January ice from your windshield, wipe your sideview mirror and even clean the back window glass. If your truck's tires were cool enough, I'd check pressures at all four corners plus the spare if accessible.

What did this cost? Nothing more than your gasoline business and, if you felt like it, you could say, "Thanks!"

The lube room was always busy, with a grease job for two dollars and fifty cents, and a lube, oil and filter running near five dollars, depending upon the filter's cost. A thorough wheel bearing repack, even on a 4x4 truck, would be less than six dollars, including the price of new seals.

For these services, I'd take out Standard Oil's lubrication chart and look up your truck model. The guide listed each grease fitting, gear case check point and fluid type. It also noted how frequently each service procedure should

0012131

Fig. 5-1. Chassis lubrication provides an excellent opportunity to inspect your truck's undercarriage. By performing such chores, you become intimately aware of your truck's needs. This is a vital part of preventive care.

be performed, and at the truck's last service, I put a dated mileage sticker on the door jamb as a reminder.

All fittings greased, the engine oil drained, gearbox and axle oil levels checked, rubber bushings dressed with rubber lube, I would inspect the clutch free-play, exhaust system and chassis. After installing a new oil pan drain plug gasket, I'd lower your truck carefully and head for the hood latch.

Armed with special data for your GM truck, I'd remove and service the oil bath air cleaner (if so equipped), check the radiator coolant with a hydrometer, inspect the steering gearbox fluid level, and carefully check brake fluid—only after vacuuming the dirty floorboard around the inspection plate (1939–59 GM trucks) and brushing all dirt away from the master cylinder fill plug or cap.

Next, I'd clean the battery case, check its water and wire brush the terminals. Since early trucks had generators and wick-oiled distributors, a squirt can of motor oil was always handy. Careful not to overfill the wicks, I'd apply oil with a light squeeze of the trigger. Then, as the engine crankcase filled from the station's five-quart copper down spout can (adding three more quarts if your truck had an inline GMC six—plus a top off for the new by-pass oil filter cartridge), I would test all lights and the turn signals—if your truck was equipped with them!

Finally, I'd spray lube each hood, door and tailgate hinge, the parking brake handle mechanism and even the ball bearing in your ash tray. Before the truck rolled out the door, I would vacuum the cab, clean all of the windows (inside and out), and check tire air pressures for all four tires and your side-mounted or under chassis spare.

Was this all that our customers came to expect? Oh, no! A free wash job went with each lube and oil change. Winter or summer, searing heat or low teens temperatures (complete with a frozen water bucket and wash mitten), I'd wash your truck thoroughly and be thankful for the $1.50 per hour that Bud paid me!

Well, times have changed. Now, I'm recommending that you do your own service. You'll be better off for it. Not only will you learn more about your favorite truck, you'll also be better equipped to handle problems afield.

Bud Berrum's training gave me a darn good foundation. My first stint as a truck fleet mechanic yielded a zero breakdown record for the organization's twenty-two vehicles. I had entered the job with a thorough grasp of preventive maintenance. If you take this whole thing half as seriously as Bud and I, your Chevrolet or GMC truck will give its all.

Defining Chassis Maintenance

Your truck's chassis, though durable and designed for longevity, requires regular maintenance. Earlier GM trucks demand more chassis service than later models, and 1939–59 models, in particular, have grease fittings at the kingpins, shackle bushings, spring anchor bolts, pedal pivots, steering linkage, shift linkage and several other wear points. Even the 1960–66 2WD/IFS and 4WD chassis is loaded with grease fittings.

Later models use zero-maintenance nylon and rubber bushings at most wear points. Such pieces still require periodic inspection and need replacement when they wear out. According to GM's maintenance schedules, most greaseable joints demand lubrication at 1,000-3,000 mile intervals. They, too, wear out, which means time for new bushings.

Minimizing wear at friction points is the overall goal of chassis maintenance. In your Chevrolet or GMC Truck factory shop manual or owner's handbook, you will find a chassis lubrication chart for your model. Pay close attention to the greases specified and service intervals.

As a home mechanic, you will likely use a hand grease gun, which minimizes grease seal damage. U-joints, in particular, require hand gun lubrication. High pressure equipment can destroy delicate seals, leaving a U-joint exposed to debris and abrasive contaminants.

Selecting Lubricants and Fluids

Various lubricants, oils, greases and fluids serve your GM truck. Proper oils and fluids are crucial to the reliability of your vehicle. Compatibility of oils, correct quantities and proper viscosities are each essential to proper maintenance.

Earlier trucks require conventional lubricants. Typically, 90-wt. gear oil fills the differentials, manual steering gearbox, manual transmission and transfer case. With the advent of chain-drive full-time 4x4 systems, automatic transmission fluid (ATF) has become common for both the automatic transmission and transfer case. Many late model manual gear cases also call for lighter lubricants.

Mixing oil brands and types is a mistake. Even when viscosity and type (GL or API rating) are the same, oil producers use different chemical additives with their base stocks. Strange chassis/wheel bearing greases, engine oils or gear oils may react adversely with your truck's existing lubricants. For this reason, the General Motors truck owner who maintains his or her own vehicle has a distinct advantage: the ability to assure consistent use of compatible fluids, greases and oils.

When changing engine oil, select a brand and stay with it. Carry a spare can or bottle of this type oil to assure availability in the field. Likewise, when draining and refilling the gearboxes or differential(s), adhere to a specific type and brand of lubricant.

0014133

Fig. 5-2. GM light trucks have specific lubrication requirements. General Motors offers special gear oils, power steering fluid and wheel bearing grease. Your best assurance of long service life is quality lubrication at recommended intervals.

Synthetic oils have generated much controversy. Synthetic lubricants will outperform conventional crude oil base stocks under heavy duty/severe service use. Regardless of your choice, beware of compatibility. Avoid mixing stocks of synthetic oil with either conventional oils or other synthetic brands.

Note your vehicle's warranty requirements as they relate to lubricants, oil types and ratings. When uncertain about the correct lubricant for a given area of your truck, refer to the owner's handbook or a factory shop manual.

Proper Greases

Lubrication greases have become simpler in recent years. Many vehicle manufacturers use a common, multi-purpose grease for all chassis, steering linkage and wheel bearing needs. I still prefer precise greases for each application: a specified chassis/steering linkage and U-joint grease or a specific wheel bearing lubricant. Use the highest grade grease when servicing your truck's wheel bearings (usually designated as a wheel bearing grease for disc brake models).

CAUTION —
Earlier 2WD GM light trucks use ball-type front wheel bearings. If your truck is so equipped, be certain that the grease you choose will work with these types of bearings. Note that ball-type wheel bearings also require special maintenance and adjustment procedures. These adjustments are critical to vehicle safety and normal bearing life. Methods for adjusting tapered roller bearings and ball-type bearings differ dramatically. (Consult your factory-level shop manual for the wheel bearing adjustment technique that applies to your model.)

Wheel bearing greases and chassis lubes have various base stocks. A major concern is compatibility of greases. Do not mix brands or types of grease. If you have just begun servicing your wheel bearings, thoroughly remove all old grease before repacking with fresh grease. (See other chapters for wheel bearing service details.)

On steering linkage and chassis joint grease fittings, simply pump fresh grease through the assembly until only new grease squeezes out. Wipe away excess with a rag. This will prevent abrasive dirt from accumulating around the joint.

Gear Oil

For gear case lubricants and oils, use a slightly different strategy. Ideally, especially if your truck has higher mileage, the gear units should be drained and refilled with a high grade gear oil. As with engine oil, gear oil viscosity and type must correspond to climate and the load on your vehicle.

Once you've selected an oil brand/type, periodic inspection and topping off will be simple. If you drive your truck extensively off-pavement or to remote reaches, squeeze bottle containers are practical, easy dispensers. Major oil companies distribute gear lube in pint or quart size plastic bottles, ideal for stowage on board.

Service Intervals

The tight factory service recommendations for early GM trucks, such as chassis lubrication each 1,000 miles, assume that users will give their vehicles a real workout. When subjected to severe environments or heavy work, older trucks, and especially 4x4s, demand closer care than later models.

Longer oil change intervals allow oil to deteriorate. The contemporary 5,000-7,500 mile oil change recommendations of many vehicle manufacturers mean that combustion contaminants will find their way into the crankcase oil for even longer periods. At recommended oil change points, with crude stock (conventional) oils, crankcase contamination can reach ten percent.

Your truck demands the best. For maximum service life and performance, adjust oil and filter change intervals to 2,000 to 3,000 miles with premium grade conventional (crude or mineral base) oil. Even with synthetic oil, light truck driving demands call for oil change intervals at 7,500 to 10,000 miles with filter changes and an oil top-off each 3,000 to 3,500 miles.

0014134

Fig. 5-3. For the 4x4 K-truck that makes stream crossings, consider extending the axle housing or transmission and transfer case vents upward onto the body. Using pipe thread nipples, oil resistant hose and insulated clamps, mount these vents well above the axle or gearbox. This reduces the risk of water entering important geartrain parts during water crossings.

Four-by-four K-model trucks have special requirements. Few vehicles submerge wheel hubs and axle housings in swift running streams. If your 4x4 sees this kind of use, regular wheel bearing service and axle housing inspection is mandatory. If you stall in a fast moving stream or suspect water seepage into the wheel hubs, clean and repack the wheel bearings immediately.

Recognizing the superior quality of modern chassis and wheel bearing greases, you can usually extend the intervals between wheel bearing and axle shaft service. Be certain that wheel hub seals, gaskets, axle and gear unit vent hoses and the one-way vent check valves can each do their job.

Building a Maintenance Schedule for Severe Service

Common sense should dictate your truck's service intervals. Years ago, service intervals were more frequent. Industrial and agricultural truck users changed gear lube each 300 hours, flushed the cooling system twice a year and fussed constantly over the amazing number of chassis lubrication points.

In industrial or farm work, oil bath air cleaner service takes place every 100 to 150 hours. (As always, dust conditions affect these figures.) If your truck has gone through twenty miles of alkaline gravel road, or at a snail's pace in high dust conditions, service the oil bath air cleaner (early GM trucks) or change your later truck's dry paper element.

0014141

Fig. 5-4. During stream fording, water drawn through the air intake snorkel can quickly pass through a paper element and into engine cylinders. If sufficient in volume, this water can act like a hydraulic ram, bending connecting rods or breaking other vital engine parts. Protect your intake system from exposure to water, and avoid use of an open faced paper filter air cleaner.

Likewise, for 4x4 trucks, stalling the vehicle for several minutes in a thirty-inch-deep, fast flowing stream raises several concerns. You will immediately need to inspect the hubs, wheel bearings, each gear unit and the engine oil for water contamination. Grease all fittings to flush out water.

Similarly, a day's play in dusty sand dunes begs a complete chassis lube and careful air cleaner service. (Keep sand from the intake area when you remove the filter.) Before performing this service, wash the chassis with a high pressure approach, like the local car wash.

2. You Can Lube Your Own Truck!

Many truck owners have developed a better knowledge of their vehicles by performing routine service. Aside from saving sublet labor costs, you can learn about how your truck works and contribute to its reliability.

The greatest benefit of routine service is that you can find a problem before it becomes costly to repair or causes an inopportune breakdown. You can inspect areas and assure that the truck's vital components are intact and properly lubricated. This, basically, is what quality preventive maintenance is all about.

You should keep an accurate account of the service you perform on the truck. Over time, various patterns emerge, and the routine begins to pay off. By keeping these records and holding onto receipts for parts purchases, you will enhance the value of your truck for resale.

Since the best way to learn routine service is by watching close-up, I have constructed a pictorial guide for basic lubrication work. (See troubleshooting and service chapters for specific details on mechanical inspection.) Compare these steps with recommended procedures found in your GM truck owner's handbook or factory shop manual.

If you follow the manufacturer's service interval guidelines, your truck will have a long and reliable life. Use the right tools to protect your hands and eyes, and always recycle or dispose of your drained fluids and other hazardous materials properly.

Engine Oil and Filter Change

Begin service by placing a drain pan beneath the engine's oil pan. Whether oil is warm or hot, wear an industrial rubber glove for protection. Drain oil is caustic and contains carcinogenic agents.

Oil filters differ depending on the year of your GM truck. Early Chevrolet and GMC light truck engines have cartridge type by-pass oil filters. A replacement cartridge fits securely within the canister. See Fig. 5-6. Earlier GMC 305 V-6s, 1957–67 Chevrolet V-8s and 1955–59 GMC/Pontiac V-8s use a full-flow type canister oil filter that mounts to the engine block, much like later full-flow spin-on filters. Chevrolet inline sixes through 1962 and GMC inline

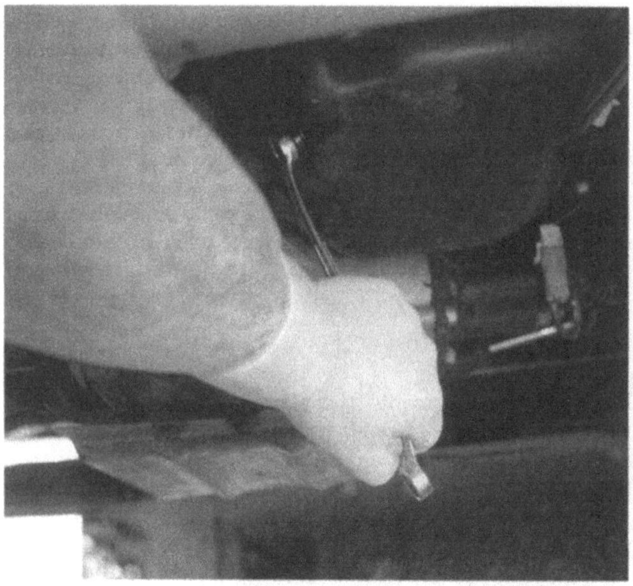

0014135

Fig. 5-5. It is better to drain engine oil when the engine is warm. To make sure all the old oil drains, leave the plug out while you perform other lube chores.

Synthetic Versus Mineral Oil Products

When the early Stovebolt and Jimmy inline OHV sixes reigned, few oil choices existed. Viscosity and detergent levels were the major considerations when picking an oil. Until the 1960s, multi-viscosity oil was virtually non-existent.

Until the advent of synthetic oils, the fundamental difference between one brand of oil and another was the additive package. Generally, we accept that a modern, multi-viscosity, high-detergent / dispersant oil will offer broader engine protection under the widest variety of engine operating conditions.

Over the last two decades, a newer debate has surfaced around mineral versus synthetic based oils and greases. This controversy will likely reign through the 1990s, but on the basis of currently available information, a higher quality synthetic oil or grease is superior to a conventional mineral or crude stock product.

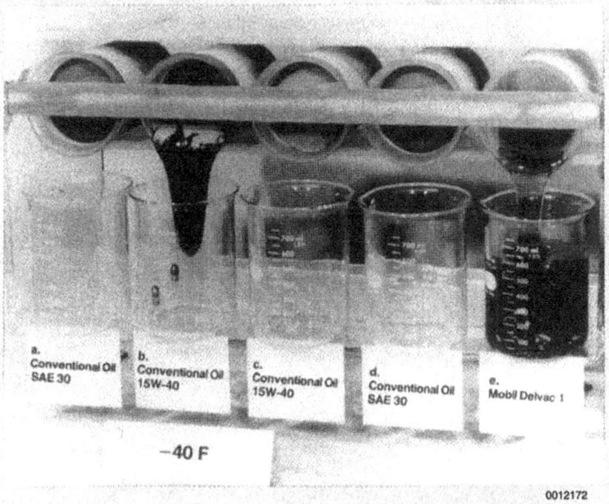

A major engine killer is sludge. Plugged or restricted oil screens mean scored bearings and engine failure. Poor oil circulation always accompanies sludge. Although changing oil is the best way to resist sludge buildup, other factors also play a role. The composition of an oil, regardless of the oil drain intervals, can contribute to sludge buildup.

High temperatures also encourage sludge buildup. Teardown of a worn truck engine generally reveals sludge in the valve covers, timing cover, and lower block or oil pan. It is easy to spot the engine's highest temperature areas; they show the greatest sludge deposits.

The typical gasoline automotive engine, for each 100 gallons of fuel burned, produces a horrifying 1 / 4 to 4 pounds of nitrogen and sulfuric acid, 1 to 2 ounces of hydrochloric acid, 90 to 120 gallons of water, and 3 to 10 gallons of unburned gasoline. For the once popular lead-additive gasolines, add 6 to 10 ounces of lead salts to this medley of pollutants. At the typical 3,000-mile drain interval, petroleum oils in the crankcase have reached a contamination level of at least four percent.

How, then, do synthetic oil manufacturers extend oil change intervals to as high as 25,000 miles? Mobil and others claim that longer term viscosity stability (due to superior control of hydrocarbon volatility), plus greater resistance to sludge formation, contribute to these longer service cycles. Superior ingredients reduce engine heat, friction and oxidation. Higher film strength and lower volatility allow many synthetic oils to last longer and protect an engine far better than any mineral base oil currently available.

The lubrication quality, engine cooling and the cleansing action of synthetics is exceptional. Even at -40° F (pictured) Mobil Delvac 1 still pours. Typical mineral based oils have already solidified. More importantly, the piston ring sealing properties of an oil largely determine the amount of contaminants that will find their way into the crankcase.

Test results show Mobil 1 can operate an engine 50° F cooler than a premium mineral based oil. As oil is responsible for cooling pistons, rings, the valvetrain, the crankshaft assembly and other critical running parts, oil temperature reduction represents a significant gain.

Under laboratory tests, high grade synthetic oils drastically reduce sludge, piston varnish, wear of metal parts and oil consumption. Prominent race engine builders confirm the merits of synthetic oils.

Notably, Smokey Yunick, quoted from a *Popular Science* interview, comments about his Indianapolis 500 engine and polyol synthetic. Upon teardown after the race, Yunick observed, "When you disassemble an engine that's been run on petroleum oil, if you examine the rings and cylinder bores with a glass, you'll see ridges and scratches—that's wear going on. With polyol (a variety of synthetic), when you take the engine apart, everything has the appearance of being chrome plated. In the engine we ran at Indianapolis, we used a polyol synthetic. When we tore the engine down, you could still see the original honing marks on the bearings...no wear at all. We put the same bearings back in because the crankshaft never touched the bearings. I've never seen that before."

Is such protection necessary for your truck? Recognizing the stresses of heavy hauling, off-road driving and harsh climates, any oil product would face hard work in a GM truck engine.

On the downside, many owners switching to synthetic oil on high mileage engines have trouble. Worn, varnish-coated seals and gaskets, suddenly faced with the high cleansing action and superior lubricity of synthetic oil, sometimes begin to leak. The synthetic oil has washed away the false sealing surfaces of built-up varnish and deposits.

Seals and gaskets may require upgrading before your truck's gear units or engine will adequately hold synthetic oil. Once seals meet normal standards, however, a synthetic oil could actually increase seal and gasket life.

Weigh the information available. If your Chevrolet or GMC truck powertrain is in top shape, relatively new or recently restored, consider use of high grade synthetic lubricants. The added protection, probability of longer component life and extension of service intervals will usually offset the higher cost of these products.

0014136

Fig. 5-6. If your filter mounts separately from the engine (arrow), with oil lines connected to the engine block, you have a by-pass oil filter. The permanently mounted steel canister has a removable top.

0014137

Fig. 5-7. While oil drains from the pan, remove the canister's top and disassemble the filter, noting the parts layout. Discard the cartridge (examples center and right, above) and wipe sludge and debris from the interior of the housing. A clean rag or shop towel, dampened lightly with solvent, will help here. At left is a spin-on oil filter for a later engine.

sixes through 1959 use by-pass type cartridge oil filtration, as do the 1955 and '56 265 Chevy V-8.

Install a new cartridge, making certain that the oil seal(s) are in place and seat squarely. Replace all pieces carefully, in the reverse order of disassembly. Re-install the mounting bolt. Install a new gasket under the mounting bolt head if wear is evident.

Chevrolet introduced spin-on oil filters with the 1963 230 and 292 inline sixes. Light truck small-block and big-block V-8s changed over in 1968, while GMC V-6s changed to spin-on filtration in 1966. See Fig. 5-8.

Use a clean shop rag to wipe the area around the filter base. Keep debris away from oil passages. Apply a small film of clean engine oil to the spin-on filter gasket before installing. Follow directions on the filter, and tighten the unit securely. Avoid overtightening, however, or you will have a very difficult time removing the filter next time.

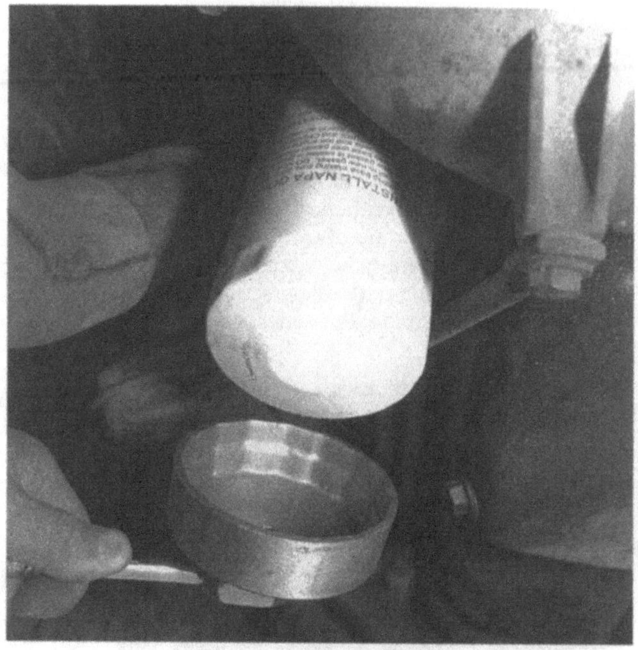

0014138

Fig. 5-8. If your GM truck engine has a spin-on oil filter, replace the unit with each oil change. Remove the oil filter carefully, using a special filter wrench.

0012140

Fig. 5-9. It's wise to stock some new gaskets if you plan to perform your own lube and oil change service. Be careful not to cross-thread the drain plug when you re-install it.

Clean and inspect the drain plug gasket. See Fig. 5-9. If the gasket is damaged or worn, replace it with a new one of the same type and size. Stock some new drain plug gaskets if you plan to perform your own lube and oil change services. Be cautious when threading the drain plug, and tighten it to specification.

Topside in the engine bay, wipe the oil fill cap/hole before removing the cap. Make sure that dirt cannot enter the engine during service. Pour oil carefully and avoid spilling by using a spout can or funnel if necessary. After filling crankcase with specified amount of oil, replace the cap and start the engine at an idle. Check for oil leaks around filter and drain plug. Shut off the engine, let it set for several minutes, then re-check oil level on dipstick. Make sure oil reaches the FULL mark. Add oil as needed.

0014140

Fig. 5-10. It's important to make sure that no dirt enters the engine through the oil filler hole. Clean the area before removing the filler cap.

Air Filter

Chevrolet and GM trucks through the years used two types of air filters. Older trucks use an oil-bath air cleaner, where the intake air is filtered through oil-soaked metal mesh. See Fig. 5-11. The second type of air cleaner is the more familiar pleated paper element.

0014142

Fig. 5-11. If your earlier GM truck engine has an oil-bath air cleaner, you should service the unit every few thousand miles or at the same time that you change engine oil.

0014144

Fig. 5-12. Oil-bath air cleaner has two components: filter element and oil cup.

0014145

Fig. 5-13. Oil fill level is indicated on the inside of oil cup section.

Whichever type, it is important to service the air cleaner regularly. A very dirty oil-bath-type air filter, unlike a paper element, will still allow reasonable engine performance. This can create the impression that the filter is okay. For maximum performance and economy, you must service the oil-bath unit more frequently when driving in dusty conditions.

To service an oil-bath air cleaner, separate the filtering element from the oil cup and remove the air cleaner assembly from the engine. See Fig. 5-12. Clean both of these components thoroughly in a suitable solvent and allow them to air dry. Do not use compressed air, as it may damage the element. Note the oil fill level, which is indicated on the inside of the oil cup. See Fig. 5-13. Use clean engine oil of the recommended viscosity (usually straight 30-wt. or a 20-wt. for cold temperature operation), and take care not to spill oil when re-installing the bulky oil-bath assembly.

If your engine uses a dry paper element, you must also check it regularly. Once impacted with dirt, the dry

Fig. 5-14. *Although dry paper elements offer exceptionally good air filtration, they quickly clog when exposed to high dust levels. Check this type of filter frequently if your truck operates in a high dust environment. Disregard normal change intervals, and change the filter if you cannot see light through paper layers. It's cheap insurance for your engine.*

paper element starves the engine for air. The result is similar to operating your engine with the choke on. Replace the filter element.

It is virtually impossible to thoroughly clean a dry paper element. Most manufacturers caution against reverse blowing (inside to outside) with compressed air, as this damages the paper matrix.

If you are uncertain whether the air cleaner will flow enough air, perform a simple field test. Remove the filter and gently tap its base on a clean, flat surface until loose debris has fallen free. Then, test the paper air filter's condition by aiming the filter toward bright sunlight or a flashlight. See Fig. 5-14. (Keep away from heat or flame—the element contains flammable gasoline fumes.) Look from the center toward the light source. Rotate the cleaner slowly. A new or functional dry paper filter will show light through its wafered layers. (Compare light flow of a new filter.) If no light is visible, or light seems scarce and intermittent, assume that filter needs replacement.

Fig. 5-15. *For paper element air cleaners, also check the sealing gasket for the cover and where it seals against the carburetor.*

Make certain that your truck's air cleaner seals properly. Abrasive dust, seeping into the engine through an air cleaner mounting gasket leak, can quickly destroy piston rings. If the air cleaner seals look weak or seat poorly, replace them immediately. Clean and ample air supply is vital to an engine's survival.

Fuel, Spark and Emission Controls

Engine service includes the fuel, spark and emission control systems. (For details on tune-up, troubleshooting and emission controls, refer to service chapters.) Closed crankcase ventilation eliminated the open road draft tube. Check the positive crankcase ventilation (PCV) valve during routine service. Periodically clean or replace the valve.

Fig. 5-16. *The positive crankcase ventilation (PCV) valve is just one part of emission control maintenance. For more information, see Chapter 8, Engine Tune-up and Emission Controls.*

Steering Gear

While beneath the hood, check the steering gear fluid. With the engine turned off and cool, begin by clearing away debris from the inspection plug on a manual steering gear (Fig. 5-17) or the power steering pump dipstick. Remove the plug or dipstick, check fluid level and top off fluid, if necessary, with recommended lubricant. If you find fluid level very low, look for leaks and make repairs.

Manual steering gears usually use conventional gear lubricant. SAE 80-wt. or equivalent was standard on many older trucks. (In a temperate or hotter climate, 90-wt. gear lube works fine in a manual steering gear.) Power steering systems require the ATF fluid type marked on the power steering reservoir or in your GM truck owner's manual.

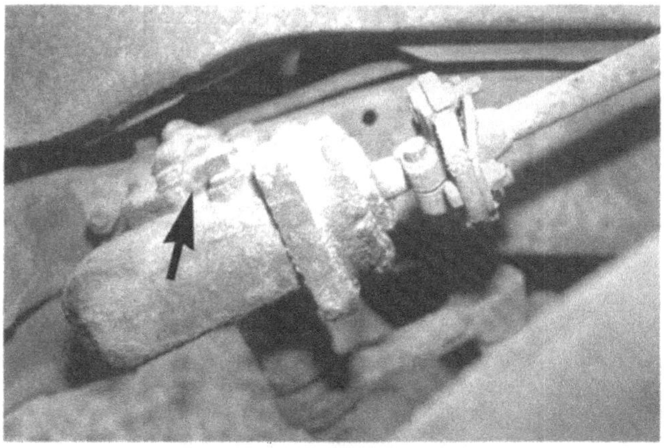

0014147

Fig. 5-17. *Manual steering gear check and fill hole (arrow).*

Other Lubrication Points

On an earlier GM truck, the generator, ignition distributor and even the starter motor may require periodic oiling. Several drops of oil, applied regularly to oil wicks, assure long service. See Fig. 5-18. Look for spring-loaded oil caps at these locations and add clean engine oil with a squirt can. GM recommends oiling every 1,000 miles. Avoid excess use of oil. Simply saturate the oil wicks.

Chassis and Driveline Lubrication

Move next to the underside of your truck. You may need to raise the vehicle. If so, always use jackstands for support.

> *WARNING —*
> *Always use jackstands to support the vehicle when raised. Never use just a jack, cinder blocks, wooden blocks, or other makeshift supports.*

0014149

Fig. 5-18. *Generator oil wick fill caps (arrows).*

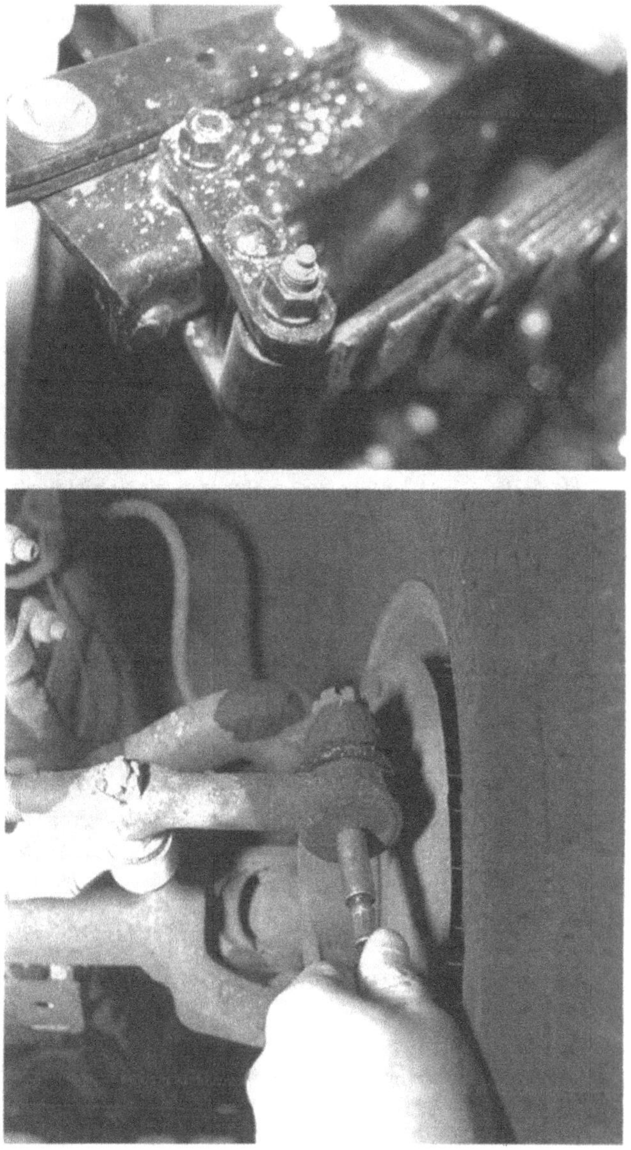

0014150 / 0014152

Fig. 5-19. *Early models require more greasing than later models. Check the leaf spring shackles, anchor pivot bushings, steering linkage, tie-rod ends, the drag link, and pitman arm joints for grease fittings.*

Chassis and driveline lubrication includes spring shackle pivots (early models), ball joints, U-joints, steering knuckles, transmission, and differential(s).

If your GM truck is an early model, the leaf spring shackles and anchor pivot bushings require grease. See Fig. 5-19. Wipe each fitting with a clean rag or shop towel, then apply fresh lubricant through the grease fitting. Watch for grease to exit the opposite end of bushing. Wipe away excess.

On leaf spring models with rubber or synthetic bushings, spray each bushing with rubber or silicone lubricant. See Fig. 5-20. This will reduce both friction and formation of surface oxidation, which will maximize the life of these materials. Avoid use of lubricant that contains petroleum distillates or other mineral/petroleum based solvents and oils. They harm rubber and cause premature wear.

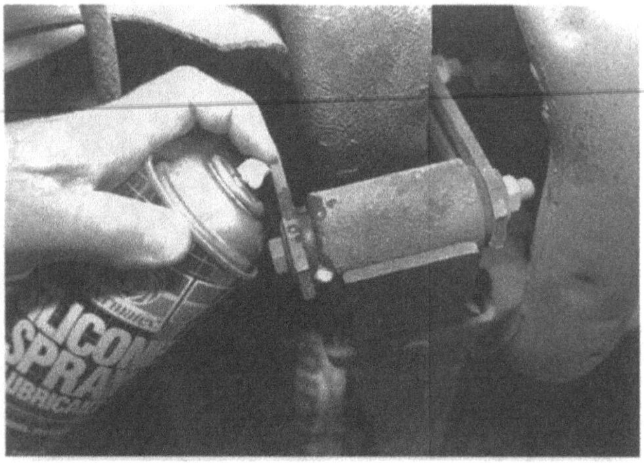

0014151

Fig. 5-20. "Maintenance free" rubber or synthetic bushings still benefit from a spray of rubber or synthetic lubricant.

0012153

Fig. 5-21. Avoid overgreasing joints, especially the splined slip collars.

Once you have greased the front spring ends and steering linkage, begin lubing all driveshaft components, including slip collars and U-joints. If the slip collar is extended, add grease modestly. Otherwise, compression of the driveshaft will displace grease. In extreme cases, overfilling a splined slip collar creates a hydraulic effect capable of damaging seals or squeezing a large amount of messy grease from the end of the driveshaft.

Move rearward. On an earlier GM truck, you will find additional grease fittings that need attention, including the clutch/brake pedal linkage, transfer case lever pivot (4WD) and column shift linkage.

On an earlier 4x4 truck with closed-knuckle steering joints, the fill hole appears much like a gear oil check point. The steering knuckle cavity contains an axle shaft joint, which calls for gear lube. Some guides recommend 90-wt. while others call for 140-wt. gear oil. Especially at high mileage, a mix of gear lube and light chassis/U-joint grease works fine and is less likely to leak past seals.

When lubing closed steering knuckles, add enough grease to lightly fill the cavity. Avoid pressurizing the knuckle with grease, which could stress seals. Closed steering knuckles are notorious for seal leaks, anyway, especially at the large inner grease seal. This seal, exposed to road debris and ice, fatigues over time.

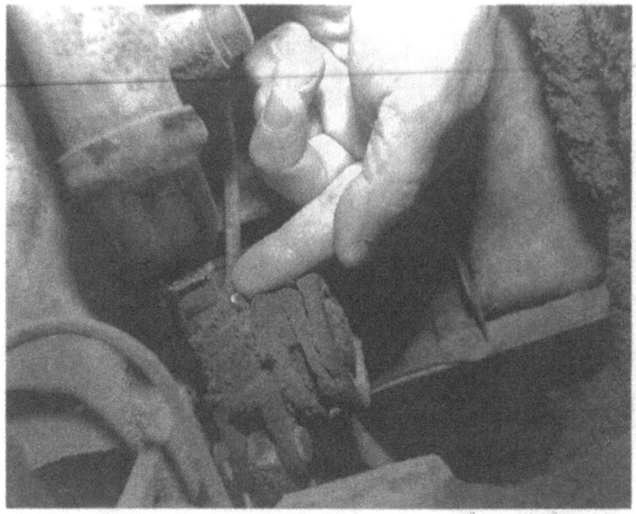

0014153

Fig. 5-22. On an earlier GM truck, you will find additional grease fittings that need attention, including the clutch/brake pedal linkage (shown) and shift linkage.

0012155

Fig. 5-23. Closed-knuckle steering joint has a fill/inspection plug. Check grease at routine intervals.

Steering knuckle lubrication assures that axle shaft joints and kingpin bearings receive grease. Periodic engagement of free-wheeling hubs is necessary to supply adequate lube for upper kingpin bearings. If your closed-knuckle front axle (NAPCO conversions and 1960–70 factory K-model 4x4s) has manual hubs, engage LOCK mode for a few miles each month. This will circulate grease for axle shaft joints and kingpin bearings and also reduce the effects of condensation.

After running on slush or ice in freezing weather, swing the front wheels to each extreme before parking your closed-knuckle equipped 4x4 truck. Knuckle wipers will sweep away debris that could otherwise freeze and damage components.

0012156

Fig. 5-24. Excessive or high pressure lubrication of closed knuckles can cause seal failure and expensive damage. Here, a large inner seal leaked badly.

4x4 front axles with closed knuckles call for periodic steering knuckle/axle shaft grease or fluid changes. Front wheel bearings often call for a repack at 6,000 miles, more frequently if you run through water. If your GM truck is a newer model with open knuckles (Fig. 5-25), you will find that wheel bearing repack intervals have been extended. For both new and older 4x4s, modern greases can lengthen periods between bearing and joint service.

Since disassembly of a closed-knuckle unit is a major job, any means for extending service intervals is practical. Intact seals and superior lubricants can serve beyond OEM service recommendation of 12,000 miles if you avoid stream crossings or running in deep water.

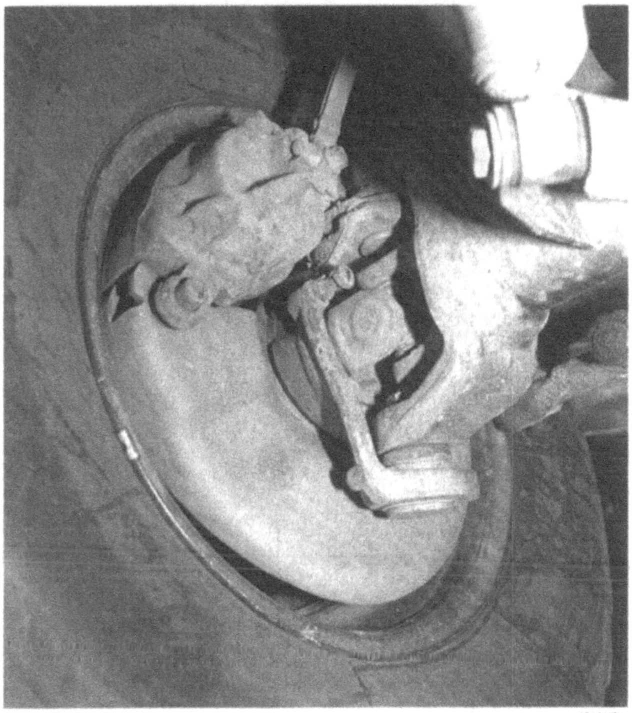

0014154

Fig. 5-25. Open-knuckle front axles have longer service intervals.

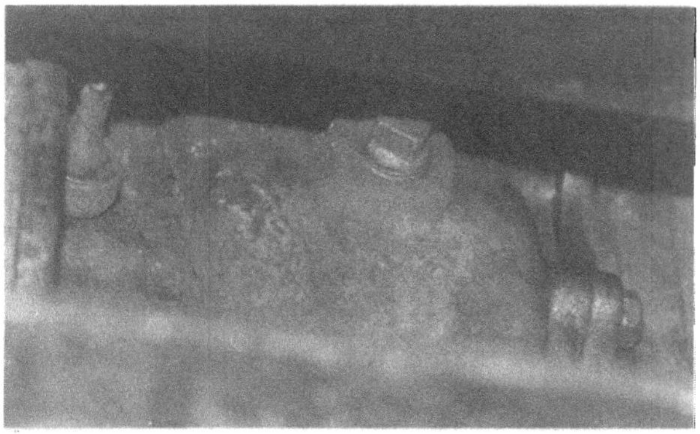

0012158 / 0012171

Fig. 5-26. Typical transmission and transfer case fill plugs.

On all GM 4x4 models, the axle differentials, transfer case and manual transmission each have oil fill plugs. The fill hole also indicates the oil full mark with the vehicle stationary and level. The recommended interval for changing hard working 4x4 gear and differential lubricant is 10,000 to 15,000 miles. You should check fluid level with each oil change or at 2,500 to 3,000 miles, and more often if seepage is apparent.

Your kind of driving and periods that the truck remains idle, which contributes to condensation and corrosion, also govern fluid change intervals. Before multi-viscosity gear oils, SAE 80-wt. (cold weather) or 90-wt. was commonly recommended for front and rear differentials (except positive traction differential units, which require special lubricant). SAE 90-wt. accommodates the typical manual transmission and transfer case top-off. Contemporary gear lubricants, like a high quality synthetic, are much more resilient. These products enable your truck to go way beyond 10,000 miles between gear lube changes.

Before removing any fill/inspection plug, clean the surrounding area. Likewise, take special care when checking an automatic transmission dipstick. Keep debris and abrasive contaminants away from openings. These are expensive gear units, responsible for taking your truck into remote back country. Cleanliness assures reliability.

With your truck on level ground, fluid should not be above the lower edge of the inspection/fill hole. If the gear unit is over full, drain it down to the lower edge of the fill hole. (Make sure your truck's chassis is level and that fluid has settled before making this determination.)

0014155

Fig. 5-27. *Powr-Lok is Spicer's trade name for a positive traction differential. Over the years, GM and others have offered Powr-Lok, the Detroit Locker/No-Spin (shown) and OEM limited slip or posi-traction differentials. Clutch units in some positive traction differentials require special lubricants and/or additives. Periodic flush-and-clean can slow clutch deterioration. Use only specified cleaners and lubricants when servicing your limited slip differential.*

0012160

Fig. 5-28. *Since the introduction of improved, multi-viscosity lubricants, 75/90-wt. and even 80/140-wt. gear oils (designed for both wide temperature range and limited slip use) have become popular. Later chain drive transfer cases, and even some manual transmissions, rely on lighter viscosity (weight) gear lubricants. Some even specify an engine oil or automatic transmission fluid (ATF). For late model transmissions and chain drive transfer cases, consult your GM truck owner's manual for recommended fluid types.*

Overfilled gear cases can raise havoc, especially on 4x4 vehicles that operate on steep angles. Excess oil can cause a leak or even drive a seal loose from the gear case. If this occurs, expensive parts can starve for oil or gear lube can find its way into the clutch lining, ruining friction material.

0014156

Fig. 5-29. *Differential lubricant fill plug (arrow).*

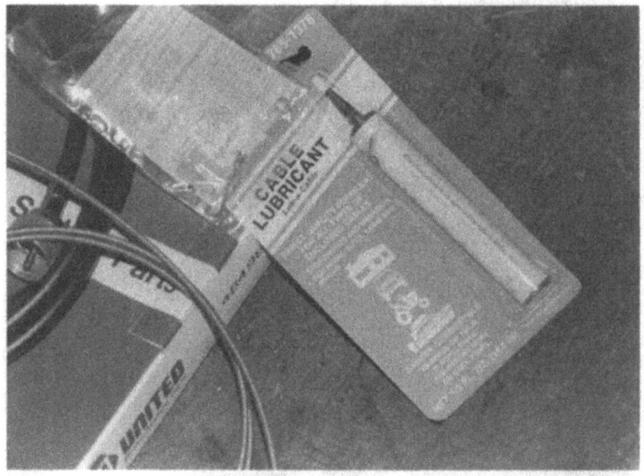

0012164

Fig. 5-30. *Even items such as the speedometer cable require periodic lubrication.*

Final Lubrication Details

Several other service points require attention. Clean the battery case and cable ends, then check and add distilled water as necessary. The manifold heat riser valve, found on many GM truck engines, requires penetrating oil. With engine cold, apply a solvent / penetrant oil, like WD-40, to the riser shaft, then test to see that it moves freely and opens smoothly as the engine warms.

Remove the speedometer cable occasionally, wipe it down and dress with speedometer cable lubricant. On early Chevrolet and GMC trucks, treat all control cables (steel conduit sleeve type) with a penetrating oil such as WD-40. Some lithium sprays work equally well. Always wipe off excess lube to avoid attracting dirt. If cables still balk, remove and clean them thoroughly, then lubricate with a suitable graphite or lithium based grease.

White lithium and silicone sprays work well on hood and tailgate hinges, latches, strikers and locks. Lithium acts more like a grease, while silicone penetrates and frees up sticky mechanisms.

3. Storing Your Truck for Long Periods

Many trucks, especially camper and trailer pulling models that serve seasonally, park for long periods of time. Some 4x4 models are strictly for snowplowing, idle for the other three seasons of the year. Arctic trucks often hibernate through deep freeze periods, immobile from early fall to the beginning of summer. A collectible 1955–58 Cameo bed pickup might undergo long storage to protect its value.

When storing your General Motors truck for long periods, consider the temperature, air quality and humidity. Major areas of concern are the engine, geartrain, cooling and electrical systems, the body and interior, fuel system, tires and brakes.

Body and Upholstery

Preserving your truck's body and upholstery involves many of the chemicals used for detailing work. For exterior painted surfaces, a heavy coat of wax, preferably buffer applied for even distribution, will help protect the finish. For long storage, apply two coats of a carnauba-base wax, buffing lightly. (A coat of cosmoline has been the long-term approach for severe climate storage or salty air.)

Vinyl upholstery, along with the dash pad, tire sidewalls and all other plastic and rubber areas, requires a liberal coating of a protectant/anti-oxidant treatment like 303. Professional rustproofing treatment, hot wax, and spray undercoatings can help protect the underside of the body and chassis.

You can apply some products at home, like rubberized spray undercoating. Whenever your truck faces exposure to corrosive environments, especially salted roads or sea air, take every precaution to eliminate oxidation of bare metal.

Once the body, frame/chassis, wheels and tires have been thoroughly protected, you should blanket the truck with a fitted cover. An enclosed garage, barn or storage shed will further protect your truck from elemental damage. Prevent exposure to bird droppings, tree sap and other corrosive hazards that might impair wax protection and destroy paint.

Engine Protection During Dormancy

Before storing your truck, change the engine oil and install a new oil filter. Run the engine to warm up and assure clean oil flow throughout the system. Install a new air filter element (paper-type), and make sure that it fits securely. If your older GM truck has an oil-bath air cleaner, thoroughly clean the unit and change the oil. Be sure belts and hoses are in top condition and apply a quality belt dressing or protectant to each drive belt.

If the engine will set for a very long period, or if high humidity and varied temperatures are factors, protect the engine's cylinder walls, valve guides, valve seats, valves and piston rings. Remove the spark plugs and squirt approximately two tablespoons of Marvel Mystery Oil or a similar fine lubricant into each cylinder.

0014159

Fig. 5-31. Removal of coil wire and rotor during storage discourages theft. After long storage period, you can crank the engine without start-up to circulate oil.

Reinstall the spark plugs, and with the coil wire disconnected or ignition rotor removed, crank the engine just a few revolutions. This will coat the cylinder walls and other bare metal in the upper cylinders with a film of highly refined oil. Leave the rotor out or ignition coil wire disconnected as a safety and anti-theft measure during storage.

After the storage period, before attempting a start-up, crank the engine over with the rotor or coil wire removed. This will pump the fine oil from the cylinders. Remove and clean the spark plugs in solvent or install a fresh set of spark plugs.

Reinstall the ignition rotor or coil wire. Start the engine, maintaining the lowest practical rpm during start-up and initial warm-up. Oil pressure should appear immediately upon start-up, quickly registering normal on the gauge.

Protect the Fuel System

If water contamination in the fuel is a concern, run a can of fuel system de-icer through the fuel tank before storing your truck. Carburetor cleaners with alcohol or other water bonding dispersants may be sprayed directly into the float bowl through the carburetor bowl's vent opening. A teaspoonful is plenty.

Cooling System and Storage

The cooling system requires fresh anti-freeze/coolant (ethylene glycol type or equivalent) with a 50/50 mixture that tests, minimally, to -34° F or lower on a hydrometer. Coolant must be thoroughly mixed, with a quality water pump lubricant/anti-rust agent added. An alternative to water pump lubricant is traditional "soluble oil," a vegetable based, non-mineral (non-petroleum) oil that can also help preserve rubber parts.

Unless the storage area will be subject to temperatures below -34° F, avoid heavier concentrations of anti-freeze. Pure anti-freeze has an insufficient expansion rate and can actually cause engine castings to crack at temperature

0014160

Fig. 5-32. Oil-bath air cleaner and sediment bowl fuel filter (arrow) are common to earlier GM trucks. Drain and clean bowl screen before long storage. This will remove trapped water that could corrode parts.

extremes. Poor expansion capability will also cause an overly concentrated coolant mixture to boil over. Follow the mixture chart and manufacturer's recommendations described on the anti-freeze container.

Tighten all hose clamps, inspect hoses for cracking or weather checking and consider installing a new thermostat if the system requires flushing or draining. When running the engine and circulating new coolant, be certain to turn on and operate the heater. Coolant/anti-freeze of proper mix must fill the heater and all hoses, or damage from freezing could result.

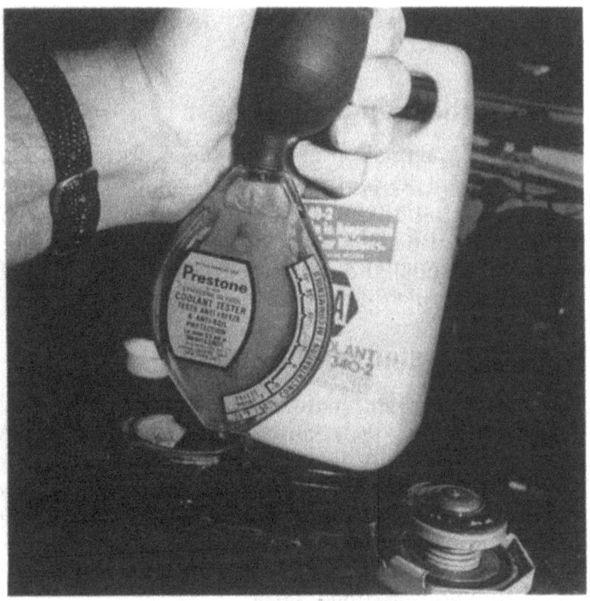

0012167

Fig. 5-33. Radiator hydrometer tests specific gravity of coolant/ anti-freeze. Weak concentrations allow freeze-up and also lower the boiling point. Excessive concentration adversely impacts the expansion rate of coolant mix.

Chassis and Geartrain Preservation

Several powertrain items require attention. Lubricate the U-joints and all other grease fittings on your truck. Force out old chassis lube and make certain new grease squeezes from each joint. Wipe off excess. Dress rubber shock absorber, spring and sway bar bushings with rubber lubricant to prevent surface oxidation and dehydration.

If you haven't repacked the wheel bearings recently, buy new front wheel hub seals and fresh grease. Remove the wheels and hubs, and inspect for any signs of moisture damage. Thoroughly clean, closely inspect and repack the bearings. Fit new seals during installation. (For details on front wheel bearing repack, see Chapter 12.)

0012168

Fig. 5-34. When greasing steering linkage, suspension or driveline parts, grease fittings sometimes fail. These fittings are replaceable. Take care not to overfill joints, as seals may rupture and allow contamination of joint or bushing.

Check fluid levels in each gear case and the axle/differential units. Note the smell and appearance of gear oil. A burnt, acrid odor indicates older and likely worn gear lube. Signs of damaging moisture are a milky, greyish appearance either in the fluid or around the housing cavity.

If signs of moisture appear in a gearcase, drain and flush the unit with a specified flushing oil, an appropriate solvent or clean kerosene. (During the flushing operation, drive the truck at minimal load for a very short distance to thoroughly wash the gear housing walls. Do not pull a load or allow gearcase to get hot.) Drain unit immediately and completely. Refill with fresh, proper grade gear oil, and drive the truck to circulate the new oil.

Major damage to expensive bearings, gears and shafts will result from unchecked water or condensation in the gear cases. Check all vents from the axle housings, transfer case and transmission. One-way check valves must be clean and seat properly to prevent moisture from entering the gearcase during the storage period.

0012169

Fig. 5-35. One-way type check valves (arrow) allow transfer case, transmission and axle housings to vent pressure. Make sure these valves are clean and seating properly to prevent moisture from entering the gear unit.

0014162

Fig. 5-36. Many GM trucks benefit from power steering. With the engine stopped, check ATF fluid at the power steering reservoir fill cap. Keep debris from entering the reservoir. Remove dipstick and wipe with a clean (lint-free) rag. Note Hot and Cold levels indicated on dipstick. Top off with ATF or power steering fluid specified for your truck.

If you are storing an automatic transmission equipped truck for a lengthy period, change the transmission fluid and filter. Operate the truck long enough to fully circulate new fluid. ATF is a high detergent oil, and fresh fluid purges older, acidic lubricant that might otherwise act on seals. Fresh fluid also helps flush varnish forming agents from the sensitive valve body and friction lining.

Prepping the Electrical System

Disconnect the battery cables to eliminate voltage drains from the clock or elsewhere. Clean the outer battery case thoroughly with a solution of warm water and baking soda. Use an inexpensive nylon paint brush.

> *WARNING —*
> *Avoid splashing cleaning solution on painted surfaces or into your eyes. Wear protective goggles. Make certain that the cleaning solution does not enter any of the battery cells. Rinse away all cleaning solution with a stream of clean water.*

If you remove the battery, make sure it rests on a non-conductive surface in a state of full charge at the time of storage. Remember that a fully discharged battery, at low enough specific gravity, can freeze and crack.

Battery specialists recommend storage of batteries in a temperate setting. If at all possible, avoid exposing the battery to extremes of heat or cold, and always store away from spark or flame sources. After storage, bring the battery slowly up to full charge with a low amperage trickle charger. (Make certain that the charger has a built-in voltage regulator to prevent overcharging.)

Brake System and Storage

Hydraulic brake fluid is hygroscopic and readily bonds with water. On domestic trucks built prior to 1967, the master cylinder vents directly to atmosphere. These brake systems are especially vulnerable to moisture contamination. Eventually, especially if you store the vehicle for long periods, moisture can seep into the system, lowering the boiling point of the brake fluid, causing oxidation damage and pitting or corroding the hydraulic brake cylinders.

As a minimal precaution, especially with these older braking systems, you should routinely flush fresh brake fluid through the hydraulic system. (A power bleeder speeds up this procedure.) The aim is to force old fluid, and any contaminants suspended in that fluid, out of the system.

The traditional, more involved method is to flush the system with denatured alcohol or a specially formulated hydraulic brake system flushing compound, then disassemble each wheel cylinder, caliper and the master cylinder. Air dry the lines and cylinders. Coat cylinder bores with special brake/rubber parts assembly lube or brake fluid, then install new rubber cups and seals. Fill/bleed the system with clean DOT 3 or higher grade brake fluid. (See service chapters for details on brake work.)

Along with a thorough flushing and installation of new rubber parts, you might consider switching to silicone brake fluid. Although expensive, silicone brake fluid nearly eliminates the water absorption problem. If you store your truck regularly, for long periods, silicone brake fluid could be practical.

When converting from conventional brake fluid to silicone, the system must be entirely purged of conventional brake fluid. (Use the silicone brake fluid during assembly of cylinder rubber parts.) Follow instructions carefully to avoid mixing incompatible chemistry. Make sure silicone brake fluid meets your vehicle's DOT brake fluid requirements.

> *WARNING —*
> *Silicone fluid and conventional brake fluid are incompatible. Do not mix or blend these substances.*

Fortunately, General Motors truck brake systems built since 1967 are less prone to absorbing moisture. Most of these trucks have master cylinder covers with bellows-type gaskets that offer far more protection from atmospheric contamination. Even with these models, I recommend periodic purging of old brake fluid using the pressure bleeding method. This will at least reduce moisture content in the brake fluid and help maintain a normal boiling point for reliable braking.

Tires and Climate

If your truck will be dormant for more than a few months, raise the chassis and place the frame safely on jack stands. (See your GM truck owner's handbook or shop manual for jacking locations and where to place stands.) Tires suffer from long storage periods, which can cause sidewall distortion and damage plies or radial belts—especially if you store the truck with a heavy cabover camper mounted in the bed. Raise the truck enough to take the weight off the tires.

Climate plays a role in the precautions you take. In desert environments, the concern is ultraviolet damage and dehydration of rubber seals and bushings. Arctic regions require protection from freezing. Moist and salt air regions call for anti-rust measures. Consider the environmental stresses that your truck will face, and prepare accordingly.

Chapter 6

Troubleshooting and Minor Adjustments

TYPICALLY, A TRUCK CAN TAKE A LOT OF ABUSE, especially when equipped with four-wheel drive and forced to carry severe loads on bad roads. While routine maintenance and inspection will enhance any truck's reliability, your talent at making emergency field repairs could mean the difference between walking or driving back to civilization.

After three decades of exposure to two- and four-wheel drive trucks, I cannot overstate the need for preventive care, those service steps that turn up potential problems. A truck will provide signs and symptoms before most parts fail, so the best tactic for preventing a breakdown is periodic inspection of the chassis and powertrain. Your lubrication and tune-up service should include a thorough look at the chassis, axle and driveline components.

Aftermath of a Hard Day's Work

The off-pavement work truck stretches over rocks and logs, stressing its chassis to the limit. Springs and shackles twist in every direction while bushings and joints battle awkward angles. As the dust settles from a day of tough work, your truck needs a thorough inspection.

0014455

Fig. 6-1. When work or recreation takes you into remote places, a thorough knowledge of your truck's powertrain and chassis will help assure your return. Troubleshooting skill is vital in remote country.

Look beneath the front bumper at the axle, steering linkage, leaf springs and front shackles or the IFS A-arm suspension system. Vulnerable items on off-pavement 4x4s include the tie-rod assembly, steering stabilizer shock and axle housing(s).

Look for oil seepage and cracks along the axle unit, especially gear lube leaking where the axle housing tubes press into the center member of a pre-Sierra 4x4 solid axle. Extreme jarring and twisting can dislodge, bend or crack an axle housing.

Note the condition of the springs. Look for broken or out-of-line leafs and bent U-bolts. If a leaf spring appears offset from its axle perch, suspect a broken center bolt. Leafs out of alignment mean loose U-bolts or distorted spring clamps. Extreme flexing and twisting is the usual cause.

The tie-rod and steering stabilizer damper are especially vulnerable on 4x4 trucks. Due to available space and the necessary position of the front driveshaft, the steering linkage mounts forward of the axle housing. Especially on 4x4s with a solid axle housing, the long tie-rod and hydraulic steering stabilizer/damper face obstacles like rocks, tree stumps and debris.

Veteran four-wheelers know where this tie-rod rides. Aware driving involves a sense for low hanging and vulnerable chassis parts. When knocking around on boulder-strewn trails, protect your truck's axle housing(s), suspension, steering, driveshafts, brakes, fuel system and other chassis/powertrain components. Become familiar with exposed, expensive pieces.

Check the stabilizer bar (if so equipped), support links and bushings. These parts really flex, especially off-pavement. Look closely at the brake hoses and other brake hardware. Brush, tree limbs and loose rock can damage sensitive components. Learn to scan along brake and fuel lines; watch for kinks or rock damage. In the worst cases, it is possible to rip whole sections of brake pipe loose from the frame or rear axle housing. Accidently backing into a rock or tree stump can crush the rear axle housing brake piping and impair brake action.

Before finishing your front end inspection, pay close attention to the steering knuckle joints. (Later in this chapter, I will share the procedure for checking knuckle joint/kingpin play and identifying damage.) A broken or loose knuckle joint will impair steering and place your safety at extreme risk. Severe off-pavement impact can break a kingpin bearing race, crack a knuckle casting or damage a steering knuckle ball joint. On closed-knuckle 4WD front ends, watch for spindle separation from the

0014177

Fig. 6-2. Until 1987, all GM 4x4s have solid Spicer/Dana or GM Corporate live front axles. 1988–91 K-30/3500 one-ton Crew Cab models and 4x4 Suburbans and Blazer/Jimmy models retain this solid axle design. These models change to the Sierra IFS 4x4 chassis design (first introduced in 1988 K1500 to K3500 models) by 1992. Solid front axles like this 1986 K2500 unit can handle a good amount of off-pavement pounding, however, severe overloading can loosen axle tubes at the housing's differential section.

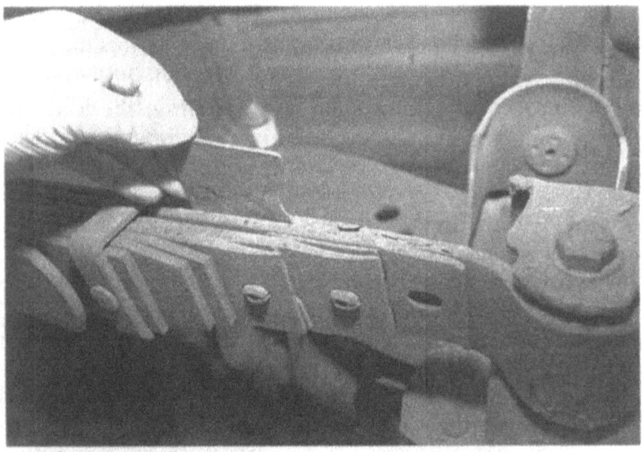

0014178

Fig. 6-3. Spring flexing loosens U-bolts and clamps. Look for misaligned leafs, broken plates and spring sag. GM light trucks, with the exception of 1960–72 coil spring equipped models, have leaf-type rear springs. Leaf springs were also popular with the pre-Sierra chassis 4WD front axles.

knuckle casting and for cracks at the spindle, especially if your truck has aftermarket wide wheels and big tires.

Inspect the rear axle housing for leaks, cracks or broken welds. Springs and spring supports demand a close look for cracks, bushing wear, fatigue and damage. Look for emergency brake cable damage, signs of water in the axle housing and evidence of mud or sand in the brake drums.

0014179

Fig. 6-4. Steering linkage, stabilizer shock and tie-rods require close inspection. On pre-Sierra solid axle 4x4s, a single tie-rod mounts in front of the axle housing, vulnerable to rocks, stumps and debris. 2WD GM light trucks built before 1960 have the advantage of a tie-rod mounted behind the solid-beam axle.

Inspect the exhaust system for leaks, dents, kinks or any other damage that might impair flow or create unsafe and noxious fumes. Tap gently on the muffler(s) with a plastic or rubber head hammer while listening for loose and rattling internal baffles.

Driveshafts, flexing and moving constantly, are also susceptible to wear and damage. If your GM truck wallows constantly along rocky trails and through creek beds, keep U-joint flanges and driveshaft tubes away from rocks and stumps. It is relatively easy to spring (bend) a driveshaft tube.

0014181

Fig. 6-5. Brake hoses and brake or fuel pipes require close inspection. Steering knuckles, kingpin trunnions/bearings or ball-joint pivotal supports are vulnerable to impact damage. Inspect these components regularly.

Memorize the original appearance of your truck's undercarriage. When inspecting the chassis, use that image as your standard. Especially when subject to off-pavement hazards, Chevrolet and GMC light truck reliability depends on good driving habits, the willingness to pick sensible travel routes and unrelenting chassis inspection. Skid plates are not enough.

1. GUIDE TO TROUBLESHOOTING

Engine failure is intimidating, especially if you use your truck in remote country or pull a heavy horse trailer or fifth wheel. Your engine can quit for many reasons, and if unprepared while in the back country, you can burn as much shoe leather over a shorted ignition module as a seized connecting rod bearing.

Maintaining your General Motors truck includes troubleshooting savvy and the means to remedy common problems. Whether you perform repairs or send the work to a qualified shop, troubleshooting skill increases self-sufficiency and heightens your understanding. (For additional details on service work, see service chapters.)

> **NOTE —**
> Overhaul of specific powertrain, geartrain and chassis components is beyond the goals of this book. For overhaul and unit repair guidelines, refer to the Chevrolet or GMC Truck factory shop manual for your model.

Lack of Engine Power

Low Compression can result from a pressure leak at one or more cylinders. Loss of compression suggests several possibilities: leaking or misadjusted intake or exhaust valves, worn or defective piston rings, a blown head gasket, casting cracks, and a severely worn camshaft and timing chain or gear set. Coolant loss into the engine oil (turning it milky) indicates a cracked cylinder head or engine block—or a leaking head gasket.

Diagnosing low compression requires a compression gauge or cylinder leakdown tester. (See other chapters for these test procedures.) A field testing method involves shorting cylinder spark leads, one at a time, and comparing the engine rpm drop per cylinder. A high rpm drop indicates a strong cylinder, while a low rpm drop reveals a cylinder that has either low compression or an ignition, fuel or vacuum related problem.

0012178

Fig. 6-6. A compression test reveals loss of cylinder pressure. When only two adjacent cylinders show low pressure, suspect a warped cylinder head or a head gasket failure.

Internal Friction indicates major engine trouble. If the engine will not crank easily, first rule out the obvious battery or starter / electrical problems. Place the transmission in neutral. Remove all spark plugs and rotate the crankshaft with an appropriate socket and ratchet. The engine should turn freely, with only the moderate resistance of the valvetrain.

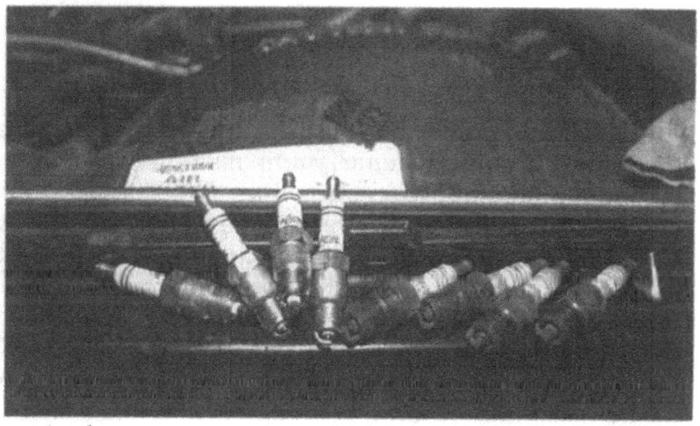

0014182

Fig. 6-7. Remove the spark plugs and rotate the crankshaft. High resistance indicates internal damage.

To rule out transmission damage as a possible cause, have a helper disengage the clutch (depress the pedal) while you rotate the crankshaft. If the engine will not turn freely, suspect bearing, piston, connecting rod or valve damage. When water (either drawn through the intake system or originating as an internal leak) prevents engine rotation, removing the spark plugs allows liquid to escape. Water exiting the cylinders suggests the possibility of severe damage, even bent connecting rods or damaged rod bearings.

Overheat/Seizure means serious trouble. If the engine will not crank or rotate after a severe overheat or running without oil, major damage has occurred. Pistons can distort from heat, gall the cylinder walls and destroy crankshaft bearings. Lubrication generally fails during a severe overheat, causing glazing and scoring as the piston rings drag on cylinder walls. Valve stems can seize in their guides, and the camshaft may seize in its bearings. Casting cracks from severe overheat are common, especially near exhaust valve seats and along cylinder walls.

The least gloomy prospect is that a cylinder head (possibly both heads on a V-8) has warped, resulting in a head gasket failure. Coolant fills the cylinders, locking up the engine. Even here, the risk of bent connecting rods and other crankshaft assembly damage remains.

0012180

Fig. 6-8. *Radiator damage, overheat and loss of coolant are more than an inconvenience. Piston/cylinder wall galling and engine bearing damage result from extreme heat. Amount of heat involved will determine the extent of damage.*

Fuel Starvation results from low fuel supply pressure or volume. In addition to fuel pump malfunctions and restrictions in the supply or return lines, EFI/TBI-equipped engines can suffer from pressure regulator defects or fouled/defective injectors. A sticking carburetor float needle, although rare, is another source of trouble for carbureted engines.

Testing fuel pump pressure requires a special gauge. Pump flow volume is easier to determine. Before suspecting the fuel pump volume, flow rate or carburetion/injection troubles, consider the fuel filter(s) or the fuel line inlet filter (sock) in the gas tank. Especially with a paper element fuel filter, a single fill-up with watery gasoline is enough to stop fuel flow.

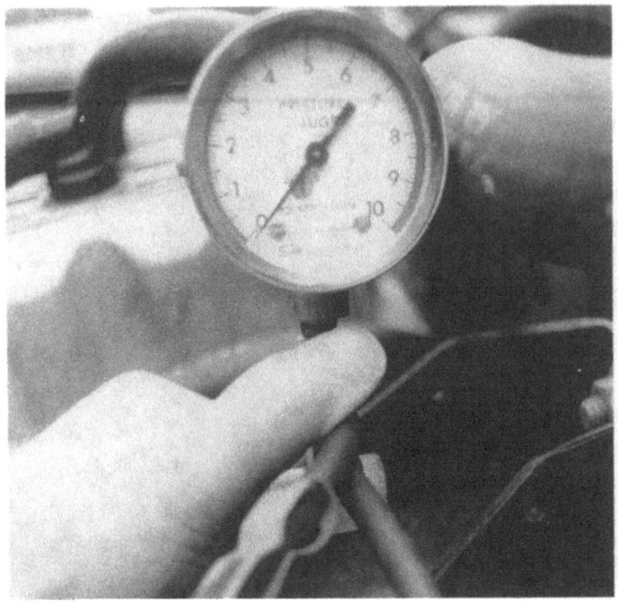

0012181

Fig. 6-9. *A fuel pump pressure gauge quickly determines pressure output. Before condemning the pump or other expensive items, look to the simpler causes, like a plugged fuel filter.*

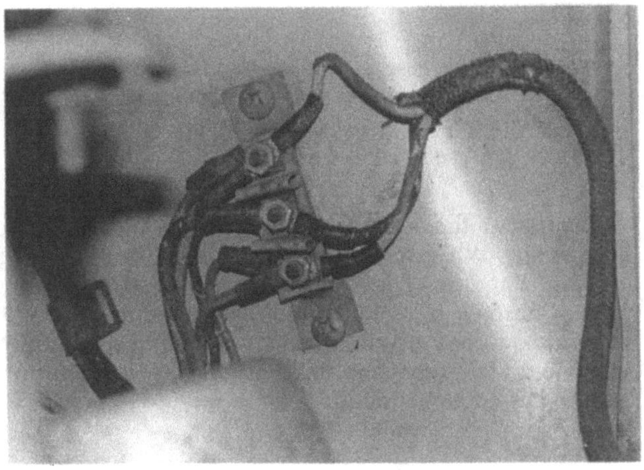

0012182

Fig. 6-10. *Wiring shorts, fraying and bad grounds cause the majority of field failures. Look closely at routed wires and connections.*

Weak Ignition creates hard-starting problems and a lack of power. On older engines with breaker points, rubbing block wear retards ignition timing, and the points resistance increases with pitting and arcing. Condenser, rotor, distributor cap and spark cable defects can also weaken spark output.

Check the distributor shaft for excess runout (sideplay), a common cause of erratic spark output and errant ignition timing. Dwell angle variance of more than 2° is a sign of distributor defects. Mechanics often condemn the coil, although a coil is far less likely to fail than the breaker points, condenser, primary or secondary wiring or a set of worn distributor shaft bushings.

Breaker point and electronic ignitions are vulnerable to wiring failures and poor connections (due to corrosion or dirt). Consider this a major cause of poor ignition performance. Check carefully for insulation breakdown and shorts to ground. Especially on very early trucks with cloth type insulation, wire failures and shorts are a very common source of trouble.

Test wires between junctions. (You can find engine and chassis wiring diagrams for your GM truck in the factory shop manual.) If an electrical or ignition problem is not readily apparent, test circuits with your volt-ohmmeter or have it done by a local service garage that has special testing equipment.

Vacuum Leaks, if severe, will prevent the engine from running. A sufficient leak creates low manifold pressure, stalling, lean air/fuel mixtures and backfire. Even small vacuum leaks can lean the air/fuel mixture, cause idle speed to drop and prevent smooth performance.

0012183

Fig. 6-11. A non-volatile spray solvent or penetrating oil helps detect engine vacuum leaks. With the engine idling, spray toward the intake manifold sealing edges and the carburetor base. If rpm changes, then there is a leak.

The engine's sudden inability to idle indicates a vacuum leak. Check the PCV valve, all vacuum hoses, the distributor advance diaphragm and the transmission vacuum modulator and hoses, if so equipped. Intake manifold bolts loosen over time, resulting in poor gasket sealing and possible vacuum loss. Torque manifold bolts and the carburetor mounting nuts or bolts. As the engine idles, spray a mist of fine penetrating oil (non-volatile) along the gasket sealing edges. Listen for a change in engine speed. This indicates a leak.

> *WARNING —*
> *Always keep volatile solvents away from hot engine parts. Use a spray substance that will not ignite if it contacts a hot surface or spark.*

Engine Timing is crucial for engine performance. The three essentials are normal compression, correct valve lift and proper valve timing. When troubleshooting reaches beyond spark timing adjustment, changing a fuel filter or basic tuning, make certain your engine meets these three requirements.

Measure compression with a compression gauge or cylinder leakdown tester. (See tune-up/service chapters for details.) If compression registers normal for each cylinder, verify valve lift by removing the valve cover or pushrod/lifter cover(s).

Depending upon the various test requirements, measure either the height of each valve stem tip from its closed position to fully open or the amount of lift at the valve lifters (OHV inline sixes). Respectively, this is the total valve or lifter/tappet lift produced by each camshaft lobe. Compare this figure to specifications found in your factory GM truck shop manual.

In addition to valve lift, make note of valve timing variances that result from a severely worn timing chain mechanism or gearset. If ignition timing has suddenly become retarded, yet the distributor housing remains securely clamped to the engine block, suspect excess slack in the timing chain or bad sprockets, which, if severe enough, can allow valve timing to jump one or more teeth.

0014183

Fig. 6-12. A worn camshaft lobe or improper valve adjustment will affect valve lift. Always check valve adjustment or tappet clearance before testing valve lift.

Clutch Slippage and related troubles are relatively easy to detect. Before testing, check and adjust the clutch at the release arm. (See service chapters for clutch adjustment tips.) Make certain that the clutch disengages and engages properly. Through the release arm opening in the bellhousing, observe whether the throwout bearing actually moves the clutch release fingers or levers.

> *WARNING —*
> *Keep your fingers away from moving linkage while an assistant depresses the clutch pedal. The force of a clutch linkage could easily crush a finger. The bellhousing's release arm opening has sharp edges that could cut your hands.*

If the clutch release arm has insufficient movement, check the linkage from the pedal all the way to the release arm. Note excessive play and correct the cause. In the case of a hydraulic linkage system, inspect the fluid level and bleed any air from the system. Repair or replace defective parts.

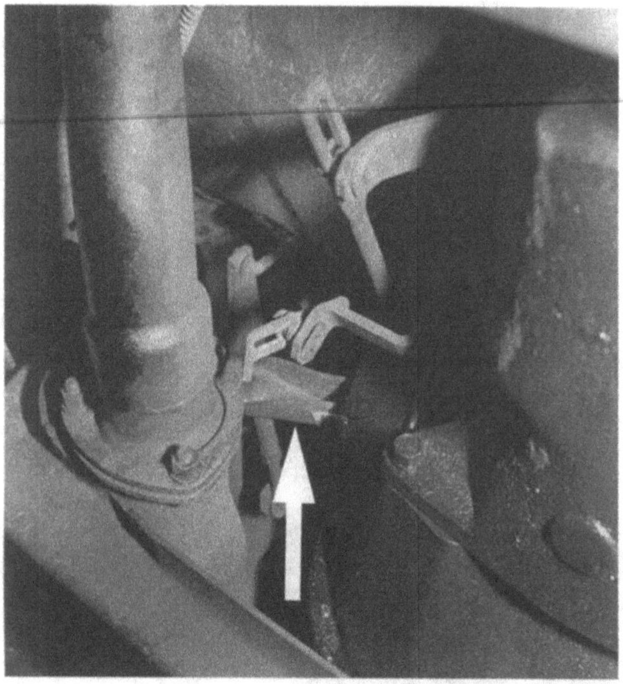

Fig. 6-13. Always check clutch adjustment at the release arm (arrow). Pedal play alone is misleading, as linkage wear can masquerade as clutch free play.

Fig. 6-14. Exhaust system restriction is a possible cause of power loss. Off-pavement use leaves tailpipes, mufflers and catalytic converters vulnerable to damage. Tap muffler gently with a rubber or sand-filled plastic hammer to test for loose baffles.

Now drive down a deserted road at 15 to 20 mph. Depress the clutch pedal, and place the transmission in high gear. Raise engine speed to 2500 rpm and rapidly release the clutch pedal. Engine rpm should drop immediately. If rpm decreases gradually, the clutch unit is probably weak. Sources of trouble could include worn clutch cover springs, a worn or glazed clutch plate, a glazed or worn flywheel face, or oil on the friction disc.

Engine Will Not Run

Tune-up Problems include faulty ignition, inadequate fuel supply, flooding or vacuum leaks. On breaker point ignitions, verify point dwell angle and resistance. Both breaker point and electronic distributors require spark timing adjustment. Fuel system troubles involve dirty filters, plugged carburetor passages, a sticky needle/seat assembly in the carburetor, a defective float or a defective fuel pump. (See service chapters for details on ignition timing procedures and other tune-related tasks.)

Isolate problems. Verify the strength of the ignition spark, check timing and ensure that the engine has an adequate fuel supply. Check vacuum circuits. Make certain that the emission control system is functional, especially the PCV and EGR valves. If indicated, remove and overhaul the carburetor with a quality rebuild kit. You will find instructions for the carburetor overhaul within the kit or a professional-level service manual.

Exhaust System Restriction has vexed plenty of troubleshooters. Check the exhaust system! Off-pavement or construction site pounding can flatten the tailpipe or muffler. Restricted exhaust can prevent the engine from starting or developing full power. A muffler or catalytic converter may show no external damage yet have broken baffles or internal restrictions.

Engine Will Not Crank

Poor Battery Maintenance/Charge Circuit Troubles remain the primary sources of starting problems. The simplest cause is dirty or corroded battery posts. Regular cleaning of the posts and battery case prevents hard starts and a stranded truck. Make certain that cables are clean and connections tight, especially on an early 6-volt electrical system with high amperage demands and a low output generator.

Generator or alternator troubles are easy to identify using a charge current induction meter or a simple volt/ohmmeter. Begin with the voltmeter OFF. Take care not to generate a spark near the battery. Securely attach the negative (black) probe to a good chassis or engine ground point. Attach the positive (red) probe to a battery current source some distance from the battery, such as the solenoid switch. Switch the voltmeter to DC.

> **NOTE —**
> On GMC 6-volt models with positive-ground polarity, reverse your voltmeter probes for a correct reading. All 6- and 12-volt Chevrolet trucks that I cover within this book use negative-ground polarity.

Measure the voltage level before cranking, during cranking and after starting the engine. Make certain that the maximum charge voltage reads within the regulator's normal charging range as listed in your GM shop manual or a professional guide.

Dead Battery Cell(s) present a difficult diagnostic problem. A high capacity battery can limp along with a dying cell for months. It takes a deep overnight freeze to bring out the worst in a battery. To avoid walking home from a chilly mountaintop, test each of your battery's cells with a hydrometer. Specific gravity should be normal and uniform at each cell.

0012187

Fig. 6-15. Battery maintenance is the best preventive care for the starting circuit. Don't buy a new starter, generator or alternator before thoroughly cleaning the battery and cables and testing specific gravity.

0012188

Fig. 6-16. A precaution, even for a battery that shows no sign of weakness, is the hydrometer test. Specific gravity of a fully charged battery should read uniformly at each cell. Perform this test before cold weather begins.

Starter Motor Problems generally give warning. A solenoid switch or starter drive unit often shows signs of weakness before it fails. Run-on, clicking and erratic cranking are signs of starter and solenoid troubles.

GM light truck engines use a variety of starter and solenoid designs, but starter principles remain universal: The solenoid acts as a relay to handle heavy amperage flow. In some designs, the solenoid actually moves the starter drive. On all but the later GM engines, starter motors are a series-wound design with brushes. Periodically inspect for water damage, clutch drive fatigue and brush wear.

0012189

Fig. 6-17. Starter defects often give warning. A clicking solenoid or erratic, dragging motor indicates trouble. An amperage draw test helps determine the condition of the starter.

Poor cranking when hot is often due to worn brushes or armature bushing wear that allows drag on the field coils. Aftermarket exhaust headers passing too close to the starter may also cause hard starting when hot. To diagnose whether your starter draws too much amperage, test the draw with an induction meter on the starter cable, or measure the voltage drop at the starter solenoid switch while cranking the engine.

Geartrain Friction or Drag can prevent cranking. (Also see section on Lack of Power.) Among geartrain items that can prevent engine cranking are seizures of a transmission input shaft bearing, a gear set or the crankshaft pilot bearing. A seized pilot bearing will not allow power to disengage between the engine and transmission. However, the engine will crank in neutral.

Seized transmission components also allow the engine to crank with the clutch disengaged, but the engine will stall when you engage the clutch. (Before suspecting a damaged transmission, check clutch adjustment and operation.) A seized transmission can result from poor lubrication, severe parts stress or excessive wear.

Cooling System Troubles

Engine cooling presents a challenge, especially with high horsepower conversion engines or trips through hot desert environments. Rock crawling in the desert at high noon is the ultimate test for any truck's cooling system.

Before troubleshooting common cooling system problems, clarify your truck's needs. For years, the two most popular buzzwords around cooling system upgrades have been "four-row" and "cross-flow" radiators. These terms are meaningless without an understanding that horsepower equals BTUs (heat). The more horsepower, the more heat your radiator and fan system must handle.

I once installed a 270-horsepower 1957 Pontiac 347 V-8 (similar by design to the 347 GMC truck engine) into a pickup that originally had a 110-horsepower engine. The stock down flow radiator had good size tanks and a very adequate looking core. However, the high gallon-per-minute (gpm) coolant flow rate of the transplant engine,

0012190

Fig. 6-18. A high performance engine or heavy duty radiator benefit from aftermarket stainless steel flex fan. This particular setup keeps engine within 5°F of thermostat setting, even under load in the hottest climates.

plus its horsepower figure of more than twice the original engine's output, thoroughly overtaxed the radiator.

A radiator specialist educated me on the gpm flow needed for the new engine. He found a larger radiator core that easily fit with the original radiator's top and bottom tanks. The engine ran cool ever after.

Sometimes the issue is fan air flow through the radiator core. A radiator may have plenty of flow capacity, tube size and fin surface area, but the fan draws too little air through the core. The cure in this case is a heavy duty mechanical fan. Well-pitched blades and a shroud may solve the cooling problem completely. (Make certain that the radiator's tube and surface area plus the mechanical fan size are adequate for your engine and the usage you anticipate.)

Heavy-pitched truck type or high performance aftermarket mechanical fans draw far more CFM air flow than an automobile type or light duty fan. Check your truck's fan blade count and pitch. Upgrade if necessary.

Make certain a shroud captures the fan's full draft without creating an air block. (See the cooling system chapter for further details.) Fortunately, most GM truck models have large grill openings, which makes the fan's job easier.

An air conditioning-application radiator provides a good design for the basically stock GM truck engine. For higher horsepower transplant engines, evaluate the heaviest duty replacement radiator available for your chassis. Order that radiator or have an adequately sized radiator built. Install a hefty mechanical (engine driven) fan. A fan clutch unit, which lessens engine load at speed, is often advisable.

Engine Overheat at Low Speeds suggests an undercapacity or restricted fan or radiator. Overheat can also result from insufficient water pump volume, cavitation or aeration problems. Air, either trapped within the cooling system or siphoned through a pinhole leak or defective water pump seal, can cause cavitation (air gaps and blocks) and drastically lowers cooling efficiency.

Another source of air in the cooling system is a slight head gasket leak that allows pressurized combustion gases to seep from a cylinder into an adjacent cooling port. This rapidly creates rust or oxidation, visible in the upper radiator and coolant recovery tank. As preventive care, you should check torque of the cylinder head bolts, tighten all hose clamps, watch the water pump bleed hole for seepage, and pressure check the cooling system.

NOTE —
Restrictions in air flow through the radiator core, like from a tall winch, will cause overheating.

0012191

Fig. 6-19. Pressure tester can check hoses, water pump, engine castings, gaskets and heater core. Radiator pressure cap must also seal properly, or boiling point will drop.

Engine Overheat at High Speeds involves incorrect coolant flow (either too fast or too slow) through the radiator, restrictions in the radiator core or an undercapacity water pump. Many of the symptoms for low speed overheat apply, so first follow those troubleshooting guidelines. Always check the thermostat, which regulates the coolant flow rate and temperature.

If coolant actually pushes from the radiator overflow at higher speeds, the water pump generates more coolant than the gallon-per-minute (gpm) capacity of the radiator core. (The core is either too small or plugged with scale.) Freeze plug failure and hose leaks are not uncommon under such conditions, as excess pressure backs through the entire cooling system.

Coolant Boil-over requires careful diagnosis. Is the coolant erupting from extreme engine heat? This means the radiator and fan cannot cool the liquid sufficiently— or that the engine/powertrain produces very high temperatures due to abnormal friction, spark timing error, low-grade fuel, improper air/fuel mixtures, automatic transmission overheat or other cooling system overloads.

0012192

Fig. 6-20. A relatively inexpensive item like the thermostat can cause major heating problems. Replace the thermostat during your periodic flush and refill of the cooling system.

NOTE —
An under-capacity radiator flow rate will cause coolant overflow from the radiator—even at normal engine temperatures.

Observe when the overflow occurs. Monitor the temperature gauge closely. If the engine runs consistently hot, suspect a sticky thermostat, plugged radiator core, obstructive block mud (accumulated rust and scale in an older engine), a defective water pump or other factors that raise coolant temperature.

Clutch and Manual Transmission

Clutch Noises tell of bad things to come. Fatal clutch noises include the abrasive whirring of the throwout bearing during disengagement, the grinding of clutch plate rivets as the clutch engages, or the rattle of broken clutch disc torsion springs. Expect that any new, persistent sound from the clutch means trouble.

A defective pilot bearing makes noise with the transmission in gear and the clutch disengaged. Clutch disc or cover assembly noises occur during engagement and disengagement. (Broken clutch cover springs cause uneven engagement and severe chatter.) Throwout or release bearing noise becomes apparent with light pressure against the clutch pedal, just enough pressure to start the bearing spinning

CAUTION —
Continued vehicle operation with a defective clutch can damage motor mounts, the flywheel and components of the transmission.

0012193

Fig. 6-21. Clutch plate (disc) torsion springs and rivets make distinct noises. Rivets grind against the flywheel or clutch cover face while torsion springs rattle in the hub.

0012194

Fig. 6-22. Shift linkage binding or failure can prevent gear engagement or power flow. In an emergency, it may be necessary to free a 4x4's transfer case linkage by manually moving the shift rails beneath the floorboard.

Gearbox noises grate and amplify according to load on the gear teeth. Coast and acceleration noises differ. Transmission bearing troubles give distinct cues, with countergear or counter bearing noises evident in the lower gears. Input or output bearing noises correspond to shaft or road speeds. Any clutch or transmission noise requires immediate repairs.

Gear Clash in a manual transmission or transfer case has several possible causes. Before condemning the transmission, check the clutch adjustment at the release arm and note any slack in the linkage. Complete travel of the linkage is necessary for disengagement of the clutch. A partially disengaged clutch causes difficult shifting and rapid wear of parts.

Another source of clash is hasty shifting to a non-synchromesh first or reverse gear. You must allow gears to quit spinning (or double-clutch on a first gear downshift) before engaging gear teeth. A defective synchromesh assembly will also produce this metallic clashing noise during gear shifts.

Use of the wrong gear lube can cause synchronizer balkiness and also make shifting difficult under various climate conditions. As such, gear clash and hard shifting will occur when using an overly stiff gear lube viscosity in winter months. Heavier gear and engine oils become rigid in extremely cold environments. Multi-viscosity synthetic gear lubricant is another cure for cold weather problems.

Synchronizers, which act much like a friction brake mechanism, wear over time. A patterned gear clash or jumping out of any gear usually indicates bearing, shift housing, shift fork or synchronizer damage. These troubles require a transmission overhaul.

Vehicle Will Not Move means several possibilities. A failed clutch is the first consideration. A clutch permanently disengaged (linkage extended and binding, disc worn completely or clutch cover springs broken) may still allow shifting of gears.

The opposite situation is damaged clutch linkage or bad contact between the throwout bearing and clutch cover fingers, which prevents disengagement of the clutch. With the truck in an open area and the engine shut off, place the transmission in low gear (also low range if a 4x4). Click or crank the starter. This should move the truck.

WARNING —
Make sure nothing is in the truck's way, as the engine may start. Be ready to shut the ignition switch off immediately.

If the clutch works, check the transmission. On a 4x4 equipped model, also check the transfer case (begin by locking the front hubs and engaging four-wheel drive). Now shift gears and try to move the truck. If your truck still will not move, power flow has stopped at the transmission or transfer case input. If the truck moves in four-wheel drive mode, suspect a broken rear transfer case output, a failed rear driveline or rear axle troubles.

When power fails to reach the axles of 4x4 trucks, defective transfer case shift linkage is a common cause. The linkage may bind or catch between gear ranges, creating a neutral effect and preventing power flow. As an emergency repair, block the wheels carefully, crawl beneath the vehicle and shift the transfer case manually at its shift rails.

WARNING —
Stop the engine and place safety blocks at each wheel before attempting to engage the transfer case. The vehicle can roll with the transfer case in neutral.

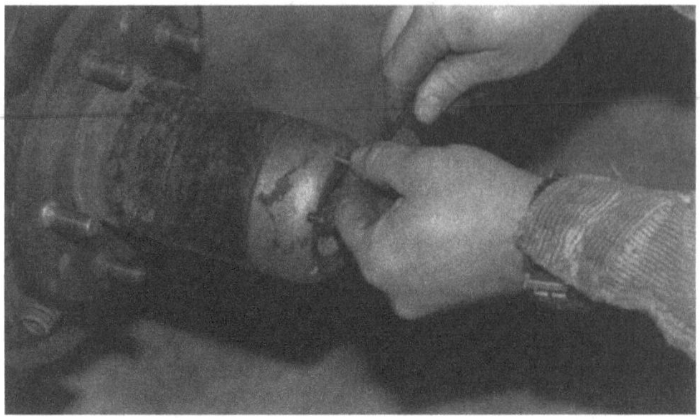

0012461

Fig. 6-23. On a 4x4 truck, power flow includes front hubs that work properly. While the engine, clutch, transmission, transfer case, driveshafts, differentials and axle shafts may work fine, a defective free-wheeling hub can prevent front axle traction.

Poor Traction/Erratic Wheel Spin is usually an axle/differential problem. On 1973–79 GM 4x4s with full-time NP203 transfer cases (common with the automatic transmission option), the transfer case's differential mechanism is much like an axle differential. Before condemning a part-time 4x4 transfer case or axle system, rule out the much simpler possibility of a defective front axle free-wheeling hub(s).

To check free-wheeling hubs, engage/lock the wheel hubs and the 4x4 drive system. (Roll forward in four-wheel drive to engage automatic free-wheeling hubs.) Jack each front wheel, one at a time, safely off the ground. By hand, rotate the raised wheel assembly with the opposite wheel still on the ground. The axle shaft should spin the front differential and cause the front driveshaft to rotate. (If your 4x4 truck has a front axle positive-traction device, the wheel assembly should rotate only slightly in each direction.)

If your GM truck has a limited slip differential at the rear, erratic handling and odd traction are often caused by wear in the differential's clutch unit. Lurching, clicking and snapping noises indicate trouble here. A failing limited slip unit shows obvious signs: poor traction with audible symptoms of trouble, most notably as the vehicle negotiates turns.

Gear bind is a common phenomenon with any 4x4 truck. If you attempt to operate your 4x4 truck on a dry, hard road surface with the front hubs locked and the transfer case in either 4WD high or low range (or lock mode on full-time 4x4 systems), the rotational speed differences between the front and rear axles will act as a counterforce within the geartrain.

Gear bind prevents disengagement of the transfer case. To overcome the binding force, gently rock your truck forward and in reverse while maintaining gentle, steady pressure on the transfer case lever. There is a point of free load, somewhere between forward and reverse, at which the bind loosens. At that moment, the transfer case lever will slide into the two-wheel drive position. Never apply excess force to the transfer case lever.

Driveshaft and Axle Woes

A common driveline problem on GM 2WD trucks and 4x4s is U-joint and constant velocity joint failure. Especially in rough and rocky terrain, the radical change angles place major loads on driveshaft U-joints and live front axle steering joints. Massive torque applied under high stress driving conditions can destroy a U-joint.

The loud, metallic snap of a breaking U-joint is hard to forget. Back country veterans of hardcore trails carry spare U-joints for such occasions. Although proper driving habits prevent the majority of mishaps, U-joint failure is still a major concern.

Another source of driveshaft trouble is torque twisting the tubes. A properly built driveshaft, operating at normal angles and in correct phase, will withstand tremendous abuse. If, however, a shaft sustains impact damage or operates at an abnormal posture, the tube and welds may fail. Inspect your truck's driveshafts regularly, and note any shake or vibration at road speeds. A bent or sprung driveshaft will create havoc, most apparent as vehicle speed increases.

0012196

Fig. 6-24. U-joints fail at inopportune times. Off-pavement, radical driveshaft angles and high torque loads place maximum stress on these components.

If your truck has a conventional, non-positive traction differential(s), an axle shaft or joint failure means an immediate loss of power flow. Although a truck equipped with four-wheel drive may still move when the front or rear differential fails, if a semi-floating rear axle shaft breaks, do not drive the truck.

On a semi-floating rear axle, like those found in all GM 1/2-ton models and many 1988–up Sierra chassis trucks, a broken axle shaft offers no stability to the wheel, tire and brake drum. If the axle shaft breaks outboard of the outer bearing, or if the bearing and its pressed-on lock collar (or an inner axle shaft C-lock) dislodges, the wheel and brake drum assembly can separate from the axle housing.

With a full-floating rear axle, it is possible to move the truck with a broken rear axle shaft. If the full-floating axle has a positive traction device, you can remove the inner section of broken axle shaft, reinstall the outer flange section, and carefully drive the truck.

On 4x4s, front axle shaft or steering joint failure is another safety risk. A broken shaft, cross-type joint or constant velocity joint may wedge in the housing or steering knuckle cavity. This could prevent rotation of the steering knuckle and wheel spindle, causing loss of vehicle control.

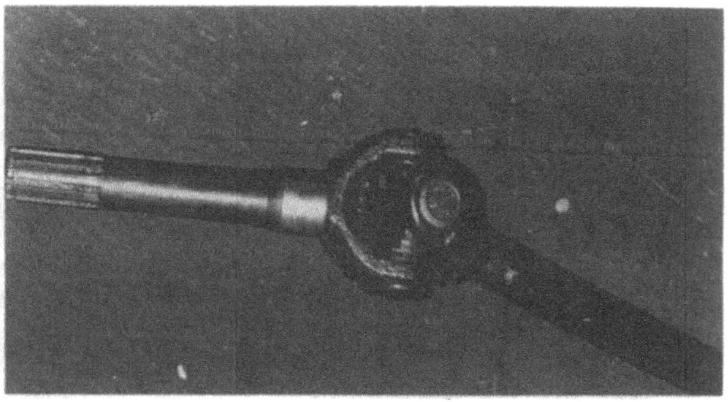

0012197

Fig. 6-25. Front axle joint failure is a dangerous situation. A broken shaft or joint can wedge in the steering knuckle and prevent the wheels from turning. Before driving the truck, check closely for such damage. If necessary, remove the axle shaft.

On solid front axle 4x4s, if the axle shafts are still safely in line and supported, you may place the transfer case in two-wheel drive mode and turn the hubs to FREE. (Disengage automatic locking hubs by placing the transfer case in 2WD mode and backing up the truck for fifteen feet.) Drive cautiously and make certain that the steering knuckles continue to pivot freely.

> **CAUTION —**
> *If you believe the defective axle shaft/joint could cause a lock-up of steering, and you must get home, remove the axle shaft assembly. Leave the transfer case in 2WD mode and the front hubs on FREE. This is a temporary fix to get home. Once back, immediately make a thorough repair.*

In any instance where your truck must operate with failed axle components, understand the extent of damage. If necessary, remove the inspection cover from the differential to locate the source of trouble. (In the field, catch drain oil in a clean container and save for refilling the differential if necessary.) Raise each wheel/tire from the ground and rotate the wheel (with both front hubs engaged) to determine whether the axle shafts and joints are intact. On an open steering knuckle axle, watch joint and driveshaft rotation.

If your 1973–79 GM truck has a full-time 4x4 system and no free-wheeling front hubs, axle shaft damage poses several driving threats, including steering impairment, risk of losing a wheel assembly, loss of braking or the possibility of increased damage to the truck. If an inner component in the axle breaks, exercise extreme caution if you must move the truck at all. Do not attempt to drive the truck if the steering knuckle, outer axle shaft, steering knuckle U-joint or wheel bearings have become severely damaged.

On such a truck, the full-floating front wheel hubs permit removal of a broken front axle shaft in an emergency. If you must move a full-time 4x4 model that has an unsafe, broken front axle shaft or joint, first remove the

0012198

Fig. 6-26. Ring and pinion gears, side gears and differential pinions can each fail. Remove the axle inspection cover to check these parts. Excess play at the pinion shaft or axle shafts can mean trouble.

0012199

Fig. 6-27. Limited slip, like a Spicer axle's Powr-Lok traction unit, features multi-plate clutches. Wear occurs over time, and traction diminishes. GM Corporate and Saginaw axles offer several types of traction differentials.

broken shaft, then the front driveshaft assembly. Set the transfer case in 4-Loc. (See axle service chapter or your GM shop manual for details on front axle shaft removal.)

During axle oil changes, with the differential cover removed, clean and inspect all parts. Look closely for abnormal tooth contact patterns on the ring and pinion gears. Check the pinion shaft for any end play or radial movement. Inspect the seals, observe side gear/pinion backlash (play) and note the condition of the carrier bearings that support the ring gear and differential carrier housing. Preventive maintenance and careful inspection remain your best safeguards against axle troubles.

Differential Troubles include clutch failure on positive traction units, broken differential side gears or small pinions and the stripping of teeth from the ring and pinion gears. Bearing failures, seal leaks and thrust washer wear are other trouble areas.

0014185

Fig. 6-28. On GM light trucks with either a 2WD or 4WD solid front axle, camber is only a concern when springs sag or an axle housing/beam fatigues or becomes bent.

Steering and Tire Troubles

Wander, the tendency for steering to either drift or follow road irregularities, is a common complaint with both two- and four-wheel drive models. The usual causes are front end misalignment, cupped tires (mostly bias-ply type), a loose steering gear, defective steering linkage, or suspension wear. Steering linkage and ball-joint or kingpin bearing/bushing wear are other problem spots.

When aligning the front wheels, service should include a caster check. Insufficient positive caster angle can cause shimmy and loss of steering control. If your GM truck needs coaxing to steer straight after a turn, check caster and toe-in. Sagging suspension or aftermarket lift kits can also affect caster angle.

For K-models with a solid 4x4 front axle, if slight caster and camber correction is necessary and no safety problem exists, slight adjustment is possible. An alignment shop can place shims between the axle and leaf springs for caster correction or install specially offset upper steering knuckle ball joint seats to correct camber and caster error.

1988–up Sierra 4x4 models and 1960–up IFS 2WD light trucks have factory adjustment provisions for caster, camber and toe-in. (See your GM shop manual for details on your truck's front end design and adjustment/alignment concerns.)

Loose steering gear and linkage result from high mileage and wear, severe loads and the rigors of off-pavement pounding. Excess play translates as wander. Depending upon your truck's front end design, inspect for wear at tie-rod ends, the steering gear, spring bushings and shackles, the centerlink assembly, idler arm, draglink, steering arms, kingpin bearings/bushings and ball-joints.

Front End Shimmy usually results from looseness in the steering knuckle (or kingpin) bearings/bushings or ball-joints. A contributing factor is looseness in the steering linkage, front wheel spindles or wheel bearings. Sagging springs and improper wheel alignment (especially caster angle) can also cause front end shimmy. Oversize tires exaggerate shimmy and so does severe tire imbal-

Fig. 6-29. Spin balancing helps guard against vibration and abnormal tire wear. In some cases, tires require truing, matching or balancing on the truck. Rotate tires every 5,000 to 7,500 miles, and check balance as needed.

ance. Any vibration or road shock can set off this potentially violent shaking of the front wheels. With manual steering, kingpin shimmy is a wrist-wrenching experience.

Perform a quick check of spindles, wheel bearings, kingpins or ball-joints by raising front wheels safely from the ground and installing jack stands beneath the axle housing on a solid axle 4WD model or the solid axle beam of a pre-1960 2WD model. (On 1960–up IFS 2WD models and the Sierra 4WD chassis, you can place jack stands beneath the lower A-arms, which also unload the spring or torsion bar tension on the ball joints.) Grab each front wheel and tire firmly at six and twelve o'clock. Rock the tire in and out with a lifting motion. Note the amount of movement.

If play exists, have a helper watch the backside of the wheel and steering knuckle. Determine whether the play is at the wheel hub (loose wheel bearings or spindle) or the knuckle support (kingpin bushings/bearings or ball-joints). When wheel bearing play is excessive, adjust the wheel bearings to specification, then repeat the inspection. (See service chapters for further details.)

Wheel Run-out and Tire Imbalance is another area of concern. Especially with oversize mud-and-snow tires, the weight mass at each wheel becomes excessive. Cleated truck tires, unlike conventional passenger car types, fall out of balance with normal wear. Periodic re-balancing and rotation are essential. (Switch in cross with bias ply, non-radial tires; ask your tire dealer for manufacturer's recommendations when rotating newer radial tires.)

Use of a quality tire gauge is essential. Your truck requires specific pressures for on- or off-highway use. Off-highway pressures below 20 psi will reduce load capacity drastically and possibly damage the tires. Always check tire pressures cold, and follow the manufacturer's recommended inflation rates for your GM truck model.

Hard-core 4x4 rock crawling can dislodge wheel weights or cause them to rotate on the rim. Tire damage, including internal belt separation of radial tires, causes vibration and shake. Bent wheel rims (runout) creates a wide range of handling and tire wear problems. The best preventive measure is periodic spin balancing of each tire and wheel. Have the technician pay close attention to rim run-out and distortion. Replace rims that show excess run-out.

Traditionally, heavy duty bias-ply tires have benefitted from truing, a procedure that trims out-of-round material from the new tread surface. Radial tires sometimes require tread and sidewall matching, a procedure that contributes to uniform tread pressure over the full circumference of the tire.

Tire imbalance usually becomes noticeable between 45 and 55 mph. Sometimes a set of tires and wheels may balance perfectly, yet the symptoms of imbalance remain. This situation may call for balancing the tires on the vehicle, with the brake drum or rotor and hub included in the rotating mass. Balancing on the truck requires re-balancing the tires each time you rotate them.

Brake Problems

Brake Pull and Grab occurs when you apply the brakes. Defects in hydraulic or mechanical parts of the brake system cause these problems. A pitted or corroded wheel cylinder or disc caliper piston bore can cause erratic piston action, while a sticking piston prevents normal movement of the brake shoes or disc pads.

An incorrectly adjusted master cylinder pushrod or dirty and corroded fluid reservoir can affect brake performance. If brake fluid cannot return to the master cylinder reservoir through the compensation port, fluid trapped in the system will keep pressure on the brakes. This can cause drag, fade and erratic braking action.

Several mechanical factors contribute to brake pull and grab. Oil on the brake lining, binding linkage, a broken shoe return spring, warped brake shoes and drums (bell mouthed or out-of-round), distorted rotors and pads, hard spots on drums or rotors and excessive lining wear each contribute to erratic braking. Poor lining quality, which leads to fade and undercapacity braking, is another source of trouble.

Slipshod brake jobs, without turning drums and rotors or rebuilding (sometimes replacing) hydraulic cylinders, can lead to problems. With exposure to water, mud and drastic climate changes, your brakes deserve quality care. Restore your brakes properly, then protect the brake system by periodically cleaning debris from shoes, backing plates, brake drums or rotors. Inspect the dust boot seals regularly.

> *WARNING —*
> *All older brake lining contains harmful asbestos. Brake vacuum equipment and special parts washers are available to prevent exposure to harmful asbestos brake dust. If you cannot safeguard yourself from asbestos, leave brake work to a professional shop. When performing brake work, inquire whether a non-asbestos lining is available for your truck.*

Failure to Stop has two symptoms: no pedal pressure or an extremely hard pedal. No pedal pressure generally means a hydraulic system failure, especially on pre-1967 trucks with single master cylinder systems. Also, if you use your truck off-pavement, it faces environmental haz-

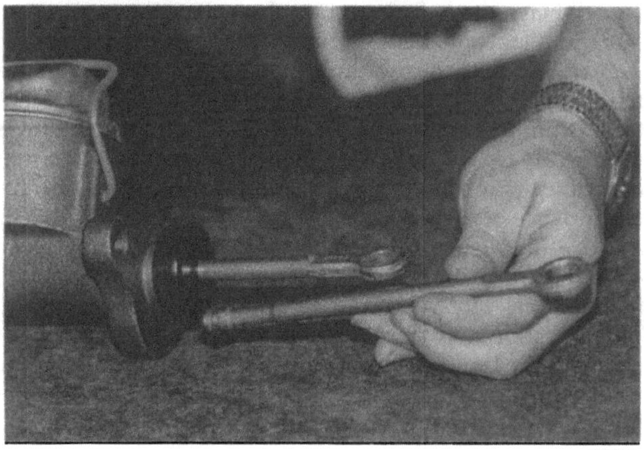

0012203

Fig. 6-30. Master cylinder pushrod clearance is crucial to safe braking. Insufficient clearance at the tip of the pushrod will prevent the piston from retracting completely.

0014188

Fig. 6-31. Glazed or contaminated brake lining, rotors and drums will increase pedal pressure. A defective outer axle shaft seal permits gear lube to saturate and ruin the brake lining.

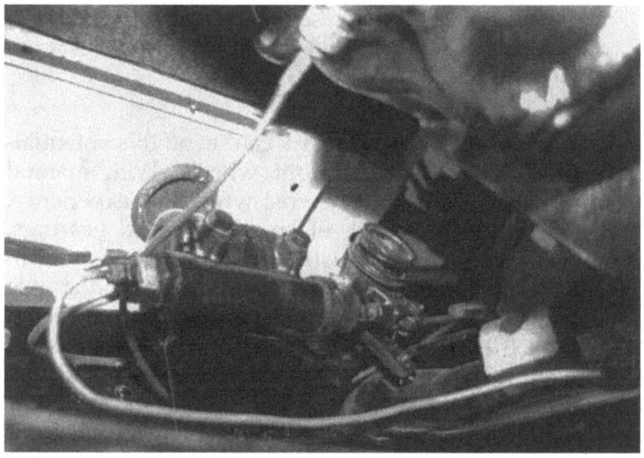

0014187

Fig. 6-32. Until 1960, the GM light truck master cylinder mounts below the floorboard. Exposed to moisture, debris and ice, the master cylinder's dust boot must seal properly. Otherwise, rust and corrosive road salts will attack the cylinder.

ards that can damage brake pipes or hoses. If fluid loss has occurred, carefully repair the hydraulic system, bleed air out, and check for leaks before driving the vehicle.

Mechanical problems like a broken brake shoe, drum, actuating linkage or defective self-adjuster mechanism will cause the master cylinder piston to fully exhaust its stroke before the brakes apply. (Actually, this too is a hydraulic failure, although a mechanical cause underlies the problem.)

Under extreme circumstances, misadjusted brake shoes, combined with major lining wear, will create the same effect. The brake pedal reaches the floor before lining reaches the drums. If your truck's brakes have no self-adjusters, you must periodically adjust the shoe-to-drum clearance and monitor the lining wear.

Normal lining wear lowers the level of fluid in the master cylinder reservoir. Check brake fluid at regular intervals to assure an adequate reserve. The master cylinder must displace a full stroke of fluid to actuate the wheel brakes. (See chapters on maintenance and brake service.)

An extremely hard pedal is usually the result of contaminated lining (oil, dirt, or water), glazed brake lining or warped drums and / or rotors. Poor brake shoe seating, often a consequence of improper shoe arc, can prevent lining from making full contact with the drums. Binding of the linkage, actuating hardware or hydraulic cylinder pistons will also increase brake pedal pressure.

In freezing weather, always check your brakes before driving the truck. Wet hardware may ice up—another cause of hard pedal. Additionally, hard pedal can result from overheated lining or fade.

There are several causes of brake fade: improper fitup of brake parts; hydraulic fluid trapped in the lines (due to a misadjusted master cylinder pushrod, bent pipe or kinked brake hose); extensive use or abuse of the brakes; excess load on the brake system; a misadjusted wheel-type emergency brake; incorrect brake shoe-to-drum clearance (too tight); and glazed / contaminated brake lining.

Chapter 7

Cooling System Service

WHEN WORKING HARD, your General Motors truck places a high demand on its cooling system. The engine must maintain normal operating temperatures, whether the air outside is -60° F or 130° above. Dusty roads pack dirt and abrasive material into a radiator core, and rocks and debris from the tires of other vehicles can damage the radiator core just as easily as they break a windshield.

For 4x4 models, a twisting back country trail, where tires hang suspended in air, can loosen a weak radiator core support. Hose flex fatigues the radiator inlet and outlet tubes. Hard impact force can drive the fan into the radiator or fan shroud.

Add to this the burden of air conditioning and an automatic transmission. Many truck owners consider creature comfort a valid part of driving. Why suffer with 120° heat inside your vehicle? The installation of a factory or aftermarket air conditioner places another obstacle in front of the cooling system, as the air conditioning condenser restricts air flow through the radiator.

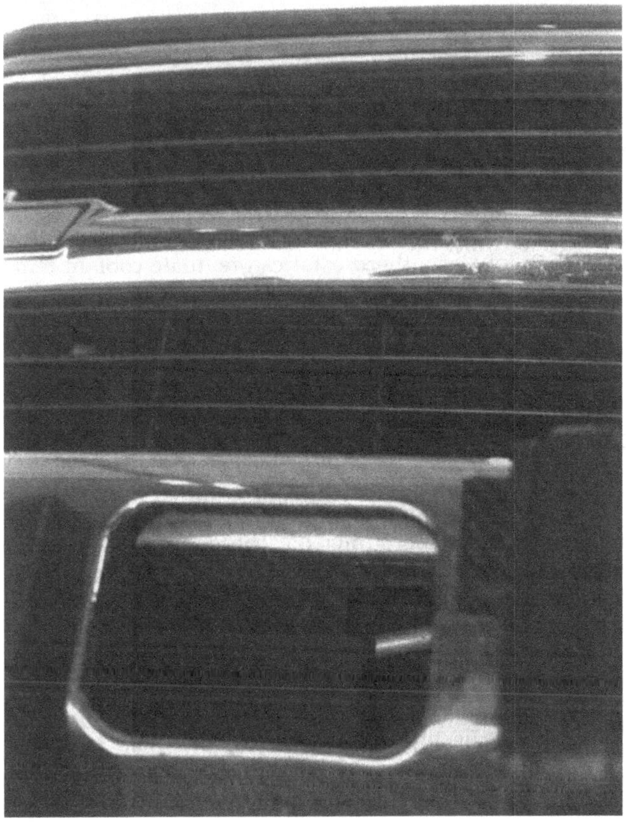

0014163

Fig. 7-1. An automatic transmission and air conditioning place an added load on the engine's cooling system. The air conditioning condenser and auxiliary transmission cooler each limit air flow through the radiator core.

Many GM trucks have an automatic transmission. All but the earliest Hydra-Matic Drive automatic transmissions cool ATF at the engine's radiator. This places an even greater load on the radiator, coolant and fan system. Likewise, an auxiliary engine or transmission oil cooler mounts within the fan's air flow. This adds extra heat that the cooling system must handle.

Another factor that increases the risk of overheat is a forward mounted winch. Often, 4x4 truck models have such an assembly or other accessories mounted just forward of the grill. Today's better winch mounting kits place the winch behind or in line with the bumper, below the grill opening. This allows vital air to flow through the radiator.

Since many light truckers pull trailers, higher horsepower engines are popular in Camper Special or trailer towing models. The ultimate cooling challenge for any truck is a high horsepower engine, which places a tremendous load on the radiator and fan system.

The simplest way to explain this equation is that each horsepower equals a certain number of British Thermal Units (BTUs). More horsepower means a higher BTU output or engine heat. The cooling system must adequately dissipate this thermal load.

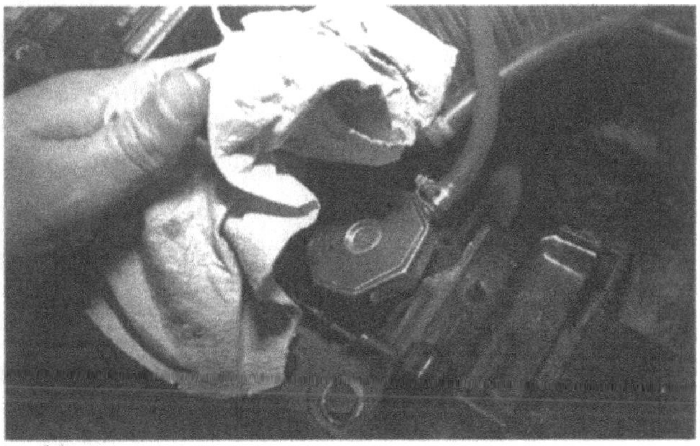

0014164

Fig. 7-2. If a hot engine has a good amount of coolant still in the system, run the engine while pouring a light stream of water over the radiator core and tanks. (Avoid hitting a hot engine with cold water, as this could crack a block, cylinder head or other castings.) The temperature will drop quickly. Allow the engine and radiator to cool completely before removing the radiator cap.

Safety Precautions: An Overheated Engine

WARNING —

- *Never remove the radiator cap when the engine is hot. Hot coolant under pressure leaves the radiator with extreme force and spews in all directions. This scalding hot liquid could cause severe bodily injury or burns.*

- *Always use extreme caution when removing a radiator cap. (Use a heat resistant rubber glove or stack of shop rags as a protective barrier.) Always shield yourself from the fill neck when removing the cap. Relieve all pressure by first holding the cap at its safety notch, if so designed.*

CAUTION —

- *Never add coolant to the engine when it is hot or overheated. If you must add coolant, leave the engine running.*

- *Coolant is poisonous to pets. Use extreme care when draining and disposing of engine coolant.*

Sufficient cooling requires maximum transfer of heat from the engine to the air. The radiator, comprised of coolant tubes and fins, handles the majority of this task. For those who like engineering formulas, here's the actual equation for engine cooling: Draw off at least 42.5 BTUs of heat per minute for each horsepower.

Since BTU heat dissipation relates directly to the area of radiator tube and fin exposure, core size is very important. Air flow and radiator core size (reflected by the number and size of the coolant tubes plus the area of the fins) will determine cooling capacity.

1. Cooling System Basics

Chronic cooling system problems usually originate at the radiator. Often, especially with larger engines, an under-capacity or clogged radiator creates trouble. Several factors apply when choosing the correct radiator, but the main issue is horsepower. Higher horsepower equates to a greater need for heat transfer, your truck radiator's principal job.

Engineers see horsepower output as the main variable when determining the capacity of a radiator or fan system. Your truck's engine loses approximately one-third of its thermal energy as heat dissipating from the radiator, the heater core and surfaces of the engine. Another one-third of the thermal energy goes out the tailpipe as hot exhaust. (This valuable energy, when harnessed to power an exhaust turbocharger, produces considerable extra horsepower.)

The actual ignition process and combustion of fuel consume the other third of this thermal energy, as the hot gases expand and drive the pistons. Moving pistons rotate the crankshaft and propel the vehicle.

0014165 / 0014166

Fig. 7-3. *Here is the difference between a 1967 or newer GM V-8 cross-flow light truck radiator (top) and an earlier GM down-flow unit. A big V-8 with air conditioning requires far more overall radiator size, more tubes and a larger core surface area than the radiator for a smaller V-8 or inline six.*

Matching Cooling System Components

Whether you are restoring an earlier model truck, retrofitting a higher horsepower engine into your truck's chassis or increasing an engine's performance, you must accurately determine the horsepower level. It's better to guess high than low, as a thermostat can regulate coolant temperatures if you install a slightly oversize radiator that cools too well. With an undersize radiator core, the engine will never run cool.

Also consider the engine's water pump volume and coolant flow rate. If the engine pumps more water into the radiator than the tubes can flow, the coolant will overflow the filler neck as engine speed increases. This is a common symptom of an inadequate radiator flow rate.

Lastly, the radiator's ability to rapidly transfer or dissipate heat must be sufficient. The engine fan plays a large role here. As an absolute minimum, you need a fan that creates an air flow rate of 725 to 1150 feet per minute through the radiator core.

Excess loads, high ambient temperatures, air restriction or unusually slow road speeds require additional fan flow and a higher radiator flow rate.

Flow rate is the amount of coolant that can move through the radiator in a given interval of time. The industry standard of measurement is gallons-per-minute flow or gpm. If your truck's original radiator won't cool a transplanted bigger engine, the cause is either a deficiency in gpm flow or too little surface area.

0012247

Fig. 7-4. A four-row core is not always bigger than a three-row. Tube size also contributes to flow rate and surface area. Pay attention to gpm flow ratings and various engine/chassis applications when selecting a high output radiator. Recyclers and radiator shops offer information on gpm flow rates and applications.

The usual cure for flow rate weaknesses is a larger radiator or radiator core. Popular four- or five-row radiators offer a thicker core with more rows of tubes. If you must adhere to the original radiator's height and width dimensions, and that radiator has two or three rows of tubes, the addition of a four-row core may provide the necessary gpm flow level.

The size of each tube is actually more important than the number of rows. Many three-row cores, with larger tubes, offer higher BTU dissipation ratings than a four-row core with small tubes. When in doubt, consult flow and BTU charts at a local radiator shop.

Fan Air Flow

If, despite adequate coolant flow and proper thermostat action, your truck's engine overheats, air flow or fan shrouding could be at fault. Especially with a narrow grill opening, fan draw becomes a major part of cooling. Poor fan location, a defective fan clutch, or an improperly shaped shroud can prevent air from passing through the radiator core.

Some truck owners make the mistake of eliminating the clutch fan unit and trying to run a non-flexing metal fan. This can actually create a blockage of air flow at high road speeds. Here, air moving through the grill and radiator can travel much faster than the draw speed of the fan. For this reason, and to reduce horsepower drain, either a fan clutch assembly or an aftermarket flexible-blade fan is frequently found on high performance engines.

0012248

Fig. 7-5. Flex-A-Lite aftermarket flex fan and spacers replace a factory fan clutch and fan. Stainless steel blades will flatten at higher engine speeds to prevent air blockage. Note reverse fan rotation, required on many late engines with serpentine drive belts.

0014167

Fig. 7-6. The location of the fan and shroud are important to cooling. Factory fan blade lies approximately halfway into the shroud opening. Shroud captures air from the entire radiator core. Late GM truck engines with a serpentine drive belt use a reverse rotation fan.

The shroud must capture the entire core area of the radiator. Ideal fan location will have half the thickness of the blades inside the shroud, the other half just rearward. (Aftermarket flex fans alter this formula slightly, so read instructions that come with any conversion fan.) This allows the fan to draw under all circumstances and prevents turbulence or an air blockage to occur within the shroud.

The last area of concern is coolant or air blockage within the cooling system Beware of improperly installed engine gaskets, especially the head gasket(s), or an upside down thermostat. When performing a valve grind or complete engine overhaul, follow engine assembly instructions carefully. Make sure all gaskets seal properly and that coolant ports align correctly.

Finding Leaks

Coolant leaks can ruin your drive or vacation. As a safeguard, check your cooling system regularly with a pressure tester. External leaks are easiest to find. With the engine shut off and cool, simply pump the tester to the cooling system's normal pressure, and watch the gauge. It should not drop. If it does, look for leaks at hoses, the intake manifold, the thermostat housing, freeze plugs, or the radiator and heater cores.

If no external leaks are present, suspect an internal engine leak, including a seeping or blown head gasket, casting cracks, or an interior intake manifold/cooling passage leak. A blown head gasket or cracked casting will either leak coolant into a cylinder or create low compression in two adjacent cylinders.

When coolant can enter a cylinder, compression gases also leak into the engine's cooling ports. Rapid overflow at the radiator filler neck or coolant recovery tank results when high pressure cylinder gases enter the cooling system.

Intake manifold gaskets leaking at the coolant crossover passages on GM V-8 and V-6 engines will drain coolant into the crankcase. So will a leaking timing cover casting or gaskets. Block or cylinder head cracks cause coolant leaks into the upper cylinders and/or crankcase, depending upon the crack's location in the casting.

There are several tests for an internal coolant leak. Securely attach a pressure tester to the radiator fill neck. Have someone start the engine while you watch the gauge. If pressure rises rapidly and pegs at the high side of the gauge, shut the engine off. This indicates that cylinder pressure has entered the cooling system and pressurized the radiator. A casting crack or blown head gasket is the cause.

CAUTION —

Cylinder gases in the cooling system will create an abrupt and dangerous rise in pressure. (Imagine 100-plus psi of pressure within a cooling system designed for 17 psi.) Protect your cooling system tester by shutting the engine off immediately if pressure starts to rise rapidly with the engine running. Use extreme care when working around a cooling system. Do not remove the cap if the engine has warmed or if the tester gauge reads high. Allow time for the system to cool and pressure to drop.

The appearance of bubbles in the radiator often indicates the presence of cylinder gases and a head gasket or casting leak. This can be deceptive, though, since other causes of aeration, including water pump malfunctions, can also introduce air bubbles into the cooling system.

0012249

Fig. 7-7. *A cooling system pressure tester is quickest check for leaks. Pump tester to normal cooling system pressure, then watch gauge. Sealing properly, no drop should occur.*

0012250

Fig. 7-8. *Strange place for an exhaust gas analyzer probe! With the engine idling at normal temperature, an exhaust infrared tester can sniff cylinder gases just above the radiator filler neck. Combustion gases will enter the cooling system through a blown head gasket(s), a cracked cylinder head or a crack in the block. Carbon monoxide (CO) is detectable here.*

An infrared exhaust analyzer can quickly confirm whether bubbles in the radiator are from leaking combustion gases. By holding the analyzer probe just above an open radiator fill neck or coolant recovery tank, a reading of carbon monoxide and hydrocarbons is possible. If you find these gases present, suspect cylinder leakage.

Automatic Transmission Load on Cooling

An automatic transmission can overtax your engine's cooling system. Automatic transmissions operate hot, well in excess of normal engine coolant temperatures, and the truck's radiator is often the only source of cooling

0012251

Fig. 7-9. An add-on auxiliary transmission cooler takes a tremendous load off the engine's cooling system. Install an auxiliary transmission cooler if your plans include trailer pulling or rock crawling in the off-pavement environment.

for the transmission. As a result, a heavily worked transmission can actually cause an engine overheat.

The original iron-cased band-type Hydra-Matics did not rely on the engine's cooling system. 1960s and later truck Powerglides (Pow-R-Flow) and TH350 or TH400 transmissions have fluid lines that run to the radiator for cooling. On downflow type radiators, the lower tank of the radiator harbors a separate cell for circulating automatic transmission fluid (ATF). Cross-flow radiators incorporate a transmission cooler in one of the side tanks. Engine coolant, moving around this cell, draws off heat from the scorching ATF.

One of the best solutions for better engine and transmission cooling is an auxiliary transmission cooler. Some GM trucks feature an optional original equipment (OEM) transmission cooler, which is usually part of a heavy duty/air conditioning or trailer pulling package. Aftermarket manufacturers build units that work either in-line with the radiator or independently.

The auxiliary transmission cooler resembles an air conditioning or refrigeration condenser. Air, either from vehicle movement or from the engine's fan, moves past the fins on the transmission cooler, drawing heat away from the transmission fluid.

If you install an aftermarket transmission cooler, position it carefully. Since so much heat passes from its surface, placing the unit in front of the radiator core is not always wise. Pre-heated air can raise the temperature of the radiator fins and tubes. Often, a better approach is to place the transmission cooler behind the radiator, or somewhere in the vehicle's air stream, without restricting the flow of radiator air.

Keeping Late Model Engines Alive

Late model light truck engines operate hot. More thorough combustion, better fuel economy plus lower CO and HC emissions result from lean fuel mixtures and higher thermostat settings; the side effect is more heat. Years ago, a truck engine came from the factory with a 180° winter thermostat. It was common practice to install a 160° thermostat in the summer months.

Today, due largely to cooling system controls and emission restrictions, engines run at 195 to 205° F thermostat settings. "Normal" operating temperature can range to 240° F—well past the boiling point of water.

One way to compensate for high operating temperatures is by using the correct radiator cap and coolant mixture. A radiator pressure cap of 15 psi can raise the boiling point of a 50/50 anti-freeze and water mixture to 265° F, while a 60/40 coolant mix is good for 270°. Each pound increase in radiator cap pressure raises the boilover point by three degrees. Make sure the cap pressure rating is right for your engine.

Also, while anti-freeze/coolant seems the cure-all for raising the boiling point, remember that there's a limit to its use. The expansion rates differ between water and anti-freeze/coolant. An excessive amount of ethylene glycol limits the solution's ability to expand within itself. Running pure anti-freeze can cause boil over—expansion right out of the system.

Too much anti-freeze/coolant also affects the freezing point. At -8° F, pure ethylene glycol anti-freeze will actually freeze, resulting in broken engine castings and/or a cracked radiator core. Never mix ethylene glycol solutions richer than the 68% maximum ratio recommended by most vehicle manufacturers. (The minimum recommended mix is usually 44%.) A 68% anti-freeze/32% water solution should provide engine protection to -90° F.

A mix of at least 40% water is considered practical in an ethylene glycol anti-freeze/coolant solution. This can be confirmed by either mixing the solution from scratch or testing the cooling system with an anti-freeze hydrometer. Make sure that the coolant has circulated (through the heater system, too) before you attempt to check its specific gravity with a hydrometer.

When to Use an Aftermarket Electric Fan

It takes far less to cool a low compression, low horsepower inline six-cylinder engine than a high compression, high horsepower V-8. The 1940 216 Stovebolt inline OHV Chevrolet six with 6.25:1 compression cranked out a modest 78 horsepower in light truck form, while a late EFI/TBI 454 V-8 produces 230 net horsepower. A modified or supercharged Chevrolet 350 V-8 engine or a heavily built up 454 V-8 can range from 300 to 600 horsepower. Remember, horsepower equals BTUs.

You can now find auxiliary electric fans in OEM truck applications. They typically serve as factory add-on devices for a heavy duty cooling or tow package. The engine driven fan assembly still provides primary cooling. Factory auxiliary electric fans meet engineering guidelines for a particular cooling system, GVWR rating and engine package.

For the conversion engine in a tight chassis bay, there's a temptation to use an electric fan in place of an engine-driven fan. On many large V-8 conversions, the engine's mechanical fan is difficult to fit within the confines of a smaller engine bay or will not line up easily with the center of the radiator core. (The 1955 Second Series and newer GM light truck chassis was built for a V-8 engine. These broad engine bays even accommodate larger big-block 396, 402, 427, 454 and the latest Gen V marine/racing V-8 engines.)

0014168

Fig. 7-10. Factory electric fans are an auxiliary source of air flow for cooling. While this type of replacement auxiliary electric fan could serve a high GVWR package that wrestles with an automatic transmission, an air conditioner and a large displacement V-8 engine, a cooling system's principal source of air flow is still the heavy duty engine-driven mechanical fan.

Some custom street rod builders believe that the mechanical (engine-driven) fan is unnecessary and that a heavy duty electric fan system, alone, can cool the engine. As a former truck fleet mechanic and long standing four-wheel drive user, I am not a supporter of aftermarket electric fans and am especially disappointed with electric fans that rely on the radiator fins for support. (These kinds of assemblies are held in place by plastic ties through the radiator core.) With enough vibration, a fin mounted electric fan can severely damage the radiator.

A mechanical fan, if centered reasonably well and shrouded properly, proves superior in all cases. A heavy-duty truck fan or any of the better aftermarket flexible (engine-driven) cooling fans provide far more pitch and air draw than the typical electric fan.

An electric fan may provide adequate cooling for light load highway use where cruise speed air flow meets the majority of cooling needs. I once tested a "high output" aftermarket electric fan on a 4x4 truck with a high horsepower conversion engine. The electric fan was the sole source of cooling air. At crawl speeds or traffic light stops, the electric fan cooled engine would heat up as if the cooling system was under capacity. When the vehicle reached 25 to 30 mph, the engine would cool rapidly, even with the electric fan turned off.

The real test of truck cooling is a high noon rock crawling episode on a mid-summer trip through the desert—or pulling a 30-foot travel trailer up a six-percent, twelve mile long grade out of El Centro, California in August—or getting stuck in the Los Angeles freeway interchange with a sailboat in tow and the ambient temperature around 100° F. Here, when used as the sole source of air flow, a heavy duty engine-driven fan serves far better than any aftermarket automotive electric fan.

0014169

Fig. 7-11. Follow factory belt tightening procedure whenever possible. If data is unavailable, adjust a V-type belt to 1/2" deflection midway between the generator/alternator pulley and fan pulley. Measure this deflection while applying firm downward thumb pressure to the belt. Correct tension will rotate generator/alternator pulley slightly as you apply pressure.

I would consider using an aftermarket electric fan to cool an auxiliary engine oil cooler or a transmission cooler. These devices often rely on the engine-driven fan for air flow, which places an added burden on the engine's own cooling system.

Tenacious Overheat Problems

Cooling problems can go beyond the radiator and fan. A dirty or corroded engine block, obstructions in the block, the wrong cylinder head(s), an improperly installed head gasket or excessive internal friction can each cause overheating. Faulty ignition timing or spark advance, excess

0014170

Fig. 7-12. Even a defective spark advance mechanism or vacuum unit (arrow) can cause engine overheating. The State of California once advocated a retrofit smog control that eliminated vacuum spark advance under most driving conditions. Engine overheat damage was so prevalent that California abandoned the measure.

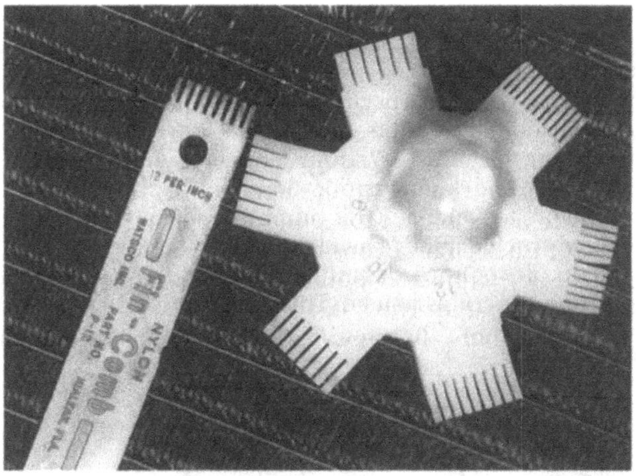

Fig. 7-13. Fin design makes a difference, with serpentine-type fins generally better for the off-highway environment. Overall, whether your oversize radiator is a downflow or crossflow design, quality construction and adequate air flow are more important than whether coolant moves horizontally or vertically.

carbon, valves ground too thin, a defective thermostat, the wrong intake manifold, cross-firing spark plug wires and an overly lean or rich carburetor mix can also cause an overheat.

Water pump defects are a common cause of trouble. The most obvious pump problem is a leaking seal. Worn pump bearings allow pulley and fan blade runout, usually visible when looking sideways at the idling engine. Improper gaskets, corroded impeller vanes or a missing water pump backing plate can also cause coolant circulation problems.

A plugged exhaust system or a stuck heat riser valve will quickly overheat an engine. Pinched or air-blocked cooling hoses, excessively hot spark plugs or a loose fan belt(s) can also cause trouble. Avoid using flex type hoses, as they can collapse or place excess stress on radiator inlet and outlet sleeves. Wherever possible, use OEM type molded hoses with wire reinforcement.

An older radiator may need boiling and rodding. This process involves removing the top and bottom tanks, boiling the radiator in caustic, then running rods through the scaly tubes. Reassembly and pressure testing complete the job. Late model truck cooling systems operate at higher pressures, which, in conjunction with anti-freeze/coolant, raise the boiling point.

A clean, pressure tested radiator, with adequate flow rate and the proper fan cooling, should keep your truck's engine running at normal temperatures. Most radiators that test leak free at 20 psi in the shop will offer long service. A 17-psi cap affords a 260-plus-degree boiling point with a 50/50 mixture of high grade anti-freeze/coolant and water.

A heavily modified engine, however, may require a special radiator. Especially challenging are the big V-8s. Here, a custom downflow or crossflow type radiator must have a large flow capacity. Also consider a heavy duty OE replacement radiator. Often, a radiator specialist can mount your original radiator tanks and brackets to a much larger new radiator core.

Fig. 7-14. Check radiator solder seams and joints for coolant seepage. Have weak or loose brackets repaired by a radiator shop.

As for specialty radiators, don't rush to buy a NASCAR or SCCA aluminum road racing radiator. Such a unit may rely on high speed air flow for cooling, a non-existent commodity when your 4x4 shares a desert floor with the lizards or your fifth wheel Doolie lugs a four-horse trailer over the Grapevine.

2. WATER PUMP SERVICE

Eventually, every engine's water pump will fail or wear out. Although water pumps often last between engine overhauls, the load and stress placed on a hard working truck can cause earlier failure. If you periodically pressure check the cooling system, maintain an adequate amount of coolant/anti-freeze and keep proper tension

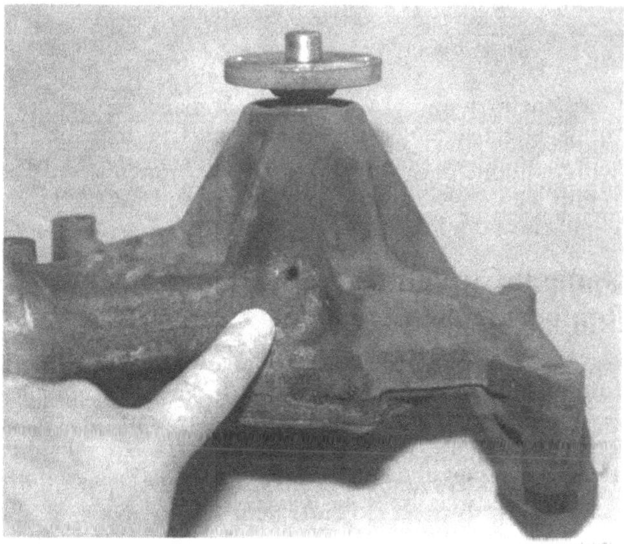

Fig. 7-15. Water pump failure seldom occurs instantly. Signs of weakness, like coolant seepage or a wobbling shaft bearing, give forewarning. Watch bleed hole at base of pump. When the seal fails, coolant will leak from bleed hole.

0014172

Fig. 7-16. In an emergency, you can change the water pump yourself. Make sure the engine is completely cool before attempting to drain coolant, and use a drain pan. Avoid prolonged skin exposure to anti-freeze, sealants or parts cleaning agents. Use adequate ventilation as indicated.

on the drive belts, you will decrease the likelihood that a failed water pump will leave you stranded.

On that note, like an extra fan belt, a bottle of radiator stop leak solution is a smart accessory for your truck's toolbox. Often, if the leak has just developed, Stop Leak can get your truck home or to a service garage. For the water pump in good condition, a water pump lubricant additive is of some value.

As a precaution, pressure check your cooling system regularly. Often, a water pump will only leak when under pressure. Also, with the engine shut off, rock the fan blade to test the water pump shaft bearings.

> *WARNING —*
> *Be extremely careful when handling an aftermarket stainless steel fan. The edges are often as sharp as a knife.*

At the first sign of water pump seepage, replace the pump. Don't take chances or attempt a permanent fix with a liquid or powder stop leak treatment. A weak pump will likely fail at a critical time, such as when the engine is under load and pulling hard.

General Guidelines for Water Pump Replacement

Prior to the advent of engine driven power options, water pump replacement was relatively easy. For later models, depending upon equipment and how many engine accessories stand in the way, this task can vary. In general, GM trucks with sixes and small-block V-8s have open engine bays and ready access to the water pump.

Power steering and other engine-driven accessories can make the water pump more difficult to access. If your engine has an alternator, power steering, air conditioning and an air injection pump(s), allow plenty of time to complete the water pump replacement.

Although the steps discussed should assist in your water pump removal-and-replacement (R & R), the job may require additional measures for your particular year, model or accessory package. If you find areas not discussed and have doubts about what steps to take, consult the GM factory service/shop manual for your specific year truck and engine application.

Before tackling a water pump change on a well-loaded GM truck engine, consider the scope of the project. If you decide to proceed, outline on paper the steps and the position of parts as you go. This sequence is crucial to correct reassembly. To avoid a "sour" job or the ultimate

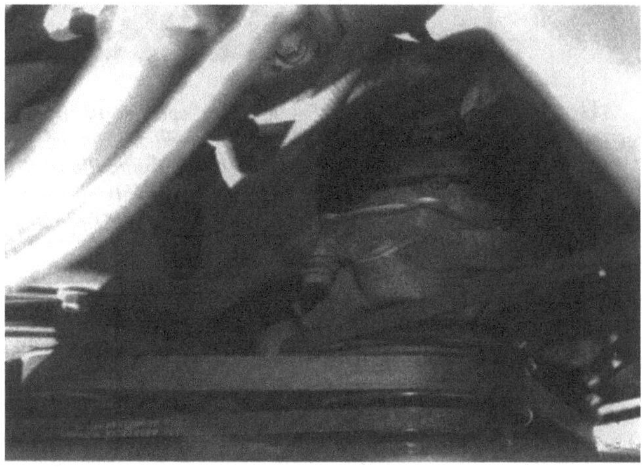

0014175

Fig. 7-17. My 1986 GMC K2500 Suburban's chassis rating exceeds 8,500 pounds GVWR, and the Sierra Classic package provides a full complement of power options. The 350 V-8's water pump lies beneath a maze of accessories and drive belts. This is the last V-8 engine to use V-belts (in conjunction with a modern serpentine belt), and I did not attempt a water pump change without first referring to steps outlined in my factory-level truck shop manual.

0014173

Fig. 7-18. Single serpentine belts have unique routings. Note the engine equipment and match to your GM light truck workshop manual chart or the decal beneath the hood of your truck. Most later fans are reverse rotation design.

frustration of re-doing the project, take time to observe how the many pieces come apart.

Begin any water pump replacement by placing a large pan beneath the radiator drain cock. With the engine cool, loosen the petcock and allow coolant to drain into the pan. (You may find that removing the radiator cap allows faster draining.) Unless this coolant is relatively new and very clean, discard it at your local recycling outlet.

Disconnect the negative battery cable if your engine requires removal of the generator or alternator and its mounting bracket. With the negative battery cable disconnected, loosen the generator/alternator belt, whether serpentine or V-groove type. For serpentine belts, make careful note of belt routing.

Unbolt and lay the generator or alternator aside, with its wires still attached if possible. Do not stretch these wires. Support the alternator or generator properly.

On all engines, remove the radiator fan shroud, fan and fan clutch where applicable. If you have not already done so, you will need to loosen and remove the generator or alternator belt or serpentine belt to perform these steps. When the engine drives power accessories, other belts may also need removal. Note their location and routing so that you can reinstall them in the proper sequence.

If you are not removing the radiator but need to remove the shroud, reinstall one screw at each side to support the radiator as the shroud is detached. On some trucks, the space between the radiator and engine is enormous, so you can replace the water pump by just removing the shroud. Take care not to damage radiator fins when removing the fan, pulley or water pump.

> **NOTE —**
> Carefully support the water pump as you remove the bolts. Pull the pump straight forward to avoid damaging the impeller. Take extreme care not to damage the radiator core if the radiator is still in place.

0014174

Fig. 7-19. *If the air conditioner interferes with pump removal, you must follow necessary steps to move the compressor and access the water pump. Power steering pumps, an alternator, air injection pumps and even vacuum fittings and electronic sensor components may interfere with a water pump removal.*

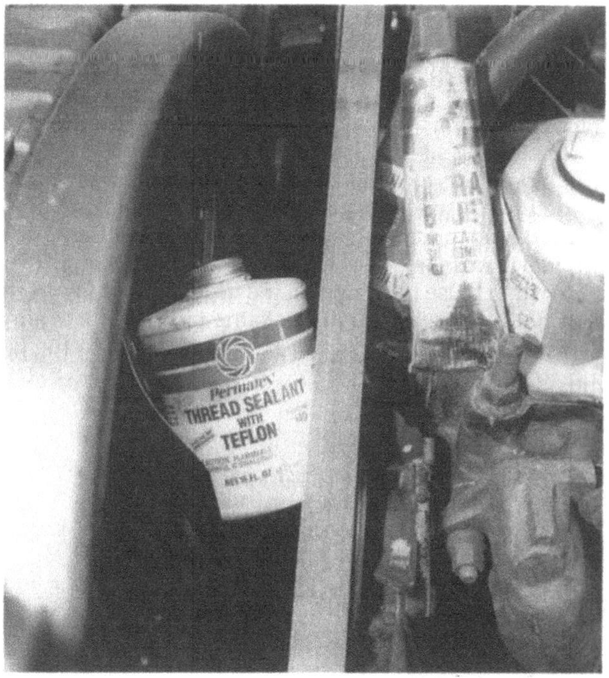

0012262

Fig. 7-20. *Use the specified gasket sealant when installing a water pump. Proper sealant is both oil and coolant resistant. Place a thin coat on each side of the gasket. Thoroughly clean bolt threads and pipe fittings, and apply thread or pipe sealant before assembly.*

If the lower radiator hose attaches to the water pump, you need to disconnect this hose at the water pump. (On some engines, you may want to remove the upper hose to allow more room to work.) Now loosen all other hoses attached to the water pump.

All water pump installations require wire brush cleaning of bolts and fasteners and close inspection of hardware and fittings for corrosion damage. Carefully scrape old gasket material from the water pump mounting surface. If surfaces are aluminum, use extreme caution when scraping to avoid nicking soft alloy.

Years ago, water pump rebuilding kits were available. Today, your local GM truck dealership or parts outlet supplies complete new or rebuilt pumps. Make certain that the replacement pump is identical to the one you have removed, and inspect the new gasket(s).

As required, transfer any reusable fittings or pipes from old pump to new pump. If fittings show excessive wear, replace with new parts of like kind and coat threads with a film of liquid Teflon sealant. Evenly coat both sides of new gasket(s) with a suitable gasket sealant. Apply sealant or liquid Teflon to bolt threads before installing the new water pump.

Find an appropriate coolant-resistant sealant approved for water pump installation. Avoid use of too much sealant on gaskets, as excess sealant finds its way into the radiator tubes. On very late model engines, anaerobic sealers sometimes take the place of a conventional gasket. Observe what kind of seal your engine parts require.

With the odd routing of serpentine drive belts, some late model engines have either forward or reverse rotation water pumps. Make note of which way your water pump and fan rotate. Be certain that the new pump's impeller vanes match the original pump's direction of rotation.

If electrolysis or erosion has weakened your water pump bolts, discard them and replace with new, properly graded hardware. Always be certain that bolts are of the same thread pitch, thread length and overall length as original hardware. Use hardware gradings equal to or better than those indicated on the heads of OEM bolts. Install new lock washers of the same kind as the original hardware, and apply coolant-resistant sealant to the bolt threads.

WARNING —
The running fan and water pump contain a lot of energy. One of the worst possible accidents is a fan coming loose and either driving through the radiator core or flying in lethal fashion from the engine bay.

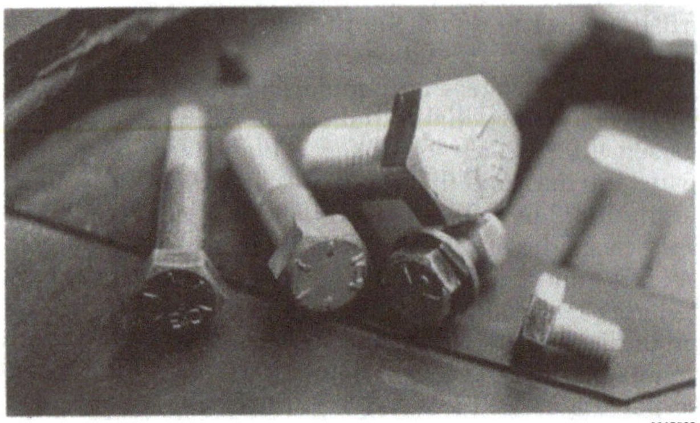

0012263

Fig. 7-21. These bolt head markings represent different grades of USS and SAE hardware. Three marks is Grade 5. Six marks is a Grade 8 bolt, a much higher tensile strength than the general purpose Grade 5.

When a specific torque setting is not available, torque bolts according to their thread size and grade standards. Many non-factory service manuals neglect the torque settings for water pump and engine accessories hardware. If

Water Pump R & R Notes For Specific Engines

Water pump installations differ by model, year and engine application. For later trucks, a Chevrolet or GMC factory Workshop Manual is available through your local Chevy or GMC Truck dealership, along with any specialty tools needed for service operations.

If your truck is older and the factory manual is no longer available through your Chevrolet or GMC Truck dealer, see the appendix at the end of this book. I have provided some sources for used and even new reprints of Genuine Chevrolet and GMC Truck shop manuals and service guides.

The following descriptions give additional details for specific engines. Look closely at your engine and its accessories. If you see distinct differences, refer to a GM factory shop manual or professional-level service guide that covers your year and model truck.

1939–62 Chevrolet 216, 235, 261 inline OHV sixes; 1939–59 GMC Truck inline OHV 228-270 sixes: The pump pulley is pressed onto the pump shaft on earlier designs. *Do not* attempt to remove the pulley unless it slides readily on and off the hub and shaft. On models where the pulley is firmly pressed onto the pump shaft, the pump and pulley come off as an assembly. Torque bolts in gradual cross sequence until all are firmly seated.

1963–87 230/250/292 inline OHV sixes: Basically, the job is much like the earlier sixes, although the fan pulley is removable. Many models have fan shrouds that must be detached for easier access to the fan and water pump.

1955–59 GMC/Pontiac V-8; 1960–69 GMC 305 V-6: There are basic similarities in fitup and design between these water pumps. They are fitted to a cast timing cover. A major advantage is that these pumps have no hoses attached and, therefore, can be simpler to change once you deal with the fan shroud and other concerns. Be cautious and do not overtighten the relatively light hardware that holds the pump housings to the timing cover.

1955–up small-block truck V-8s (265, 283, 327, 307, 350, 400, 305); big-block Chevrolet light truck V-8s (396, 400/402, 454); late 4.3L V-6 engines: By design, this is one of the easiest water pumps to remove and replace. You will spend far more time disconnecting the radiator hose, heater hose(s) and by-pass hose (included on many engine applications) than removing the pump. Early V-8s have few engine-driven accessories, and you will find the water pump very accessible. As power options, air conditioning and emission equipment add up, so do the obstacles to this otherwise simple water pump replacement. My 1986 350 V-8 is a glaring example of an application that requires step-by-step shop manual procedures.

Diesel V-8s: The 350 (Oldsmobile design) diesel, 6.2L V-8 and 6.5L V-8 water pumps each mount to a water pump plate. These pumps have several hoses attached, including a by-pass hose. With the 350 V-8, the water pump unbolts from the timing cover plate and can be carefully removed without disturbing the timing cover. On the 6.2L and 6.5L V-8s, there is a cast timing cover that supports the water pump and its backing plate. The water pump backing plate comes off during water pump removal and requires a special anaerobic sealant for re-installation. Clean the plate thoroughly before mounting the new pump, and follow your factory shop manual steps when putting hardware into place. Torque specifications are also found in your Chevrolet or GMC Truck factory shop manual.

you cannot find a torque setting, see the appendix of this book for a general purpose torque/tightening chart and an explanation of grade markings. Be aware that aluminum casting threads take less tightening torque than cast iron.

Reinstall and torque power-driven accessory hardware to the settings found in your factory or professional-level shop manual. Much of the hardware that you remove during a water pump installation supports components that are under stress when the engine is running. Setting proper torque is essential.

Unless otherwise specified, other parts go back in place by simply reversing the step sequence used for removing the old pump. Once you've secured the water pump, pulley and fan, install a new fan belt or serpentine drive belt (if wear exists) and tighten securely. Follow the factory belt tightening procedure. In some cases, a special belt tensioner or a torque wrench is necessary to meet OE requirements.

If no data or special tools are available, a V-groove belt should deflect about 1/2" when you apply heavy thumb force midway between the pulleys. (The alternator or generator pulley should rotate very slightly as you press firmly on the belt.) Serpentine belts require a large amount of tightening force, and the above rule does not necessarily apply.

With coolant drained, this is also a good time to replace the thermostat. During replacement, carefully scrape old gasket material from the mounting surfaces, taking care not to scrape gasket material into the cooling ports. (If old gasket material circulates to the radiator tubes, it can restrict coolant flow and inhibit cooling.)

Examine the radiator for rust and scale, seepage at solder seams and signs of corrosion. Consider sending the radiator unit for a boil out and pressure testing, even if no leaks are apparent. You only want to do this job once, so consider any parts that could fail in service.

Put a light coat of suitable sealant on the inner ends of hoses and outside the hose fitting threads. Install hoses with new clamps centered carefully. (Where applicable, make sure the coil of wire is in place within each radiator hose. This prevents the hose from collapsing.) Tighten clamps securely.

Make certain the radiator draincock is shut snugly. Pour anti-freeze/coolant and correct water mix into the radiator. Allow the coolant to settle, and keep filling until liquid reaches full level. Top off as necessary. On closed coolant systems with an overflow tank, fill radiator to the top of the filler neck, then seal with the radiator cap. Add coolant to the overflow tank's COLD line.

Install the radiator cap, turn the heater controls to HOT, and start the engine. Let the engine reach operating temperature, then turn it off and allow to cool completely. Once cool, slowly open the radiator cap.

Since the coolant has circulated thoroughly with the heater on, you can check the coolant mixture with a hydrometer. This will help you decide whether to top off with straight coolant, water or a mixture of both. Unless your climate has arctic temperatures, strive for a 50/50 coolant/water ratio, which will read around -34° F protection with an ethylene glycol anti-freeze solution.

Now, with the engine shut off and cool, you should recheck torque on all hardware and the hose clamps. Also check closely for leaks. If you suspect a leak, pressure check the system.

Chapter 8

Engine Tune-up and Emission Controls

TUNED CORRECTLY, a properly equipped Chevrolet or GMC pickup can easily tow a weighty trailer over Colorado's Loveland Pass or California's infamous Grapevine. At construction sites and timberlands, GM 4x4 work trucks spend the bulk of their service life hauling maximum payloads over bad roads and up severe grades. For top performance, dependable service and decent fuel economy, your GM truck's engine requires routine tune-ups and preventive maintenance.

Tuning demands have changed dramatically since 1939. Until 1975, GM light truck engines had breaker point ignitions. Beginning in 1975, the HEI (High Energy Ignition) and electronically activated spark gained prominence, with enhanced and more complete ignition plus lower maintenance requirements.

Through 1986, all GM light truck gasoline engines have carburetors, some later versions featuring electronic feedback circuits. Beginning in 1987, GM light truck engines benefit from electronic fuel injection with oxygen sensed fuel ratio adjustments and instantaneous computer controlled spark timing.

Earlier mechanical and vacuum advance ignition distributors and carburetor fuel systems often require tuning or adjustments for altitude changes and lower grade fuels. Later GM engines with electronic fuel and spark management automatically adjust for altitude, poor fuel grades and a wide range of loads and driver demands.

If your truck's engine has carburetion and a breaker point or conventional (mechanical/centrifugal and vacuum) spark advance electronic ignition, precise tuning can make a difference. Understanding your truck's tune-up needs, including the fuel, spark and emission control systems, will also improve your skills at troubleshooting and field repairs.

Moreover, tune-up skills provide a cornerstone for off-highway survival. Back country travel, effectively carrying a heavy cargo and your truck's trailer pulling ability each rely upon proper ignition and fuel system tune.

By design, your GM light truck gasoline engine is a vacuum pump. Both the ignition and fuel systems affect vacuum quality. Tools that you will find useful for fine tuning range in complexity from an inexpensive vacuum

0014202

Fig. 8-1. My 1986 GMC Suburban 3/4-ton 4WD features the last four-barrel carbureted 350 V-8. An HEI ignition, two air pumps buried at the right side of engine and a heavy duty emissions package provide a tuning challenge.

0014205

Fig. 8-2. I find the Denco Step a handy item for tuning GM full-size 4x4 truck engines. For my tall 1986 GMC, the step adjusts easily to match 245R75/16 tires. Using a fender cover, you can work on a V-8 without marring the truck's paint.

gauge to electronic infrared scope analyzers that operate in conjunction with a chassis dynamometer.

Either of these tools can reveal fundamental engine problems. Become familiar with these and other automotive diagnostic tools. Know your engine's normal manifold vacuum and watch for changes or fluctuations in this reading. (See other sections for details on vacuum tests.)

Emission Controls and Tune-up

Emission control service, which has become an increasingly larger part of engine maintenance, also affects your truck's performance, especially with V-8 engines that use more systems to reduce tailpipe pollution. For EPA (49-State) purposes, emission regulations become important with 1968 and newer vehicles.

For basic tuning, the exhaust gas recirculation (EGR) circuit and closed crankcase ventilation (PCV) system are primary concerns. (GM light trucks offered optional and retrofit closed crankcase devices in the early 1950s. California mandated devices emerged in the early 1960s.) Always service or replace the positive crankcase ventilation (PCV) valve when tuning your truck's engine.

California still requires a closed crankcase retrofit on 1955–up vehicles and biennial smog inspection on many model years of light trucks. Other states and local areas, designated as "non-compliant" or poor in air quality, now have similar annual or biennial inspection requirements.

To pass a visual inspection in California and the many other states and local areas that require emission compliance and testing, all OEM (factory) emission controls must be in place and operative. Your truck can fail a smog test for simply not having the flexible aluminum heat tube between the exhaust manifold and air cleaner intake. Assuming that your engine is in good condition, a tune-up will assure compliance and help pass the smog test. V-8 engines, especially 1971 to mid-1980s carbureted models, have given up a good deal of horsepower to comply with Federal and California emission standards.

Reclaiming such latent horsepower is possible, in some cases, through the use of aftermarket performance parts that have California E.O. (exemption) numbers. (See the engine performance chapter.) As a rule, however, if you want your truck to comply with emission laws and contribute to clean air, you need to preserve OEM emission controls. Emission control maintenance helps assure a successful tune-up.

Later in this chapter, you will find details on emission controls and service. If you intend to service a 1965 or newer engine, familiarize yourself with the emission control section before attempting a major tune-up.

Fundamental Engine Requirements

The best tune-up cannot compensate for internal engine defects, wear or damage. As an adult education automotive and diesel mechanics instructor, I fielded many questions about engine needs and tuning. In response, I devised a simple formula called "The Four Basics." An engine must meet these requirements before tuning can be a success. The Four Basics are:

- Normal compression
- Correct valve lift and valve opening duration
- Correct valve timing
- Normal oil pressure

Additionally, the engine must operate at its normal coolant temperature.

Normal compression depends on proper piston ring, valve and gasket sealing. The valvetrain and camshaft

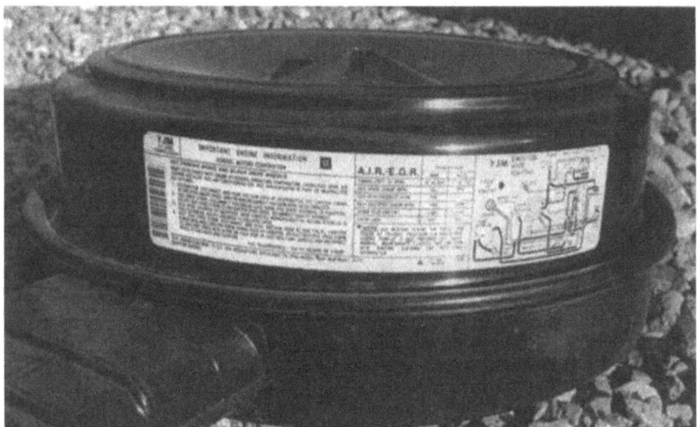

0014203

Fig. 8-3. Your V-8's tune-up decal offers valuable details about emission features and tune-up specifications. On this GM 350, decal is affixed to air cleaner shell.

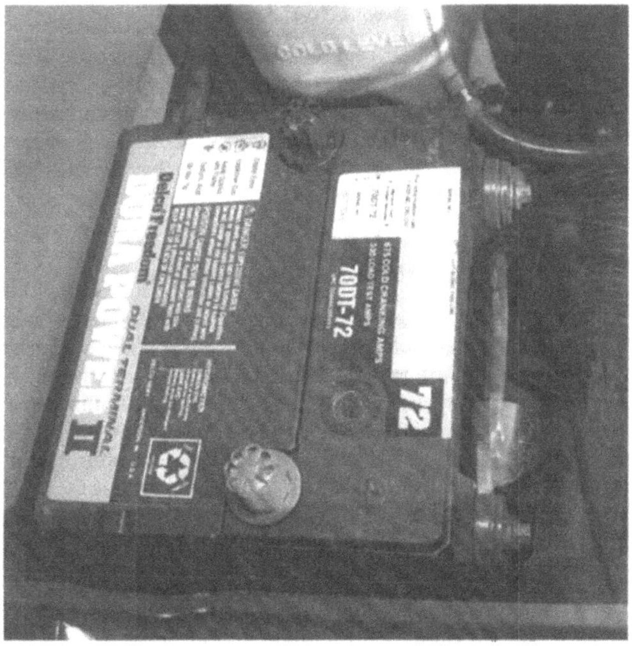

0014204

Fig. 8-4. *Often overlooked during tune-up is the battery. Ignition and electronic fuel systems require precise battery and charge voltages. Checking overall battery condition is easy with modern dash voltmeter gauge. Simply turn on key without starting engine and read voltage on dash gauge. Check drive belt tensions and clean battery posts regularly.*

condition determine proper valve lift, valve opening duration and valve timing. Valvetrain troubles include wear at camshaft lobes, the timing chain, the timing sprockets or gears and the valve springs. Oil pressure relies on good engine bearings, polished and true bearing journal surfaces, a sound oil pump and unobstructed oil passages.

For tuning purposes, you can add steady vacuum to the checklist. If your engine meets the four basic requirements and has no vacuum leaks, your tuning efforts will be successful.

1. ENGINE ORIENTATION

When I brought an older General Motors truck into the shop for periodic (routine) engine service, lubrication and tuning, the first steps were a complete chassis lube, checking all gearbox fluid levels and setting the valves with the engine still thoroughly warm. With the engine speed adjusted to a very slow idle, I could set the running valves with a minimal amount of oil spillage.

Next I drained the oil and changed the oil filter, then filled the crankcase. Installation of new ignition points, a condenser and rotor followed, and I set the points with a dwell meter before disconnecting and plugging the distributor vacuum advance line to check the base timing.

As these engines had manual chokes, I serviced the air cleaner and made sure that the choke was operating freely. After reinstalling the air cleaner, the final step was to set the carburetor idle mixture and idle speed with the engine warmed completely.

Aside from the time spent adjusting valves, changing the valve cover gasket and setting the points with a dwell

0014220

Fig. 8-5. *These parts functioned reasonably well before the tune-up. Keep them for your off-pavement excursions to the back country. A good coil, spare module (or breaker point set and condenser), usable distributor cap and rotor provide valuable backup parts.*

meter, the accessibility of engine parts was so good on early engines that a tune-up went quickly and always proved satisfying. Later engines have different needs. The following section outlines some of the basics of tuning each engine family.

Inline OHV Sixes, 1937 to 1986

These engines provide an ideal place to learn tune-up work. All distributors mount at the side of the engine block, easily accessible and simple to service. Carburetors vary in design, yet most are one-barrel. (1979-84 emissions 250/4.1L inline sixes have two-barrel carburetors.) Reaching air and fuel filters is easy, and earlier versions of these trucks were simple to fix alongside the road. The

0014189

Fig. 8-6. *The 216 (shown) and early 235 cubic inch inline OHV Chevrolet sixes changed little between 1937 and 1953. In 1954, the later 235 engine came on line and was available through 1962 models. 1939–59 GMC inline OHV sixes look similar. On all of these engines, the ignition distributor location provides easy maintenance.*

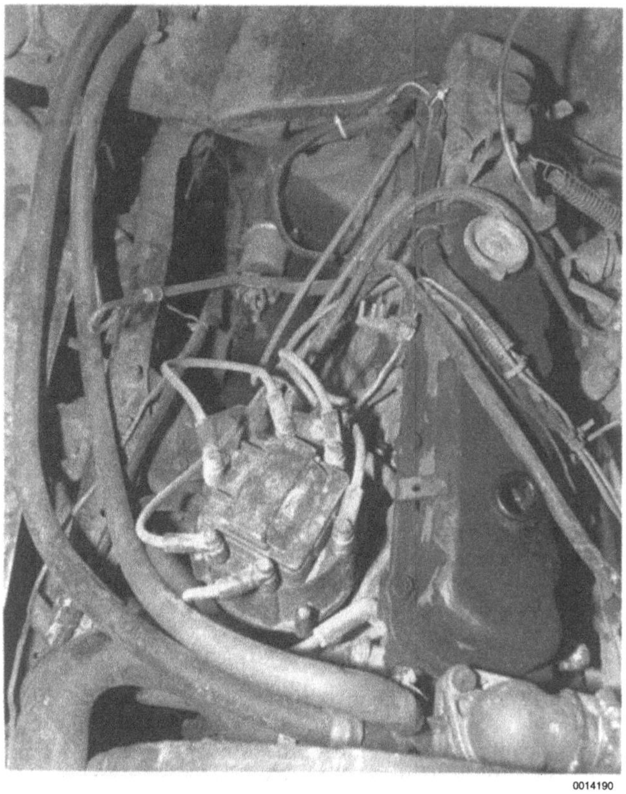

Fig. 8-7. Early Chevrolet and GMC OHV inline sixes were four main bearing types. In 1963, the seven main bearing 230 and 292 cubic inch inline sixes came on line. Well suited for truck service, the basic 230, 250 and 292 design survives to 1986 (last available in 292 form). Although 1975–up sixes have HEI electronic ignitions (shown), all of these engines use carburetors.

emission control era takes its toll on these engines, as the simple 250 or 292 OHV inline six becomes a service and troubleshooting handful in its final form. Nearly all inline OHV sixes built before 1963 have solid lifters that require periodic valve adjustment. (Watch out for the 1954–62 235 passenger car engine with hydraulic valve lifters that often winds up as a light truck replacement.) The rare 1956–57 Blue Flame 235 truck engines use hydraulic valve lifters.

Small-/Big-block Chevrolet V-8s, Late Vortec V-6, 1955–59 Pontiac/GMC V-8s

Unlike the simpler inline sixes, the V-8 or V-6 distributor is at the back of the engine, near the firewall. Servicing the distributor requires some stretching and the use of fender pads. The earliest (1955–56) Chevrolet and GMC V-8 distributors require removal of the distributor cap to adjust breaker point dwell angle. In 1957, the job gets easier with the window cap distributor design. Servicing a 1975–86 HEI V-8 distributor is, fortunately, an infrequent chore. You will find the larger diameter distributor cap and the internal module awkward to reach. Finding the four distributor cap clamp hooks takes time.

1960–69 GMC 305 V-6s

These engines feature a rear mounted distributor with a window cap for external adjustment of the breaker points. This is a very simple and fundamental engine to tune, although periodic valve adjustment adds time. One- and two-barrel carburetors used on the various 305 V-6s range from the simple to the simplest designs offered in GM light trucks.

350, 6.2L and 6.5L Diesel V-8s

Diesels also require tune-up type maintenance. Fuel filters, O-ring seal leaks, air cleaner service, injector cleaning and glow plug repairs are typical jobs. For the 6.2L and 6.5L, fuel savings and overall reliability remain tops, however, the 350 offers far less longevity. If your early 350 diesel does break or wear out, find a new or rebuilt later 350 with the "DX" block casting for a replacement.

> **NOTE —**
> Although interior or in-depth repair on your General Motors 5.7L, 6.2L or 6.5L diesel V-8 is beyond the scope of this book or the skill level of many home-based mechanics, there are several routine services that you can perform.

Fig. 8-8. The now famous 265 Chevrolet V-8 was the first small-block. Available in 1955 Second Series models, the original design had a by-pass oil filter option and a closed cap distributor at the back of the engine. By 1957, the 265 featured a full-flow, block mounted oil filter and the revolutionary Delco-Remy window cap distributor. Tune-up became much easier, despite rear location of ignition distributor.

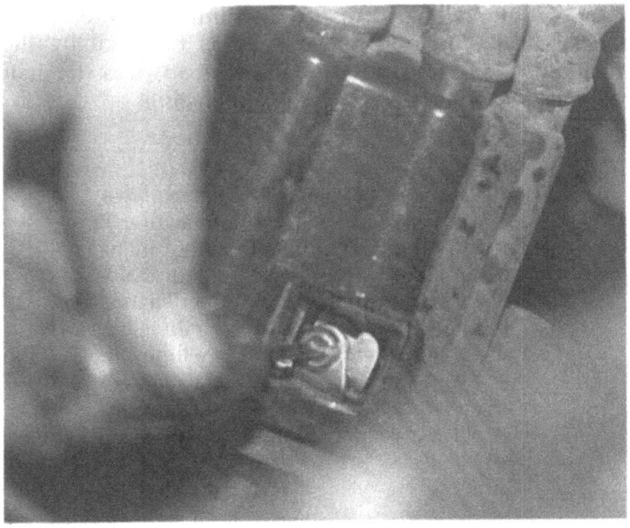

0014456

Fig. 8-9. The window cap distributor, introduced in 1957 Chevrolet and GMC light truck V-8s, is a milestone for ignition tuning. You can make fine adjustments of the breaker points with an Allen wrench while the engine is running. This enables quick and easy dwell angle setting. Pre-window cap distributors require setting the points with the distributor cap removed and engine cranking, a procedure that often requires several trial adjustments.

0014191

Fig. 8-10. The 396, 402 (big-block 400) and 454 light truck engines each performed in passenger cars before their release in light trucks. Despite their larger size, these big-block engines share tune-up procedures and ignition components with the small-block V-8s. While an ultra high compression LS7 454 high performance car or Corvette engine rates 460 horsepower, the first (1973) 454 light truck version netted only 240 horses but plenty of torque.

0014192

Fig. 8-11. The small-block 265 V-8 forms the basic design for the later 283, 327, 307, 350, 400 and 305 engines. Light in weight and very rugged, these engines have a tremendous range of uses. Lower compression truck versions, like this 327, offer economy and exceptional longevity when tuned and maintained properly.

0014245

Fig. 8-12. The 6.2L and newer 6.5L diesel V-8s have worked very well in GM light trucks. Many users like their brutish torque, good fuel economy and low maintenance needs. Routine filter changes can ensure long engine life and reliable service. Shown is a 6.5L turbo-diesel.

Filter changes are very important with your diesel engine, especially fuel filters. Diesel fuel has a very high water content, and this contributes to everything from corrosive damage to the actual emergence of living bacteria cultures in your fuel system.

Frequent fuel filter changes and use of a quality water trap filter will help preserve your diesel V-8 and ensure good performance. Become familiar with service on the water trap filter. Anti-fungal agents are available for your truck's fuel system if you suspect that a culture is alive and growing within the system.

0014246

Fig. 8-13. *Glow plug failure is not uncommon to higher mileage diesel engines. When left on too long, as when a relay sticks, glow plugs can burn out.*

> NOTE —
> At this time, the reduction of diesel fuel sulphur content to lower tailpipe pollution is a topical issue for diesel engines. The lack of lubricity found with the fuel hydrogenation process (one method of eliminating sulphur) can lead to injector O-ring damage and mechanical fuel pump diaphragm failure, most frequently in engines with higher mileage.

An area that sometimes requires attention is the glow plug system. Failure of the glow plug regulator/controller can cause excessive glow plug operation and failure of the expensive glow plugs. Whether you service your GM diesel or sublet the work, make certain that the glow plug relays and regulator/controller are operative and functioning properly.

Beyond these concerns and occasional service to the fuel injection system, the GM diesel V-8 is content with regular oil changes and filter service. If you intend to perform major work on your injector system or in-depth repairs on the engine unit, invest in the GM factory shop manual that covers these service operations.

A Look at Electronically Fuel Injected Gasoline Engines

GM trucks began using electronic/Throttle Body fuel injection (EFI/TBI) with the 1987 V-8 and V-6 engines. (The last carbureted engines appeared in 1986.) Although the special skills and requisite tools for servicing TBI have kept many consumers from servicing their own engines, you can work on various aspects of this system.

Professional mechanics often lament new technology. When the electronic (transistor) ignitions came into vogue in the 1960s and early 1970s, a trip to the parts house would invariably turn up a seasoned mechanic who complained about the lack of reliability and huge expenses involved with electronic ignition parts—not to mention that these mysterious solid state devices would surely fail when we least expected and leave us stranded!

Today, few argue that archaic breaker points make more sense than a high voltage, precisely timed and fully electronic ignition system. I can recall working with exotic dual point high performance distributors that required constant tinkering with dwell angle, followed by the mandatory re-timing of the engine on every occasion that the breaker points needed "minor" adjusting.

> NOTE —
> Failure of an EFI/spark management system is covered under the manufacturer's warranty and also under federally mandated pollution control laws. If your truck has received proper routine maintenance (replacement of serviceable parts like spark plugs, filters, etc.) and is within the time frame/mileage for either coverage, see your GM truck dealership. You may have warranty against some or all of the repair expenses.

Yes, there was a time when some electronic ignitions had marginal components, and the repair and maintenance of electronic fuel injection once meant the equivalent of an extra monthly vehicle payment for owners of high mileage cars. That has changed. General Motors' Rochester TBI (Throttle Body Injection) and CPI (Central-Point Injection, a system introduced on the L35 4.3L Vortec V-6) provide exceptional fuel economy, low tailpipe emissions and improved performance.

0014327

Fig. 8-14. *Throttle Body Injection is easy to access. Here, air cleaner cover removed, is an 1984 Corvette dual TBI Cross-Fire assembly. The Corvette and the Camaro/Firebird pioneered 350 V-8 TBI in 1982.*

TBI Operation

Throttle body fuel injection relies on a series of interrelated sub-systems. Engine sensors take into account the climate, altitude, coolant temperature, cargo loads and the driver's throttle input. In the exhaust stream, an oxygen sensor performs much like an infrared scope analyzer, noting oxygen content in the burned fuel and instantly telling the engine's computer the air/fuel ratio. The Engine Computer Module (ECM), in turn, instantaneously adjusts fuel flow to maintain air/fuel ratio.

Throttle body injector units deliver fuel at the intake manifold. Similar to port injection, TBI injectors are sole-

0014229

Fig. 8-15. *Manifold absolute pressure (MAP) sensor provides crucial information to ECM. A CCC component that originated with 1981 carbureted models, MAP sensor signal helps ECM adjust for altitude and load.*

0014336

Fig. 8-16. *A full range of sensors help ECM make informed decisions about fuel management and spark timing needs. Detonation, overrich fuel mixtures and other anomalies of earlier carburetion and mechanical spark timing devices became obsolete with GM's TBI/EST truck engines.*

0014334

Fig. 8-17. *Throttle position sensor (TPS), attaches to TBI throttle shaft (rear TBI unit of Cross-Fire engines). TPS sends crucial voltage signal to ECM. Angle of throttle valve translates to an electrical reading that the ECM weighs with a host of other sensory data.*

noid-activated, and open when a conical ball lifts from its seat. The ECM controls the opening of the solenoid. With pressurized fuel waiting for an outlet, a conical spray pattern flows instantly through the nozzle. Since pressure remains constant during the spray cycle, the *duration* of the solenoid opening determines the quantity of fuel delivered.

Coolant temperature sensors enable the ECM to understand whether the engine requires cold start fuel enrichment. Initial prime pulses accompany engine start-ups. When the engine is cold, the ECM generates longer pulse widths. Once the engine has fired, ignition distributor signals take over the injector pulsing. A delicate air/fuel ratio balance takes its additional cue from the throttle position opening as the engine warms up.

If an engine floods on start-up, holding the throttle wide open generally alleviates the problem. Air/fuel calibration leans out to 20:1 with the throttle in this position, accomplished by a relatively short injector pulse width. Once the engine fires and registers 600 or more rpm, the ECM readjusts the air/fuel ratio. While warming, the engine relies on temperature and manifold absolute pressure (MAP) signals that are fed to the ECM. This is open loop operation.

Once warm, optimal closed loop air/fuel ratios of 14.7:1 result from ECM monitoring of the oxygen sensor data. At a constant A/F ratio of 14.7:1 (stoichiometric or ideal burn mixture for a gasoline engine), the engine runs with peak efficiency yet delivers maximum fuel economy. This is the major contribution of TBI and other EFI systems.

To match the accelerator pump boost found with carburetion, the ECM responds to manifold pressure (MAP) signals and the throttle position (TPS signal). During hard acceleration, the ECM temporarily enrichens the A/F ratio by lengthening the injector pulse width. In deceleration, signals from the MAP and TPS sensors simply instruct the ECM to cut off the fuel supply—instantly.

To regulate fuel pressure at the TBI unit, a pressure regulator balances injector pressure with atmospheric pressure. Maintenance of close to 10 psi in the system is essential. Pressure is maintained by controlling how much fuel flows back to the fuel tank.

The fuel system's safety backup interacts closely with the fuel pump relay. When the ignition switches ON, a relay timer allocates 1 1/2 seconds for fuel pump priming of the injection system. As the engine cranks, reference pulses from the distributor tell the ECM that the engine has attempted to start. If the engine fails to start, the fuel pump relay resets, affording another 1-1/2 seconds of fuel priming. The fuel relay cutoff helps impede raw fuel pooling in the intake plenum or engine's cylinders.

Idle speed depends on IAC motor changes. Various IAC valve positions meter air volume around the throttle

0014333

Fig. 8-18. Pressure regulator (arrow) of TBI assembly provides a constant 10 psi fuel supply to adjacent injector. ECM, fed data from a variety of sensors, controls electromagnetic solenoids that open fuel nozzles. With system constantly under pressure, injector nozzles open for timed intervals that vary under different load conditions and driving demands.

0014332

Fig. 8-19. An idle air control (IAC) motor (arrow) mounts on the TBI unit. Activated by the ECM, the motor opens a bypass airway, permitting air to flow around the throttle valve. The ECM establishes an idle based upon voltage, temperature, load and rpm data.

plate. More air, resulting from retraction of the IAC valve, increases the idle speed. When idle is too fast, the IAC motor extends the valve, restricting air flow around the throttle plate.

Early in the development of electronic fuel injection, ECM units acquired the nickname "brain." The Electronic Spark Timing (EST) system, also ECM supported, assumes the crucial task of adjusting spark timing. Incredibly, EST provides an infinite number of spark timing curves, responding to the exact load and performance demands placed on the engine.

For 1987–up GM truck owners, EFI/TBI has meant huge savings in fuel, precise start-ups in the coldest weather conditions and the ability to pull a load without stressing the engine. Smooth travel at any altitude, plus successful use of the current rash of low octane fuels, are major accomplishments of EFI/TBI and electronic spark

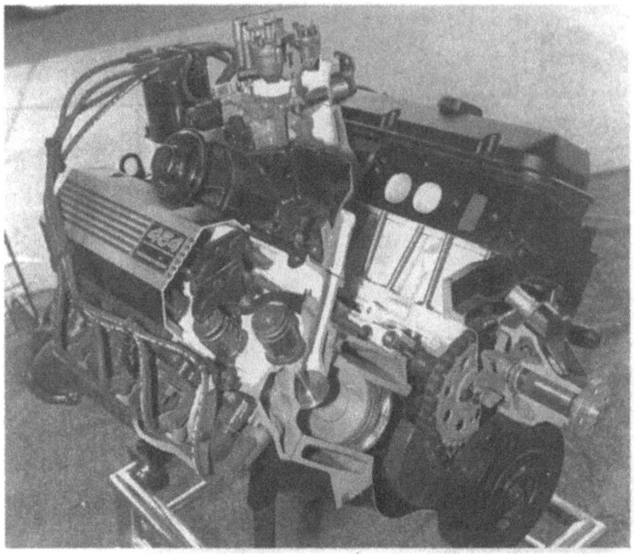

0014335

Fig. 8-20. Electronic Spark Timing (EST) complements Throttle Body Injection. Outwardly, ignition distributor looks much other GM HEI units—sans the vacuum advance unit. Circuited to ECM, spark timing is infinitely variable and instantly regulated by engine sensory input.

0014331

Fig. 8-21. Familiar emission control devices from the carburetor era appear on light truck TBI engines. Ported vacuum and solenoid/vacuum-operated EGR valve and traditional PCV valve are seen on these systems.

0014250

Fig. 8-22. Diverter valve and anti-backfire check valves are central to emission control air injection system on TBI truck engines. Similar components served on carbureted models of the emission era.

timing management. The fact that horsepower and torque output have increased, along with greater fuel efficiency, says much for electronic fuel and spark management systems.

Moreover, EFI has enabled the internal combustion piston engine to meet the challenge of increasingly higher air quality standards. Newer GM trucks with EFI/TBI emit less than 1/20th the tailpipe pollution of their counterpart 1968 light truck engines. And these newer EFI engines require no periodic adjustments or tinkering. Routine tuning has become obsolete.

EFI/TBI Tuning Needs

Although all ignition and fuel adjustments are pre-set at the factory, the EFI engine does have tuning needs. Air cleaner changes and periodic fuel filter changes are crucial to performance and quality service from these engine designs. The most common fuel injection troubles involve the fuel filter(s).

Aside from the more accessible in-line fuel filters, GM EFI engines also use a pickup filter in the fuel tank. If you know the tank has corrosives and debris that could plug a pickup screen, refer to your GM truck shop manual for recommended procedures and service steps to remove the fuel tank and/or pickup screen.

Despite the high level of reliability of modern computer and electronic components, parts failures and some adjustment needs do occur. The idle speed controls, secondary ignition pieces (distributor cap, rotor, spark plugs and spark cables), even the injectors and their O-ring seals, can require attention. Beyond this, EFI components either work properly or they don't.

Demystifying the TBI system can bolster your confidence and off-pavement sense of security. When the Badlands loom for miles ahead, and your TBI engine has stumbled to an unceremonious halt, the obvious goal is to get the engine running. Although you may not have in-depth test equipment in your toolbox, you can get the engine to start and run sufficiently, then drive to a qualified service center or your better equipped home shop. Some automotive wire, a set of spare fuses, and an assortment of electrical connectors may be enough to revive a downed TBI engine.

Several TBI diagnostic procedures call for specialized equipment. Kent-Moore provides the Chevrolet/GMC dealership network and service garages with several tools for TBI service. For common TBI troubleshooting procedures, a *digital* voltmeter is a must, necessary for addressing the narrow voltage parameters of devices like the throttle position sensor.

The voltmeter doubles as an AC/DC voltage tester and a continuity checker as well. An inexpensive volt/ohmmeter serves a multitude of purposes, and once you become familiar with the device, a test light and other electrical testers will be unnecessary. (See Chapter 14, Electrical System Basics.)

Is It the TBI System?

Before condemning expensive EFI/TBI parts, check the simpler possibilities. Assuming that cylinder compression and valve timing are normal, the engine should run. If not, ignition or TBI trouble is likely.

0014339

Fig. 8-23. Routine service should include new fuel and air filters. Troubleshooting begins with confirming the fuel level in the tank before condemning the ignition or TBI/EFI systems.

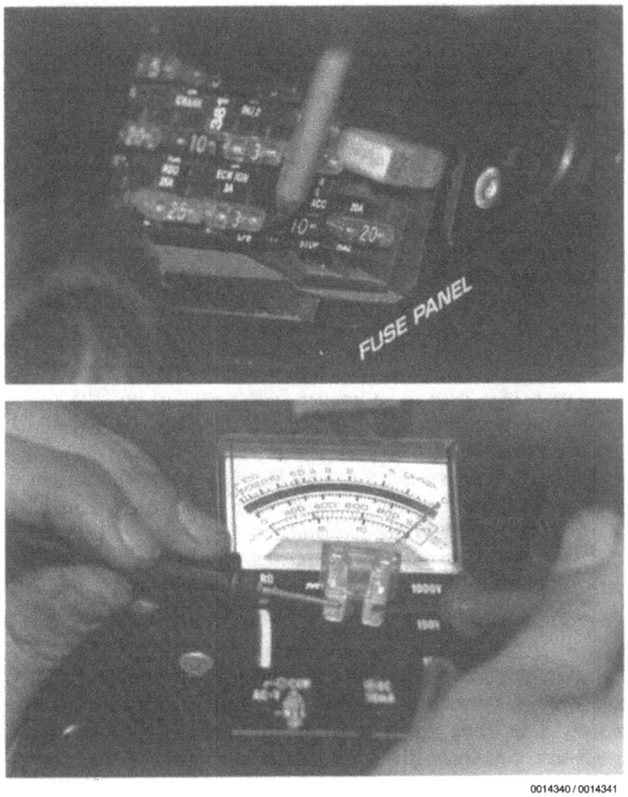

0014340 / 0014341

Fig. 8-24. The fuse should be checked first. Fuel pump circuit fuse must be functional. To avoid possibility of overlooking a bad fuse, remove and test with your volt-ohmmeter. Check for ohms-resistance/continuity.

Next, be certain that the ignition functions properly. Many owners have faced untimely roadside stops as HEI module/coil failures cause backfire, sputtering and, ultimately, engine dying. When testing for ignition spark, check at least *two* cylinders. Although removing the distributor cap takes effort, roadside module or coil replacement is possible.

0014342

Fig. 8-25. A sticking throttle position sensor can cause a number of troubles. Engine roughness is a common complaint. Open the throttle and observe movement of all linkage.

0014351

Fig. 8-26. With three jumper leads installed on TPS, test probes measure voltage between middle and lower wires. A digital voltmeter is necessary for accurate readout of required current. Turn the ignition switch ON, and with the engine stopped, check for the specified range (typically 0.450 to 0.600 volt) at closed throttle. Loosening the TPS screws allows adjustment. As a roadside emergency measure, a non-digital volt/ohmmeter will suffice. Later, a digital voltmeter can provide more accurate, precise settings.

Wiring, ground leads and vacuum hose leaks cause a variety of problems. Make a systematic check of the wires. The fuel pump mounts in the fuel tank. During start-up, you should hear the pump operate. If the pump is not active, check the fuel pump relay, fuses and wiring. Even simple troubles, like a poor battery connection, can throw the computer into a frenzy. Check for secure, clean battery connections before suspecting the TBI/EFI.

Contrary to the views of skeptics, one of the least likely items to fail is the computer. Connectors, however, often become faulty or create too much resistance, which can radically distort the computer's sensory signals. This system depends upon critical signals from sensors. Generally, concealed wiring harnesses remain intact. Check the more vulnerable exposed wires and connectors.

When bad tune or poor engine operation occurs, you can perform necessary troubleshooting, replace faulty sensors or repair those parts that test as defective. You may earnestly want to understand, diagnose and repair

0014329

Fig. 8-27. This step involves a helper. With injector's wire connector loose, crank engine. No fuel should drip from the injector. Dribbling indicates a leak.

0014343

Fig. 8-28. Hard starting can often be traced to a faulty coolant sensor.

0014330

Fig. 8-29. Normal injector spray pattern is a conical mist that fills throat. Quick camera shutter caught this instant of inception. Even at idle, flow is so fast that it appears as a steady stream.

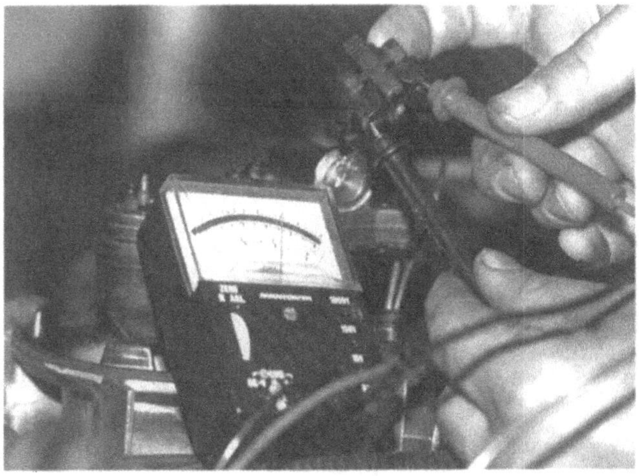

0014345

Fig. 8-30. *Volt/ohmmeter works in place of test lamp to test injector pulse current while cranking. Actually, a digital meter is required for accuracy. This compact needle meter easily fits toolbox, however, and doubles as a continuity tester. If meter shows steady voltage during engine cranking, check for a short to ground on the injector leads.*

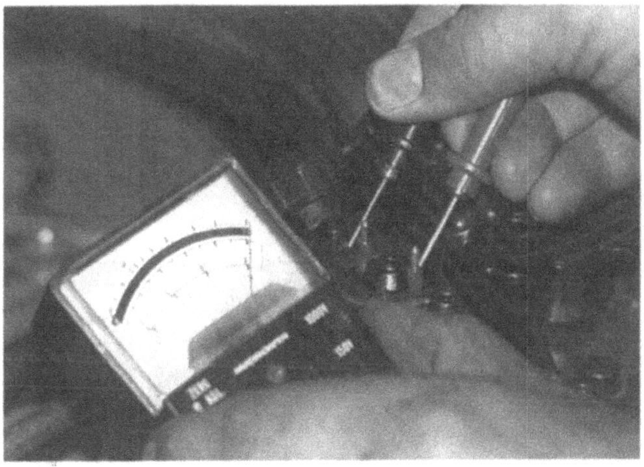

0014346

Fig. 8-31. *A volt/ohmmeter reading across injector poles verifies the resistance. Check factory limits for your year truck and engine type, specified as a minimum resistance figure.*

your GM truck's EFI and spark management system. The best way to increase your diagnostic skills to the level of a professional EFI technician is through carefully reading the GM truck shop manual that covers your model.

Although the term *tune-up* would today apply mostly to routine parts replacement, EFI/TBI engine performance issues require concise, sequential tests and measures. For me, the only limiting factors to performing EFI/TBI service are availability of specialty tools and whether I care to invest in some of the expensive diagnostic equipment required for troubleshooting and testing the circuits and devices. Professional service guides describe the tools needed for each procedure, so you can make an informed decision about whether or not to do the work. Such insight will pay for your GM truck shop manual(s) many times over.

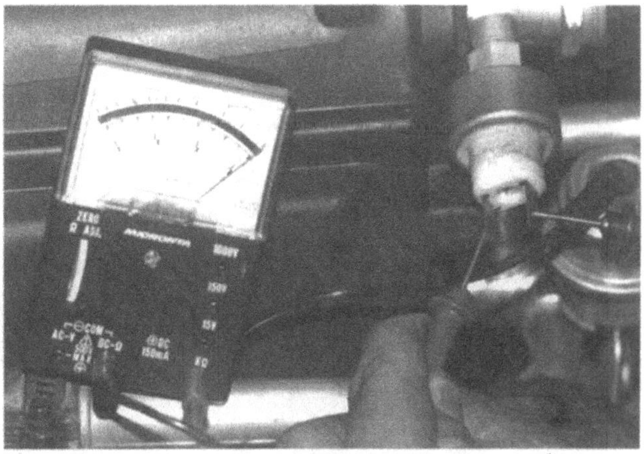

0014347

Fig. 8-32. *Switches may also be checked with volt/ohmmeter. Voltage levels, opens and grounded leads read on meter. This is a great troubleshooting aid, easily packed in your toolbox, ready for follow up tests after reading Engine Check codes.*

0014348

Fig. 8-33. *If your custom GM truck has an 1982–84 Corvette, Camaro or Firebird dual-TBI engine transplant, the need to balance the two TBI units is rare. Factory spot weld at this bolt is obstacle to adjustment. Once this weld is broken, thread-locking liquid will prevent unwanted loosening of adjuster screw. Adjustment is similar to dual carburetors, with use of a manometer to check air flow.*

2. IGNITION TUNE-UP

Spark plugs, the distributor cap, rotor, coil and plug cables make up the ignition's secondary circuit. The rotor and spark plugs require periodic service. Less frequently, the distributor cap and spark cables will need replacement.

GM truck ignition distributors are either the older style breaker point units or electronic (HEI) designs. In 1975, GM advanced from the breaker point era to efficient HEI. Owners of earlier V-8 GM trucks or the 1963–up seven main-bearing 230/250/292 inline sixes can install a later model HEI distributor or an aftermarket electronic conversion kit to replace the earlier breaker point ignition.

The primary ignition circuit consists of the breaker point set and condenser (on earlier trucks) or the module on an electronic ignition. During routine tune-up service, the breaker points, condenser and rotor require replacement. Inspect the distributor cap for corrosion at the con-

ALCL Engine Check Tests

Diagnosing engine problems on late GM trucks has become easier. A by-product of sophisticated electronic computer controls and sensors, the factory Assembly Line Communication Link (ALCL) provides troubleshooting memory capability. Later GM trucks have ALCL diagnostic plugs and quick access to trouble information. A dealership or qualified shop has special diagnostic equipment to read the trouble codes. For roadside service, however, there is a simple factory backup that suffices.

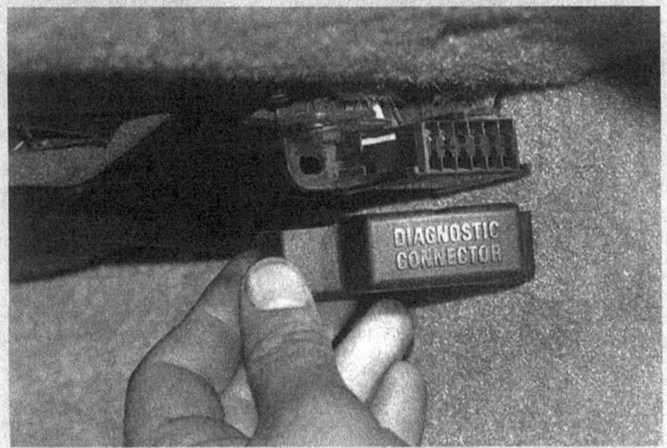

0014338

Tests involving the ALCL system begin at this connector. Concise trouble codes appear at the Check Engine light.

0014502

Rinda Technologies offers an affordable software and interlink program for for troubleshooting and tuning 1981-93 GM engines. Information feeds through an ALCL connector to a personal computer and is displayed like on analyzers costing 50 times as much!

Trouble codes for your particular year and model truck appear in the factory shop manual for your vehicle, and these codes are attainable by simply turning the ignition switch to the ON position (engine not running) and jumping the A and B terminals of the ALCL plug together with a spade lug. This will trigger the code test.

> *CAUTION —*
> *Before attempting a readout, consult your GM factory shop manual to determine the proper procedure and which ALCL terminals to jump across.*

Once jumped, watch the Check Engine light. If it flashes, that means there is a trouble code stored. The code is indicated by the flashes. Twelve would be one flash, followed by a pause, then two flashes. The system will wait, then repeat itself two more times. Any stored trouble code appears as a flash or flashes for the first digit, a pause, then flash(es) for the second digit.

These codes translate to useful data. All engine sensors, the Idle Air Control, Electronic Spark Timing, PROM/MECAL, fuel pump, and even the ECM itself, send information to memory. Test results also reflect various load and operating conditions. A factory service data chart of these codes and a readout of memory data is a good starting point.

When you have restored your truck's TBI engine to peak performance, reset the ECM memory banks. Clear any stored memory data and ready the computer for future diagnostic chores. (Consult your factory truck shop manual to confirm the procedure for clearing the ECM memory for your year and model engine.)

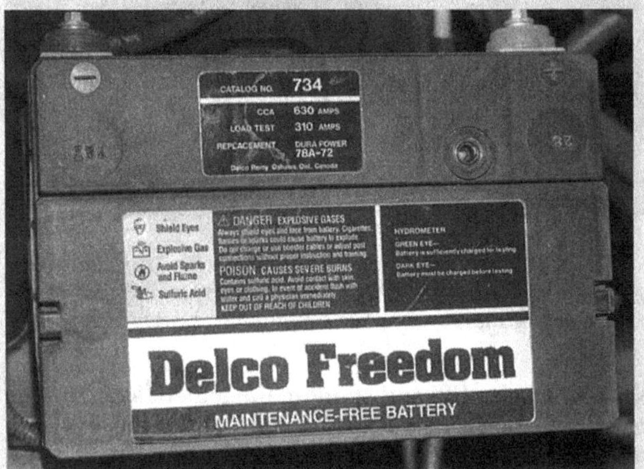

0014337

Disconnecting the battery ground cuts battery current to ECM. In a few moments, all memories vanish. Once the cable is reattached, computer takes a fresh look at engine operation.

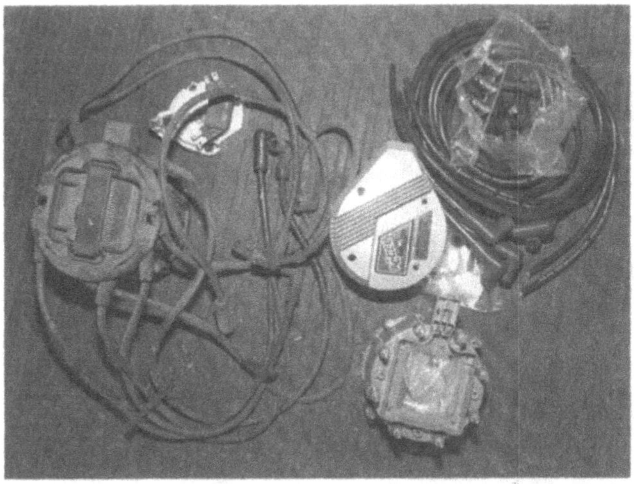

0014207

Fig. 8-34. Difficulty reaching these HEI components encourages replacement with high quality parts. At nearly 80,000 miles, I renewed the distributor cap and built-in HEI coil, rotor and plug wires. In this case, Accel's Super HEI Coil, Super Stock wires and U-groove spark plugs assured lasting tune. OEM Delco-Remy replacement parts also deliver long service.

0014196

Fig. 8-35. Ignition and other service parts are available through your GM truck dealership. Use high quality OEM or aftermarket parts like NAPA/Echlin (premium grade) and Standard Blue Streak. When it comes to parts, if you pay more, you get more.

tacts. If you believe the wires have wear, an ohmmeter can test individual plug wires for end-to-end resistance.

If an engine oscilloscope is available, you can quickly determine the condition of the distributor cap, spark cables and spark plugs. Better oscilloscopes can even simulate a load on the engine, which proves helpful for assessing spark output under real world conditions.

When testing the output of an HEI or other electronic ignitions, use a commercial tester plug or fabricate a similar device. The idea is to keep the plug shell grounded to the engine block and not allow any spark wire to arc directly to ground. This tool is also handy for back country troubleshooting, enabling a fast and graphic look at spark output.

If you test spark with a plug wire removed, the misfire of one cylinder creates a rich mixture in the exhaust stream. On late engines, this can send a confusing signal to the oxygen sensor and also load up the catalytic converter with raw fuel. Do not test ignition spark output for long.

0012272

Fig. 8-36. This commercial tester plug is a necessity with high energy (HEI) electronic ignitions. Never create a spark arc to ground. Ignition damage could result.

Spark Plug Service

Begin an engine tune-up by cleaning debris from the area around the spark plugs, then remove the wires. Use a clean socket to avoid dropping grit into the cylinders. A flex handle spark plug ratchet serves well with awkward spark plug locations.

On engines with carbon-core spark plug wires, use a spark cable pliers to prevent damage when removing the wires. Grip the plug insulator, not the wire section.

Use an air compressor and nozzle to blow debris away from the base of the spark plugs. Remove spark plugs carefully.

> *WARNING —*
> *Wear protective goggles when blowing debris from the spark plug area.*

"Read" the spark plugs. Fouled spark plugs provide a valuable insight. Oily plugs generally mean worn valve guides or piston rings. A sooty black or wet plug surface indicates gasoline fouling, unless ash from burnt oil is also present. Oily plugs are usually due to either valve guide, guide seal, or piston ring wear.

If caught quickly, gasoline fouling is less ominous than oil fouling. Gas fouling of only one or a few cylinders usually indicates a worn spark cable(s) or an ignition system problem such as a defective rotor, distributor cap, breaker points, condenser, coil, electronic ignition module or faulty wiring.

0012273

Fig. 8-37. *Use of a spark cable pliers is always wise. Grip the plug insulator firmly. Avoid tugging on the wires, as carbon-core will separate.*

0012274

Fig. 8-38. *Spark plug cleaning machines were once very popular. However, you need a spark plug tester or engine oscilloscope analyzer to verify a used spark plug's ability to fire. Avoid trouble. Replace your spark plugs with each tune-up or at General Motors' recommended intervals.*

If all spark plugs appear gas fouled, yet the ignition tests okay, suspect a carburetion or fuel injection problem. The plugs may also show other kinds of damage, including broken porcelain. When this occurs, check for detonation or pre-ignition. On unleaded fuel engines, overly advanced spark timing or the use of very low octane (highly volatile) fuel can also cause plug damage.

As spark plugs are relatively inexpensive, replacement of worn plugs is the best protection against misfire and poor starting. Before installing new spark plugs, verify that each plug has the correct part number and heat range for your engine. Especially on pre-electronic breaker point ignitions, a slightly hotter (stick within one heat range) spark plug may work better during extremely cold weather, when long warm-up periods tend to carbon foul plugs.

On engine designs with high-energy (HEI) ignition systems and stringent emission standards, the correct spark plug heat range and gap are crucial to engine survival. For many engines, the underhood emission control decal provides tune-up data and spark plug information.

Check each plug gap carefully. Correct spark plug gaps assure proper firing accuracy and spark *duration*. Follow suggested gaps for your engine and distributor type.

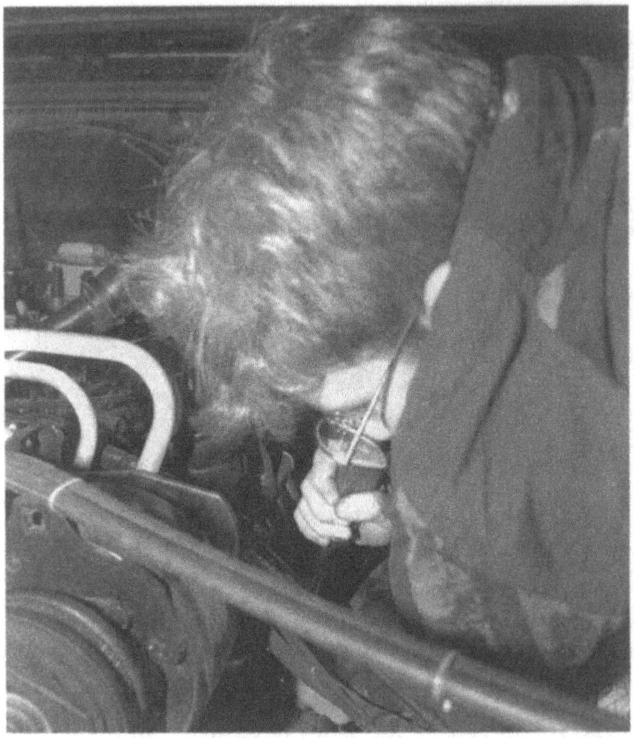

0014390

Fig. 8-39. *My son, Jacob, has started young. Here he sets spark plug torque with a torque wrench. Smaller hands work well for these tight access spark plugs.*

0014394

Fig. 8-40. *Detonation (ping) is always a symptom of engine stress. Worse yet is pre-ignition, which burns up pistons, shatters rings and even breaks connecting rods.*

I prefer a plug gapping tool that provides a flat and parallel gap surface. Many home mechanics, however, achieve good results with a round wire gauge set. Bend the side electrode strap carefully. Never attempt to move the center electrode.

In the heyday of the Stovebolt and Jimmy OHV inline sixes, it was popular to clean and reuse spark plugs. Most mechanics have abandoned this practice. Clean plugs may look good, but they may also have lost their firing capability. The only way to test a used plug is with an oscilloscope or plug tester. New plugs eliminate costly troubleshooting problems.

0014208

Fig. 8-41. Spark plug gapper is ideal tool for setting new plugs. This tool adjusts strap and sets parallel gap surfaces. Check service specifications before gapping plugs. (Do not use this tool on platinum-type spark plugs.)

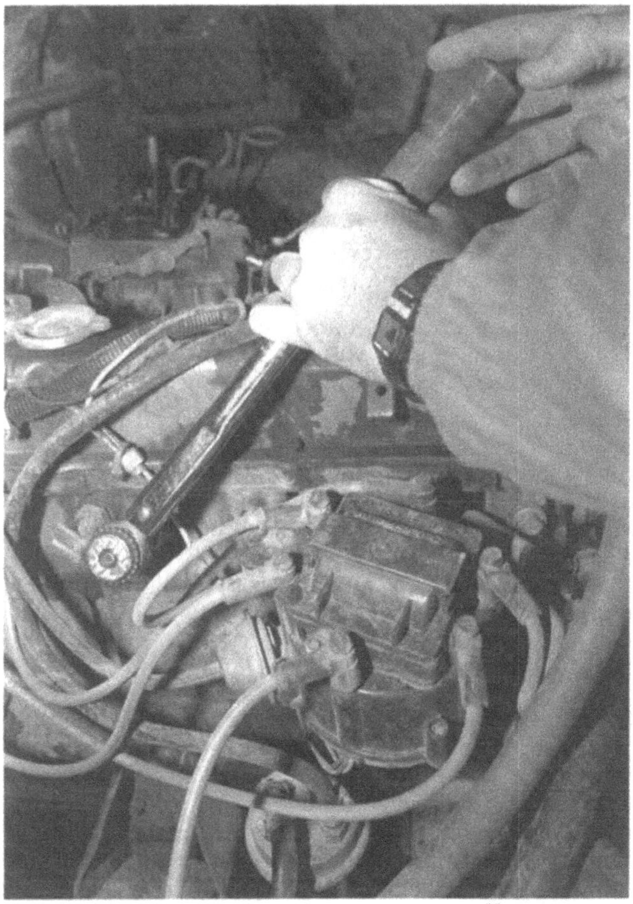

0014459

Fig. 8-42. If you have limited experience with tightening spark plugs, use a torque wrench. Overtightening can distort the spark gap or damage the plug or cylinder head.

If you have limited experience at tightening spark plugs, use a torque wrench. Too loose and the plug could unscrew and blow out. Overtightening may distort the spark gap or damage the plug.

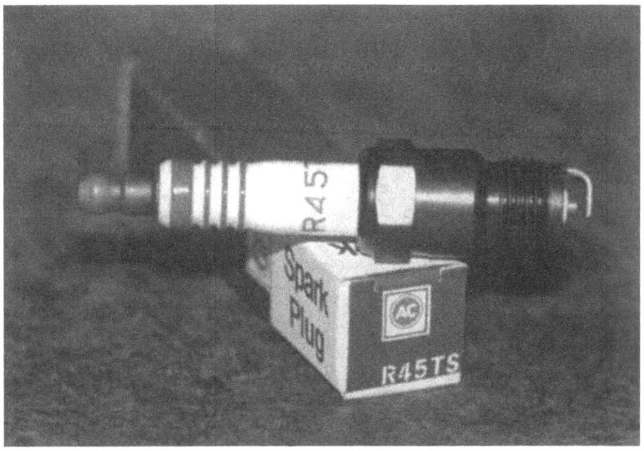

0014457

Fig. 8-43. Traditionally, AC spark plugs have been OEM in GM light truck engines. Platinum plugs have become popular in some late model engines with long service intervals. GM has used a variety of spark plug seat designs. Note tapered seat on this GM truck spark plug application. Earlier engines use a square-shoulder plug seat with a sealing gasket/washer.

Prior to the introduction of electronic ignitions in 1975 GM light trucks, spark plug gaps and torque settings were very consistent. GM light truck spark plug gaps and torque settings can be found in a service manual that covers your year and model engine.

From the late 1960s onward, mandatory tune-up decals for anti-pollution law compliance have been in effect. Your late 1960s or newer GM light truck has such a decal within the engine bay, usually located on the radiator core support, air cleaner housing or underside of the hood. The spark plug gap is included with this data, along with point gap and timing specifications.

The 1975–up high voltage electronic spark systems (HEI) require much wider plug gaps. Your underhood decal furnishes information on tuning the engine, including the type of spark plug recommended and its proper gap.

If your GM truck engine has the older 14mm thread, gasket seat spark plugs, the torque setting is a maximum of 25 ft-lbs. From 1970 onward, many GM truck engines change spark plug design, offering the newer tapered seat spark plugs that torque to a maximum of either 15 ft-lbs (1970–78) or 22 ft-lbs (1979–up).

Due largely to the exceptional degree of GM truck parts interchangeability, complete engine transplants and cylinder head exchanges are common within the repair industry. If you have any doubts about your engine's spark plug gap or torque setting, first verify the cylinder head type and the recommended spark plug design, including thread diameter, thread length, seat type and heat range.

Wires and Distributor Cap

Because modern spark cables have a carbon core to suppress radio interference, your truck's ignition wires require periodic testing for ohms resistance and shorts. The simplest volt/ohmmeter comes in handy here, providing a quick means for checking resistance between the ends of each lead. As a yardstick, longer leads typically require

0012278

Fig. 8-44. *Check plug wires with a volt/ohmmeter. Attach leads to each end of the wire and read resistance. While testing resistance, coil the wire very gently and loosely to turn up shorts without damaging the sensitive carbon core.*

a minimum resistance of 4,000 ohms and maximum of 15,000 ohms.

As you check the spark cables, twist and coil each wire gently. This will reveal opens or defective segments of wire. Also look at the insulation. Carefully route wires to prevent nicks and melted insulation.

> **CAUTION —**
> *Never puncture or use a pinpoint probe on carbon core wire insulation.*

0014194

Fig. 8-45. *The aluminum contacts on the distributor cap can oxidize and corrode. Replace distributor cap and rotor when corrosion or arcing has caused damage. If available, a high quality replacement cap with brass contacts makes a good investment.*

0014197

Fig. 8-46. *V-8 HEI distributor lies at back of engine. Four retaining clips hold cap in place. When installing this type of distributor cap, center the cap carefully and make sure each clip seats completely in its notch below the distributor housing.*

A quick preliminary test of plug wire condition is possible with a strobe timing light—preferably the induction type. Hook up the timing light lead to one spark cable at a time. With the engine idling, observe the consistency of the spark while also listening to the smoothness of the engine. Ideally, the spark should appear steady, without misfire, pause or interruption.

There are other causes of misfire, too, including lean or rich fuel mixtures, a fouled spark plug, a defective distributor or a worn ignition coil. Remove the suspected wire and test it with your ohmmeter before investing in an expensive set of spark cables.

The spark plugs and cables are part of the secondary ignition circuit. In addition to these components, the distributor cap and rotor require attention. Replace the distributor cap when you see wear, cracks, carbon tracking (a cause of cross-firing between cylinders) or corroded electrical contacts. During routine service, I inspect the cap for cracks, examine the rotor contacts and clean the cable sockets with a distributor brush.

On HEI and other GM high energy ignitions, high voltage will eventually erode the rotor. If not corrected, electricity can short to ground through the distributor shaft. Inspect the rotor carefully. Replace the rotor if arcing, heat damage or wear is evident.

Primary Ignition System

On earlier non-electronic ignition systems, the points and condenser require periodic replacement. As for when you should replace the breaker points, consider several symptoms: point misalignment, severe rubbing block wear, pitting, arcing, blue discoloration or contact surfaces showing a peaked buildup of metal on one side (which can also mean condenser trouble).

When I entered the field of automotive mechanics, ignition point service was still popular. Light contact filing, performing spring tension tests and re-adjusting the breaker gap were routine procedures.

Today, we regard breaker points as a disposable item. At routine intervals, usually 8,000 to 12,000 miles, most mechanics simply install a new set of points and a condenser. Years ago, if the condenser tested okay and the points showed even wear, reuse was an acceptable prac-

Fig. 8-47. This breaker point spring gauge, still a part of my breaker point tuning tools, helps set correct tension. Proper spring tension reduces point bounce at high rpm and also assures normal rubbing block and contact wear. Filing and regapping ignition points extends parts life and service. Use a special points file, and clean all filings away with an electrical contact cleaner. When I began performance tuning Chevrolet V-8s, Mallory's famous dual point distributor was a popular aftermarket item.

tice. In fact, if the condenser tested within specification, it was often better than many new ones out of the box.

Better engineered breaker point sets have eliminated the need to adjust point spring tension. However, setting the breaker point cam angle or dwell remains crucial to peak performance. Proper dwell allows full coil saturation for a hot, crisp spark and also assures good engine starts, smooth performance and long point set life. (Dwell is the number of distributor cam degrees between the spot where the breaker points close and just where they begin to open again.)

A prominent source of ignition trouble is defective primary circuit wiring. Especially on early trucks with 6-volt systems, cloth wire can fray and short to ground against the engine block or distributor housing. Insulators on the distributor wire terminal block also wear, allowing the stud or wires to short.

Take care when installing the points and condenser. Failure to fully isolate the point spring from the distributor housing can cause hard starts, misfire or total shorting out of the ignition.

Route and attach primary wires and spark plug cables securely. Imagine your truck jostling in rough terrain. Will the breaker plate move with the vacuum advance and cause a wire short to ground? Will wires stay in

Fig. 8-48. Loose, frayed or broken primary wires will cause ignition trouble. On earlier six-volt electrical systems with cloth wire insulation, shorts to ground become common as the wires age. Wire leads through the distributor housing wear and deteriorate. Shorts cause engine misfiring and ignition failure. Check leads whenever you service the distributor.

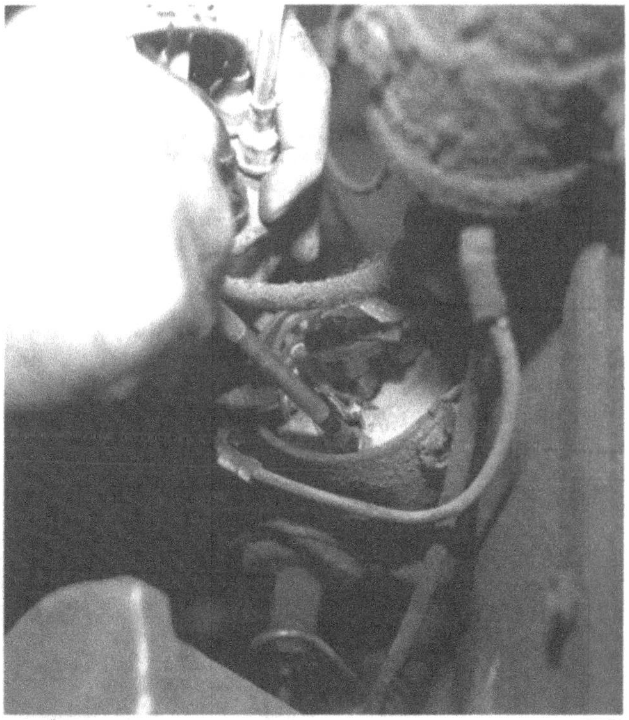

Fig. 8-49. Place the point/condenser set carefully on the breaker plate. (Do not drop screws, or you will be fishing for hardware.) A spring-loaded screw holder helps.

place, come loose or short to ground? Before condemning your coil or other parts, look for wiring problems.

Remove the distributor cap to service the primary ignition parts (points and condenser) and the rotor. For GM ignition distributors equipped with a centrifugal advance mechanism, the centrifugal weights and springs mount beneath the breaker plate on earlier breaker point distributors and beneath the rotor on 1957–up window cap distributors and the later electronic HEI units.

0014458

Fig. 8-50. Place cam lubricant in this recess. As the distributor cam rotates, grease will press against the rubbing block. Grease applied to the opposite side of the rubbing block will pull away, possibly fouling the points.

All 1939–up GM light trucks with breaker point distributors use both centrifugal and vacuum spark advance mechanisms. This highly effective system can accurately meet both the low and high speed load requirements of the engine.

If spark timing tests reveal a sluggish or erratic mechanical/centrifugal spark advance, you may need to remove the distributor for disassembly and overhaul. While some distributor vacuum advance units are adjustable or replaceable with the distributor still mounted in the engine, you will find that centrifugal advance mechanism repairs are more easily done on your work bench.

When you suspect spark advance troubles with this type of distributor, consult your GM truck shop manual for repair and rebuilding procedures. You may decide to overhaul your distributor. Perhaps wear is so severe that installing a rebuilt or new distributor assembly makes better sense or will prove cost effective.

0014206

Fig. 8-51. On window cap and most HEI distributors, remove rotor to access centrifugal flyweights and springs. Apply high-temp grease to base of weights and pivots. Make sure unit moves freely. When installing a new module, apply film of special insulation gel to base of module during installation.

During breaker point installation, wipe old grease from the cam and apply a thin film of fresh lubricant. Use a special point rubbing block lubricant, applied to the thrust side (toward the direction of the distributor cam rotation) of the rubbing block.

> NOTE —
> When you apply the grease correctly, the rotation of the breaker cam will push the grease into the rubbing block, rather than pull grease away and scatter it.

Always reset the ignition timing after you install new points or make a dwell adjustment. Any change in the point gap or the point set's location on the breaker plate will alter the spark timing.

Dwell Meter and Setting Points

When installing or adjusting breaker points, a feeler gauge is far less accurate than a dwell meter. Using a dwell meter to adjust the breaker points will assure adequate coil saturation for high speed operation plus enough spark for easy starting. Use of a dwell meter will also extend breaker point life.

Breaker Point Tips

Breaker points act as an electrical switch and they require periodic attention. The gap set between the contacts determines the coil's spark output at various engine speeds.

Although you initially set the point gap with a feeler gauge, the real concern is dwell or cam-angle, which translates as the *number of distributor degrees between the time the points close and when they open.*

Dwell is critical, since a coil needs saturation of its windings to yield a snappy spark each time the points open. Wide point gaps *decrease* cam angle or dwell; narrow gaps *increase* dwell. Although it would seem that the long dwell associated with narrow gaps is desirable, narrow gaps cause unwanted arcing of spark while the points are open and excessive heat buildup in the contacts. Arcing can also cause firing of spark plugs at the wrong time.

A traditional means for increasing dwell, without risk of re-arc or short contact point life, is the use of *two* sets of breaker points. Dual-point distributors overlap the opening and closing times of the two sets, using one set to open the circuit, the other to close it. These points, gapped at wider widths, provide high dwell degrees, allow for better coil saturation at high rpm and permit good starting.

Although none of the GM light truck engines have ever offered a dual point distributor as OEM equipment, many Chevrolet Corvettes use them. Years ago, a high performance engine buildup for a Chevrolet V-8 truck engine would often include a retrofit Corvette dual point distributor. Transistor and HEI distributors made dual points obsolete.

Use the ignition feeler gauge to set the points for initial start-up. Once the engine starts, you can take a dwell reading and readjust the points as needed. Since some GM truck engines with non-window cap distributors require removal of the distributor cap to readjust points, you will want to make accurate changes based on your dwell meter reading.

Window cap distributors, introduced in 1957 truck V-8s, allow breaker point adjustment without the need to remove the distributor cap. You may need to set the initial gap with a feeler gauge before starting the engine and checking dwell. When the engine starts, you can finely adjust dwell, with the engine running, by carefully inserting an Allen head driver through the distributor cap window and into the points adjusting screw. To avoid electrical shock, don't miss the screw.

If the engine will not start with a feeler gauge setting, check all wires and connections. (Check insulators where wires attach to the points and be sure you installed these insulators in correct order.) If necessary, have an assistant crank the engine with the distributor cap removed and your dwell meter turned on. Observe spark across the points and read dwell during cranking. No spark across the points and no dwell meter reading mean either a bad electrical connection or a defective condenser. Correct this problem before setting or changing the point dwell.

WARNING —
Do not open the points with a non-insulated screwdriver while cranking the engine, or you may get a severe electrical shock from the condenser.

By tightening the mounting screws just enough to still allow movement of the breaker set, you can adjust the points as the engine cranks. Move the point set (change gap) by rotating a screwdriver either clockwise or counter-clockwise at the adjusting slot or the eccentric adjusting screw on an early distributor. Once you adjust the

0014196

Fig. 8-52. *A dwell meter measures the cam angle from breaker point closure to reopening. Check the dwell angle specs for your engine, and use a dwell meter for best results. I bought my RAC tach/dwell meter 25 years ago and still find occasional opportunities to use it. Here, Joe Menesini checks dwell on his vintage GMC engine.*

0014199

Fig. 8-53. *The rear distributor location on all 1955–up Chevrolet V-8s and the 1955–59 Pontiac/GMC V-8s makes service awkward. Window cap distributor was a significant breakthrough in 1957, allowing easy dwell adjustment. You can come close to specification by simply turning the adjusting screw clockwise until the engine just begins to run roughly, then back the screw out exactly 180° (1/2 turn). Typical dwell setting for V-8s is 28–32°, and I like to set new points at 29-1/2° for a run-in setting of 30°. Warning: Watch where you insert the Allen wrench. There's plenty of high voltage spark inside the window.*

dwell to within specification, tighten the mounting screws securely and confirm that dwell is still correct.

Years ago, mechanics removed the distributor from the engine and used a stroboscopic distributor machine as a testbed for routine service and repairs. You may want to sublet your distributor to a shop that has such a machine. They can test and restore the advance mechanism(s), install new points and set dwell. You would then reinstall the distributor unit and set the base timing. (See timing section for instructions.)

Watch carefully for distributor shaft bushing wear. If your distributor shows a dwell variance of more than two degrees cam angle, check the shaft bushings. With the rotor removed and points open on a cam lobe, press gently against the shaft. Note the point gap. Now pull on the shaft lightly. Again measure the point gap.

The difference between these figures helps indicate distributor shaft bushing wear. When your distributor shows wear, you need to overhaul the unit or install a new or rebuilt distributor. (See performance chapter for aftermarket replacement/upgrade distributor units.)

Breaker gap and dwell angle settings vary on the GM light truck engines built from 1939–74. Consult your truck shop manual for details. You may need to verify the Delco-Remy part number on the distributor to confirm which unit your truck uses.

Early Stovebolt 216 sixes require a point gap of 0.018 inch to achieve correct point dwell. Unfortunately, the original GM factory shop manuals neglect to share what that desired dwell angle is. GM simply recommends that you adjust new points wide (between 0.020 and 0.022 inch), which allows for fiber rubbing block wear. (Modern point rubbing block materials offset this wear factor to a large degree.) I find that 1957–up window cap point sets will close the gap approximately 1/2° of dwell angle between installation and break-in.

Remember, while gap settings will start the engine and provide adequate service, accurately setting the dwell angle will gain even better performance and longer service from your tune-up.

Electronic Primary Ignition System

On 1975 and later GM truck engines, removing the distributor cap provides access to the electronic ignition parts. The GM electronic ignition systems begin with the original Delco-Remy HEI (High Energy Ignition) distributor. This unit is distinguishable by its large distributor cap that actually contains the coil.

The original HEI design incorporates a vacuum advance unit and a centrifugal advance much like the window cap distributors. In place of the traditional breaker point set and condenser, the HEI distributor uses a replaceable module and relies on a timer core and pickup coil.

The conventional HEI distributor offers tremendous reliability, tuning potential and mechanical sense. Much like an earlier window cap distributor, the centrifugal flyweights and springs are beneath the rotor and easily serviceable—even changeable. Likewise, the vacuum advance canister can be replaced with a service unit or, if desired, a unit with improved spark advance characteristics.

You can build performance modifications into any conventional HEI unit, and this is why the design enjoys a loyal following. Aftermarket parts can upgrade an HEI distributor to offer the same type of spark advance curves as a distributor found on high performance engines. Tuning for maximum horsepower or economy—or a reasonable point somewhere in between—is possible. (See performance chapter for further details.)

0014489

Fig. 8-54. Beginning with the HEI distributors of 1975, all later GM V-8s and sixes have simpler routine tune-up requirements. Spark plugs, cap, wire, rotor and new fuel filters are the customary fare.

The high firing voltages of HEI distributors, well in excess of 50,000 peak volts in stock form, make this design well suited to the emission control era. Long duration spark and more complete fuel burn is possible, and the HEI can easily fire across wider spark plug gaps like 0.045 to 0.060 inch.

The module is a primary troubleshooting spot when the HEI ignition fails. Testing electronic ignition components requires use of a sensitive digital volt/ohmmeter and other equipment, including an oscilloscope in some instances. For service and repairs beyond basic tuning, refer to your GM truck shop manual.

Before condemning a module or any other electronic ignition component, check all wiring circuits and connections. Wires can fray, short and develop loose connections. Module leads can wear out, especially on vacuum advance equipped distributors. Check your engine's wiring carefully, and replace defective wires or plug connectors as needed.

NOTE —
Distributor modules mounted near hot engine components and on the distributor housing usually require a special silicone heat insulating gel supplied with the new module. An even coating on the back of the module helps isolate this sensitive component from engine heat.

Spark Timing

If the right quantity of current reaches fresh spark plugs, the other concern is *timing*. For older engines, the mechanical (centrifugal) advance mechanism and a vacuum advance unit require routine inspection and service.

NOTE —
On later engines with electronic fuel and spark management (EFI), spark timing is electronically controlled. The engine computer receives timing signals from the ignition distributor and several other engine sensors. Once you verify the correct initial (idle) timing setting, there's no other timing consideration.

The vacuum advance unit has a diaphragm inside, set to move at a specific vacuum pull. Vacuum can be tested with a vacuum hand pump. Look up the correct vacuum setting in your GM truck shop manual or a professional service guidebook that covers your engine, then test the vacuum advance by watching the module plate (HEI ignitions) or breaker point plate move as you apply vacuum. If you perform this test with the distributor cap removed, note the vacuum level where the plate *just begins to move.*

After inspecting the vacuum advance, look closely at the mechanical advance mechanism. (This is easier on window cap and later GM distributors where you find the advance weights and springs mounted beneath the rotor.) Lube the base and pivots for each flyweight with high-temp grease and check for wear.

Be certain that the centrifugal advance unit moves easily and that the springs have tension. Once the engine is running, you can use a timing light with built-in advance to determine whether the distributor's mechanical and vacuum advance mechanisms perform properly.

> **NOTE —**
> When timing the engine, check the centrifugal advance and vacuum advance systems separately. Disconnect and tape off the distributor vacuum line before testing the centrifugal advance.

If spark advance works correctly, set the ignition *initial* advance to specification. This is generally done with the vacuum advance *disconnected,* unless otherwise specified in your GM truck shop manual, a professional service guide or on the underhood tune-up sticker. Base timing is set with an engine at a specific idle speed.

Before you start the engine to verify spark timing, check the tightening torque on fan and water pump mounting hardware. Make sure the water pump shaft and bearings do not have play or wobble. When timing your engine, stay away from moving parts.

> *WARNING —*
> *Do not race the engine, as the fan is more likely to come loose on a stationary vehicle than when air is moving through the radiator at road speed. Make sure your hands, clothing and tools are well away from moving parts. Never operate the engine beyond 2,500 rpm during service work.*

Always perform initial or base spark timing with the engine at its curb (fully warmed) idle speed. This means the choke is fully open, and the engine is running slowly enough to prevent the centrifugal/mechanical advance from altering the reading. Even a slight opening of the throttle will cause the vacuum advance to operate.

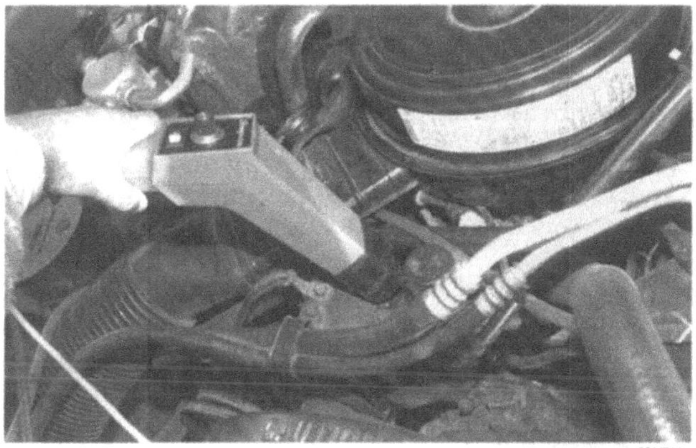

0014214

Fig. 8-55. *Timing lights with built-in advance will check performance of the spark advance mechanism. If you add initial timing degrees to the specified distributor advance degrees for a given engine rpm, the adjusted strobe light should index with the 0 (TDC) mark. This set-up proves handy for checking vacuum and centrifugal advance mechanisms.*

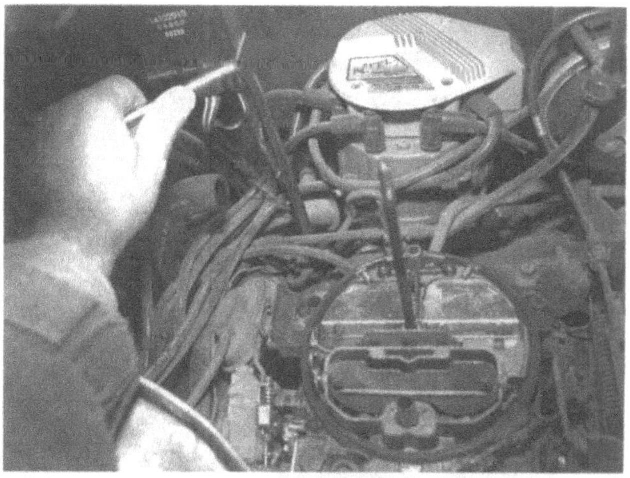

0014223

Fig. 8-56. *A distributor wrench allows easier access to the adjuster clamp nut. Loosen the bolt slightly, just enough to move the housing. The movable distributor housing permits timing corrections. On many current engines, the distributor clamps in a fixed location for emission compliance. Unlike the conventional HEI ignition (shown here), timing changes come from the engine management computer.*

Initial spark advance settings are generally with the vacuum advance hose(s) disconnected and taped and the engine at its recommended curb (warm) idle speed. On emission controlled engines, read the underhood decal carefully, as you may need to use special procedures or keep certain vacuum lines connected as you adjust base timing.

> **NOTE —**
> Emissions law requires that an engine operate at the vehicle manufacturer's recommended setting. When you tune your engine for an emissions test, be aware that many states and local areas require a check of spark timing. Set the timing correctly to avoid failing a smog test.

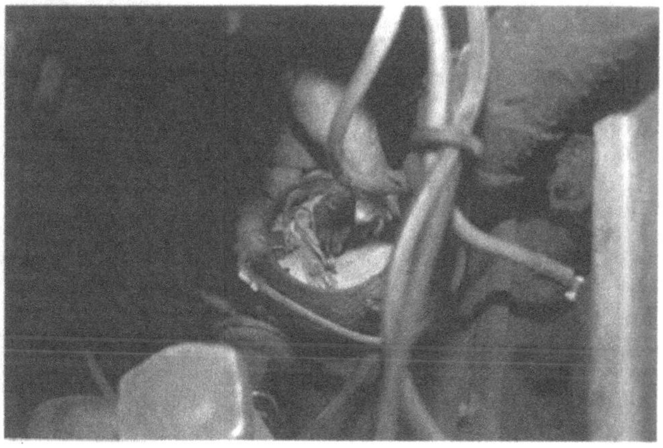

0014221

Fig. 8-57. *Rotate the distributor housing with the ignition switch ON, making sure your hand is away from the primary wire or stud terminal. First rotate in direction of shaft rotation, then reverse toward #1 cylinder firing position.*

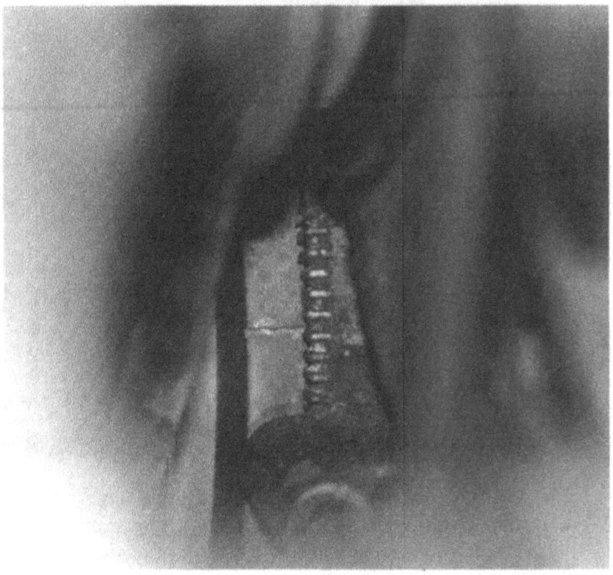

0012292

Fig. 8-58. You will find timing marks at the engine's front timing cover. The tab is likely dirty from road debris and engine grease. With the engine shut off, carefully wipe the tab clean. You will index the correct marker point with the correct crankshaft line as described in a workshop manual.

0012293

Fig. 8-59. Most settings call for the engine at an idle with the distributor vacuum line disconnected and plugged. Your timing light attaches to the #1 cylinder's spark plug wire. Disconnect and plug or tape off vacuum advance line before verifying base timing.

Use a stroboscopic timing light for best results. I like the latest induction type lights for their ease of hookup and brightness.

The GM truck shop manual or a professional-series service guidebook lists the timing mark location and initial (base or idle speed) timing specifications for your engine. With the ignition switch in the OFF position, verify the timing mark on your engine. Timing marks vary from a ball on the flywheel (early inline sixes) to a notch or lines on the crankshaft pulley. Some timing tabs mount on the engine's front cover, just above the crankshaft pulley. Become familiar with how your indexing marks or pointer align, and also know how many crankshaft degrees of timing each mark on the timing tab or crankshaft pulley represents. When you need to set the engine timing, you will be carefully observing the tab, pointer or indexing marks.

0012295

Fig. 8-60. If the mark is difficult to distinguish, clean the timing tab and notch thoroughly before starting the engine to verify timing. A dab of white or yellow indelible paint helps locate the mark with your timing light.

Your strobe timing light will attach to the #1 spark plug wire. Know which wire in the distributor cap is for the #1 cylinder. With a knowledge of the firing order and the cylinder numbering order (plus the direction that the distributor shaft rotates), you can also verify whether each spark plug wire is attached to the correct cylinder.

Static Timing

If you need to service your engine in the wilds, I have a static timing technique that can prove very useful on breaker point type distributors. (Electronic ignitions cannot be static timed, due to the need to generate electrical signals with a rotating distributor armature.)

Begin by locating the distributor wire lead to the #1 cylinder. Remove the distributor cap and spark plugs. Manually turn the engine over in its normal direction of rotation. Watch the rotor as it approaches the #1 cylinder firing position.

Rotate the crankshaft slowly, and stop exactly where the timing marker indexes with the correct initial advance mark. On your truck's engine, the marks and pointer will be visible at the crankshaft damper/pulley and timing cover. (An exception is the earlier GM inline six cylinder with a pointer and timing mark at the bellhousing.) You may need to wipe grease off the pointer or pulley to clarify the marks.

Turn the ignition switch to the ON position. With the distributor clamped loosely, move the housing in the direction that the distributor shaft normally rotates during cranking.

NOTE —
All Chevrolet and GMC truck distributors rotate clockwise with the exception of the 1955–59 Pontiac/GMC V-8s, which rotate counter-clockwise. You can determine the direction of rotation by observing which way the distributor shaft turns during cranking.

Move the housing well past the #1 cylinder distributor lobe. Now, very slowly rotate the housing in the opposite direction of the distributor shaft rotation, toward the #1 cylinder firing position. Watch the point contacts carefully.

WARNING —
Avoid electrical shock by keeping your hand away from the primary coil wire. When the condenser unloads, the primary wire receives a good voltage spike. Make sure your hand isn't the ground source.

At the exact moment the points arc, you will have set timing at the number of advance degrees indicated on the pulley and timing marker. When you start the engine and verify the timing with a timing light, you may find a slight difference. This is due to camshaft and distributor drive gear lash. For start-up purposes, however, this method serves well. (When I rebuild an engine, static timing assures an immediate start-up.)

A variation on static timing also works well. With spark plugs removed from the engine, rotate the crankshaft to locate the timing marks as before. Now, reinstall the distributor cap. Place an old spark plug on the #1 plug wire and ground the plug's metal shell carefully. Loosen the distributor housing clamp.

Turn the ignition switch to ON. Rotate the distributor housing in the same direction as the shaft rotates, well past the #1 cylinder firing point. Then, slowly rotate the housing in the opposite direction of shaft rotation until a spark fires across the test plug. If you tighten the distributor at this exact point, accurate static timing will result. If you pass the firing point, repeat the procedure.

By rotating the distributor first in the same direction as shaft/rotor rotation, and then in the opposite direction, you will prevent the advance mechanism from distorting your static timing results. If you overshoot the firing point, repeat the whole process to assure an accurate setting.

When you need to remove the distributor, carefully note the rotor position and scribe the distributor housing location at the block before pulling the unit. Upon reinstalling the distributor, immediately verify timing with your induction timing light.

Use of Timing Light with Built-in Advance

An easier approach to spark timing is possible with a timing light that has adjustable advance. Simply dial the advance until you index the timing cover marker with the 0, TDC or dot/groove on the crankshaft pulley (or the bellhousing pointer and flywheel ball marker on early GM inline sixes). Read the timing light's scale. If the reading equals the correct timing specification, the engine's spark is in time.

The built-in advance light is ideal for verifying the performance of the spark advance mechanism. For engines with a centrifugal and/or vacuum advance system (without electronic computer overrides), you can use an advance timing light much like a stroboscopic distributor test machine.

You can quickly test the vacuum advance unit with a vacuum pump. (In your GM truck shop manual or a professional service book, you will find specifications for the vacuum and centrifugal advance units.) With the engine idling, disconnect and plug the vacuum line and read the degrees of spark timing advance.

Hook the vacuum pump to the advance unit and apply the number of vacuum inches (in/hg) described in the service guidelines.(If the idle speed picks up, lower the idle speed to prevent the mechanical advance from interfering with the advance reading.) Note the degrees of timing advance that now appear at the crankshaft pulley/damper and timing marker. When assessing the results, note whether the service book describes "distributor degrees" or "crankshaft degrees."

Distributor Degrees Versus Crankshaft Degrees

Your professional service manual has specifications on where the vacuum or centrifugal advance unit should just begin to move and how many total degrees it should advance at full apply vacuum or a given rpm. Be aware that most service guidebook distributor specifications read in distributor rpm and distributor degrees.

These figures are exactly one-half the number of engine crankshaft degrees and one-half the crankshaft/engine rpm. When you read degrees of timing advance at the crankshaft, what you see is *twice* the distributor degrees, *plus* the number of degrees of initial spark advance. Likewise, engine speed is *twice* that of distributor rpm.

Example 1: Initial timing calls for 0 or TDC. Centrifugal advance specifications call for 5 distributor degrees of spark advance at 1250 distributor rpm. With the vacuum advance hose blocked off, timing will read 10 crankshaft degrees of spark advance at 2500 crankshaft/engine rpm.

Example 2: Vacuum advance specifications call for 8 degrees of distributor advance at 13 in/hg vacuum. With the engine at an idle, you apply 13 in/hg vacuum to the vacuum diaphragm. Timing should increase 16 crankshaft degrees (possibly a bit more if the engine rpm rises enough for the centrifugal advance to swing).

Consider sending out the distributor for testing if you suspect an inoperative centrifugal advance mechanism. When removing the distributor, mark the housing and rotor location. Have a shop test the advance mechanism(s) in a distributor test machine. These machines are now somewhat rare in this era of rebuilt/exchange parts, but they were popular in the breaker point distributor era.

Vacuum Versus Mechanical/Centrifugal Advance

Many GM light truck distributors use a very slow or mild centrifugal advance curve, relying heavily on vacuum advance for extra spark timing and power at low engine speeds. Vacuum advance works well for truck engines because under severe loads, the engine needs spark advance quickly. By contrast, centrifugal advance requires engine speed in order to work, and that's not often easy when the truck lugs a heavy load.

Vacuum provides the necessary spark advance for low speed power. As speed increases, a centrifugal (weight and spring) advance unit can offer an engine speed related advance. At this stage, as the throttle opening widens and neither engine vacuum nor ported carburetor vacuum can assist, engine speed alone can regulate the degrees of centrifugal spark timing advance.

Ported Versus Manifold Vacuum

When a distributor uses ported vacuum, the vacuum source is a channel just above the carburetor's throttle plate. As the throttle valve begins to open, this port becomes exposed and receives a high rate of engine vacuum, causing the spark timing to advance substantially. Ported vacuum declines gradually as the throttle valve opens further.

Manifold vacuum, which is sometimes used in a single or dual diaphragm vacuum advance system, is the vacuum from within the engine's intake plenum. Manifold vacuum is highest at an idle, remains relatively high at light loads and throttle settings, and drops as the throttle opening and engine load increase. At wide open throttle under load, manifold vacuum reaches its lowest point.

Fuel economy is best at higher manifold vacuum readings. Sluggish spark timing advance reduces manifold vacuum. Adequate spark timing advance, whether vacuum or centrifugal, maintains the best manifold vacuum. This contributes to better performance and optimal fuel economy.

3. CARBURETOR TUNE-UP

Carburetor adjustment is another aspect of your tune-up. Vacuum leaks, normal wear and dirt can inhibit a carburetor's performance. Tuning may include setting idle mixture, idle speed and adjusting choke operation.

Before setting the idle mixture, make certain that the fuel pump provides an adequate supply of gasoline. Change the disposable filter(s) on later model engines and clean the fuel pump's sediment bowl filter on earlier engines.

> *WARNING —*
> *During many fuel system procedures fuel will be discharged or exposed. Do not smoke or work near heaters or other fire hazards. Have a fire extinguisher handy.*

A plugged fuel filter will restrict fuel flow and affect engine idle. If flooding, starvation or other problems exist, consult your GM truck shop manual or a professional-level service guidebook for carburetor overhaul procedures. You can also find detailed carburetor overhaul procedures in the instructions that come with a quality carburetor rebuild kit. For GM carburetors, I like the Delco-Rochester or Echlin kits.

Altitude changes will alter the idle mixture. If you plan to operate an older GM carbureted truck at a higher or lower altitude than your home, for an extended period of time, expect to adjust the idle mix.

0014460

Fig. 8-61. *GMC 305 V-6 engines use this Stromberg two-barrel carburetor. Fuel economy of the earlier one barrel-equipped 305 V-6 was notoriously poor. Two-barrel delivers better performance and economy.*

GM trucks use a variety of carburetors. The list and description of specific carburetors would make a full length service guidebook in itself. Rather than writing a second volume to this book, I suggest that you seek out a quality resource such as Motor's *Truck* or Mitchell's *Domestic Light Truck Tune-up Manual*, the GM truck shop manual for your specific year vehicle, or service guidebooks or pamphlets available directly from the carburetor manufacturers.

> *CAUTION —*
> *Overhauling and repairing some of the later GM truck carburetors requires expertise and special gauges, an accurate vacuum pump and exacting service data. Unless you have a good background in carburetor overhaul, either sublet your carburetor to a specialist for overhaul or purchase a rebuilt/exchange or new unit. (See performance chapter for tips on replacement carburetors.)*

> NOTE —
> If your truck's engine runs roughly or responds poorly under acceleration (has a flat spot), suspect dirty carburetor jets, a defective accelerator pump or an ignition mis-fire. Once you rule out ignition problems, vacuum leaks, low compression or a worn timing chain, consider a carburetor overhaul.

Before seeking specifications to reset the float or adjust any linkages, solenoids or the idle mixture, verify your carburetor's type and its identification, list or tag number. For later vehicles from the emissions era, the underhood emissions/tuning decal is also a reliable tuning aid.

You cannot correct some types of carburetor wear. Consider the age of the carburetor and its general condition. Check for throttle plate wear at the throttle shaft, corrosion in the float bowl area, and warpage of main

Fig. 8-62. Change air and fuel filter elements as part of routine service. On engines with a carburetor inlet filter, change this filter annually or at a maximum of 15,000 miles. Flare nut on fuel line inlet requires care. When changing the inlet fuel filter on this type of GM carburetor, use a special flarenut wrench (top). Hold inlet fitting steady with an open end wrench and loosen flarenut carefully. When flare nut is too tight for flarenut wrench, this small version of plumber's chain wrench (bottom) can save the day.

Fig. 8-63. If your older carburetor has a warped or corroded body, or a loose throttle shaft, consider a new or rebuilt replacement unit. Rochester two- and four-barrel carburetors have served many GM truck V-8s. Reliable and serviceable, these carburetors prove durable and respond readily to an overhaul.

Fig. 8-64. Troubleshooting your electronic fuel and spark management system requires a precise digital volt/ohmmeter. For feedback/closed-loop carburetors and EFI/TBI, tenths and hundredths of a volt make a difference.

body parts. Also look for missing linkage pieces or loose and worn components. A new or rebuilt replacement carburetor can often prove practical.

On later emission control era truck engines, the carburetor has no provision for adjustment. Idle screw limiter caps or, even more recently, the complete elimination of idle screws make emission control carburetors more difficult to tune. There is a factory service procedure for accessing the adjuster screws on some engines. However, these steps must be followed in strict accord with Federal laws. (See performance chapter for information on legal replacement carburetors that can enhance or restore performance.)

Fig. 8-65. *This fuel pump pressure gauge verifies volume and pressure. During tests, route fuel away from the engine's spark and heat sources to avoid a fire.*

NOTE —
Generally, when these carburetors function correctly and the idle is still poor, other problems exist—usually a vacuum leak, low compression, late valve timing (bad chain) or ignition defects.

Consult a factory or professional service book before adjusting or servicing a closed-loop/feedback or emissions calibrated carburetor. The system may include a vacuum actuator and idle solenoid that interact with your truck's electrical accessory circuits, such as air conditioning. The curb idle speed and fast idle may be adjustable. Use your emissions and tune-up underhood decal as a guide for these rpm settings.

The mechanical fuel pumps on earlier GM truck engines are either single or dual diaphragm types. Single-diaphragm pumps serve only as a fuel supply for the carburetor. A dual-diaphragm fuel pump functions as both the fuel supply and as a vacuum source for the windshield wipers. Early GM trucks have vacuum powered wipers.

Carburetor Tuning Tips

Minor carburetor tune-up consists of nothing more than setting the choke linkage to specification (with the engine very cold and ignition switched off), then adjusting the choke-on fast idle. If the carburetor has idle mixture screws, warm the engine and adjust the curb idle. This is the hot engine idle speed with the choke completely open.

Carburetor specifications often vary between models. See your GM truck shop manual or a professional service guide for precise adjustment specifications that apply to your engine and carburetor.

Check for vacuum leaks before adjusting the carburetor. Scan all hose connections and make sure the PCV valve works. This inexpensive, replaceable valve can cause serious idle problems when stuck open—or excessive crankcase pressure when stuck closed or plugged. If in doubt, replace it.

Always set ignition timing before adjusting the idle speed or mixture screws. Also check the torque of manifold and carburetor mounting bolts.

For adjusting the fast idle, attach a portable tachometer, open the throttle and release it completely, then start the engine. Without opening the throttle, immediately adjust the fast idle speed to specification. Do not allow the choke to move the fast idle linkage and cam until you have made your speed setting.

Watch the choke open. If the vacuum pull-off (or brake) is working correctly (periodically check it with a vacuum hand pump), a blip of the throttle should immediately tug the choke valve open slightly. As the engine warms, the choke valve should gradually open to the straight-up position. Should your choke be old or its plunger sticky, you can usually clean or overhaul the choke unit without removing the carburetor.

CAUTION —
Avoid burning your fingers when working around a heated choke assembly.

After servicing the choke, thoroughly warm the engine. You can now set the hot (curb) idle speed. Note that the emission requirements will dictate which adjustment procedure is correct for engines built since the late 1960s. You will find instructions on the underhood decal or in your GM truck shop manual.

Performance wise, the best idle mixtures produce the highest vacuum reading. Unless another method is specified (lean drop, propane enrichment, etc.), I always use a vacuum gauge for setting hot idle mixtures. High and steady manifold vacuum at an idle indicates an engine with proper compression seal, a quality ignition system and complete combustion. In the tune-up realm, an overly lean or rich carburetor setting—or retarded spark timing—will create a low manifold vacuum reading.

Finally, test the stroke and squirt of the carburetor's accelerator pump. Too little pump discharge causes engine stumbling and starvation on acceleration. Some accelerator pumps have a leaner high altitude setting for operating the engine at higher elevations. If you plan to run your truck for a long period at higher elevations, consider using the high altitude pump arm setting.

Refer to the emission control section for insight into the many emission control defects that cause rough idle and other troubles. For example, an EGR valve that cannot seat properly creates symptoms just like carburetor trouble—so can the simple PCV valve, an inexpensive and routinely replaced item. Even a plugged exhaust system can be easily overlooked.

0014224

Fig. 8-66. Early GM truck engines feature a sediment bowl (arrow) on the fuel pump or carburetor fuel line. The serviceable sediment screen traps debris and functions much like a modern fuel filter. During service, avoid exposure to gasoline.

Before condemning either the carburetor or fuel pump, check the bolts that secure these parts to the manifold and engine block. Also check the manifold mounting hardware and for possible vacuum leaks. Look for kinks in the fuel pipes and hoses. On early fuel pumps with a glass sediment bowl, tighten the bail nut carefully to avoid breaking the glass bowl.

Float Settings and Fuel Pressure

When your truck's engine floods with gasoline or bucks during high speed runs, check the carburetor float setting. You can find float specifications in your GM truck shop manual or a professional service manual. Also use the manual for checking the float drop setting.

If the carburetor has a removable air horn, like the popular Rochester units, you may need to loosen the fuel pipe for access to the carburetor air horn and float(s). Loosen the air horn screws, then remove and invert the air horn. Hold it level as you measure the float height.

> NOTE —
> Although Chevrolet trucks most frequently use Rochester or Carter carburetors, earlier GMC truck engines rely on Zenith, Holley and Stromberg carburetors. Refer to your GM truck shop manual or a professional-level service guide that covers your truck model and engine.

0014227

Fig. 8-67. Rochester carburetors require removal of air horn (top section) for adjusting float. Invert the air horn and check height. Turn air horn upright to check float drop. Compare measurement against specifications found in your GM truck shop manual or a professional guide.

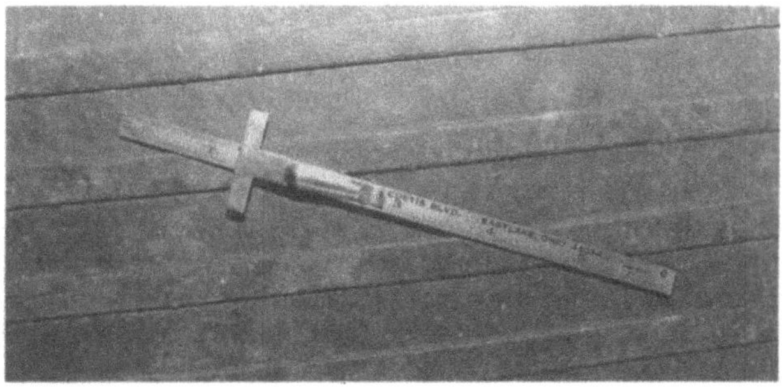

0012308

Fig. 8-68. T-gauge rule is a common carburetor overhaul tool. Better quality overhaul kits come with detailed instructions for your carburetor model and a plastic gauge for setting the float.

On Holley 1904-series one-barrel carburetors used on GMC inline sixes, you can check the float height without removing major pieces. On these carburetors, you can remove the economizer diaphragm and measure the fuel level with a depth ruler. The correct fuel level is usually 3/4" below the machined surface. (Set the gauge's cross rail just flush with the opening in the casting. Use the height specification found in your GMC truck shop manual.) The engine should be level and idling.

To reset these one-barrel floats, however, requires removal of the float bowl and careful bending of the float adjusting tab. Refer to your GMC truck shop manual or a professional-level service guidebook for float adjustment specifications.

> *CAUTION —*
> *Take care not to press the float needle into its seat. Damage could result, causing erratic performance.*

0014160

Fig. 8-69. The mechanical fuel pump can wear over time. More often, a defective or clogged filter will cause trouble, mimicking the symptoms of a worn fuel pump. Change filters before condemning the pump, especially on applications where the fuel pump is difficult to reach.

Fuel Pump Pressure/Output

If the float level is correct and fuel starvation persists, check the fuel pump output. Correct pump pressure varies between models and pump designs. Verify your engine's requirements in a factory-level service manual. Before suspecting fuel pump pressure or volume troubles, check all fuel lines from the tank forward, and also the dual tank switching valve / solenoid if your truck is so equipped. Look for leaks, loose connections or kinks.

The fuel pump is a common trouble spot. Some early GM truck fuel pumps are rebuildable. Repair kits were once a common item at the local retail auto supply. Today, however, rebuilt or new replacement pumps are available. It is wise to carry an extra fuel pump and needle / seat kit on extended trips into back country.

CAUTION —
When testing fuel pump volume, make certain that your container is unbreakable and able to catch all of the gasoline. Route gas away from spark sources or hot engine parts. Spark from the ignition or engine heat could ignite fuel and cause a serious fire.

An older, fatigued fuel pump diaphragm will stretch or rupture. Look closely for fuel dilution in the engine's crankcase or leaks around the pump. If the cause of low pressure / volume is unclear, remove the pump and check the condition of the camshaft lobe or eccentric disc that operates the pump arm.

Idle Mixture Setting

Before adjusting the carburetor, look down its throat for carbon and debris. A spray type carburetor and choke cleaner can remove accessible varnish and carbon. Short of an overhaul, these solvents work well for periodic cleaning. If dust or grime is present, suspect an inadequate air cleaner seal. Correct the problem.

You can also shoot spray cleaner directly into the float chamber vent. The alcohol present in most cleaners will absorb water sediment and carry it from the float bowl to the engine's combustion chambers. Run the engine at a fast idle to clear washed down debris; then allow the engine to cool before installing new spark plugs.

CAUTION —
Make sure your spray carburetor cleaner will not damage the sensitive oxygen sensor, if so equipped. Read labels and use these products sparingly.

A professional service guidebook will describe overhaul procedures and give the preliminary idle mixture settings for your carburetor. If your engine has run reasonably well, turn the engine off and carefully screw the mixture adjusters clockwise while counting each turn carefully.

CAUTION —
Turn the mixture screw/needle gently. Overtightening the mixture screw can seriously damage the needle end of the screw.

0014209

Fig. 8-70. A quality spray carburetor cleaner will remove accessible debris. This will allow cleaner to work inside the float bowl. Environmentally friendly Permatex Choke and Carburetor Cleaner made quick sweep of carburetor. Note that gummy varnish disappeared and linkages are now clean. Read directions, spray down primary and secondary throats, and concentrate on the venturi and exposed jet areas. Try to wash exposed bleed holes and spray cleaner into the air horn vent.

0014461

Fig. 8-71. Many GM trucks with lighter GVWR packages require emission equipment like the closed-loop computer carburetor. Designed for strict emission compliance, these fuel systems provide little room for adjustment.

See how close the current adjustments come to the settings recommended in your GM truck shop manual or a professional level service guidebook. If there is a large difference between these two settings, suspect a vacuum leak or other problems. Return the needles to the current settings, then correct any obvious problems. (Look for a vacuum leak, loose carburetor mounting or air horn screws, a defective EGR valve, etc.)

Before adjusting the idle mixture, run the engine until completely warm, watching the choke through its whole opening cycle. Make sure the exhaust heat riser valve also opens properly, along with the coolant thermostat. Bring coolant to normal operating temperature—and make certain that the choke valve is fully open before adjusting the idle mix.

Always be certain the choke remains fully open while adjusting a carburetor's idle mixture. Do not allow the engine to idle for long periods during adjustment, or the spark plugs may foul and distort engine performance.

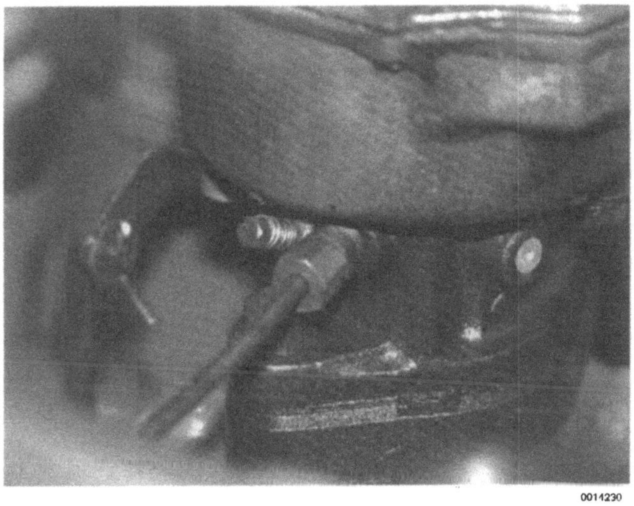

0014230

Fig. 8-72. On earlier models, idle mixture screws are easy to access. For the later emission control era, many carburetors have limiter caps on their adjuster screws or depend upon electronic controls for adjustment. On emission carburetors, cleanliness and frequent filter changes make the difference.

0014493

Fig. 8-73. Both two- and four-barrel V-8 carburetors have twin idle mixture screws. Clockwise leans mixture; counterclockwise enriches. Adjust one screw at a time. Shown here is a popular earlier GM truck Rochester two-barrel carburetor.

If you have difficulty judging the engine's smoothness, use a tachometer and vacuum gauge while you set the carburetor mixture screws. Strive for smooth running and the highest vacuum reading at a normal curb idle speed.

Try to adjust the engine to a "lean best" setting to help meet clean air standards. This is the leanest point for each adjuster screw that still allows the engine to run without mis-firing or stumbling.

On a fully warmed engine, begin the idle adjustment by turning the idle mixture screw(s) slowly clockwise. (One at a time in the case of two- and four-barrel carburetors.) A noticeable lean misfire should occur. Stop here. (If no lean mis-fire occurs as the mixture screw reaches its closed position, suspect dirty carburetor air bleeds or other troubles.)

Slowly back the idle mixture screw out (counterclockwise). Just when a smooth idle occurs, the setting is correct unless your emission decal calls for a "lean drop setting." (*Lean drop* means to turn the screws inward, toward a leaner mix, dropping the rpm a specific amount.) If the idle speed is incorrect at this point, reset the throttle or curb idle stop screw, then repeat the idle mixture adjustment if necessary.

Mechanical Fuel Pump Installation

Fuel pump installation begins with cleaning the area around the fuel pump. Carefully detach the fuel lines at the pump. Cap the fuel inlet line to prevent fuel leakage during service.

> *WARNING —*
> *Fuel will be exposed during this procedure. Do not smoke or create sparks. Have an approved fire extinguisher handy.*

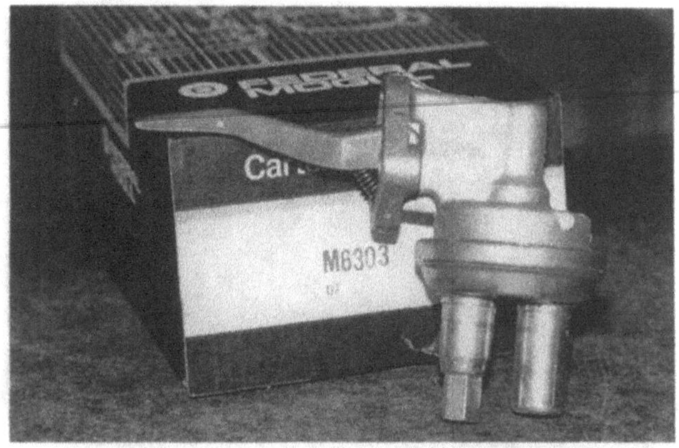

0012312

Fig. 8-74. Loosen and tighten V-8 and V-6 fuel pump bolts evenly to prevent cocking or binding of a long fuel pump arm or pushrod. Damage to the pump or misalignment with the lobe/eccentric or pushrod will otherwise result.

Loosen the fuel pump mounting bolts evenly and remove the pump and gasket. Look closely at the camshaft lobe, eccentric cam or pushrod (Chevrolet V-8s) that operates the pump arm. Make certain a worn camshaft lobe, loose eccentric or worn pushrod is not your problem.

Clean the gasket surface on the engine block thoroughly. Do not allow debris to fall into the engine. Rotate the engine to place the pump's camshaft lobe or eccentric on the lowest (heel) side to reduce pressure.

On the typical Chevrolet V-8, you must hold the fuel pump pushrod in place while installing the pump. Some recommend removing the upper adapter plate bolt and temporarily installing a longer bolt to lock the pushrod in place during the pump installation. I prefer Chevrolet's recommendation: Put a small amount of heavy grease on the pushrod end and insert the pushrod. The grease will hold the rod in place against the camshaft lobe as you align the fuel pump arm. Keep the pump straight at all times during installation.

Use a suitable gasket sealant, applied to both sides of the new gasket. Put sealant on the mounting bolt threads. Insert the bolts into the pump. Set the gasket, pump and bolts in place.

Carefully place the rubbing surface of the pump arm against the lobe or pushrod. Start the bolt threads with caution, holding the pump squarely toward the block surface. Tighten the bolts evenly until the pump is secure.

> **CAUTION —**
> *Make certain the fuel pump arm remains in place and straight during installation. Wedging the pump to one side can damage the lever or housing.*

4. MAJOR ENGINE DIAGNOSIS

If you suspect major engine trouble or your fuel and spark tune-up has little effect on performance, you need to perform further diagnosis.

On emission era truck engines (approximately 1966 forward), the emission controls can cause trouble. A defective EGR valve, for example, often creates the same symptoms as carburetor and fuel supply problems. Defective electronic closed-loop carburetion sensors or fuel/spark management components can also mimic these kinds of symptoms.

Although PCV and air injection came on some of the early emission era engines, the emission control packages were simple and not likely to cause much trouble. From the late 1970s onward, emission controls play an increasingly larger role in engine performance and tune.

After years of exposure to tune-up and engine overhaul diagnostics, I now use a compression gauge only for quick referencing. A low reading usually requires squirting motor oil into the cylinder to distinguish piston ring wear from valve troubles. I go further than this and use a leakdown tester for pinpoint diagnosis.

A leak of more than 10% in any cylinder raises questions of wear, although many engines will offer reasonable service up to 20% leakage. High performance demands, such as turbocharging, require 10% or less leak in any cylinder.

Compression Seal and Testing

For quick diagnosis, a compression gauge is very handy. I prefer a threaded hose gauge, which allows one-person operation. Clean the spark plug areas, then remove all of the spark plugs. Screw the gauge end into the #1 cylinder's spark plug threads. With the gauge secure, visible and lying away from rotating engine parts, open the throttle wide.

Consult your service guide for normal cranking compression readings. Crank the engine several revolutions, until the highest stable reading occurs. Record the reading. Repeat these steps for each cylinder.

If you get a low reading and want to pinpoint the problem with a compression gauge, squirt a tablespoon of oil in the spark plug hole for that cylinder and crank the engine again. If compression comes up to normal, you likely have an engine with defective piston rings. If no change occurs, valve or head gasket leakage is likely.

0012313

Fig. 8-75. A cylinder leakdown test of this freshly rebuilt engine reveals normal seal. A compression gauge reading is nowhere near as accurate. Leakdown tests foretell trouble long before a compression gauge.

Assessing Compression Readings

According to current guidelines, engine balance depends upon a maximum variance of 25% between the highest and lowest cylinder. I believe this is too great for satisfactory performance and fuel economy. Smooth operation, especially off-highway or when pulling a heavy trailer or load, demands better cylinder balance than this. A more traditional factor, 10% difference between the highest and lowest cylinder, still serves as my standard.

Higher compression readings mean carbon buildup. Excess carbon is very hard on the piston rings and valves. At its worst, carbon buildup contributes to deadly pre-ignition, the premature ignition of fuel by glowing material in the cylinders. Pre-ignition can break pistons and bend connecting rods.

Low compression readings indicate either worn rings, valve wear, a blown head gasket or cracked castings. Improper valve clearance also causes low readings. Although most service guidebooks list valve adjustment as a possible cure for low compression, this is very seldom the case.

After more than twenty-five years of exposure to engine repair and machine shop work, I find that running an engine with valves that do not seat completely will cause permanent damage to valve faces and seats. If valve clearances are so far out of adjustment that compression is low, damage has likely occurred already.

A valve adjustment cannot remove hard carbon buildup, pitting and burnout from valve faces and seats. For these problems, only a valve grind or cylinder head rebuild can restore performance. If adjusting valves does not restore compression, assume that the valves need repair.

Tight valve adjustment is a product of normal wear on engines without hydraulic valve lifters. As the valve faces wear into their seats, a process called valve seat recession occurs.

On all GM truck engines equipped with hydraulic lifters, valve clearance should remain stable between major overhauls. The lifters, set to proper clearance upon assembly of the engine, should be able to compensate for normal valve seat wear between engine rebuilds or valve grinding. At time of overhaul, the valves, lifters and pushrods on hydraulic lifter engines must be fitted to achieve proper plunger height/clearance within the hydraulic lifter.

> **NOTE —**
> On 1955–59 GMC/Pontiac V-8s, valve adjustment requires re-setting the rocker arm stud heights to achieve correct valve adjustment. When you grind the valves on any of the GM truck engines, always verify and re-set the valve clearance.

Unleaded Fuel and Valve Recession

Unleaded fuel aggravates valve recession, especially in engines designed during the leaded gas era. Older, more heavily leaded fuels lubricated the valve seats, faces and stems. For older leaded fuel era truck engines, the problems of unleaded gasoline and valve seat recession have a remedy. An automotive machine shop can retrofit hardened steel (replacement) exhaust valve seats into the head(s) of most OHV engines. Hardened exhaust valve seats will offset the effects of heat and reduce valve wear caused by the use of unleaded fuels.

The octane requirements for an engine are also crucial to the prevention of detonation (ping). Your GM truck owner's handbook describes octane requirements for your engine. Under current fuel standards, your older engine may need high test fuel to deliver top performance. If you must run your truck on 87–88 octane fuel, retard the timing a few degrees if harmful detonation occurs. Power may suffer some, but the engine will last longer.

Re-torque the Cylinder Head(s)

When you find a low compression reading, re-torquing cylinder head bolts may help remedy slight gasket seal or head warpage problems. (You will find the torque settings and sequence for tightening bolts in your GM truck shop manual or a professional-level service guidebook.) Re-check cranking compression when you finish. If compression is still low, suspect head or gasket damage—or other low compression related problems.

Since you are re-torquing a head that has already been in service, one pull at the full torque setting should be enough. I like to go through the sequence a second time, as bolts will often yield slightly.

If you remove a cylinder head for service and install a new gasket with proper sealant on both the gasket and freshly cleaned bolt threads, follow the three-step torque method: In sequence, 1) bring all bolts up to a snug setting, 2) advance to a firm setting just below final torque, and 3) finish with your final setting. Some gaskets require re-torquing after the engine warms.

You will find the two- or three-stage torque figures in your GM truck shop manual. If unavailable, they usually run as first stage: 2/3 of final torque; second stage: 5/6 of the final torque figure; third stage: final torque. Let the engine set for a while after final torque, then re-tighten again at the final torque setting. Always tighten bolts in the recommended sequence.

5. VALVE ADJUSTMENT

Once the head is re-torqued, you can adjust the valves on mechanical tappet engines. If the camshaft lobe profiles are normal, a valve adjustment of just a few thousandths of an inch will restore valve lift and valve opening points. Valve adjustment can reduce noise and improve engine performance.

> **NOTE —**
> The rare 1956–57 Blue Flame inline truck sixes are the only 235 engines that use hydraulic lifters. However, many of the passenger car 235s use hydraulic lifters. Since it has been common practice to retrofit passenger car engines into light truck chassis, make certain which type of lifters your 235 OHV inline six cylinder engine uses.

0014240

Fig. 8-76. Periodic valve adjustment decreases the chance of burning valves. Always re-torque the cylinder head and rocker shaft assembly support bolts/nuts (where applicable) before adjusting valves.

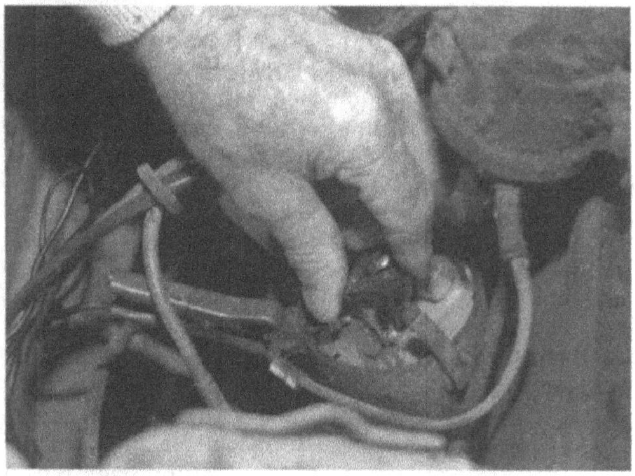

0014241

Fig. 8-77. On six cylinder engines, #1 and #6 cylinders both align with TDC. For this reason, you must look at the rotor and distributor cap alignment to see which cylinder is up to fire.

Normally, hydraulic lifters eliminate the need for a valve adjustment between engine overhauls. If your engine has noisy hydraulic lifters, suspect poor oiling, a defective lifter(s), improper valve clearances or a camshaft with worn lobes.

Chevrolet 216/235/261 and GMC 228 to 270 OHV Inline Sixes, GMC 305 V-6

Since these mechanical lifter Chevrolet and GMC engines each call for a hot valve adjustment, I prefer running the engine to check the valves. Optional methods will also work, even without the engine running. In either case, warm the engine completely before beginning—GM truck shop manuals recommend running the engine for at least thirty minutes.

The static method, or even the two- or three-crankshaft position method, requires that you shut off the engine and remove the spark plugs, then rotate the engine very slowly while following the cylinder firing order. (Watch the position of the ignition distributor's rotor as you bring each piston to top-dead-center or TDC.) Make sure each piston is at its firing point (TDC on the compression stroke) before setting the valve clearances on that cylinder's intake and exhaust valves. The process of hand cranking is slow, and by the time you approach the last cylinders, the engine has likely cooled down considerably.

I prefer a hot *running* set, despite the oily mess. Although also hard on tappet gauge blades, the results reflect your engine in its running mode, which is far more reliable than a static adjustment. The main advantages of hot adjustments are: 1) a better feel for valve action and lift under real operating conditions, and 2) an end to tedious hand rotation of the engine while you set the valves. This method is faster; however, you must guard your knuckles from bruising on moving parts. (Wearing work gloves makes sense here.)

With the engine warmed completely, my method involves slowing the idle speed to the minimum point that the engine will continue to run. This reduces oil spray and difficulty when handling the moving parts. If possible, shield the engine bay from oil spray.

0014242

Fig. 8-78. Special tools simplify valve adjustment. For the earlier Chevrolet/GMC inline OHV sixes, this Snap-On tool has been popular for decades. Later (1963–up) inline sixes have hydraulic lifters and V-8 type rocker arms.

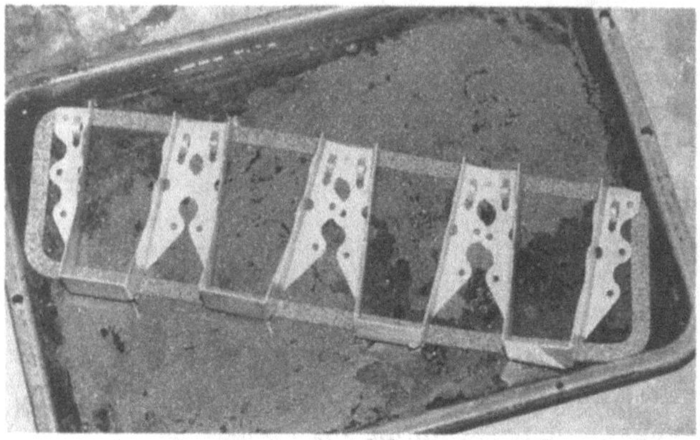

0012323

Fig. 8-79. Cork gaskets often shrink and distort in storage. To restore a side cover or valve cover gasket, soak in water until completely pliant.

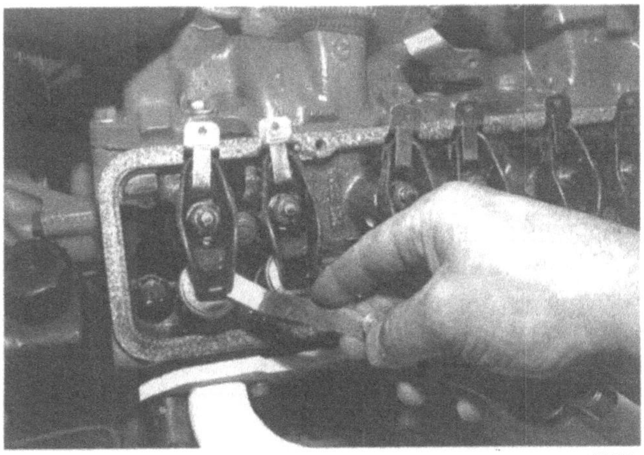

0014243

Fig. 8-80. Flat blade tappet gauges have various thicknesses. Check your service guide for correct gap thickness, and identify the intake and exhaust valve. Make certain the blade lays flat and squarely between the rocker arm end and valve stem tip. Although rougher on gauges, adjusting valves on a running engine produces highly accurate results.

0014244

Fig. 8-81. For static valve adjustment, follow the distributor rotor and firing order sequence. Watch rocker arm movement. If the piston is at or near TDC on its firing cycle, both valves will be completely closed. Here, valve clearance is at its widest point. The easiest way to identify intake and exhaust valves is by looking at the manifolds.

> WARNING —
> *Keep cloth and covers away from the hot exhaust manifolds, or a fire could erupt. Remove the valve cover carefully, without burning your fingers and hands.*

Shut off the engine, and check the cylinder head bolt and rocker shaft support bolt torque. Then, with your valve adjusting tools ready, start the engine.

Identify the intake valves by looking at the intake manifold ports. Check the intake tappet clearances by inserting the feeler gauge between each intake valve stem and its rocker arm.

Start the engine. While the engine ticks over slowly, lay the clean gauge flat and squarely between the valve stem tip and the rocker arm end. Correct settings will allow a very slight drag as you gently pull and push the feeler gauge. (You are actually feeling for the moment of widest tappet clearance.)

There is a point at which the gauge blade can slide freely. If you are uncertain what this feels like, loosen the self-locking rocker adjuster on 305 GMC V-6s or the lock nut and adjuster on early inline OHV sixes—very slightly. Slide the gauge in and out again.

Once you can feel where the gauge measures *clearance*, unaffected by the opening and closing movement of the valve, you can easily determine whether the setting is tight, loose or just right.

When right, the screw-and-lock nut adjusters require that you tighten the lock nut while holding the screw. You will find that by tightening the nut, the adjuster screw may move or pull up slightly in its threads.

This could be enough to distort the setting and require re-adjustment of the valve. If so, re-adjust the clearance, compensating for the distortion, and tighten the lock nut. Again check the clearance. When intake valves are all adjusted, move to the exhaust valves with your other tappet gauge.

On GMC 305 V-6 engines with self-locking adjusters, the job is faster and easier. For screw-and-lock nut adjusters, a valve adjusting tool is available that both secures the lock nut and provides a screw driver. (See Fig. 8-78)

Such tools were popular during the era of adjustable tappets and come in different nut sizes for various engine applications. Snap-On, K-D Tools, Eastwood Company or your local NAPA dealer are good sources for these kinds of specialty items. Blade tappet gauges are also available from these sources.

Valve Clearance Chart

Engine	Years	Valve Clearance (in.) Hot
Chevrolet 216/early 235 Inline six	1939–53	Intake: 0.006 Exhaust: 0.013
Chevrolet late 235 Inline six	1954–55 1956–62	Intake: 0.006 Exhaust: 0.016 Intake: 0.006 Exhaust: 0.018
Chevrolet 261 Inline six	1954–62	Intake: 0.006 Exhaust: 0.020
GMC 228/248/270 Inline six	1939–59	Intake: 0.012 Exhaust: 0.020
GMC 305 V-6	1960–69	Intake: 0.012 Exhaust: 0.018

> NOTE —
> All of these valve settings are for a fully warmed up engine, and they reflect Hot or H settings. Run engine to operating temperature to normalize the expansion of metal parts. These specifications will provide top performance with minimal engine noise.

Adjusting Hydraulic Lifters

In most cases, once the initial valve adjustment takes place, you should never need to re-adjust the hydraulic lifters on a Chevrolet light truck engine. Sometimes, however, service work (like changing lifters or pushrods) or a post-overhaul checkout may call for valve adjustment.

> ***CAUTION —***
> *Make sure that your 235 six (or any other Chevrolet engine) has hydraulic lifters before adjusting the valves to hydraulic lifter specifications. Severe engine damage (valve head interference with the piston crowns) will result if you adjust mechanical lifters to hydraulic lifter specifications. Most 235 Chevrolet truck sixes have mechanical lifters, and only the rarer 1956–57 Blue Flame version of the 235 uses hydraulic lifters. The 1956–57 Thriftmaster 235 and 261 truck sixes use mechanical lifters.*

I prefer a hot running setting. On V-8s, the Vortec 4.3L V-6 and 1963–up inline sixes, you will need oil clips to adjust the valves. The rocker arms oil through the hollow pushrods on these engines, and the volume and pressure of the oil is exceptional. Without clips (available from NAPA and other tool sources) and rags, the oil spray would quickly cover the engine bay and drain the crankcase of precious oil.

Consult your shop guide for valve clearance/lifter pre-load settings. You do not need a set of feeler gauges for setting hydraulic valve lifters, as the specification calls for zero lash plus a given amount of preload on the lifter plunger.

On early 235 Blue Flame sixes with hydraulic lifters, the setting is zero lash plus one-and-one-half (1-1/2) turns. Most Chevrolet engines with stamped rocker arms (V-8s, the Vortec V-6 and the 1963–up inline sixes) call for zero lash plus 3/4 or one full turn of the adjuster nut. On high speed engines or for high performance and racing purposes, many of us use zero lash plus 1/2 turn as a setting for hydraulic lifters on Chevrolet V-8s and the 1963–up sixes with stamped steel rocker arms.

Warm up the engine by driving for at least thirty minutes, then shut the engine off and remove the valve cover(s), taking extreme care not to burn your hands on the hot manifolds and other parts. Install the oil clips. Start the engine. Sequencing is unimportant. Pick a cylinder or cylinder bank and begin with the first valve.

On early (pre-1963) 235 Blue Flame sixes, loosen the adjuster lock nut. On all engines, back off the adjuster screw or adjuster nut slowly until you can hear the tappet clearance. This noise is very distinctive, and by backing off the adjuster just a bit further, you will quickly be able to distinguish the sound.

Turn the adjuster screw slowly, just to the point that the tappet noise stops. This is zero lash. Now you can set the pre-load amount recommended in your shop manual.

When adjusting the valves with a running engine, never turn the adjuster quickly. I like to use 1/8 to 1/4 turn at a time, listening for the engine to roughen up then completely stabilize before turning the adjuster screw or nut further. Count turns carefully to assure correct setting.

TUNE-UP SPECIFICATIONS FOR MY GM TRUCK ENGINE

IDLE SPEED: ______________________

INITIAL (LOW SPEED OR IDLE) SPARK TIMING @ ________RPM:________-DEGREES

HIGHER SPEED (2500 CRANKSHAFT RPM) SPARK TIMING__________-DEGREES

CARBURETOR IDLE MIXTURE ADJUSTMENT PROCEDURE (IF ADJUSTABLE):

____

AIR FILTER PART NUMBER______________

FUEL FILTER(S) PART NUMBER____________

SPARK PLUG TYPE AND NUMBER__________

BREAKER POINT OR MODULE PART NUMBER __________

BREAKER POINT GAP OR MODULE AIR GAP SETTING______________

BREAKER POINT DWELL ANGLE__________

DISTRIBUTOR CAP PART NUMBER __________

Fig. 8-82. Sample of a quick reference chart for tuning your truck engine. Keep a copy of these specifications with your on-board tool kit or in your glovebox.

> ***CAUTION —***
> *Especially with a high lift or racing camshaft, rotating the hydraulic lifter adjuster nut or screw quickly can unseat the valve too far and cause the valve to interfere with the moving piston.*

When you attain the precise turn(s) specified, secure the lock nut on 235 sixes while holding the adjuster screw still. (Stamped rocker arms use self-locking adjuster nuts that do not require a lock nut.) You can now proceed to the next valve and repeat the procedure.

6. Emission Controls

Since the 1960s, all manufactured motor vehicles must comply with federal and state tailpipe emission standards. GM light truck engines have required factory installed emission control devices, designed to combat air pollution. Some emission control devices help the engine achieve more complete combustion, while others work directly at reducing tailpipe pollutants.

Emission control components vary, depending upon the model year and requirements. Your truck's emission control package may include the ignition spark timing, the carburetor or EFI and a series of devices to reduce three major exhaust pollutants: 1) the poisonous gas, carbon monoxide (CO); 2) raw, unburned hydrocarbons

0014265

Fig. 8-83. When performing emissions control service, inspect the vacuum hoses. A principal energy source for emission control switches is vacuum. Hose routing and quality are critical to peak performance. Leaks reduce performance and create tune-up problems.

0014268

Fig. 8-84. Inspect the warm air vacuum motor (arrow) on the thermal air cleaner. Make certain this device works properly. If the flexible heat tube shows evidence of leakage or poor fitup, replace tube.

(HC); and 3) oxides of nitrogen (NOx), the building block of visible smog.

Many engine emission controls focus on peak performance, fuel efficiency and longer engine life. The care and maintenance of these devices remains an important part of servicing your truck. Even tuning your engine requires a working knowledge of emission control components, as the idle, acceleration, gas mileage and overall performance depend upon a fully operational emission control system.

Emission Control Basics and Service

In the early 1960s, U.S. vehicle manufacturers began installing Positive Crankcase Ventilation (PCV) systems on engines to comply with California emissions requirements. (GM offered retrofit PCV kits for trucks a decade earlier.) The simple concept aimed at purging the engine crankcase of combustion blow-by and fumes.

Prior to 1961, most engines vented blow-by to the atmosphere through a road draft tube. These devices were simply open pipes with their tips cut on an angle toward the rear of the vehicle.

0014273

Fig. 8-85. The modern carburetor is plumbed for emission devices. Several vacuum sources (manifold or ported) may be built into an OEM carburetor.

The road draft tube relies on low pressure vacuum, created as the vehicle moves forward, to purge the crankcase. Primitive and inefficient, an engine with a road draft tube pollutes the environment and permits condensation and corrosive agents to build sludge in the crankcase.

The modern PCV system allows manifold vacuum, regulated by a spring-balanced valve, to draw crankcase blow-by back through the intake manifold. This closed crankcase system continuously removes and recycles harmful combustion by-products. A PCV valve and closed crankcase contribute to better performance and longer engine life.

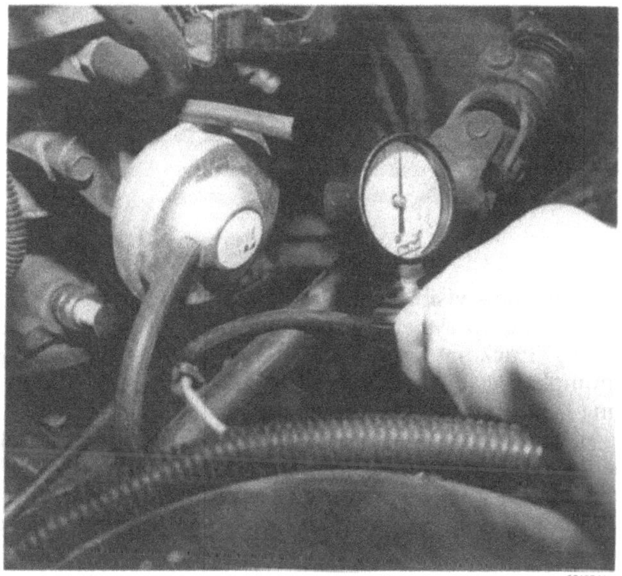

0012341

Fig. 8-86. A very popular tool with emission control specialists is the hand vacuum pump and pressure tester. Use the tester to check EGR valves, vacuum diaphragms, vacuum hose circuits and thermal vacuum switches.

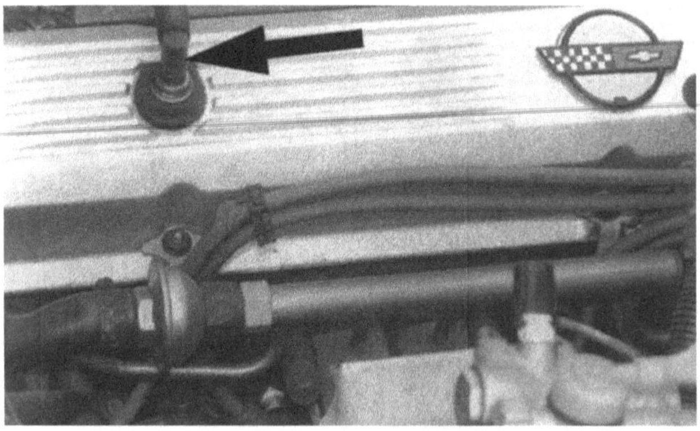

0014266

Fig. 8-87. The simple PCV valve on your truck's engine contributes to engine longevity by actively fighting sludge and the formation of crankcase condensation. Additionally, a closed crankcase prevents water from entering the engine during stream fording. Change the PCV valve with each spark plug replacement (30,000 miles maximum for late engines). On some engines, the spark plug and PCV change interval is 12,000 miles. Also make sure that hoses and grommets seal properly.

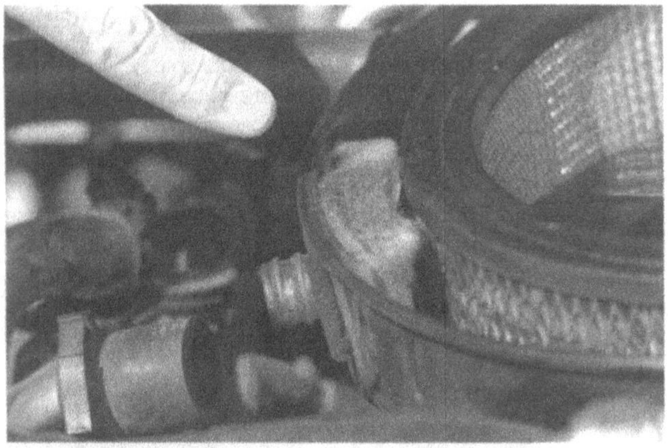

0014463

Fig. 8-88. This clean-air filter lies just inside the air cleaner canister on most closed crankcase engines. Manifold vacuum through the PCV valve creates low pressure in the crankcase. Clean air enters the engine from the filter. Without an adequate source of fresh air through the breather filter, PCV vacuum could damage engine seals and gaskets.

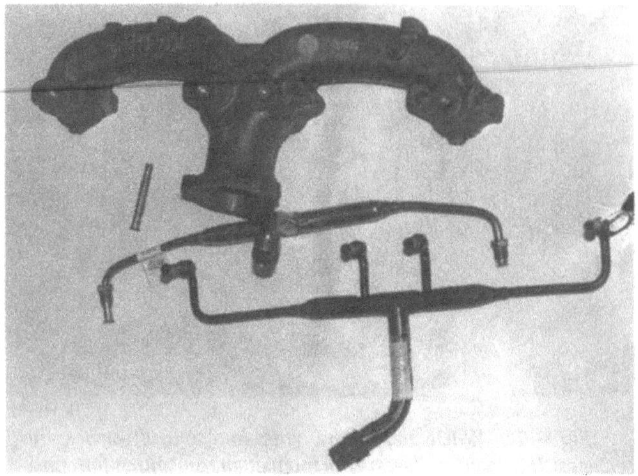

0014252

Fig. 8-89. Distribution tubes direct clean air into the exhaust manifold(s) or the cylinder head exhaust ports. GM light truck emission control systems are very typical and resemble passenger car designs.

0014251

Fig. 8-90. One-way or anti-backfire check valves prevent hot exhaust from reaching the air injection pump and hoses. Dangerously charred hoses and a burned pump can result from a defective check valve.

Air Injection System

The most visible emission control device is the air injection pump system. Found as original equipment on many truck engines since the mid-1960s, the smog pump's ungainly physical features and maze of plumbing have attracted unwarranted criticism.

Air injection is an external emission control. It has no effect on either the fuel/induction or ignition system and creates a negligible amount of exhaust back pressure. Although the engine drives this pump, power loss is less than one-half horsepower—hardly noticed by a V-8 or six cylinder truck engine. Since the air injection system is relatively passive, removal of the pump system does not improve performance.

The principle of air injection is simple: Inject oxygen into the exhaust stream near the engine exhaust ports and/or directly into a catalytic converter. Given this fresh source of oxygen, the combustion of unburned hot hydrocarbons and carbon monoxide can continue.

Your truck engine's air injection system requires little maintenance. Pump bearings are permanently lubricated and the drive belt seldom requires adjustment. The rest of the air injection system consists of a diverter/bypass valve, anti-backfire check valves, and manifold or cylinder head distribution tubes.

Air Bypass Systems

The diverter or bypass valve receives a high manifold vacuum signal during engine deceleration, as carburetor venturi effect causes an over-rich fuel mixture. The valve opens, allowing pump air to vent into the atmosphere. Without a diverter valve, air pumped into rich, unburned exhaust stream gases would cause spontaneous combustion. The exhaust system could be severely damaged.

Fig. 8-91. The air pump drive belt requires periodic adjustment and replacement. Relatively light load of this device assures long belt life. Tampering with the air injection pump system can prevent cool air from reaching the exhaust valves, manifolds and air injection tubes. Heat damage to your truck's engine will result. Maintain your air injection system.

Fig. 8-92. The diverter/bypass valve directs air away from the exhaust stream during deceleration. This pollution control device prevents an over-rich mixture of unburned fuel from igniting and damaging the exhaust system.

Additionally, the engine's exhaust valves, manifold(s) and even the air injection tubes rely on pump air for cooling. When an air injection system is defective, or a mechanic disables the engine's emission devices, melted injection tubes, damage to exhaust valves or a cracked manifold often result.

Fig. 8-93. Examine the rubber air injection hoses for signs of charring. Check the vacuum line to the diverter. On a fully warmed engine, snap the throttle open and shut and observe whether air exits the bypass/diverter valve under deceleration. If the valve functions properly, air should bypass.

Exhaust Gas Recirculation

Lean fuel mixtures reduce CO and HC emissions. These lean fuel mixtures, however, also increase combustion temperatures and raise NOx emissions. In the early 1970s, engineers applied a simple, effective means for lowering combustion temperatures: recycle the exhaust gases.

Recirculating exhaust through the intake stream dilutes fresh fuel mixtures yet has little effect on the air/fuel ratio. These cooler combustion temperatures also enhance performance.

The exhaust gas recirculation (EGR) system permits the use of leaner air/fuel ratios without compromising cylinder temperatures. EGR valves serve a useful function on any engine that runs low octane fuel, requires a mild spark advance curve or operates with lean air/fuel mixtures.

Unfortunately, ill-informed mechanics see the EGR as a source of trouble or a horsepower thief. This false reasoning overlooks the EGR system's ability to lower scorching combustion temperatures (which run as high as 4800° F

Fig. 8-94. An EGR valve can lower upper cylinder temperatures by as much as 2000° F! Lower temperatures reduce oxides of nitrogen (NOx) emissions, the key component in visible smog. The EGR valve, effective from off-idle through cruise rpm, typically operates via a ported vacuum source.

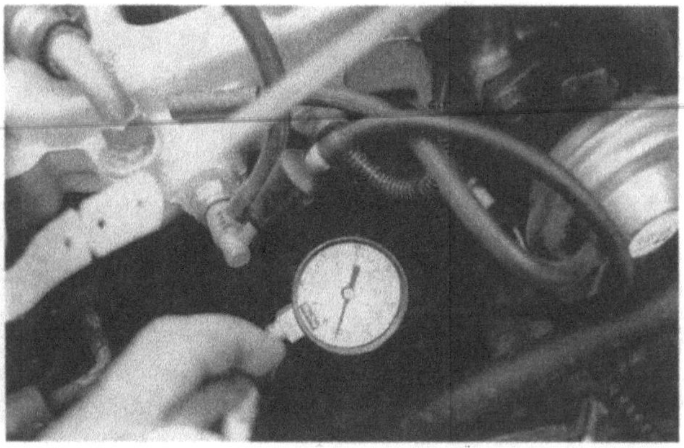

0012333

Fig. 8-95. EGR valve inspection is simple. Attach a vacuum pump to the valve. With the engine idling, unseat the valve by applying vacuum. Idle should get rough, often enough to stall the engine. Watch the gauge to be certain the EGR valve diaphragm holds vacuum.

without an EGR system) to below 2500°. Operating properly, the EGR system eliminates most detonation or ping. If, after tossing the EGR valve in the dumpster, your truck's engine now suffers severe ping, look here for the problem.

Catalytic Converter

Another anti-pollution device, found on many light truck engines since 1975, is the catalytic converter. Simply a muffler-like device, the converter operates a small chemical processing plant in your exhaust system.

Oxidizing catalysts (usually platinum and palladium) in the converter react with carbon monoxide and hydrocarbons. The by-products of this catalyzing process are harmless carbon dioxide and water. Reducing catalysts also take the oxygen out of NOx, leaving harmless free nitrogen to pass out the tailpipe.

Although the catalytic converter emits sulfuric acid and an annoying rotten egg smell during rich fuel conditions, the only cost in performance is exhaust system back pressure. Aftermarket high performance catalytic converters are now available to reduce this back pressure.

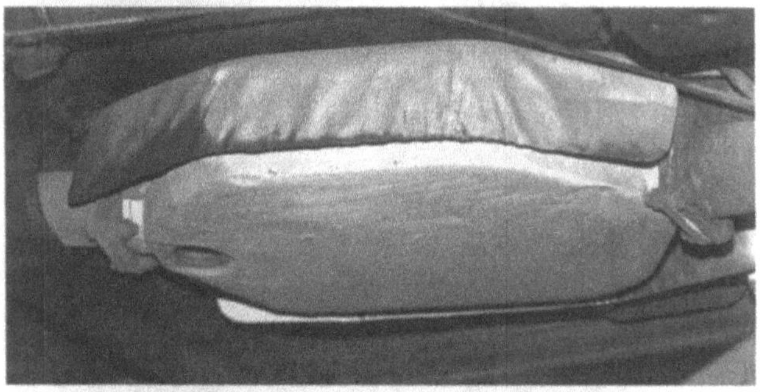

0014248

Fig. 8-96. Catalytic converters resemble a muffler. These small chemical processing plants reduce carbon monoxide, hydrocarbon and oxides of nitrogen. Consider the very high temperatures generated by a catalytic converter. Avoid touching the converter during service work, and never park your truck in tall, dry brush.

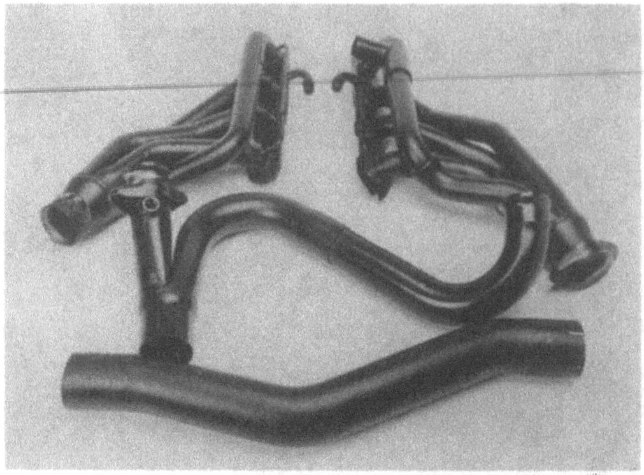

0014254

Fig. 8-97. An emission-legal aftermarket high performance exhaust system, like Edelbrock's big-block truck kit, can reduce back pressure. Do your share for clean air, even if high performance is your goal. Be sure your exhaust system complies with federal and state emission regulations.

Cold-start and Warm-up Devices

All gasoline engines require cold-start systems. A carburetor's choke or an EFI engine's cold start enrichment cycle must meet both cold start-up and emission control needs.

For low tailpipe emissions, the choke should open as quickly as the engine can accept leaner air/fuel mixtures. To accomplish this, a number of devices come into play. The air cleaner assembly doubles as the thermal air system to direct heated air from the outside surface of the exhaust manifold into the intake inlet of the air cleaner.

Light truck engine chokes come in a variety of shapes and sizes. Early GM truck models rely on manual, cable controlled choke valves. Later carbureted engines feature either a bi-metallic spring (engine heated) type or electric automatic choke.

Observe choke operation and timing. Spray all carburetor linkages with a quality cleaner. Clean the choke valve, choke housing and vacuum piston if there is any evidence of choke stickiness. The choke should move freely when unloaded.

Fuel injected (EFI) engines benefit from a computer controlled cold start enrichment system that maintains precise air/fuel ratios and driveability during the entire engine warm-up cycle.

Additionally, many carburetors rely on a vacuum signaled choke pull-off to allow quicker vehicle operation during warm-up. The choke pull-off or brake unit consists of a vacuum diaphragm and choke release linkage operated by either manifold vacuum or ported vacuum.

On many emission engines, a thermal air cleaner (TAC) provides a vacuum-actuated warm air valve. The vacuum motor receives signals from a thermal vacuum switch and/or bi-metallic valve. The motor opens and closes the warm air door at the air cleaner intake.

When the engine warms sufficiently, the vacuum motor closes the warm air door, permitting cooler, fresh air to enter the air cleaner. Your engine's thermal air cleaner allows quicker choke opening and better driveability.

0014255

Fig. 8-98. *The conventional manual or automatic choke must open quickly to maintain low tailpipe emissions. Adjust your truck engine's choke for driveability and lower pollution levels. (For proper settings, see your truck's underhood emission decal, the GM truck shop manual or a professional service guide.) Make sure vacuum pull-off/brake works properly.*

0014256

Fig. 8-99. *Some automatic chokes operate as manifold heat reaches a bi-metallic coil spring. Others open via a heated electrical coil, activated as the ignition circuit opens. Signals from engine coolant temperature open some chokes.*

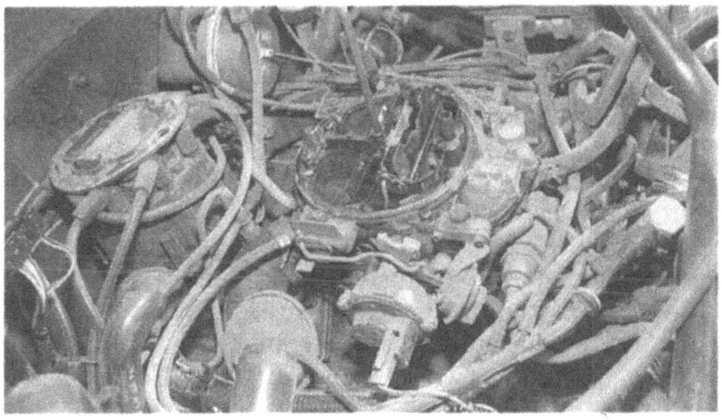

0014202

Fig. 8-100. *Many chokes open electrically, including this GM Rochester Quadrajet unit on a GM 350 V-8. Check the current flow to the choke unit with a voltmeter. Chokes quickly become too hot to touch. Take care not to burn your fingers.*

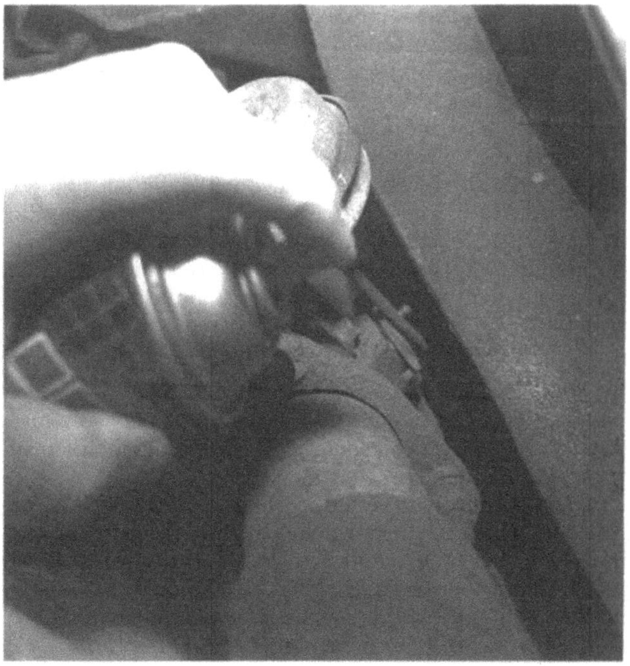

0014269

Fig. 8-101. *The heat riser valve plays an important role during engine warm-up and choke operation. A heat riser stuck shut creates severe back pressure and reduces engine power. A heat riser stuck open causes the choke to stay on too long, affecting performance and fuel economy.*

0014258

Fig. 8-102. *Heat risers can have one of several power sources. One style is this vacuum operated type, which uses engine coolant temperature as a signal and a TVS to apply vacuum. For earlier GM truck engines, a bi-metallic spring expands and opens with engine heat.*

Exhaust Heat Riser

The heat riser, usually eliminated with the installation of aftermarket exhaust headers, also serves a vital function. During cold start-up, the riser valve stays closed, redirecting hot exhaust through a passage in the intake manifold of V-type engines or to the base of the intake manifold on an inline engine. This heated section of the manifold sometimes houses a stove well for the choke.

This heat warms the area under the carburetor, permitting better atomization of fuel and more thorough combustion. It is important that the manifold heat passage remain clear. Often, especially on V-type engines, the passage clogs as carbon builds up.

Some riser valves open with a vacuum diaphragm and motor, while others rely on a heated bi-metallic spring.

To service the heat riser, on a cold engine, spray the heat riser valve with a suitable penetrant and oil. Make certain that the valve moves freely and the bimetallic spring or vacuum diaphragm is intact and functional.

Switches, Valves and Vacuum Controls

Your truck engine's emission control devices must know when to work and usually require energy to work. A variety of electrical and vacuum switches help meet those requirements.

The ignition switch often serves as the trigger for a fuel shut-off solenoid. Other switches, such as the thermal vacuum switch (TVS), control vacuum to the distributor spark advance or an EGR valve. Most TVS switches rely on the engine coolant temperature to expand an enclosed wax pellet, which opens one or more vacuum ports.

GM trucks popularized the use of TCS (Transmission Controlled Spark). In the early years of federal emission requirements, these devices would prevent the distributor's vacuum spark advance from operating while the transmission operated in lower gears. This pollution control measure, which essentially held back the spark timing, also lowered vehicle performance substantially.

On your truck's engine, vacuum serves as a very powerful and economical source of energy. Vacuum switches, valves and motors, like those that open and close the thermal air cleaner intake flap, can serve quickly and efficiently.

Vacuum- or electrically operated throttle positioners serve a variety of roles. Some raise the idle speed to compensate for extra loads like the air conditioner. Others serve as a dashpot, relying on a spring and resistance diaphragm to slow the throttle return. On carbureted engines, a dashpot helps reduce over-rich fuel flow (venturi effect) during deceleration.

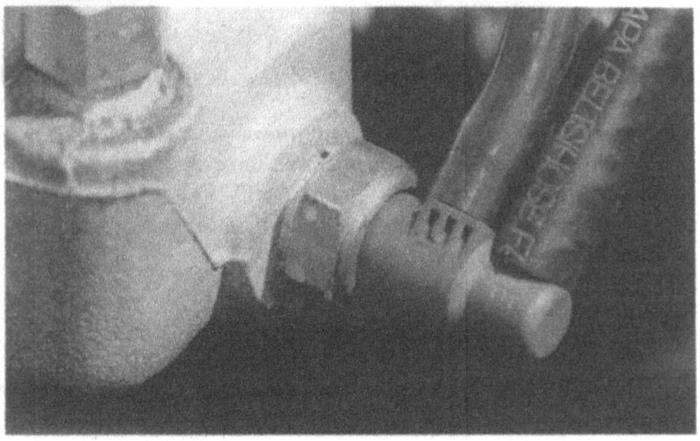

0012348

Fig. 8-103. *Thermal vacuum switches (TVS) are useful. On many truck engines, they activate the thermal air cleaner or EGR valve. At a preset temperature, the valve opens ports, directing vacuum to devices. Check your engine's vacuum circuit diagram to determine the role of the TVS switch.*

0014259

Fig. 8-104. *Vacuum powers a number of engine devices. Some emission carburetor designs rely on a vacuum-actuated throttle positioner. Vacuum provides ignition spark advance on all pre-emission era GM engines and many emissions era engines as well. Emission service always includes inspection of vacuum hose circuits. Shown is a 1957-74 era window cap distributor with vacuum advance*

Fuel Tank and Carburetor Fumes

The raw fumes from gasoline are another source of air pollution. To contain these vapors, light trucks have incorporated evaporative emission control devices since the early 1970s. Although storage methods vary, vacuum helps capture float bowl, crankcase and fuel tank fumes, eventually recycling them through the engine's intake system.

When servicing or repairing your truck's fuel system, you must route vacuum and ventilation hoses very carefully. Follow a factory or professional-level guide for your model.

Inspect the evaporative canister and hoses. If the canister smells heavily like gasoline or feels weighted with liquid, safely drain the gas and replace the canister with a new unit. Evaporative canisters have check valves and require careful routing of hoses to the carburetor or EFI unit, the vacuum source and fuel tank.

WARNING —
Gasoline fumes are highly volatile. Use extreme caution when working with the evaporative emission control system. All parts must fit according to design, including the gasoline cap.

0014272

Fig. 8-105. Evaporative emission controls include a vapor canister. Typically, the replaceable canister is plastic with a granulated carbon element inside. The fuel tank, carburetor vent and other vapor sources each feed the evaporative emission system. Correct hose routing is critical to performance.

Conversion Engines and Emissions

Many earlier GM trucks have conversion engines. The low horsepower output of early six-cylinder engines has encouraged swapping to larger, more powerful powerplants. Since the late 1950s, a number of manufacturers have produced parts for engine and transmission swaps into the early GM light truck chassis.

Engine conversions come under Federal emission control compliance laws and statutes in many states. Whether your truck now has a conversion engine or you plan such a change, be certain of emission control laws. (You will find further information on engine conversions and emission control compliance in the performance chapters of the book.)

0014261

Fig. 8-106. OHV V-8 transplants into an early truck chassis became a popular practice in the 1960s. An entire industry developed around improving the performance of light trucks. (See Chapter 16, GM Engine Performance for further details.)

Passing an Emission Test

Although California has the strictest motor vehicle pollution laws in the United States, many vehicles that fail California's smog tests have sufficiently low tailpipe emissions. They fail the visual inspection part of the test.

During the visual inspection, before the engine has a chance to show how cleanly it burns, the inspector takes a close look at the emission control system and vehicle chassis. Any missing/modified parts are cause for failure.

This is a tough test. All vacuum hoses, flexible heat tubes, the smog pump drive belt, vacuum switches, the EGR valve (if required) and closed crankcase devices must be intact and function properly. The inspector, using a detailed manual and the emission decal found under your truck's hood, checks your engine and chassis equipment against the OEM requirements.

The vehicle can fail visual inspection for something as simple as a missing two-dollar section of aluminum flex hose at the thermal air cleaner. Although many aftermarket performance parts immediately fail the visual test, some pieces comply with California Air Resources Board standards.

0014262

Fig. 8-107. The underhood emission and tune-up decal is important. It describes the standards for tuning your truck's engine and also the emission control package assigned to the vehicle. The decal often describes smog devices and vacuum hose circuits.

Approved aftermarket parts bear a special number (E.O. Number) allowing your truck to be inspected at a regular California smog station. Such products even include retrofit superchargers like the Vortec, Whipple/Sprintex, Weiand and Paxton units designed for certain GM light truck V-8s.

Increasing numbers of aftermarket high performance engine components, including intake manifolds and a number of ignition devices and exhaust pieces, also meet CARB standards. (Lists of these devices are available from the California Department of Consumer Affairs, Bureau of Automotive Repairs.)

NOTE —
Aftermarket components described as "not legal for use on California highways," hold a good chance of getting your engine an F on the smog inspection test. California has essentially become a model for Federal and 49-State emission control policy.

The cold-start circuit is among the many items considered during the visual inspection. Although this system operates for only minutes during the warm-up cycle, every component is essential.

A hand choke retrofit kit to replace an automatic choke, a missing vacuum hose and a discarded thermal air cleaner are each causes for failure. Even raising the air cleaner bonnet with a thicker filter element results in an F, as the open canister compromises both the cold-start and closed crankcase systems.

Well tuned and running properly, your engine will meet hydrocarbon, carbon monoxide and NOx standards at both an idle and the currently required 2500 rpm. Bonafide defects, such as vacuum leaks, carburetor flooding, bad ignition cables, fouled spark plugs or a defective EGR valve, will result in a tailpipe test failure. Ignition timing must match OEM specifications for the engine.

When a California Smog Chek inspector suspects that the wrong engine is in a chassis, he or she may examine the block and/or cylinder head casting numbers. If your engine is not original for the truck, you'll receive a noncompliance certificate and referral to a referee.

0012331

Fig. 8-108. *Many 1975 and newer U.S.-sold light trucks require unleaded gasoline. Note that this truck's fuel filler neck has a restrictor. In California and other states, smog inspection includes a look at fuel filler.*

0014166

Fig. 8-109. *By California and U.S. EPA standards, this engine, despite a closed crankcase, EGR valve, enhanced ignition and precise tuning, is not legal. Handsome aftermarket chrome air cleaner, without a thermal air system, would immediately fail visual smog inspection.*

0014263

Fig. 8-110. *Use of this Edelbrock Performer intake manifold is acceptable. The dual-plane design, provision for an EGR valve and no increase in tailpipe emissions help determine emissions law compliance.*

The referee station identifies the engine by casting or serial numbers, determining the age and OEM emission requirements for both the engine and the chassis. (You may need sales documentation for the engine.)

The referee compiles a list of necessary emission control devices for both your truck's chassis and the conversion engine. A visual engine and chassis inspection confirms whether the needed devices are in place. If not, the referee recommends which devices will bring your truck into compliance.

After meeting compliance, the vehicle receives a certification tag noting the required emission control devices. Currently, this enables the owner to take the truck to any Smog Chek station for either a biennial or change of ownership inspection. If the truck complies, you only need to see the referee once.

For emission compliance by California legal criteria, your engine must fit a given range of years (be the same year or newer than your truck's chassis), and meet either OEM or state-approved aftermarket parts requirements. The chassis requires such original equipment as the catalytic converter(s) and the gas tank unleaded fuel restrictor if so equipped.

Lastly, your engine must meet specific tailpipe emission standards—equal to or better than the truck's original engine in good operating condition.

Exhaust System

A truck's exhaust system is subject to severe abuse. Off-highway debris, harsh climates, corrosion, freezing, scorching temperature extremes and a variety of other hazards impact your truck's exhaust system. Aside from emission related components, like the catalytic converter, the system has several other replaceable components.

The exhaust system begins at the exhaust manifold flange and heat riser (if so equipped). The exhaust pipe leads from the manifold to either the catalytic converter or a muffler. If your truck requires a catalytic converter, a pipe exits the converter and connects to the muffler. After the muffler, a tailpipe continues to the rear of the truck.

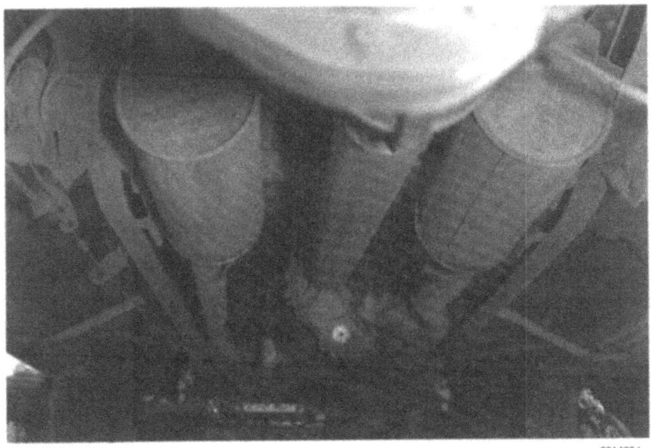

Fig. 8-111. Dual exhaust system conversions for V-8 engines help reduce back pressure. Better economy and performance result. A correct installation has tailpipes exiting at the rear of the truck, just like original equipment system. Keep exhaust fumes away from the cab and bed areas. Check state and federal requirements before converting to dual exhausts on catalytic systems. Shown is the legal, factory-installed dual exhaust system on my 1986 Suburban. The truck has a 49-state, over 8500-lb. GVWR chassis, the last non-catalyst GM light truck model.

NOTE —
Pre-1975 trucks have no catalytic converter. Some light trucks through the mid-1980s have no required cat system, either. These cat exempted trucks have heavier chassis ratings. You can determine this requirement by looking at the underhood decal for the terms CAT, catalyst or catalytic converter.

The majority of GM light trucks use a single exhaust system. V-type engines use a Y-shaped exhaust pipe that leads to the catalytic converter or muffler. These single exhaust systems restrict the flow of gases on V-type engines, and many owners of V-8 powered trucks have converted their exhaust systems to dual exhaust.

The obstacle to a dual exhaust conversion is legality. Interpretation of the 1990 Federal Clean Air Act has varied. One view states that if your cat-controlled truck has a single exhaust system, you cannot convert to dual exhaust—period. Under this judgement, no muffler shop can install a two-cat, dual exhaust system on a single exhaust equipped truck. If the truck were converted before the 1990 revision of the act (and receipts are available to prove this fact) a shop can service and repair the two-cat, dual exhaust system.

If your state requires visual inspection of the emission control system, discuss the dual exhaust option with an emission control inspector or contact the state bureau. When periodic inspection is necessary, make sure your new system is smog legal as well as functional.

Always replace any worn or damaged exhaust parts. Your exhaust system inspection should take place with each lube job. Especially on short wheelbase models or those equipped with a bed cap or camper unit, a leak-proof system is a must. Backflow of exhaust and seeping fumes present a health hazard to vehicle occupants.

By design, light truck tailpipes have always exited to the rear of the truck, as it allows fumes to flow away from the truck's body. Some owners, however, choose to shorten their exhaust systems, thinking that less length will improve performance. Such pipes usually exit just forward of the rear wheels. This is a significant health hazard, as exhaust fumes roll upward from the sides of the truck and into the cab, especially on shorter wheelbase models.

If a muffler shop suggests short dual exhaust pipes that exit out the truck's sides, insist that the tailpipes continue to the rear of the truck. An experienced muffler technician can bend and twist pipes to fit the contours of your truck's chassis. Dual tailpipes can always exit the rear of the truck—even if both pipes must fit along the same side of the chassis.

Chapter 9

Clutch and Transmission Service

CLUTCH AND TRANSMISSION PROBLEMS are sometimes difficult to separate. The high cost of a clutch replacement or transmission overhaul makes diagnosis very important. Transmission wear is often mistaken for a bad clutch and vice versa. As troubleshooting skill is the best mechanical resource you can muster, I'd like to help you understand various clutch and transmission problems.

Troubles first appear as driving quirks. As an accurate troubleshooter, you must isolate each symptom and determine its cause.

1. CLUTCH AND TRANSMISSION TROUBLESHOOTING

WARNING —
The clutch disc may contain asbestos fibers. Asbestos materials can cause asbestosis. Always wear an approved respirator and protective clothing when handling components containing asbestos. Do not use compressed air, do not grind, heat, weld or sand on or near any asbestos materials. Only approved cleaning methods should be used to service the clutch disc or areas containing asbestos dust or asbestos fibers.

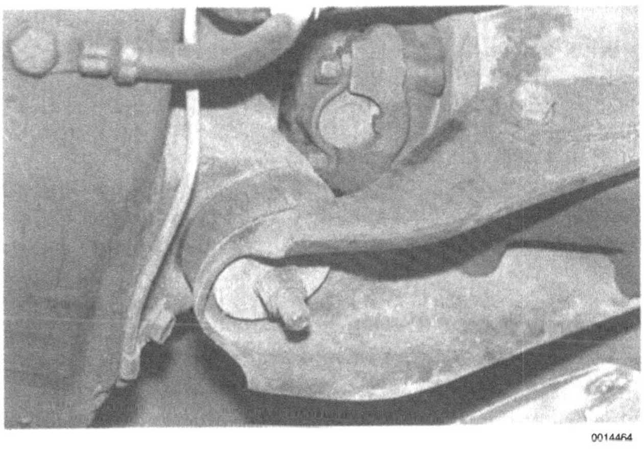

Fig. 9-1. *Engine mounts and transmission mounts can create clutch chatter symptoms, especially on suspended pedal models with mechanical clutch linkage. Inspect all mounts before condemning your clutch assembly.*

Clutch Chatter

You release the clutch pedal, and the powertrain shudders, sometimes violently, as clutch engagement begins. If the problem has developed suddenly, especially after an unusually hard day of trailer pulling or pounding a rocky trail, examine the engine mounts and, on 4x4 models, the transmission/transfer case mount. (On some models, a torque arm helps limit transfer case torque twist. Check this bracket along with the mounts.)

If none of these points appear troubled, look to the clutch unit. Disc wear, clutch damage or oil on the disc are common causes of chatter. Especially with 4x4 trucks operated at odd angles, an engine oil leak from the rear main seal or pan gasket can find its way into the clutch assembly and saturate the disc.

An attempt to burn off the oil by riding the clutch to generate friction is a waste of time and could prove dangerous. Clutches can explode under extreme stress or

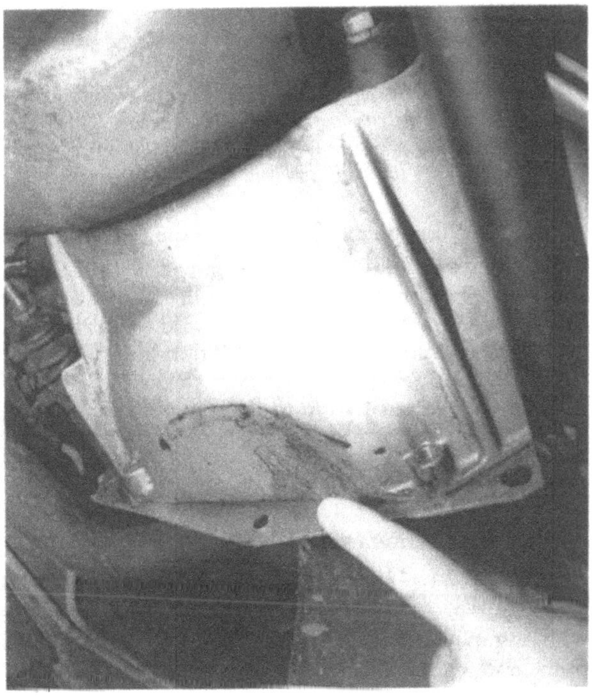

Fig. 9-2. *An engine oil leak at the rear main seal or pan gaskets can cause clutch damage. Oil saturates the clutch disc and causes chatter, slippage and failure. The only cure is clutch replacement.*

from overrevving. There's no sure way to clean the disc in the truck, either. If oil has entered the clutch housing and soaked the disc thoroughly, the disc is ruined.

Another source of oil on the clutch is from the transmission. The front bearing retainer seal is responsible for keeping oil within the gearcase. These seals wear, and on rare occasions, the retainer may crack or leak around its sealing gasket(s). Gear oil, acidic and tenacious, has a devastating effect on a clutch disc.

A common cause of clutch chatter is a distorted clutch cover or broken springs. Excess heat and overworking the clutch can warp a clutch cover. Springs break from fatigue or abuse. Heat also weakens springs, making them exert uneven force. Simply put, clutch chatter results from uneven application of pressure. Loose clutch cover bolts, broken torsional springs in the disk hub or a warped disc will cause chatter.

0012355

Fig. 9-3. *As the clutch disc wears thin, clamping force decreases. (The clutch cover springs compress less, which reduces their apply pressure.) This is why a high mileage clutch cannot deliver the same performance as a new assembly.*

Clutch slippage symptoms are obvious. In gear, the engine revs up, yet the truck does not accelerate. Slippage and chatter often have common causes. In either case, clutch cover apply pressure cannot hold the disc firmly

Slippage results from oil saturation of the disc or extreme wear of either the friction disc or clutch cover springs. The faintest sound of rivets grating on the flywheel face or pressure plate is a sure sign of major wear. Replace the clutch assembly immediately before the flywheel is irreparably damaged.

Unwanted Clutch Noises

Truck owners become accustomed to particular powertrain and geartrain noises, those rhythms and pitches of whirring machinery that accompany us on long interstate pulls and dusty trails. An abnormal sound from the clutch area immediately draws attention.

A defective clutch sends a clear message. A warped or severely worn disc will grate or transmit a metallic sound as the disc engages. Broken torsional springs around the disc hub also transmit noise. The more common clutch region noises, however, are bearing defects.

0012356

Fig. 9-4. *There are three types of pilot bearings and bushings available for various GM truck applications: the solid bronze bushing, a needle bearing assembly and a caged, permanently lubricated ball bearing. In some cases, you will have a choice of designs. Needle and ball bearings offer less friction, while bronze bushings have a reputation for long, trouble-free service.*

The pilot bearing supports the forward end of the transmission input shaft. Pressed into the center bore of the crankshaft flange, the pilot bearing allows the clutch or input gear to rotate independently of the crankshaft during clutch disengagement. GM trucks have used needle and caged ball-type pilot bearings and also bronze bushings. While some pilot bearings have permanently sealed cases, others require lubrication during installation.

> ***CAUTION —***
> *A needle or ball bearing should never be used with an input gear designed for a bronze bushing. Heat treatment of gears differ, and needle bearings will damage a shaft end designed for use with a bronze bushing.*

The pilot bearing or bushing should only need service during clutch replacement. A dry pilot bearing, however, is common to trucks that perform "submarine duty." Running in surf or stream crossings and other water traps can wash grease from the pilot bearing. Dry, the bearing wears quickly and sets up a howling noise distinct from any other. With the clutch disengaged and the transmission in a gear, pilot noise is obvious.

Loss of lubricant can cause the pilot bearing to seize on the clutch/input gear nose end. This mimics symptoms of a clutch disc and pressure plate that won't disengage properly.

On rare occasions, debris from a backwoods trail enters the clutch housing. Protective plates, tinware and a rubber clutch fork boot should prevent this from happening, but in extreme cases, gravel or other abrasive material seeps through and becomes embedded or trapped in the clutch disc. The symptoms are chatter, clutch slippage and metallic grating. (Twigs or rocks make a raking or rattling sound against the spinning faces of the flywheel or clutch pressure plate.)

A time-honored clutch noise is the worn release or throwout bearing. These bearings often fail before the

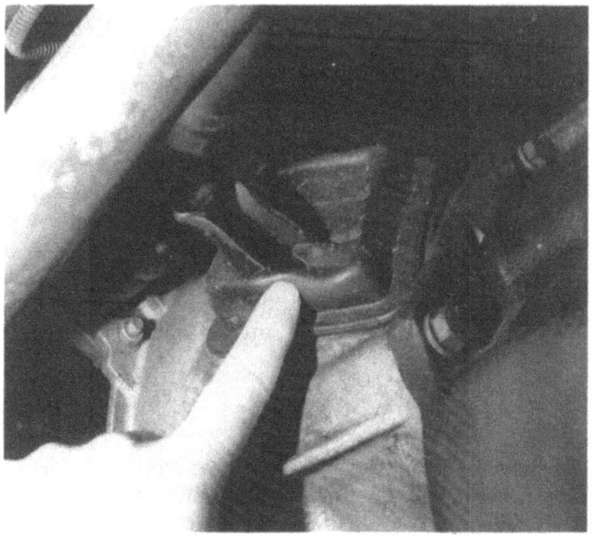

Fig. 9-5. The dust boot at the clutch fork is a vital part. Water and debris entering your truck's clutch housing can damage parts. Water can wash vital grease from the pilot bearing or transmission front bearing retainer surface. Keep seals, plates and tinware in good condition.

disc and clutch cover, and the noise is easy to distinguish. First, make certain that the clutch is adjusted properly, as described later in this chapter, and that free play exists between the clutch release fingers and the throwout bearing. At this point, with the engine running and the pedal fully released, the throwout bearing cannot make noise.

Now apply very light pedal pressure, just enough to bring the bearing against the fingers. The bearing will begin spinning and allow noise to develop. It may require firmer pressure before the bearing transmits sound. Also, to avoid confusing throwout bearing noise with pilot bearing noise, leave the transmission in neutral (with the clutch engaged) so the clutch / input gear can turn in unison with the pilot bearing.

With your transmission in neutral, the clutch fully engaged and the throwout bearing clear of the release fingers, clutch pilot and throwout bearing noise should disappear. If you hear bearing sounds now, look to the transmission for trouble.

Difficulty Shifting Gears

The simpler causes of hard shifting are a misadjusted clutch or insufficient clutch linkage travel. Begin troubleshooting by adjusting the clutch properly and examining linkage from the release fork all the way to the pedal. You need full pedal travel and proper fitup at the various links. If your truck's clutch linkage has a pivoting bellcrank, replace worn bushings and eliminate any excess play. Each link must provide full movement when you depress the clutch pedal.

Any obstacle to complete clutch disengagement will cause hard shifting. This includes a warped disc or pressure plate, a clutch disc bound on the input gear splines, a seizing pilot bearing or debris wedged between the clutch disc and pressure plate or flywheel.

NOTE —
For smooth shifts and complete clutch disengagement, the clutch pressure plate must move away from the disc and allow the disc to rotate freely and independently of the flywheel.

On trucks with hydraulic clutch linkage, look first to hydraulic system troubles. Aside from proper pushrod and pedal height adjustments, the hydraulic system requires a full stroke of fluid to release the clutch completely. This means that the master cylinder piston must retract completely, and the clutch slave cylinder piston must have ample travel in its bore.

The clutch master cylinder piston must return to its stop when you release the pedal. Adjust the pushrod and / or pedal height to achieve correct piston-to-pushrod clearance and travel. Assuming that the master cylinder has a full fluid reservoir (check fluid first), check the pushrod and pedal height adjustments. (See adjustment section of this chapter.)

If the fluid has run low, the system may require bleeding. Like a hydraulic brake system, the hydraulic lines can trap air, causing a loss of piston movement at the slave cylinder. Flush and bleed the system periodically with clean brake fluid to purge sludge, accumulated moisture and any air. If the system draws air regularly or loses fluid, overhaul the master cylinder and slave cylinder. (See the brake section of the book for tips on hydraulic cylinder overhaul.)

In good operating condition, bled properly and full of fresh brake fluid, the hydraulic clutch system will move the clutch release arm enough distance to disengage the clutch. If your clutch still drags, consider other causes.

Manual Transmission Troubleshooting

GM light trucks have used a variety of manual transmission types. (See earlier chapters.) If you have the skill and tools necessary to overhaul your transmission, your GM truck shop manual provides an excellent, in-depth guide for rebuilding.

CAUTION —
Never work on your truck's transmission without first reviewing a professional-level service manual. Subtle differences between synchronizer assemblies and other parts make transmission designs unique. A professional guide will provide correct step-by-step instruction, outline critical clearances and suggest the tools you need. You'll find the job rewarding and a great confidence builder.

As hard shifting is a symptom shared with clutch troubles, take the time to distinguish causes. Begin by adjusting the clutch and transmission linkage, if possible. Although many GM truck transmission shifters are within the control housing and inaccessible to adjustment, many three-speed transmission trucks have column shift linkage.

On three-speed models with column shift, the neutral gate and shift linkage alignment are crucial to shifting ease. (Refer to the shift linkage adjustment section of this chapter.) Periodically clean away all debris and lubricate the linkage.

Hard Shifts, Jumping Out of Gear, and Other Woes

Binding shift linkage is always a concern. Your truck is subject to twisting and off-highway stress, and the effects are often felt at linkages and pivotal supports. Eliminate any binding in the shifter or clutch linkage.

Before disassembling the transmission in pursuit of a shift problem, consider the gear lubricant. In many late model trucks, lighter oils, including ATF, have replaced traditional 80- or 90-weight gear lube. Make sure your truck has clean, proper viscosity lubricant. Synthetic gear lubricants replace traditional 90-weight, generally claiming easier shifts and a working temperature down to -50° F—allowing one oil to serve year round.

If your manual transmission has the wrong gear lubricant and the weather gets cold, expect trouble. The braking action and movement of synchronizers becomes difficult, and in some cases, the effect is so severe that gear clash makes cold shifting impossible.

Perfectly good clutches come under suspicion because a transmission won't shift into the lower gears when cold. The cause is often an improper viscosity lubricant which prevents normal synchronizer action.

Refer to your GM truck lubrication specifications when selecting correct lube—summer and winter. In extreme climates, it may be necessary to change oil in the fall and spring. If the linkage, lubricant and clutch check okay, look to possible transmission problems.

Hard shifting is rarely a transmission shift fork problem, although you cannot rule out this defect. Broken shift rail detents and other shift mechanism troubles are possibilities, although that likelihood is again slim. The most common hard shift problem is a defective synchronizer assembly.

Synchronizers wear over time. The balky shift common to high mileage transmissions is usually a synchronizer problem. The tendency for a transmission to slide out of second, third or any other synchronized gear is often caused by a synchronizer assembly defect.

Loose transmission bearings, worn synchronizer parts and excessive clearances can cause a transmission to slip out of gear. (Before condemning the transmission on column shift models, check shift linkage adjustment for full travel and smooth operation.) Worn or chipped gear teeth, excessive shaft end play, and drive gear pilot bearing wear are also causes of hard shifting and jumping out of gear. Other possibilities include a loose or misaligned clutch housing, worn motor or transmission mounts, a broken torque brace or a defective crankshaft pilot bearing.

Synchronizer interlock springs, detent keys and shift rail poppet springs each help keep the transmission in gear. Wear or defects here require a transmission teardown.

If you have isolated your trouble to the transmission, prepare for considerable expense. An overhaul must be thorough, replacing all worn pieces. If severe growling or gear whine noises have developed, you may wish to compare the cost of a major overhaul to that of a recycled or new transmission.

Burnt gear oil is a sign of major trouble. If fried oil and various metals come from the drain hole, expect to find heat-discolored shafts, damaged gears and failed (expensive!) bearings.

Transmissions contain hard steel gear and shaft parts, bronze thrust washers and in some later units, nylon shift fork slippers. When you service your transmission, examine the lubricant carefully for the presence of these materials. Powdery bronze thrust washer material, in small quantities, is normal. These washers wear very slowly over time. However, a high degree of bronze, or the presence of harder metal pieces, means trouble.

2. CLUTCH SERVICE

A truck clutch will eventually fail or wear out. Fortunately, a clutch rarely breaks without warning. The key to getting the most from your clutch is to exercise reasonable driving habits, avoiding severe powertrain shock loads or continuous clutch overheating.

Although many accessories speed up clutch wear, oversize tires have the heaviest impact. Big wheels and tires have the same effect as installing a taller (numerically lower) set of axle gears. Unless you change axle gearing to match the new tire diameter, the new gearing will take its toll on the clutch.

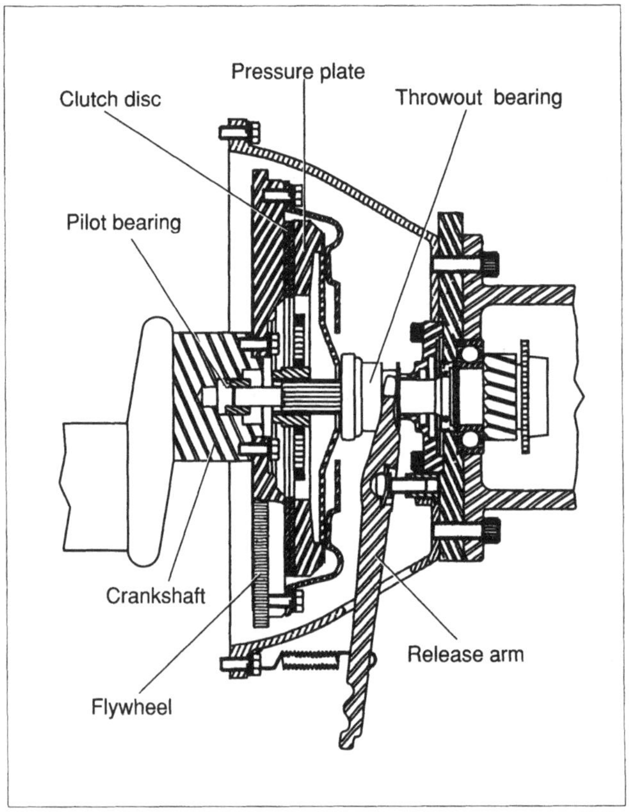

Fig. 9-6. The spring loaded clutch pressure plate sandwiches the clutch disc face against the flywheel. As the disc's friction material wears, spring apply pressure weakens. This accounts for the slippage common with higher mileage clutch units.

A variety of causes lead to clutch slippage. Misadjusted clearance between the throwout bearing and pressure plate, overloading, slipping the clutch and other bad driving techniques usually speed up the process. Even under ideal circumstances, the clutch disc wears, becoming progressively thinner and seriously weakening the clutch cover apply pressure.

The best way to reduce clutch wear is to reduce the amount of time that the clutch plate slips during engagement. Beyond this, proper use of your gears can help. (See chapter on operating techniques.)

Clutch wear is obvious. Slippage will occur as you release the pedal, when the truck climbs steep inclines and during low speed lugging of the engine. If your clutch isn't noticeably weak, you can push the test further: Place the shifter in high gear at 15 to 20 mph. Disengage the clutch, and, as you hold the clutch pedal to the floor, bring the engine speed to about 2500 rpm and quickly release the clutch pedal.

Assuming that clutch free play has been adjusted correctly, one of two things will happen. When the clutch is in good condition, releasing the pedal will cause an immediate and noticeable drop in engine rpm, sometimes enough to nearly stall the engine. If the clutch has excessive wear, such as glazed friction lining or weak pressure plate springs, the engine speed will either remain high for several seconds or drop slowly.

Sooner or later your truck's clutch will fail this test. When it does, a variety of rebuilt and new clutch assembly options exist to restore or improve your truck.

An improved aftermarket clutch design can work with no modifications to your truck's existing flywheel, clutch linkage, or other clutch-related parts. A clutch replacement offers an excellent opportunity to upgrade your truck.

Identifying Your Clutch

There are several clutch types used in GM light trucks: the original GM diaphragm type, Borg & Beck, Long-type, and other diaphragm designs. All clutch discs have torsional springs and composition friction material.

The earlier GM light trucks use GM's own diaphragm type clutch assemblies. Later Borg and Beck (B&B) type clutches have a multi-spring clutch cover design with three release fingers. Between 1939 and the present, various GM truck models have used diaphragm spring, direct pressure and semi-centrifugal design clutches.

Years ago, clutch covers with coil springs and adjustable release fingers could be rebuilt by a well equipped shop. It was common for a general repair shop to rebuild a cover or adjust the release finger height. Today, neither the three-finger types nor multi-finger diaphragm clutches require field service. Auto parts retailers and your local GM truck dealership sell fully adjusted (rebuilt or new) clutch cover/pressure plate assemblies.

When your GM truck needs a clutch replacement, consider installing the largest diameter unit that will fit your engine's flywheel and safely within the bellhousing. When seeking such a clutch, you will find that diameter usually increases with larger displacement engines or higher GVWRs.

Since many Chevrolet truck engines share the same flywheel design and even the same bellhousing, you can usually find a larger clutch assembly that will fit your engine. Light GM trucks commonly use a 10", 10-1/2", 11" or a larger 12" diameter clutch disc. Torque, horsepower, load, and transmission type will determine the original clutch size that GMC or Chevrolet assigned.

If you increase the engine performance level or the load placed on the clutch, a heavier duty unit is often necessary. When buying a new clutch assembly, you will need to match your clutch disc diameter (unless a larger unit will fit properly), the hub spline configuration and the clutch cover design.

GM trucks have used a variety of manual transmissions. The clutch splines and input shaft diameter can vary between designs. Identify your transmission whenever ordering parts.

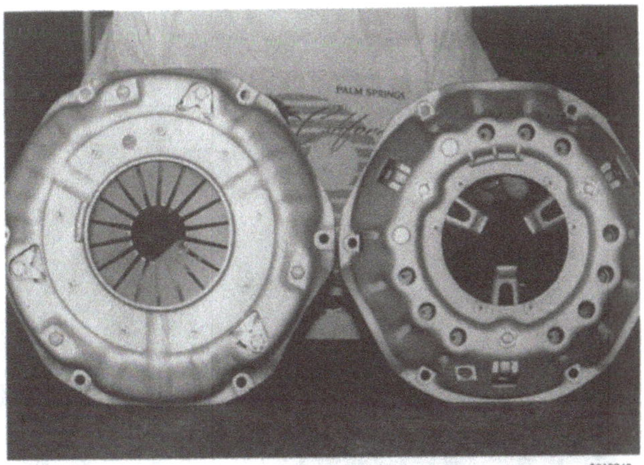

0012748

Fig. 9-7. *Early GM trucks use the common GM diaphragm type clutch/pressure plate (left) with its full radius of non-adjustable release fingers. Clutch disc diameter is an indication of stamina and strength. In many cases, your GM truck flywheel and clutch housing will accept a larger diameter clutch disc and cover. This is a way to upgrade the system.*

0012360

Fig. 9-8. *Borg & Beck clutches are common to many GM trucks. This Borg & Beck three-finger release type unit offers good clamping force and smooth operation. These clutches deliver quality service.*

0012361

Fig. 9-9. Aside from the clutch diameter, the spline configuration must match the transmission input gear. It's good practice to take your complete clutch unit to the parts house. Always avoid inhalation of asbestos fibers from the disc.

Clutch Linkage Repairs

Many GM trucks have mechanical clutch linkage. These systems require periodic service, as bushing wear leads to unwanted play. The rods and levers that actuate the clutch will wear and fatigue at the pivot points. Nylon bushings wear out, along with the pedal stops and return springs. You must replace parts when wear develops.

Hydraulic clutch systems consist of a master cylinder, hydraulic hose and pipe, and a clutch slave (release) cylinder. In most cases, the slave cylinder actuates a release fork/arm, much like a mechanical clutch linkage system.

0014279

Fig. 9-10. Mechanical clutch linkage requires regular inspection for wear and excessive play. Older models with through-the-floor pedals have the advantage of chassis mounted linkage. This reduces flex, distortion and binding.

(Some contemporary clutch systems use a hydraulically actuated throwout bearing in place of traditional release arm linkage.) Similar to your truck's braking system, cleanliness and fresh hydraulic brake fluid assure longer service.

When performing work on the hydraulic clutch system, you need clean hands, free of any grease, oils or abrasive contaminants. Repair kits are sometimes available for the master and slave cylinders, or you can replace these parts if they show excess wear.

0012373

Fig. 9-11. Hydraulic clutch linkage eliminates many problems. Twisting and body/frame flex off-highway can raise havoc with mechanical clutch linkage, especially models with suspended pedals. By contrast, a hydraulic cylinder mounts solidly to the bellhousing, maintaining constant alignment with the release arm.

Judge cylinder wear as you would a brake cylinder. Consult your GM truck shop manual for tolerances and rebuilding details. Do not take chances here, as a clutch linkage failure could strand your truck or cause clutch and transmission damage.

Look closely at the hydraulic hose. Again, like brake hose, this is a wear item. If embrittlement or dehydration has occurred, replace the hose. Use DOT 3 or higher grade brake fluid. (See the brake section of this book for further details on hydraulic system repairs.)

Clutch Adjustment

A manual transmission truck may require periodic clutch adjustment. On later models, the clutch adjustment is automatic, and the hydraulic clutch linkage readily compensates for wear. (Actually, GM light truck hydraulic clutch linkage dates back to the 1960–63 period, although these earlier trucks *do* require periodic clutch adjustment.) GM trucks reintroduced hydraulic clutch linkage in the 1980s. Other GM truck models use mechanical linkage to actuate the clutch.

You will need to work beneath the truck to adjust linkage at the clutch release arm or rod. After setting the parking brake and blocking the wheels, crawl beneath the truck with a set of wrenches. Remember to loosen locknuts before attempting adjustments. Tighten lock nuts when done.

0014274

Fig. 9-12. GM light trucks first used hydraulic clutch linkage in 1960, with a tandem clutch/brake master cylinder. The early hydraulic linkage was a reliable and popular design used from 1960–62 (through 1963 on K-10 4x4s), then replaced in 1963 by mechanical linkage. On these early hydraulic clutch models, the clutch release arm is at the right side of the bellhousing.

WARNING —
Always set the parking brake and block the wheels before crawling beneath your truck.

Since the hydraulic linkage slave cylinder mounts firmly to the engine/clutch housing, smooth clutch engagement is possible under all operating conditions, a distinct advantage over mechanical linkage. With mechanical linkage, engine torque can twist and shake the release rods, and this translates as jerky clutch engagement. Especially for trucks that operate with heavy loads or off-pavement, hydraulic clutch linkage is superior.

Always begin your clutch adjustment by checking freeplay at the release arm. Although proper clutch operation demands sufficient pedal travel and freeplay, release arm movement provides the only true measurement of the throwout bearing-to-clutch clearance. Maintaining the required gap between the clutch release fingers and the throwout bearing face assures full engagement of the clutch and a long life for the throwout bearing.

On models with adjustable clutch linkage, normal clutch wear will decrease the clearance between the clutch release fingers and the throwout bearing. If wear becomes excessive, the throwout bearing will actually ride on the fingers. This can cause premature failure of the bearing or damage to the release fingers.

If wear continues beyond the point of contact, the throwout bearing will not allow the clutch to engage completely. Slippage occurs, resulting in heat buildup and friction. The clutch will wear rapidly when adjusted too tightly and ruin a perfectly good clutch or release bearing.

NOTE —
Your truck's clutch can be costly and difficult to access (especially 4WD models), taking considerable labor to replace. Avoid trouble. Inspect clutch linkage and check the clutch adjustment periodically.

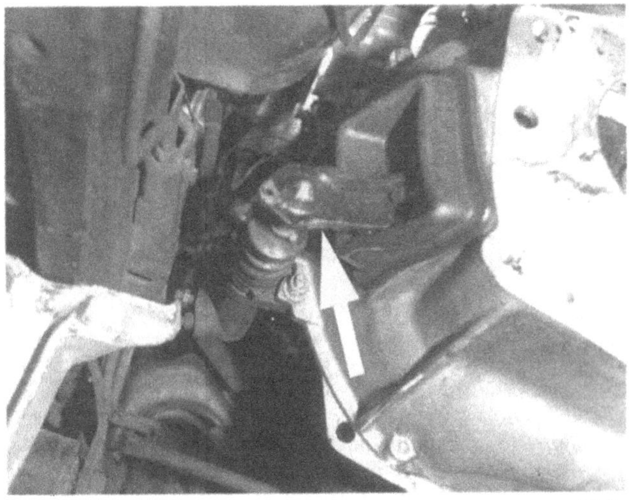

0014465

Fig. 9-13. Always check clutch freeplay at the release arm (arrow). Note relationship of throwout bearing and clutch release fingers. Linkage wear can make freeplay measurement at the pedal inaccurate.

0014275

Fig. 9-14. Even though it is a hydraulic linkage, the early 1960s release rod (arrow) is much like mechanical linkage. You need to periodically adjust the clutch on these earlier hydraulic systems.

Clutch Adjustment: Early Models

On 1939–59 light truck models with the diaphragm type clutch, the clutch adjustment is 3/4-inch to 1-inch free play (movement before the throwout bearing contacts clutch fingers) measured at the clutch pedal. Use a light finger touch here and not your foot.

This method of adjustment assumes that linkage is in good condition and the return springs pull the pedal to the top of its travel. When linkage wear exists or return springs are weak, a false reading will result.

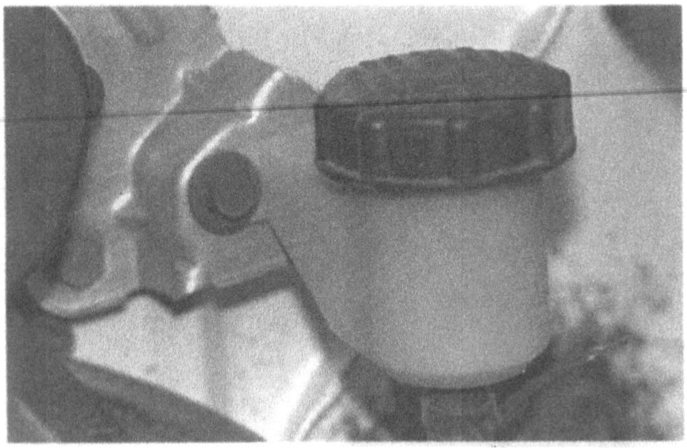

0014276

Fig. 9-15. Beginning in 1985, GM C- and K-model trucks use hydraulic clutch linkage. There is no need to adjust this kind of clutch linkage. However, you should check the clutch master cylinder's fluid level regularly and change the fluid at appropriate intervals. Proper pedal height is essential. (See service section in this chapter.)

0014277

Fig. 9-16. Clutch linkage on 1939–59 GM trucks is through-the-floor pedal type. The clutch release rod requires periodic adjustment to achieve proper pedal freeplay. Watch for wear at pivots and rod fatigue, as this kind of linkage is a high friction design.

Heavier duty Second Series 1955–59 applications, including the GMC light trucks with Pontiac-design V-8s, use a three-finger 11-inch diameter Borg & Beck type clutch. On these models, pedal freeplay is 1-1/2-inches.

You will find that pedal freeplay figures strive for clearance between the clutch cover/pressure plate fingers and throwout bearing face. Despite the pedal travel specifications, make sure that at least 1/16-inch of freeplay exists between the release bearing face and clutch release fingers (observed through the release arm opening in bellhousing).

Check for throwout bearing movement by moving the release arm and observing the bearing-to-finger relationship within the bellhousing. These early GM trucks use a clutch linkage/pedal return spring at the release arm or rod. Make sure the springs work properly so that pedal weight does not cause the throwout bearing to ride on the clutch cover fingers.

Clutch Adjustment: 1960–63 with Hydraulic Linkage

On 1960–62 (plus the 1963 K-10/1500 4WD) GM light trucks with hydraulic clutch linkage, the adjustment is more involved. Clutch adjustment takes place at the release arm linkage near the clutch housing.

First make sure the master cylinder is full, and bleed any air from the slave cylinder.

Next, verify the clutch pedal rod-to-master cylinder piston clearance. The rod must allow the piston to retract completely when the pedal rests against its bumper stop. (The clutch pedal should be level with the brake pedal.) From 1/32" to 1/16" clearance between the rod's tip and the fully retracted piston will work fine.

If clearance is incorrect, the pushrod attaches to the pedal with an eccentric bolt on some models. On other models, the pushrod length is adjustable. For models with eccentric bolts, you can loosen the lock nut and rotate the eccentric bolt to attain the correct pedal rod-to-master cylinder piston clearance.

On models with an adjustable pushrod, slide the dust boot back, taking care not to allow debris to enter the backside of the master cylinder or the boot. Loosen the lock nut and adjust the length of the pushrod to establish proper clearance; then reinstall the boot carefully.

> **NOTE —**
> Pedal/pushrod adjustment is rare and generally addresses long term chassis wear. Subsequent clutch adjustment(s) will likely require nothing more than an adjustment at the clutch release arm.

Now you can go beneath the truck and check/adjust the clutch release arm clearance. With the clutch return spring detached, push the release arm pushrod into the slave cylinder until the pushrod stops (piston bottomed). Hold the pushrod here, and move the clutch release arm fork away from the pushrod until the throwout bearing stops against the clutch cover fingers.

You set clearance by turning the adjuster nut while holding the pushrod with a second wrench. Strive for a 5/32-inch space on Chevrolet models with the diaphragm type clutch and 1/4-inch to 5/16-inch spacing on V-6 GMCs and other models equipped with the Borg & Beck type three-finger clutch. Measure between the V-block fulcrum's pointed end and the release arm.

Reattach the return spring, which must be in good condition. Work the clutch pedal several times, then check the pedal free travel again. This should be approximately 1/8-inch of pedal movement (measured at the pedal foot pad center) before the pushrod begins to push the master cylinder piston. (You may need to either slide the dust boot back to see this or grip the pushrod through the boot and feel for play. Keep dirt and debris from entering the backside of the master cylinder or the boot.)

Secure each locknut after adjustment, and always recheck the release bearing-to-clutch finger clearance after driving the truck.

Clutch Adjustment: 1963–84 Mechanical Linkage with Suspended Pedals

Pedal height and the pedal-to-cross shaft rod length is adjustable on these models. If you need to confirm or adjust the pedal height or pedal-to-cross-shaft lever rod length, consult your shop manual. Unless damage or wear has occurred, adjusting the pedal height is usually unnecessary. If you need to make this adjustment, follow up by checking and resetting the clutch release arm freeplay as required.

1963–84 GM trucks with mechanical clutch linkage provide for clutch adjustment at the push rod near the clutch release arm. Once you know that your clutch pedal and upper linkage is adjusted properly, you can adjust the clutch linkage at the release arm. This task requires use of clearance specifications given in your GM truck shop manual or a professional service guidebook.

Although the specifications may call for a certain pedal free-travel, make sure that there is adequate freeplay between the throwout (clutch release) bearing and the fingers of the pressure plate. On mechanical clutch linkage systems, I strive for a minimum of 1/16" of clearance here. This translates as approximately 1/4-inch of freeplay at the release arm and rod.

Be aware that worn linkage can create a false pedal freeplay reading. Check the linkage, bushings and adjustments from the pedal to the clutch release arm. Correct for any wear before measuring pedal freeplay. Regardless of the pedal travel and freeplay, the actual concern is clearance between the throwout bearing face and the clutch cover release fingers.

Clutch Adjustment: 1985–up Hydraulic Linkage

Later hydraulic clutch linkage designs omit the use of a release arm spring. This design relies on the rotational force of the clutch to thrust the release bearing slightly away from the clutch fingers when the driver releases the pedal. These systems self-adjust, requiring no type of adjustment between clutch replacements. Check clutch reservoir fluid with regular maintenance.

Assuming that pedal height is correct and the clutch cylinders work properly, this type of hydraulic clutch linkage provides enough piston travel to compensate for normal wear of the clutch disc and other parts. The system simply compensates for wear, providing correct release bearing clearance for the normal service life of the clutch.

Hydraulic systems occasionally need bleeding, and a periodic bleed/flush will provide fresh fluid and remove moisture or other contaminants. (Bleeding procedure is much the same as for hydraulic brakes.) Always use fresh DOT 3 or higher grade brake fluid and maintain cleanliness. Keep all contaminants out of the system. Clean fluid will help protect the release mechanism from premature failure.

CAUTION —
As with a brake system, clean debris from around the fluid reservoir before removing the cap. Prevent contaminants and dirt from entering the hydraulic clutch system. Always use clean brake fluid.

Clutch Replacement Tips

Replacing your truck's clutch is a major job. Before condemning your clutch, try a simple adjustment first and make sure that the mechanical linkage or hydraulic cylinder operation is correct. A hydraulic seal leak can limit the clutch release arm travel, prevent full release of the clutch and cause symptoms of a defective clutch.

Also, clutch wear or failure symptoms are often mimicked by troubles like loose or broken motor mounts, a worn limited slip axle/differential or binding clutch linkage. When clutch failure or a diagnosis like "worn out" is premature, consider other possibilities.

WARNING —
The clutch disc may contain asbestos fibers. Asbestos materials can cause asbestosis. Always wear an approved respirator and protective clothing when handling components containing asbestos. Do not use compressed air, do not grind, heat, weld or sand on or near any asbestos materials. Only approved cleaning methods should be used to service the clutch disc or areas containing asbestos dust or asbestos fibers.

When your truck requires a clutch replacement, the factory shop manual for your model will clearly outline the steps. Rather than provide step-by-step instructions for the clutch replacement, this section provides the footnotes that OEM and professional workshop manuals, written for journey-level mechanics, often omit.

The clutch in your truck mounts on the flywheel, at the back of the engine and in front of the transmission. On 4WD equipped trucks, the removal of the transmission involves far more work than on a 2WD truck.

Two-wheel drive trucks require driveshaft and transmission removal for clutch replacement. On a 4x4, the front and rear driveshafts attach to the transfer case, and clutch replacement means removing the transfer case, plus numerous components that connect to it, before removing the transmission.

0014494

Fig. 9-17. Examine engine mounts and other areas before condemning the clutch. Mounts sag, break, loosen and become oil saturated. A 4x4 GM truck clutch job is a major task, done only when necessary.

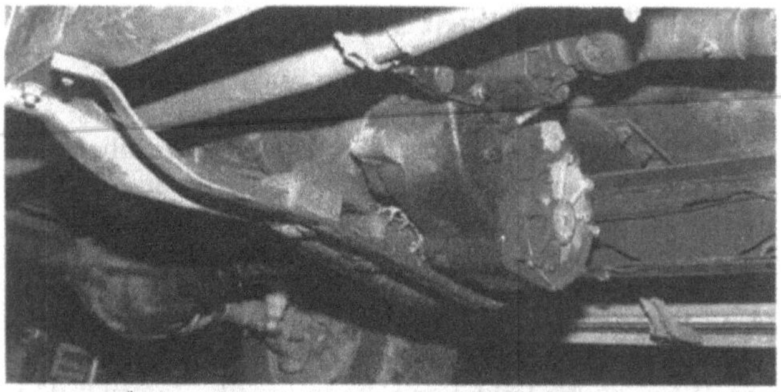

0014278

Fig. 9-18. A 4x4 GM truck clutch replacement calls for transmission and even transfer case removal. In some cases, it may be easier to remove the radiator, detach and move the engine forward, and leave the rest of the powertrain in place. Support the transmission/transfer case carefully.

0012368

Fig. 9-19. A massive truck four-speed, coupled to an iron transfer case, can weigh in excess of 250 pounds. Separate these components and use a special transmission jack to remove and install the sub-assemblies. Here, transfer case has been removed with a transmission jack. Floor jack shown supports engine and transmission.

Obviously, if you have any good reason to remove the engine, consider performing a clutch replacement at the same time, especially on 4WD trucks. This is simply good insurance.

Clutch replacement can be done in concert with other repairs. For example, if your 4WD's radiator needs repair when the clutch also begs attention, consider doing both jobs simultaneously. Once the radiator is out, you have added engine bay space. This could make it possible to separate the engine from the bellhousing and, with an engine hoist, *partially* remove the engine to access the clutch.

If changing the clutch in this manner makes sense, securely support the transmission before moving the engine forward. This method is an alternative to the customary routine of removing the two drivelines, the transfer case and the transmission assembly.

The choice is yours. First read the factory procedure for removing the engine, then the steps for replacing the clutch. Assess your truck, the available tools, and your working conditions. Some later model engines have a mass of accessories and confusing A/C plumbing, special wiring considerations and a maze of vacuum hoses that could make engine removal less practical.

When removing and installing powertrain components, understand that they are very hefty and cumbersome. Use appropriate jacks and any other safety equipment to protect yourself from injury. If you cannot afford a transmission jack, rent one. This will save time, make the job easier and prevent damage to vital parts. Aligning the transmission and transfer case with the clutch is an awkward job, even with a special jack.

A Muncie 465 truck four-speed coupled to an NP205 iron transfer case can weigh near 250 pounds—enough to pin you to the garage floor for good. Use extreme caution with this type of bulk, as no clutch job is worth a permanent injury. Use a hoist, hydraulic transmission jack or special lifting devices.

For saving time and protecting vital parts, always use clutch aligning tools. More trouble occurs during attempts to align the transmission with the clutch disc hub than any other operation. To avoid clutch disc damage, never hang weight off the clutch hub.

Take care to tighten clutch cover bolts gradually, evenly and in cross sequence, following factory guidelines. Warping a brand new clutch cover can ruin the whole job, plus require a teardown to correct the clutch shudder.

Inspect the flywheel surface for heat cracks, glazing and possible warpage. Again, with the magnitude of this task, don't try to cut corners. Mark the flywheel's location on the crankshaft and remove the flywheel. Send the flywheel to a quality automotive machine shop. Let them inspect the flywheel and resurface its face. If the flywheel's starter ring gear shows any damage, replace either the ring gear or the entire flywheel.

Flywheel thickness is important for normal clutch operation, engine balance and correct positioning of the release bearing. Make sure flywheel thickness is within factory specifications.

0012370

Fig. 9-20. Check the flywheel for heat cracks, blue discoloration and glazing. If you find any of these symptoms, sublet the flywheel to an automotive machine shop for service.

The Parts List

The job is tough, and you don't want to do it over. When you make your list of necessary parts, begin with the clutch cover (pressure plate), clutch disc and throwout or release bearing. Closely inspect the crankshaft pilot bearing and clutch release arm for wear. If in doubt, replace these parts.

For most trucks, weather and age take their toll. The release arm sealing boot can deteriorate or be in rough shape. If worn at all, replace it. Any saggy return springs need replacement. Look closely at the clutch linkage; inspect for wear, fatigue and life expectancy. Inspect the transmission's front bearing retainer that supports the throwout bearing. If you find galling or wear, replace the retainer.

Replace all seals that are leaking or could soon leak. This includes the front bearing retainer seal and gasket. (On some transmissions, like the NP435 four-speed, the retainer gasket is a selective fit to control bearing end play. Read your service guidebook for clearances before replacing this gasket.) Use your imagination; visualize where a leak could develop and which parts would be especially hard to access.

Toss out any worn fastening hardware and replace with equivalent grade bolts, nuts and locking devices. Know your grading (see appendix charts) and upgrade if necessary. If you remove the flywheel, install new original equipment (OE) type replacement flywheel bolts. The same with the clutch cover. Replace all locking hardware and/or washers, and clean or chase threads to assure proper torque settings.

WARNING —
Use properly graded hardware, identical to OE design. Engineers often design bolts to serve a particular function. Match hardware perfectly, and do not install generic hardware in place of specially configured bolts. Always replace hardware with identical parts. Match bolt shoulder length, thread pitch, grading, lock washer design and other details. Do not replace specialized hardware with generic fasteners.

0012424

Fig. 9-21. The transmission front bearing retainer also supports the throwout bearing. Galling or a rough surface can cause erratic clutch operation, including chatter during engagement. If you find wear here, replace the retainer.

Tools

For a quality job, you'll need several specialty tools. Removal of the pilot bearing generally requires a special puller. For solid bushing type pilots, you might try this alternative, which I learned from a Stovebolt-era mechanic: Pack the pilot cavity with grease. Find a steel shaft or an old transmission input gear with the same diameter nose as the pilot bushing bore. Tap the shaft into the pilot bore.

WARNING —
Cushion your blows with a block of wood or a plastic hammer, and wear eye protection.

The shaft acts like a hydraulic ram. As you tap, grease will create impact force at the back side of the pilot bushing and drive the bushing out. This only works with bronze bushings, not with bearings, and the driver shaft must fit snugly into the bore.

A clutch aligning tool is a must. An old transmission input gear with the same splines will also serve to align the clutch disc as you secure the clutch cover to the flywheel.

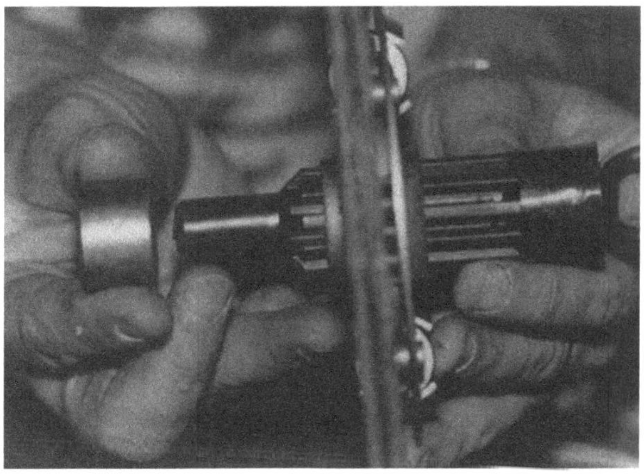
0012371

Fig. 9-22. A clutch disc aligning tool is a must when fitting a new disc. Always install a new pilot bearing/bushing and clutch throwout bearing when replacing the clutch disc and pressure plate.

Over the years, I have accumulated a drawer full of alignment dowels for the two upper bolt holes of various clutch housings. To make your own transmission alignment dowels, simply cut the heads off long bolts of the proper thread size. For simpler removal, make a screwdriver slot at the end of each dowel and keep threads clean.

By installing dowel pins, you can keep the transmission aligned and on center as you slide the assembly into position. Once you've installed the lower transmission bolts, unscrew one pin at a time and replace each dowel with a transmission mounting bolt. Tighten all bolts in sequence, and establish final settings with a torque wrench.

Prevent damage to the transmission case, bearing retainer, clutch hub and pilot bearing. Carefully maintain transmission alignment during installation. Always support the transmission with a jack until all upper and lower mounting bolts are secure.

0014495

Fig. 9-23. Column shift linkage will wear, stretch and fatigue, and worn parts require replacement. Periodically clean linkage and thoroughly lubricate this assembly. (See the lubrication chapter.) Normal wear requires periodic adjustment of column shift linkage. Shown is a 50's Chevrolet with Hydra-Matic shift linkage.

You will want some high melting point grease for the inside collar of the throwout bearing. Some manufacturers package the bearing with grease. Never clean a new throwout bearing in solvent, as this will remove grease.

Make sure you have proper sealant if you intend to remove the front bearing retainer and install a new gasket. As I commented earlier, transmissions like the NP435 four-speed have selective fit bearing retainer gaskets (shims) for precisely adjusting the end play of the input gear and bearing.

> **CAUTION —**
> *Do not alter the thickness of selective fit shim/gaskets. If necessary, use a micrometer to confirm the original thickness and match this figure with the new gasket stack. The NP435 calls for a dial indicator check of input shaft endplay, then use of proper gaskets to restore or correct the endplay.*

Be sure you have plenty of parts cleaner and shop towels. This is a very messy job, especially on a 4x4 or truck that runs off-pavement. (Before you start work, thoroughly clean the chassis and powertrain.) You will also need the best hand cleaner available. You'll be very oily when this job is done.

3. TRANSMISSION ADJUSTMENTS

For GM truck manual transmissions, the need for linkage adjustments is limited to three-speed column shift models. Other gearboxes feature removable control housing assemblies, generally considered part of the transmission assembly. Rarely does a control housing require overhaul, although in many models, you can perform such service without removing the complete transmission unit.

The 1947 (late) Advance Design trucks began using column shift linkage on the lighter duty three-speed transmissions. 1939–early 1947 (pre-Advance Design) light trucks were equipped with floor shifted light duty and heavy duty three-speeds or a four-speed (spur gear) transmission.

Advance Design models also introduced the far more versatile Muncie SM420 option, a floor shifted four-speed gearbox. This rugged gearbox served light truck customers in need of a heavy duty transmission with synchromesh on second through fourth gears. For light service use, the column shift three-speed transmission remained a Chevrolet and GMC light duty truck standard well into the 1970s.

Although a GM truck shop manual or professional service guide provides details for adjusting the column shift linkage on your truck, I will share some basic aims.

Two rods reach from the transmission's control levers to pivoting arms at the steering column (just forward of the engine cowl). The driver controlled shifter lever moves fore and aft through a neutral gate. This aligns the shifter lever with one or the other pivoting arm.

One pivot arm works the first and reverse gears, while the other attaches to the second and high gear control lever. Adjustment consists of aligning these two pivoting arms so that the shifter moves smoothly from the first / reverse gear path, then through the neutral gate and into the second / high gear shift path.

You will find specific adjustment procedures in your GM truck shop manual or a professional-level service manual. Three objectives apply: 1) the rod adjustments should place the steering column pivot arms in perfect alignment through the neutral gate; 2) for driver convenience, the column shifter should swing through a comfortable range; and 3) rods must move freely and permit complete engagement of reverse, first, second and third gears.

This last point is crucial. The only place to verify proper gear engagement is to block the wheels, set the parking brake and crawl beneath the truck (with the engine turned off and cold so the exhaust system won't scorch your hands) and have an assistant move the shift linkage through each gear.

Make sure that the transmission control lever moves completely into each gear position indicated. If you are uncertain, remove the shift rod at the transmission control lever and note whether the lever is completely in gear.

Automatic Transmission Adjustments

Your GM truck's automatic transmission requires periodic service. Look for fluid leaks, the condition of vacuum hoses to the modulator, if so equipped, and perform periodic fluid and filter changes. Cleanliness in the service of your transmission cannot be overstated—guidelines call for lint-free shop towels when working around an automatic transmission's valve body.

There are some basic adjustments for your automatic transmission. Later trucks have sophisticated electrical and electronic controls, yet the rules remain similar. First, the manual (shift) valve requires proper adjustment. This measure cannot be overstated.

A manual valve out of adjustment may direct an inadequate flow of hydraulic fluid within the transmission. Incorrect manual valve adjustment can cause weak shifts, incomplete apply pressure, slipping clutch packs and

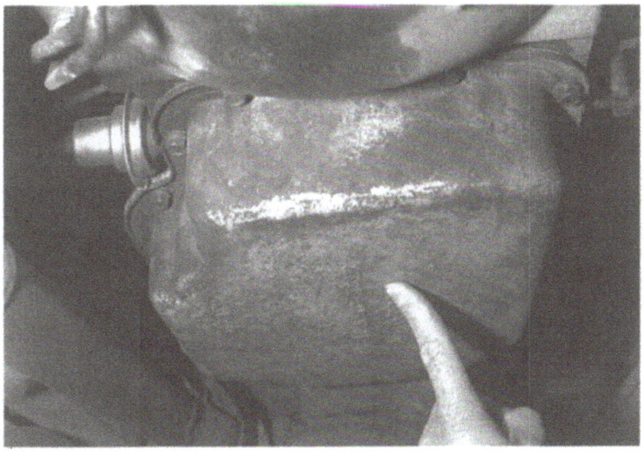

Fig. 9-24. *When servicing your automatic transmission, cleanliness is crucial. Dirt, even lint, in the valve body can cause shifting irregularities and other problems that lead to an overhaul. When changing the filter, use extreme care to keep contaminants out.*

Fig. 9-25. *A full service on your automatic transmission includes a fluid and filter change, adjustment of the shift and kickdown linkage or electric switch, and adjustment of the ignition neutral/park safety switch.*

weak band application. Damage or complete transmission failure can result from incorrectly adjusted shift linkage.

The second automatic transmission adjustment is the kickdown or downshift linkage. Mechanical linkage found on GM's earlier four-speed iron-case Hydramatic and Powerglide (Pow-R-Flo) transmissions, or the electrical kickdown switches used on later Turbo-Hydramatic

Fig. 9-26. *A defective vacuum modulator can cause shifting irregularities that mimic symptoms of more serious problems. If you catch a defective modulator before other damage occurs, the cure is relatively inexpensive. The modulator can be changed easily on most automatics.*

transmissions, link the throttle to the transmission. On the latest models, this task is performed by way of an electronic module and the engine management computer.

For three-speed automatics, the electrical switch or mechanical linkage causes a downshift from Drive (third gear) to second gear at full throttle if the vehicle speed is less than the limit set for the truck's axle gearing and OEM tire size.

If your transmission has a vacuum modulator, this can also affect shifts. The modulator helps dictate upshift and downshift points. An automatic transmission that shifts erratically can suffer from either a defective governor or a bad vacuum modulator.

On the early GM band-type iron Hydramatic and the Powerglide/Pow-R-Flo automatic transmissions, periodic band adjustment is a requirement. These types of transmissions, described in the GM light truck shop manuals for their respective model years, depend upon proper band clearances in order to shift properly and hold planetary members securely. If excessive clearance develops, poor shifts and slippage on upshifts will occur. This can rapidly damage the transmission's clutch packs and other expensive parts.

Before condemning your whole transmission, perform a full service. Change the fluid and filter. Adjust the manual linkage, centering the shift indicator for neutral and park. Readjust the neutral safety switch, if necessary, to assure that the engine will start only in neutral or park. On adjustable band-type units, adjust the bands.

Adjust carburetor linkage on models with manual detent/kickdown controls. Check the adjustment of electrical kickdown switches on later transmissions. Change the vacuum modulator, if suspect, and make certain that leak-free vacuum signals reach the modulator.

If none of these measures improve your automatic transmission's performance, accept the likelihood that the unit needs in-depth repairs or a major overhaul. Like a manual clutch, automatic transmission parts wear over time. During an overhaul, you can upgrade most GM automatics. Improvements include use of heavy duty or high performance clutch packs and hard parts. High performance torque converters are also available.

Chapter 10

Transfer Case, Driveshafts, Axles and Hubs

GM TRUCKS HAVE A STRONG WORK ETHIC. Whether moving a loaded fifth wheel travel trailer or hauling supplies to a minesite or logging camp, a GM light truck will earn its keep. The rugged four-wheel drive K-models, once the beasts of burden for primitive worksites and agricultural use, have gained popularity among suburban and urban non-commercial users.

GM 4WDs can grapple with mud and snow, inch their way up steep grades and slosh through swampy bogs. Such a wide variety of chores requires auxiliary gearsets, and the two-speed transfer case has provided the solution. All 1950s NAPCO conversion 4x4s and the 1960 to present factory K-models feature a two-speed transfer case with provision for 4WD low range mode.

1. TRANSFER CASES

The GM transfer case mounts rearward of the transmission and divides power between the front and rear axles. A two-speed transfer case offers low range, essentially an extra gearset available for four-wheel drive mode and heavy off-pavement pulling chores.

On GM 4WD truck geartrains, the transmission output shaft drives the transfer case input. NAPCO conversions and first generation (1960–66) K-models, which mount the transfer case separately, require a short driveshaft between the transmission and transfer case. Later versions attach the transmission to the transfer case via a cast adapter housing, which doubles as a pedestal for the transmission and transfer case mount.

0014469

Fig. 10-1. Muncie SM420 (1947–67) and Muncie 465 (1968–91, pictured here) four-speed truck transmissions have been a durable mainstay for GM light through medium duty trucks. First gear is a non-synchromesh compound low. Engineered by General Motors for rugged service, these transmissions are among the best units ever built.

Beginning with GM's earliest Spicer and Rockwell transfer cases, the rear driveshaft's output yoke is in line with the transfer case input shaft. Power within the transfer case flows downward to the intermediate gearset and power take-off (PTO) gear, then to the front output shaft, which rides low in the case.

Known as a "through-drive" transfer case design, these auxiliary gearboxes have a driver operated shift lever (twin-levers on some NAPCO conversions) that engages 2WD High, 4WD-High, Neutral (PTO mode) and 4WD Low ranges. Two sliding forks provide the necessary power flow and engagement of the front axle output shaft (four-wheel drive), low range and a neutral mode for PTO use.

For rock crawling or heavy off-pavement pulling in low range, the Spicer, Rockwell and NP205 (gear drive) and NP203 (chain drive) transfer cases accomplish speed reduction through engagement of a gear on the intermediate shaft. When you move the lever toward low range, a sliding gear or sliding clutch releases the high-range gear, then moves further to engage the low-range gear.

0014473

Fig. 10-2. 1960–66 GM K-model 4WD trucks have "divorced" transfer cases. In 1967, along with a major 4x4 chassis change, GM began mating the transfer case to the transmission with an adapter. Switching from the Rockwell to Spicer/Dana units, then the New Process NP205 (part-time) and NP203 (full-time) transfer cases, GM built a solid string of formidable 4x4 models through 1979. In 1980, like other manufacturers, GM K-models switched to the chain drive style NP208 part-time transfer case.

0014117

Fig. 10-3. This type of New Process transfer chain-drive case unit serves early 1980s GM trucks and other makes. They are lightweight, easy to shift and feature chain drive.

CAUTION —
These units have no synchromesh between high range and low range. You must stop your truck before engaging low range, although most transfer cases can shift from 2WD High to 4WD High without stopping the truck. (For details, see earlier chapter on operating your truck.)

The gear drive transfer cases and even the 1973–79 NP203 chain drive transfer case can easily meet the requirements of GM truck users. A through-drive transfer case proves superior to side drive types like the Spicer Model 18 unit found in pre-1972 Jeep CJ and earlier Willys truck models.

As GM four-wheel drive trucks evolved from utility vehicles into multi-purpose vehicles and SUV types, the transfer case design also changed. As 4x4s began to spend more time on the highway than off, simultaneously facing stiffer emission and fuel economy standards, GM reduced the two-wheel drive mode wear and frictional losses by changing to chain drive part-time 4x4 transfer cases.

In 1980, GM K-trucks began using the New Process NP208 chain drive transfer case. Although these units definitely reduce friction, with planetary gear systems acting in place of hefty gearsets, many buyers regretted the passage of iron-cased gear drive units like the NP205. (K-30 series one-ton trucks retain the NP205 through the 1991 Crew Cab models.)

For stamina and a remarkably long service life, there is no substitute for a gear drive (iron-case) transfer case. In particular, the industrial strength New Process 205 unit is my number one choice of all light truck transfer cases built to this date. GM began using the NP205 as early as 1969. (Some late 1960s to mid-1970s GM K-models use the durable Spicer/Dana 20 unit.) Use of the NP205 stopped after 1979 on half- and three-quarter ton models. Even the pre-1980 Blazer, Jimmy and Suburban 4WD trucks were equipped with this transfer case.

Full- Versus Part-time Four Wheeling

During the 1970s, a series of chain drive full-time transfer case systems appeared. Jeep used Warner's Quadra-Trac, while Dodge, Ford and GM trucks adopted the massive chain-drive, full-time New Process 203 unit.

A full-time four-wheel drive transfer case prevents use of front locking hubs and provides four-wheel traction at all times. These systems use an internal differentiating system which allows proportional power flow to the front and rear axles.

On the early types, the differential system is similar to a spider gear arrangement in a drive axle assembly. The design continuously delivers power to both the front and rear axles. A hefty chain connects the two drive outputs, while a gearset provides low range. High- and low-range Lock mode overrides the transfer case's differential system for off-pavement or loose traction driving.

Excess parts wear and poor gas mileage encouraged most light truck manufacturers to abandon full-time four-wheel drive by 1980. The return to part-time four-wheel drive, however, did not signal a change back to the rugged NP205 or Dana 20 and Spicer/Dana 24 gear drive (iron-case) units. Instead, most American full-size trucks switched to the New Process 208 chain drive part-time unit.

The NP208 transfer case is a lightweight aluminum housed design. An NP208 design allows quick, easy shifting (on-the-fly) between 2WD high and 4WD high ranges. Although some would assume that drive chain life is a weakness with these designs, chains and sprockets are, in fact, very durable.

On early NP208 transfer cases, wear is most often at the shifting forks and nylon fork channels. As many of these units use thin ATF for a lubricant, seal and case leakage is another area of concern.

Lightweight Part-time Systems

Chain drive transfer cases have proven far less durable than earlier iron-cased gear drive transfer cases. Shift mechanism failures and leaks plague many aluminum chain drive transfer case units. A major overhaul is necessary to correct these problems.

Those 1969–91 K-models equipped with the New Process 205 transfer case still offer the best stamina. To date, iron cases and durable gear drives have proven superior to all other designs. The vehicle manufacturers argue that weight savings and reduced friction encourage the use of lighter transfer units. I argue that a Spicer/Dana 20 or 24 and the New Process 205 gear drive transfer case mechanisms could easily be fitted within a high-strength and lightweight alloy case. A number of Japanese truck transfer cases have taken this design tack, most notably the formidable Toyota FJ models.

Most four-wheelers are fully capable of pulling a lever, twisting a manual hub or reading an instruction decal. Overall reliability and off-pavement survival suggest the need for heavy duty factory options—choices like a bulletproof New Process 205 transfer case that can give trouble-free service well in excess of 150,000 miles.

Transfer Case Troubleshooting

Overhauling your truck's transfer case is a job much like a manual transmission overhaul. If you need to do such work, you will find step-by-step overhaul procedures in the GM truck shop manual or a professional-level service manual. Within the scope and aims of this book, I outline some general troubleshooting guidelines for common transfer case problems. This should help you determine what measures to take. Your shop manual can help with step-by-step removal/installation (R & R) and overhaul.

The most frequent transfer case trouble is hard shifting. Often, the remedy is really simple, requiring nothing more than cleaning the linkage and properly lubricating these parts. Sometimes the problem is bent or damaged linkage, the result of off-pavement abuse.

If external linkage is not the problem and your transfer case slips out of gear or front wheel drive, anticipate more serious trouble. Before condemning the transfer case unit, I would suggest that you check the transfer case-to-transmission attaching hardware. A loose transfer case housing can cause gear binding and internal side loads or pressure on the gears.

Deeper Troubles

Service manuals list the shift mechanism among the possible causes of transfer case problems. Poppet balls and springs are of concern in earlier transfer case shift mechanisms, but noises, jumping out of gear and difficult shifting usually indicate more serious troubles.

Before removing the transfer case from your truck for overhaul, it's always prudent to check the condition of the shift rail springs and poppet balls. There are instances when a worn or broken spring does cause trouble, but more likely the culprit is bearing damage, a bent shift fork or other internal defects.

If your high-mileage transfer case has never been through an overhaul, suspect bearing fatigue at the very least. Although gear drive transfer cases have a solid record for longevity, you should always replace worn bearings, as excessive gear clearance and poor tooth contact can quickly cause gear failure and expensive parts damage.

Chain Drive Transfer Case Troubles

Failure of a fork or shift mechanism can leave your 4x4 stranded. With the NP208 and similar later units, trouble symptoms include jumping out of gear, failure to engage the low, high or neutral range or noisy operation. Before tearing into the unit, however, check the easy possibilities.

Fluid deserves a look. (Various applications use ATF or motor oil, so check your truck's requirements.) Leaks develop at seals, case halves, and castings. Pay close attention. Shift linkage sometimes needs adjustment or alignment. Make certain the linkage does not bind or interfere with the body parts. When these simpler cures fail, plan to remove the transfer case unit for overhaul.

Removing the NP208 for Rebuilding

The NP208 transfer case is usually simple to remove. General procedure includes placing the shifter in 4H and draining the fluid. Disconnect all cables, linkages and driveshaft joints.

Drain all fluid, then separate yokes from the input and output shafts. See whether the exhaust pipe or brake cable interferes, and check the top of the transfer case for switch wires.

Once you have disconnected all external parts, place a transmission jack beneath the transfer case. Now unbolt the case from the transmission adapter. In minutes, with the use of a floor jack or the help of a stout friend, you can free the transfer case from the adapter.

Keep all parts level until the input shaft completely clears the transfer case. Place the transfer case on your workbench. Level the ends, and lay the unit with the case's split lying parallel to the benchtop.

Remember to replace all seals, including yoke seals. Always refer to your GM truck shop manual or a professional-level service manual for detailed procedures on the removal, overhaul and reinstallation of your transfer case.

> *CAUTION —*
> *When towing a 4x4 truck, consult the owner's handbook for special towing instructions that apply to the model and transfer case design. Severe geartrain damage can result from failure to observe the manufacturer's requirements.*

2. DRIVESHAFTS

A light truck's driveshaft(s) take tremendous punishment. On 4WD models, excessive suspension travel, weighty loads, radically changing driveshaft angles and modifications like an overly zealous suspension lift kit can tear your U-joints and driveshafts to pieces.

Often, the cause of a U-joint failure is misconstrued. Sure, wear takes a rapid toll on trucks that ford streams, flex their springs to the maximum and crawl through tor-

0012431

Fig. 10-4. A variety of U-joint failures directly relate to poor maintenance or bad driveshaft angularity.

Fig. 10-5. *Trent Alford at M.I.T. in El Cajon, California aligns hefty replacement parts for a heavy duty rear driveshaft that will increase a truck's stamina.*

Fig. 10-6. *Longer wheelbase trucks use a mid-shaft bearing. Wear here will cause severe driveline vibration.*

tuous rocks with massive torque applied through low range gears. On 2WD models that pull trailers or campers, the loads on drivelines also become excessive.

Poorly fitted driveshafts also provide a major cause of failure. Shafts pieced together out-of-phase or badly angled are the worst culprits. Wear in the rear driveshaft slip yoke, stub spline or mid-shaft bearing can produce an unusual vibrating sound during a float condition (period between acceleration load and deceleration). This is especially noticeable on heavier duty trucks with driveline-mounted parking brakes, as the brake drum amplifies the noise.

A driveshaft's U-joints must also be "in phase" with each other. As a simple maintenance concern, proper grease intervals and grease gun pressures contribute to driveshaft longevity.

Beyond these factors, driveshaft survival depends mostly on torque loads. These include the weight placed

Fig. 10-7. *Although they look similar, replacement U-joint at left fits one-ton trucks. Middle joint is size found in most half- and 3/4-ton models. At right, the small size joint fits driveshaft of a compact 4x4. Bigger is better.*

Fig. 10-8. *Use of a hefty custom built driveshaft assures resistance to torque loads. With a truck-type four-speed and low gearing, reduction ratios in excess of 70:1 are possible! Such torque is tremendous.*

on the vehicle, the amount of engine torque applied to the joints and also the departure and receiving angles between the driving and driven yokes of the driveshaft.

(continued)

Driveshaft Angularity

Angles and rotational arcs make or break U-joints and driveshafts. While torque load determines the proper size U-joint to use, engineers design driveshafts for an 85% efficiency factor. To understand the highest load placed upon your driveshafts, the formula is: Lowest Gear Torque = Net Engine Torque X Transmission Low Gear Ratio X Transfer Case Low Range Ratio (if a 4x4 with low range) X 0.85.

Two angles affect a driveshaft: side-view drop and plane-view shift. Side view is simply the angle that the driveshaft slopes downward from the transfer case to each axle's differential. Plane view is the lateral angle of the driveshaft, viewed from directly above the frame.

For your truck's driveshafts to live, the angles on each end of the driveshaft (the side-view drop combined with the plane-view shift) must create as little non-uniform motion as possible. U-joint angles, in simple terms, must rotate on nearly identical arcs, with the vertical faces of the U-joint flanges nearly parallel. (Spicer/Dana recommends that the limit of inequality must not exceed that of a single U-joint operating at a 3° angle.)

The included U-joint angles should remain identical on each end of the driveshaft. When the shaft rotates, joints should move in similar arcs, with bearing cross shafts each running at the same tilt.

Speed dictates maximum allowable driveshaft angles. A driveshaft rotating 5000 rpm (somewhat obscure for a 4x4 truck unless flat out in a desert race) tolerates no more than 3 degrees, 15 seconds of operating angle, while the same shaft spinning 1500 rpm will work at an 11-degree, 30-second angle. Driveshaft length affects this formula, too, with longer driveshafts tolerating more operating angle.

Owners who lift their trucks with shackle kits or springs must also consider that a 3/4° change in the differential pinion angle will change the U-joint operating angle about 1/4°.

Shimming the axle housing at the spring perches is a common method for restoring the pinion angle and U-joint operating angles. Driveline specialists insist that appropriate steel shims be used or, if the angle is radically off, cut the spring perches from the axle housing, reposition to the correct angle and re-weld the perches in place. Brass and aluminum shims tend to pound flat during off-road bashing.

Before hybridizing your engine, transmission or transfer case angles, take accurate measurements of the shaft angles. When lifting a 4x4, the side angles of the driveshafts also change. Small changes are acceptable, as long as the axle swings up and down on its original arc of movement. Problems begin when the side angle becomes excessive.

An excellent source of information, including formulas and professional driveshaft service tips, is Spicer/Dana's *Trouble Shooting Guideline*, available through Spicer distributors or Dana Corporation, Drivetrain Service Division, P.O. Box 321, Toledo, Ohio 43691. This quick reference guide and the *Spicer Universal Joints and Driveshafts Service Manual* are the last word on professional driveshaft service, maintenance and construction techniques.

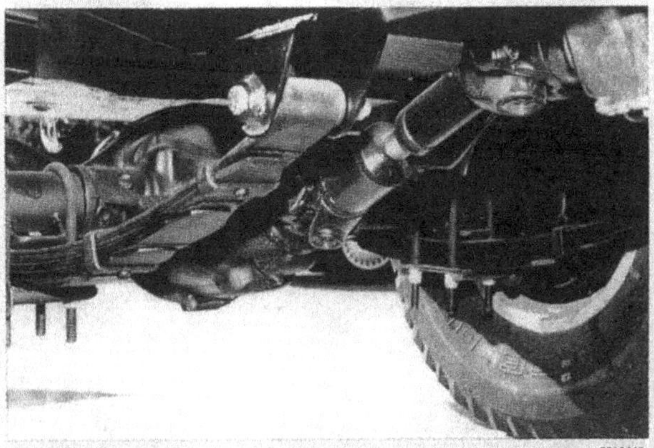

0012445

Looking upward from below the rear driveshaft, the line between the U-joint flanges is evident. A short shaft demands precise side and plane angles.

0012446

Side-view angle shows the relationship between the sloping driveshaft and the U-joint flanges. Note that flange centerlines are parallel.

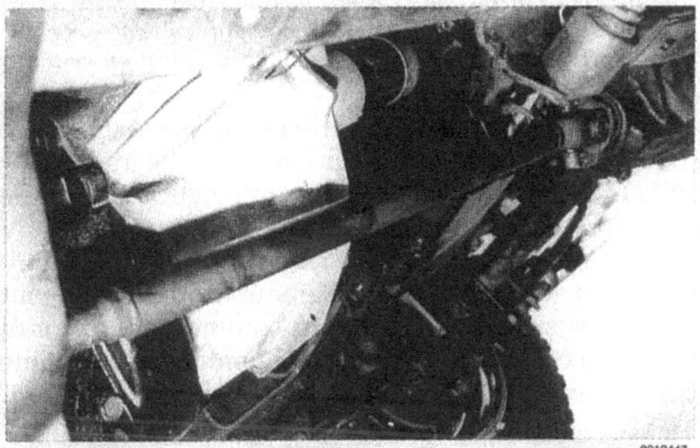

0012447

Short wheelbase 4x4s sometimes boast a long front driveshaft with very slight slope (side-view angularity). As length reduces torque load, this heavy duty replacement shaft will easily handle the chores.

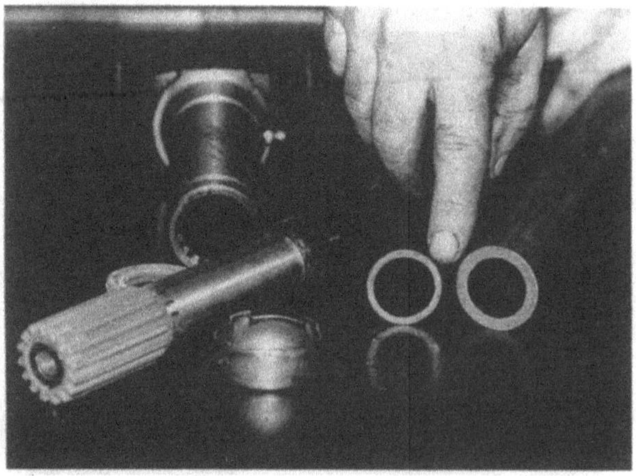

0012436

Fig. 10-9. Dramatic difference between an OEM front driveshaft tube section and a replacement heavier wall thickness tube is obvious.

0012438

Fig. 10-11. Before MIG wire-feed welding, the shaft is carefully tapped into alignment. The builder will work this section until total runout is less than 0.005 inch! Such tolerances are necessary for vibration-free results and illustrate the importance of protecting your driveshafts from bashing.

0012437

Fig. 10-10. This step is critical during driveshaft construction. Proper driveshaft phasing requires that U-joint cross yokes are absolutely in line. Before welding, a spirit level or protractor and a perfectly flat benchtop assure alignment.

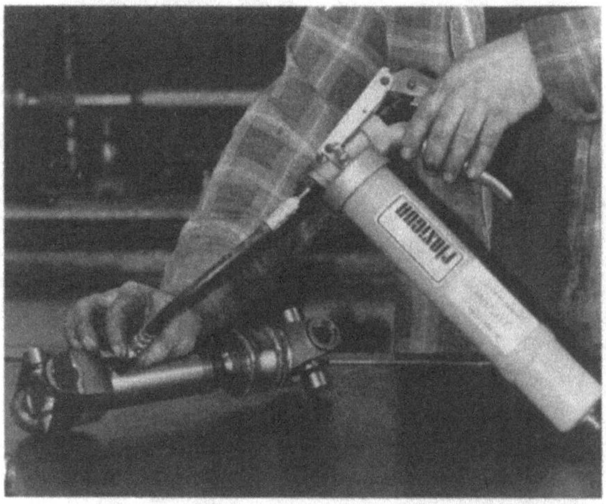

0012439

Fig. 10-12. U-joint failure usually follows loss of grease. Worn seals allowed moisture into these joints. Brindling resulted from lack of grease.

A common problem with trucks that have a suspension/spring lift kit is too much angle on the joints. This results from the radical difference in height between the axle pinion shafts and the transfer case output shafts.

Rotating the axle pinion shaft upward is a shoddy method that some lift kit installers use to reduce U-joint angles. This approach can lead to another crop of problems, those caused by unmatched U-joint angles. U-joints rotating on widely dissimilar arcs can create enough rotational vibration and stress to break a gear case housing!

Your truck's driveshaft survival depends upon joint size, tubing diameter and wall thickness, plus the ability of the assembly to compensate for speed, length and angle changes. Often, a driveshaft that would work perfectly well in its original mode cannot handle a chassis lift or increased horsepower loads. Here, a custom heavy duty driveshaft is necessary.

Proper Lubrication

U-joint survival depends upon correct lubrication. Stream crossings, wintry highways and sandy deserts take their toll. Assuming that U-joint dust seals are in top shape, you can follow Spicer's on/off-highway lubrication guidelines: 5,000 to 8,000 miles or every three months (far more often if your truck is subject to either severe service or exposure to water). A high-quality lube gun is a prerequisite to preserving U-joints and their delicate seals.

When selecting U-joint and driveshaft greases, follow Spicer's guidelines. Use only National Lubricating Grease Institute (NLGI) Extreme Pressure Grade 1 or 2. Avoid heavier greases. Severe service requires lithium soap base or EP grease with a temperature range of +325° to -10° F.

U-joint Service and Repair Tips

U-joint replacement always begins with driveshaft removal. Before loosening a driveshaft, mark the shaft's order of assembly. Drivelines must be in-phase, with couplers kept in line with their original splines.

> **NOTE —**
> If your driveshaft has two pieces, scribe an indexing line on each section. Reassembly in the original position will assure satisfactory service, alignment, and balance.

Cleanliness is essential, regardless of the locale in which you make the repairs. (I and others have replaced U-joints on the tailgate of a pickup and even atop granite boulders.) If the work area is particularly gritty, beware. New U-joints, freshly coated with grease, attract dirt like a horseshoe magnet draws pig iron from beach sand. Assuming that the shaft isn't damaged, you can make a permanent U-joint installation in the field if you approach the job with professional expectations.

The tools needed to remove and replace a U-joint are minimal. In the field, a good mechanic's hammer, solid punch, blade screwdriver, a variety of sockets and a set of pliers can handle the job. Specialty or homemade tools

Fig. 10-13. Coupler types and U-joints vary. Double Cardan (constant velocity) joints have become common on 4x4 driveshafts. Joint-to-yoke attaching methods also vary.

Fig. 10-14. Disassembling a joint requires few tools. On Spicer-type U-joints, you must remove two external snap rings.

Fig. 10-15. Clean the driveshaft for close inspection and reassembly. This will assure proper fitup of parts.

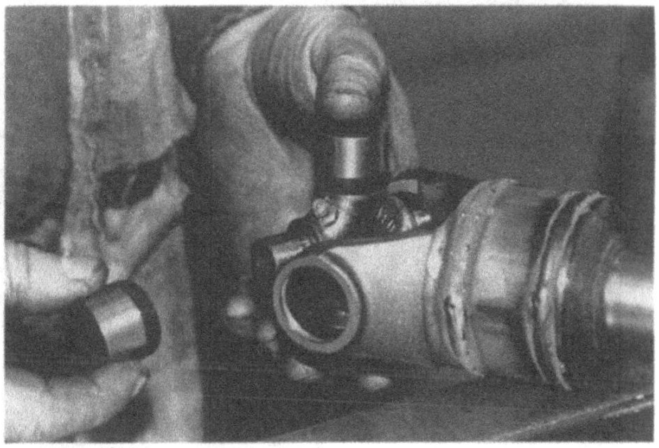

Fig. 10-16. Once both bearing caps are free of the driveshaft, you can separate the U-joint.

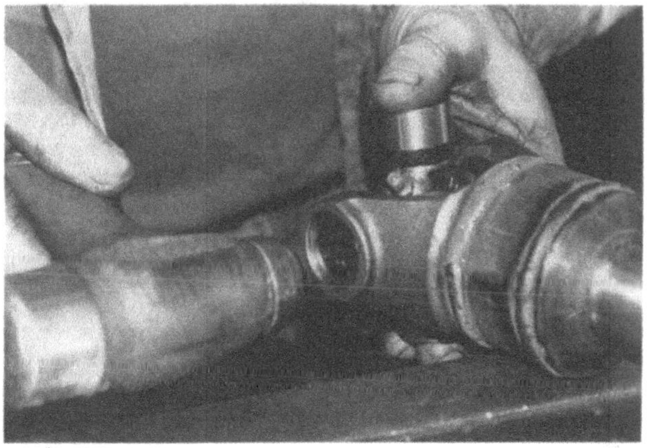

Fig. 10-17. Protect these snap ring grooves during service. Striking a groove with a hammer or punch could cause permanent driveshaft damage.

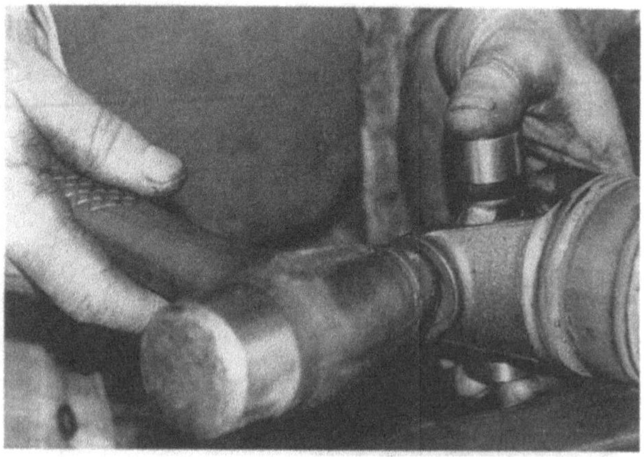

Fig. 10-18. Install the first bearing cap. Use the hammer carefully and support the bearing needles with the cross section of the U-joint. If you doubt your hammer skills, use a socket to drive the bearing cap into its recess. Install the cap far enough to insert the snap ring. Install the second cap. Again, carefully keep the cross section centered to hold needle bearings in place. If all needles remain intact, the second bearing cap will just clear its snap ring groove. Install the snap ring. Make sure snap rings seat completely.

Fig. 10-19. New U-joints come with snap rings and a grease fitting. Make sure needle bearings stay in place during assembly. Always align the grease fitting to permit easy access and service. Field lubrication of double Cardan joints requires special grease gun tip.

can ease the job further, although the principles remain the same.

If your technique is correct, even the most trying environment will not prevent a quality job. Find a solid surface to work on, preferably steel plate (the bumper, a front winch mounting plate, or a hefty wooden board in a pickup bed). Get out of the weather if gale winds prevail, and plan on several minutes of painstaking work.

Fig. 10-20. A constant velocity, double Cardan U-joint has a precise assembly sequence. Be aware of the spring, which must be in place when installing the new joints. Reassemble in exactly the reverse sequence of disassembly.

Fig. 10-21. By contrast, Detroit type U-Joints utilize internal snap rings. Straps hold the joint to the yoke.

U-joint Installation

Although a press or specialized U-joint tools are helpful, don't be misled. Some of the best craftsmen in the automotive repair industry still replace U-joints with basic hand tools. The reason? U-joint bearing caps fit precisely into their saddles and bores, and the slightest cocking of a cap during installation can ruin a driveshaft. Presses and hefty tools eliminate the *feel* of the cap moving into its bore. Hand tools maintain your awareness of fit.

Once you have completed the U-joint replacement and reinstalled the driveshaft, grease the U-joints. Do not grease a U-joint before bolting it into the yoke, as you will force the bearing caps out of position. (See your factory service manual for torque specifications.)

If you left the grease gun home, new joints usually contain enough grease for the drive back. Permanently sealed joints, in fact, have high quality grease and seals, and require no further greasing. Other joints, equipped with grease fittings, require periodic lubrication.

3. AXLE ASSEMBLIES

The mysteries within the axle housing, the maze of gears and bearings, are responsible for turning horsepower into motion. How that happens is as significant as any other aspect of your truck's powertrain. Although axle overhaul is beyond the scope of this book, your knowledge of tell-tale wear signs could prevent serious trouble, reduce damage and contain the repair costs. Let's begin with some axle basics.

Engine power flows through the clutch or torque converter, transmission, transfer case (4WD models) and driveline(s). The driveshaft rotates the axle's pinion shaft/gear (attached to the U-joint companion flange) to carry power into the axle. Supported by bearings in the axle housing, the pinion shaft's bevel gearhead transfers power to a matching ring gear, which changes the direction of the power flow by 90°.

Together, the ring and pinion gears serve two functions: 1) changing the power flow direction, and 2) increasing torque, proportionally, by reducing the rotational speed of the axle shafts. A 4.10 gear ratio (41

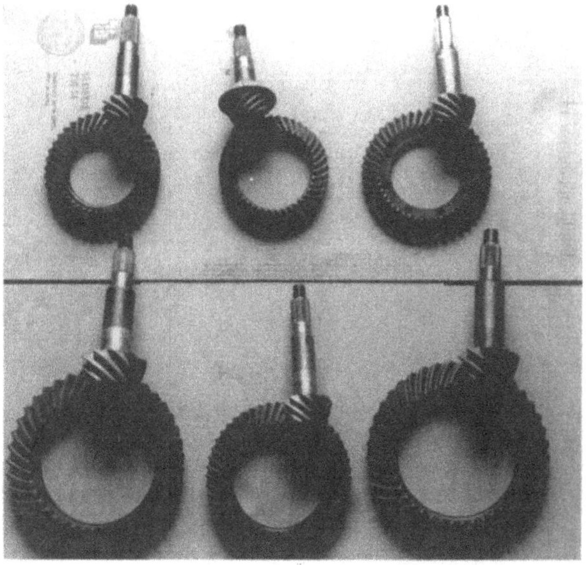

0012452

Fig. 10-23. *Comparison of ring and pinion gears says it all. Top row, left to right, is a Spicer 27, a light duty Dana 28, and a WWII vintage Jeep MB Model Spicer 25. Bottom row of Dana gears shows the 60, 44 and 70 sets. The Spicer/Dana 44 is a popular front axle on full-sized 4x4 1/2-tons and some 3/4-tons, also used at the rear of many half-ton GMC trucks from 1955 Second Series through the 1960s (called the Spicer 45 in this application). The two larger gearsets fit 3/4-ton and one-ton capacity trucks.*

0014470

Fig. 10-22. *This early Spicer integral front axle housing features pressed-in and welded axle tubes and closed steering knuckles. An integral axle overhaul takes place in the chassis. The job requires a special spreader to remove the differential carrier from the axle housing.*

Fig. 10-24. Compare the Dana 70 differential side gear with that of the 44. Note the axle splines inside each gear, indicating the size difference between a one-ton truck's axle shaft and a full-sized 1/2-ton's. GM's own Corporate 14-bolt rear axle, in its full-floating form, boasts a 10.5-inch diameter ring gear.

teeth on the ring gear and 10 on the pinion) rotates axle shafts with nearly four-and-one-tenth times the torque of the driveshaft—and at slightly less than one-fourth of the driveshaft's speed.

The ring gear bolts to a case, generally called the differential carrier. Bearings support the differential carrier in either the hypoid axle housing or a removable third member housing. Chevrolet and GMC trucks have used both the integral-type hypoid axle housing and the removable carrier design. The removable carrier (also called the third-member or center-section) was a popular approach from the 1930s through 1972, especially on Chevrolet models.

If the axle shafts connected directly to the ring gear's case, both wheels would spin continuously at the speed of the ring gear. Such a locked rear end or spool, although maximizing traction, is incapable of adjusting for the vehicle's left or right turns.

All four-wheeled vehicles require unequal wheel speed to negotiate a turn. The inside wheels rotate slower than the outside wheels. If all four wheels turned at equal speed, serious trouble would result. Tires would skid and axle shafts would work against each other.

Here the differential becomes important. The speed of the right side wheels needs to vary from those on the left. In a straight ahead mode, the ring gear turns both shafts at equal speed, that speed determined by the axle ratio and engine rpm. For turns, however, the individual axle shaft speeds adjust for smooth traction at each wheel.

Imagine your truck's driveshaft(s) rotating at 2000 rpm. With 10 teeth on the pinion gear and 40 teeth on the ring gear, the axle shafts will spin at 500 rpm. Although useful for illustration purposes, an axle ratio of 4-to-1 would cause the pinion gear teeth to continuously find the same ring gear teeth, an undesirable tendency. Instead, engineers devise ratios like 4.10, with a 41/10 tooth arrangement that constantly renews tooth contact.

Differential Action

As your truck enters a corner, the inside wheel turns slower than the outside wheel. The speed at each wheel must differ. To allow for the speed change, the differential contains a series of gears inside the rotating carrier case. While ring and pinion speeds are constant, the differential gears allow axle shaft speeds to vary.

The differential carrier housing is hollow, and the axles slide through the space in the housing, entering from each side. Splines on the inner ends of the axle shafts engage the differential side gears. These side gears, in non-locking differentials, also have bevel teeth, meshing with two smaller gears, called pinions or spider gears.

The spider gear teeth, facing inward toward the center of the carrier case, engage with the side gear teeth. The spiders float on a pinion shaft, which mounts rigidly through the center of the carrier case. Effectively, the four gears can move independently of the carrier.

The result: 1) If road speed at both wheels remains the same, the gears all rotate like a solid unit in unison with the differential carrier case; 2) when turning a corner, the four gears can rotate at the speed necessary to apply more rpm at the outside wheel and proportionately less at the inside wheel; and 3) at times, discouragingly, the conventional differential mechanism directs power to the wheel with the least resistance. This last point remains the primary shortcoming of conventional, non-locking differentials.

When watching a 2WD truck negotiate rocks, sand and loose terrain, it's easy to distinguish the conventional rear axle. One wheel will often spin furiously, while the opposite wheel, with solid traction, stands still. Four-wheel drive models, even with conventional axles, fare much better than a 2WD truck.

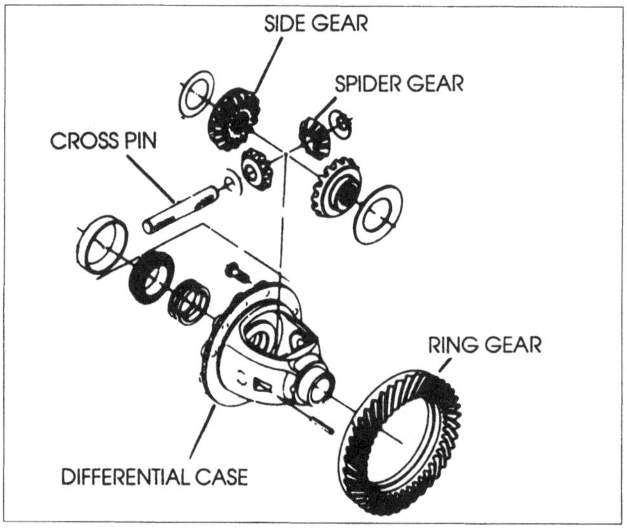

Fig. 10-25. Exploded view of conventional differential shows gear locations.

Controlling Wheelspin

Traction loss is a serious problem. The other extreme is damage caused when no differential action takes place. A truck's handling with a permanently locked rear axle would be very dangerous, too. For this reason, we depend upon systems that provide more positive traction but still allow differential action.

GM light truck limited slip differentials enjoy a variety of trade names. Several aftermarket performance systems have also been developed, many suited for street, drag strip and off-pavement use. (See the performance section of the book for detailed information on aftermarket traction devices.)

Typically, a limited slip unit is built around a clutching mechanism within the differential. Simply put, the clutching device enables torque delivery to the axle and wheel with traction. The basic difference between factory limited slip and aftermarket locker differentials is the design of the clutching or lock-up mechanism.

By design, the clutch type limited slip unit can still allow variance of wheel speed on corners. The differential behaves in much the same manner as a conventional unit, permitting the inner wheel to rotate slower.

> *WARNING —*
> *Use caution with any limited slip or positive traction differential. Your truck will tend to go sideways when both wheels of an axle lose traction at the same time. On ice or slick pavement, locked traction at both wheels of an axle can cause sideward motion of the vehicle, most often toward the low side of the road. (See chapter on driving techniques for details.)*

Axle Types

Although integral housing hypoid axles require more tools for disassembly, they generally provide substantial ring and pinion support. While Spicer's integral-type axles have served many GMC trucks, Chevrolet light trucks have most often stayed with the GM Corporate and Saginaw axles.

The Spicer/Dana 44, 60, 60 HD and the Spicer/Dana 70 have been popular rear axles over the years on a variety of models. Based upon GVWR package, light GM truck 4x4 front axles include GM's own 10-bolt axle plus the ever-popular Spicer/Dana 44 and the Dana 60 units.

A similar integral rear axle design is the GM/Saginaw 10-, 12- and 14-bolt types. The semi-floating 12-bolt was a Chevrolet 1/2-ton model mainstay from the mid-1960s until the late 1970s and boasts a large ring gear diameter and plenty of stamina. In my estimation, this is a good match for the legendary Ford 9-inch axle. The 10-bolt GM light truck axle also offers good performance in light-duty applications.

Semi- Versus Full-floating Axles

Semi-floating axles offer less ruggedness than full-floating axles. On the semi-floater, a single outer wheel bearing supports the axle shaft, while the splined inner end of the axle shaft relies on the differential side gear for support. A broken axle shaft can cause real trouble.

Most semi-floating axles rely upon bearing retainer plates at the outer bearing to hold the axle in place. If the axle shaft should break in the wrong place, the broken axle shaft, hub and wheel can slide out.

Many semi-floating axles use a C-lock at the inner end of each axle shaft, but the risk of losing an axle remains. C-locks and the inner axle shaft end can wear out, or the axle shaft could break and come loose, much like an axle shaft without a C-lock.

Full-floating axle shafts, by contrast, act simply as a drive bar. The wheel and hub ride on bearings much like on the front end of a conventional 4x4 truck. A retaining nut provides for hub bearing adjustment and also holds the wheel hub on the spindle.

The spindle is a component part of the axle housing, and the axle shaft fits through the spindle's bore. Engaging the side gear at its inner end, the axle shaft's outer flange bolts to the wheel hub. If an axle shaft breaks, the hub and wheel continue to rotate on the spindle.

To remove the broken shaft, you unbolt its flange from the wheel hub and fish out the broken section. The wheel and tire remain on the ground, supported by the wheel hub bearings, so there is no need to even jack up the truck.

> NOTE —
> Since a broken front axle shaft or steering knuckle joint could impair steering and cause further axle damage, it's best to remove the axle shaft assembly before moving the vehicle.

Conventional (non-Sierra solid front axle chassis) GM 4x4 light trucks featured full-floating type front axles. The 1988 Sierra truck introduced a durable semi-floating IFS system signaling the end to semi-floating front axle use.

All years of half-ton trucks and many of the 3/4-ton models built since the early 1980s have featured semi-floating type rear axles. Until the early 1980s, all 3/4-ton (3600-Series and the C/K-20 models) use full-floating rear axles. Since 1986, however, only heavy duty applications like the rugged one-ton C/K-30/3500 models consistently use the full-floating rear axle design, though some C/K-20/2500 models are again being so equipped. For truck use, especially hauling cargos, carrying a fifth-wheel trailer or working off pavement, the added stamina of a full-floating type axle is significant.

GM 4x4 Front Axle Types

Two primary changes have occurred in GM 4x4 front axles. The shift to open steering knuckles with ball-joints began in 1971, when the K-10/1500, K-20/2500 models and the K-5 Blazer/Jimmy began using this design. The change to independent front suspension (IFS) on 1988 Sierra chassis 4WDs was the second major engineering change.

Free-wheeling manual locking hubs, which serve the full-floating conventional solid front axle 4x4s, remain available to 1991 on the K-5 Blazer/Jimmy, K-Suburban and K-30/3500 Crew Cab. Automatic locking hubs became available in 1980 and continue through the last solid axle 4x4s.

> NOTE —
> Full-floating front wheel hubs plus manual or automatic locking hubs provide the only means for completely eliminating excess front axle and driveline wear. I have always opted for rugged and reliable manual locking hubs.

Closed-knuckle front ends use kingpin bearings (tapered roller type) or conical bronze bushings. Open knuckles use ball-joints or pivot pins and bushings. Prior to 1971, all GM 4x4s featured closed steering knuckles.

The closed-knuckle axle system features fully enclosed front axle shaft joints (Rzeppa/constant velocity type on NAPCO conversions and GM 4x4 models through 1959; Spicer cross type joints on 1960–70 GM K-models) that receive grease from the sealed knuckle cavity. The later open-knuckle axle joints are also Spicer-type U-joints; most often these joints are factory filled with grease and permanently sealed.

> **NOTE —**
> Permanently sealed joints are easy to distinguish. They have no provision for a grease fitting. Always replace these joints with a sealed joint of the same OEM design. Driveshaft U-joints with a grease fitting often lack the torque capacity of sealed joints.

Drive Axle Troubleshooting

Before suspecting trouble with your truck's axle(s), check the fluid levels and also the type of gear lubricant required. On limited slip units or the GM governor-lock differentials, special lubes prevent multi-plate clutches and other components from sticking together. If you introduce a non-specified oil to these axles, symptoms of differential trouble can result.

Try to isolate the noise. Tire sounds, front or rear wheel bearing noises, engine and transmission troubles and even the type of road surface can confuse the situation. Especially with oversize tires, light trucks often develop noises that have nothing to do with the differential or any other axle component, yet the sound comes from that area. Check each of these other possibilities before condemning your axle(s).

A clicking or patterned ratcheting noise at the rear wheels is a possible wheel bearing problem. By supporting the rear axle safely on jack stands, you can rotate each wheel by hand and feel for bearing roughness. (See other chapters of the book for front wheel bearing inspection and service.)

If you detect an actual wheel bearing problem, consult your GM truck shop manual or a professional-level service manual for details on axle shaft removal and wheel bearing service.

Differential side gear and small pinion (spider) gear noises are most often heard when the vehicle turns. If your truck has a conventional or limited slip rear axle that makes noises as the vehicle negotiates a corner, suspect differential trouble. Similar front axle noises, especially with the hubs engaged and the transfer case in 4WD, also suggest differential trouble, although a defective axle shaft joint can mimic these sounds.

A continuous grating noise that varies with vehicle speed suggests pinion bearing failure. Trucks that run in deep water without frequent changes of gear lubricant are vulnerable to ring gear, pinion gear or bearing failure.

Ring and pinion noise is distinguishable under various driving conditions: coast, drive or float. Deceleration creates coast noises. Drive noises are detectable as you accelerate the truck. Float noise occurs under light throttle situations and easy loads that keep the ring and pinion gears spinning with the least amount of pressure.

When your truck's axle gear lubricant smells badly burned, remove the inspection cover and examine the gear teeth and bearings. Blue discoloration usually indicates extreme heat, fatigue and poor lubrication.

> ***CAUTION —***
> *If lubricant is very low for any length of time, the axle is subject to major damage. Always watch for seal leaks or other symptoms of fluid loss. Proper fluid levels are crucial to axle survival.*

Seal Leaks

Seal failure is a primary cause of fluid loss on truck axles. Look closely for fluid loss at the axles whenever you service your truck, and watch for oil drips when you park the vehicle. The locations for axle seal leaks are easy to monitor, beginning with the pinion shaft seal, the ventilation valve (if so equipped) and the axle shaft seals.

The pinion shaft seal is very easy to locate. Follow the driveshaft to the U-joint flange, then note the point at which the pinion shaft enters the axle housing. The seal that surrounds the shaft at the entrance to the axle housing is the pinion shaft seal.

Axle shaft seal leaks appear as oil dripping from the bottom of the rear brake backing plates or at the steering knuckle on an open-knuckle front end. Axle seal leaks on closed-knuckle front ends can lead to dangerously diluted wheel bearing lubricant. Often the closed-knuckle system's large diameter inner axle housing seal will leak visibly. (See brake section for details on parts damage from leaking axle seals.)

When a seal leak occurs, first check the lubricant levels. Overfilled steering knuckles or differentials will cause leaks and can even dislodge a seal by hydraulic pressure. Again, a common leak on all closed-knuckle front ends is the large inner oil seal. This seal at the inner side of the steering knuckle will leak grease from the knuckle cavity. You can replace this seal without removing the entire steering knuckle.

0012456

Fig. 10-26. *A pinion seal leak is easy to spot. Loss of lubrication can lead to expensive parts damage.*

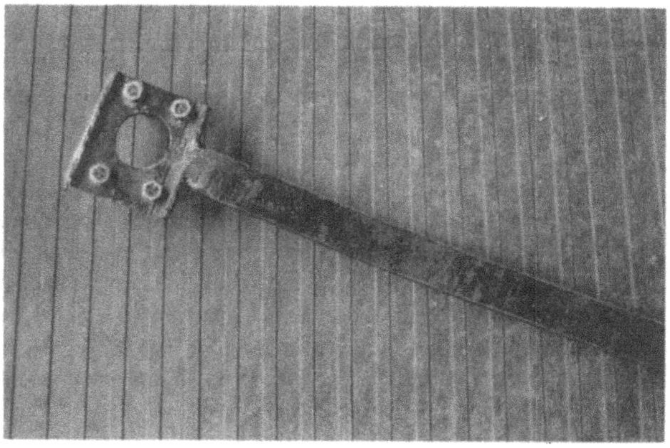

0012457

Fig. 10-27. This tool, fabricated twenty years ago with simple materials, holds the U-joint flange. The pinion shaft nut torque is very high, and heavy leverage is necessary. Today, the option for most mechanics is an air impact gun. Always set and check final torque with a torque wrench.

Axle Seal Installation Tips

Front drive axle seals are difficult to replace. Rear axle seals are also a handful. You'll want to do the job right the first time. Axle pinion seal replacement requires a holding tool to keep the U-joint flange from rotating while you loosen its nut. As an option, mechanics usually use an air impact gun when performing this work.

Before installing a pinion seal, clean the housing bore thoroughly. Be certain to apply a thin film of gasket sealant to the outer edge of the seal. Coat the inner lip of the seal with light grease. (Early models use leather seals that require soaking the seal in oil before installation. Neoprene replacement seals are now available.)

Tap the seal gently and evenly in cross. I like to use a rubber or plastic sand head hammer to avoid damaging or distorting the steel portion of the seal. Although I've always had access to special seal drivers, I feel that carefully placed hammer taps can produce the same results—and often better. Without a solid driver, you can maintain the *feel* for what you're doing by using a soft headed hammer and a light touch.

Coat the backside of the pinion flange washer with a thin film of gasket sealant, and install a new self-locking nut and crush/adjusting sleeve if required. Torque the nut to OEM specifications.

Other seals, including the front and rear axle shaft seals, are more difficult to access. Fortunately, seal replacement is relatively easy on the GM drop-in center section (semi-floating type) rear axles and semi-floating Spicer type axles found in earlier light duty half ton trucks. Later model axles with C-locks on the inner ends of the axle shafts can be a much messier job.

Front Axle and Knuckle Seals

By careful seal placement and use of sealant, you can change a closed-knuckle inner split ring seal and felt without removing the steering knuckle. The closed-knuckle inner felt seal can be carefully cut on a diagonal. (See my step-by-step illustrations or your shop manual for details.)

After carefully sliding the split seal/wiper into place, the sealant, cut felt and retainer halves can also fit around the axle housing's tube and against the ball end. Follow the illustrations for this procedure.

> **NOTE —**
> When servicing the closed-knuckle front end, be aware that spindle bolts have a nasty habit of loosening on the steering knuckle and shredding the spindle gasket (if so equipped). Once loose, a very unsafe condition exists, with the risk of shearing the bolts or threads that attach the spindle to the knuckle casting.

Some remedies for this chronic spindle bolt problem include 1) drilling and wire tying the bolt heads to aircraft standards; 2) replacing the bolts with Grade 8 studs secured with thread locking compound, then using aircraft Grade 8 self-locking nuts to secure the spindle; or 3) installing special aftermarket buttonhead (aircraft tensile strength) studs that have a serrated shoulder and compact round head. The studs pass from inside the knuckle through the thread holes and face outward to receive the spindle, looking much like the later open-knuckle type. The spindle then attaches with self-locking aircraft nuts.

> **NOTE —**
> While some Spicer/Dana OEM spindles attach with bolts and split lockwashers, others use conical washers. I prefer the conical washer for its full locking surface and long service life, plus a dose of Loctite 242 on cleaned threads to provide added insurance.

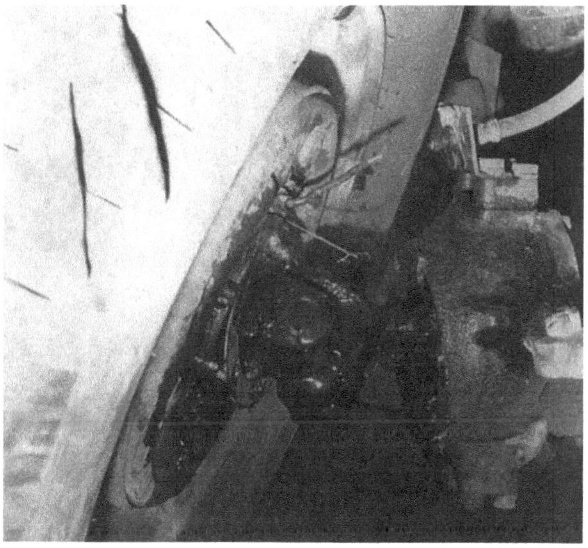

0012458

Fig. 10-28. An early closed-knuckle front axle trait: the spindle's six bolts have ripped cleanly from the threaded holes in the steering knuckle.

Closed-knuckle Steering Rebuild

The original 4x4 live front axles all had closed-knuckle steering mechanisms. A popular GM 4x4 front axle was the closed-knuckle Spicer/Dana 44, used from 1960 through 1970. A traditional Spicer full-floating design, these closed-knuckle units now have many miles on them, and most have fallen victim to fatigue and wear.

0012459

Fig. 10-29. *Closed-knuckle steering served Spicer live axles from 1941 until mid-1970s. Axle U-joint is within the spherical housing end, enclosed by steering knuckle casting. Knuckles pivot on pins and tapered roller bearings or bronze conical bushings. Wear occurs at pivot pin bearings or bushings, seals and steering linkage. GM's use of open-knuckle design began with Dana 44 axles on the 1971 K-model trucks.*

0012460

Fig. 10-30. *Rebuild begins with removing tie-rod assembly and drag link. Inspect for wear and replace any worn pieces.*

Before the ball-joint or open-knuckle era, these axles provided the rugged service and stamina that a 4x4 needed. In the interest of your truck's steering integrity and for resistance to leaks, here is an illustrated restoration/rebuild that I performed on a common closed-knuckle Dana 44 front axle.

Individual model years require different specifications. This how-to provides an overview of the closed-knuckle Spicer/Dana axle's steering wear points, repair needs and general overhaul requirements. See your shop manual for specifications and recommendations for your truck's live front axle. Overhauled and serviced properly, you can expect another 100,000-plus miles service from your Spicer/Dana 44 closed knuckle.

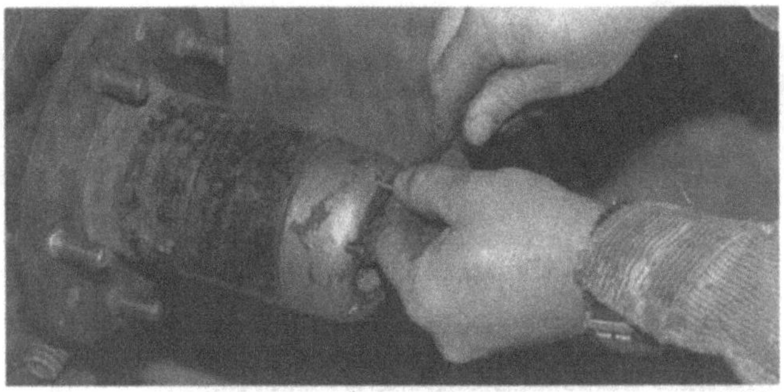

0012461

Fig. 10-31. *First part of this job resembles wheel bearing repack. Remove brake drum and free-wheeling hub. In applications where time has frozen parts together, it will be easier to remove drum-and-wheel hubs as an assembly. (Closed-knuckle live front axles have drum brakes.)*

0012462 / 0012659

Fig. 10-32. *Some wheel bearing applications use double hex nuts and a lock plate; others use two special nuts with a locating pin and indexing lock ring. Consult your OEM-level service manual for details on wheel bearing service and adjustment.*

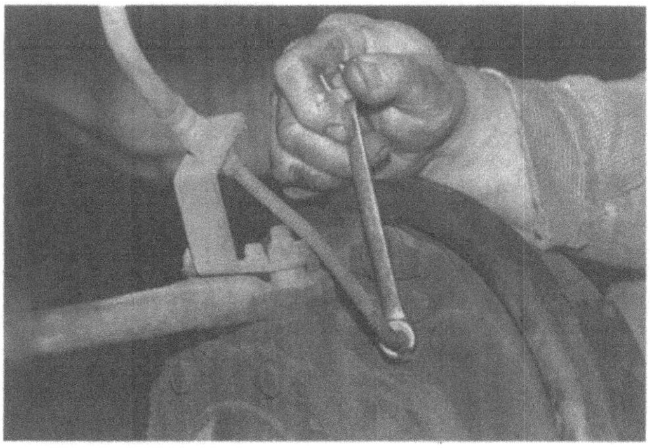

0012463

Fig. 10-33. Disconnect brake pipes or hoses before removing brake backing plate. Use a flare nut wrench and be sure to keep debris out of the brake system. Seal pipe end with a clean cap.

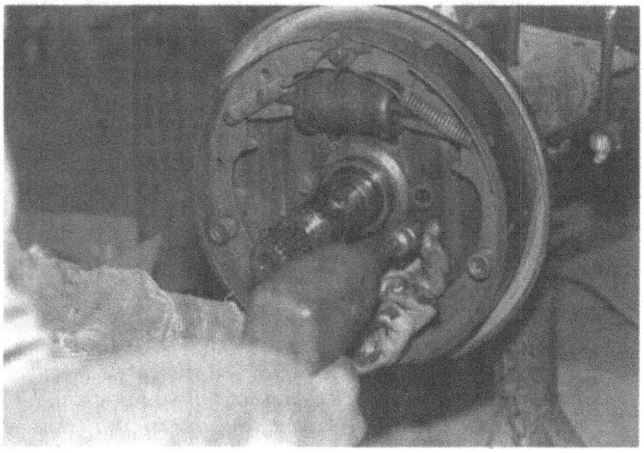

0012464

Fig. 10-34. Unbolt wheel hub spindle and remove brake backing plate and spindle. Avoid getting grease on brake lining.

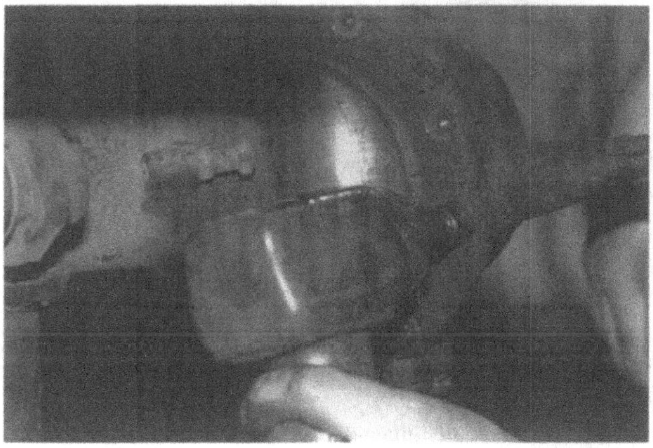

0012465

Fig. 10-35. Remove retainer plates, felt seal and rear knuckle seal. Plates, felt and large steel reinforced neoprene seal will come loose once you remove these screws.

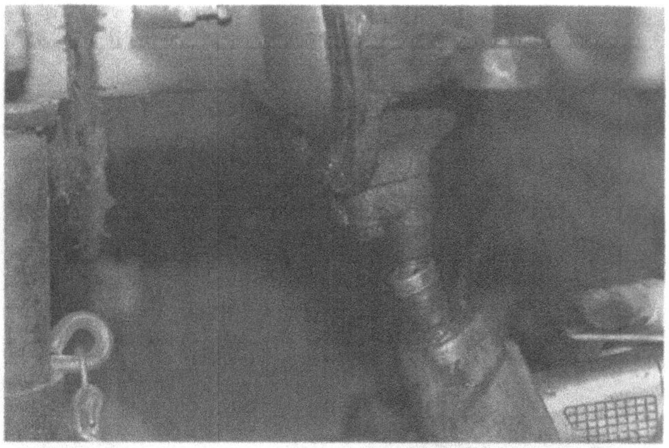

0012466

Fig. 10-36. With seals loose, remove lower bearing cap bolts. Keep cap and shims together, as these shims are selective fit and set the proper preload on pivot pin bearings.

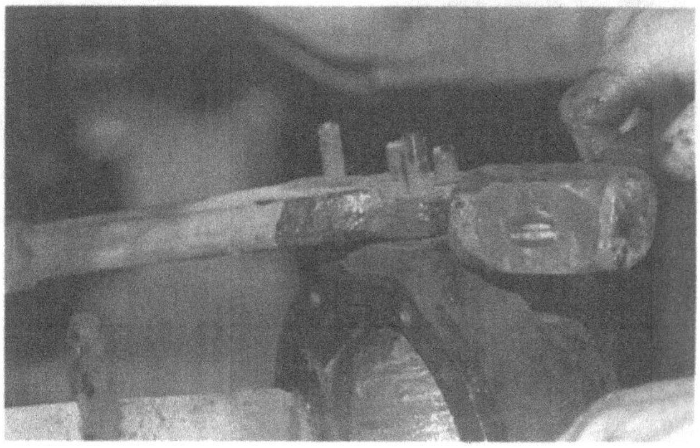

0012467

Fig. 10-37. At steering arm, studs and nuts are centered with split ring cone washers. Tap side of arm with a plastic or brass hammer to unseat cones. Pry cones out before attempting to remove arm. Knuckle is now free. (Axle shaft will slide easily from the housing once wheel spindle is removed.) Slide axle shaft very carefully to avoid damage to axle shaft seals.

0012468

Fig. 10-38. Clean and inspect all parts. Replace worn or damaged bearings and castings. Check for cracks and fatigue. Take this opportunity to repaint outer hub, knuckle and brake drum's outer surface with high temp engine paint.

0012469

Fig. 10-39. Drive bearing cups carefully from axle housing seats. Avoid damage to axle casting and inspect housing ends for cracks or damage. Clean housing end and use crocus cloth to eliminate burrs or scratches to machined ball-shaped seal surfaces. Install new cups squarely with a cup driver.

0012470

Fig. 10-40. Bearing cups show reason for sloppy front knuckle and excessive play. This 44 application uses conical bushings at top pivot pins and tapered roller bearing cones at bottom. Conical bushings wore, and lower bearing rollers pounded bearing cups. (Some applications use tapered roller bearings at both upper and lower pivot pins.)

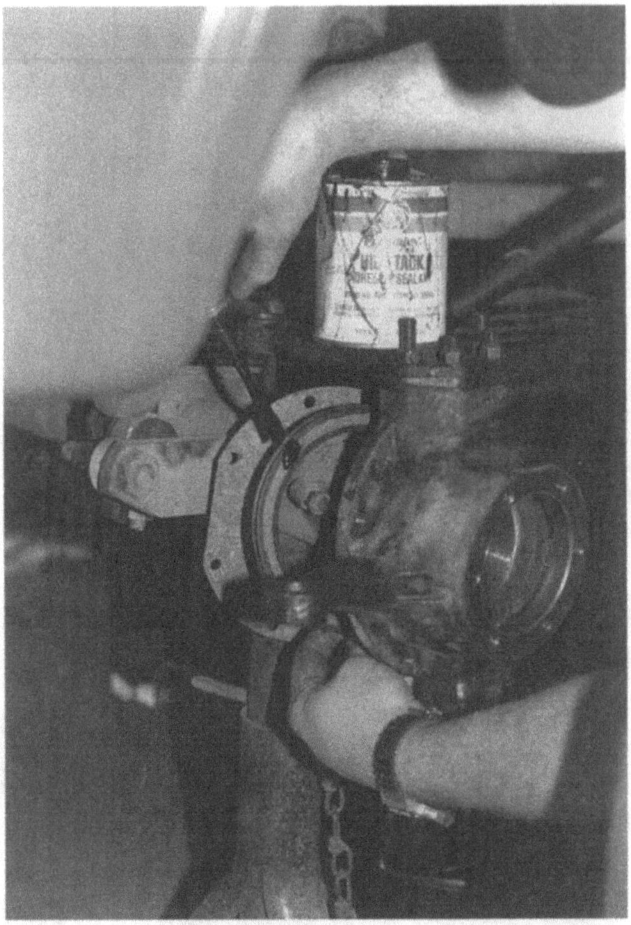

0012471

Fig. 10-41. Although some cut felt seal straight for installation, I make a diagonal cut and place split at top of knuckle with Permatex High Tack sealant applied at cut point. Diagonal cut resists moisture penetration at the split.

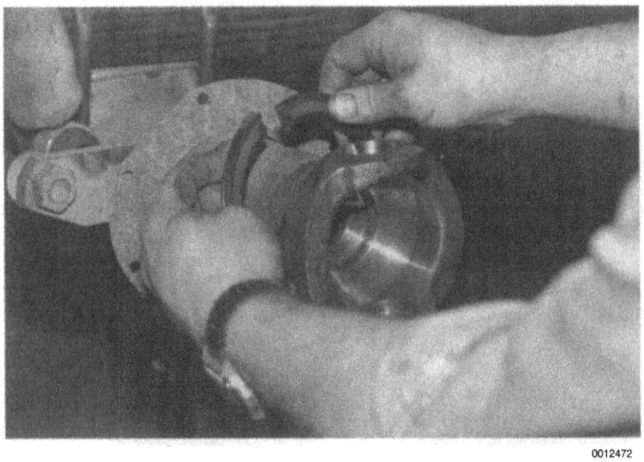

0012472

Fig. 10-42. Carefully spread neoprene seal, just enough to twist sideways around inner side of axle spherical end. Once walked around housing tube, seal can be straightened for seating at back of knuckle. Apply High Tack at split.

0012473

Fig. 10-43. *Straighten tin plates where bolts attach. Do not overtorque these bolts. (See your shop manual for tightening specifications.) Plates secure felt and large neoprene seal.*

0012474

Fig. 10-44. *Packed with grease, upper conical bushing fits into newly installed bearing cup. Conical bushings need light coaxing (plastic hammer or wood block) onto pivot pin. Make certain bearing cups are firmly seated into axle housing for accurate preload adjustment. Then hand pack tapered roller bearings with suitable wheel bearing grease.*

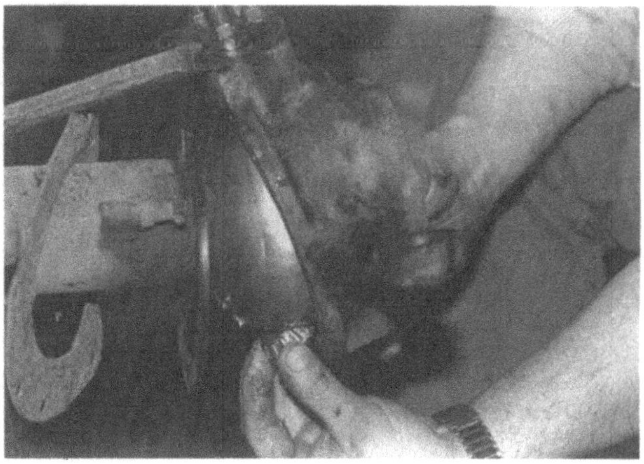

0012475

Fig. 10-45. *Set top shim(s) into place and attach upper bearing cap or steering arm. (You may need to tap bronze conical bushing onto pivot pin before installing cap. If this design, carefully align teeth or locating key during installation.) Set grease-packed lower bearing into its bearing cup. Slip knuckle onto upper bearing cup. Swing knuckle over lower bearing.*

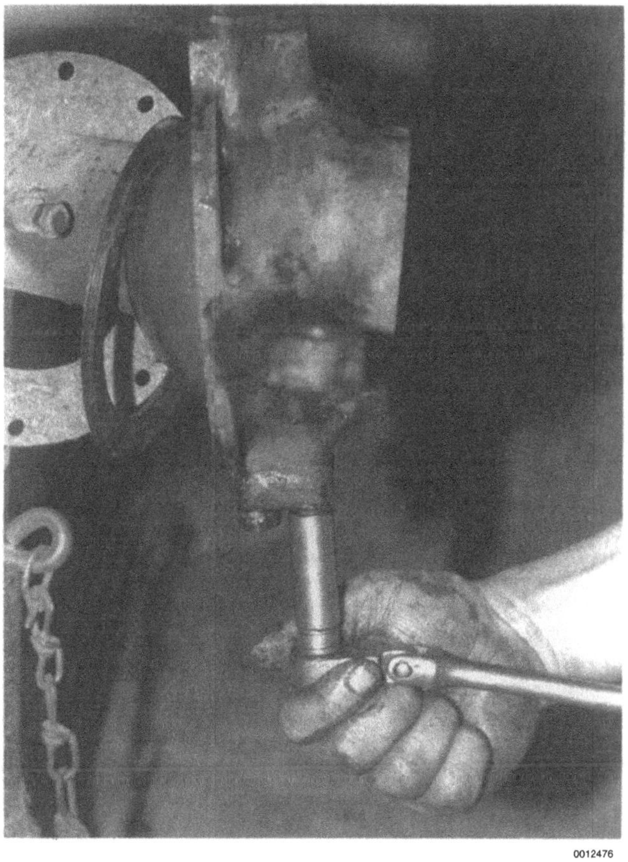

0012476

Fig. 10-46. *Use the original shims between lower bearing cap and knuckle. Tighten slowly, moving knuckle as you attempt to seat bolts. Stop if knuckle will not move, and increase shim pack thickness. Too loose, you will need to decrease shim thickness. Check your OEM-level shop manual for recommendations on the placement and thickness of upper and lower shims.*

Fig. 10-47. When upper and lower bearing cap fasteners are torqued to specification, you can check steering knuckle drag (bearing preload). Rotate knuckle at bearing cap studs and read torque. Note that inner seal and steering linkage are not attached during this check. Your truck shop manual will give required torque specifications. As an alternative, some Spicer axles call for spring scale test. Hook scale into tie-rod socket and move knuckle. Read amount of torque required to keep knuckle moving through its arc.

Fig. 10-48. Oil the felt lightly with a quality penetrating oil. You should apply Permatex High Tack to split at upper end of felt seal and carefully align the split during its assembly. Apply High Tack to split in neoprene seal. Install felt and retainer plate halves carefully, making sure neoprene seal and felt each seat properly into place. Torque bolts to specification or snugly, in a manner that will not warp plates or distort the felt seal.

Fig. 10-49. Grease or oil splined inner end of axle, and carefully keep axle shaft centered during installation to avoid damaging axle shaft seals within housing tubes. Axle shaft will slide through knuckle opening. Backing plate and spindle will slide into place. Bolts that retain backing plate and spindle to knuckle housing have a habit of loosening. Some replace OEM hardware with pre-drilled aircraft Grade 8 bolts and wire ties. I opt for heavy duty OEM-type conical washers and Grade 8 bolts, cleaning threads with Loctite Kleen & Prime, then applying liberal amount of Loctite 242 onto bolt threads.

Fig. 10-50. Always tighten spindle bolts in cross, then set final torque with a torque wrench. See your GM truck shop manual for correct tightening specifications. Final step is to refill knuckles with recommended lubricant or grease, the type noted in your shop manual or glovebox owner's handbook.

4. FREE-WHEEL LOCKING HUBS

Free-wheeling hubs stretch drivetrain component life by thousands of miles. Manual or automatic locking hubs eliminate front axle shaft rotation during two-wheel drive operation. Hubs save wear on front axle joints, seals, the differential assembly and front driveshaft components. Drag, especially in cold weather, translates to added engine wear, increased clutch effort and a loss of fuel economy.

On most 4x4 full-floating front wheel spindles and hub castings, you can install retrofit manual or automatic locking hubs. By design, a full-floating system affords operation and rotation of the wheels, with or without an intact axle shaft. This type of spindle and hub flange also allows use of free-wheeling hubs.

0012481

Fig. 10-51. Aftermarket free-wheeling hubs have existed since the 1940s. Hubs come in many shapes and sizes to fit various axle splines and wheel hub flanges.

0012482

Fig. 10-52. This very early Warn system was clearly manual. The hub cap bolted in place of an OEM drive flange and permitted wheel hubs to rotate without turning the axle shafts. By 1960, when GM introduced its first non-NAPCO type 4x4 K-trucks, Warn hubs had evolved far past this design and were a 4WD industry standard.

Full-floating wheel hubs, supported by inner and outer wheel bearings, ride on the spindle. The axle shaft fits through the hollow recess of this spindle, and the spindle attaches to the steering knuckle.

At the splined outer end of the axle shaft, a drive flange attaches to the wheel hub casting, much like the systems found on older 3/4-ton and larger truck rear axles. Here, the axle delivers its rotational force to the wheel hub, wheel and tire.

All early 4x4 locking hub systems were manual. Highly dependable, manual hub designs survive to this day. Although locking mechanisms differ between manufacturers, each design disconnects power flow from the axle shafts to the front wheel hub flanges. Providing a means to disconnect rotational force, free-wheel/locking hubs allow the wheel hub, wheel and tire to free-wheel on the spindle.

Automatic locking hubs came in the wake of troublesome full-time four-wheel drive. The full-time 4x4 systems, which proved costly to maintain and taxing to fuel economy, eliminated free-wheeling hubs.

While many owners appreciated the convenience of having no hubs to operate, they were glad to see an end to full-time 4x4. Bridging the gap, automatic hubs provide easier operation for a part-time four-wheel drive system. I still prefer manual locking hubs, despite the inconvenience. (See chapter on vehicle operation for tips on making manual hub use easier.)

Maintaining Your Locking Hubs

Many four-wheelers wrestle with their front wheel locking hubs. Some go to extremes, fabricating special tools for muscling the manual hub knob. Whenever more than light hand force is necessary, there's something wrong with the hub mechanism or its installation.

Laid out, these pieces can include a clutch mechanism, springs, locking clips or drive plates. Manual hubs utilize sleeve bushings, needle bearings, ball or roller bearings. Periodic bench stripping and service of the front hubs will assure free movement and proper lubrication of all parts.

Free-wheeling hub bearings and bushings cannot tolerate the rotational loads of parts running at speed. If pressed into such service, as when one hub is accidently left in LOCK while the other is on FREE, a free-wheeling hub assembly will quickly fail. Periodic disassembly and cleaning help reduce the risk of dragging hubs.

Servicing hubs is relatively simple and should accompany every front wheel bearing repack. Repeated or prolonged submersion of your 4x4 truck in deep, fast-running water requires immediate hub disassembly and inspection for water damage. The sealing areas of hubs deteriorate over time, another reason for periodic inspection and service.

Service Work

Servicing front wheel locking hubs is well within a competent mechanic's ability. Hub disassembly requires basic handtools, including a torque wrench and snap ring pliers. As always, seek out a service guidebook. A detailed schematic of the hubs will eliminate guesswork as you inventory parts.

Servicing hubs requires cleanliness and order. Remove parts carefully, noting their relationship to each other. Lay pieces on clean newspaper or shop towels. Clean pieces carefully in solvent. (Avoid harsh cleaners that affect plastic parts.) Clean grease will not adhere properly to solvent coated parts. Rinse away solvent with a dish detergent solution and a clean water rinse, then air dry (preferably with compressed air) before regreasing parts.

> **CAUTION —**
> *Never spin a bearing with compressed air. High speed, friction and stress could score the bearings or cause the assembly to explode.*

Use a grease recommended for your hubs. If wheel bearing type is acceptable, use the same grease that you use for your front wheel bearings. This often falls into the category of high temp wheel bearing grease, recommended for disc brake equipped applications. Such greases have excellent heat resistance yet afford the viscosity needed for free hub movement on those -40° F mornings in North Dakota. Avoid mixing unknown grease types—perform a major wheel bearing repack at the same time.

Service kits are inexpensive and provide cheap insurance against hub sealing problems. The O-ring or paper gasket that looks marginal is a risk. For a few dollars, new seals and other hardware will keep water out of your hubs and wheel bearings. Properly and sparingly applied, a silicone compound like Permatex Ultra-Blue can provide additional protection in areas that require gasket sealant.

As with any mechanism, inspect parts carefully. Look for bushing wear, galling, scoring and binding of parts. Include emery cloth in your service tools for light touch-up of rough or scratched pieces. Clean thoroughly after sanding. Dry before repacking.

0012483

Fig. 10-53. For ease of maintenance, most hub manufacturers offer service kits for their hubs. Warn's kits consist of paper gaskets, snap rings, O-rings, new Allen head screws, and bolt lock tabs if required.

0012484

Fig. 10-54. First step in overhaul of Warn hub is removal of free-wheeling hub unit from the wheel hub flange.

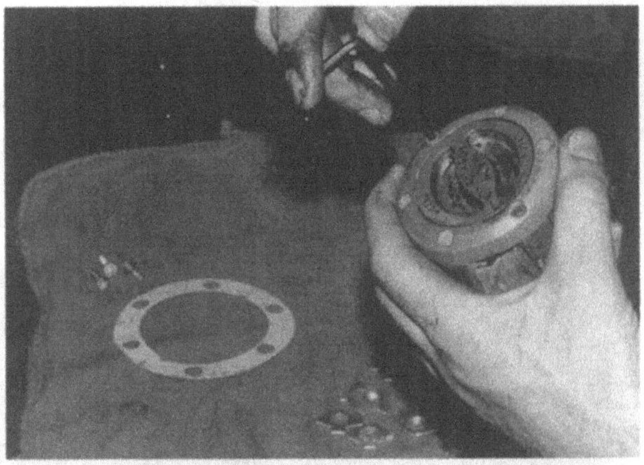

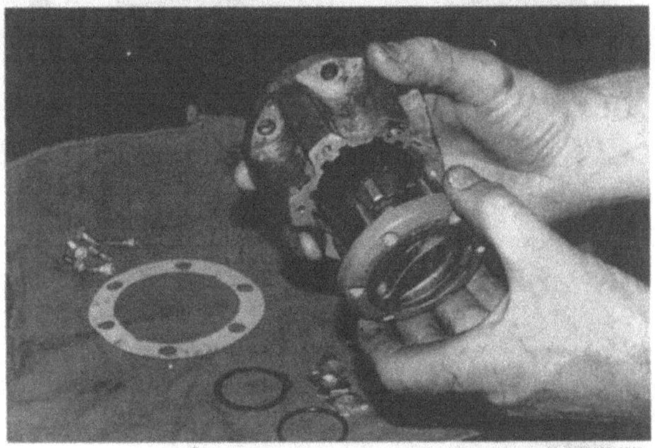

0012485 / 0012660

Fig. 10-55. Disassembly begins with clutch mechanism flange screws.

0012486

Fig. 10-56. *Drive hub rides in needle bearings on this early Warn hub design. Watch out for falling needle bearings!*

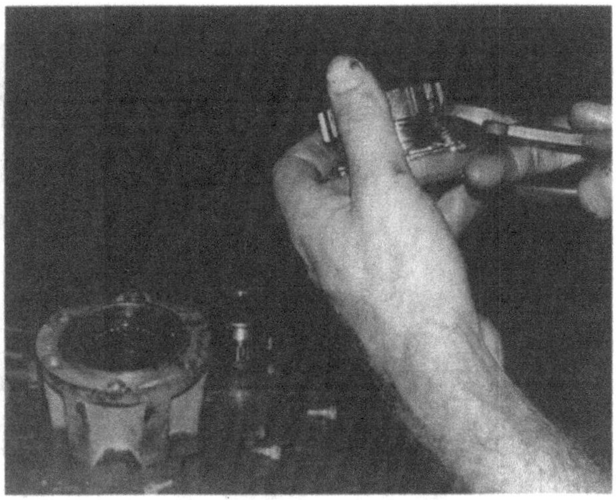

0012487

Fig. 10-57. *Spring roll pin locks clutch unit to flange.*

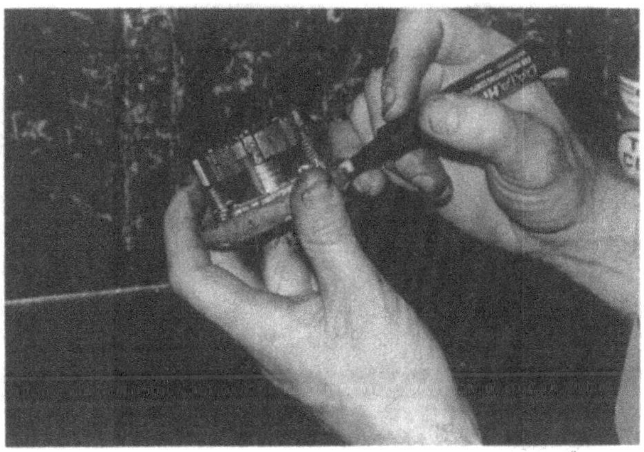

0012488

Fig. 10-58. *Mark or scribe location of plate to flange.*

0012489

Fig. 10-59. *Now remove the spring clutch mechanism.*

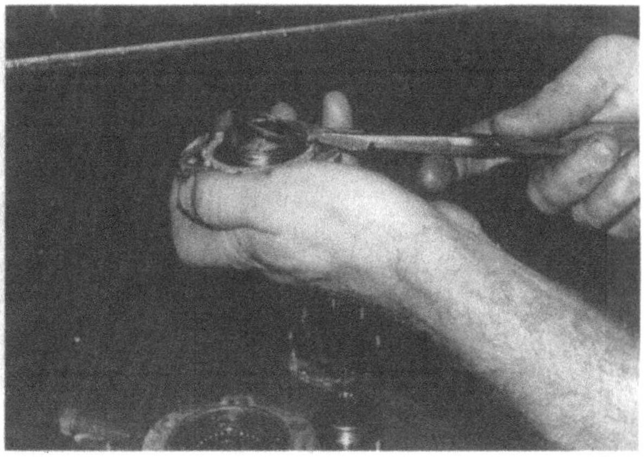

0012490

Fig. 10-60. *Snap ring holds hub knob to flange.*

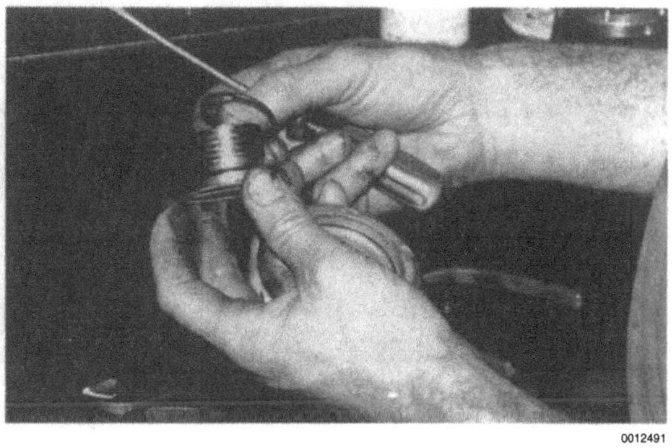

0012491

Fig. 10-61. *With knob removed, important O-ring is accessible. Here's where water often seeps into hub units.*

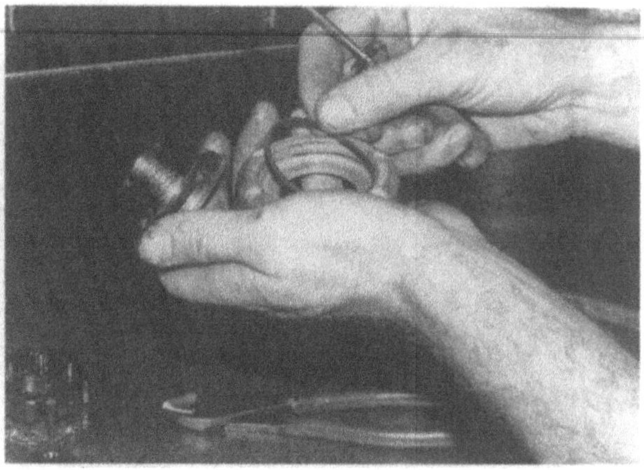

0012492

Fig. 10-62. Another critical O-ring is found here.

0012493

Fig. 10-63. Scrape gasket material from surfaces before thoroughly cleaning parts.

0012494

Fig. 10-64. After a hot tank dip, thorough rinse and air blow drying, these clean pieces can go back together.

0012495

Fig. 10-65. Pack the cavity of the needle bearing bore with a compatible wheel bearing grease. Needles are carefully replaced. Last bearing holds set together by keystone effect.

0012496

Fig. 10-66. Drive hub, with proper spacer/thrust washers in place, goes easily into bearing bore.

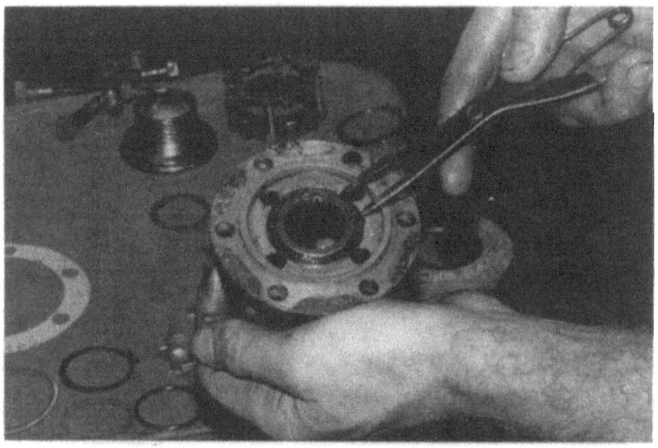

0012497

Fig. 10-67. Snap ring secures drive hub.

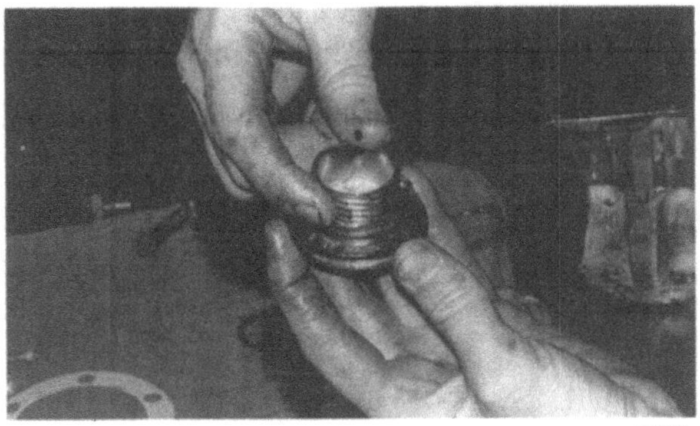

0012498

Fig. 10-68. *Install new O-rings, greased lightly, to base of brass knob assembly and to cover.*

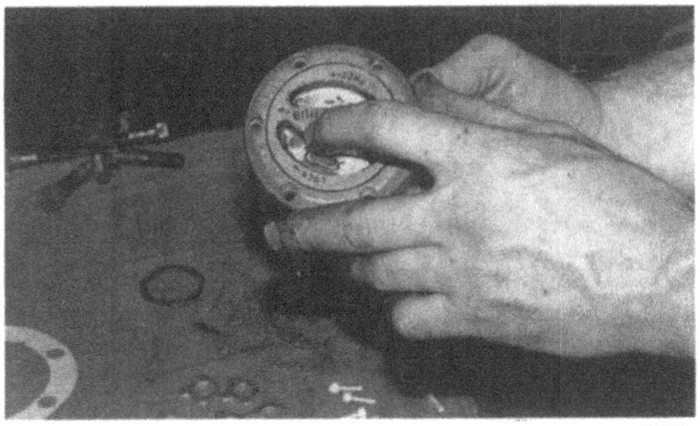

0012499

Fig. 10-69. *Install the hub knob and place in FREE position.*

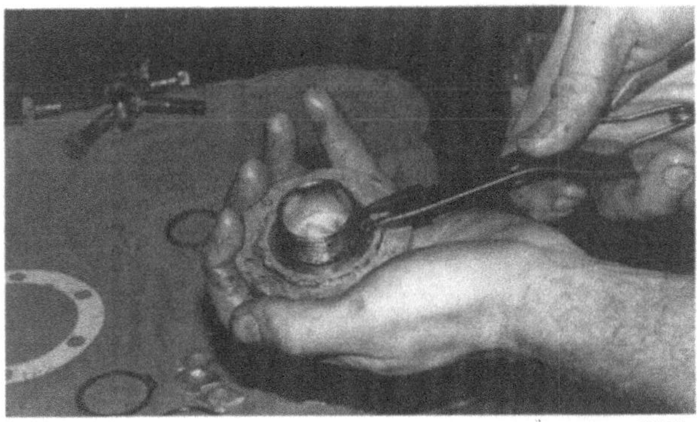

0012500

Fig. 10-70. *New snap ring, provided in Warn service kit, fits at base of knob.*

Once clean, the hubs reassemble easily on the workbench. After putting each unit back together, make certain that the finger control works freely and smoothly. Hubs that test friction-free on the bench should provide easy operation on the vehicle.

Before reinstalling the hubs, carefully inspect the wheel hub mounting flange. Internal splines must be free of debris, rough edges or galling. High-grade hardware, specified for this installation, is necessary. The mounting bolts are subject to tremendous stress, so tighten them in sequence. Recheck final torque before securing new lock

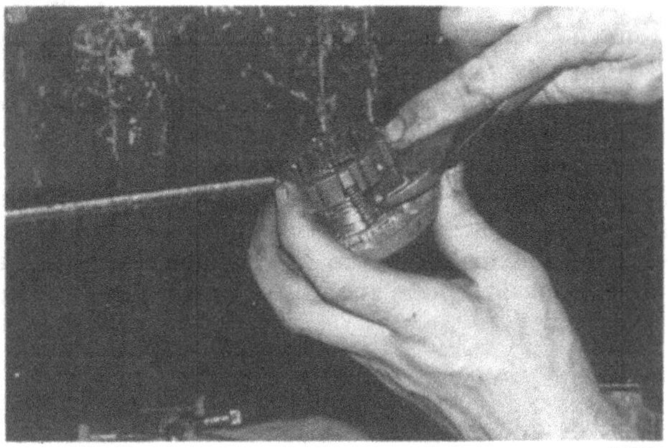

0012501

Fig. 10-71. *With clutch spring mechanism screwed into place, reinstall spring roll pin.*

0012502

Fig. 10-72. *Check clutch movement by rotating hub knob to LOCK; then slide clutch mechanism into the clean, lightly greased hub body bore. Careful fitup, torquing bolts, and bending lock tabs will help assure proper operation.*

tabs. Some bolt applications require wire tying, Loctite thread locking compound or special lock washers.

Hub mounting bolts on some applications may loosen or even shear. One remedy is the installation of Grade 8 studs set with thread locking compound and using aircraft grade self-locking nuts. In severe operation, this has prevented many hub and casting failures.

Lastly, especially if your 4x4 truck was purchased used, be certain that all locking hub parts are present. Often, after several services, small pieces get lost. Find a blow up schematic in a service guide, parts catalog or manufacturer's literature. Compare your pieces with those required, and restore the hubs accordingly.

Retrofitting New Hubs

Eventually, your truck's free-wheeling hubs will wear out. The effects of weather, age and abuse take their toll. (Late model automatic locking hubs may simply fail to meet your requirements.) Fortunately, you can retrofit a set of quality manual hubs.

A variety of new hubs are available through aftermarket suppliers. When selecting new hubs, consider your driving habits and intended use of the truck. Although price often influences your decision, weigh the cost against the inconvenience of walking home from a remote mountain range or the desert.

Since free-wheeling hubs require the same stamina as the differential, transfer case or transmission, consider upgrading your equipment. The controversy around automatic locking hubs continues. I maintain a singular view on the subject: Unless you need automatic hubs to offset a physical disability or other medical problem, forget them!

Whenever possible, I request new test vehicles with manual hubs or a delete-automatic-hubs option. I always retrofit manual hubs if I buy a used 4x4 equipped with automatic hubs. To me, stepping from the truck to twist manual hubs into LOCK mode is worth it. At least I'm certain the hubs have engaged.

Chapter 11

Suspension and Steering

SEVERAL YEARS AGO, my journalist's duties had me interviewing Jim Sickles at Downey Off-Road. When my questions shifted to worn suspension parts, Jim commented, "Springs are a perishable commodity." No vehicle proves this point better than a light truck, whether 2WD or a 4x4.

Fatigue, owner upgrades and modifications limit the life-span of springs, shock absorbers, shackles, bushings and steering linkage. Changes in tire diameter or the need to carry an extra load can also demand more body clearance.

1. SPRINGS

Three criteria govern your truck's spring height and rates: 1) the necessary eye-to-eye length of leaf springs, 2) arch of leaf springs, and 3) plate thickness for each spring leaf. Coil springs, like those found on front ends of 1963–up 2WD models, have specific wire diameters and free length/height. (So do 1960-72 rear coil springs.)

Leaf spring arch or coil spring length also determines your truck's ride height, while leaf plate thickness and taper control the spring rate, as does coil spring wire diameter. For serious off-pavement use, special spring rates can offer an advantage.

For light truck trailer pulling, heavy cargos or off-pavement four-wheel drive use, custom springs and shock absorbers can remedy a multitude of quirks. Often you can order such products with your new truck. In other cases your truck may need special suspension products, available through aftermarket vendors or a custom spring shop.

Although inexpensive modifications meet some tire clearance and ride height needs, the right springs offer a much better solution. For oversized tire clearance, a properly engineered lift spring set or custom coil spring kit can raise chassis/body height without compromising axle caster or pinion/driveshaft angles.

A reputable aftermarket spring/suspension installation kit can meet most OE engineering requirements for your truck and still provide a responsible and moderate amount of lift. When spring age and fatigue become a problem, a traditional spring/blacksmith shop can also fabricate stock-type replacement springs that will improve both the suspension longevity and ride quality.

0014283

Fig. 11-1. Rear leaf springs are common on most GM light trucks. However, from 1960–72 many GM 1/2- and 3/4-ton models use coil springs. Note support for working on the truck, a set of 5-ton (per stand) rated jackstands. Don't compromise here. Your life and limbs are at stake.

> *WARNING —*
> *Front axle spacer blocks and homemade lift kits are not only unsafe but also illegal in most states. GM 2WD and 4WD IFS models are especially vulnerable to handling quirks when lifted incorrectly. See the suspension upgrade chapter for details on kits and what to seek when modifying your truck chassis.*

Shackles and their Bushings

The leaf springs on your truck move in a shackle. Early models use bronze bushings and serviceable shackles. Later models use low-maintenance rubber bushings. Eventually, either type of shackle bushing will wear out.

Always replace the shackle bushings when noticeable wear develops. Even with proper lubrication, all greaseable (look for a grease fitting at the joint) bronze bushings will wear out. If the bushings have not received grease for a long time, wear has likely occurred. A grease job often turns up loose and worn parts.

> *CAUTION —*
> *Spring bushings and frame hanger designs vary. Each type requires specific torque settings for both the pivot bolts and shackle nuts. Refer to your GM truck shop manual for further details on spring assembly methods and torque settings.*

0014472

Fig. 11-2. *Leaf springs attach to frame at either end with bushings and shackles. U-bolts hold axle to spring.*

Installing New Leaf Springs

Leaf spring replacement is relatively simple. Unlike torsion bar and coil spring installations, there is no threat of a loaded spring flailing out of its socket like a missile. Although awkward, truck leaf spring replacement is reasonably easy.

When aligning the parts, mount the spring in the frame anchor first, then secure the hardware. Attach the shackle assembly at the opposite end of the spring, tightening all hardware to specifications found in your GM truck shop manual.

You may find it easier to bend out a slight amount of arch from the spring before clamping the axle U-bolts into place. (Compress the spring slightly with a safe garage-type floor jack beneath the axle, just enough for the axle's spring pad to drop into place at the spring center bolt.)

0012208

Fig. 11-3. *When installing U-bolts, tighten nuts evenly and in a cross pattern. At final torque, all exposed threads should be of equal length. Re-check torque periodically.*

Especially with new lift springs, spring compression may be necessary to achieve spring conformation at the original axle center point. Use a garage-type floor jack, which will place you safely away from the axle and the loaded spring.

Attach the U-bolts carefully, tightening U-bolt nuts uniformly. Watch the exposed thread lengths to determine equal tightening. Torque nuts in sequence. (See your GM truck shop manual for tightening specifications.) Gradually tighten each nut until you have reached full torque value and the bolt threads extend evenly past the nuts. Properly installed springs often live well past 100,000 miles, depending on how and where you drive your truck.

> NOTE —
> After driving a few miles, re-torque these spring U-bolt nuts. It's also a smart policy to re-check U-bolt torque periodically, especially on 4x4 models.

Torsion Bar and Coil Spring Front Suspension

GM introduced independent torsion bar front suspension (IFS) with the 1960 2WD models. In 1963, the 2WD trucks switch to coil front springs. IFS survives today in the Sierra 2WD (coil) and 4WD (torsion bar) front ends. Although 1960–91 conventional K-model 4x4s use leaf springs with a solid front axle, the 1988 Sierra IFS truck changed 4WD design dramatically.

> NOTE —
> Conventional (solid front axle) 4x4s include the Blazer/Jimmy, Suburban and Crew Cab K-30/3500 models through 1991. These well built models carry the earlier technology into the era of the Sierra chassis. By 1992, all GM light trucks are of Sierra chassis design.

0014471

Fig. 11-4. In 1960, GM trucks from 1/2-ton to 40-Series models pioneered the first truck use of independent front suspension (double A-arm type IFS) with torsion bars. By 1963 GM substituted coil front springs for the torsion bars. IFS improved ride quality without compromising durability.

The GM IFS 2WD and 4WD front end systems use double A-arms at each front wheel. This is a popular method of suspension that allows excellent wheel and tire alignment in all steering and wheel travel positions. GM's system provides superior ride quality, improved handling characteristics and an excellent reliability record.

By basic design, the coil spring and torsion bar IFS system has changed only slightly since the early 1960s. Key components include 1) the double A-arms of unequal length, 2) spindles attached to the A-arms by pivoting ball-joints, 3) the hefty chassis / frame front crossmember for supporting the A-arms and coil springs and 4) steering linkage that accommodates the movement of paired independent A-arms at each front wheel. A-arms pivot on bushings mounted at the control arm shafts on all 2WD IFS and Sierra 4WD IFS trucks.

IFS Wear Points

The 1960–up GM light trucks with independent front suspension have several wear points. Control arm (shaft) bushings, spindle / knuckle ball-joints and steering linkage components deteriorate over time, a factor that affects wheel alignment, handling and safety.

Most IFS front ends have greaseable ball-joints and steering linkage components. Knuckle / spindle ball-joints, whether permanently sealed or greaseable, require routine inspection for wear. When greasing the ball-joints and other steering components, I prefer a hand grease gun, as the dust boots are vulnerable to rupture when too much grease is applied too quickly.

Do not overfill joints. On non-sealed boots (those boots with an open flap edge), apply just enough grease to force old lube out. On joints with a grease plug and a fully sealed boot, do not add more grease than enough to slightly swell the boot. Any more grease than this will cause the boot to rupture and create a need for parts replacement.

Whether your 2WD GM truck has kingpins or ball-joints, either design is prone to wear and requires replacement service at high mileage. The GM truck shop manual describes the procedure for replacing kingpins, which requires access to a machine shop for pressing the bushings in and out of the steering spindle / knuckle. Reaming / fitting new bushings is also a machine shop procedure.

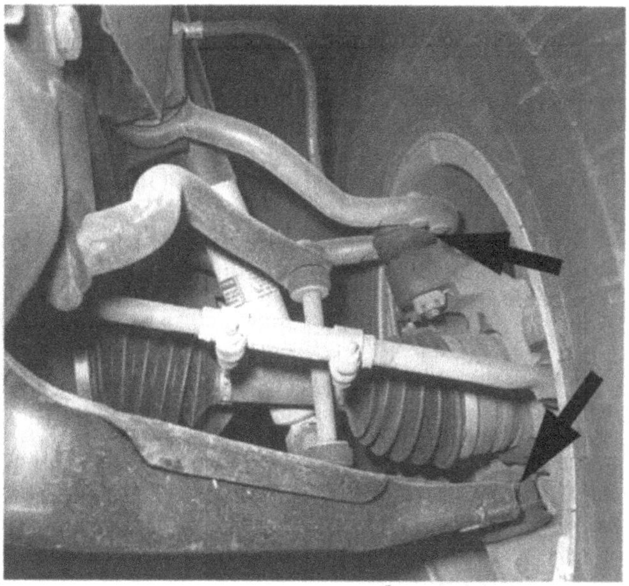

0014284

Fig. 11-5. Spindle/knuckle ball-joint and steering linkage wear can cause looseness in the steering. This affects wheel alignment and handling. Always consider these wear points when your GM light truck with IFS wanders or tracks poorly.

> *CAUTION —*
> *Older or high mileage I-beam axle kingpins are likely frozen in the axle beam. Use caution and protective eyewear when driving old kingpins from position. The kingpin is exceptionally hard steel. Avoid flattening its end — use a plastic head hammer if possible. Most truck owners prefer to send this job to a well equipped front end and frame shop.*

The procedure for changing ball-joints on 2WD and 4x4 models, plus information about alignment corrections, is within the GM truck shop manual for your model or a professional-level service guidebook. Review this task before proceeding. You may decide that subletting such work is appropriate. (Also see illustrations for 4x4 ball-joint replacement in this chapter.)

Frame Damage

Off-pavement pounding and heavy hauling can damage your truck's frame. All GM light trucks feature a driveable chassis or ladder frame. Subject to severe twisting and overload, frame damage is possible.

During routine service, inspect your truck's frame. Look closely for tears, cracks, wrinkles, loose rivets or damaged fasteners. Inspect axle housing mounts and spring hangers. All pivot bolts and other friction points require a close look. Make certain crossmembers are intact. On 4x4 models, consider the skid plates and transmission crossmember an integral part of the frame. Structural support and frame stiffness depend on intact crossmembers.

One area of frame fatigue on pre-1967 4x4 GM truck models with leaf front springs, especially rigs with histories of hard use off-pavement, is just behind the front spring anchor points. The anchor (rear) end of the springs receives a great deal of punishment, as road and trail obstacles want to drive the front axle from beneath the truck. The frame, sadly, receives the brunt of the punishment and can crack.

Another area of concern is the power steering gear attaching point on 1969–up 4x4s with the solid front axle. When abused severely, the frame can crack near the gear, as the integral power steering unit exerts a very powerful force.

Under the most severe service, spring shackles on a leaf spring 4x4 can break, along with the front spring shackle upper frame supports. When such a truck twists in the off-pavement environment, harsh push and pull on the upper shackle supports can break the bracket or frame rail. (See suspension upgrade chapter for more details.)

WARNING —
Fatigued or stress damaged spring shackles, frame brackets or spring hangers pose a safety hazard. Broken leaf springs can cause complete loss of vehicle control. Inspect your truck's frame and spring supports regularly.

2. SHOCK ABSORBERS

Single, dual and gas shocks—the market seems glutted with shock absorbers! What do you need? Which shock design works best? Is there a formula for choosing the right shock absorbers? You bet!

Shock absorbers make a major contribution to your truck's handling, ride, braking and safety. As shocks wear and fatigue, they lose their effectiveness. On most off-highway vehicles, the original shock absorber set fails before any other chassis item. Shocks deteriorate rapidly under excessive heat, friction and overwork. Due to wear over time, shock absorbers are another perishable item.

Anatomy of a Shock Absorber

All shock absorbers meet the same goals: 1) damping the oscillating motion of the vehicle frame and body, 2) limiting the rebound effects as uneven loads affect each wheel, and 3) keeping the wheels on the ground when suspension moves violently, like over rough washboard roads.

Off-pavement, your truck's suspension travels constantly, from full extension to pounding compression. Damping such forces, the shock absorbers pay the price, often succumbing to leakage or faulty performance. A bone jarring ride, squeaks and rattles develop when shock absorbers fail.

Of the two common shock absorber designs, single tube and twin tube, most truck manufacturers install the lighter duty single tube types, avoiding the more expensive and dependable twin tube or gas filled designs. Original equipment shocks concentrate on highway ride and driver comfort.

A single tube shock absorber has a machined steel cylinder and a rod/piston assembly. The body of the shock absorber holds an oil (plus freon or nitrogen on gas filled types) that resists the force of the moving piston. Precise valving in the piston controls the flow of oil, which helps regulate the movement of the rod.

0012211

Fig. 11-6. Laid out, twin tube shock absorber components consist of an outer tube, inner tube and cylinder, plus the rod and valve assembly. Fluid fills the reservoir of this sealed Doetsch Tech unit.

0012212

Fig. 11-7. Piston head and cylinder have valves and precisely metered orifices. Doetsch Tech's Pre-Runner shocks boast progressive valving.

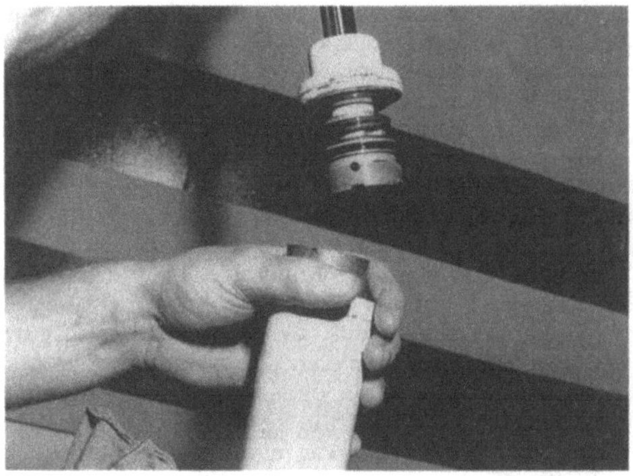

0012213

Fig. 11-8. O-ring sealing on these valves is sign of better quality.

Twin tube shock absorbers provide the added benefit of a second valving and reservoir system. Beyond the valves on the piston head, these shocks provide a bottom check valve, permanently affixed to an inner, machined cylinder. Valving in the piston head allows fluid to bypass during shock absorber compression and rebound. The second, fixed valve enhances damping sensitivity. Located between the inside cylinder tube and outer shell reservoir of the shock absorber body, this valve enables fluid or gas pressure to act as an additional damping force.

When resistance against the piston is too great, the suspension cannot move. Too little damping will cause serious handling and ride problems. Therefore, the most important job for your truck's shock absorbers is to sense road forces and continually work to control them. The heat generated during rapid movement of the piston compounds that task by weakening the damping ability. Fluid fade directly corresponds to the velocity of the piston.

Shock absorber valving faces its greatest challenge when your truck tackles a washboard road. The better shock designs, which boast as many as ten stages of valving, compensate for the varying fluid velocities and heat demands found in severe off-pavement conditions.

Gas Shocks

Foaming (aeration) of fluid inhibits shock absorber action by creating gaps that cause erratic shock behavior or fade. The best counter measures employ gases such as freon (now outlawed as an environmental hazard) and nitrogen. These substances offset many of the troubles associated with hydraulic oils, including heat buildup.

When high performance and constant pounding demand real shock action, gas shocks do the job. Non-gas shocks suffer from oil thinning. They operate best under moderate piston velocities. By contrast, nitrogen gas keeps shocks cooler and foam-free, allowing valves and fluid to continue working, even at extreme piston velocities.

Popular nitrogen gas shocks come in two varieties: low and high pressure. As gas filled shocks place high loads on the rod and piston, many recreational and off-pavement users prefer low pressure gas shocks. (By contrast, desert racing demands high pressure, 200 psi-plus nitrogen gas damping.) Due largely to their off-pavement superiority, reliability and predictable behavior, gas filled shocks have become a popular aftermarket item.

Selecting a Quality Shock Absorber

Most OEM shocks feature one- to 1-1/8-inch piston diameters. I feel that the minimum piston size for overall good performance should be 1-5/16". Popular for many years, the even larger 1-3/8" piston head satisfies all but the most brutal off-pavement maulers and heavyweight haulers.

> **NOTE —**
> Some GM light trucks come with optional gas-filled or heavy duty shock absorbers. If your truck is so equipped, be certain to replace these shocks with a similar type at replacement time.

A typical high performance shock is Rancho's RS-7000 series, a gas cell design with 1-5/8" piston diameters. The operating pressures of these shocks hover around 200 psi with chrome-hardened 17.3 millimeter rods. Sealing ability contributes to the life expectancy of shock absorbers. (See suspension upgrade chapter for additional details on performance shock absorbers.)

Pistons should be O-ring sealed, and the cylinder requires a tough double wall. Oversize fluid reservoirs provide better cooling and more resistance to fading. Refinement of the valve mechanism, that ability to sense terrain and load demands, will determine a shock absorber's worth. Proper shock damping serves as a primary element in a truck's suspension system.

Lastly, shock mounting grommets and eyes must hold up to road and load demands. A shock absorber is useless when detached or loose. A weak set of grommets allows wasted movement and undamped travel.

3. 4x4 Steering and Front End

Off-highway driving can punish your truck's steering and suspension components. On 4x4 equipped trucks, the live front axle design, especially with full-time 4x4, adds extra wear to the steering knuckle ball joints (open-knuckle models) or kingpin bearings (earlier models).

Replacing a steering knuckle ball joint is a major job, requiring removal of the wheel hub assembly, spindle, axle shaft and steering knuckle. For repairs on your live front axle unit, including axle shaft removal, refer to the GM truck shop manual or a professional service manual.

Rebuilding a Battered Ball-joint Steering Knuckle

My friend Greg Williams is a veteran race truck suspension mechanic with a wealth of front end and suspension experience. At his East County Alignment day job, Greg rebuilds 4x4 steering and suspension systems regularly.

As an enhancement for this chapter, Greg helps illustrate repairs on a GM solid axle 4x4 with open knuckles. Here, a U-joint has blown apart, and Greg's work includes straightening the frame before making axle repairs. After removing the automatic locking hub and the rotor/wheel hub and bearing assembly, Greg tackles the steering knuckle removal.

> ***CAUTION —***
> *Do not re-use any fasteners that are worn or deformed in normal use. Many fasteners are designed to be used only once and become unreliable and may fail when used a second time. This includes, but is not limited to, nuts, bolts, washers, self-locking nuts or bolts, circlips and cotter pins. For replacement always use new part(s) of OEM grade and quality.*

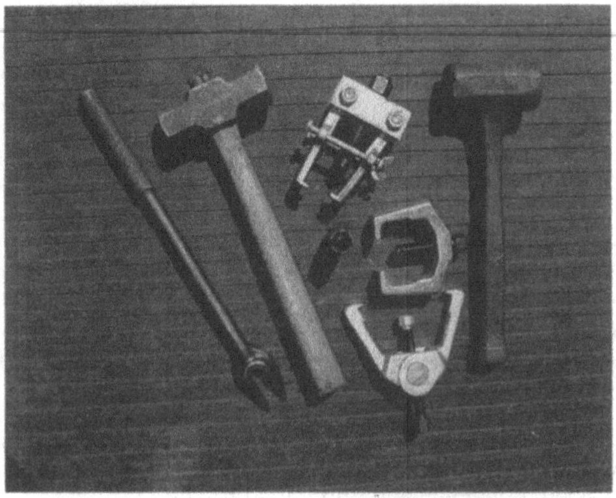

0012214

Fig. 11-9. *Use of proper tools is crucial to safe, dependable work. Steering knuckle replacement requires each of these tools. For many applications, a spring scale is also necessary.*

0012216

Fig. 11-11. *Loosen tie-rod nut, leaving a few threads in place to prevent tie-rod from falling. As joint will not be reused, insert a pickle fork between tie-rod joint and steering arm to separate the ball stud from its tapered seat in the arm. (Never use pickle fork if you plan to reuse the ball-joint.)*

NOTE —
Some OEM guides suggest loosening the upper and lower ball joint nuts until the top of the nut is flush with the end of its stud. Rap the top of the upper stud/nut squarely with a lead, brass or sand head hammer to unseat both joints. Consult your shop manual for approved methods.

0012217

Fig. 11-12. *Alternate method for loosening tie-rods is a pair of hefty hammers. Place one at the back of the steering arm's tie-rod seat and rap the other hammer on the front of the arm. A sharp rap will dislodge the tapered ball stud from its seat. Take care not to damage the steering arm or tie-rod threads.*

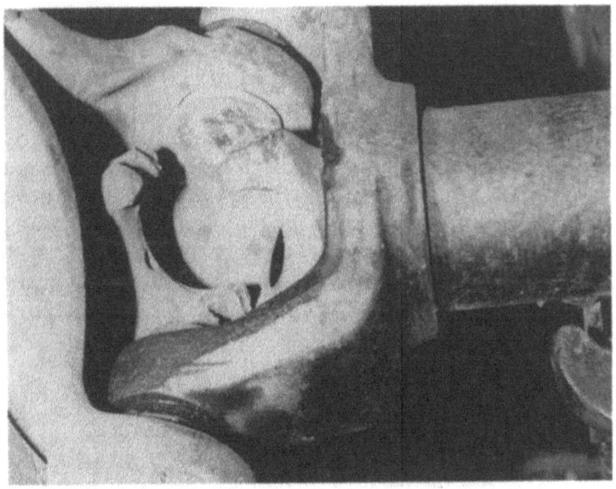

0012215

Fig. 11-10. *This Dana 44 front axle provides an excellent example of U-joint failure. The steering knuckle now needs replacement as a result of the damage.*

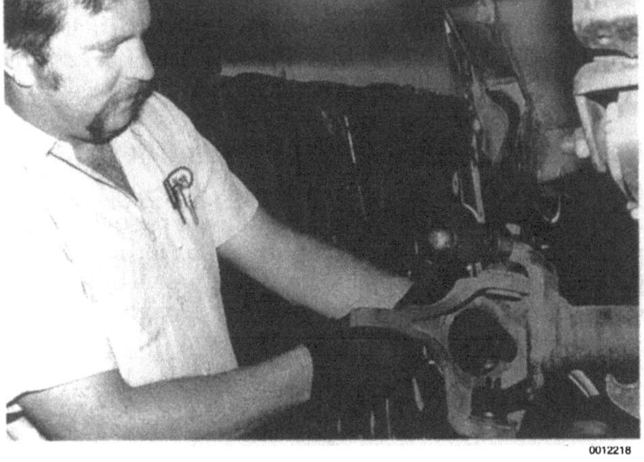

0012218

Fig. 11-13. *Another method for loosening ball stud is to simply strike the flange near ball stud. With a few solid blows directed at flange, ball joint drops. (Lower ball joint nut is loose, but still in place to prevent spindle from falling to the ground.) Follow by removing upper ball joint adjusting sleeve using a specially keyed socket.*

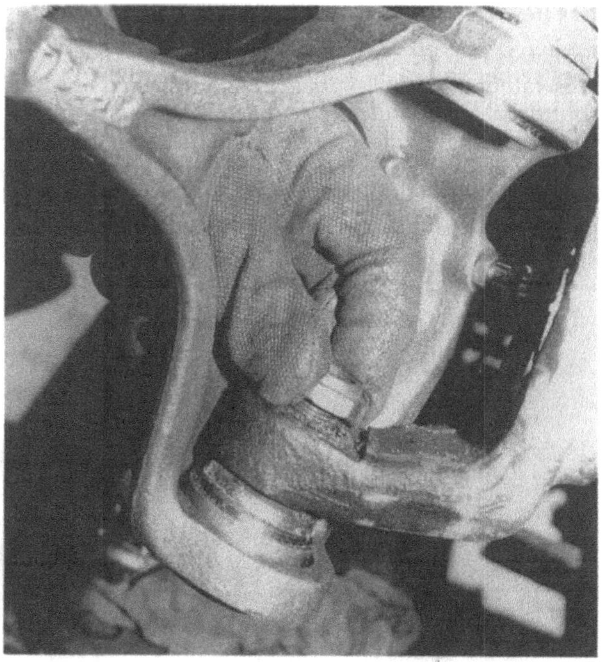

0012219

Fig. 11-14. *The self-locking nuts should be replaced during reassembly. Spindle nuts and lower ball-joint nuts are self-locking and should be replaced with new self-locking nuts during assembly.*

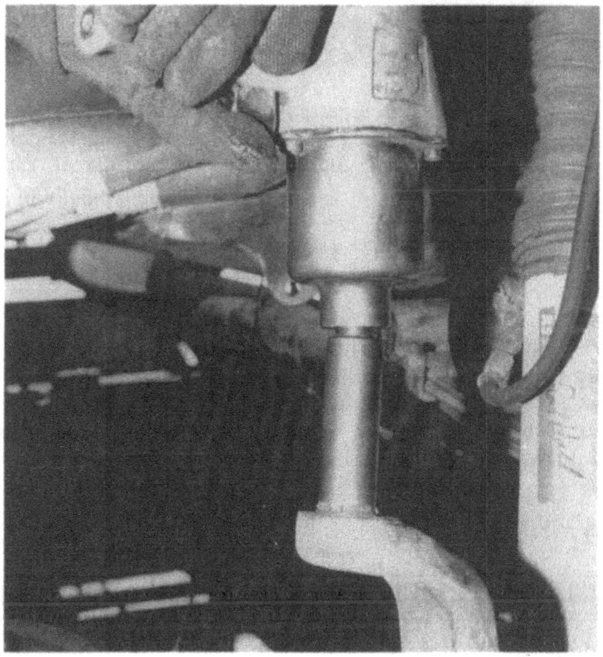

0012220

Fig. 11-15. *Installation of a new steering knuckle and adjuster sleeve is straightforward. Install adjuster sleeve loosely to allow tightening of lower ball-joint.*

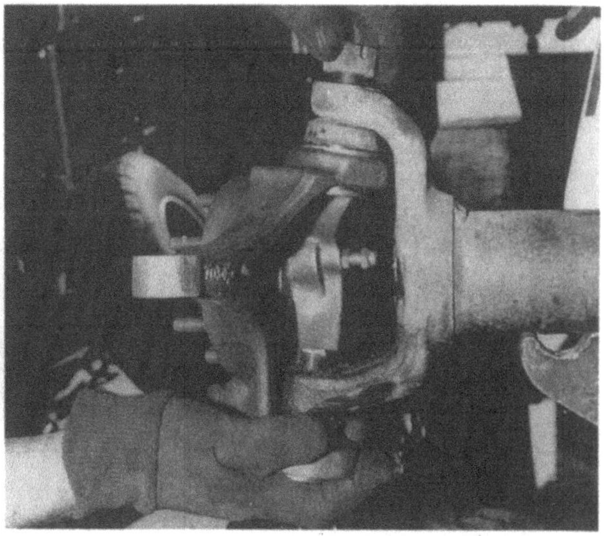

0012221

Fig. 11-16. *Finger tighten the castellated upper nut to hold the knuckle in position while torquing the lower self-locking nut to specification. Now set the adjuster sleeve for proper pre-load on the ball joints, followed by final tightening of the upper nut. The castellated nut requires a new cotter pin. Replace self-locking nuts with new identical OEM hardware.*

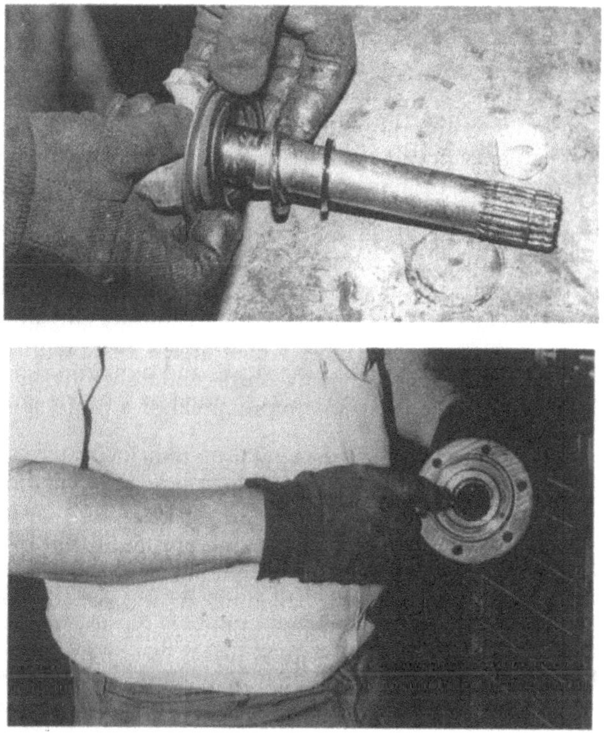

0012222 / 0012223

Fig. 11-17. *The axle shaft seals must be placed in order on the new axle. Use the original pieces as an example, or better yet, consult the GM truck shop manual's illustrations. Before installing the spindle, repack the needle bearing with fresh grease.*

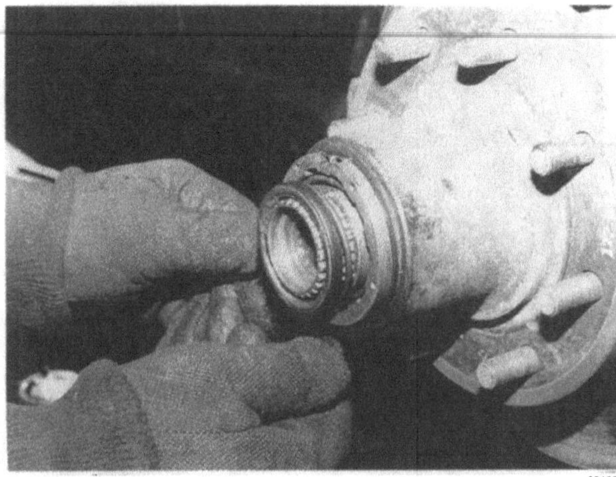

0012224

Fig. 11-18. Once the spindle is secure on the steering knuckle, proceed with wheel bearing service and assembly. (See next chapter or the GM truck shop manual for details.) With wheel hub/rotor assembly installed, mount disc brake caliper and tie-rod. Torque bolts and tie-rod nut to specification, then install new cotter pin at tie-rod nut.

Knuckle Assembly and Tie-rod Footnotes

The tapered and threaded upper ball joint seat is a critical part, responsible for setting a slight load on the ball joints for steering control and proper wear. Upon reassembly, adjust the new sleeve slightly loose until the lower ball joint is secure. While supporting the knuckle, torque the new self-locking nut to the lower ball joint stud.

Now, torque the adjusting sleeve at the upper ball joint to specification. (Find specs in the GM truck shop manual or a professional-level service manual.) Lastly, torque the castellated ball stud nut to spec, completing the job with the installation of a new cotter pin.

Reassemble the remaining parts in the reverse order of disassembly. This is also a good time for a wheel bearing repack. Assemble wheel bearings carefully and adjust to spec. Include new inner wheel grease seals with the bearing pack. Follow the procedures and tightening specs outlined in the GM truck shop manual or a professional service guide.

Always use new self-locking nuts, new lock tabs or retainers and new cotter pins. Clean assembly methods during fit-up of parts, proper use of tools, and correct procedures for cleaning, re-packing and adjusting bearings will assure a proper job. If you intend to reuse parts, don't bang directly on the ball joints, tie-rod ends or their studs. Aim your sharp hammer blows carefully and protect the dust boots. Never use a pickle fork if you intend to reuse the ball-joints and their dust boots.

When adjusting wheel alignment or installing new steering linkage pieces, always center the tie-rod ends in the tie-rod sleeve. The ball studs and their sockets should line up evenly before you tighten the sleeve clamps. Make sure each tie-rod end has its full range of motion.

4x4 Closed-knuckle Axle with Kingpin Pivots

Earlier 4x4s with closed-knuckle axles use kingpin bearings rather than ball joints. At the bearing caps, shims control steering knuckle preload. When your early 4x4 truck has high mileage, the kingpin bearing clearance may increase enough to cause looseness at the knuckles or a "kingpin shimmy." If inspection reveals excessive play, consider replacing the bearings and their races.

> *WARNING —*
> *When a large amount of kingpin play appears suddenly, suspect that kingpin bearing race or knuckle damage has occurred. Immediately repair the problem.*

0012225

Fig. 11-19. Shims beneath the bearing caps on closed knuckles control the steering knuckle preload. Proper placement of shims is crucial. If these bearings need adjustment, use a spring scale or torque wrench as per guidelines found in an OEM-level shop manual. (See previous chapter for more details on closed-knuckle steering rebuild.)

You will find additional information on inspection and rebuilding procedures for a 4x4 closed-knuckle steering system in the chapter on axle and 4WD service. I cover routine lubrication service in the maintenance and lubrication chapter.

4. STEERING

Whether your truck serves utility needs, lugs a travel trailer or plies recreational back country, vehicle control depends on a reliable steering system. GM light truck steering system layouts differ widely, both in design and function.

Your truck's suspension and steering linkage design dictate the location of the steering gear, while driving requirements and engineering intent determine the speed or ratio of the steering gear. Responsive handling results from correctly matching the suspension, steering linkage and steering gear, while a chassis lift and other suspension modifications often compromise the steering geometry.

NOTE —
Bump steer and other handling anomalies result from the misalignment of suspension and steering linkage. See chapter on suspension upgrades for details.

Production trucks, especially older models with manual steering systems, have slower steering and suspension response than passenger cars. Concerned about safety and liability, truck manufacturers de-tune suspension to meet a wider audience of drivers. Later models feature quicker power steering ratios, which give the light truck a sportier feel, nimbler parking habits and easier trailer backing ability.

Types of Steering Gears

General Motors pioneered the use of improved recirculating ball-and-nut manual steering gears. By 1941, GM light trucks switched from the higher friction worm-and-sector type steering gears to the much smoother and highly durable ball-and-nut design.

This breakthrough set a standard that, today, all other light domestic truck manufacturers follow. In fact, the popularity and superior quality of GM's Saginaw recirculating ball-and-nut gears—both manual and integral power piston types—have made these units widely sought by other truck manufacturers.

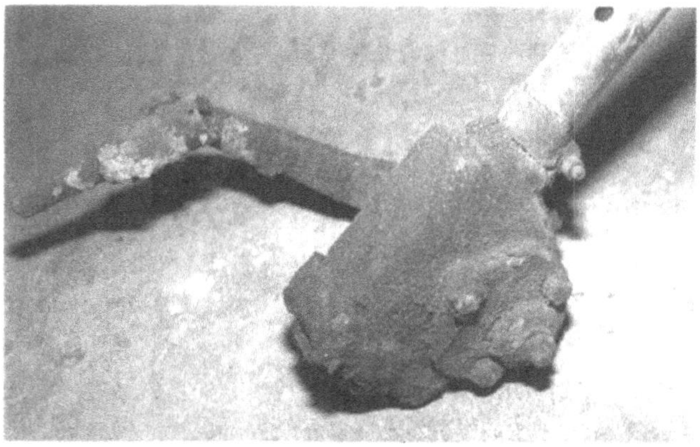

0014474

Fig. 11-20. By the early 1940s, GM phased out the more primitive worm-and-sector steering gears and switched to its new recirculating ball-and-nut steering unit design in light trucks. This engineering breakthrough revolutionized the safety and driving ease of trucks, and GM's patented design was decades ahead of all competition.

NOTE —
A common cause of steering parts damage is from towing a pre-1941 GM light truck that has worm-and-sector type steering. (Construction companies often did this.) The gear design does poorly with reverse flow of energy, like when the road causes the primitive Pitman shaft teeth to turn the worm shaft. If you must transport a truck that does not have recirculating ball-and-nut steering, consider using a low-bed car hauling trailer.

0014286

Fig. 11-21. On 1960–up IFS models, the Pitman arm and steering linkage move laterally. On solid front axle models with leaf springs, the draglink and Pitman arm move fore-and-aft as shown here.

On all GM steering gears, the Pitman arm attaches at the outer end of the sector or cross-shaft. Clockwise and counterclockwise rotation of the sector- or cross-shaft translates as the fore and aft swing of the Pitman arm on pre-1960 GM light trucks and all 4x4s with the solid front axle. By contrast, the 1960–up IFS models rely on lateral movement of the Pitman arm.

The manual recirculating ball-and-nut gears drastically reduce friction. A ball nut, machined internally to form the top half of a ball race, rides on ball bearings. These ball bearings run in the worm shaft's precisely machined groove. The machined groove serves as the inner half of the ball bearing race.

Machined teeth on the outer surface of the ball nut engage teeth on the Pitman (cross/sector) shaft. Steering wheel/worm shaft rotation translates as up and down movement of the ball nut. This movement of the sector teeth rotates the sector shaft and Pitman arm.

CAUTION —
A steering gear that needs a significant amount of adjustment always suggests internal damage and time for a complete overhaul. Service adjustment, although rare with ball-and-nut gears, focuses solely on the mesh between the ball nut's teeth and the Pitman/sector shaft teeth. Worm shaft bearing pre-load is also adjustable, although this procedure is also rare between steering gear overhauls. Never attempt a steering gear adjustment without instructions from an OEM-level shop manual.

The major gain of recirculating ball-and-nut steering gear designs is the reduction of stress and friction. Gliding motion of the ball nut, up and down the worm shaft, takes place with ball bearing smoothness. Wrist wrenching steering kickback is drastically reduced with a ball-and-nut design, especially the integral power assist type. Moreover, even with severe four-wheel drive use, these gears can survive.

The antiquated worm-and-sector gears suffer from sector teeth and worm gear chipping and, in the worst cases, seizure from jammed tooth debris. Friction and shock loads translate to wear that requires periodic adjustment. Unseen damage often follows hard use. My experience with both the earlier Ford and Dodge truck type

Gemmer worm-and-roller gears and the early GM worm-and-sector truck steering gears has taught me that any steering gearbox with an excessive amount of play deserves a teardown for inspection and replacement of defective parts.

The Power Steering Option

Power steering, once considered a horsepower-robbing accessory for lazy drivers, is now a light truck standard feature. Major design breakthroughs, especially the switch to integral power steering gears, popularized light truck power steering by the late 1960s. GM's first light truck use of integral power steering came about in 1968 2WD models.

GM K-model 4x4 models did not offer integral power steering until 1969. Prior to this time, linkage-assist power steering was available, an add-on looking option that dated to the 1950s. Linkage power steering was widely used on models ranging from the light trucks to passenger cars. (Corvettes use this design through the 1983 models.) GM passenger cars (aside from the Corvette) switched to Saginaw's modern integral power steering gears in 1965.

Before integral power steering gearboxes, power steering was a cumbersome affair. Linkage-type power assist, with a hydraulic power ram and an awkward network of hoses, uses a conventional (manual) steering gearbox. A control valve, mounted at the drag link/Pitman arm socket, senses the steering wheel apply pressure. Hydraulic force directs ram pressure for either left or right turn power assist.

Linkage type power steering is an add-on device that simply reduces steering effort. Beyond its negative features, like attracting debris and becoming easily damaged by trail obstacles, linkage power steering offers benefits, particularly driving ease and reduction of road kickback at the steering wheel.

Saginaw Power Steering Gears

The reliability found in GM's Saginaw manual and power steering gears is legend. Power/integral gears were first introduced to 2WD light trucks in 1968, followed by 4x4s in 1969. This is the premier steering gear of modern light trucks.

A Saginaw integral power gear provides the best features and attributes found in light truck power steering. For this reason, I am offering a description of the Saginaw integral power gear.

The Saginaw integral power gear employs a rotary valve that opens ports and directs high pressure fluid to help during turns. The degree of assist corresponds directly to the driver's steering wheel effort.

Some Saginaw integral units offer a unique variable ratio, produced by using unequal length teeth on the Pitman/sector shaft and rack piston. As you steer full left or right, the Pitman shaft speed increases, quickening the steering. Straight ahead, steering is very stable, with a slower ratio giving more road feel.

0012228

Fig. 11-22. *Saginaw's recirculating ball-and-nut technology carries to the integral power steering gears. Every U.S. truck manufacturer has benefitted from the use of these rugged Saginaw power steering gears.*

Saginaw integral power steering gears are sensitive, precise mechanisms operating under close tolerances and very high fluid pressures. Service on a power gear is rare, but when necessary, requires intricate preload adjustments and special assembly tools. Your safety depends upon proper fit-up of parts.

> **NOTE —**
> Despite basic similarities between recirculating ball-and-nut manual gears and the Saginaw integral power units, you need much greater skill to service a power gear.

GM truck owners sometimes retrofit Saginaw integral power gears to an early truck chassis (2WD street truck or vintage 4x4). Such a conversion project requires skill, however, plus a thorough knowledge of steering and chassis fabrication requirements.

> *CAUTION —*
> *Do not attempt such a conversion without the requisite skill level. The most common mistakes that inexperienced installers make are 1) misalignment of steering linkage (causing bump steer or limiting travel), 2) failure to make sure that the steering gear is in its center position when the vehicle's wheels aim straight ahead, and 3) not setting the steering knuckle/wheel stops properly, which could allow the steering gear's ball nut to hyper-extend at the extremes of its travel and severely damage the gear assembly.*

Advance Adapters and others make conversion kits for retrofitting a Saginaw recirculating ball type integral power steering gear to an earlier truck chassis. (See the suspension upgrade chapter of the book.) The few horsepower lost in running a power steering pump are sometimes worth the trade-off: smooth and easy modern steering.

Steering Linkage and Control

Although lock-to-lock steering ratios affect turning quickness, the true blueprint for off- and on-highway handling is the precise delivery of steering signals. The wheels must respond readily to linkage movement.

Later 4x4 model steering linkage often includes a stabilizer shock designed to eliminate severe road kickback. Although an OE or aftermarket stabilizer is a major asset, it's not a substitute for replacing worn steering components. Before tackling steering wander, eliminate worn or dangerously loose linkage.

If your truck wanders, check for excess play at the wheel bearings, steering knuckle joints, kingpins or the steering linkage. The Pitman arm, draglink, tie-rod ends, idler arm, steering knuckle ball joints and kingpin bearings are acute wear areas.

Begin your inspection with the wheel bearings and knuckle joints or kingpins. Next, check the steering linkage. Worn tie-rod ends and other joints cause steering looseness, road wander, and the risk of losing steering control.

Suspension frame mounts, control or link arm bushings and spring shackles are also wear points that can cause poor vehicle handling and loss of control. Especially on a 4x4 model or a truck used extensively off-pavement, off-road pounding can stress the steering system to its limits.

Rear spring position also affects steering control. Check for misaligned springs, loose U-bolts, broken spring center bolts, and worn or defective spring bushings. Wander and "rear wheel steer" can result from rear suspension defects.

0012229

Fig. 11-23. *The best procedure for checking steering linkage, ball-joint, kingpin or wheel bearing play is to shake the tire and wheel assembly. Jack and secure the front end safely off the floor. Grip each front tire at six and twelve o'clock to check ball joints, kingpins or wheel bearings. Lower one tire to the floor, then shake the raised tire from a three and nine o'clock position to note steering linkage wear. Have a partner watch for play at each tie-rod end and the other joints while applying a shaking, back-and-forth force.*

0012230

Fig. 11-24. *Excess spring movement contributes to wander. Always inspect spring bushings for wear. OE-type hard rubber bushings can wear over time and leave your front end wobbly and unstable.*

Worn steering linkage parts are generally not serviceable. When defective, you must replace them. (The pre-1960 GM truck draglink assemblies are rebuildable.) Parts removal requires care and should follow professional service guidelines found in a shop manual.

> *CAUTION —*
> *You may need special tools, including pullers. Cleanliness is essential. Debris must not interfere with the tight fitup of tapered ball studs on tie-rod ends and ball joints. You must torque self-locking and castellated nuts to factory specs. (Always install a correctly sized new cotter pin on the castellated nut.)*

Periodic steering linkage maintenance is simple, consisting of wiping dirt from fittings, then greasing joints with clean chassis lube through a hand greasegun. Safety inspection should include dust boots, joint wear, and straightness of rods. Always replace bent steering linkage components. Straightening a bent tie-rod compromises safety. Stretched one way, then the other, tie-rod tubes and steel rods can weaken and fail.

Inspecting the Steering System

Restoration of steering linkage, knuckle joints, kingpins and wheel bearings usually eliminates steering play. If looseness remains, make certain that the frame, spring bolts and spring attachments are intact and that hardware is secure.

Tires and front end alignment are also a concern, as wander often occurs when tires have abnormal wear patterns. On GM trucks with solid I-beam front axles and kingpin type knuckle pivots (or closed- and open-knuckle 4x4 solid front axles), wheel alignment is simple. Unless you've bent the axle beam/housing or the truck's frame, alignment consists only of setting the toe-in.

> **NOTE —**
> As mentioned earlier in this book, on a solid axle 4x4 with open-knuckle ball-joint steering, you can make slight camber/caster adjustments with an aftermarket upper ball-joint adjusting sleeve. On leaf spring front suspension 4x4s, you can also set caster with wedge shims between the axle and leaf stack.

If steering play still exists, suspect the steering gearbox. For a quick check, center the steering and carefully rotate the worm or steering shaft. (This may require a helper on the early trucks with an enclosed steering shaft/column.) Note the amount of rotational movement necessary to just move the Pitman arm.

Fig. 11-25. Sway/stabilizer bar bushings are also perishable. On later trucks, inspect these pieces for wear, looseness and deterioration. Too loose, the bar serves no purpose. Control in corners benefits greatly from the sway bar. Here is bushing wear at sway bar link.

Fig. 11-26. Inspect ball-joint supported steering knuckles. Excess play here causes kingpin shimmy, characterized by a violent shake of the steering wheel and the entire front end. Kingpin bearing shims on early models and upper ball joint adjustment sleeves on open-knuckle axles allow for minor adjustment. Greater looseness calls for parts replacement or knuckle rebuilding. (See previous chapter.)

Fig. 11-27. The coupler above the steering gear (arrow) is also a wear point. An open column and coupler enable a quick check for steering gear damage and excess backlash.

On later trucks with exposed steering shafts, this operation is very easy. Park your truck with the wheels straight ahead. Turn the shaft at the input end of the steering gear while holding the Pitman arm with your other hand. It's easy to detect Pitman movement by gently rotating the steering shaft.

Be sensitive to the exact point at which the Pitman arm responds to the steering shaft movement. Rotate the shaft in the opposite direction to determine the degree of play. If wear or play is evident, either steering gear adjustment or overhaul is necessary.

Note that the steering gear must be in its center position when checking for play. Steering gears have a high point in the exact center position that creates a very slight pre-load in the straight ahead driving position. Turned left or right of this point, sector play or backlash will increase. If you suspect a mis-centered steering gear, disconnect the steering linkage at the Pitman arm and very gently rotate the steering to one extreme.

Now count the exact turns back to the opposite extreme, then divide that number by two. Turn the wheel back this amount, and your steering gearbox will be on center. Check for play and over-center (high point) preload at this position. (Never turn the shaft hard against its extremes, as damage to ball races could occur.)

Signs of Steering Gearbox Trouble

Sudden development of steering gear play or symptoms of wander, clicking noises or binding imply internal damage to the gear. Although later steering gears have great resiliency, hard-core abuse or four-wheeling can damage even the best steering unit.

Unless high mileage dictates a minor readjustment to compensate for wear, any more than a slight amount of steering gear play suggests internal gear damage. Since the gear's inner workings are invisible without a teardown, you must make a judgement call here.

WARNING —
Never adjust a gear that has substantial play. Under such circumstances, removal and teardown of the gear is mandatory.

Before considering a steering gear teardown, review the GM truck shop manual for your model. Understand the complex tools, close tolerances and sequence of disassembly and reassembly.

Power steering gears, in particular, require special care and clean work habits. Consider a new, factory rebuilt or undamaged (low mileage) recycled gear. Sometimes a rebuilt/exchange unit proves cost effective. Individual power steering gear pieces get very expensive.

However, unless you find a recycled truck with well under 100,000 original and easy miles on the odometer, the manual or power steering gear likely has substantial wear. If you have a manual unit and decide to rebuild it, always install new parts in a sound housing. Always use new seals, bushings, bearings, a new worm shaft, a new ball-nut and a new Pitman/sector shaft assembly. Never mix or fit up old and new parts, especially gear pieces. If you cannot find parts at your local GM dealer, try for NOS (new original stock) pieces through a vintage truck restorer's outlet.

Steering Linkage and Suspension Damage

Normal wear over time and the common off-pavement use of light trucks can affect wheel alignment. Rough terrain and obstacles like rocks, stumps, slick mud, and streambeds each threaten the chassis and front end system. Damaged steering linkage and badly misaligned front wheels can ruin a brand new set of tires in just a few miles.

Off-pavement pounding can cause serious suspension trouble. Especially sensitive are the leaf spring centering bolts and the spring U-bolts (which shear or break and allow the axle to shift out of alignment). GM coil springs ride above the control or link arms, and unless stressed to the limit, these coils seldom break, even under tight off-pavement twisting. Coil springs can dislodge, however, from serious suspension bashing.

Steering linkage is a major area of concern. Steering linkage must move with the axle to maintain wheel alignment. Generally, a solid axle tie rod lies just above the axle centerline, making this linkage the most vulnerable steering component. On 4x4 solid axle models, the drivetrain layout has the front driveshaft angling from the transfer case to the backside of the front axle. Here, the steering linkage must ride in front of the axle.

Tree stumps can easily damage the tie rod(s) or a steering stabilizer. If the stabilizer shock damper (found on most 4x4 models) becomes bent, steering bind is possible. If obvious damage exists, remove the stabilizer shock damper. Other than some wander and possible shakiness, the truck can get home without this unit. Replace with a new stabilizer shock damper immediately.

5. Wheel Alignment

Subjected to normal wear-and-tear or off-pavement pounding, your truck demands regular steering system inspection and front wheel alignment. Whenever you suspect poor tire wear or plan to replace the front tires, have the front wheel alignment checked and re-set if necessary. The longevity of expensive tires and your safety both depend on proper front wheel tracking.

0012234

Fig. 11-28. *Toe-set is a regular part of chassis service. Especially on vehicles subjected to off-pavement pounding, tire life depends on periodic checks of front wheel toe-set. Radial tires have different toe-set requirements than bias-ply types. Adjust toe-in when installing new tires. On solid front axles, toe-in is normally the only adjustment required. Caster or camber changes result from axle, chassis or suspension damage and wear.*

0012235

Fig. 11-29. *Note use of a special tie-rod sleeve wrench. After rain, slush, mud, and water crossings, joints require fresh chassis grease to displace water and foreign matter.*

Fig. 11-30. Caster and camber gauges clamp to the wheel. Once on a centerline with the wheel spindle, levels indicate steering and wheel tilt angles.

Front end alignment also reveals defective steering and suspension components. Consider wheel alignment an important part of your truck's preventive maintenance program.

Steering Geometry

For the light GM truck, periodic front end alignment always includes toe-in. Toe-in is the measurement between the centerlines of the tire tread at the tire's horizontal midline.

Imagine lines scribed at the center of your front tire treads, running the full circumference of the tire. Each line references 360° of tire tread surface and offers an easy measurement at the front and rear of the tire. The object when setting toe-in is to properly distance these two reference points.

Vehicle manufacturers establish toe settings with consideration for rolling resistance and chassis geometry. Generally, older bias ply tires require a slight (1/32" to 1/8") toe-in. Modern radial tires have less rolling resistance and need only minimal inward toe. They often call for a zero-degree/inch toe-set, or tires that run perfectly parallel in the straight ahead mode.

Normal steering and reasonable tire wear also depend upon correct caster and camber geometry. Camber is simply the upright angle or tilt of the tire. The camber angle can change when an axle housing, I-beam, steering spindle or steering knuckle becomes bent or excess wear develops at the knuckle pivots (kingpins, pivots or balljoints).

Caster is trickier to define. The caster angle is the tilt of an imaginary line drawn through the centerline of the steering kingpins. On ball-joint front ends like 4x4 solid open-knuckle axles or GM's IFS designs, we draw this line through the orbital centerline of the upper and lower ball joints.

This line's angle tilts rearward (positive caster) or forward (negative caster). Its purpose is to encourage straight ahead orientation of the wheels—the feature that causes the steering wheel to center naturally as we exit a turn. Caster also helps prevent kingpin shimmy, the violent back-and-forth shaking of the front wheels.

The last front end geometry issue is steering axis inclination. Effectively, steering axis inclination is two angles (caster and camber) in one, with the steering spindle angled to maintain a specified arc during turns. Steering axis inclination depends upon the condition and integrity of the steering knuckle and spindle. If axis of inclination has changed, yet the caster, camber and toe-in remain correct, suspect a bent or defective steering knuckle or spindle.

Many manufacturers and specialists assert that caster and camber should never be adjusted by bending a solid axle beam (hot, cold or otherwise). If these measurements are beyond specification, look for bent, worn or damaged parts. Don't overlook sagging springs and ride height. You will find chassis, alignment and ride height measurements in the GM truck shop manual for your model.

Wheel Alignment Features

GM IFS double A-arm front suspension systems allow both caster and camber adjustments by adjusting the kingpin centerline inboard (negative camber) or outboard (positive camber) from its vertical axis. Such systems also provide fore and aft adjustment of the kingpin centerline for setting caster. IFS models with torsion bars have the added benefit of adjustable ride height.

Solid live front axle 4x4s and kingpin-type (non-balljoint) 2WD I-beam axle systems have no provision for camber or caster adjustment. You can, however, set caster by placing accurately degreed, wedge-shaped shims between the axle and front springs.

CAUTION —
Camber on older solid-beam axles and closed-knuckle solid 4x4 front axles is non-adjustable. It is not advisable to bend the axle beam or housing to make a caster or camber correction.

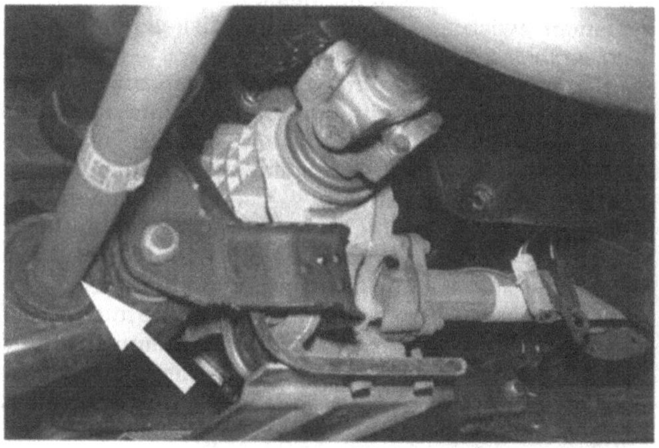

Fig. 11-31. 1960–up 2WDs and the late GM Sierra IFS 4x4 front ends have provision for caster and camber adjustment. On torsion bar models (arrow), ride height is also adjustable. Solid front axle leaf spring 2WD and 4x4 models are restricted here. All models allow for toe-in setting.

For ball-joint pivot open-knuckle 4x4 solid front axle assemblies that have no apparent damage, you can make minor camber and caster corrections by replacing the threaded upper ball-joint seat with an aftermarket (threaded) correction sleeve. These sleeves offer a precise off-set angle and are available for slight caster and camber corrections. (See your local alignment shop or NAPA store for these parts.)

> NOTE —
> See a local frame and wheel alignment shop or your NAPA store for leaf spring shims, offset ball-joint mounting sleeves and 4WD spindle shims to correct wheel alignment on solid front axles. Before installing such parts, be absolutely certain that none of your truck's suspension or steering components have become damaged. Never compensate for collision or wear damage with the use of shims or adjuster sleeves. Replacing defective parts should correct the caster or camber error.

Field Fix to Get Home

A front end alignment is a good safeguard after any serious off-pavement pounding or hard bout with washboard. In an emergency, you can restore toe-in in the field—at least close enough to keep your precious tire rubber from peeling away like an apple's skin.

Back woods straightening of the tie rod could save a walk home and allow your truck to track reasonably straight. As for the permanence of such a fix, realize that any straightened steering linkage part should be replaced as soon as possible.

> *CAUTION —*
> *Many frame and axle specialists can skillfully straighten a slightly bent I-beam or solid axle (and even pull out several degrees of frame kink). No professional, however, will reuse a bent piece of steering linkage.*

For just getting back to civilization, be very cautious not to break the parts as you straighten them. Use care to distribute force over a broad area, while centering the pull at the bent section. If the kink is at the threaded portion of a tie rod, leave it alone. Threads respond badly to stretching, and breakage is very likely.

Attach a tow strap to an immovable object—like the tree stump that caused all this trouble. Use the truck's power to gently pull the tie rod straight.

If your truck has a winch, a tree and a snatch block provide an ideal alternative. Park the truck in low range and low gear (manual transmission) or Park (automatic) and low range. Shut off the engine, set the parking brake and block the wheels securely.

> *CAUTION —*
> *Never use only Park mode in your automatic transmission when you winch a heavy load. Severe loading of the chassis could break the tiny parking pawl within the transmission. Always set the parking brake.*

Anchor the snatch block securely. Run the cable forward, and loop it 180° through the snatch block. Attach the hook to the tie-rod. Use your winch remote control to operate the winch while watching the tie-rod from a safe distance.

Straighten the tie rod only enough to provide clearance for moving parts and approximate wheel alignment. Once you straighten the tube or sleeve, adjust toe-in if possible.

When adjusting wheel alignment or installing new steering linkage pieces, always center the tie-rod ends. The ball studs and their sockets should align correctly before you tighten the sleeve clamps. Make sure each tie-rod end has its full range of motion. Also be sure that each tie-rod end is threaded into the sleeve.

A Wooded Backdrop for Your Alignment Shop

Temporary toe-in can be set with a few hand tools, a tie-rod sleeve wrench, a tape measure, and an axle or frame jack. Center the steering (Pitman arm) before beginning. Set the steering wheel for normal, straight ahead driving, then jack one front wheel slightly off the ground. Without a toe adjusting bar and scribe for drawing lines around the tire centerlines, the next best tool for a primitive "get home only" alignment is a piece of chalk.

Carefully note the tread pattern of your front tires. Find reference niches that are easy to identify. Hold the tape measure level, close to the mid-point of each tire's

0012238

Fig. 11-32. *After straightening the tie-rod with a tow strap, the Lantern Alignment Shop opens. Raise the driver's side wheel slightly from the ground and reference mark the front tire tread. Keeping the steering wheel straight ahead, measure between the front treads of the tires and the rear reference marks. This will indicate the degree of misalignment.*

0012239

Fig. 11-33. Loosen the tie rod clamps and stabilizer mount, then turn the tie rod tube or sleeve to adjust its length. The adjusting tube, often stubborn from rust and scale at the tie rod threads, may require a pipe wrench(s) or sleeve adjuster tool to rotate.

0012240

Fig. 11-34. Carefully position the sleeve clamps after confirming the final measurement. Clamps must not interfere with steering linkage movement or other components.

diameter. Make sure that the tape does not interfere with suspension parts, and pull it snugly from the opposite tire's mark.

If you encounter an obstacle while pulling the tape straight, drop the level of the tape, re-match the tread pattern, and try again. Once the tape is level, make an accurate note of the length between your two niche marks.

Perform the same procedure at the rear of the front tires. Again, attempt to draw a level line, close to the tires horizontal mid-line without parts interference. Note the length between these tread pattern niches. (Make sure your chosen tread patterns match those used at the front.)

0012241

Fig. 11-35. Make sure plenty of tie rod thread remains within the sleeve/tube ends. Tighten clamps and make certain that parts move freely as you turn the steering wheel. Envision suspension movement, and make sure of adequate clearance when the chassis, control arms or axle beam moves.

These two measurements form the basis for your toe-in alignment. For simplicity, use an emergency toe-in spec of zero. Both front and rear measurements should read the same. (Were our goal 1/8" toe-in, the rear measurement would be 1/8" longer than the front. Simple? Well, with practice it gets easier.)

A bent tie rod shortens the distance between the steering arms. On a solid axle 4x4 truck with its steering linkage forward of the axle housing, this toes the front wheels inward. Under such conditions, the bend will cause a long measurement at the backside tread. The exact opposite is true of a pre-1960 2WD I-beam axle model with its tie-rod mounted behind the axle.

To shorten or lengthen the tie rod, loosen the tie rod end clamps to allow rotation of the adjusting tube/sleeve. Note the left-hand or right-hand threads at each end of the tube, and also the amount of thread screwed into each sleeve end. If you must lengthen the tie rod, be careful not to un-thread the tube so far that the tie-rod thread fitup becomes too shallow and unsafe.

The tube may not rotate easily. Moisture, rust and scale cause seizure of tie-rod end threads. A rust penetrant will sometimes help. Rotate the tube, checking the fore and aft tire measurements often. When the measurement is correct, tighten the clamps securely.

Many of us have been fortunate enough not to hit tree stumps or rocks. It's wise, however, to travel prepared. Whether we experience trouble or find ourselves able to help others, survival skills help. A slow drive to pavement with a temporary field fix sure beats walking. Success can sometimes be a twelve-mph trip to civilization—with your truck's heater humming, windshield wipers swishing and headlights leading the way.

Chapter 12

Brakes and Wheel Bearings

PROPERLY FUNCTIONING WHEEL BEARINGS and brakes are essential to safe driving. Inspect your truck's wheel bearings and brakes regularly. Perform all brake work with careful attention to cleanliness, correct specifications and proper working procedures.

> *WARNING —*
>
> • *Brake friction materials such as brake linings or brake pads may contain asbestos fibers. Do not create dust by grinding, sanding or cleaning the pads with compressed air. Avoid breathing any asbestos fibers or dust. Breathing asbestos can cause serious diseases such as asbestosis or cancer, and may result in death. Use only approved methods to clean brake components containing asbestos.*
>
> • *Brake fluid is poisonous. Wear safety glasses when working with brake fluid, and wear rubber gloves to prevent brake fluid from entering your bloodstream through cuts and scratches. Do not siphon brake fluid with your mouth.*

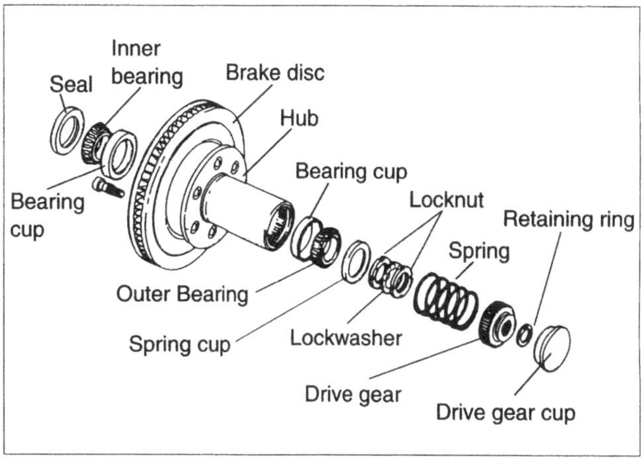

Fig. 12-1. *Unlike ball bearings that require a light pre-load, tapered roller front wheel bearings require end play adjustment. On trucks with inner and outer tapered roller front wheel bearings, a specified in and out movement of the bearing assemblies provides proper running tolerance. GM 1/2-ton 2WD light trucks began using tapered roller front wheel bearings in 1962. (All 4WD models use tapered bearings.)*

1. Wheel Bearings

GM light trucks built before 1962 had ball-type front wheel bearings. 1962 is the first year for tapered roller type bearings on 1/2-ton models.

Tapered roller bearings provide for slight float. While maintaining the vehicle load, properly adjusted rollers can still move laterally (axially) within the clearances of the inner and outer bearing races. Ball bearings, by contrast, cannot tolerate any axial play and require a pre-load rather than end play adjustment.

Any type of rolling bearing will micro-slip (slide or scuff) slightly, and all bearings suffer chronic wear at their rollers, balls and races. The most common bearing race, roller or ball steel is a chromium-alloy, usually SAE 52100 bearing race steel.

This is tough stuff (ranging between 60 and 68 on the Rockwell C scale tests for hardness). These materials furnish high rolling mileage, but the hardness makes races vulnerable to impact damage and pitting from abrasive contaminants. For this reason, thorough cleaning, inspection, and periodic bearing repacking with a suitable grease is necessary.

0012531

Fig. 12-2. *The disc rotor and wheel hub rotate as an integral unit. Correct disc brake rotor lateral runout is critical. Trueness of rotor and proper adjustment of the wheel bearings provide acceptable runout.*

Front Wheel Bearing Fundamentals

Although wheel bearing service procedures and exact adjusting specifications differ among models, some general

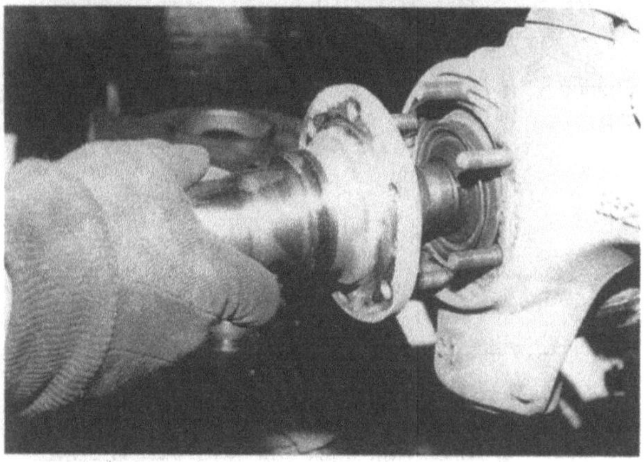

0012532 / 0012662

Fig. 12-3. Inspect the spindle surface where the wheel bearings ride. On both 2WD and 4x4 front spindles, any wear, galling or play will affect the adjustment of the bearings. Check closely for cracks, especially if your truck has overly wide aftermarket wheels and oversize tires. Always replace worn parts.

points apply to all GM light truck models. (Adjustment standards and methods for your truck are available in the GM truck shop manual or an OEM/professional-level service guide.)

For tapered roller wheel bearings, precise wheel bearing adjustment takes end play into account. End play is measurable with a dial indicator attached to the wheel hub, outer brake drum face or rotor. Push the brake drum or rotor straight inward with both hands. (Push evenly to avoid cocking the hub to one side). Take a dial indicator reading, aiming straight toward the spindle.

The dial indicator measures end play when you pull the hub outward. Do not rock the drum or rotor, or a false reading will result. End play is the straight inward and outward (lateral) movement of the hub along the spindle's axis.

Bearing Survival

The two most common causes of bearing failure are poor maintenance and abuse. Poor maintenance includes neglecting periodic cleaning or failure to repack and properly adjust the bearings.

For 4x4 trucks, abuse takes on several additional forms. Such a truck may sport oversized custom wheels

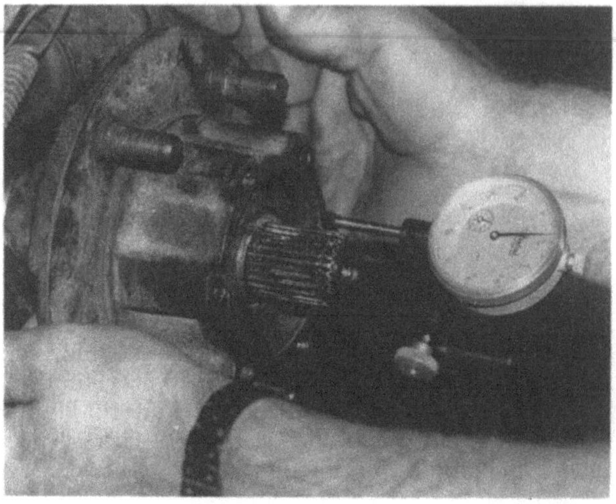

0012533

Fig. 12-4. Dial indicator on magnetic stand measures wheel bearing end play on models with tapered roller wheel bearings. This measurement addresses the acceptable range of bearing roller movement (axially) on the races. Holding the hub flange at nine and three o'clock, push the hub straight in and pull straight out while measuring end play. Check your OEM-level service manual for proper end play specifications.

and tires, or perhaps a change in weight on the front end, the result of a larger V-8 transplant or a cabover camper. (This can also apply to 2WD trucks.) Operating the truck with either too much load on the bearings or excessive lateral stress can cause damage.

Often, bearing failure results from using radically offset (reversed) custom wheels. Shifting the tire centerline outboard from the stock location causes vehicle weight to act as leverage against the wheel hub and bearings. With a front mounted winch or a hefty V-8 engine, even more weight bears directly on each wheel hub. If that same weight applies with the tire centerlines located further outboard, the bearings must now resist an added amount of leverage force.

Wheel Bearing Service Notes

Always service wheel bearings with the correct grease. All wheel bearing greases are not the same. Mixing grease types can severely damage parts and compromise your safety.

> **NOTE —**
> Use the recommended wheel bearing grease for your model and type of wheel bearings. Disc brake equipped vehicles demand exacting wheel bearing adjustments and highly heat resistant lubricant.

When repacking your truck's front wheel bearings, begin with a thorough solvent cleaning. Make certain that no solvent residue remains on the bearings before repacking them. Also clean the spindle, inner wheel hub and races. Wash, wipe and dry all parts thoroughly to remove any traces of solvent before repacking the bearings with fresh, clean grease.

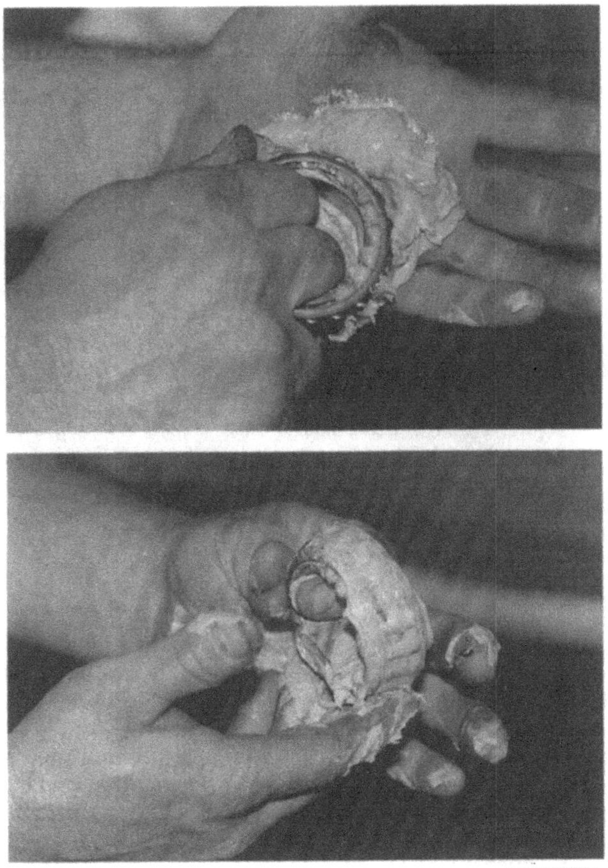

0012534 / 0012663

Fig. 12-5. Wheel bearing packers make this job easy and assure complete grease penetration of the rollers. When hand packing a bearing, squeeze the grease between the wider end of the bearing cage and the inner bearing race. Make sure grease flows out the opposite end of the rollers. Go around the entire bearing assembly at least two full times to assure thorough saturation. Once grease fills all spaces between the rollers, spread a generous film of grease around the outer face of the bearing and cage.

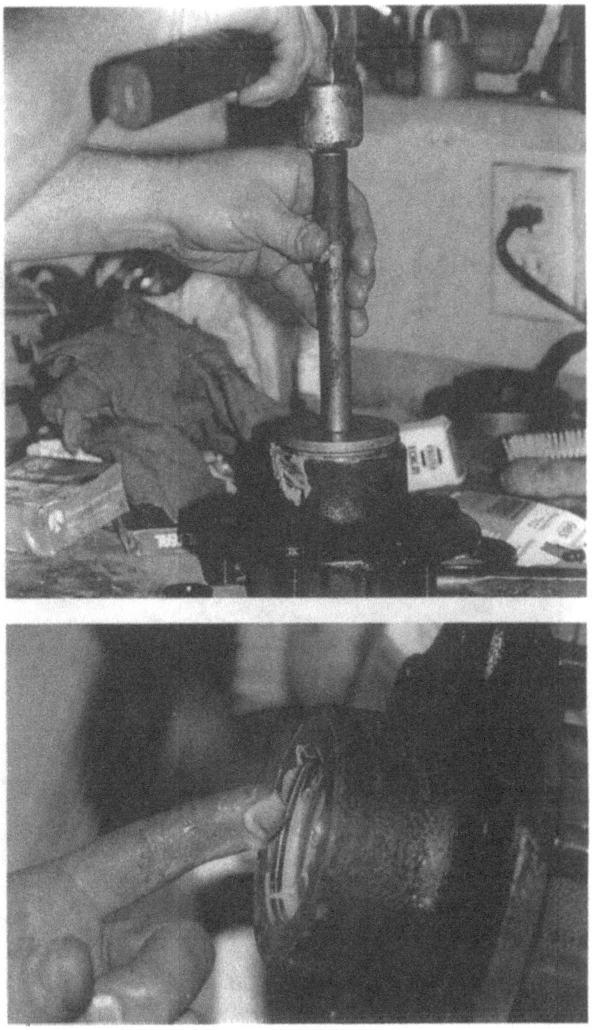

0012535 / 0012665

Fig. 12-6. After cleaning and thoroughly drying the hub and rotor assembly, swab clean grease against the walls of the hub's inner cavity. Grease should fill the hub's grease recess and provide a dam to prevent hot grease from leaving the inner sides of the bearings. Install the freshly packed inner wheel bearing and a new grease seal. The hub is now ready for installation on the spindle. Keep grease away from brake linings. (Shown here is an early Spicer/Dana-type 4x4 front hub assembly.)

> **WARNING —**
> *Never spin bearings with compressed air. Severe bodily harm could result from a bearing assembly flying apart at speed.*

Always replace grease seals. Do not attempt to reuse them. Installing new front or rear wheel seals lowers the risk of parts failure. At the front wheel hubs, they prevent moisture and dirt from entering the hub assembly. Rear axle seals prevent grease or gear lubricant from ruining brake lining and causing failure of the rear brakes.

Use proper tools, refer to your OEM- or professional-level repair guidebook, and take your time when servicing your wheel bearings. On early 4x4 models with a bendable locking washer between the two spindle nuts, install a new washer whenever fatigue is obvious. On 2WD models, always install a new cotter pin after adjusting the castellated or adjuster nut and aligning the retainer (if so equipped) with the cotter pin hole.

On later 4x4 spindles with an inner pinned adjuster, a lock washer with indexing holes and an outer lock nut, make certain that the washer seats securely when tightening the outer lock nut. Done properly, a wheel bearing repack and seal replacement will last for many miles.

> **CAUTION —**
> *Wheel bearing service and adjustment is a critical part of your vehicle maintenance. Your safety and the truck's reliability depend upon proper bearing adjustment. Always follow the adjusting procedure and specifications described in your GM truck shop manual or a professional-level service guidebook. On models so equipped, use the correct size and type of cotter pin, and secure the cotter pin properly.*

0012536

Fig. 12-7. *Install the repacked outer wheel bearing. Build a dam of additional grease between outer side of bearing and thrust face of spindle nut.*

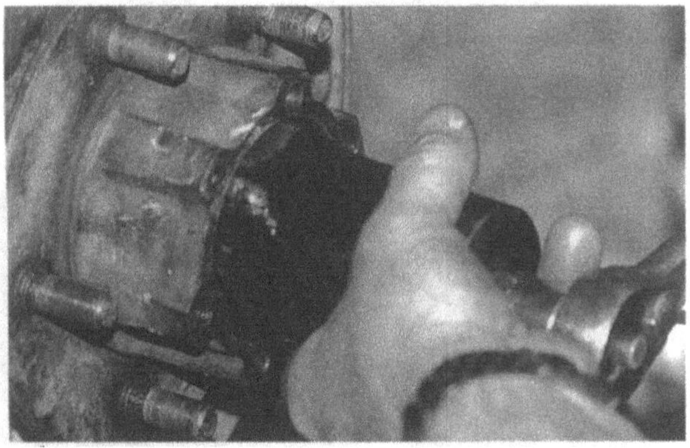

0012537

Fig. 12-8. *Thread the adjuster nut carefully onto the spindle. 4x4 front axles require a special spindle nut wrench. (Consult your GM truck shop manual for adjustment procedure and torque figures.) Note that later model 4x4 hubs have a small locating pin on the inner adjuster nut. Make sure the pin faces outward to receive the multi-holed indexing washer.*

0012538

Fig. 12-9. *Confirm the order of parts assembly in your GM truck shop manual. Carefully install the retaining lockwasher (early 4x4 models) or multi-holed indexing washer (later model solid-axle 4x4s), then install and torque the outer lock nut to specification before measuring hub end play with a dial indicator.*

0012539

Fig. 12-10. *Once end play is correct, bend the early style lockwasher tab (shown here) to secure the nuts. Earlier GM 4x4 axles with hex nuts use this type of lock washer.*

2. THE BRAKING SYSTEM

All GM light truck models covered in this book (1939–up) have brakes that actuate by hydraulic pressure. The basic hydraulic apply system begins with a brake pedal and master cylinder. 1939–59 GM light truck brake systems have a single reservoir master cylinder mounted beneath the floorboard. 1960 was the first year that GM light trucks had a firewall mounted master cylinder with a suspended pedal.

In 1967, the U.S. Department of Transportation invoked safety standards requiring dual hydraulic circuits on the master cylinder. All U.S. built trucks from that year forward have separate hydraulic supply lines for the rear and front brakes. If either end of the system should fail, brakes still operate at the opposite axle.

For light trucks, the dual brake system was a major advancement, eliminating the risk of total brake loss in the event of a fluid leak. For the many truck chassis exposed to fallen trees, jagged rocks and raw terrain, the pre-1967 single braking system offers little protection. If a brake hose snaps or a steel pipe tears, the system loses pressure and the brakes fail completely.

> *WARNING —*
> *Brake friction materials such as brake linings or brake pads may contain asbestos fibers. Do not create dust by grinding, sanding, or cleaning the pads with compressed air. Avoid breathing any asbestos fibers or dust. Breathing asbestos can cause serious diseases such as asbestosis or cancer, and may result in death. Use only approved methods to clean brake components containing asbestos.*

Pedal Warning Signals

A spongy brake pedal is caused by air in the hydraulic system or low brake fluid level. This leads to poor braking action and rust within the system. Check for leaks and bleed any air from the system.

Low fluid can be due to normal lining wear. Periodically verify the thickness of lining, check for proper lining to-drum clearance, and top off fluid after adjusting the brakes. Make sure that the emergency / parking brake has been released before adjusting the wheel brakes.

Another sign of trouble is the pulsating brake pedal, characterized by a rhythmical pumping action during braking. On your truck, causes could include warped drums or rotors, defective brake hardware, a bent front spindle or rear axle shaft and loose wheel bearings. These symptoms can occur suddenly, often following an off-road pounding or submersion in water.

> NOTE —
> Old brake fluid has likely drawn moisture, especially in an early model truck with an atmospherically vented master cylinder. (Conventional brake fluid is "hygroscopic.") This lowers the boiling point of brake fluid, increasing the risk of brake fluid failure under hard braking. Overheated brakes and old brake fluid make deadly companions.

Trailer pullers and those who use their GM truck for hauling heavy cargos should change brake fluid periodically and avoid overheating the brakes whenever possible. (Recreational or tow vehicles that set for long off-season periods are especially vulnerable to brake fluid moisture contamination.) Always use lower gears on a steep downgrade to relieve the load on your truck's brakes. Let the brakes cool down thoroughly when severe heat-up has occurred. Any pedal fade is a sure sign of trouble.

High pedal pressure accompanied by increased stopping distance is brake fade. Fade suggests poor lining quality, drum or rotor warpage, contaminated brake fluid, excessive rotor runout or materials that have fatigued severely.

0014391

Fig. 12-11. *On earlier truck models without self-adjusting brake mechanisms, you must periodically adjust the drum brake lining to avoid a low pedal. On most GM light trucks, the rear brakes double as the parking/emergency brake. Watch for oil, grit and contaminants that will make your wheel brakes—and parking brake—ineffective. Also check and lube the parking brake cable frequently. Shown is a 1986 GM rear brake system with self-adjusting mechanism.*

Brake pull, another common trouble symptom, results from contaminated brake lining, misadjusted shoes or sticky hydraulic cylinders. If brake pads or shoes require replacement, always change lining at both wheels of that axle to avoid uneven braking. Ideally, you should change lining and renew the brake cylinders at all four wheels (both axles) for optimal braking efficiency.

Other Brake Woes

Metallic brake noise signals danger. Generally, metal-on-metal sounds imply total loss of lining and the dragging of shoes or pad backs against a drum or rotor. These symptoms quickly degenerate into damaged rotors or drums, often beyond the point of repair.

Periodic inspection of your truck's brakes can help prevent this trouble. Check for leaks, worn lining and heat damage. Look closely at hoses and brake pipes, especially in those areas exposed to debris and trail abuse. Periodically, remove all brake drums to assess lining wear.

Brake Fluid Precautions

Safety is at stake when you replenish your truck's fluids. Accidental use of mineral-based oils in the hydraulic brake or clutch system can cause swelling of rubber seals and complete failure of the brakes or clutch.

> *WARNING —*
> • *Brake fluid is poisonous. Wear safety glasses when working with brake fluid, and wear rubber gloves to prevent brake fluid from entering the bloodstream through cuts and scratches. Do not siphon brake fluid with your mouth.*
>
> • *Always use DOT 3 or higher rating brake fluid in the master cylinder/braking system or hydraulic clutch system of your truck. Never add motor oil or any substance other than brake fluid to a hydraulic brake system. Do not mix silicone brake fluid with conventional brake fluid.*

Clean, moisture-free brake fluid is fundamental to brake safety. The master cylinder cover must seal tightly. When topping off fluid, use clean brake fluid with the DOT rating specified by General Motors—or better.

Exposed to the atmosphere, brake fluid has a short shelf life. Keep lids sealed snugly and never store fluid in an open container. DOT 3 fluid, fresh out of a new can, boils at 401° F or higher, while the absorption of only 3% moisture reduces the boiling point to 284° F. This is ample justification for the annual flush and replenishment with clean brake fluid.

Apply special care when handling brake service parts and brake fluid. Since brake fluid has an affinity for water, store a tightly resealed brake fluid container in a dry location. The need for cleanliness cannot be overstated, as hydraulic brake cylinders will fail when exposed to abrasive debris or mineral / petroleum based oils, solvents and greases.

Chapter 12

Brake Fluid Service

Your truck's brakes require regular attention. Routine concerns include checking the hydraulic brake fluid, inspecting hoses and steel pipes for damage and noting the lining left on disc brake pads and brake shoes. With clean hands and a clean master cylinder cap, check the brake fluid level at each lubrication interval.

Dusty trails, stream crossings, slush and snow expose various brake parts to water, abrasive dirt and road salts. Older trucks, with master cylinders mounted beneath the floorboard, have atmospherically vented filler caps. These models face the risk of contaminants and moisture entering the reservoir.

> **NOTE —**
> Take care when checking the fluid. Especially on models with floorboard inspection covers, make certain that debris and grit cannot fall from the floorboard into the open brake fluid reservoir. Before removing the master cylinder fill plug, clean the area thoroughly—with a shop vacuum cleaner if necessary.

The early master cylinder design also raises other service issues. The air vent in the master cylinder cap often draws dust and moisture into the master cylinder reservoir. It is common for abrasive mud to accumulate in the base of the master cylinder reservoir. A complete system flush and overhaul of each cylinder is the only remedy for this problem.

A 1939–59 GM truck model with an under-the-floorboard master cylinder faces even greater hazards. Submerging the chassis in running stream water, or driving through a flooded roadway, can contaminate the hydraulic braking system.

0012541

Fig. 12-12. *Before checking brake fluid on a 1939–59 GM light truck, vacuum or brush dirt away from the inspection plate hole (here seen through the passenger compartment floor boards) and the master cylinder fill plug area. Carefully remove the plug to verify the correct fluid level, which you will find listed in your GM truck shop manual.*

0014289

Fig. 12-13. *1967 and newer GM trucks feature tandem master cylinders, mounted high on the firewall, a sensible distance from debris and water. Still, always clean around the master cylinder assembly before removing the inspection cap.*

Most truck owners and mechanics ignore flushing the hydraulic brake system. Years ago, brake parts manufacturers recommended pressure flushing with a special flushing compound (usually containing denatured alcohol) or pumping clean brake fluid through the brake system annually. Replacement of all rubber cups, seals and boots would follow.

For the pre-1967 GM truck (single master cylinder with atmospheric vent) that sets for long periods, or the 1939–59 truck that drives through streams regularly, periodic flushing of the system is still a good idea. At the very least, you should pump fresh brake fluid through the system annually and bleed out all air.

Make certain that enough brake fluid passes through to carry away most of the stale fluid. If your truck has an under-floorboard master cylinder with a cap that vents the reservoir to atmosphere, periodic inspection and service of your hydraulic system will contribute to the preservation of expensive brake parts.

1967–up braking systems have much less trouble with atmospheric contamination of brake fluid. Later master cylinder covers provide a sealed rubber bellows to accommodate pressure and fluid level changes. This eliminates the need for a vent hole from the reservoir to atmosphere. Despite these design improvements, moisture still enters the hydraulic brake system at approximately 3% volume per year.

For details on servicing, flushing or bleeding air from the hydraulic brake system, consult the GM truck shop manual for your model. GM truck brake systems vary, and modern brake designs, especially the newer Antilock Braking System (ABS), call for much different service procedures and precautions than earlier models.

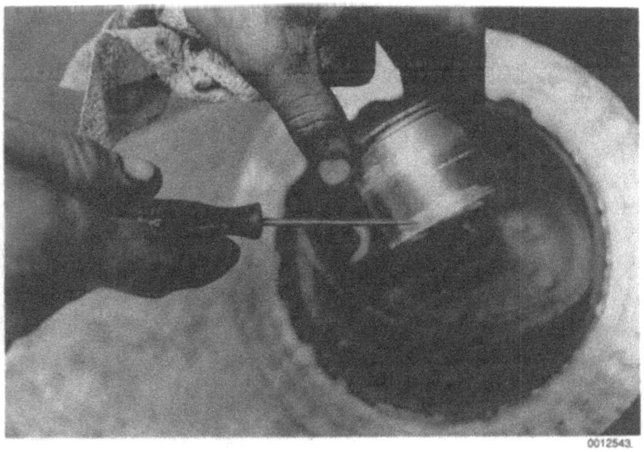

Fig. 12-14. Disc caliper piston scoring resulted from the severe heat generated as a rotor disintegrated. Piston seizure can cause brake lockup or severe brake pull.

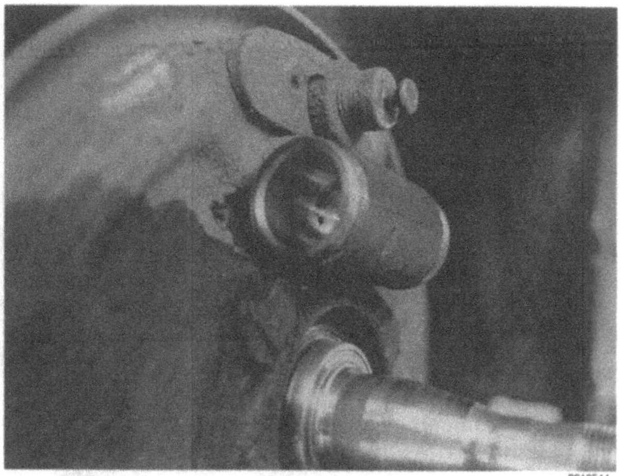

Fig. 12-15. Wheel cylinders cannot tolerate scoring. If honed, this cylinder will lose too much material. Pitting and scoring result from moisture and wear. Periodic flushing could have prevented this pitting.

Fig. 12-16. Many late model master cylinders have aluminum housings. Most shops regard such assemblies as a throwaway item, finding them ill-suited for overhaul. Scratches and scoring, common traits when these parts require service, can render such a master cylinder useless. Never hone an aluminum brake cylinder. Follow factory service guidelines.

Brake Service and Overhaul Tips

Avoid introducing contaminants or abrasive foreign material into the hydraulic reservoir(s). Such debris damages sensitive rubber parts within the master cylinder and hydraulic system. Late model trucks with aluminum master cylinder bores are especially vulnerable to scoring.

During brake system overhauls, check the labels on brake parts cleaners. Many contain petroleum solvents or distillates. These cleaners work fine as metal parts degreasers. However, petroleum- or mineral-based solvents and oils can cause the wheel cylinder, caliper and master cylinder rubber parts to swell up and fail.

> *WARNING —*
> *Never use mineral- or petroleum-based solvents or oils around rubber parts.*

Denatured alcohol and automotive brake fluid are among the few substances that will not destroy rubber. The traditional cleaner for critical brake parts is denatured alcohol. (Allow alcohol to evaporate completely before filling the system with brake fluid.) Your GM truck shop manual will indicate which cleaning substances to use. Read safety precautions before handling any of these cleaning substances.

> *CAUTION —*
> *Due to changes in metal types and factory bore finishing methods, manufacturers do not recommend honing certain hydraulic cylinders. Consult a factory workshop manual for recommended service procedures that apply to your model and year vehicle. Follow factory guidelines when servicing a master cylinder, wheel cylinders and disc brake calipers.*

Always inspect hydraulic brake cylinders for pits, scratches, scoring, and corrosion. If in doubt, replace the cylinder. If rebuildable, remove the cylinder from the system. When recommended in the factory workshop manual covering your model and year vehicle, hone the cylinder's bore lightly with a suitable brake cylinder hone.

Hone as described in the factory workshop manual. Be certain not to leave debris or abrasive material in the cylinder. Carefully measure the bore diameter. If within factory tolerance, the cylinder must be thoroughly cleaned in the manner noted within the factory shop manual for your model. Assemble new rubber parts with clean brake fluid or special brake rubber parts assembly lube.

When servicing disc brakes, make certain that floating (self-centering) caliper assemblies and pistons

Fig. 12-17. Overhauling disc brake calipers requires cleanliness, care and proper tools. Here, a new seal seats in a reconditioned bore.

slide freely. If signs of friction exist, overhaul or replace the caliper.

If four-wheeling or off-pavement bashing has caused damage to your truck's hydraulic brake lines or fittings, replace parts only with DOT-approved brake hardware. Tees, hoses, junction blocks and valving should meet or exceed your vehicle's original equipment brake standards.

Use pre-formed steel brake pipe. This tubing, cut to length and double-flared at each end, comes complete with flare nuts and ready to install. Once you have shaped the new tubing with a tubing bender, use a flare nut wrench to remove and replace the brake pipes. Torque flare nuts to the manufacturer's specifications listed in the GM truck shop manual.

WARNING —
Avoid introducing debris or contaminants into the hydraulic system when changing brake hoses or pipes. Always bleed air from the system and check for leaks before driving.

While servicing your brakes, inspect the wheel bearings and axle seals. A leaky rear axle seal can ruin new brake lining quickly. Preserve your truck's braking system. Apply preventive care wherever possible. This is your best safeguard against losing your brakes.

Brake Linings

Whether your GM truck is bone stock or highly modified, brake performance is important. Although we refine our engines, transmissions and axles, brakes often get overlooked.

WARNING —
Brake friction materials such as brake linings or brake pads may contain asbestos fibers. Do not create dust by grinding, sanding, or cleaning the pads with compressed air. Avoid breathing any asbestos fibers or dust. Breathing asbestos can cause serious diseases such as asbestosis or cancer, and may result in death. Use only approved methods to clean brake components containing asbestos.

Fig. 12-18. Age, fatigue and overheating cause brake lining failure. Thinner lining loses heat resistance, as witnessed by these heat-cracked disc brake pads.

Improving your truck's brake system begins with brake lining. Organic friction materials use asbestos, usually in a phenolic-resin compound. Asbestos, an environmental hazard, places the brake mechanic at risk. Use of an approved respirator and protective wear has become mandatory for asbestos and brake industry workers.

The brake and clutch industry's attraction to asbestos has been its exceptional heat resistance, low wear and minimal noise. Asbestos health risks outweigh benefits, however, and asbestos-bearing organic friction materials now border on extinction.

Bendix, a respected industry supplier of quality brake parts, advises several precautions when purchasing new brake lining: 1) If your truck has semi-metallic brake pads, always refit with semi-metallic lining; 2) Replace asbestos/organic pads and shoes with comparable lining; and 3) Don't replace OEM organic or organic/asbestos lining with semi-metallic lining—unless sanctioned by the vehicle manufacturer.

Fig. 12-19. Thinned brake lining shows heat crack formation. Replace parts now to avoid the risk of lining separation.

0012549

Fig. 12-20. *New brake lining has code marks. Many states require edge coding, which helps consumers determine lining type and quality.*

0012551

Fig. 12-22. *Non-directional finish of rotors assures semi-metallic lining break-in. Some manufacturers recommend a brake lathe grinder for this task, while others find a hand held drill motor and disc sander acceptable. Wear an approved particle mask, or a federally approved respirator if you suspect presence of asbestos, and safety goggles.*

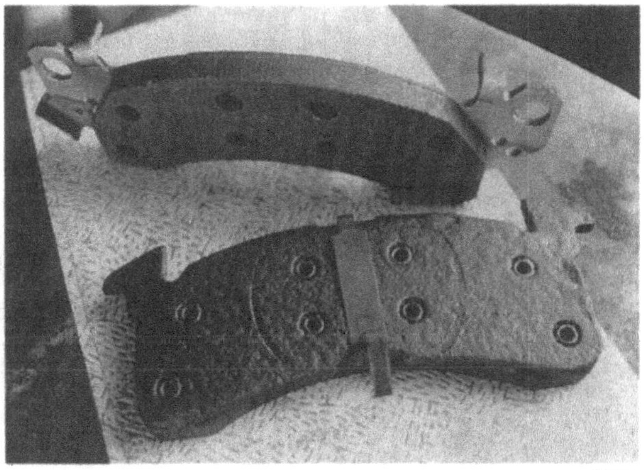

0012550

Fig. 12-21. *Coat new pad backs before installation. Special silicone grease dries quickly and helps prevent brake squeal.*

As of this book's publication, asbestos is still legal for some applications. All manufacturers, however, will stop using asbestos as suitable non-asbestos products become available. Stay informed on this issue, and avoid using asbestos products whenever possible.

Semi-metallic brake lining, suited for front disc pad material, provides cooler operation. Under severe braking conditions and heavy loading, semi-metallic lining rapidly draws heat away from the rotors. Excessive heat, the cause of fade and pad/rotor damage, is less likely with semi-metallic brake materials.

Manufacturers recommend that replacement brake lining match the OEM material standards. Poor braking, short pad life, and rotor scoring or warping will otherwise result. Fade usually leads to complete brake failure. If you have questions about your truck's original equipment brake lining, consult your local GM light truck dealership or a brake parts supplier for guidelines.

Semi-metallic Brake Pad Break-in

If your truck can use semi-metallic disc pads, special preparation of the rotors is necessary. When resurfacing your rotors, Bendix recommends a satin-smooth final cut, followed by a non-directional finish. Correct rotor finish will eliminate squeal and hard pedal action.

Semi-metallic pad replacement always includes rotor resurfacing—even if very minor work is necessary to true the rotor and condition the surfaces. The final non-directional finish assures quieter operation and quick seating of pads.

Like engines and other automotive components, brakes require break-in. For semi-metallic brake pads, Bendix recommends light use of the brakes for the first 150 to 200 miles. When pads are new, avoid panic stops if possible. Instead of hard burn-ins, Bendix suggests 15 to 20 slow stops from about 30 mph. Use light to moderate brake pedal pressure and allow at least 30 seconds of recovery between each stop.

As another consideration, semi-metallic lining requires heavier pedal pressure when cold or wet. Some disc brake trucks with heavier (integral with the wheel hub) front rotors will dissipate heat so effectively that a semi-metallic retrofit lining cannot work at peak efficiency.

Reciprocally, a less expensive organic lining will overheat and wear rapidly when installed on a late model, lightweight rotor system designed for semi-metallic lining. This is one more reason to stick with original equipment recommendations.

Drums and Rotors

The trueness of a rotor or drum is essential. Drums and rotors should be checked for scoring, hard spots, warpage and proper inside diameter (drums) or thickness (rotors). Micrometers for this task are common to brake shops and automotive machine shops. If the rotor or drum surface is at all suspect, resurfacing on a brake lathe is necessary.

CAUTION —
A common cause of disc brake rotor damage is over-torquing the wheel lug nuts. Wheel lugs too loose or tight, or tightened out of sequence, can warp a rotor.Use of an impact gun is the easiest way to overtighten lug nuts. Aside from the risk of breaking lug studs, overtightening enlarges wheel holes and warps disc rotors. Improperly torqued lugs can warp a rotor enough to cause pulsation of the brake pedal and premature pad wear.

0012552

Fig. 12-23. *Before disassembly, check your truck's hub/drums or disc rotors for lateral runout, warpage and thickness variance.*

0012553

Fig. 12-24. *Read the thickness and wear of the rotor with an outside micrometer. Determine whether to cut the rotors or buy a new pair. Better ventilated, lightweight rotors are often candidates for semi-metallic pads. Your local GM truck dealership's parts department can verify which type of lining is acceptable.*

0012554

Fig. 12-25. *A badly scored rotor cannot be reused. Here, disc brake lining and rivets wore into the rotor, destroying its surface and causing complete front brake failure.*

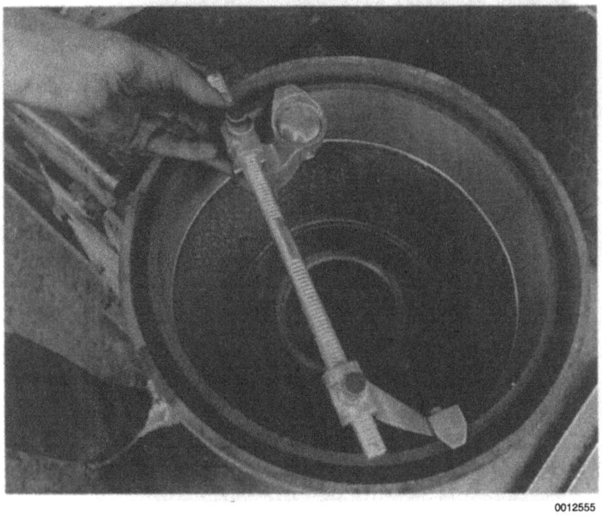

0012555

Fig. 12-26. *Resurfaced rear brake drum assures a quality brake job. Lining will wear-in better and offer complete contact with the drum surface. Service opposite wheel's brakes at the same time. (On a four-wheel drum brake system, service all four wheels at the same time.)*

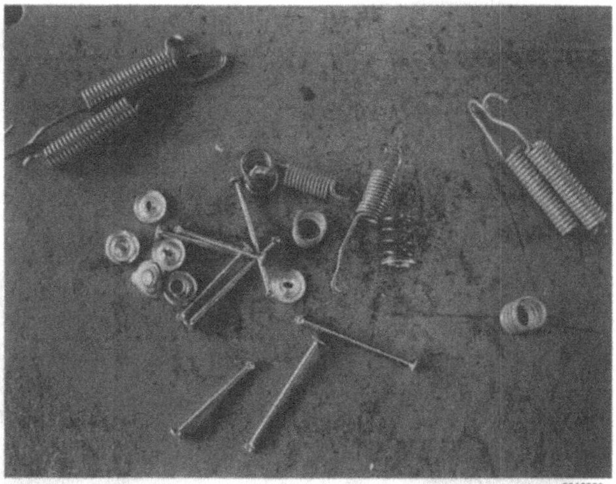

Fig. 12-27. Professionals install hardware kits with every brake overhaul. Old springs and retainers fatigue from heat, while new pieces ensure proper shoe alignment and action.

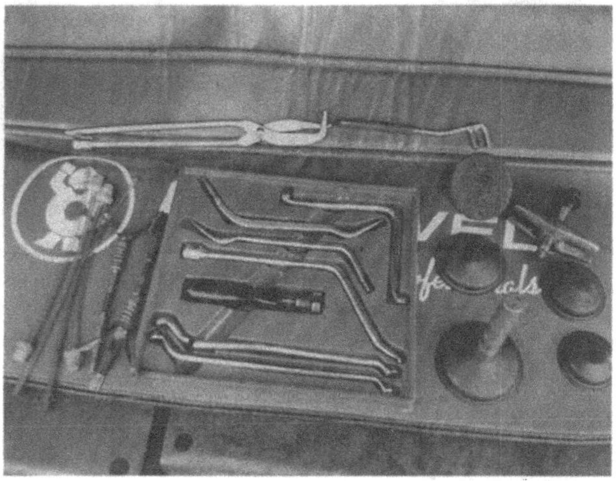

Fig. 12-28. Specialty tools used for brake work include seal drivers, piston removal tools, adjuster spoons, bleeder wrenches, spring pliers and retainer/removal tool. Seen also is a set of master cylinder bench bleeding hoses.

Rotors, drums and lining are expensive. Care should be taken to tighten each set of lugs gradually and in cross. Whenever possible, use a torque wrench for final tightening.

Always recheck air gun tightened lugs when you have new tires mounted commercially. If too tight, jack up the wheel, loosen the whole set of nuts, and retightened properly. If too loose, bring nuts to specification in cross sequence.

Fig. 12-29. Wheel cylinder cups and dust boots are available in a variety of sizes. Replace these parts at each brake overhaul. Older trucks called for an annual brake system flush and periodic replacement of cups and boots. The GM light truck shop manual for your model describes the service procedure .

Fig. 12-30. Other damage, like these over-torqued and broken wheel studs, adds to restoration cost. Broken studs usually result from overtorquing during wheel installation.

0012560

Fig. 12-31. Here is a common cause of premature rear brake lining failure. This semi-floating axle's bearing seal has leaked. Gear oil saturated the brake shoes and rubber dust boots.

0012561

Fig. 12-32. Resurfacing the brake drums is an important part of a brake job. The GM light truck shop manual provides safe machining limits. Rivet heads, steel pad backings and metal shoe backs cause the worst damage.

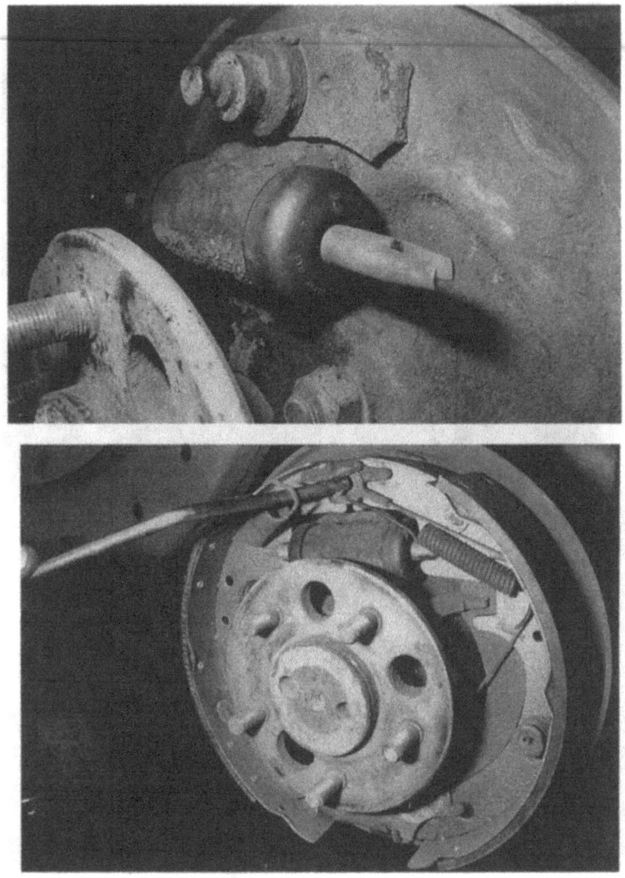

0012562 / 0012686

Fig. 12-33. New wheel cylinder boots protect against moisture and debris. Once the cylinder overhaul is complete, new brake shoes and hardware fit into place.

Chapter 13

Body and Detailing

HARSH CLIMATES, BRUSH SCRATCHES and off-pavement bashing tear unmercifully at your truck's body. Over the years, a truck also accumulates its share of oxidation. The battle against rust is an endless vigil. You must watch constantly for fresh scratches and exposed metal. In salt air regions, including areas with corrosive salt spread on winter roadways, truck bodies are especially vulnerable. Bright metal, chrome and painted surfaces can oxidize rapidly.

1. BATTLING RUST

Sadly, hundreds of thousands of otherwise restorable GM trucks have wound up as rusty hulks at recycling yards. Rust is a chronic problem for any truck, even more so for the 4x4 models.

In addition to environmental hazards, some truck bodies have weak sheet metal areas or a section that provides very poor water drainage. Mid-1980s and newer models, with more extensive use of galvanized (zinc treated) metals, plastic and rubberized trim, can resist rust much better than older trucks.

Ironically, rust was not a major issue with the 1939 to 1955 (First Series) GM trucks. Many restorers discover these early models still much intact, with a minimal amount of rust. Despite their age, the oldest GM trucks with separate running boards feature strong gauge sheetmetal and few body areas that collect mud, road salt and other corrosives.

By contrast, the most susceptible models for rust are the 1955 (Second Series)–59 and 1960–66 GM light trucks, the first two body designs without running boards but with deep door sill step areas. Recycling yards, body shops and sheetmetal parts vendors have done a thriving business around replacement body panels for these trucks—and even the 1967 to mid-1980s models.

In fairness to General Motors, this era also represents the most significant use of winter road salt in U.S. history, and the Midwestern trucks have suffered the worst. In drier climates, GM light trucks have resisted rust and proven as durable as any other truck make.

The more persistent rust areas are the front fenders, door sill/step areas, the floorboards, tailgate area and the bed. Rust forms at hood hinges and other parts of the body where paint can wear thin. Bare metal on inner fender panels, the cowl, floorboards, grill shell and front fenders will rust quickly in corrosive or moist air.

With the body and chassis thoroughly cleaned, inspect your truck for rust. Pay close attention to areas with add-on accessories, which can expose bare sheetmetal. Look for poor sealing and exfoliation (bubbling), an indication of rust formation beneath the paint.

0014475

Fig. 13-1. Proper care and detailing has kept my family's 1986 Suburban in showroom condition. Periodic detail work helps prevent paint oxidation, rust, and road salt damage. Protect your truck's value—clean and detail on a regular basis.

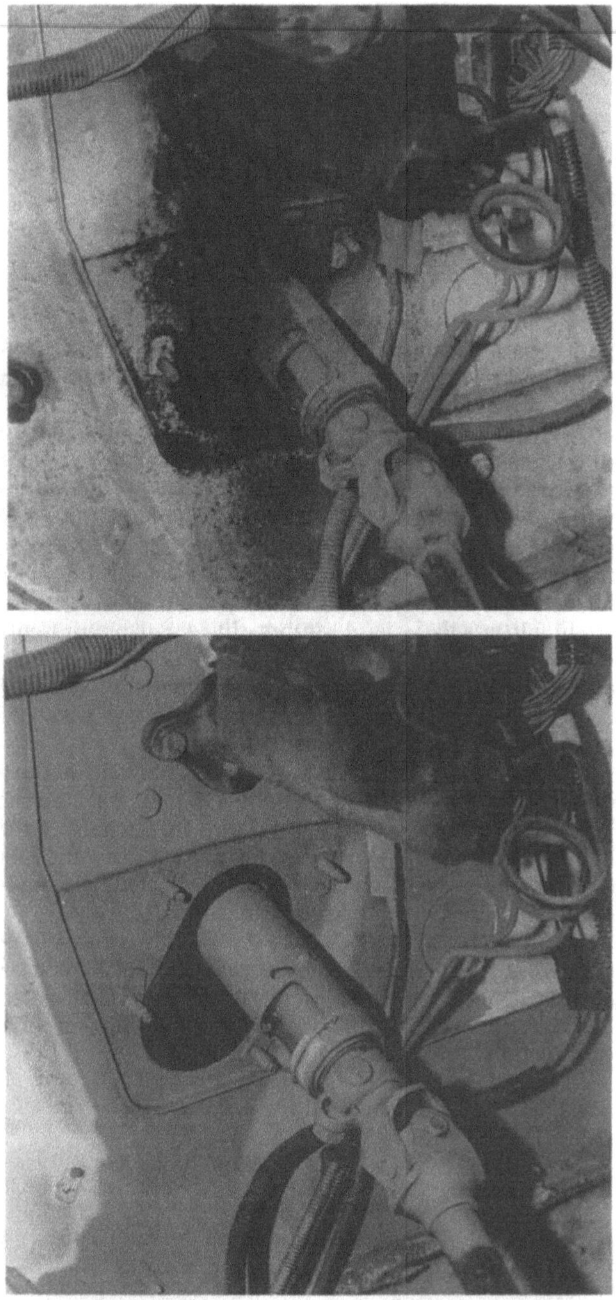

0012565 / 0012667

Fig. 13-2. This area may look ominous because of its surface rust. A professional body worker sees this as salvageable. Sandblasting of firewall will restore this metal. Surface rust, although unsightly, does not effect the integrity of base sheetmetal. Sandblasting reveals that underlying metal is strong and serviceable.

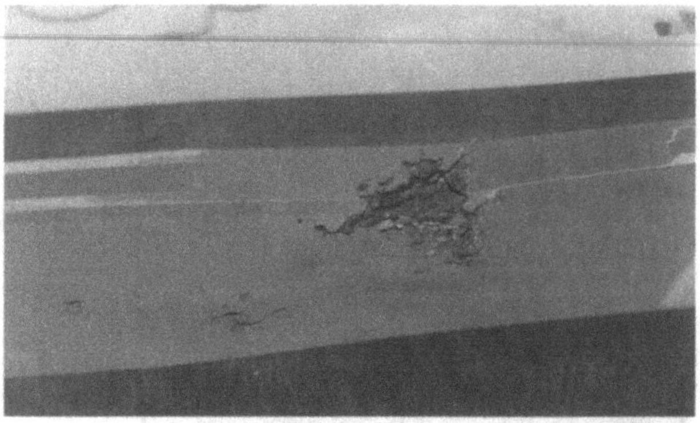

0012566

Fig. 13-3. This is insidious rust. Watch for high spots like this. Hidden behind an inside trim panel, rust worked its way through the body and now presses through the sheetmetal.

0012564

Fig. 13-4. When the carpet rolls back, so can the metal! The small bulges at the outer body surface never suggested this major rust. On older GM trucks, floorboard and door sill rust is a major problem. If your truck or a prospective buy needs restoration, look closely for rust. You must always seal around any drilled holes. Carpets may hide an area where water can accumulate and menacing rust forms. Always take rust bubbles or exfoliation seriously.

If you suspect rust, remove the accessory and treat the area with thorough sanding, primer/sealing and paint as needed. When damage is excessive, consult a local body shop.

Fix It Yourself

The flatter panels on a truck body make a good place to enhance your metalwork and painting skills. Restoration and maintenance can include sealing, priming and painting your truck.

As for your GM light truck's frame, although made of metals which resist rust perforation, frames also build up surface oxidation. Wear a particle mask and safety goggles, and clean rust with a drill-powered wire brush. Prime and paint surfaces to prevent further problems, using a rust inhibiting primer or paint.

0012567

Fig. 13-5. Sandblasting at this metal bulge tells a broader tale. Hidden between an aftermarket trim panel and interior carpet, major rust damage resulted from improper metal seal during installation of the add-on roll bar.

Rust Repairs

Louie Russo, Jr., owner of L. J. Russo's Paint and Body Shop at Lakeside, California, is an auto body and paint master. If your truck restoration includes rust removal, Louie's step-by-step rust repair system provides a good lesson.

Consider these procedures carefully before tackling your truck's rust. Techniques shown here provide a like-new fix and prepare the truck for a quality paint job.

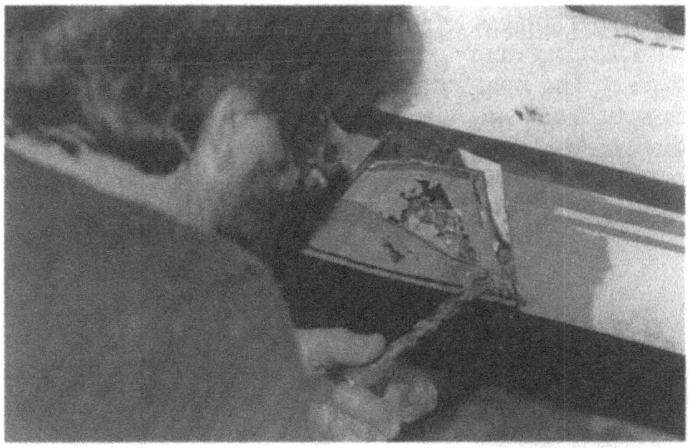

0012568

Fig. 13-6. Factory rivets drilled, Louie Russo separates floorpan from the interior body brace. Extent of rust is still deceptive at this point.

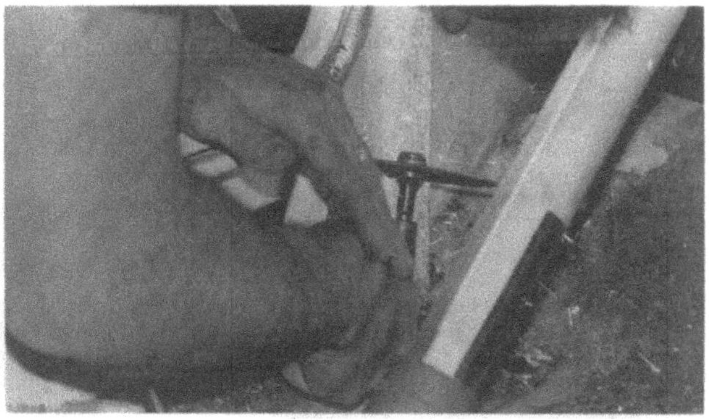

0012569

Fig. 13-7. Louie carefully removes rotted metal. Here, a carbide disc cuts quickly through the sheetmetal brace. Structural integrity of the body is a consideration with this repair. Use an approved particle mask or respirator and goggles around carbide grinding.

0012570

Fig. 13-8. Remove or treat all rust-affected metal. At this point, wire brushing and sandblasting will determine strength of metal and pinholes to fill.

0012571

Fig. 13-9. Heavy-gauge metal section from an ancient truck fender has become a replacement piece for the OEM brace. Louie welds the hand-formed repair section into place. Note use of salvageable segment of the original brace. This small portion of metal helps maintain alignment and contours.

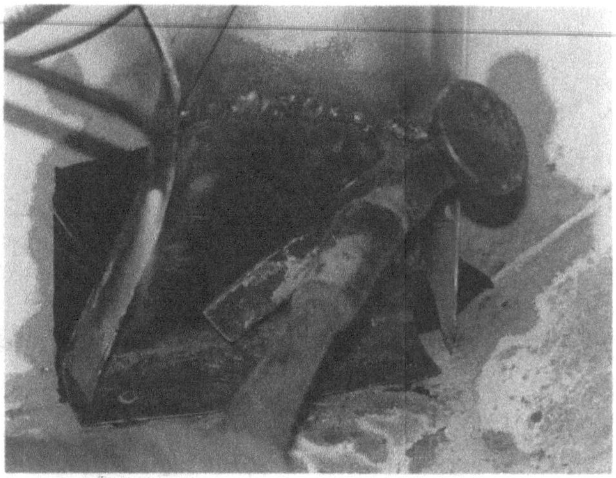

Fig. 13-10. *MIG welded into place, section now fits against the cleaned floorpan. Heat applied to lower bracket flange allows shaping with a body hammer until new brace matches OE fit perfectly. Louie also welded pinholes in floorpan. Surface grinding of welds will restore original appearance.*

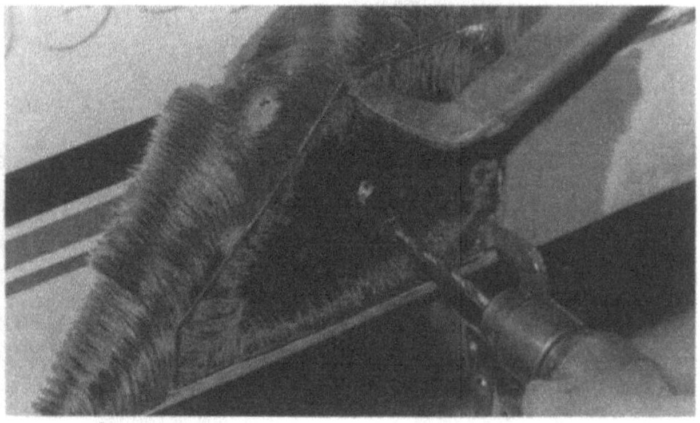

Fig. 13-11. *Louie cuts and forms flat piece of sheetmetal to fit cutout. He purposely keeps the original lower roll of body lip to avoid having to reform edge. Drilling and spot-welding outer panel to inner brace duplicates OE engineering. MIG confines heat. Louie strategically lays down welds while carefully quenching hot sheetmetal to maintain shape.*

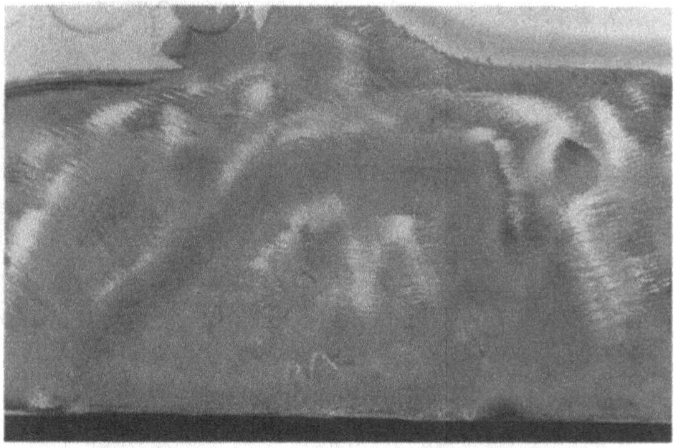

Fig. 13-12. *Surface grinding reveals Louie's careful handling of metal. Masterful heat isolation, shrink/stretch control and correct heat diffusion results in near perfect surface straightness.*

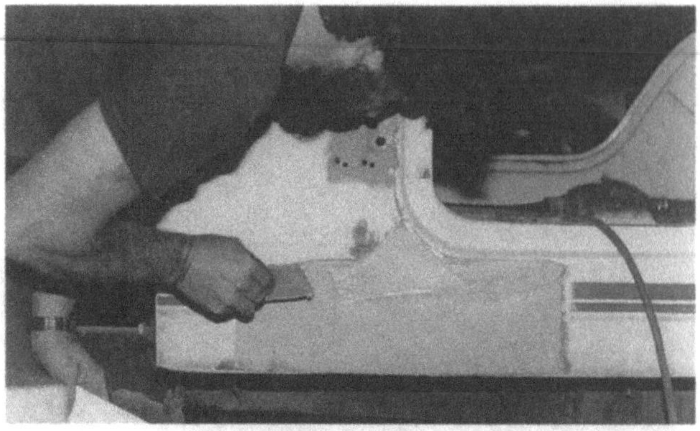

Fig. 13-13. *Louie applies a light coat of plastic body filler to sanding scratches and very slight depressions. Once shaped and sanded, only a tiny amount of plastic will remain. Louie Russo prefers the challenge of metal working to the simpler, plastic fill approach. His work shows good-as-new quality.*

2. BODY DETAILING

As a light truck owner, get to know your local self-service car wash. Here, the combination of soap and high pressure spray can transform a mud-caked truck into respectable suburban driveway material. In minutes, pounds of mud and debris will stream from the body, wheel wells, frame, axles and suspension.

Detailing your truck begins with a thorough wash. Many trucks face as much dirt, sun and abrasive wind as a desert camel, yet there's no protective hair or hide to seal the elements from your truck's paint finish. Magnetic abrasives cling tenaciously to the paint pores, while scorching sun and road salts oxidize the trim and rubber. A cleaner must be gentle enough to leave healthy paint intact, yet still cut and flush the grit from the paint.

There are many commercial car wash solutions on the market. The main objective with any good car soap is to dissolve road oils and gently flush dirt away. Although dishwashing liquids work well, commercial products might be part of a complete cleaning system, chemically engineered to work with specific waxes or polishes.

Fig. 13-14. *Local car wash or a home pressure washer will remove major debris after a hard day's work or off-roading.*

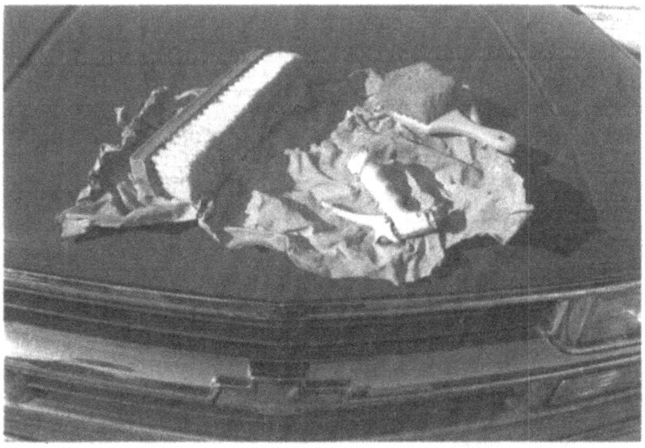

0014451

Fig. 13-15. A spray nozzle, car wash solution, horse hair brush and a genuine English chamois are tools for a quality wash job.

0012578

Fig. 13-16. Eastwood Company's mail order catalog features products for a show-winning appearance.

Even more important is your washing technique. For a quality wash job around grit and abrasives, avoid scratching the finish. A sponge or wash cloth is hazardous. Special car wash mitts work much better, but hand pressure can still cause grit to press into the paint or drag across the surface.

I always begin with a thorough wash-down using a high pressure washer that attaches to an air compressor source and garden hose. This washer can easily clean dirty engine bays, inner fender wells and the chassis.

For hand washing, the gentle bristles and cushion provided by a horse hair brush reduce the risk of scratches yet still massages foaming soap into paint pores. Your truck's panels will cleanse easily, followed by a gentle rinse of clear water. Use a quality, rubber-nosed faucet nozzle, capable of controlling pressure while protecting the vehicle's finish.

Why Fight Your Paint Finish?

Most truck owners can find better things to do with their weekends than wash and polish a vehicle. Playing in the backwoods and seasonal four-wheeling hold a lot more fun than performing a wax job. In recent years, however, professional detailing equipment has drastically sped up detailing work. Shifting away from disc-sander type buffers, the orbital polishers now appear everywhere—and for good reason.

Traditional buffing methods, especially hand or disc polishing, can leave the paint finish full of swirls. Worse yet, the risk of buffing right through the paint edges scares most non-professional detailers from even attempting to use a disc-type buffer. The gentle orbital buffers, by contrast, offer the first-time user a chance to do a professional polishing job without ruining an expensive paint finish.

As for the risk of paint removal from orbital buffing, I once interviewed Loren E. Doppelt, Senior Product Manager for Waxmaster/Chamberlain. Loren noted, "I've buffed and polished a sample hood at car shows. The hood receives 1,000 buffings before we routinely re-paint it.... Frankly, even then, there's no evidence that the paint is damaged."

0012579

Fig. 13-17. A random orbital waxer/polisher is your best investment and incentive for detail work. The Chamberlain/Waxmaster and other units are available from retail suppliers.

0012580

Fig. 13-18. *This buffer bonnet's grey debris came from a fully cured new paint job after a thorough wash. An orbital buffer, used with a wide range of detailing chemicals, can strip/clean, apply wax or polish and buff the finish to a high luster. Uniform results make hand or disc-type polishing obsolete.*

0012581

Fig. 13-19. *An orbital buffer works with any number of specialized products. Shown are Waxmaster and Mothers brands of waxes and polishes.*

Your First Orbital Buffing Job

When your new paint finish turns dull from road film and caked mud, don't panic. Armed with the right detailing chemicals and a quality orbital buffer, you can produce a professional wax job in less than an hour. Park your truck in the shade, and begin by washing it thoroughly. With the metal cool, apply a smooth coating of wax.

The body contours and accessory hardware on many trucks can pose a nightmare for buffing. A steep sloping cab, trailer pulling mirrors and abutments sticking out everywhere create a real challenge for an orbital buffer. Still, the promise of uniform buffing action, as opposed to sluggish, ineffective hand waxing, will spur your polishing job forward.

Carnauba based semi-paste wax, mixed with a liquid polish, works best with the orbital buffer. Although the buffer easily works with other chemical products, the combination polish and wax allows a faster, more thorough job. Carnauba based waxes provide better paint breathing and protection from atmospheric hazards.

Apply the wax and polish solution simultaneously to the terry cloth buffing bonnet. Movement of the orbital buffer is easy to master. The technique is much like operating a floor polisher. Application of wax/polish will take approximately thirty to forty minutes on a light truck, including the exterior surface of the bed.

The buffer will lay down a uniform blend of wax. Hard to reach and hand applied areas rub easily with the remaining wax/polish on the polishing bonnet. Install a clean cloth and begin buffing. In minutes, the surface will glisten from every angle. Hand buffing with a terry cloth towel brings the inaccessible areas to a high lustre.

Orbital buffing leaves your truck's finish with a protective, penetrating coat of Carnauba wax. Surface oxidized material has transferred to the buffing pads.

Conventional hand waxing, a tedious, unfulfilling task, is now passe. An orbital buffer produces professional results, the first time out. For a sharp appearance that lasts for years, treat your truck to quarterly polish jobs with a random orbital buffer and a quality Carnauba wax/polish.

Weather-beaten Paint

A grossly oxidized finish may still respond to a finishing compound buff out. Seek a quality compound that lifts dead paint by chemical action, not abrasion, and leaves no swirl marks. Follow buffing with a careful polish and wax job.

Badly oxidized finishes may take a full morning and several orbital buffer pads to fix. Bonnets are washable and reusable if you keep them wet after use.

Finishes raked with disc buffer swirls respond impressively to orbital buffing with a quality swirl remover. Applied directly to the buffer pad, this non-scratching substance is more like a polish than a rubbing compound. I've played with ultra-fine sanding scratches left by 1200 grit wet-sanding paper and found that an orbital buffer can remove all traces in minutes—without cutting into the finish.

The Rest of the Details

When your truck's paint finish comes back to life, a sparkling surface with deeply colored lustre, there's a real incentive to complete the detailing chores. Here, too, I recommend fast, high quality chemical products for highlighting the interior and exterior trim.

Flat stainless steel and chrome moldings respond readily to the gentle buffing action of the orbital machine, and the balance of the stainless hardware will polish easily by hand. Rubber and vinyl, the two most vulnerable materials after paint, require a hand-applied combination cleaner/protectant product that will counter oxidation.

The principle cause of oxidation on your truck's paint surface and rubber is sunlight. Use of a protective UV-blocker agent on vinyl, leather and plastic trim extends the life of these materials. I get good results with 303 Protectant.

Quick Tips to a Better Detail Job

1) Wash your truck thoroughly. Use bug and tar remover and other specially formulated chemicals to treat problem areas.

2) When using a buffer, make sure your polish and waxes are compatible. Chemical bases differ, and some chemicals react adversely when mixed.

3) Use several terrycloth towels when hand waxing. Don't apply towels used for buffing the sides and rocker panels to the upper body surfaces. Avoid introducing road oxidants and corrosives to the upper panels.

4) Wax your truck in the shade. Many polishes and waxes have chemistry that will evaporate rapidly in direct sunlight. A hot paint surface is also more vulnerable to damage.

5) Apply polish to the cloth or bonnet. Pouring it onto the painted surface may cause uneven chemical action, including stains.

6) Avoid use of any product that seals paint permanently. Such materials may prevent normal expansion and contraction of paint and seldom offer protection against UV radiation. Auto painters lament the fish-eye effect that results when repainting finishes sealed with permanent protectants.

7) Invest in the miracles of modern science. Special detailing chemicals not only leave more time for recreation, but they often provide superior results.

8) Allow vinyl surfaces to breathe. Most vinyl has a chemically engineered top-coat that needs protection. Choose your vinyl treatment carefully.

9) Use a small detail brush to reach difficult areas. A freshly polished finish draws attention to those small crevices and crannies that you miss. A few extra minutes makes the difference between a show-stopper and a shoddy job.

10) Pay attention to quality. There's a reason for higher priced products, and all waxes are not the same. The longest lasting stuff may not serve your paint finish best. Look for breathable Carnaubas and anti-oxidants. They can extend the life of your truck's finish.

A gentle cleaner, 303 claims to provide a protective barrier against oxidation without damaging the vinyl's top-coat chemistry. Sensitive vinyl surfaces must flex and breathe. Any coating that either draws away the special surface chemistry or seals the top-coat from breathing will eventually cause embrittlement. According to Orvis, the noted fishing tackle company, 303 will also lengthen your flyline cast as much as 30 feet!

CAUTION —
Avoid silicone oils and other chemistry that leave a "wet" look on vinyl.

Wheel cleanup is simple on most truck models. Painted steel rims respond readily to a light coat of Carnauba

0012582

Fig. 13-20. *The boating and outdoor equipment industries highly recommend 303 Protectant for vinyl and fiberglass. 303 can protect tires, dash pads, door rubber seals and bumper inserts.*

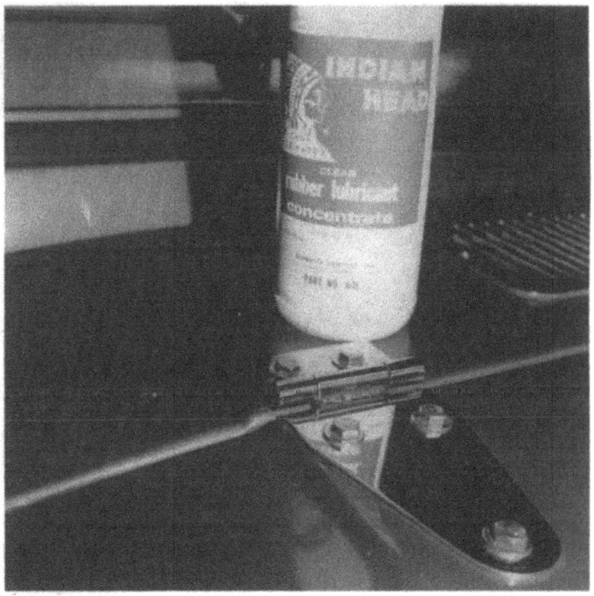

0012583

Fig. 13-21. *Permatex's Indian Head Rubber Lubricant has a long history. Claims have it harmless to vinyl, rubber and canvas, with many uses around your truck. This substance also works as an emergency tire mounting lubricant. Used regularly on shock bushings, sway bar bushings and other chassis rubber, this lubricant enhances service life.*

wax. If wheels are chrome or alloy and dull, hand rubbing with a metal polish such as Simichrome does the trick. If the wheel surface has oxidized, polishing with a die-grinder driven buffer pad will restore its surface.

NOTE —
A light coat of Carnauba-based wax will allow porous surfaces to flex and breathe. This prevents UV absorption and permanent dulling, yellowing or damage.

Paint Scratch Repairs

Light trucks and four-wheel drive utility vehicles have close scrapes with trees, limbs and brush. Scratches detract from the appearance of your truck, and brush-on touch up paints often leave ugly scars.

Armed with a random orbital buffer, some brush touch-up paint, a sheet of 1200-grit color sanding paper, a 3M Soft Hand Pad and some swirl remover, here's my formula for a super-fast, professional scratch repair:

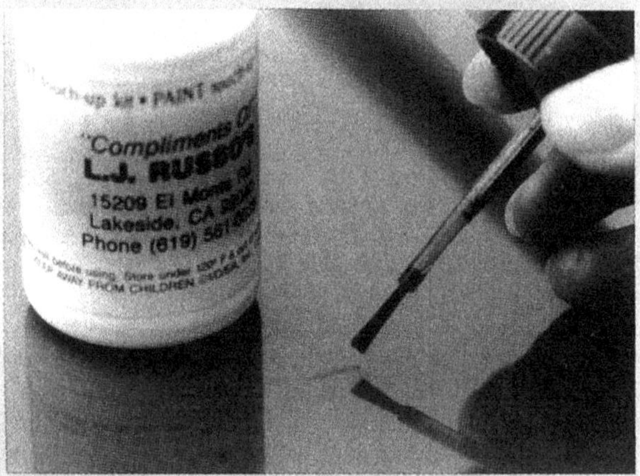

0012584 / 0012804

9:00 a.m.—Slight scratch in hood surface is carefully cleaned and filled with touch-up paint. (5 minutes)

11:00 a.m.—Left in direct sunlight, touch up is completely dry. Move the truck into the shade.

11:30 a.m.—Gently color sand with 1200-grit paper and 3M pad, confining your sanding to the crown of the touch-up paint. Sanding stops when adjacent paint shows signs of ultra-fine, uniform discoloration. (10 minutes)

11:40 a.m.—Swirl remover is applied to orbital buffer pad. Buffing the discolored area, focus directly on the repair. Light use of the buffer edge will concentrate the polishing effort. (2 minutes or less buffing time)

11:48 a.m.—Wipe away remaining swirl remover. Treat the beautifully matched surface to a new coat of wax/polish. (6 minutes)

12:00 p.m.—Load fishing poles into the cab, bed or cargo area of your truck. Grin broadly and drive to the hottest local angling spot. Catch your limit before heading for camp. Note: Releasing fish is optional, if such is your ethic. (Time involved depends on fishing action.)

The final step in detailing your truck is interior clean-up. Professional shampoos, cleaners and specialized chemicals work quickly on the interior. Carpet stains and other tough challenges respond best to professional cleaners.

Stripping Film and Wax Buildup

Improperly applied waxes and polishes, particularly those which seal the paint surface, will permit oxidation and yellowing. The worst example is a dull, sun-bleached truck with a color base coat and a clear-coat finish.

Some aftermarket paint sealant/protectant products also pose a threat to paint. Claiming long term paint protection and ease of maintenance, many of these products actually smother the original paint. Sealed and unable to breathe, the treated paint or clear coat surface succumbs to cracking, weather checking and other damage caused by ultraviolet sunlight.

The most common cause of wax buildup is poor application technique. The paint finish likely had untreated surface oxidation, and uneven hand rubbing has built up successive layers of wax. Although most one-step waxes and polishes employ a cleaner to cut through and loosen the old layer of wax, this chemistry often fails.

After using a random orbital buffer and professional chemical products, it's obvious why hand polishing leads to wax buildup. A truck waxed regularly by hand will turn a terrycloth buffer bonnet blacker than the tire sidewalls. Successive layers of wax simply seal off the paint. Paint cracking or severe fade then develops. A proper wax job should lightly coat the surface and allow paint to breathe.

Use a chemical finishing compound and an orbital buffer to reverse the damage of wax buildup. (Avoid the use of rubbing compounds. They are abrasive and remove paint.) The goal is to eliminate old wax and gently lift oxidized, dead paint from below the wax. (Yellow simply means that oxidation has occurred.)

Once the finishing or cleaning compound has removed wax and oxidized paint, the surface will regain its luster. The fresh finish can receive a coat of quality polish or wax.

3. Pickup Bed and Tub Liners

Did your pickup truck go off to work, only to return all bashed and battle scarred? Does your cargo bed rattle with tools, jacks and other menacing items? Forget the dents and raw paint. An aftermarket slide-in bed liner or sprayed-in polyurethane bed coating can prevent utility bed damage. Both the looks of your truck and its resale value will benefit from bed protection.

The traditional plastic tub liners now compete with a new generation of spray-in materials. Advocates of tub liners assert that the liner is replaceable (or removable on resale of the truck), while spray-in materials are permanent.

By contrast, a spray-in polyurethane coating will rust-proof far better than a slide-in tub. Polyurethane sprays adhere to every square inch of the pickup bed or the cab's floor, one of the other areas that can benefit greatly from this material.

0014292

Fig. 13-22. Slide-in tub liners have the advantage of easy removal if you sell the truck. If you use this kind of liner, periodically remove the tub and check for rust. A heavy coat of wax on the bed floor can help prevent the formation of rust on sheetmetal beneath the liner/tub.

This last point is important. A major concern with slide-in bedliner installations is that moisture can creep beneath the liner. Once there, collected water waits patiently for bare metal to appear. Hidden rust forms, spreading beneath the bedliner. Often, rust perforation through the bottom of the bed is the first clue that oxidation has occurred.

If a bedliner is installed in a new truck, the odds of rust formation can be drastically reduced. Most rustout develops when owners install bed protection after scratches and seam spreading have already scarred the bed. For a bedliner installation in a used truck, first eliminate all rust, caulk or seal each seam, and prime any repaired or scratched surfaces.

Tub or polyurethane spray-in bedliners offer protection against chemicals, corrosives and denting. For loading and handling materials, however, another factor should also influence your choice of a liner: anti-skid protection.

0012586

Fig. 13-23. Spray-in polyurethane bed coatings have gained popularity. This material, applied properly, offers durability and anti-corrosion protection, plus a waterproof barrier against rust. When textured, the coating has anti-skid quality. Color can be added to coordinate with your truck's paint scheme.

Chemistry 101 for Detailers

Effective detailing is knowing which chemicals to use on a given surface. For washing your truck, look for solutions that prevent streaking. Professional car soaps remove very little wax and allow several cleanings between re-wax jobs. Tar and spot removers are actually high-grade cleaning solvents designed for work around interior and exterior finishes.

> *CAUTION —*
> *Tar and spot remover may affect the top-coat of some vinyl and plastic items. Read labels carefully. These chemicals are also useful for removing wax and silicone before painting stripes or applying touchup.*

Rubber dressing and protectants generally have a polymer or silicone base. Renewing tires, moldings, floor mats, pedal pads, dashpads, vinyl materials and other items is as easy as applying the right chemistry to the surface. Some materials require slight hand buffing.

Rubbing and finishing compounds meet several uses. Cleaning or cutting into the painted surface, these materials remove dull paint, "orange peel" and water spots. Often, new paint or even clear coatings require color sanding, which leaves a mildly scratched, dull surface. Power (orbital) buffing with non-abrasive chemical compounds can make the finish smooth and shiny.

Products like Carecraft's Swirl Remover fit a special niche. Carecraft calls its product a buffing cleaner capable of removing fine scratches and oxidation. Swirl Remover contains no wax or silicone, yet it lubricates the buffer pad. As a follow-up to rubbing compound or a poor detail job, Swirl Remover has no harsh abrasives and can be a mild, effective alternative for restoring a slightly oxidized finish.

Additionally, there are treatments and cleaners for upholstery, rugs, chrome, stainless steel and every other material found on a truck. The concern here is chemical compatibility. With questionable materials, always test chemicals first. Discoloration and damage can result from improper use or poor mixing of chemicals.

Let modern tools and chemistry do the work. Save your time and energy for family, friends and outdoor recreational pursuits.

My choice is a spray-in polyurethane coating that offers a permanent barrier to rust. In many parts of the United States, a moist climate or harsh and wet winters make a slide-in bedliner unwise.

By comparison, if the bed is prepared properly and sprayed correctly with a quality polyurethane bedliner material, rust is no longer an issue. An aftermarket spray-in bedliner can preserve your bed and prevent rust formation.

These spray-in bed coatings require special equipment and spray booths for installation. They adhere so well that it would be virtually impossible to remove the

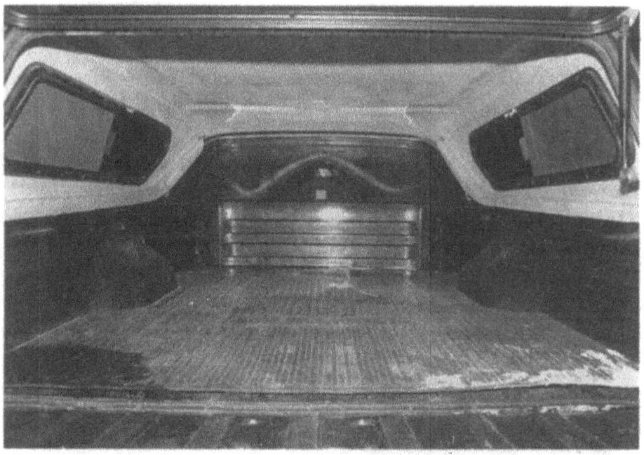

0012587

Fig. 13-24. This bed mat provides ample protection plus an oil resistant surface that has a non-skid texture. Easily removed or exchanged between vehicles, bed mats are practical for many light truck and utility applications.

cured material without damaging paint—and possibly the bed metal. If damaged, the coating can be retouched.

An alternative to the permanent tub or spray foam installation is a bed mat. Bed mats, custom fitted to cover the entire floor of your truck, provide substantial protection. Better mats offer skid resistance and a cushioned cargo surface.

Mats insulate the bed or floor from cargo damage. Additionally, you can remove a quality mat periodically to thoroughly clean and wax the bed to reduce the risk of rust formation. Better quality bed mats are resistant to oil, chemicals and marring. They provide years of service.

Chapter 14

Electrical System Basics

TRUCK RESTORATION AND MAINTENANCE include the electrical system and wiring. Repair work and routine service frequently mean the renewal of wiring and changing connectors. Often, the frame-up restoration of an older truck chassis (especially six-volt systems with cloth wrapped wiring) requires wiring the truck from scratch.

A successful wiring job can be gratifying. I well remember my first job as a truck fleet mechanic. My employer bought a two-ton capacity stake truck. The vehicle came really cheap, via a U.S. government surplus source, as someone had cut every wire behind the instrument/dash panel and left the truck paralyzed!

My first task was to re-wire the entire chassis and engine electrical system. Armed with a wiring schematic from the local truck dealership, I chose the proper wire gauge for each circuit and carefully began routing the scores of new wires.

When I finished and turned the key, the engine started—and the lights, turn signals, wipers, accessories and all instrument gauges worked, too. In fact, everything operated safely, as I had routed all circuits through an OEM fuse panel for reliable service. The truck had a fine six-cylinder engine and rugged geartrain, and we got excellent service from the workhorse chassis.

Fig. 14-1. 1941 GM truck electrical system and wiring was simple and functional. Unless the cloth insulation has deteriorated, early wiring presents few problems. Modern trucks feature computers and intricate wiring that need a precise voltage supply and exact system resistances.

Your truck works dependably when the lights glow, turn signals flash, heater blows, starter spins, wipers swish, spark plugs fire, alternator charges and electric fuel pump pulses. Understanding the dynamics of a truck's electrical system can enhance your troubleshooting skills, a vital asset when traveling through remote country.

1. The Electrical System

Light truck electrical systems vary in voltage layouts. Until Second Series 1955 models, all GM light trucks had 6-volt electrical systems, either positively grounded (GMC) or negatively grounded (Chevrolet). Early wiring was the infamous cloth-wrapped design, heavier in gauge and lighter in life-span.

Beginning in the mid-1950s, GM and other vehicle manufacturers switched to plastic wrapped wiring. GM light trucks gained their first 12-volt electrical systems with Second Series 1955 models, which improved the performance of accessories, the starting circuit and lighting.

> **NOTE —**
> Both cloth and plastic wiring insulation deteriorate over time. Trucks used off-pavement, in agriculture, harsh climates or around corrosive industrial settings are ongoing candidates for electrical wire repairs.

System Overview

Depending on the chassis year, a 6-volt or 12-volt wet storage battery supplies current for the electrical system. GM trucks have used a variety of starter motor designs, however, the most tenacious and popular types are the GM/Delco-Remy "direct contact" and "solenoid" applications.

Early on, GM light trucks used the direct contact starter. This is a reasonably fail-safe two-phase system that relies on a mechanical floorboard start pedal/lever to 1) engage the starter drive, and 2) close a switch that allows high amperage current to spin the motor.

Beginning with 1954 6-volt HydraMatic Drive models and the 1955 Second Series 12-volt V-8 models, the solenoid type starter system assigns the starting operation to the key switch. The solenoid unit, which mounts atop the

0014477 / 0014298

Fig. 14-2. Early 216 Chevrolet starter (arrow) has foot-operated direct contact switch. More modern Delco-Remy starter features a piggyback solenoid and key action.

starter motor, engages the starter drive and also delivers current to the starter motor.

Solenoid activation begins when low amperage current flows from the key switch's start pole to the solenoid. As magnetism moves the solenoid plunger, the drive gear engages and high amperage current flows to the starter motor.

Traditional GM truck starter motors were of conventional field coil/pole shoe series wound armature type. Lighter weight permanent magnet motors have gained popularity in recent years.

The solenoid switch doubles as a junction block terminal for the main leads of the electrical system. (Floor pedal starters also use the starter mounted switch as the main electrical junction.) As the starter draws more amperage than any other item in the electrical system, the battery's hot lead cable attaches directly to the solenoid switch (or the pedal activated starter switch on earlier models) to minimize resistance.

General Motors' Delco-Remy Division has remained a mainstay source for GM light truck electrical components. Reliable and easily serviceable Delco-Remy generators served the charging needs of 6-volt models and well into the 12-volt era, while quality Delco-Remy Delcotron alternators became standard equipment in 1963 models.

What Is an Alternator?

Although alternator designs have evolved since the early 1960s, their operation remains much the same. Typically, as the ignition switch turns ON, a wire lead with 12-volt current feeds to the alternator or external regulator. Through transistor and diode switching, current reaches a field coil. While the engine cranks, a high field current is generated to increase available voltage. This is the precharging mode.

Once the engine starts, the alternator's rotor spins at speed, with alternating current produced within the stator winding. Typically, the stator sends AC current to an internal rectifier bridge and diodes, which convert the AC current to usable 12-volt DC current. Diodes also prevent battery current from draining at the alternator.

The battery (BAT) pole on the alternator or regulator can perform two roles: 1) act as a route for charging current returning to the battery, and 2) serve as an information source for the battery's state of charge or electrical loads on the system.

During normal operation, all amperage drains on the battery send a voltage reading to the alternator's regulator. (Later trucks feature voltmeters on the instrument panel. The voltmeter signals the correlation between battery drain and volts.)

While the engine cranks, a 12-volt battery reads approximately 9 or 10 volts. At times, an electric winch load can equal this rating. Headlights, air conditioning or any other electrical demand will also drop voltage at the battery.

0014478

Fig. 14-3. Modern Delco-Remy alternator is compact and packed with amperage (140 or more amps in some applications). Voltage is regulated internally.

How the Alternator Charges the Battery

When your truck's battery has a low state of charge, the alternator returns high amperage current to the battery. Although this current flowing from the battery is actually a quantity of *amperage*, the battery and regulator interpret the flow in terms of *voltage*.

Charging a 12-volt battery requires meeting a range of voltages at various temperatures. At very low temperatures, for example, the regulator may test at 14.9 to 15.9 volts of current. The same regulator at 80° F may operate between 13.9 and 14.6 volts, while 140° F ambient temperature produces 13.3 to 13.9 volts. Above 140° F, the same regulator may offer 13.6 volts.

Since a fully charged battery reads approximately 12.6 volts, the charging circuit must at least maintain that voltage. This requires enough current flow to recharge the battery plus the amperage necessary to operate the entire range of electrical accessories and lights while the engine is running.

For generator-equipped vehicles, and even into the early alternator era, accessories like air conditioning place an exceptional load on the charging circuit and battery. Often, such charging systems cannot keep up with battery drain at an idle. Today's 120- to 140-plus ampere hour alternators can easily meet these engine idling requirements. When ordering a new truck, a high output alternator/battery system is well worth any additional expense.

Charge Circuit Routine Service

Battery condition and state of charge are very important to your truck's performance. Later models with electronic fuel and spark management systems depend upon very accurate voltage readings and a strong current supply. All trucks, regardless of the environment in which they operate, require a quality battery in premium condition.

> **NOTE —**
> The new generation of high cold cranking amperage (CCA) batteries exceeds older OEM requirements by a good margin. (For details on battery service, see the lubrication/service chapters.)

Earlier Delco-Remy truck generators require periodic bearing lubrication. Drive belt condition is always crucial, and a spare belt is a mandatory item for back country trips. All GM/Delco-Remy generator systems have external voltage regulators, which are adjustable. Most mechanics, however, prefer to replace a unit that reads out of range.

Polarity is a concern when servicing or replacing either the generator or generator regulator. You must polarize the generator/regulator to prevent damage and permit charging. As the regulator adjusts current flow back to the battery, correct wiring of the charging system is essential. The different types of automotive regulators (6-volt or 12-volt with either an internally or externally grounded field) require different polarizing procedures.

> *CAUTION —*
> • *1939–55 (First Series) GMC trucks with 6-volt electrical systems use a* positive *ground. Chevrolet 6-volt systems have the more common* negative *ground polarity. Beginning with 12-volt 1955 Second Series electrics, all GM truck systems are negative ground. This is important when installing a new battery or polarizing the generator/regulator.*
>
> • *Know which type of regulator your GM truck uses, and consult the GM truck shop manual for instructions on how to polarize the generator system when you install a new or rebuilt generator or regulator.*

The Lights and Other Circuits

Truck lighting is basic, with current simply flowing through switches, fuses/relays, then to the headlights, tail lamps, turn and brake lights, warning lights and interior lamps. To avoid shorts and unreliable service, your truck's lighting system requires safe routing of wire, correct wire size and secure connections.

Aftermarket accessories pose a challenge. Sound systems, add-on lighting, auxiliary fuel pumps and other additions to your truck's electrical system demand careful consideration. Where should components source their current supply? What wire gauges are suitable? How do you route wires safely? (You'll find more information about these issues in Chapter 15, Accessories.)

Your truck's OEM electrical system follows a layout common to other U.S. built trucks and cars. Earlier GM trucks have very simple electrical systems, built around common components still available at any auto supply house. Later 12-volt era models boast modern electrical systems, with more complex switches and power accessories. By the late 1970s, the automotive electronic era emerged, introducing the first use of modules and computer components that depend on constant voltage levels, perfect wire connections and secure grounds.

The modern light truck electrical system proves very demanding. Air conditioning, closed loop emission controls and electronic fuel, spark and automatic transmission shifting systems create a maze of wires. ABS braking has its own demanding circuits, with speed sensors and other components dependent upon the integrity of the chassis wires.

Work on a late model GM light truck electrical system involves use of accurate wiring diagrams, an understanding of wire gauge requirements and a clear sense for wire routing. Electrical wire shorts and poor ground connections can leave your truck stranded or cause expensive damage.

Relays

Relays began to appear with the 12-volt era. The main advantage of relays is that minor amounts of current can control major power flow. For heavy amperage (a measurement of electrical resistance), this is useful.

Relays have two basic designs, each with a different function. Electro-*magnetic* relays tend to control circuits with large current flows. The relay, activated by a low am-

0012589

Fig. 14-4. Relays and fuses come in a variety of sizes and meet various needs. Circuit or reset breakers work well with vehicles that are temporarily exposed to shorts or grounding, especially a 4x4 model that wades through streams.

0012590

Fig. 14-5. This unique fuse/relay holder, available through Wrangler Power Products, features popular ATO-type fuses and circuit breakers that fit ATO sockets.

perage current, directs high amperage current to systems like the horn and starter motor. Smaller gauge wiring from the horn button activates the relay, then current flows through a higher amperage (heavier wire gauge) from the battery to the horn. The starter solenoid, which must deliver very high amperage battery current directly to the starter motor, receives its activating signal by way of a much lighter gauge ignition/starter switch wire.

Electro-magnetic relays are a practical way to perform mechanical tasks. The fuel cut-off solenoid or similar device uses electrical current to magnetize and move a plunger.

Electro-*thermal* relays receive and deliver current to a bi-metallic contact set. After exposure for a given interval of heat, the switch opens, stopping current flow. As the contacts cool down, the switch closes. The traditional turn signal flasher switch is this type of relay.

Volt/Ohmmeter: The Perfect Troubleshooting Tool

Of all my automotive testing equipment, one of the most valued tools is a combination volt/ohmmeter (VOM). The ohmmeter can read circuit continuity levels and ohms resistance. A voltmeter reads the actual voltage available at a given circuit. Adjusted for alternating current (AC) or direct current (DC), a voltmeter can measure line voltage between any two points. For automotive electrical troubleshooting, these tools provide a wealth of useful information.

Ohms, a measurement of electrical resistance, follows the engineering formula: 1 ohm = 1/siemens = 1 volt/ampere. Simply, each ohm is a precise increment of resistance to current flow. Conductive liquids or solids (such as electrical wiring) serve as mediums through which we can measure ohms resistance.

Aside from testing alternator diodes or components in a fuel injection or electronic ignition system, most automotive electrical troubleshooting centers around continuity of current flow and availability of voltage.

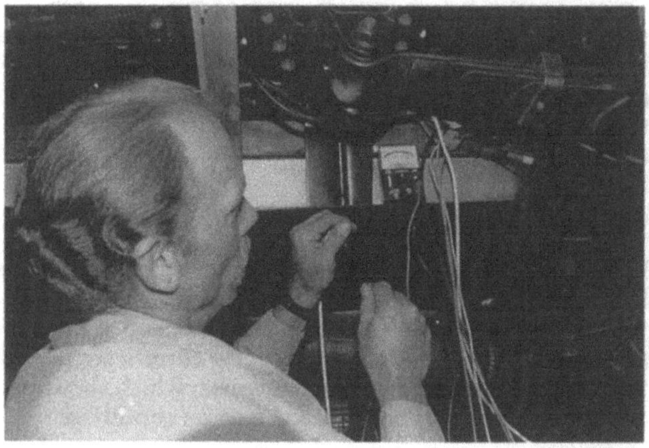

0012591

Fig. 14-6. Grounds are as important as hot sources. Ohmmeters take the guesswork out of testing your truck's engine, chassis and body grounds.

0012592

Fig. 14-7. Trailer connectors demand more than a test lamp check. You can detect insufficient current flow or resistance at a ground lead with your volt/ohmmeter.

The ohms segment of a VOM will quickly satisfy a wide range of these continuity checks, helping you find shorts and either partially or fully open circuits.

An inexpensive needle meter can handle basic voltage and resistance tests. For less than twenty-five dollars, you can buy a quality pocket-size tester. (My Radio Shack tester, purchased in 1982 for $10, still functions flawlessly.)

Designed for light use, these handy testers can perform a wide range of effective tests and still fit neatly into your truck's on-board toolbox. For testing fuel injection and other electronic components, however, you must use a more precise digital voltmeter.

CAUTION —

- *Connect or disconnect multiple connectors and test leads only with the ignition off. Switch the multimeter functions or measurement ranges only with the test leads disconnected.*
- *On later model vehicles with sensitive electronic components, do not use a continuity/test lamp with an incandescent bulb to test circuits containing electronic components. Use only an LED (light emitting diode) test lamp. Do not use an analog (swing-needle) VOM to check circuit resistance or continuity on electronic (solid state) components. Use only a high quality digital multimeter with a high input impedance rating (at least 10 meg-ohms).*

2. ELECTRICAL TROUBLESHOOTING

Four things are required for current to flow in any electrical circuit: a voltage source, wires or connections to transport the voltage, a consumer or device that uses the electricity, and a connection to ground. For trouble-free operation, the ground connections, including the battery ground cable and the body ground strap, must remain clean and free from corrosion.

NOTE —
Most problems can be found using only a multimeter (volt/ohm/amp meter) to check for voltage supply, for breaks in the wiring (infinite resistance/no continuity and such) or for a path to ground that completes the circuit.

Electric current is logical in its flow, always moving from the voltage source toward ground. Keeping this in mind, electrical faults can be located through a process of elimination. When troubleshooting a complex circuit, separate the circuit into smaller parts. The general tests outlined here may be helpful in finding electrical problems. This information is even more valuable when used in conjunction with OEM wiring diagrams for your truck.

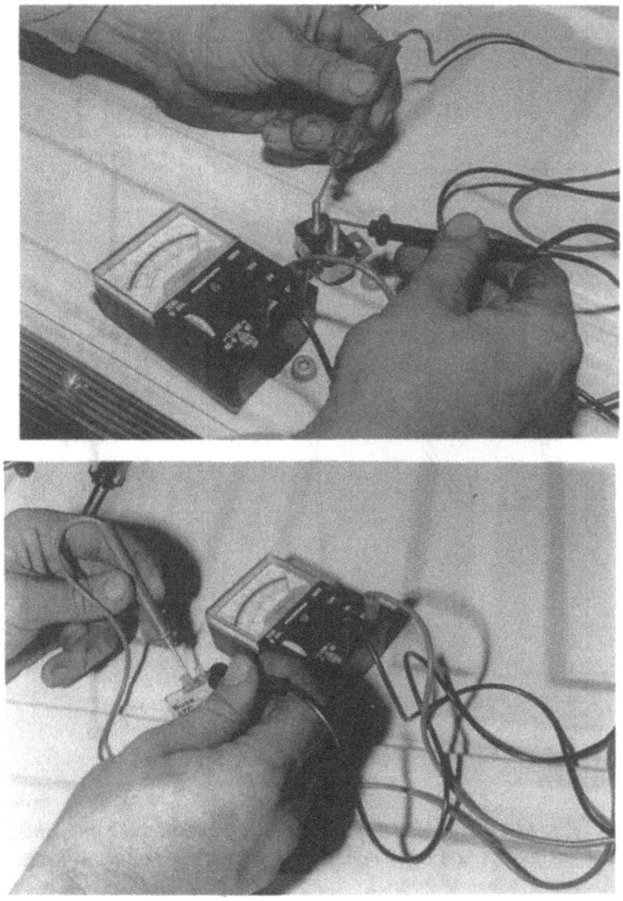

0012593 / 0012805

Fig. 14-8. *This 20 amp breaker and a late ATO style Buss fuse each pass the ohmmeter test. Test any suspect circuits and switches for high resistance readings.*

0012594

Fig. 14-9. *Test variable voltage devices with the voltmeter. Although most trailer brake controllers are now electronic, they still send voltage signals to the trailer brakes, much like earlier rheostat devices.*

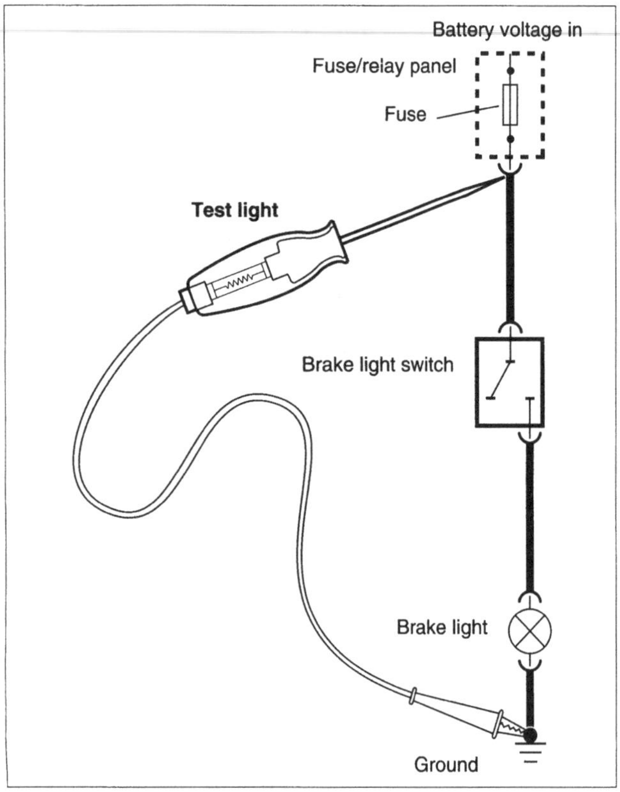

Fig. 14-10. This is a test light set-up for checking available current. A test light makes a quick check of voltage sources and a complete ground.

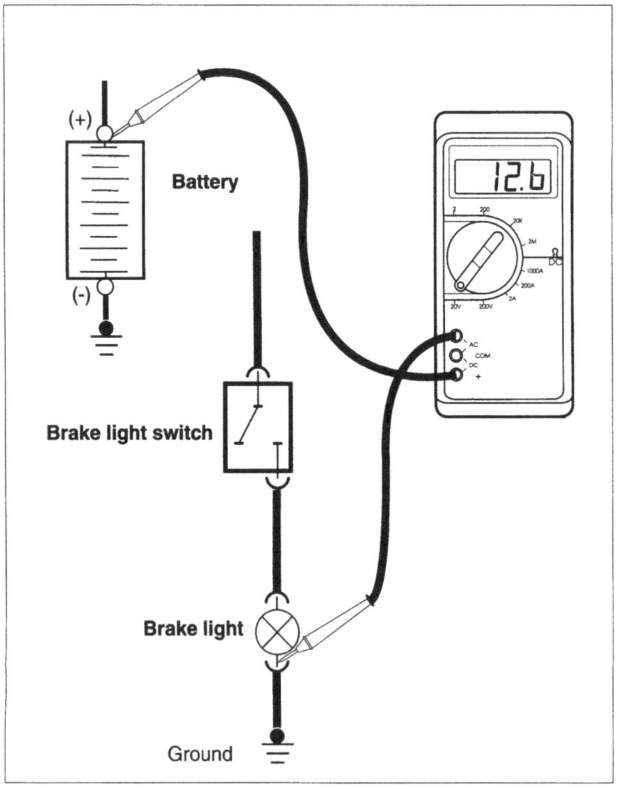

Fig. 14-11. Here, a voltmeter checks for proper ground.

Testing for Voltage and Ground

The most useful and fundamental electrical troubleshooting technique is checking for voltage and ground. A voltmeter or a simple test light should be used for this test. For example, if a parking light does not work, checking for voltage at the bulb socket will determine if the circuit is functioning correctly or if the bulb itself is faulty.

To check for battery voltage using a test light, connect the test light wire to a clean, unpainted metal part of the truck or a known good ground. Use the pointed end of the light to probe the hot lead of the connector or socket.

To check for continuity to ground, connect the test light wire to the positive (+) battery post or a battery source. (Use the negative (-) post on early GMC Truck systems with 6-volt positive ground polarity.) Now use the pointed end of the light to probe the connector/socket's ground lead. In either case, the test lamp should light up.

> *WARNING —*
> *Never create electrical sparks at or near the battery. A hot or defective battery emits explosive gases.*

> *CAUTION —*
> *Do not use the pointed end of the test light to pierce a wire's insulation. This could lead to later electrical problems.*

> NOTE —
> A test light only determines if voltage or a ground is present. It does not determine how much voltage or the quality of the path to ground. If the voltage reading is important, such as when you test a battery or when you need a precise reading of a circuit's voltage, use a digital voltmeter. To check the condition of a ground connection, check for voltage drop on the suspected connection as described below.

To check for voltage using a voltmeter, set the meter to DCV and the correct scale. On all 12-volt GM systems or early 6-volt Chevrolet trucks, connect the negative (-) test lead to the negative (-) battery terminal or a known good ground. Touch the positive (+) test lead to the positive wire or connector. (Use the opposite approach with an early GMC Truck's 6-volt positive ground system.)

Again, on a 6- or 12-volt negative ground system check for ground, connect the positive (+) test lead to the positive (+) battery terminal or voltage source. Touch the negative (-) test lead to the wire leading to ground. The meter should read battery voltage. (Reverse this approach on an early GMC Truck's 6-volt positive ground electrical system.)

> NOTE —
> When using an analog (swing needle) voltmeter, be careful not to reverse the test leads. Reversing the polarity may damage the meter.

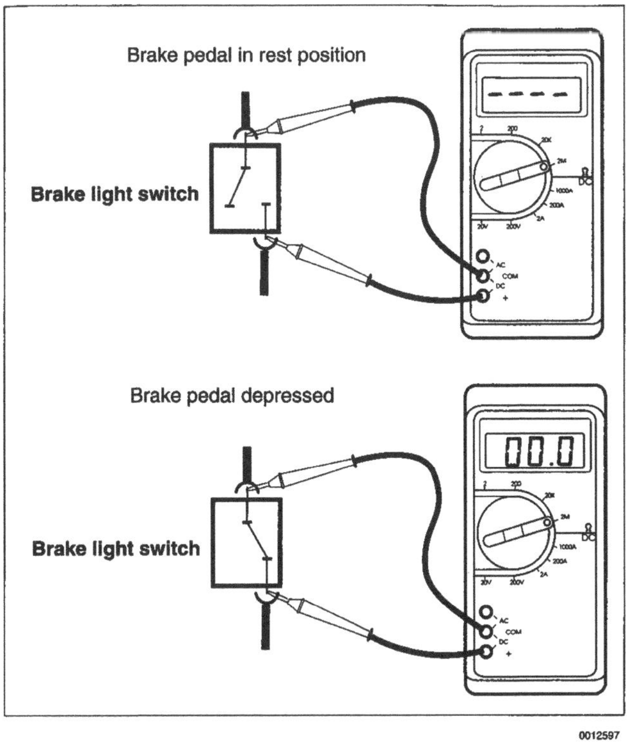

Fig. 14-12. This is a brake light switch being tested for continuity. With the brake pedal in a resting position (switch open), the test reveals no continuity. With brake pedal depressed (switch closed), there is continuity.

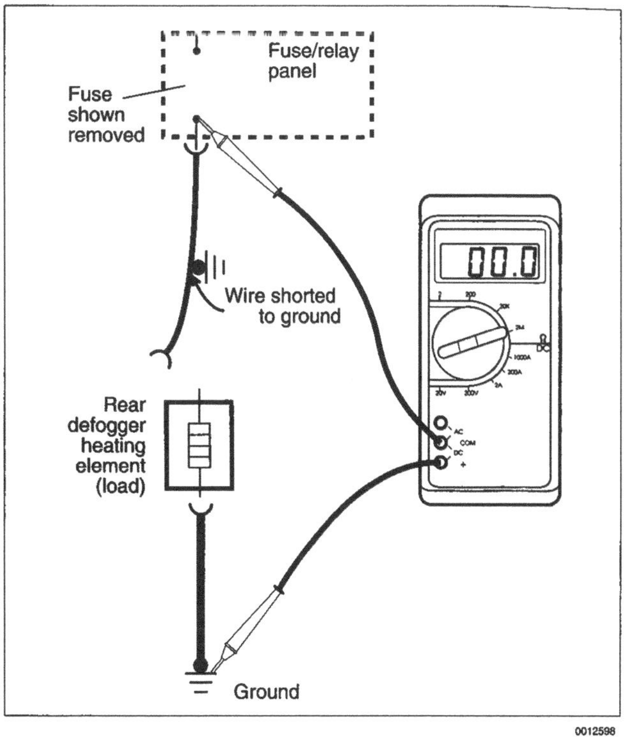

Fig. 14-13. Ohmmeter being used to check for short circuit to ground.

Continuity Test

The continuity test can be used to check a circuit or switch. Because most automotive circuits are designed to have little or no resistance, a circuit or part of a circuit can be easily checked for faults using an ohmmeter or a self-powered test light. An open circuit or a circuit with high resistance will not allow current to flow. A circuit with little or no resistance allows current to flow easily.

When checking continuity, keep the ignition off. On circuits that are always powered, disconnect the battery. Using the appropriate wiring diagram, a continuity test can easily find faulty connections, defective wires, bad switches, defective relays and malfunctioning engine sensors.

Short Circuit Test

A short circuit is exactly what the name implies. The circuit simply takes a shorter path than intended. The most common short that causes problems is a short to ground where the insulation on a hot lead wire wears away, and the metal wire becomes exposed. If the exposed wire is live (positive battery voltage on a 6- or 12-volt GM negative ground system; negative battery voltage on a 6-volt GMC Truck system with positive ground), either a fuse will blow or the circuit may become damaged.

Shorts to ground can be located with a voltmeter, a test light, or an ohmmeter. However, these shorted circuits are often difficult to locate. Therefore, it is important that you use the correct wiring diagram when troubleshooting your truck's electrical system.

CAUTION —
On circuits protected with large fuses (25 amp and greater), the wires or circuit components may be damaged before the fuse blows. Always check for damage before replacing fuses of this rating. Always use replacement fuses of the same rating.

Short circuits can be found using a logical approach based on the path that current follows. To check for a short circuit to ground, remove the blown fuse from the circuit and disconnect the cables from the battery. Disconnect the harness connector from the circuit's load or consumer. Using a self-powered test light or an ohmmeter, connect one test lead to the load side fuse terminal (terminal leading to the circuit) and the other test lead to ground.

A short circuit can also be located using a test light or a voltmeter. Connect the instrument's test leads across the fuse terminals (fuse removed) and turn the circuit on. If necessary, check the wiring diagram to determine under which circumstances the circuit should be live.

Working from the wire harness nearest to the fuse/relay panel, move or wiggle the wires while observing the test light or your meter. Continue to move down the harness until the test light blinks or the meter displays a reading. This will pinpoint the location of the short.

Visually inspect the wire harness at this point for any faults. If no faults are visible, carefully slice open the harness cover or the wire insulation for further inspection. Make sure that you find the trouble. Repair the defects to OEM standards.

> **NOTE —**
> On critical circuits, like the EFI system, you will likely need a new harness to ensure circuit integrity and the quality of connections. Consult the GM truck shop manual for recommendations on repairing a particular electrical circuit.

Voltage Drop Test

The wires, connectors, and switches that carry current have very low resistance so that current can flow with a minimum loss of voltage. A voltage drop results from higher than normal resistance in a circuit. This additional resistance actually decreases or stops the flow of current.

A voltage drop produces symptoms and problems ranging from dim headlights to sluggish wipers. Some common sources of voltage drop are faulty wires or switches, dirty or corroded connections or contacts, and loose or corroded ground wires and ground connections.

Voltage drop can only be checked when current is running through the circuit, such as by operating the starter motor or turning on the headlights. Making a voltage drop test requires measuring the voltage in the circuit and comparing that reading to what the voltage should be. Since these measurements are usually small, a digital voltmeter must be used to ensure accurate readings. If you suspect a voltage drop, turn the circuit on and measure the voltage when the circuit is under load.

A voltage drop test is generally more accurate than a simple resistance check because the resistances involved are often too small to measure with most ohmmeters. For example, a resistance as small as 0.02 ohms results in a 3 volt drop in a typical 150 amp starter circuit (150 amps x 0.02 ohms = 3 volts).

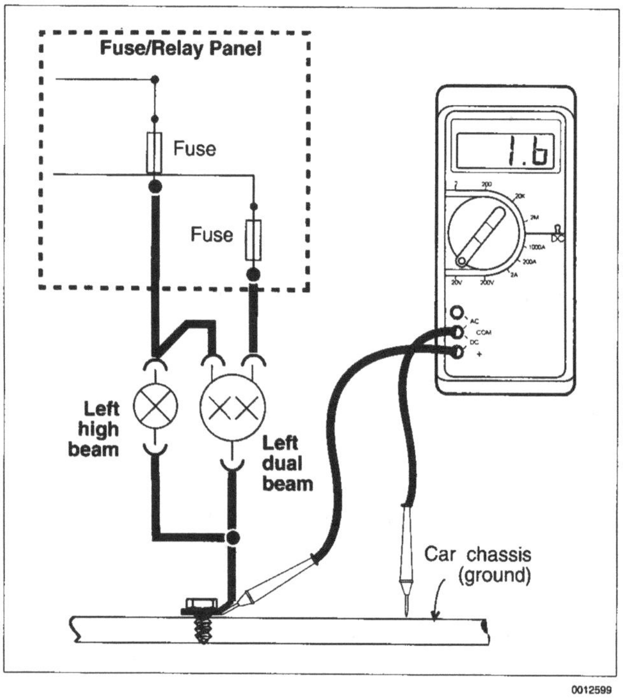

Fig. 14-14. Example of voltage drop test on dim headlights. Voltmeter showed 1.6-volt drop between ground connector and chassis ground. After removing and cleaning headlight ground, voltage drop returned to normal and headlights gained brightness.

Keep in mind that voltage with the key on and voltage with the engine running are not the same. With the ignition on and the engine off, full charge battery voltage should be approximately 12.6 volts. With the engine running (charging voltage), voltage should be approximately 14.5 volts. For exact measurements, first measure voltage at the battery with the ignition on, then with the engine running.

> *WARNING —*
> *Do not create a spark near a hot or possibly defective battery. An explosion could result. If necessary, take your battery voltage reading at the primary battery terminal block (typically at the starter solenoid), away from the battery.*

The maximum voltage drop, as recommended by the Society of Automotive Engineers (SAE), is: 0 volt for small wire connections; 0.1 volt for high-current connections; 0.2 volt for high-current cables; and 0.3 volt for switch or solenoid contacts. On longer wires or cables, the drop may be slightly higher. In any case, a voltage drop of more than 1.0 volt usually indicates a problem.

3. TESTING BATTERY AND CHARGING SYSTEM

When checking the battery and charging circuits, be careful and considerate of battery hazards. High amperage applied to a defective battery is, literally, a potential bombshell. When you know your truck's charging system is functional yet the battery acts dead, proceed with extreme caution.

> *WARNING —*
> *A minute spark near an overcharged or defective battery is a safety hazard. Avoid the risk of igniting explosive hydrogen gas. Always unplug your battery charger before connecting or disconnecting the clamp leads. If in doubt, make voltohmmeter tests well away from the battery, at the alternator, a factory wire junction or the fuse/breaker panel.*

Find a good ground, and attach the correct meter probe (based on your system's polarity). Attach the other probe to the hot wire source and read battery voltage. If you get a reading of 12.30 or fewer volts on a 12-volt system, with all known current drains (including lights, ignition and accessories) shut off, the battery's state of charge is at 50% capacity or lower. This indicates poor electrical connections, weak generator/alternator output, excessive current drain from accessories or a defective battery.

You can check each of these possible problems with the VOM. Start the engine and begin at the alternator. The battery signal to the voltage regulator should say, "I'm low on voltage, flow some current my way!"

In response, the normal charge circuit will call for a heavy amperage flow. Use the voltmeter mode of the

0014497

Fig. 14-15. The solenoid junction block and other points that lie well away from the battery provide alternate battery testing sources. Avoid direct voltage checks at the battery, especially after heavy charging from the alternator or a battery charger. Explosive hydrogen gas can surround the battery and ignite from the slightest spark.

tester, and probe the charge wire at the alternator or generator with the positive lead on trucks with a negative ground system—use the negative probe on 6-volt GMC Truck systems. On negative ground systems, attach the negative lead to ground; on a positive ground system, attach the positive lead to ground.

Charging properly, the alternator should now read well over 12.6 volts on a 12-volt system. (See the GM truck shop manual for your model to determine regulator settings or correct readings for an earlier 6-volt system.) With current flowing toward the battery, voltage could read 14.8 volts or higher, depending upon the parameters of the voltage regulator and output capacity of a 12-volt generator or alternator.

If you see no increase in voltage from your static battery test level, the alternator or regulator is not performing properly. However, before condemning these expensive parts, troubleshoot further.

Shut the engine off and leave the meter set for the 12-volt range. Touch the heavy (BATTERY or BAT) lead at the 12-volt system's alternator or generator with the positive (red) meter probe. Using a quality engine ground for the negative probe, again read available voltage at the alternator or generator. This should be approximately the same as the battery's voltage reading.

If you cannot read voltage here, a wiring or fusible link problem exists. Trace the route of the alternator BAT lead. At the first junction between the alternator and the battery, your ohmmeter test can begin.

Zero the meter and set for DC-Ohms and K-Ohms. Check the wire for continuity and conductivity by holding a probe at each end of the wire and reading the scale. If no opens or shorts exist, the meter will rest happily at the zero line. If there is too much resistance, as with a slight open in the lead or a poor connection, the needle will read upward on the scale. An actual open in the wire prevents the needle from registering at all.

Repeat this procedure along the wire path toward the battery. Eventually, you will locate the short or open. Resistance readings help locate corrosion within wire leads, too. Battery cables or terminal clamp connections often develop such problems. Unseen in a visual inspection, a current blockage cannot fool your ohmmeter. The force necessary to keep current flowing is measurable.

When the generator/alternator unit is defective, your OEM-level shop manual will provide test information and overhaul procedures. Most bench tests of alternators, generators, starters, coils and ignition modules involve a VOM. You can also test headlight and dimmer switches, relays, breakers, fuses, and turn signal switches with the meter. Tracing poor ground wires, troubleshooting faulty gauges, finding nuisance shorts, isolating worn spark plug cables and most other electrical tests are well within the VOM's ability.

Getting a Charge Out of Your Alternator

Alternator and generator output tests are similar. (For simplicity, I use the term *alternator* for this section.) If your earlier truck has a generator, you will find the majority of these troubleshooting and test suggestions useful and applicable.

Any concern about alternator output should begin with checking the drive belt tension. Next, inspect all wire connections. To test the alternator and regulator output, test the current flow from the alternator with an induction ammeter. Compare the ammeter flow to the OEM specifications for your truck, beginning at an idle, then 1500 engine rpm, then finally 2000 engine rpm.

> **NOTE —**
> Perform the induction meter test with the battery charge low. You want the alternator near its maximum output.

An induction ammeter, although not as accurate as more expensive test equipment, provides a quick sense for alternator output. These handy tools fit easily in your truck's on-board tool box. Since the meter simply fits over the cable or wire insulation, you can test without removing any electrical component. (Note: Make certain that magnetic interference from adjacent wires does not influence the readings.)

My two alternator (charging) and starter (draw) induction meters have served for over twenty years. If your equipment includes an ohms-resistance meter, you can perform additional field tests. When you suspect an alternator problem but cannot find its source, sublet the alternator and regulator to an automotive electrical repair shop. The shop can help distinguish regulator troubles from alternator defects.

Your GM truck shop manual or a professional service manual will detail the troubleshooting guidelines for your generator/alternator and regulator. Most public libraries maintain a reference section that contains automotive and light truck service manuals.

Shorts and Voltage Leak-off

If starter and alternator circuits check okay and the battery's cells read normal specific gravity at a full charge, then chronic low battery voltage is still possible. Accessories like the clock or the improper hook-up of an aftermarket sound system can cause the battery to go dead. Be sure to wire your sound system through a fused and ignition switched accessories (ACC) source.

A defect in the ignition switch, air conditioning clutch, lighting equipment, the turn signal switch, a radio, tape deck or hazard lamp can each draw excessive current from the battery. The dome, underhood and hazard lamps operate without the ignition switch on, so check these areas first. When an aftermarket accessory taps directly to a battery source, disconnect the accessory and see if the problem resolves.

If a current drain persists, suspect the ignition switch. A shorted ignition switch can deliver current, even when the key is in the off position. Current may be passing to the coil, ignition module or EFI computer (on later truck models). You can confirm current flow at each of these areas by taking voltage readings with your VOM.

Testing Ignition and Fuel System Components

Most automotive tool boxes include test lamp type continuity and hot lead testers. The VOM serves far beyond these tools, however, giving precise readings about the underlying condition of your truck's electrical system.

For example, spark plug misfires or engine balking under load are often the result of excessive resistance in the primary or secondary ignition circuits. Here, the VOM can provide an ideal tool for diagnostic work.

Many ignition and late model fuel system parts rely on electrical switches and electronic components. Given the ohms-resistance values for these pieces, you can easily test them with your meter. The troubleshooting and service guidelines in your OEM-level shop manual can provide useful test criteria.

Ballast resistors, spark plug wires and electronic ignition modules each have specified tests. Voltage and ohms-resistance readings at the ends of a ballast resistor can determine whether the unit works properly. Likewise, an ignition coil has a specified resistance in its winding. Ohms resistance tests of a coil can identify most shorts and internal defects.

0014295

Fig. 14-16. Check your ignition cables periodically with an ohmmeter. Late electronic ignitions with higher firing voltages place more stress on high tension carbon cables.

> **NOTE —**
> When worn excessively, electronic ignition rotors can short to ground through the distributor shaft. You may experience this problem on a GM/Delco-Remy HEI ignition.

Used imaginatively, the tests performed with a VOM often serve the same purpose as diagnostic analyzers that cost a thousand times more. Although fancy oscilloscope patterns and digital electronic readouts are valuable, the VOM's simple, pragmatic answers often serve better than expensive and bulkier diagnostic equipment. Besides, you can't tow an oscilloscope engine analyzer along a 4x4 trail!

4. The Starter Motor

Engines resist cranking as compression, valve spring tension and spinning belt-driven components fight the starter motor's efforts. Toss in a bit too much ignition spark advance, and it's clear why some starter drive housings break.

A 12-volt starter is a high torque electric motor, with or without an internal gear reduction drive. Very heavy "lock test" amperage draw, well in excess of 450 amps on many large V-8 engine applications, is normal.

Such a starter may demand over 100 amps just to spin freely on a bench test. A defective starter motor may draw over 500 amps while cranking the engine, enough to fry both the battery and its cables. The typical engine with a modest compression ratio still requires a starter cranking draw of 150 to 210 amps.

A 12-volt automotive starter motor can spin as high as 8500 rpm on the bench. However, while cranking the engine at 160 crankshaft rpm, with an 18-to-1 flywheel-to-starter drive tooth ratio, this same starter motor might spin 2900 rpm. Considering the amperage necessary to rotate the flywheel or flexplate, the starter motor has a major job.

Brush-type starters consist of typical electrical motor components: an armature, field coils and brushes that ride on the armature's commutator. From a service standpoint, these motors require nothing more than periodic brush changes and replacement of the armature end bushings. There are other wear factors, however, that can also retire the starter motor from service.

Starter Solenoid

For massive current flow to reach the starter, without cooking the wiring circuits, the starter utilizes a solenoid switch. Simply put, the solenoid is an electrical switch that handles heavy current flow. The switch receives its signal from the ignition/starter switch via a small wire. On Delco-Remy systems, the ignition/start mode current causes magnetism to move the plunger inside the solenoid.

0014392

Fig. 14-17. GM/Delco-Remy use of a starter motor mounted solenoid dates back four decades. Unit shown is very common 1957 or newer GM truck application. This part is available at every GM dealership and most local auto supply outlets.

When the plunger moves (engaging the drive gear), the circuit closes between the solenoid's heavy battery pole and the starter motor's hot lead. Battery cable current now flows to the starter motor. This sequence is such that the starter drive gear engages the flywheel or flexplate ring gear teeth before the starter spins. To prevent severe clash of teeth or starter motor damage, starter drives have a one-way overrunning clutch mechanism.

Starter Drive

There are two types of starter drives common to the GM light truck models described within this book. One design engages when the electro-magnetic solenoid switch moves a shift lever. The other starter drive, found on the earliest GM truck starter motors, is foot pedal (manually) activated.

The early manually operated starter motor has a gear drive much like the later solenoid actuated units. As the driver depresses the start pedal, a lever moves the drive to engage the flywheel ring gear teeth. As the pedal moves slightly further, an electrical switch, mounted atop the starter motor, closes. This sends high amperage current to the starter motor and spins the drive.

Models with the electro-magnetic solenoid also use a lever actuated starter drive. The lever attaches to the solenoid's plunger. When the ignition switch's start mode flows current to the solenoid (mounted astride the starter motor), two events occur: 1) The plunger moves the starter drive toward the flywheel teeth, and 2) just upon tooth engagement, a second phase begins as the solenoid closes the heavy amperage switch and battery current flows to the starter motor.

The common wear points in these Delco-Remy starters are the solenoid, brushes, armature bushings, engagement shift lever and clutch/drive gear assembly. Although each of these components can be readily serviced in the field, most of today's owners and mechanics simply exchange a worn or defective starter motor assembly and solenoid switch for a relatively inexpensive rebuilt starter and a new or rebuilt solenoid switch.

0012602

Fig. 14-18. Release lever relationship is clear here. The solenoid's magnetic core draws the lever and also closes a high amp current switch. Forward of lever is drive clutch and drive gear.

> **NOTE —**
> Your starter motor may spin but not engage the flywheel or flexplate gear properly. This sounds like a high speed electric motor whir without the engine cranking over. (Or perhaps the drive only partially engages, causing a raucous grating noise as the gear teeth gnash.) Usually, the culprit is a worn starter drive/shift lever.

All starters must compensate for drive gear shock. Torque loads at the point of gear tooth mesh is where most starter housing damage occurs.

Starter housing nose end breakage, especially on big-block Chevrolet V-8s, is often the result of poor starter motor mounting or bracing methods. This problem is less significant on earlier V-8 truck engines, as the starter motor bolts/studs attach to the front face of the iron clutch housing, holding the starter more securely and helping to keep it on a straight plane.

If your GM truck has a high output V-8 and a starter that mounts to the engine block, be aware that the starter motor requires a metal brace between its endplate (commutator end frame) and the side of the engine block. If this brace is either missing or not attached properly, the starter motor can flex. This movement usually breaks the aluminum nose or drive housing of the starter.

CHAPTER 14

Starter Motor Troubleshooting

Assuming that your truck's engine won't crank over, you need to answer a few questions. Does the starter solenoid click? Is the starter motor turning too slowly? Can you hear the starter motor spin, but the engine isn't cranking? Always check the neutral safety or clutch pedal start switch before condemning the starter motor or starter solenoid switch.

If the battery and cables check okay and the solenoid simply clicks, the trouble is either 1) a defective solenoid, or 2) a defective starter motor (bad brushes, armature, or internal windings). Also check the starter drive shift lever or fork.

When the starter motor turns too slowly, you must consider internal engine problems. With the ignition switch turned off and the coil high tension lead disconnected, rotate the engine by hand and observe any friction. If the crankshaft turns okay, the trouble is likely within the starter motor assembly or solenoid switch.

There are two exceptions to this conclusion: 1) a jammed starter drive or 2) water in the engine's cylinders (hydro-lock). Either will prevent the engine from rotating. If you suspect water in the engine, remove the spark plugs and crank again. (If you find that internal engine friction keeps the engine from turning freely, refer to the troubleshooting chapter.)

Attach a starter motor induction meter to the heavy starter cable, and observe the amount of current flow necessary to crank the engine. If an abnormally high amp draw is evident (above the level of 150-210 amps), remove the starter motor for a bench test and determine the damage. Should the starter motor spin quickly and loudly, without rotating the engine, suspect a defective starter drive.

On those starters with the solenoid mounted at the motor housing, the starter drive or the starter shift lever could be faulty. Noise also suggests teeth missing from ei-

Fig. 14-19. Induction ammeter can check starter current flow. Without removing the starter or any other parts, place the meter over the battery cable's insulation. Used in conjunction with a VOM, the induction ammeter can help pinpoint defects and malfunctions by showing excessive current draw while the engine cranks over.

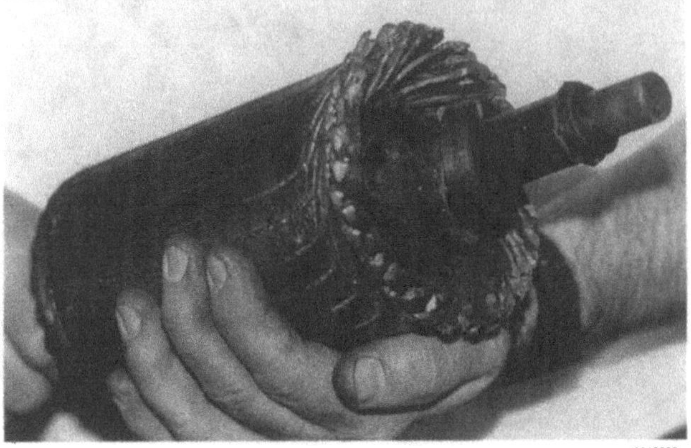

Fig. 14-20. Here, a worn GM/Delco-Remy solenoid welded its contacts and kept the drive and starter motor engaged. The motor winding unraveled from the heat—not a healthy prospect for a truck used in back country. This type of failure is very uncommon.

Fig. 14-21. Crumbliss test bench at North County Rebuilders tests this V-8 starter motor. If you suspect trouble with your truck's starter, an auto electric shop can assess the unit's performance.

ther the starter drive, flexplate or flywheel ring gear. The latter prospect is costly and difficult to repair.

Replacing a damaged starter ring gear (flywheel or flexplate type) requires removal of the transmission and clutch or the torque converter. In the ranking order of starter motor related repair costs, a solenoid switch is the least expensive item next to brushes and armature bushings.

For popular GM truck engines, rebuilt starter motors are available and inexpensive. However, if you have modified your engine with performance parts, a generic rebuilt starter may not handle the cranking load of a modified engine. You may need a starter application that serves a high compression/high output engine or perhaps an aftermarket high-torque starter.

If the field coils and armature are intact, your starter's major overhaul should include new end bushings, properly installed and reamed to fit. New brushes, re-dressing (cleaning and resurfacing) of the commutator, replacement of a worn starter shift lever/fork, a renewed solenoid and general clean-up of components will complete the job.

Starter Motor Overhaul

Your truck's reliability depends on an engine that will crank and start readily. Especially with an automatic transmission model that cannot be "bump" or push started, starter performance is critical. Depicted in these photos are starter motor rebuilding procedures that apply to most Delco-Remy truck starters. For specific details on your truck's starter motor and electrical system, refer to the shop manual that covers your model.

0012607

Fig. 14-22. *On this starter design, overhaul begins with solenoid switch removal. This particular V-8 starter has a GM/Delco-Remy type solenoid that mounts to the nose section.*

0012608

Fig. 14-23. *Brush inspection is possible once you remove the end plate. You will likely replace brushes and the end plate bushing during a starter repair, as these parts are readily available and inexpensive.*

0014296

Fig. 14-24. *Brushes are accessible with the commutator end frame (end plate) removed. At this point, brushes can be easily replaced by removing the brush holder pins and brush holders. Lay parts out carefully and in order. Note the way wires attach to brushes.*

0012610

Fig. 14-25. *This commutator and armature show wear. Note the angle of the shaft (arrow), an indication of end bushing wear.*

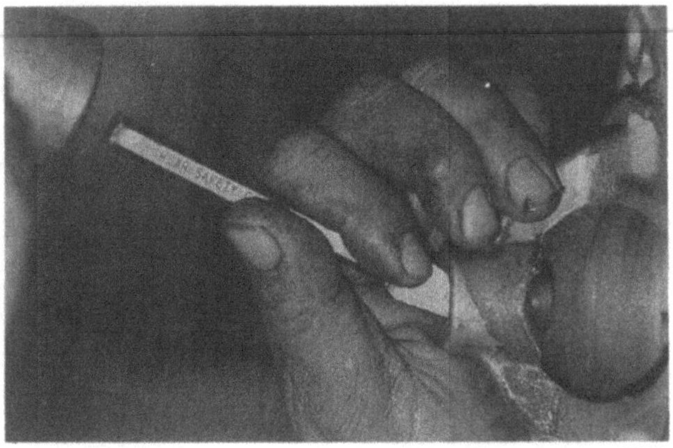

0012612

Fig. 14-26. End bushing replacement is a standard procedure.

0012613

Fig. 14-27. Loosening brushes precedes field coil removal. An impact driver or special tool is necessary for removing field coil screws (arrows). These screws are really seated firmly and should only be removed if field coils require service.

0012614

Fig. 14-28. Bench tester charges armature. Time-honored hacksaw blade test indicates shorts or opens. I recall performing this test as a fleet truck mechanic during the 1960s. The procedure was already old at that time.

0012615

Fig. 14-29. Commutator receives resurfacing in a metal lathe. This operation requires professional skill. Sublet the work to a local starter rebuilding shop.

0012616

Fig. 14-30. A new or rebuilt drive is a must. This item wears over time.

0014297

Fig. 14-31. Starter parts for GM light trucks remain available through most channels. Parts like the gear drive shift lever are generally a truck dealership or Delco-Remy dealer item. This kit would overhaul a modestly worn starter. Brushes, a new drive and end bushings make up the necessary pieces. A new or rebuilt solenoid unit will round out the rebuild unless the coils or armature show damage.

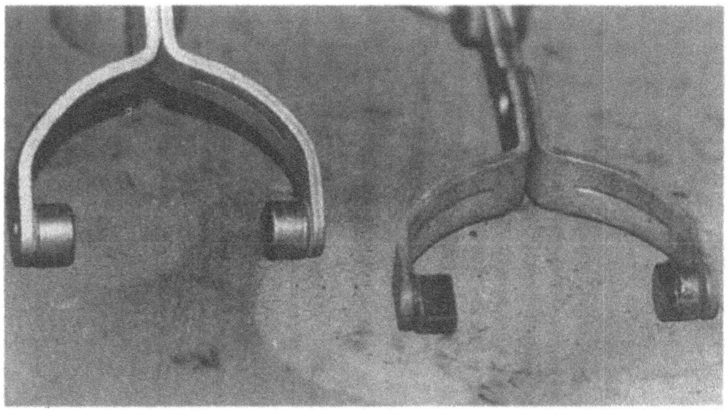

0012619

Fig. 14-32. Release fork wear is evident at right. This fork needs replacement to assure starter's reliability.

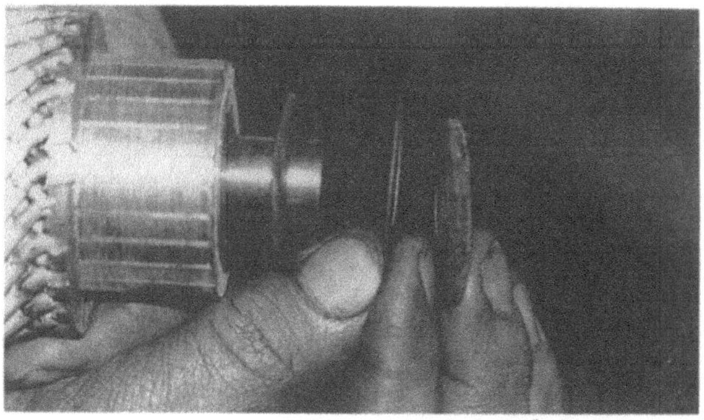

0012618

Fig. 14-33. On some applications, a selective fit thrust washer(s) controls end play of the armature. Consult the GM truck shop manual or a professional-level service manual for end play specifications.

0012620

Fig. 14-34. Rebuilt solenoids are not all the same. On the right is a cheap replacement item of approximately 80 winds. 140-wind wire at left is a high quality rebuilt, similar to a new OE unit.

Chapter 15

Accessories

As early as the post-World War I era, GM light truck accessories were a booming industry. Many of the original Chevrolet and GMC trucks were themselves the product of aftermarket coach and body builders. Rolling out of GM plants in cab-and-chassis form, early Chevrolet and GMC truck models set a precedent for today's custom utility beds and motorhome coach bodies.

GM Light Truck Accessorization

In the period just prior to World War II, and especially in the early years of the postwar era, huge numbers of light trucks rolled out of the GM plants. Buyers immediately began personalizing their vehicles. The WWII years of rationing encouraged owners to stick with their trucks and make them work better. Spare tire carriers, trailer towing hitches and military-style tow hooks, auxiliary lighting and add-on safety equipment were common products that carried forth into the postwar era. From custom bodies to turn signals and auxiliary heaters, GM trucks offered plenty of room for accessories.

Many items went on a new truck before it left the dealership. Auxiliary heaters, electric wiper motors, spare gas can holders and power take-off (PTO) driven accessories expanded the versatility of GM trucks. For specialized off-pavement needs, aftermarket and pre-delivery NAPCO four-wheel drive conversion packages became available by the early 1950s.

Add-on traction devices became popular GM light truck improvements, as OE limited slip and locking axles were still a decade away. Postwar suburban consumers found more time and resources for outdoor recreation,

0014299

Fig. 15-1. The light truck aftermarket has developed along two distinct paths. While commercial fleets create a demand for utility products, a growing number of recreational and multipurpose users now personalize their trucks with cosmetic, utility and convenience accessories.

Fig. 15-2. The versatile and affordable GM light trucks helped many families gain access to outdoor recreation. Models like the Suburban/Carryall revolutionized the concept of a station wagon, providing a genuine truck chassis as the platform for a rugged personnel and cargo hauler. (Photo courtesy of General Motors Corporation)

Fig. 15-4. NAPCO furnished aftermarket 4WD conversion kits to GM truck dealers. From the early 1950s until the 1960 introduction of factory K-model 4x4s, NAPCO made four-wheel drive available to GM light truck owners.

which created wide interest in camping, amateur mineral prospecting, touring ghost towns, fishing and hunting.

Popular aftermarket items often become original equipment or factory options on later truck models. As a GM light truck owner, you can select from a huge array of aftermarket upgrades, including safety enhancements, high performance components, specialized wheels and tires, utility products and cosmetic accessories.

If your GM truck needs more personality, better onboard work tools, styling improvements or a less spartan interior, there's likely an aftermarket solution. In some cases, an older truck can provide the features and conveniences of a later model by simply adding the right accessories.

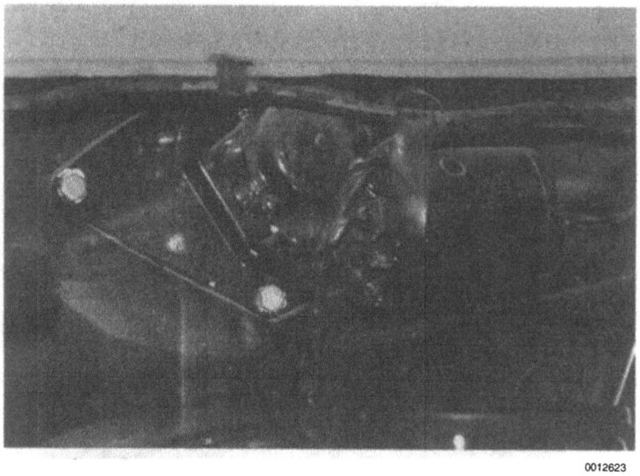

Fig. 15-3. Early GM trucks had vacuum windshield wipers. Even a dual diaphragm (combination) fuel pump seldom provides enough vacuum to operate the wipers under all driving conditions. For better service, the aftermarket has provided replacement electric wiper motors. By the mid-1950s, light GM trucks offered OE electric wipers.

1. WINCHES

Nearly as important as optional four-wheel drive systems, power winches have enhanced truck utility for half a century. Pioneered by Claude C. Ramsey, front mounted power take-off (PTO) winches were the first truck designs. By 1948, Ramsey's winch popularity was widespread. A recognized dealer-installed option, Ramsey winch systems were often factory-approved products offered through U.S. truck dealerships.

Early truck winches relied solely on engine power. Many light truck transmissions and transfer case designs feature a power take-off (PTO) drive, and tapping into such a gearbox gives access to all forward speeds and a reverse gear. Power flows to a front mounted winch gearbox via an accessory PTO driveshaft.

Fig. 15-5. Truck transmissions have PTO drive access. This convenient feature became the power source for Ramsey's early winch units. GM's latest NV-4500 series transmission still boasts PTO capability.

Koenig Iron Works also offered PTO winches. In the 1930s, Emil Koenig had furnished oil field trucks with power drive winches. His entry into the postwar power winch field targeted both commercial and recreational users. Koenig's King winches were suitable for front, rear and bed-mounted use, which gave Koenig, like Ramsey, access to the commercial hoisting and tow truck markets.

The Koenig/King and Ramsey PTO product lines drowned in the wave of electric winch sales. By the early 1970s, the bulky PTO winches, with scores of moving parts and a massive installation task, made the PTO winch far less attractive than the growing number of electric winches.

Ramsey Winch Company made a successful transition to electric winches. The respected Koenig Iron Works, however, disappeared from the recreational accessory market. Today, PTO-driven winches are still available, although their use is largely limited to commercial and utility company service.

Electric Winches

Since the late 1960s, a heated debate has waged between PTO winch advocates and electric winch users. PTO buffs argue that battery power limits the usage of the electric winch. Stranded in a stream, will the battery last long enough to pull the truck free? Electric winch advocates counter with the argument that a stalled engine can't spin a PTO shaft. Either way, the operator is in trouble.

0012625

Fig. 15-6. Warn's XD-9000 winch is an electric planetary design. Compact and inconspicuous, the unit ranks a hefty 9000 lbs. single line rating. This winch is rated to pull twice the weight of a K-1500 4x4 truck. Select a winch capable of pulling at least 1.5 times your truck's gross weight.

Dual battery installations, isolators and high output alternators have virtually eliminated the shortfalls of electric winches. Today, electric winches furnish the quality—and quantity—of service that users demand. Notable manufacturers in the truck mounted electric winch market include Ramsey, Warn and Superwinch. Contemporary winch marketing emphasizes gear and motor design, integrity of components, amperage draw, load capacity and utility.

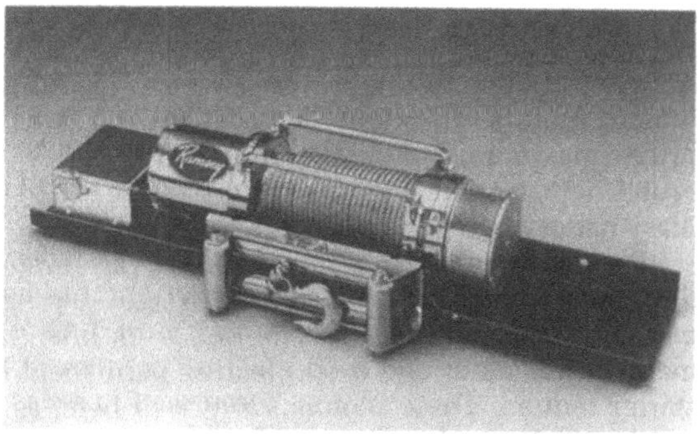

0012626

Fig. 15-7. Ramsey REP 8000 is a popular winch unit. Optional roller fairlead is shown. This is one of Ramsey's heaviest duty planetary gear models, weighing 61 lbs. RE 8000 and heavier RE 10000 or 12000 models feature worm gear drives and choice of Hawse or roller fairleads.

Determining Your Winch Needs

Electric winches have a variety of ratings. Speed (defined as feet-per-minute or fpm spooling) results from the gear reduction ratio and electric motor speed. Popular electric winch designs feature worm, spur or planetary gear systems.

The vehicle's battery (and/or an auxiliary battery) powers the winch motor, which basically resembles the motor portion of an automotive starter. In turn, the winch motor spins either a drive gear, worm shaft or sun gear.

Worm-and-gear systems rotate the worm gear inside a bull gear. Typically, the bull gear attaches to the cable spool drum. A major advantage of the worm drive is its ability to stop abruptly or load-reverse when power flow ceases. Planetary and spur gear arrangements, by contrast, require a brake mechanism to prevent reverse rotation when the motor stops spinning.

Worm gear systems have a low efficiency factor (the ability to transmit energy from one gear to another). By contrast, if a winch gear system could develop 100% efficiency, it would spool in either direction with equal ease, whether loaded or unloaded.

Gear efficiency of less than 45% creates a self-locking capability. Here, the relationship and ratios of the gears create a lesser incentive for free-spooling, even with a load on the cable. Worm gear systems, although extremely strong, offer only 35 to 40% efficiency, and need no brake.

Spur gear drives like Warn's Model M8274 work at 75% efficiency, which is why it requires a braking mechanism to prevent load-reversal. Similarly, the popular planetary gear systems offer 65% efficiency. One variation, the compound planetary gear, produces 40% efficiency, which provides for self-braking action. The compound planetary gear system requires a high speed motor, generally in the 4000 to 5000 rpm range.

The planetary systems provide both strength and smooth operation. Compact planetary winches have good resistance to torque loads. Direct power flow through the sun gear permits lighter weight, a low profile and high output.

Winch Motors

At present, the heaviest duty winches feature series wound motors. These provide maximum torque with a price: maximum amperage draw. The series wound brutes demand a heavy duty battery or the use of an auxiliary battery.

Permanent magnet motors require far fewer amps, draw less battery power, and save weight. On light and medium load winches, these motors work fine. After all, many newer autos and trucks feature permanent magnet starter motors. These motors serve well here, as engine cranking takes a short time and seldom generates excess heat.

The arguable disadvantage of permanent magnet motors is overheat. Under sustained and heavy loads, the permanent magnet motor tends to overheat. The operator needs to monitor the winching effort and time involved, allowing the motor to cool at regular intervals. (Most winch motors have circuit breaker protection against extreme overload.)

Winching and R.V. Batteries

Modern batteries offer higher cold cranking amperage or CCA. These types of batteries are far more practical for series wound motors. A dual battery system, once mandatory for high output winch systems, remains an option.

If your truck's battery rates above 650 CCA (preferably 850 CCA or higher), the normal needs of a high output series wound winch motor could be met with a single battery. For extreme duty use or very long winch pulls, consider a second battery and an automatic battery isolator. The isolator prevents draining your main battery below the level necessary to start the engine.

Selecting a Winch

Determine your truck's gross vehicle weight (GVW) before choosing a winch. This is the combined weight of the truck, your cargo, fuel, oil and any other items on board. Include your spare tools, the mounted winch and any accessories attached to the truck.

Also account for the other guy. As a rescue or emergency tool, your truck (especially a 4x4 model) has a wide range of uses. Consider not only your GVW but also the weight of other vehicles that you might assist.

Engineers compute the winch safety factor at 1.5 times the working GVW of your truck. Working GVW is the real world, loaded version of your vehicle. If in doubt, take your fully loaded vehicle to a local truck scale, and have it weighed. Multiply the amount of working GVW by 1.5. Example: If your fully loaded truck weighs 4,000 lbs., the minimum winch capacity should be 4000 x 1.5, or 6,000 lbs.

Many buyers, even those who own lighter half-ton rated trucks, seek 8,000-pound or higher capacity winches. The added margin of safety is obvious with a high output winch. A winch motor rated to pull heavier loads than you have planned will last longer and hold up better when worked hard.

Also be clear of a winch's rating method. "Single line pull" or "double" makes a major difference. Applying the physics of a snatch block (making a 180-degree turn of the cable and coming back to a tow hook near the winch) provides almost twice as much pulling strength and far less strain on your winch unit.

0012627

Fig. 15-8. *A snatch block and 180-degree reversal of the cable can reduce load on the winch motor by nearly one-half. Always allow a 15% safety margin.*

> ***CAUTION —***
> *Although physics shows nearly a doubling of pulling power, engineers advise a 15% safety factor. If your winch's single line pull is rated 6,000 lbs., a 180-degree turn of the cable should increase pulling power by 85% or 5,100 lbs. This would make your total pull rate 11,100 lbs. Any deviation from the 180-degree pull angle will reduce load capacity. Also, always consider the cable's load limit when using a snatch block.*

Although doubling and even tripling the cable is possible, the cable length eventually becomes an issue. Also, it is very hard on larger wire cables to bend them 180-degrees around a snatch block pulley. Even with a high output winch, conservative loads make a good strategy.

Mounting a Winch

Mounting position is important. Winches that mount at or above the frame/bumper height seem better suited to off-pavement use. Often, when you most need a winch, the front of the truck is low to the ground. If above the bumper height, the cable and spool will still be easy to reach.

In the worst instance, a below bumper mount could actually become buried in snow, mud or a creek. As with any front bumper extension, the truck's approach angle may also suffer from a below-the-bumper mount. A winch near the ground increases the likelihood of dragging the cable during pulls.

Many truck owners, however, prefer hiding the winch behind the bumper. An open grill frontal area is important. In very hot climates, under severe loads, a high mount winch may compromise the truck's engine and automatic transmission cooling system. Decreased air flow over the radiator core can reduce radiator efficiency.

Options are another factor when selecting your winch. Winch manufacturers frequently offer extra equipment. A roller fairlead, winch cover, remote controls, a portable/receiver mount, handtools or a wiring harness may be items you'll want—either when you purchase your winch or later.

Mechanical engineers design winch mounts to match a given winch installation. As life, limb and expensive property are at stake, proper installation is a necessity. Your wisest strategy is a manufactured winch mount. Installation kits available from the winch manufacturer will fit the frame and vehicle requirements of your truck. Mount kits address load points, the strength of frame attachments and the ease of access to the winch. Engineers take the rated load capacity of the winch and apply that force to the truck's frame.

WARNING —
Eliminating any part of a winch installation package could compromise safety and load capacity. Use only the graded and designated hardware included in the kit. If your truck has modifications that make a winch kit difficult to install, consult the winch manufacturer for possible solutions.

Sadly, operators often underestimate the load forces involved with winching. A cable drawn to maximum load capacity must transfer force to the frame. This concern goes beyond the winch mount and hardware.

0014480

Fig. 15-9. *Warn Industries offers quality electric winches and carefully engineered mounting kits. Here, winch mounts neatly behind a custom "Enforcer" front bumper. (See Fig. 15-1 for installed view.)*

If the winch attaches to the OEM bumper or brackets, that hardware must also be at factory standards. If the bumper has been removed, make certain that the attaching bolts and nuts meet or exceed OEM standards for your truck. Winch kit engineering assumes that the truck's frame will meet or exceed OEM guidelines.

Portable Winches

A recent development in winch mounting is the portable winch receiver. Recognizing the versatility of a detachable front or rear mounted winch, manufacturers now build winches and winch frames that fit a Class III (2" square) trailer receiver.

0012629

Fig. 15-10. *Portable winches allow quick removal. A Class III or stronger frame mounted receiver serves at either end of your truck. The portable winch is highly versatile for recovery work.*

Using a quick disconnect electrical cable and pin-type receiver hitch, these winches install and disconnect in minutes. The main advantage of a quality portable winch is out of the way storage. Protected from theft and foul weather, the winch can stow in a covered pickup bed or bed tool box. Ready for an emergency, the winch assembly is free of ice, mud or rusted cable. Additionally, the portable winch is useful at either end of the vehicle.

Portable winches rely on the integrity of your truck's receiver mount or hitch kit. Commercially made, most frame mounted hitches that have a two-inch receiver rate as Class III or higher. The load (tow) capacity of a properly installed Class III hitch is 5,000 lbs., with a maximum tongue weight of 500 lbs. Graded bolts and reinforcement plates generally accompany a frame mount hitch kit.

WARNING —
Failure to install a safe hitch is hazardous. Under heavy load, a bumper-mounted hitch could break away, causing personal injury. Cosmetic tube bumpers seldom rate even Class II hitch status. Many homemade and poorly installed hitches fall short of Class III standards. If you plan to install a portable winch, have your hitch inspected by a specialist or install an approved frame mounted hitch with the correct class rating recommended by the winch manufacturer.

Winch Controls and Installation

Winch installation kits offer either direct or remote controls. The remote cable allows control of the winch feed from twenty or more feet away, well away from the cable, spool and gearworks. This gives an optimal view of the pull without your standing in line with the load.

Carry-on Winch Accessories

Once you've mounted and wired your new winch, it's ready for work. A few accessory items, handily stored in your truck, will help your winch perform at maximum capacity.

Accessory kits offer compact storage for important winching gear. Warn's kit includes a snatch block, forged steel shackle, tree protector, leather work gloves and a carrying bag. Ramsey and other winch manufacturers also offer such kits.

An industrial or logging supply provides an excellent assortment of high grade snatch blocks, pulleys, shackles and swivels. Swivels protect cable from twisting under load, a major source of damage. Load rated assortments of hooks are also available. Watch for rough inner edge of hooks. Protect your nylon tree saver and recovery straps by carefully bevelling forging scars with a grinder or file.

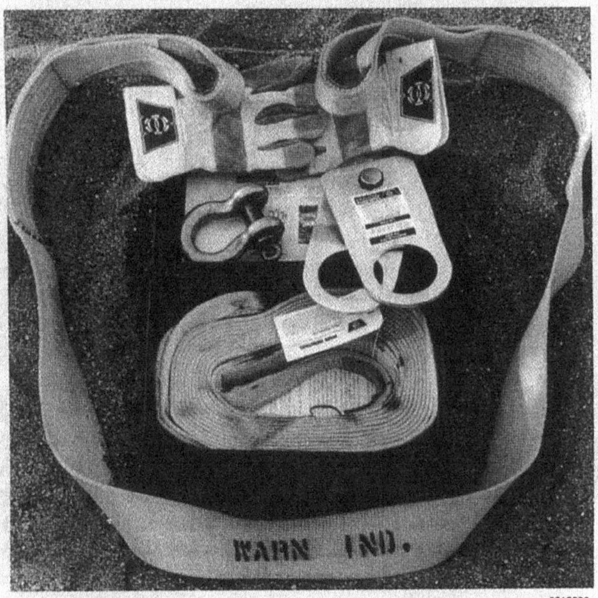

0012630

Recovery Strap. Quality winch accessory kits always include a recovery or tow strap. Often, you can free a stuck vehicle with a tug rather than setting up your winch. Many strap designs provide controlled stretch, which reduces shock loads.

Snatch Block. Known in other circles as a pulley block or block and tackle, the snatch block is an anchor plate with a pulley inside. Attached in front of the truck with a 180-degree return of the line, the snatch block offers 85% (with safety factored) load reduction when the cable hook attaches near the winch.

Choker Chain. A term familiar to woodsmen and loggers, the choker is a high tensile strength link chain with hooks at each end. The chain is very versatile, acting as a vehicle recovery tool or reinforcement between two anchor points. You'll find it handy for wrapping around huge rocks, truck frames or other anchor points. You can easily store a six- to ten-foot choker in your truck.

Tow Hooks. Factory or aftermarket front and rear frame mounted tow hooks require high tensile strength bolts and self-locking aircraft quality nuts. Attaching points and hardware must meet OE frame requirements. Never mount a tow hook directly to the bumper. Hooks are available with spring clips to prevent straps from slipping off. These are especially useful for one-person operation. Mounted upward, downward or sideways, tow hook bolts should align in the direction of pull. Mount the hook(s) at frame height and remember that the safest pull is a straight line. If possible, avoid welding tow hooks into place. These hooks may need replacement at some time.

D-Shackle. Most popular winch accessory kits include a D-shackle and pin. This is a highly versatile device for attaching and joining straps, rings, chain and even cable. When using a D-shackle with straps, make certain that nylon material rubs against the inside of the smooth looped end. Otherwise, fraying and damage to the strap will result. Tighten threaded bolt, then back off 1/2-turn to prevent thread seizure during heavy pulling.

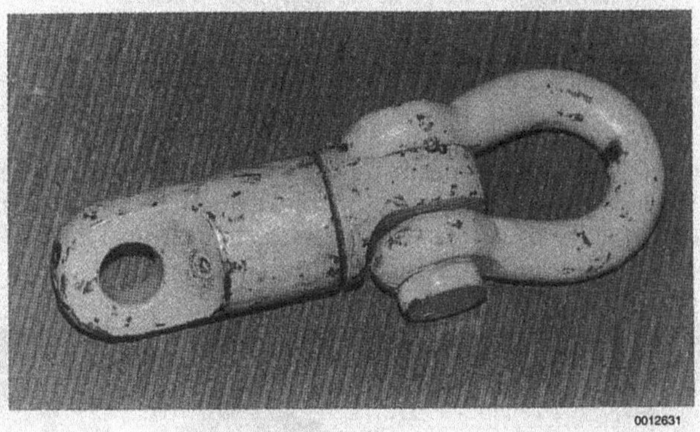

0012631

Gloves. Every accessory kit should include a pair of hefty (preferably leather) work gloves. These gloves must resist weather, cable friction burns, scraps and abrasions. Frayed cable and sharp sheet metal edges can cut fingers to the bone. Wear gloves.

Tree Saver Strap. This is vital. For attaching a winch cable or anchoring your vehicle to a tree, the tree saver strap protects the bark and live sections. The eyes of the saver strap provide an attachment point for your D-shackle, which in turn becomes the snatch block anchor.

Shovel and Hand Tools. A simple, often overlooked tool is the folding shovel. Vital hours are wasted when shovels, handyman jacks and proper handtools get left at home. Many winches provide the framework for mounting a shovel, axe and jack. Also, bring along strong wire cutters, as a broken cable can easily wrap up in the winch or the truck's chassis. The MAX multi-purpose tool kit and a High Lift or Handyman jack are must items for serious off-pavement adventures.

0012633

Fig. 15-11. The remote winch control is a must. Never stand in the line of a winch cable. If the cable breaks and recoils under load, severe bodily injury could result.

When mounting the control box, follow the suggestions of the manufacturer. Since distance equates to amperage loss and resistance, many control units have a specified location. The switch box should be easily accessible, in an airy space, preferably out of the weather.

Modern electric winch controls include solenoids, breakers or relays. In most instances, the control box is a plastic case, sealed from the weather. Since relays and/or solenoids flow constant battery current, you must isolate them from moisture. If ice, snow or sleet were to freeze inside the switch box, a current drain could sap your battery. Likewise, operating the winch under such conditions could create a short circuit.

A properly grounded electrical system is fundamental, and the issue becomes more critical with a winch. A 400- to 600-amp resistance load, even for a brief time, will tax your truck's electrical system to its limit. Poor grounding is a fast way to establish a power robbing voltage drop.

Grounds and Winch Wiring

As a rule, the best ground system takes the 12-volt battery negative cable directly to the engine block. Next, the alternator housing, or its ground post, connects to the engine, with a ground strap from the engine block to the frame completing the circuit. (To assure a good body ground, add a strap from the frame or engine to the cab.) The winch system may now ground directly to the block or frame.

Each manufacturer furnishes specific electrical requirements for its various winch models. Consult your kit instructions for details. As an additional item, consider an accessible master disconnect switch. Mount the switch in an easy to reach place, out of line from the winch.

NOTE —
Under extreme load, winch motors and the electrical system can overheat. An accessible master switch allows shutting the system down completely without placing your limbs in jeopardy.

If your winch electrics interface with a complex electrical system (sound system, lights and an extra battery), you may need a complete, high amperage cable and wiring harness.

Using a Winch

Before operating your winch, raise the hood. A broken winch cable is potentially lethal and could easily break your truck's windshield. (For this reason, a brush/grill guard makes a smart addition to a winch mount.) Make sure that the cable can spool evenly onto the drum, and attach the hook to a substantial anchor point.

If possible, stand far to the side when winching, well outside the cable's path. Many operators lay a blanket over the cable, assuming that this will reduce recoil if the cable breaks.

Although a cover or blanket may help contain the cable, no cloth blanket can absorb the immense force of a snapping cable under load. Pull as straight as possible, and always use leather work gloves when handling wire cable.

Always leave a reasonable length of cable on the winch spool. Your winch manufacturer has guidelines for the necessary length. Paint the cable red from the starting wrap to the length specified. This will signal when the maximum length of cable has spooled out.

0014302

Fig. 15-12. Loads on cables are fully capable of launching a tow hook, clevis, snatch block, bumper section, bumper bracket or frame piece through the windshield of a vehicle. Never stand in the line of a loaded cable. Many truck owners raise their hoods to protect the windshield in the event of a cable failure. Use your remote winch control to keep clear of the cable.

0012635

Fig. 15-13. A sensible anchor point for your tow chain or strap is the receiver of a quality mounted hitch. A Class III hitch/receiver rates a 5,000 pound load capacity and will withstand the stress of moving another light vehicle. Avoid use of elastic or bungie cord-type recovery straps. The load of a stretched cord places far too much stress on tow hooks and attachment points.

WARNING —
Always assume that a loaded winch cable is dangerous. Imagine the path a snapped cable might take. Stay out of that space.

Freeing a vehicle often will require more than one run of the cable's length. If the vehicle wants to roll faster than the cable spools, apply slight brake pressure. Many winches operate at both a minimum and maximum operating load. Proper cable spooling depends upon working within this load range.

When winching, keep in mind that the winch's maximum pulling ability is rated as the first few wraps of cable. As the cable spools in, the larger diameter wraps offer less load capacity than the first wraps. For this reason, you should spool out as far as possible when moving a heavy load. If necessary, use a snatch block and 180-degree cable return (back to the vehicle's tow hook) to reduce cable length and add pulling power.

Preventive Maintenance For Your Winch

Your winch is a safety device and lifeline. When a four-wheeling trip requires the use of your winch, you're way out there! A secluded box canyon or a muddy creekbed is no place for winching errors or a poorly maintained winch.

The modern electric winch is easy to maintain. Unlike PTO winches, with their oil-filled transmissions and mechanical driveshafts, the electric winch requires simple service.

Cable Inspection. The major wear item is the cable. Properly used, the wire winch line will last for years. One careless moment, however, can weaken or kink the cable. If a night time or blizzard winching episode leaves your winch cable coiled wrong, free-spool the cable entirely and check for damage. Kinks, broken outer strands and twists that leave the cable distorted are all signs of weakness. Clean the cable thoroughly to allow close inspection.

Lubrication. Your winch may have grease fittings and require periodic lubrication. If you have an oil bath drive (usually on PTO winches), the gear oil must be clean and up to the full level. Check for seal leaks. If your winch operates in a dusty and wet environment, always wipe zirk fittings clean before greasing. Use the manufacturer's recommended grease or a water-resistant chassis / bearing lube. Cable friction leads to fatigue and unnecessary stress. Many users lube the cable with special cable lubricants.

As greases often attract unwanted dirt and dust, special lubricants are available for use on cables. Industrial supplies sell chain and cable lubricants that cure like cosmoline. This reduces messy handling and resists dirt accumulation. Such lubes also work well on clevis pins, hook pivots and the snatch block. They provide a good moisture barrier against rust, too.

Mounts, Hooks, Pulleys and Straps. Inspect your hooks and straps. Make certain clevis pins are free of moisture and lubricate them lightly. Dry out your nylon straps before storing them. Check tow hook and winch mount bolts and nuts for tightness and signs of fatigue. Inspect parts closely for bending or possible fatigue cracks. Clean and lubricate pulleys and the snatch block at regular intervals.

Electrical System. Inspect your remote control cable, control box and all cable leads to the winch. Insulation on these leads must be in good condition and free from nicks. Amperage passing through the winch motor cables is high enough to weld metal. If a hot cable shorts to ground, a fire or severe damage might result. Inspect the cable routing to make certain no cable lays across sharp metal edges. You can reduce the effects of moisture through the use of silicone sprays and dispersing chemicals. Make certain that the control box and remote connectors are free of debris and corrosives.

2. Electrical System Upgrades

Automotive electrical wire must meet various current loads. Amperage requirements determine the proper wire gauge for each area of your truck. Since resistance increases with distance, longer runs of wire require heavier gauge sizes.

Wire for 6-volt accessories and components is substantially heavier than wiring found in later 12-volt systems. This is an advantage when converting an early GM truck's 6-volt system to 12-volts. Factory wires, if in good condition, are usually more than ample.

For rewiring and repair work, safety standards must apply. Heavy duty devices demand more amperage draw and larger wire sizing. OEM standards assume a specific distance between the current source and each device.

As a rule, 12-volt ignitions draw between 1.5 and 3.5 amps. A pair of horns draw 18 to 20 amps, while electric wipers demand 3 to 6 amps. A pair of back-up lights drain 3.5 to 4 amps, while an air conditioner drains 13 to 20 amps.

On a 12-volt and four-lamp system, headlights demand 8 to 9 amps on low beam and 13 to 15 additional amps for high beam operation. Assume slightly less draw if your truck has a two-headlight system.

The cigar lighter, often used for plug-in accessories, drains 10 to 12 amps from the battery. A radio draws up to 4 amps (tape decks more), while power antennas drain 6 to 10 amperes. Instrument lamps, engine gauges, a clock or dome light each pull from 1 to 3 amps, a relatively mild load. Wire type ranges accordingly, and gauge size increases with wire length.

0012632

Fig. 15-14. A heavy duty engine, alternator, frame and winch ground system assures full power. Here, Wrangler Power Products' custom 1/0 welding type cables provide both positive and negative battery current and the complete ground circuit.

By contrast, the 12-volt starter motor, requiring an arc welding size lead from the battery, draws 150 to 450 amps during cranking. (This is a generalized range for modern automotive engines. An OEM-level shop manual offers specific data for your truck's engine and starter.) These amperage requirements demand safe wire sizes.

Determining Wire Gauge

Distance also fits into the wiring equation. A device demanding 10 amperes of current requires a minimum 18-guage wire for a seven foot flow. The same device needs a heavy 10-gauge wire at 75 feet.

> **NOTE —**
> When choosing wire, the higher the wire's AWG number, the smaller the wire size.

Undercapacity wire creates an excess voltage drop (the inherent loss of current due to a wire's resistance), causing lights to burn dimly, motors to turn slowly or accessories to operate below capacity. If the wires are grossly undersize, resistance rises to the point that the insulation melts, usually followed by a short to the closest chassis or body ground.

For auxiliary lighting (lightbars, emergency lights, floods, halogen lamps and such), look closely at the Watt ratings. Manufacturers list the Watt output, and there's a simple formula for converting Watts to amperage: Wattage divided by voltage = amperage.

Example: On a 12-volt electrical system, a 100W lamp equals 100W divided by 12, or 8-1/3 amps. Therefore, an exotic string of ten 100W lamps draws 83.3 amps.

For computing your electrical needs, consider the typical amperage draws for various accessory and OEM items on your truck. Add up the on-line components, and build your charging and battery system around these guidelines.

Wire, available at local auto supplies, usually comes in spool lengths of 25 to 100 feet. Once you determine the proper amperage draw for each electrical component in your truck's system, select wire by gauge size.

Carry the amperage needs through the fuses and relays, those safety devices that will prevent wires from frying in the event of an overload or short. When matching fuses to electrical components, each fuse should allow little more amperage flow than the device requires. Allow a slight margin for upstart surges and hot operation (when amperage draw increases slightly).

> ***CAUTION —***
> *Never install a higher amp fuse as a cure for an OE circuit that keeps blowing fuses. Always find the reason for the overload. (See electrical chapter for details on troubleshooting.)*

Fuses blow for valid reasons: a defective electrical component, a bare wire short in the circuit, a weak ground, loose connections, or a charging circuit defect. Resolve the problem and install the correct fuse. A small volt/ohmmeter makes the ideal tool for troubleshooting resistance and the continuity of wiring circuits. (See chapter on electrical system.)

The backside of an early GM truck dash is readily accessible. This reflects the utility and ease of service found in older light trucks. 1960–up GM truck electrical systems become increasingly more complex and difficult to access.

CHAPTER 15

Matching Accessories and Wiring

When selecting the right wire gauge for your add-on accessories, note the relationship between amperage draw, Watt ratings, candle power and length of the wire runs.

Auxiliary lights, a sound system or a winch each have an assigned amperage draw. Cover that rating with a safety margin. You can always go bigger. Wherever possible, use fuses or circuit breakers. Protect higher amp items and wiring with reset breakers. Protective devices are available from 1.0 amp to 250 amp ratings and higher.

A winch's current draw is similar to a starter motor. Route cables very carefully to avoid high amperage shorts and possible fire. Review the winch manufacturer's guidelines for circuit protection and cable routing.

Remember, more wire means added resistance. Resistance raises amperage. Note the length of wire feeding each accessory. Select the recommended amperage ratings from an automotive wire manufacturer's guidebook, and match wire size accordingly. Account for the entire distance that current will flow, from the battery source to the accessory.

If your truck has a camper or aftermarket fiberglass body panels, you must run a ground wire to any accessory mounted on non-conductive material (fiberglass, plastic, wood, etc.). In this case, choose a wire gauge that satisfies the *total length of the power lead and ground wire*. A ground lead must always match the gauge size of the power lead.

0012636

Fig. 15-15. *Wrangler Power Products at Prescott, Arizona offers this crimping tool for the do-it-yourselfer. These crimps in heavy duty copper battery terminals offer maximum conductivity and a long-lasting cure for resistance problems.*

High Work Standards

Safe routing of the long wires that run from the front to the rear of your truck is essential. A quality wiring job ensures that vibration and road shake will not separate or damage wires.

> ***CAUTION —***
> *Improperly installed plastic wire ties, clamps and straps have a nasty habit of wearing through wire insulation.*

A yardstick I like to apply is the worst case scenario. (Some call this Murphy's Law, but I don't believe Murphy or anyone else can stake sole claim to the concept!) Assume that the wire you're routing will face tension, heat and friction. Are there sharp metal edges just waiting to whittle at your vital wiring loom? Can engine heat melt the plastic off wires? Will chassis movement tear a crucial connection apart?

You must depend on your wiring in blizzards, on remote desert moonscapes, atop craggy and windswept mountains—and even in the fast lane of the freeway during rush hour. Take the time to route, shield, tape and secure all wires.

Wire Looms and Connections

For assuring quality work, use universal plastic wire shields, quality wire connectors, ties and straps. Rewiring and repairs often involve use of insulated, solderless connectors. These connectors match wire gauge sizes. When using solderless connectors, be certain to select the correct size for the wire involved.

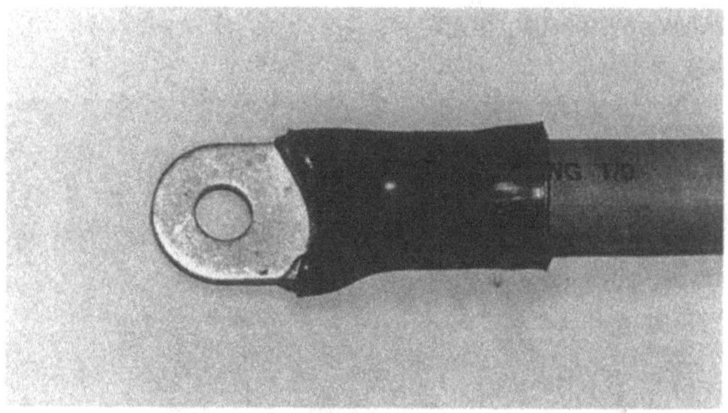

0012637

Fig. 15-16. *This is a quality wire connection. After crimping, the copper terminal receives a coating of special adhesive-lined heat shrink tubing.*

Color coded solderless connectors have become popular over the last three decades. They are easy to fit, quick to secure in tight places and offer long service life. A special crimping pliers is necessary for installation. Don't cut corners when buying this tool. Tight, neat connections depend on professional caliber tools.

Expect to waste a few connectors practicing your crimping skills. Too tight or loose won't do. On connectors and crimp terminal ends with seams on the metal sleeves, make certain your crimp is on the solid side, not the seam.

The factory (OE) wire connections are often solder type, with molded insulation. In some cases, aftermarket pigtails are available to restore OE integrity to electrical connections. Some fitups, however, benefit from the use

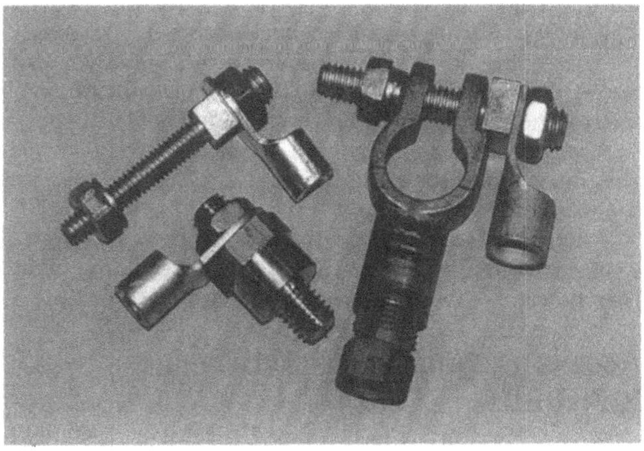

0012638

Fig. 15-17. Various types of battery attachments are available. Shown are two crimp type terminals and a unique compression nut clamp. Each meets high industrial/automotive standards and features durable, high quality copper.

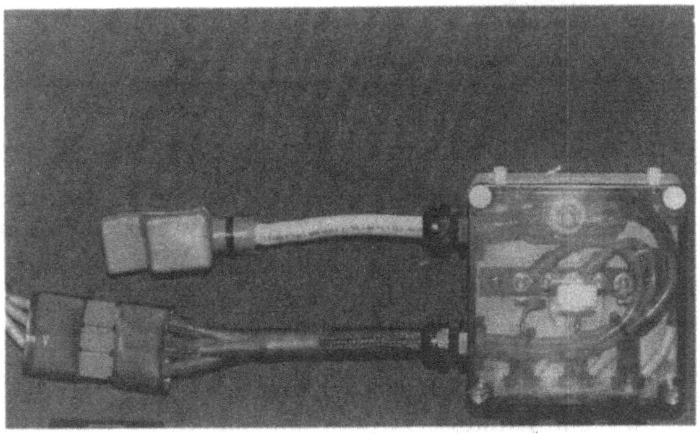

0012639

Fig. 15-18. This arrangement from Wrangler Power Products offers major protection and a high quality appearance. Imagine these junction boxes beneath the hood of your truck.

of an entire OE wiring harness, tailored to your truck's needs. Pre-formed harnesses, insulated properly, provide the best connections possible.

> **NOTE —**
> Late model GM trucks with electronic components depend upon proper circuit resistance and voltage signals. On such a system, it may be necessary to repair damaged wiring with the installation of a complete new harness. Consult the GM truck shop manual before attempting wire repairs on a late model truck.

Some forethought and a factory schematic of your truck's electrical system will contribute to a quality wiring job. Electrical work, done properly, is very gratifying. It also provides a better understanding of how your truck operates. Armed with this knowledge, you'll feel more confident about traveling to isolated regions.

Consider the Load

When amperage load rises, so does the need for a high performance electrical system. Light trucks, and especially four-wheel drive models, offer more room for accessorization than any other vehicle. These trucks press their electrical systems to the limit.

Installation of an aftermarket high output alternator can serve your high amperage charging needs. Along with high amps from the alternator, you must consider the wiring and safety devices needed to support such a high output charging and accessory system.

Protecting Your Electrical System

Once you've selected the right alternator to meet your amperage needs, heavy duty wiring can begin. In external regulator systems, wiring starts with the alternator-to-regulator harness. Needs here include proper wire sizing and use of quality terminals. If the alternator unit has an integral regulator, an adequate charge wire, routed directly to the battery, is necessary.

If your alternator delivers 130 or fewer amps, the appropriate (minimum) requirement for a 10-foot or less length alternator lead is 4-gauge wire. A positive battery cable with the proper ring size end for the alternator output stud is more than adequate. (Protect this lead with a 150 amp circuit breaker or fusible link.)

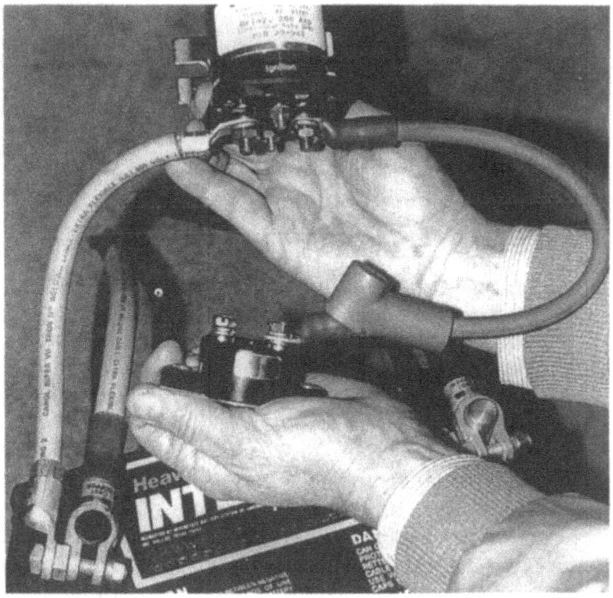

0012640

Fig 15-19. In-line relays are available in high amperage ratings. These devices service heavy accessory circuits.

For the battery cable or a higher output alternator charge lead, premium 1/0 size copper welding-type cable is more than adequate. The fine strands of the welding cable, with quality crimped or compression clamped ends, will easily handle high resistance loads.

Unlike battery cables, which are relatively rigid and of lower grade, welding wire meets the highest industrial standards for carrying amperage. Fine-strand wire permits oversizing without excessive resistance, voltage drop or false battery / current signals to the voltage regulator.

When building the charging / battery wiring with 1/0 welding cable, make sure you also use 1/0 cable for all grounds, including the engine-to-frame and battery. The 6- or 12-volt battery system of a GM truck is direct current (DC), and this means the ground circuit wire gauge must match both charging and starter draw demands.

Dual Battery Electrical Needs

Many truck owners with heavy duty electric winches add an extra battery to their system. For electrical systems with auxiliary batteries, I recommend use of Wrangler Power Products' Battery Management System.

The system provides an automatic low voltage battery response designed to disconnect the current flow from the auxiliary battery when voltage drops to a critical level. This prevents abuse of your truck's expensive accessories and also protects the auxiliary battery from severe discharge. Upon recharging the battery to a full state of charge, the system reconnects the circuit.

0012641

Fig. 15-20. Dual batteries require a quality management system. Wrangler Power Products' Battery Manager System is a driver switched dual battery circuit controller. The reliable battery isolator and switching components make it virtually impossible to get stranded by a discharged battery. This is my choice for a reliable dual battery management system.

A quality dual or auxiliary battery management system performs two functions: 1) delivers maximum battery current for starting, and 2) charge system protection. In the event that the chassis main battery(s) become low, a management system reads the voltage level of the auxiliary battery and brings that current on line to help start the engine.

The system monitors the two batteries once the engine starts, applying current solely to the main battery until it reaches a full charge state. Then the management system reads the charge state of the auxiliary or winch battery and feeds current to both batteries as required.

Other types of battery isolators are also available. Both electronic and electro-magnetic / mechanical relays, ranging in amperage limits from 100 to 200 amps, can handle major current flow chores. A hefty 250 amp battery switch will also meet heavy current requirements.

Circuit breaking relays, gaining popularity over traditional fuses, work very well on truck electrical systems. In environments where temporary shorting is likely, such as submersion in a running stream of water, a circuit breaker will reset when the hazard passes and the components dry—a helpful prospect.

Circuit breakers range from huge devices to small two-spade ATO fuse size relays. The latter conveniently fit in place of the original fuses in later model trucks.

Assessing Your Electrical System's Reliability

Building a first class wiring system involves use of high grade copper terminals and wire products. Regardless of style, judge switches by two criteria: amperage load capacity and a switch's designated number of service cycles.

> **NOTE —**
> Better quality switches have amperage load and service cycle ratings. You will find these switches listed in automotive and electrical / industrial parts catalogs.

If you want maximum performance from your truck's electrical system, each piece of hardware, including crimped and compression terminals, should bear either a military, commercial or industrial (UL) rating. The switches found at discount auto supply outlets seldom have these ratings.

For heavy duty purposes, be suspect of any electrical component without a recognizable rating. When in doubt, seek out an industrial / commercial supplier or high quality automotive sources like NAPA's Belden line or Wrangler Power Products. (See appendix for parts sources.)

High grade hardware, including both brass and copper battery attachments and wire terminals, eliminates trouble in heavily worked electrical systems. Protection from battery acid and the corrosion of salty winters is a must. Underhood heat becomes your nemesis in desert climates, gnawing away at wire insulation and taxing the voltage regulator and other relays. Quality electrical hardware is the best protective measure.

Some Unusual Electrical Hardware

Among the electrical specialty items that fit a light truck owners' needs is a battery jumper system that mounts permanently to the front or rear of your truck. Quick connect cables can serve easily in emergencies, enabling your truck to park nose-to-nose with a stalled vehicle.

Quick disconnect jumper cables help you avoid the hazard of hanging your truck out in the road or running over a cliff while trying to pull alongside a vehicle. The best system I've found yet comes from Wrangler Power Products. These kits feature 1/0 welding cable, copper terminals and industrial grade connectors.

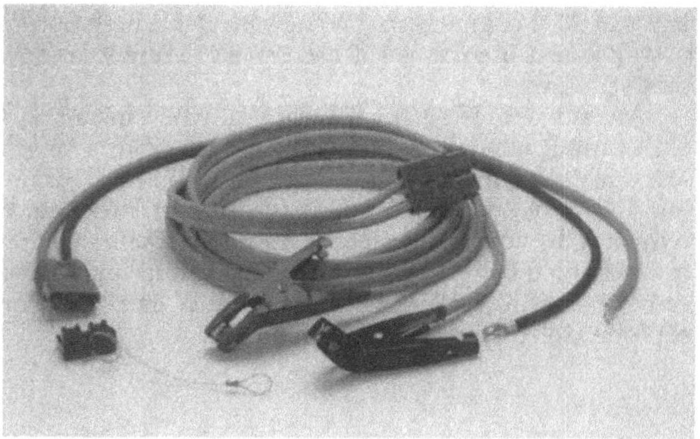

0012642

Fig. 15-21. Here is the best way yet to jump batteries, with special quick-connect system that terminates at front bumper. This avoids the spark-and-explosion risk of hooking jumper cables directly to a battery.

Selecting a Battery

Each battery has an ampere hour rating and cold cranking capacity. The engine and electrical system dictate their needs, with air conditioning, power options, the engine size and compression ratio determining the necessary battery group size.

An under-capacity battery will discharge quickly and require excessive, high amperage recharging. Such recycling leads to short battery life. If your truck has a heavy electrical load, or has been hybridized with an engine transplant, battery selection should favor the engine.

Find a listing for a car or truck equipped with your engine and approximately the same accessory package, and note its battery size. Select a similarly rated battery that will fit your battery box, if possible, or change boxes to an adequate size. Secure the battery safely, and use the best battery cable connections available.

A 12-volt battery will operate best above 12.3 volts. (A full state of charge is 12.6 volts.) When you crank the engine for a long period or the headlights have burned without the engine running, the battery voltage actually drops below 12 volts. Healthy batteries will recover some voltage if left alone for a while (regain a "surface charge"); however, to completely restore a battery's state of charge, the generator or alternator must flow amperes.

Maintaining and Monitoring Battery Charge

Earlier GM truck charge systems (both generator and alternator versions) have ammeters that read the amperes of electrical current that flow either toward or away from the battery. Current flow is regulated by an external voltage regulator. It acts as an electrical current monitor, directing charge flow to the battery. The regulator receives battery voltage signals and adjusts current to achieve a full charge.

Later trucks have voltmeters instead of ammeters. Voltmeters show the battery's actual state of charge, or the charge state as current flows from the alternator to the battery. Most truck owners prefer a voltmeter and find it more useful. I certainly do.

A worn battery with bad cells loses more voltage while spinning the starter motor. When this occurs, the alternator floods the battery with heavy amps of current, and a vicious cycle begins. The already tired battery suffers from this fast charge, which heats the battery and reduces its life even further. Soon, the worn battery is nothing more than a source of lead for recycling.

Likewise, an engine rebuild or performance modifications may finish off a lighter duty or worn out battery. Heavy voltage depletion followed by maximum charging after each engine start-up will quickly ruin any battery. Battery drain from heavy lighting or an electric winch can also create a high-rate charging situation. This can quickly destroy the battery.

High Performance Charging System

A high output alternator can restore the battery's state of charge in minutes. OE alternator output usually improves with power options like air conditioning, electric door locks and power window lifts.

Even with a high output factory alternator, however, truck owners find ways to overwhelm their electrical system. Auxiliary lighting, an electric winch, high Watt sound systems, and dual-battery installations leave the alternator with a heavy burden. Worse yet, high amp draw auxiliary lighting or a winch often operate with the engine either idling or stopped.

The alternator's strongest advantage over older generator designs is its ability to produce a higher charge rate at slower speeds. Alternators can meet the demands of a vehicle that idles in traffic with air conditioning and other luxury accessories gnawing at the battery.

Late OEM alternators have outstanding charge rates at an idle. By comparison, trucks built before the 1980s, even with high output factory alternators, lag at lower

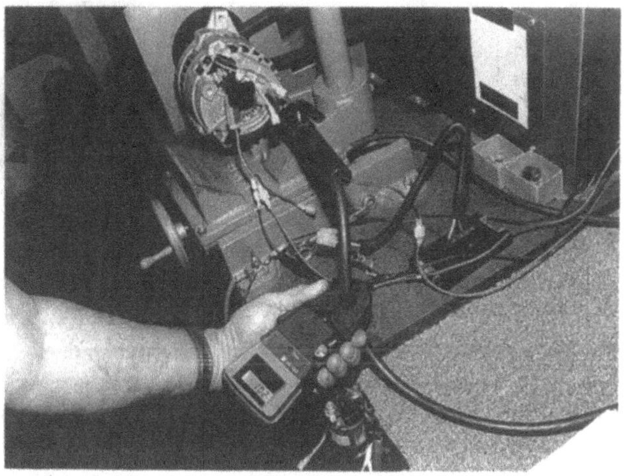

0012643

Fig. 15-22. OEM GM CS-130 style alternator is potent. This Delco-Remy unit, capable of 100 amps at an equivalent of 1500 crankshaft rpm, tests a top end output of 103 amps. Characteristic of many late model alternators, the CS-130's most impressive attribute is 61 amp output at an engine idle.

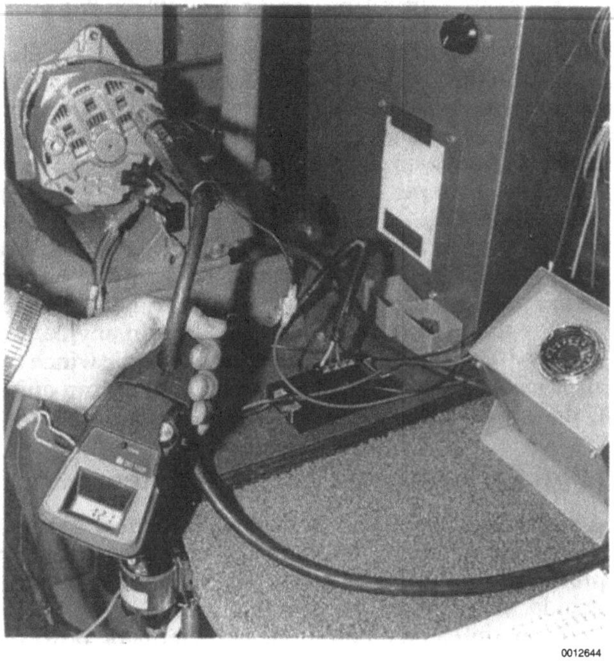

Fig. 15-23. *Wrangler Power Products tests a GM factory CS-144 alternator, which stormed to a 121 ampere output by 5000 rotor rpm. Idle speed amperage read 61. Wrangler builds the GM CS-133 or CS-144 alternators into even higher output 140 and 160 amp systems.*

Fig. 15-24. *Here are high quality components for building longevity into a charging system. Your new alternator is just the beginning. Shown is a junction block for high amperage, battery size leads.*

rpm. The typical high output alternator of early 1970s vintage produces 55 amps @ 6500 alternator/rotor rpm but only 9 amps at an engine idle. In fairness, this alternator at 1500 engine rpm jumps to a 44 amp output, but the message is clear: At a curb idle, or when you're crawling off-pavement in the desert, the older alternator has limited output.

As a high output OE alternator retrofit for your truck, consider the features of later factory alternators. By 1982, a popular 80 amp Delco-Remy alternator produces 55 amps at 2000 engine rpm. The newest Delco high output units produce in excess of 60 amps at a 675 rpm idle. Now that's progress!

Always upgrade your battery size when installing a high output alternator. Running a winch from a single, low ampere hour battery is dangerous. Completely draining a battery, then forcing massive current back into it (which is the voltage regulator's normal response to a fully discharged battery) will heat up the battery plates and cause their failure. Weak batteries produce gases that can explode violently under such conditions.

An On-board Welder

We were five tortuous, rock crawling hours into the Rubicon. In our whole group, only one rig had given us mechanical trouble. Compared to the two guys now standing in the trail, the trip was a breeze.

A powerful Saginaw power steering gear, manhandled by two burly arms, had ripped out the section of frame rail that supports the steering gearbox. In three hours time, the CJ model Jeep had moved only a couple of healthy stone's throws.

As much as we wanted to help these guys, our tools fell short. What we really needed was a welder. An alternator-powered frequency welder takes a fabrication welder wherever your truck goes. Mounted either underhood or in the bed, the compact unit is powerful stuff.

Better frequency welders perform serious welding, including the use of 5/32" rod on heavy steel plate. Since the principle is frequency, not amperage, cable length/distance is no barrier. Some designs also provide a 110-volt DC outlet with enough wattage to run brush motor power tools or a string of camp lamps. A battery booster mode assists stranded vehicles in minutes.

A high-output alternator is at the core of a frequency welder system. At 1500 engine rpm, the alternator reaches 135 or more amps, enough to deliver peak welding voltage.

Options include all welding accessories and even TIG (heliarc) or MIG (wire weld) equipment. From my view, this is the ultimate tool for the serious outback traveler. (See Appendix for sources.)

3. ROLL BARS

By design, light trucks need ground clearance, which means that your truck has a higher center of gravity than modern passenger cars. Concerns about a hazardous rollover are valid, with taller 4x4 models especially vulnerable.

> *WARNING —*
> *A cabover camper raises the vehicle's roll center and also impacts center of gravity. When you carry such a load, your truck should have stabilizer bars and other devices to offset the risk of rollover. Wheel and tire width also play a role here. For ideas on how to reduce risk, see the chapter on chassis/suspension upgrades.*

It's unnerving when a trail or roadway shifts off-camber and your truck's tilt meter runs off the safe zone. When you drive in these kinds of environments, the best protection against bodily injury and major vehicular damage is a roll cage and ample seat belt/harnesses.

Greater concern for product liability has encouraged aftermarket manufacturers to classify cab bars and other steel tubular assemblies into distinct classes: the bonafide roll bar (chassis or cab mounted), and a group of lighter weight, largely cosmetic tube or bed bars.

Cab cages, built for light trucks and multi-purpose sport/utility 4x4s, resemble race truck protection. The critical differences between a hard-core Baja race truck cage and a manufactured cab cage are the bracing and attachment methods.

A Racing Roll Cage

Off-road racing is the best test for roll cages. The standards set by the High Desert Racing Association (HDRA) and SCORE say a lot about our safety needs. Whether you are building your own truck roll cage or shopping for quality aftermarket rollover protection, racing requirements offer the highest standards.

0012648

Fig. 15-25. Where does the roll cage/frame end and the suspension begin? On desert race trucks and stadium race trucks, the line is thin. Bracing angles reflect Nature's strongest design, the triangle. This shape repeats itself throughout the chassis and cage.

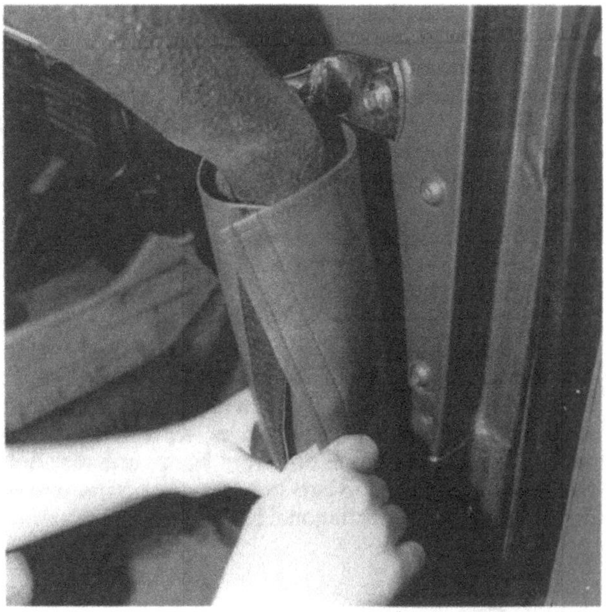

0012649

Fig. 15-26. Roll bars require padding. If your bars are shaped oddly or you want a custom pad, Bar Glove by the Off-Road Factory is one such accessory.

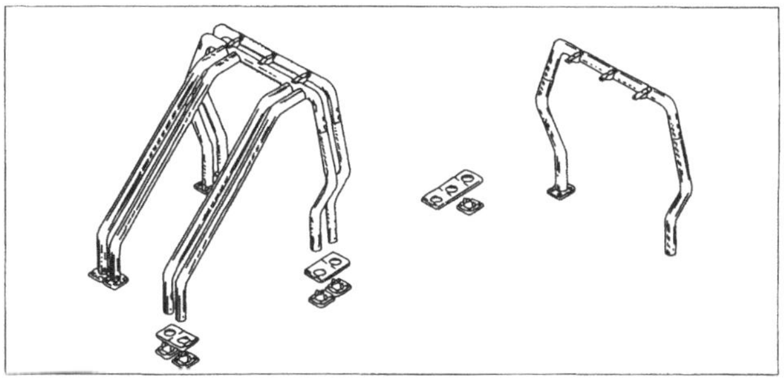

0012650

Fig. 15-27. Hobrecht, Grizzly, Smittybilt and others make attractive truck bars for pickup beds. These bars provide mounts for lighting and minimal protection. Mounted to the bed sheet metal, they do not qualify as bonafide roll bars. Hobrect and Smittybilt also offer more protective cab cages for pickups.

For racing, the minimum tubing size for a 2,000–3,000 lb. truck is 1-3/4" diameter for open cockpits and 1-1/2" for closed cabs. Tubing wall thickness is a minimum 0.120". A 3,000–4,000 lb. race vehicle requires 2" x 0.120" for open cockpits and 1-3/4" x 0.120" for a closed cab. In trucks over 4,000 lbs., tubing size increases to 2-1/4" x 0.120" for open cockpits and 2" x 0.120" for closed cabs.

Materials and construction follow strict guidelines. HDRA/SCORE recommends CRW, DOM, WHR, or WCR mild carbon steel or 4130 Chromoly steel. Light weight and high strength make 4130 popular.

According to official rules, "All welded intersections should be stress relieved by flame annealing. Welds must be high quality with good penetration and no undercutting of the parent metal. No oxy-acetylene brazing on roll cage tubing is permissible. No square tubing is permitted. Use of other materials is subject to prior HDRA/SCORE approval."

Along with these minimum material standards, HDRA/SCORE has strict construction guidelines. The cage must mount securely to the frame or body. All intersection points must have gussets and bracing.

Officially, "Cab or body mounted cages must not be attached to the body structure by direct welding, but must be bolted through and attached by the use of doubler plates (one on either side) with a minimum thickness of 3/16"...Roll cage terminal ends must be located to a frame or body structure that will support maximum impact and not shear...."

The required tubing sizes apply to front and rear hoops, front and rear hoop interconnecting bars, rear down braces and all lateral bracing. Minimum bolt size for any attachments is 3/8", with Grade 5 or better strength. A minimum requirement for HDRA/SCORE racing is a roll cage with one front hoop, one rear hoop, two interconnecting top bars between the hoops, two rear down braces and one diagonal brace.

> **NOTE —**
> Gussets are mandatory at all welded intersections on the main cage and down braces. Fabricators must also use gussets at any single weld where a fracture could affect driver safety.

Triangular gussets at the top corners may be halves of a 3" x 3" x 1/8" flat plate. Another approach is split, formed and welded corner tubing, or tubing gussets the same thickness as the main cage material. When making the rear down braces and diagonal bracing, the angle cannot be less than 30 degrees from a vertical plane.

HDRA/SCORE rules provide another valuable insight. If a race truck has no steel doors to protect the driver and co-driver, side bars are mandatory. A minimum of one bar per side, as near parallel with the ground as possible, must provide protection yet allow the driver and co-driver (i.e., passenger) to get in and out of the vehicle quickly.

The side bars, formed from the same tubing as the roll cage, must attach to the front and rear hoops of the cage. Gussets and other such braces are also necessary. Sure, it might be tougher to crawl in and out of such a truck, but if rocky terrain or high speed in the desert is part of your game plan, the added protection could prevent severe injury in a rollover or T-bone accident.

Racing rules also state that the roll cage bars must be at least 3" in any direction from the driver's or co-driver's helmets while in their normal driving or riding positions. Poorly constructed cages have many back country four-wheelers knocking themselves silly against their roll bars. For off-pavement driving, bar padding is a must.

In addition to the roll cage requirements, HDRA/SCORE requires head and neck restraints to minimize whiplash. The restraint is usually 36 square-inches with at least 2" of padding. Rules also call for padding at all areas of the roll bar or bracing that the occupants' helmets might reach. For an off-pavement or race truck, full padding of the whole interior cage is practical.

Practical Alternatives

Few drivers will ever experience a rollover at high speed or the catastrophic impact forces that regularly threaten desert racers. For reasonable use, short of a racing-specification cage, manufactured cab cage systems will often suffice. Better manufactured kits have the advantage of pre-fabricated pieces, with all necessary bends in place. Manufacturers like Smittybilt and Hobrecht work hard to assure proper fitup and ease of installation.

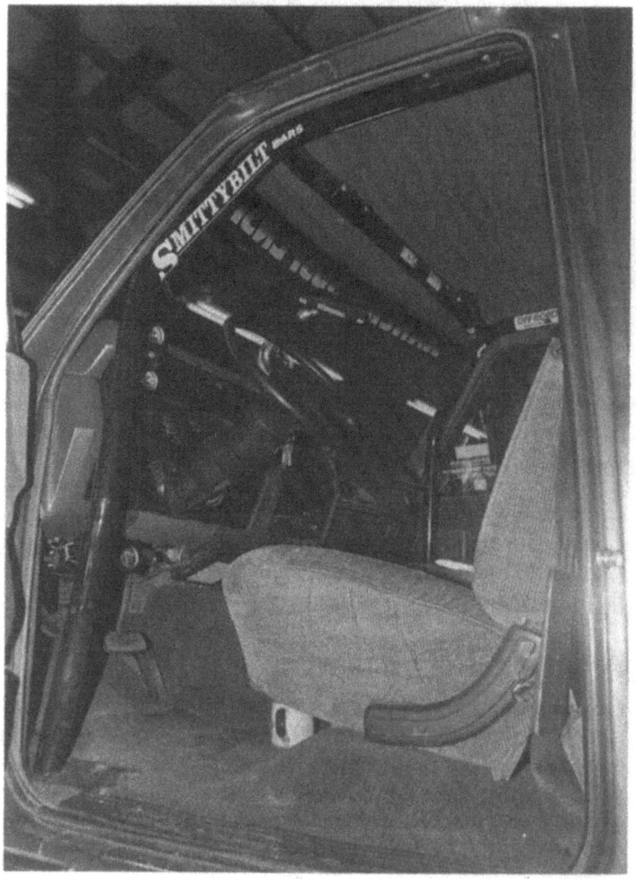

0012651

Fig. 15-28. Cab cages like the one in this 4x4 pickup truck can serve well in a crisis. Smittybilt kit makes installation easier, with minimal amount of assembly time. Carpet and seat removal are part of the installation.

While HDRA/SCORE standards assure maximum protection, less elaborate designs can serve most off-highway situations. At lower speeds, especially while rock crawling, a rollover is generally the less extreme matter of slowly laying a truck on its side. Here, a quality roll cage with side protection, proper seat mounts and secure belts will meet most needs.

> *WARNING —*
> *An often overlooked issue is flying objects, like tool boxes, metal jacks and jack handles, which can become lethal weapons during a rollover. A bolted down and latched or locking box to contain these pieces is a very important off-pavement accessory.*

4. Seat Belts and Safety Harnesses

Rough terrain driving means odd angles and plenty of bounce. Vehicles can roll over, even at a snail's pace. With very few exceptions, an occupant is safest when securely seat belted within the truck.

If, however, your truck faces a situation like rolling off the edge of a ledge above a steep cliff or into a deep and swift running body of water, consider getting out. (The same rule applies if you might be crushed or impaled by an object in your path as the truck heads for a very low speed rollover.)

> *WARNING —*
> *Faced with such a foreboding choice, be sure to exit your truck as safely as possible, at the point furthest away from the hazard. Avoid being crushed or trapped by your vehicle as it rolls over. Use extreme caution if you choose to jump from the vehicle. This is always a tough call to make—and on extremely short notice.*

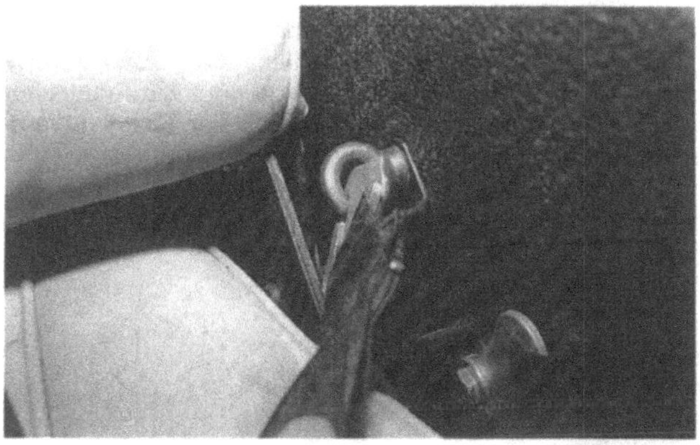

0012653

Fig. 15-29. *Grade 8 or better quality hardware, including this eye loop anchor from Filler Safety, assures strong seat belt and harness attachments. A 3" square reinforcement plate backs up sheet metal where harness tail strap attaches.*

0012652

Fig. 15-30. *Factory seat belt anchors are quality attachment points for lap belts. OE engineering accounts for high strength and proper angles.*

Beyond these kinds of situations, you're better off seat belted within the protection of your cab and, optimally, a roll cage. That's why you have one.

Racing Harnesses

HDRA/SCORE racing standards provide an excellent yardstick for measuring seat belt and harness quality. The minimum standard for racing is a five-point fast release seat belt and shoulder harness assembly. Buckles must be metal-to-metal, with the single anti-submarine strap attached "as close to the front edge of the seat as practical so that it will exert maximum restraint to the upward movement of the belt and harness."

Seat lap belts are 3" width, the submarine belt 2", and shoulder straps must be 2" to 3". Harness materials must be Nylon or Dacron Polyester and in new or perfect condition with no cuts or frayed layers, chemical stains or excessive dirt.

HDRA/SCORE recommends that belts be changed after one year of use. They *must* be changed three years from the date of manufacture. The mounting position of the shoulder harnesses is approximately 4" below the top of the driver's and co-driver's shoulders. This issue is critical, as severe injury can result from poorly positioned belt anchor points.

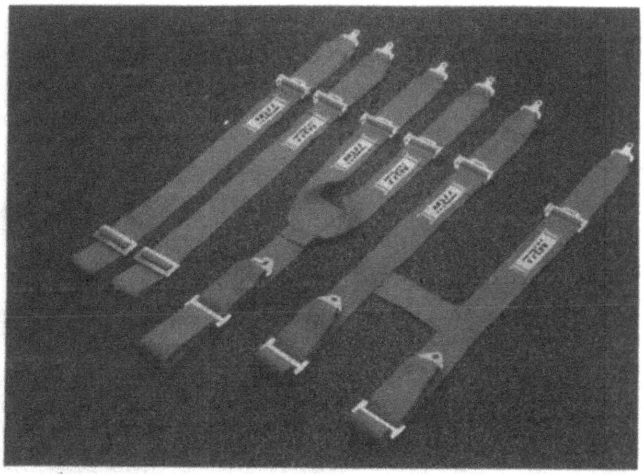

0012654

Fig. 15-31. *TRW shoulder harnesses demonstrate two popular styles: H and Y types. TRW is popular in off-road and other forms of sanctioned racing.*

By HDRA/SCORE guidelines, "Lap belts should be kept at a minimum at least 2-1/2" forward of seat and backrest intersection. All belts must be mounted directly to a main structure member with the strength at least 1-1/2" x 0.090" tubing with gussets." HDRA/SCORE also recommends keeping adjustment buckles a minimum distance of 1-1/2" from the seat to prevent accidental loosening or chafing.

Avoid Submarining

Submarining is your body sliding beneath the lap belt during a frontal impact. In desert racing, submarining also occurs when a truck or buggy flies over a rise and lands nose first in a silt bed or the edge of a streambed.

Spinal and head injuries can result from submarining. By sliding down into the seat, the body's alignment during the recoil-phase (when the body slams rearward after impact) is awkward. Your head may hit the space between the headrest and seat back, causing severe neck injury.

A series of factors cause submarining: poor design of the safety-belt, bad location of the belt's attachment points and the wrong seat configuration.

Many shoulder belt designs actually pull the lap belt up during a collision. Schroth, a major producer of rally and racing seat belts, discovered that evenly distributed loads on the shoulder belts were more likely to pull the lap belt up and cause submarining.

As a remedy, Schroth's ASM (AntiSubMarining) system is designed to allow one shoulder belt to readjust very slightly on impact, turning the body a few degrees. The slight shift in body position causes the lower body to press into the lap belt earlier (approximately 20 milliseconds sooner). This tiny delay before the shoulder belts begin to pull is just enough time to tighten against the lap belt.

Using a precalculated energy change also cushions head and shoulder force as the belts begin to tighten. An additional benefit, Schroth notes, is that the design prevents hard pressure on the sternum and breastbone.

WARNING —
Like all other seat belts or harnesses, once the ASM shoulder belts have experienced a heavy frontal impact shift (enough to lengthen the belt), they require replacement.

Filler Safety Products, very popular with racers, also stresses the importance of proper seat belt mounting. On 5- and 6-point harnesses, Filler recommends that lap belts angle 45 to 55 degrees to the tangent line of the thigh. Filler shoulder harness tailstraps require a 45° angle from the seat top, tying to a roll bar cross brace 4-inches below the shoulder line.

The lap belt anchors 2" forward of the point where the driver's back line and the floor intersect, or 2-1/2" forward of the intersect point of the seat and backrest. Belts should attach to the floor at the same width as the occupant, with brackets aimed in the direction of belt pull. The crotch strap should anchor in line with the driver's chest. Filler's guidelines comply with HDRA/SCORE rules.

Engineers work continuously to improve seat belt and roll bar systems. Light truck and four-wheel drive users have a lot to gain from that effort. If you and your truck have an appetite for the rough stuff, give yourself a fighting chance.

5. TRAILERING

My trailering experience includes two- and four-wheel drive light trucks and 4WD SUVs. (I once pulled a tandem axle travel trailer with a 90-inch wheelbase 4x4 utility model.) In my experience, trucks and SUVs with a wheelbase shorter than 110 inches are poor candidates for pulling a sizable trailer. For towing stability, I always choose a hefty, long wheelbase truck chassis.

0014303

Fig. 15-32. *Arden Rogers' 1976 K-20 Chevrolet 4x4 has factory and aftermarket equipment that serves trailer pulling demands. Hauling and trailering require special accessories and upgrades.*

As a rule, short wheelbase vehicles don't track well in front of long framed trailers. Even without a trailer, a short wheelbase vehicle can be a handful on ice, slick pavement or when turning at excess speed.

The shorter the wheelbase, the tighter the turning radius, though, and that's where some mini/compact 4x4 pickups and sport utility (SUV) models reign. These shorty SUVs and light 4x4 trucks are often ideal for a tight, twisty off-pavement trail. Once such a vehicle crosses up or skids sideways on a firm roadway surface, however, they're in big trouble.

> *WARNING* —
> *When a short wheelbase truck starts to skid, with steering way out of control, directional stability has already been lost. Events will happen very quickly with a shorter wheelbase and frame. A full spinout or rollover is possible.*

When towing a trailer, steering control is the main drawback for a shorter wheelbase vehicle. Trucks under 110-inch wheelbase have insufficient frame length for absorbing the side sway and whip of a trailer. Additionally, a lightweight truck chassis is easily overrun by a bigger trailer during braking.

A truck's higher center of gravity adds to the short wheelbase problem, making risk of a rollover even greater with a trailer out of control. A two-ton load pushing at the rear bumper centerline of a light duty, short wheelbase truck will tax both the vehicle's design and intent.

For the truck better suited to towing, a set of beefier springs, heavy duty shock absorbers, sway controls and an increased tread width can help add stability. A wider-than-stock tread width, accomplished with appropriate wheel rims and oversized tires, can improve the vehicle's directional control. (See suspension/chassis upgrade chapter for details about wheels and tires.)

0012655

Fig. 15-33. *Drawtite equalizer and EAZ-Lift Sway Control provide ingenious means for stabilizing a trailer in tow. The trailer and truck chassis move in unison, offsetting road forces while distributing the load.*

0012657

Fig. 15-34. *A Class III fabricated hitch rates strong enough for a 5,000-lb. tow load. These hitches accommodate Warn and Ramsey portable winches. Similar hitches are available from your local GM truck dealership or most RV outlets.*

Stable Hitch Assemblies and Equalizers

Equalizers have revolutionized trailer towing. An equalizer is the ultimate torsion bar suspension system, designed to neutralize chassis load on the tow vehicle.

The equalizer looks inconspicuous enough, basically two unassuming bars that trail rearward from the truck hitch's ball mount. They swing in their hitch mounting sockets, attached by link chains to brackets that mount on the trailer frame. The adjusting links of the chain are significant, actually loading tension between the truck's hitch and the trailer frame.

The theory is ingenious. As you load the bars, the tongue weight that would otherwise push downward at the rear of the truck becomes "equalized" by the torsion bar tension. When properly adjusted, the trailer's weight becomes distributed over the entire length (each of the axles' spring sets) of both the trailer and truck frames. Incredibly, your truck can set almost exactly at its unloaded ball height with a thirty-foot travel trailer attached.

Now visualize pulling such a trailer without the equalizer. Imagine hard braking with a 3,500-lb. trailer rocking forward. Consider the interaction between the two chassis when your truck encounters dips. Picture the truck loaded with additional gear in the back, its front tires too light to steer and the rear springs slamming against the bump stops.

The equalizer apparatus attacks each of these problems, allowing the truck and trailer chassis to move together. These torsion bars aren't just responsible for balancing the load, they also exert a counterforce as they flex.

An equalizer assembly works effectively to counter uncontrolled chassis movement. With an equalizer hitch assembly, the truck and trailer frames can move closely together on nearly the same plane.

Sturdy Hitches

Pre-fabricated trailer hitches are available for all popular light truck models. Your local GM truck dealership or a trailering/RV center can supply a bolt-on assembly that

Fig. 15-35. *This platform hitch rates 10,000 pounds only when used with a weight distributing (or equalizing) hitch. For serious trailer loads, you should use an equalizing hitch and frame-mounted platform.*

Fig. 15-36. *Hefty Drawtite receiver ball mount adjusts horizontally and also for tilt angle. Massive sockets for equalizer torsion bars can be seen here. The welded miniature ball bracket holds a sway control ball head. Sway control and equalizer assemblies make the whole package work. Without these devices, a light truck and trailer could wind up in serious trouble.*

meets a wide range of needs and load ratings. In some cases, however, a custom hitch will better suit your trailer or the truck's needs.

A capable shop can build the right hitch for your truck. When choosing a custom trailer hitch, look carefully. You want a well-equipped shop, with all the necessary tools, welding apparatus, and quality steel for building a good hitch.

The highest grade steel, 1/4" thick, should be used for braces and gussets. two inch square, 0.188" wall thickness rectangular tubing is best for the hitch framework. To prevent stresses inherent to heat-and-bend methods, tubing bends should be made on a press. Likewise, all construction welds and actual frame attachment welds should follow rigid standards for reducing heat stress to frame members and other vital parts.

Trucks and 4x4s used off-pavement occasionally bury their rear bumpers in the dirt. For this reason, a receiver-type hitch, tucked in close to the rear frame member, works well.

Big League Trailering

If a 1,500-pound or larger trailer fits your vacation or utility needs, consider towing with a GM truck of 114" or longer wheelbase. (I prefer the 127-inch or longer 3/4-ton or larger Suburban or full-size truck wheelbases.) The strikes against shorter wheelbase models are not only the wheelbase but also their lighter duty braking capacity, weaker axle sizing and lower spring rates.

Good trailer brakes, a frame-mounted Class III or better hitch and an equalizer (load distributing) assembly can help bring your truck and trailer to a quick, straight stop. Add a sway control (basically a friction brake mounted between the trailer tongue and hitch) to reduce the effects of cross winds and whip on curvy roads. Most trailer whip can be controlled with a matched equalizer assembly and sway control.

You can remove the detachable ball mount assembly when the trailer is not in use. This will reduce rear departure angle hang ups and also discourage theft of expensive pieces. Use of a pin-and-clip disconnect on the ball mount, with a nut welded to the side of the receiver to accept an anti-rattle bolt, provides for quick installation and removal of the ball mount.

Years ago, when doing a magazine assignment on trailer hitches, I met Rick Preston, owner of Rick's R.V. Center and Hitch Shop at El Cajon, California. Rick is one of the best hitch fabricators around, an experienced and innovative designer of custom built towing hitches.

When Rick's crew builds a custom hitch, they often incorporate two rearward facing side gussets, triangular in shape. Safety chain-holed plates brace the receiver. The trailer's safety chains, which can route through the hitch and index with chain slots, help meet mandated safety requirements.

Final fitup includes strategically placed welds for the frame mounts, then installation of cross-bracing and support. (Added braces can raise the class rating of the hitch.) A trailer electrical connector bracket and glossy black engine enamel complete the job.

Before towing any trailer with your truck, get an expert opinion about the vehicle's towing equipment. Shops like Rick's R.V. Center know the requirements and can quickly identify unsafe hitches.

Chapter 16

GM Engine Performance: From Trail to Track

1. Engine Performance and Smog Legal Modifications

The United States Clean Air Act of 1990 was a watershed measure to curb environmental pollution. "This landmark bill will result in deep and lasting reductions in acid rain, of toxic industrial air pollutants and urban smog," President George Bush noted. "It also will limit U.S. greenhouse gas emissions and sharply reduce our potential contribution to climate change."

The President expressed this nation's commitment to protect the environment and added, "While national governments have an important role to play, progress in protecting our environment is also made community by community, street by street, person by person." Targeting engine modifications that defeat pollution controls, the U.S. Environmental Protection Agency (EPA) has given aftermarket performance manufacturers a higher level of accountability. Product disclaimers that read "off-highway use only" are no longer enough.

The Message Is Clear

The California Air Resources Board and the U.S. EPA mean business. Cars and trucks manufactured and licensed for public road use must comply with clean air standards and emission control guidelines.

0014305

Fig. 16-1. Performance has a long history among GM truck owners. This vintage model boasts a radically built 235 inline six. The Bow-Tie has meant "power" since the advent of the stovebolt and GMC's Jimmy inline OHV sixes.

An EPA letter addressed to automotive parts manufacturers, distributors, retailers and installers clarifies the amended government policy: "The Clean Air Act now prohibits any person from manufacturing, selling, offering for sale, or installing any part or component intended for use with, or as part of, any motor vehicle, where a principal effect of the part or component is to bypass, defeat, or render inoperative any device or element of design, and where the person knows or should know the part or component is being put to such use."

As an example, the letter notes, "...EPA has determined that a catalytic converter replacement pipe, also known as a test pipe, is a part or component intended for use with a motor vehicle for which a principal effect is to bypass, defeat, or render inoperative a vehicle's catalytic converter...EPA believes it is illegal for any person to manufacture, sell, offer for sale or install a catalytic converter replacement pipe...The penalty for violations is up to $2500 for each such device which is manufactured, sold, offered for sale or installed on a motor vehicle."

Ignorance is no excuse. Simply saying that the pipe cannot be used on pollution controlled vehicles won't satisfy the law. The manufacturer of such a device must now take full responsibility for the actual use of the product. The EPA warns, "We intend to focus our enforcement efforts not only on the manufacturers of these defeat devices, but also on auto parts houses and repair facilities who stock, sell or install such devices."

Taboos under The Law

How does this new policy affect your GM truck? Using the catalytic converter as an example, you cannot remove the converter for off-road driving. According to the EPA, "The federal tampering prohibition pertains to motor vehicles, which are defined by section 216(2) of the Act as 'any self-propelled vehicle[s] designed for transporting persons or property on a street or highway.' "

The EPA emphasizes that in each model year, vehicle manufacturers certify engine-chassis configurations to meet certain tailpipe emission standards. Under the 1990 mandates, "...it is not legal for anyone to de-certify a motor vehicle for off-road use." This means that General Motors Corporation has certified your vehicle model. You cannot compromise any part of your truck's pollution control system.

This same law says that swapping an earlier non-catalyst engine into a later, catalytic-equipped chassis is illegal. The chassis still requires the use of a catalytic converter, and the engine must be either the same year or newer than your GM truck. Shops are now held accountable for knowing whether a vehicle originally required a catalytic converter.

Importantly, a muffler shop cannot install a non-certified (termed "non-exempt" in California) dual exhaust system in place of a single exhaust system—even if the shop installs dual catalytic mufflers. If your truck was originally a single exhaust model, certified by General Motors in that mode, the new EPA law restricts any kind of non-certified modification by a muffler shop.

So strong is this ruling that the only current exception is a vehicle already converted to dual exhausts with double catalytic converters. Although the EPA encourages a shop to retrofit an OEM style single exhaust system in such cases, the agency currently allows shops to install replacement catalytic converters and pipes on a previously retrofit dual exhaust system. The shop must be able to prove, however, that they did not replace the OEM single system with a dual exhaust setup.

Catalytic converter rulings are just the beginning. EPA has adopted California's standards for exemption or certification of aftermarket engine parts. Components that the California Air Resources Board (CARB) finds acceptable also earn a federal stamp of approval. An Executive Order (EO number) from California indicates that an aftermarket part has undergone the testing necessary to meet or exceed OEM tailpipe emission standards.

Legally Exempted Components

Before you limit the utility of your smog-compliance GM truck, consider the legal alternatives. The EPA and CARB each approve (exempt) many engine components that meet clean air requirements. There are also legally recognized components that have no impact whatsoever on tailpipe emissions. A high output water pump, an improved cooling system, a high capacity charging circuit or chrome valve covers will not fail the emissions test.

Equally important, engine rebuilding can legally include many upgrade parts that will increase the reliability of your engine. Components like stronger pushrods, hardened exhaust valve seats, better bearings, improved piston rings, quality (stock compression ratio) pistons and a heavy duty timing chain have no effect on tailpipe emissions.

The point here is tailpipe emissions. Changing the camshaft to a long duration grind for maximum mid-range and top end power is a sure way to raise measurable hydrocarbon and carbon monoxide output at lower engine speeds. (California-type biennial smog inspection tests traditionally have taken place at an idle and 2500 rpm.) Likewise, a non-approved high performance retrofit carburetor could raise your truck's tailpipe emissions.

NOTE —
A non-approved replacement carburetor will immediately fail the visual portion of the California-standard smog inspection test.

Many aftermarket manufacturers have taken their components through the California emission certification process. Some performance items qualify as OEM replacement parts. Most of Edelbrock's Performer dual-plane manifolds, for example, provide a mount for the EGR valve.

Although these Edelbrock manifolds improve flow and engine efficiency, they will not increase tailpipe pollution. Several exhaust header and ignition component manufacturers have also passed the CARB tests and received executive order (EO) exemption numbers for their products.

For electronic fuel injected and turbocharged engines, a variety of aftermarket improvements in air flow and induction tuning parts have met certification standards. If a part has an official California exemption number for use on your specific engine, you can install these parts without violating the law.

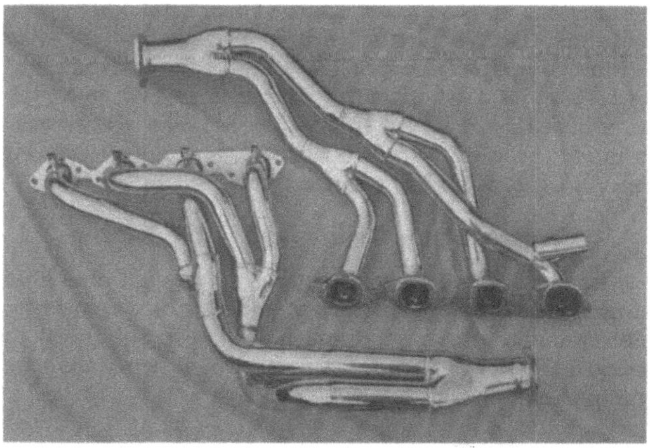

0014311

Fig. 16-2. For a 454 powered, multi-purpose light GM truck or tow vehicle, Doug Thorley's street/emission legal Tri-Y type headers contribute to a low restriction, highly efficient dual exhaust system. 2-1/4-inch exhaust piping from the header collectors rearward also improves performance.

0014213

Fig. 16-3. This Accel HEI Super Coil (on top of distributor) has a California EO number. Decal installed above distributor allows smog inspection at any Smog Chek station. If you upgrade your ignition, stick with emission legal parts.

Clean Air High Performance

Under the amended Clean Air Act of 1991, aftermarket manufacturers must certify any induction system component, ignition system piece, performance camshaft or exhaust device that differs from the OEM design or engineering standards. Additionally, each state has statutes or regulations that prohibit defeating or tampering with the pollution control equipment on a certified motor vehicle. The EPA emphasizes, "Vehicle owners who tamper with their own vehicles may be subject to substantial penalties under both federal and State law."

These laws, however, encourage lower tailpipe emissions. For this reason, California has no objection to replacing the carbureted 305 V-8 in your 1980 K-5 Blazer chassis with a late model Chevrolet TBI or even TPI 350 V-8. Despite the increase in horsepower and torque, the tailpipe pollution from a late EFI engine is a fraction of that allowed for a 1980 vehicle.

NOTE —
A late EFI conversion engine must include its OEM computer and all factory engine sensors. You must swap all parts that make up the OEM engine/emissions package.

Buy Legal Performance

A wide range of aftermarket parts have California EO exemptions ("50-State legal" status). An exemption means the part will not defeat the design or intent of your engine's emission control system.

When you find EO exempted parts, make sure that pieces have approval for use on your particular year and model engine. Some parts might fit your engine but still do not meet the emission requirements. EO exemptions apply to a specific year/model, chassis type and engine application. There are a variety of devices that have EO numbers. Currently, the EPA accepts CARB tests and exemption criteria. Parts that have California exemption status also meet Federal/EPA standards.

NOTE —
A complete list of California exempted components is available from the California Air Resources Board or local motor vehicle emissions testing stations throughout the State of California.

A Bright Future

Improvements in engine technology mean more likelihood of swapping late EFI engines into earlier GM truck chassis. Electronic fuel injection overcomes sidehill flooding and the negative effects of altitude. Also, without exception, later EFI engines have lower tailpipe emissions and potentially better fuel efficiency than earlier carbureted versions of these same engine designs.

California has provided a referee program for smog certification of vehicles with engine conversions. Referees determine whether you have made a complete conversion, including all necessary emission equipment.

NOTE —
Tailpipe emissions from your new, upgraded engine must not exceed those of the original GM truck engine in good operating condition. For details, contact the California Consumer Affairs Department for referral to your local Bureau of Automotive Repairs referee station.

Imagine the performance of a late 350 TBI V-8 with an aftermarket Whipple/Sprintex, Paxton or Vortech (50-State legal) supercharger—in place of the 307 V-8 in a 1971 Chevrolet or GMC pickup. How about a stout late model 454 TBI/EFI V-8 engine in place of a 1980 350 carbureted V-8 smog motor in a 4x4 Camper Special model? Your earlier GM truck would gain both torque and fuel efficiency, yet produce far less tailpipe pollution.

Aftermarket manufacturers have responded to the EPA requirements. Crane Cams has tested and received California Air Resources Board EO numbers for several camshaft profiles. Crane camshafts with EO numbers have 50-State legal status when used in specific engines. Gene Ezzell, President and CEO at Crane Cams, credits the Specialty Equipment Market Association (SEMA) for encouraging the aftermarket to build California/EPA legal products. SEMA's effort helps assure the stability and future of the automotive performance aftermarket.

As an active supporter of TREAD LIGHTLY! and the Clean Air Act standards, I encourage you to protect the environment. Use those aftermarket performance parts with California EO numbers or EPA/50-States Legal status. At the very least, make sure that your truck is emission legal.

2. Bow-Tie and Jimmy Power: An Overview

Building a truck engine strictly for horsepower, a valid goal for desert racing, may actually inhibit low speed torque output and diminish trail running and rock crawling ability. Careful planning and selection of components can give your engine more usable torque, better breathing characteristics and greater stamina for tortuous off-pavement lugging and climbs.

CAUTION —

- *Many engine modifications are illegal for street or public highway use. If your truck must comply with vehicle registration and public highway requirements, make certain that aftermarket parts have California and federal EPA approval. It is illegal to remove, modify or degrade pollution control devices on vehicles licensed for use on public highways.*

- *When making major engine modifications, the rest of the truck's powertrain must be able to withstand the added torque. A light duty transmission, transfer case and drive axle(s) often fail when subjected to great increases in horsepower. Beware. You may need a host of geartrain modifications.*

High Performance Begins with the Valvetrain

The typical valve-in-head (OHV) engine's valvetrain consists of the camshaft, camshaft followers (lifters), pushrods, rocker arms, valve springs and valves.

On all 1939–up OHV GM light truck engines, the valves and springs fit in a removable cylinder head. Camshaft followers or lifters ride on lobes of the camshaft. Pushrods link the lifters to the rocker arms, which pivot and press against the valve stem ends. The intake and exhaust valves open and close the ports, allowing gases to enter and leave each cylinder.

The camshaft has an important job. Lobes, carefully shaped to open and close the valves at precise times, rotate at one-half the speed of the crankshaft. Each two turns of the crankshaft, the camshaft will open and close each valve, doing so for the entire service life of the engine.

Tension between a camshaft lobe and the lifter's convex base is the highest pounds-per-square-inch load within your truck's engine. Hardness of the camshaft material and its compatibility with the lifter will affect the overall reliability of the engine. The severity of lobe contours or "profiles" also dictates the degree of stress placed upon pushrods, rocker arms and valve springs.

Camshaft Lobe Profiles and Valve Timing

Each truck engine type requires a camshaft of unique dimensions. Lobe profiles vary, and careful engineering determines the correct shape from low point (heel) to peak lift. Lifter design limitations also influence the lobe ramp shape.

CAUTION —
Radically tall lobe contours increase stress and wear between the lobe and the lifter base. Very tall valve lift requires roller lifters, special valve springs and other valvetrain upgrades. (See camshaft manufacturer's recommendations.)

The three basic elements in camshaft design are the total valve lift (over the full range of lifter movement), valve opening duration (the number of crankshaft degrees that the valve stays open) and valve timing (essentially the opening and closing points for the valves). The correct replacement camshaft will have proper valve lift and opening duration with the right valve timing.

Selecting Your Camshaft

Some general rules apply when meeting off-pavement and heavy duty pulling chores. For general four-wheeling and trailer towing, your engine will operate over a broad rpm range, needing power from just off idle to at least 4000 rpm. Here, the long duration performance-street camshaft is incorrect, as valve timing has excessive overlap.

Valve overlap is the exhaust valve still closing while the intake valve has already begun to open. Excess valve overlap creates two fundamental problems for an off-pavement 4x4 or towing engine: 1) rough idle and poor low speed throttle response, and 2) low manifold vacuum at slower engine rpm.

Manifold vacuum is crucial to truck pulling power, proper combustion, and fuel economy. In effect, an automotive gasoline engine is a vacuum pump. Your truck engine's operating cycle begins with the vacuum characteristics of the intake stroke.

If you plan serious rock crawling and trailer pulling, or want low speed economy and good throttle response, high manifold vacuum will be on top of your priority list. Especially at higher altitudes, engine breathing depends upon efficient manifold vacuum.

NOTE —
Before considering a camshaft change, assess your engine's overall condition. Check the carburetor, hunt down vacuum leaks, measure compression and analyze the ignition timing and spark. Confirm the manifold vacuum. These are each areas where good performance is won or lost.

Off-pavement and Towing Camshaft Profiles

The back country truck engine needs a camshaft that works well at highway cruising speeds (generally 2000 to 3000 engine rpm) and still can crawl through your favorite rockpile. Likewise, a truck that tows a trailer or carries heavy loads will require strong low speed performance and low- to mid-range strength.

If light duty use, highway cruising, occasional trailer pulling and modestly good fuel economy are your goals, a camshaft close to the OEM specs will likely work fine. The formula for hardcore off-pavement or trailering success, however, requires more low-rpm torque response and a relatively low speed horsepower peak. This typically requires more valve lift than many OE truck camshafts provide.

Most early camshaft grinds were much the same as passenger car profiles. The last decade of engine/camshaft development has produced higher torque and more horsepower at lower engine rpm. This is a substantial improvement.

Controllable power in an off-idle rock crawl situation relies more on torque than horsepower. (Good low speed torque is often the product of increased valve lift and a mild valve opening duration.) As lugging the engine can prevent wheelspin, the engine must have good low-end torque at very light or tip-in throttle. (For driving details, see the chapter on operating your truck.)

Traditionally, gasoline engines have realized their full horsepower potential in the mid- to top-end rpm range, speeds upward of 3600 rpm. However, when your truck's tires need a solid grip and rock shale threatens the sidewalls, running the engine at 3600 or more rpm is not only unsafe but also abusive to the engine, geartrain and environment.

Low rpm control requires immediate off-idle torque, the product of healthy valve lift. I always use manifold vacuum as a guide for selecting a utility truck camshaft, looking for a grind capable of delivering at least 16 (preferably 18 or more) inches of manifold vacuum at an idle.

Such an RV, trailer towing or economy camshaft grind will work well with milder carburetion or EFI. Four-wheeling and trailer towing always benefit from the strong torque characteristics of a camshaft that delivers good idle and higher manifold vacuum at low speeds.

In general, I look for a camshaft with slightly more valve lift than the OEM profile. (OE specifications are generally available in your OEM truck shop manual.) I stay conservative with both the valve opening duration (total degrees) and valve timing.

Aftermarket Camshaft Options

For high torque within a reasonable rpm range, several camshaft profiles have worked well in GM truck engines. For the 292 cubic inch inline OHV six, a real torque monster with seven-main-bearing crankshaft support and a healthy stroke, it's easy to extract serious stump pulling power.

For the 250/292 inline truck sixes, a hydraulic cam of approximately .444" gross lift and 264° duration will work well. Assuming that your Chevrolet or GMC six has a reasonable compression ratio (around 9.2:1 or less), the idle with this kind of camshaft is smooth, and your engine can develop usable low-end torque and respectable mid-range (2000 to 3500 rpm) horsepower. Expect this type of camshaft's power curve to drop abruptly above 4500 rpm.

If towing or heavy cargo power is desirable, consider an RV type camshaft with good lift and a mild valve opening duration. For GM light truck gas V-8s, I like Competition Cams' 252H grind for an automatic transmission application or the 260H grind when using a manual transmission and lower (numerically higher) axle gearing.

These two camshafts will set a lower ceiling on rpm; however, a non-racing or relatively stock small- or big-block V-8 engine works best to a maximum of 5000 to 5500 rpm anyway. The correct tow vehicle camshaft will peak horsepower between 4000 and 4500 rpm, provide massive low end torque and lugging power, plus offer considerable manifold vacuum at low speeds.

For towing, camper loads and cargo hauling, select a compression ratio between 8.5:1 and 9:1 (preferably 8.5 to 8.7:1). At these compression ratios, your engine will work well with a milder RV camshaft grind. Fuel economy will also benefit, and you can run low octane fuels without harmful detonation. As Chevrolet and Pontiac V-8 (same as 1950s GMC design) racing buffs recall, the highest performance engines tolerate far more valve opening duration and valve lift than an RV camshaft provides. However, in order to make 300 to 460 horsepower, as GM's mammoth Muscle Era engines produced, you need a compression ratio in excess of 10:1. Today's low octane fuel will not support such ratios.

For GM truck carbureted V-8 engines, lift is again useful. Two good overall camshaft profiles that I like for true towing power are Competition Cams' High Energy 252H or 260H types.

The 260H has more multi-purpose and light duty uses and would also satisfy the 305 or 350 builder who wants low (numerically higher) axle gearing. Similarly, the Competition Cams 268H can work well for a 454 big-block trailer puller with low axle gearing, although fuel economy will suffer when compared to the 260H profile.

A 252H and proper gearing will deliver exceptional fuel economy and lugging power. For a relatively stock 350 travel trailer puller, I like this camshaft with 4.10:1 axle gearing and 31-inch diameter tires. The 252H produces great low end torque, high manifold vacuum and good horsepower at cruise rpm. Expect a noticeable power drop above 4200 rpm.

NOTE —
Whenever you upgrade the camshaft, install new lifters and make certain that the valve springs are in top shape. The valve lifts I recommend here are relatively mild, and they only require that your OEM components be in good condition. Install a high quality roller timing chain and sprocket set, and carefully follow the camshaft manufacturer's recommendations for setting camshaft/valve timing.

Camshafts of this type satisfy rock crawling needs, help pull a light trailer and deliver good gas mileage. On a pre-EFI engine, you can use OEM-type carburetion or an improved carburetor with near stock cubic-feet-per-minute (CFM) flow rate.

For carbureted engines, my manifold of choice for a 4200 rpm ceiling and 350 or larger V-8 is either a stock OEM four-barrel design or Edelbrock's Performer dual-plane design. (Most Performer applications are emission legal.) For any Chevrolet V-8, the GM Quadrajet carburetor works well for towing and general all-around use. Edelbrock is now offering Quadrajet-type replacement carburetors by Weber. Holley also makes a Q-jet replacement.

I like several of the GM OEM truck camshafts: the 261 OHV inline six camshaft that fits 1954–62 Chevrolet 235/261 inline sixes; the 283/327/350 V-8 truck camshafts of the pre-emission era; and the 396 and earliest 454 truck (Federal/49-State emissions) camshafts. These will work fine for trailer pulling and overall performance. An aftermarket camshaft grind for any of these engines may enhance their performance but not necessarily improve economy or trailer pulling power. If you rebuild an engine of this type for towing or hauling, consider a stock truck replacement camshaft grind.

Variable Duration Lifters

Few camshafts can satisfy a truck owner's every need. Some cams deliver strong bottom end power but weak performance from 3600 rpm upward. Others offer more mid-range and top-end power while sacrificing crucial idle and low speed power. For some engine designs, the solution is a set of variable duration valve lifters.

Jack Rhoads pioneered such a hydraulic lifter. The Rhoads Lifter bleeds down at low rpm and allows valve lift to drop 0.020" to 0.030" with milder valve opening duration. In essence, the precisely metered bleed down makes several camshaft profiles out of one. Rhoads, Crane and others now offer variable duration lifters for many engine designs.

The reduction in lift and duration creates a tolerable idle and good low speed response, even with a slightly racy camshaft. Using variable duration lifters, a V-8 performance camshaft of 270 (*total*) degrees or more of valve opening duration can work in many truck applications.

Similarly, valve lift can be extended well beyond 0.435". Better low-end torque, reasonable manifold vacuum at low speeds and great mid-range and top-end pow-

Crane's Emission Legal EFI Performance Camshafts

Since the early-1980s, EFI and carbureted high performance engines owe their much improved performance levels to the wizardry of electronic fuel and spark management. Production engines now meet stringent tailpipe emission and fuel economy standards while horsepower has continued to increase.

For nearly a decade, the aftermarket stood patiently aside, waiting for the OEMs to stabilize their EFI technology. When horsepower gains peaked, even with the more efficient roller camshafts, it was clear that a plateau had been reached.

Focus on What You Know Best

At that point, Crane (a prominent camshaft builder since the dawn of OHV V-8 high performance) saw the many attributes of factory computer technology. Rather than pursue computer modifications, like other aftermarket performance researchers, Crane went after improvements in camshaft valve timing, lift and duration.

Crane believed that camshaft changes could take advantage of factory programmed spark and fuel variables. The OEM computers produced reasonable performance, driveability and fuel economy. Why mess with a good thing? Crane also discovered that the factory computers could compensate for minor camshaft changes.

One of the secrets to Crane's success is the preservation of high manifold vacuum. Manifold pressure sensors, which heavily influence computer decisions, need a strong vacuum signal at engine idle and low speeds. Crane worked with this need, not against it. Instead of overloading the feedback loops with low manifold vacuum readings and overrich signals from the oxygen sensor, Crane designed the cam lobes to provide even more lift and a larger flow area.

Center of the Action

Crane determined that if intake valves lifted from their seats more quickly and seated at a faster rate, valve timing improvements were possible—without a sacrifice in vital manifold vacuum.

Crane tightened the camshaft lobe centerlines. On the average, a Crane CompuCam 2000 profile has a 4° tighter lobe center than the factory camshaft. Coupled with a mild lift increase of around 0.030" at each valve, these Crane camshafts deliver increased low-end to mid-range torque and more horsepower at a higher rpm. The CompuCam also retards the exhaust valve timing slightly, yet holds the exhaust valves open slightly longer. Better exhaust scavenging results.

The intake lobe, meanwhile, advances valve timing very mildly. This usually requires more intake/exhaust lobe center spread, but here the key to this design's success is quick acceleration of the intake valve from its seat. The effective lift and duration give much better performance, yet the computer believes that all is normal. The vacuum and valve timing events continue to deliver the right computer signals. (The OEM shift to roller lifter camshaft profiles pursues a strategy similar to Crane's CompuCam 2000 designs.)

The Target

For the computer car or truck owner unhappy with sluggish acceleration and poor economy, the Crane CompuCam 2000 program could be the fix. CompuCam 2000 is a new breed of tuned valve control that can match the sophistication of factory electronic fuel and spark management. Within their specified design aims, these emission legal camshafts can make a difference.

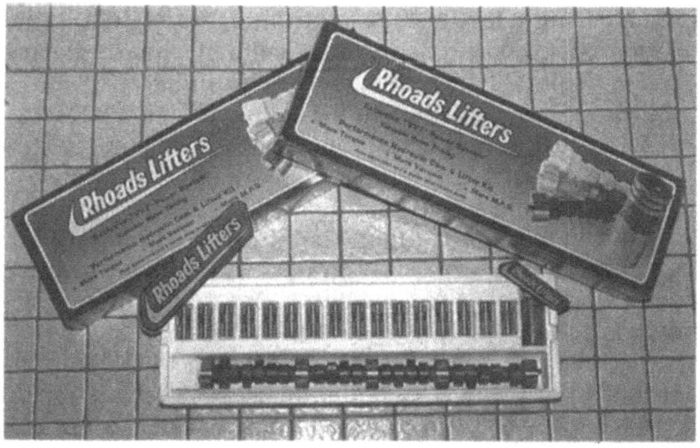

0014326

Fig. 16-4. Rhoads pioneered "variable duration" lifters. A decrease in valve lift and opening duration at idle and lower speeds allows use of a slightly hotter camshaft. Result is good manifold vacuum for the brake booster plus better fuel economy. Warmer camshaft profile takes effect as lifters reach maximum lift/duration near 3500 rpm.

er are all possible from the same camshaft grind. The only downside to variable duration lifters is that they often create more valvetrain noise than stock hydraulic lifters.

Axle Gearing for Your Camshaft

When making a camshaft selection, consider your axle gearing and tire diameter. These two factors determine the cruising rpm and low-speed responsiveness of your truck's engine.

Unless the tire diameter is oversize, very low axle ratios (like 4.27:1 to 5.38:1) will substantially raise the highway cruising rpm. Likewise, mid-1970s and later trucks often have taller axle ratios (3.08:1 to 3.73:1).

Taller axle ratios or oversize tires can drop the truck's highway/cruising rpm range to below 2,000 rpm. This will not work with a mid-range or top-end camshaft grind. You would need a milder camshaft or lower axle gear ratios.

Tall gearing (numerically low) and oversize tires require a camshaft that delivers plenty of low end torque. Forget about 5,000 rpm performance. For a truck with 3.08:1 gearing, 33" diameter tires and a non-overdrive transmission, the engine spins 1,882 rpm in high gear at 60 mph. For the engine that develops peak torque at 3,000 rpm or maximum horsepower around 5,000 rpm, this could impede performance and hamper fuel economy.

By dramatic contrast, a truck with 5.38:1 gears and 30" diameter tires would have the engine spinning 3617 rpm at 60 mph. Making an engine's horsepower available and useful is the primary concern of axle gearing and tire diameter choices. With careful planning, your truck can make substantial performance and fuel economy gains off-pavement or at highway cruise speeds.

Hot and Reliable Ignition Spark

A high performance or working truck engine requires top ignition performance. Spark cannot falter, as a misfire at the wrong moment could prove catastrophic. Battling weather, high altitude, extreme climates, precarious road surfaces and marginal fuel grades, your truck's engine needs a quality ignition system.

An excellent starting point for GM ignitions is the original equipment HEI system that came into the field in 1975. For GM/Delco-Remy HEI and EST era ignitions, the aftermarket offers enhanced ignition coils, complete distributors, rev limiters and interface devices that will not compromise even the latest electronic fuel and spark management systems. For durability and quality assurance, you can build an ignition around these 1975 and newer factory units.

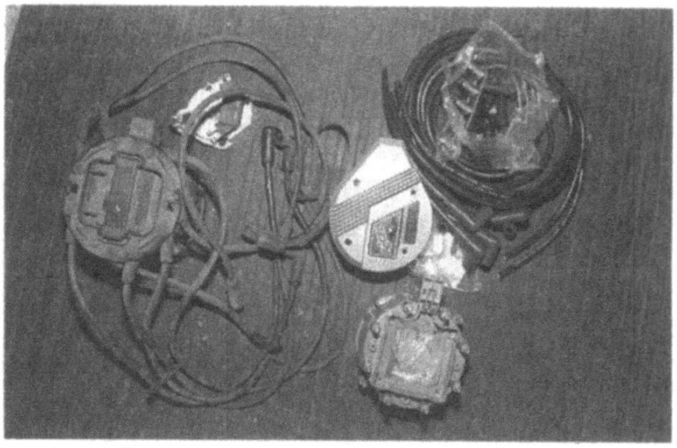

0014207

Fig. 16-5. Factory HEI distributor assemblies can fit all Chevrolet V-6s, V-8s and seven main bearing inline six-cylinder GM engines. Custom drives, advance spring kits, spark cable kits and special distributor caps are available through Chevrolet and a variety of aftermarket sources.

Accel Performance Products also offers a wide range of high performance ignition components. Racing Coils, the Super Coil and HEI intensifier kits are designed to work in conjunction with various OEM GM ignition systems. Super Stock Coils can replace several OEM types.

Electrical accessories, including ballast resistors and coil brackets, round out OE replacement components. Accel is also serious about racing, and a number of all-out performance distributors are available. A 37-Series Dual-Point provides performance to 9,000 rpm. The 43-Series Magnetic NASCAR-developed distributor has an adjustable spark curve, making it useful for many applications. Accel's 44-Series Direct Drive distributor, with rigid timing, ranks well as a sand drag or mud bog ignition.

Accel Crankshaft Trigger Kits for Chevrolet V-8s offer greater spark timing accuracy, while milder needs revolve around the 34-Series Super Stock dual point distributors. Less racing oriented, the 34-Series units offer a vacuum advance option.

Off-pavement truck users find the Accel 41-Series electronic distributor attractive and available in optional vacuum mechanical/vacuum advance form. In an off-road emergency, a common GM HEI module and Chrysler distributor cap can bring your rig home.

Allison, which is now a division of Crane Cams, has a long record of quality ignition products. Popular is the 50-State legal XR-700 electronic ignition conversion for older breaker point ignitions. This system allows use of your stock distributor with all the benefits of an electronic high energy spark. For pre-electronic GM ignitions, the XR-700 kit can upgrade the ignition performance and eliminate breaker points.

Allison claims performance and mileage gains, along with easier starting than the original breaker points. The XR-700 kits are about as simple to install as OEM breaker points. In addition to a lifetime warranty, the XR-700 conversion offers the ideal off-pavement backup system: an OE set of points and condenser. If the electronic parts fail in the field, simply reinstall the OE ignition parts.

Mallory pioneered high performance ignitions. Racing and high performance distributors, coils, electronic conversion kits, modules, rev limiters and much, much more make Mallory a strong choice for your spark needs. The Mallory catalog covers OE replacement upgrades, computer chips and a traditional line of accessories. The popular Unilite breakerless distributors or a Unilite conversion kit provide plenty of dependable spark. Racing dual-point and Unilite units are also popular.

MSD is distinguished by a full line of high quality ignition distributors and all-out racing hardware. Many MSD electronic devices interface with OEM, aftermarket or the complete MSD ignitions. Adjustable timing controls provide more complete combustion and a cure for high altitude and poor fuel grades. Want to compensate for thin air or Mexican gasoline? The MSD timing controls place spark timing at your fingertips.

Performance Distributors provide completely reworked OE-type HEI units that wield a whopping spark. Performance Distributors claim nearly twice the fire of a magneto, reach the 9000 crankshaft rpm range, offer a custom spark curve to meet your exact engine needs and undergo thorough pre-testing before shipment.

Spark Knock Cures

Trailer pulling and hauling heavy loads can stress your truck's engine to its limit. This kind of use boosts cylinder pressures and creates risk. Running hot, at extremely high cylinder pressures, your spark-ignited engine's worst enemy is detonation (premature ignition or rapid burning of volatile fuel). Detonation is far more than an annoying rattle or "ping." If severe enough, detonation can damage pistons, rings, valve faces, and even the crankshaft.

The only reliable means to reduce detonation is to delay the point of fuel ignition. While late (more retarded) spark timing does decrease detonation, it also lowers the engine's horsepower and torque output. Loss of spark advance can translate as sluggish performance and poor fuel economy.

The more advanced engines with fuel and spark management (like the EFI systems in GM trucks) meet low emission standards and also cope with the limitations of low octane fuel by using engine mounted knock sensors. Knock sensors "listen" for spark knock, then retard spark timing for all cylinders until the noise disappears, keeping the engine close to its detonation point for maximum performance.

Aftermarket Knock Fix

Aftermarket devices can now rival or exceed the performance of most OEM systems. I have tested J&S Electronics' device on several engines and can say that this is a significant breakthrough in aftermarket ignition engineering.

The 50-State legal SafeGuard senses spark knock and then seeks out the *individual* culprit cylinder(s). A pre-programmed computer/module reduces spark advance in small increments until detonation just disappears.

As an option, the kit offers a Retard Display monitor that reads the number of spark retard degrees necessary to stop engine ping and piston rattle. The monitor also features an Air/Fuel Ratio Display that interprets signals from an oxygen sensor mounted in the exhaust stream. Various SafeGuard kits can interface with a conventional, fully electronic or even an older breaker point ignition.

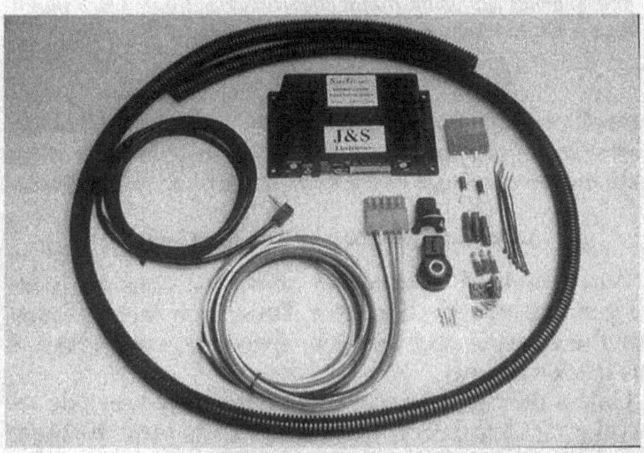

0012673

J&S's SafeGuard device is 50-State legal. Well crafted electronic module provides settings for knock sensitivity plus an adjustable engine rpm limiter. Mode settings can retard either all cylinders simultaneously or just those cylinders that knock.

Included in the kit is a high quality solid-state electronic module, a full wiring harness of high grade wire with molded aircraft quality terminal ends, an OEM style knock sensor for your particular engine application, and easy to follow instructions.

Hook-up requires few tools and only a basic understanding of automotive wiring. My installations, which involve extra care when routing wires and mounting hardware, have taken a maximum of 3-1/2 hours. Drilling and welding for the oxygen sensor plug takes some additional time. The simple sensitivity adjustment, which requires driving your truck under load conditions, takes an extra half hour.

SafeGuard is capable of twenty crankshaft degrees retard per detonating cylinder. Aside from dramatic gains in fuel economy and performance, SafeGuard has a distinct advantage over the typical OEM spark management system. OEM systems pull back on timing for all cylinders just to eliminate the pinging of a few. SafeGuard, by retarding spark for individual cylinders, keeps the other cylinders developing peak performance.

Running 0.050–0.055" recommended spark plug gaps, these new distributors yield tremendous gains from idle through high rpm. A bronze terminal cap and racing coil accompany each distributor. Performance Distributors can rework a popular GM HEI electronic distributor unit to meet your high performance standards or specific needs.

Quadrajet Performance Tuning

Recognized by its spread-bore design, the Rochester Quadrajet ranks as one of the most popular OEM carburetors. From the late-1960s through the 1986 models, nearly all GM light trucks with four-barrel V-8s came with a Quadrajet.

Often overlooked as a high performance item, the Quadrajet has tremendous potential. These carburetors have met the needs of engines ranging from the 231 Buick

0014231

Fig. 16-6. Quadrajet spread-bore design revolutionized four-barrel carburetion. Huge secondary bores, seen here from throttle plate side, allow maximum acceleration and maximum CFM flow on demand. Small primary bores act like a tiny two-barrel for light throttle economy.

0014232

Fig. 16-7. Air valve (arrow) above the secondary throttle plates is vacuum and spring tension operated, and enables smooth transitions onto the secondary circuit. Air/fuel flow in the secondary cannot begin until the air valve opens. This means that manifold vacuum and engine load determine when the engine can receive more air/fuel. Quadrajets are noted for exceptional ability to flow fuel, in direct response to throttle position, manifold vacuum and venturi velocity.

0014235

Fig. 16-8. View down primary throats with choke valve open shows simple air flow during cold starts. Secondaries will not open until the choke unloader moves. This prevents excess air/fuel flow before the engine warms.

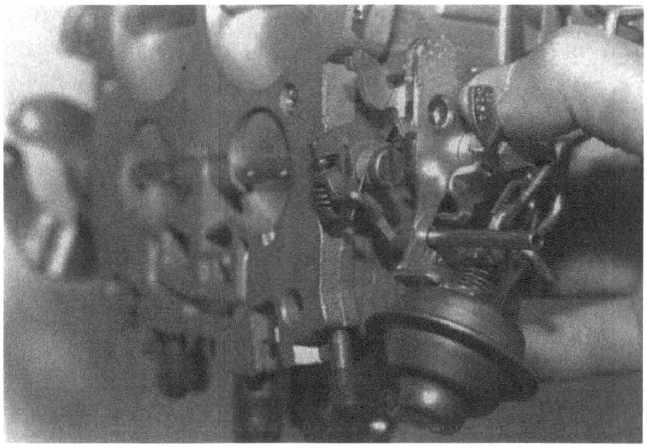

0014236

Fig. 16-9. Vacuum brake unit allows secondary air valve to open under hard acceleration. As manifold vacuum drops, spring pressure in the vacuum brake assembly moves a rod that allows the secondary air valve to open. The throttle plates, opened mechanically by the throttle linkage, allow manifold vacuum to pull the air valve open.

V-6 to 500 cubic inch Cadillacs, with only modest design variations between the applications.

The most striking feature of the original Rochester Quadrajet model was its revolutionary use of two small primary and two large secondary throats. The various Quadrajet carburetors provide a smooth idle and optimal fuel economy at cruise speeds, yet deliver outstanding acceleration and top end performance.

On all but late closed loop computer applications, the separate idle circuit can be adjusted by simply setting the idle mixture screws at the front of the carburetor's throttle body (on those carburetors that provide adjusting screws).

NOTE —

State and Federal emission control laws prevent any carburetor modification that could adversely impact your vehicle's tailpipe emissions.

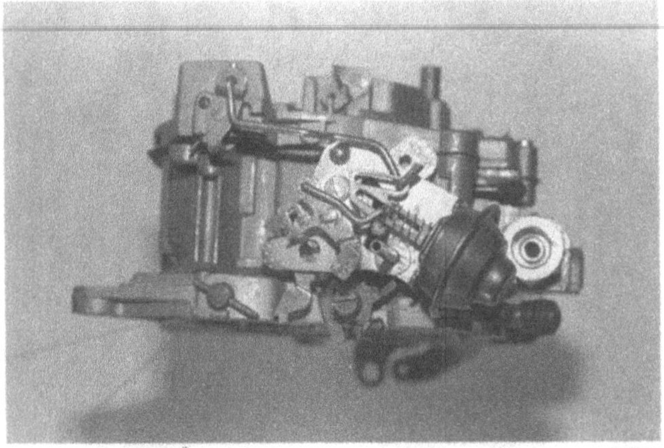

Fig. 16-10. Relationship between vacuum brake assembly and secondary air valve is clear. Choke, choke unloader, fast idle cam and linkage all center here. Correct adjustments are crucial, and each has a trickle down effect.

Fig. 16-11. Both the air valve rod and choke pull-off rod attach to a single vacuum brake plunger on this application. Some Quadrajets use a separate vacuum brake for the choke and air valve damping.

Quadrajet Tuning Options

The use of replaceable primary jets and sized metering rods on each bore means that a basic Quadrajet body can be fitted for a wide range of engine modifications. On modified engines, a properly built Quadrajet can perform as well as most other aftermarket high performance carburetors.

Q-Jet bench stripping is more complex than the popular 4150 or 4160 series Holley four-barrel. However, fine tuning jets and metering rods are available from Rochester/Delco dealers.

> NOTE —
> Since 1978 the EPA has scrutinized the sale of carburetor parts in an effort to prevent pollution control tampering. Unless you can supply a specific carburetor identification, parts may be difficult to buy.

The Quadrajet float, which pivots from the front, is ideal for off-pavement use. This design meets sidehills, steep rises and instant acceleration needs without hesitation. In addition to these fuel bowl advantages, Q-jet throttle bodies and other parts are very durable. Unlike many other carburetor types, a properly staged Quadrajet will hold tune indefinitely.

> NOTE —
> As a basic upgrade, always install an aftermarket brass float in place of the plastic OEM item.

By removing the air horn and float, you can replace the primary main jets or change the metering rods by simply lifting the power piston from its bore.

Once you remove the metering rods, the primary jets can be replaced. Quadrajet secondary metering rods are simple to reach although they seldom require replacement and do not use removable jets.

A Quadrajet's primary fuel circuit depends on the float, idle, main metering, power piston and accelerator pump systems. With each of these systems operating properly, you can fine tune with primary jetting.

The Quadrajet primary main metering system shares a common fuel supply with the secondaries. Most tuning takes place at the primary main jets/rods. The primary jets and metering rods play a crucial role in fuel mixing from off-idle to wide open throttle.

By design, primary main metering rods restrict fuel flow during high manifold vacuum (cruise and light engine loads) and increase fuel flow as heavier throttle demand lowers manifold vacuum. As the power piston's spring tension overcomes the lighter vacuum pull, the primary rods move upward, opening the jet orifices. The power piston and metering rods operate between spring tension and the pull of manifold vacuum.

When an engine runs lean at cruise and under light loads, use of a smaller diameter rod will allow more fuel flow through the jet. This smaller diameter rod can also correct leanness on acceleration. A larger jet size likewise resolves fuel starvation. Each 0.001" jet change also affects full throttle (combined primary and secondary) mixture by approximately one-and-one-half percent.

Blueprinting Your Quadrajet

Before changing primary main metering jets or rods on a Quadrajet, you should strip, clean and "blueprint" the unit during reassembly. Use a comprehensive service guidebook, preferably a GM truck shop manual or professional service manual, that covers your carburetor.

Blueprinting includes adjustments of every linkage and primary/secondary interlink. Once you have checked all settings (linkages, float, accelerator pump stroke, warm idle mixture, etc.), you can consider re-jetting and changing metering rods.

Choosing Primary Main Metering Jets and Rods

Jet changes affect performance in different ways. Lean or rich primary jetting is noticeable just off-idle. Rich jetting affects cruise, light throttle and hard acceleration.

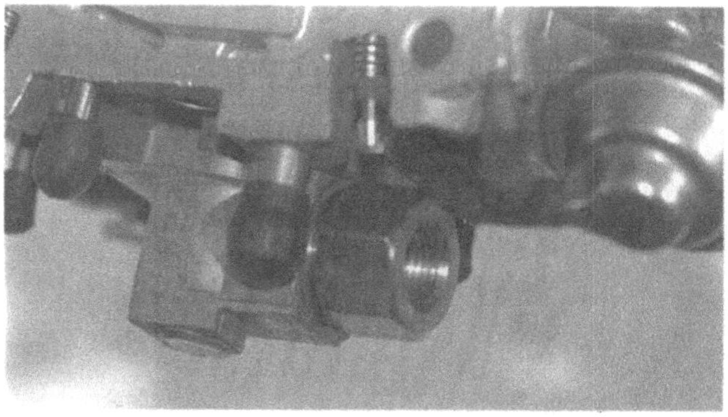

Fig. 16-12. On most Quadrajets and some of the other Rochester carburetor designs, a fuel inlet filter inserts behind this fitting. GM/Rochester carburetor fuel inlet fitting threads are sensitive. Simply removing the fitting can take the threads with it. Heli-Coil makes a high quality repair kit for re-threading the inlet and saving an expensive carburetor body.

For testing, you need enough throttle valve opening to get past the idle circuit. Your goal is to bring the engine to the stage where manifold vacuum and the power piston spring tension begin their balancing act. This usually means 2000 to 2500 rpm, under light load, on flat ground, holding the throttle steady.

A chassis dynamometer with tailpipe probes and an infrared scope is the ideal tool for carburetor jetting tests. Oxygen-sensor driven air/fuel ratio meters, available from various sources, are useful on-board tools for accurately reading air/fuel ratios during the operation of each carburetor circuit, during transitions and at cruise.

> NOTE —
> Always make certain that ignition spark, spark timing mechanisms and the EGR system function properly before running air/fuel ratio tests.

You can make a rough test of primary jetting with the truck parked (in neutral or Park) and the wheels blocked. Stay completely clear of the engine fan, as if testing the ignition spark advance or tailpipe emissions.

Run the engine until fully warm, then remove the air cleaner and open the throttle slowly to 2500 rpm. Watch the tach and avoid over-revving the engine. Hold this throttle position, and gradually close the choke valve. Watch the tach.

If rpm *increases*, the primary main metering system is flowing too lean; with very lean metering, rpm will continue to increase past 3/4 closure of the choke. If immediate *stumbling* or *reduced* rpm (over-choking or enrichment) is evident as the choke valve begins to close, the jets/rods are flowing too much fuel at cruise.

Usually a rod and/or jet of the nearest size will make a noticeable improvement. When choosing between slightly *lean* or slightly *rich*, choose rich. Very minor enrichment has a cooling effect and curbs detonation. Excessively lean mixes will cause heat buildup, harmful detonation and misfire, which actually raises pollutants.

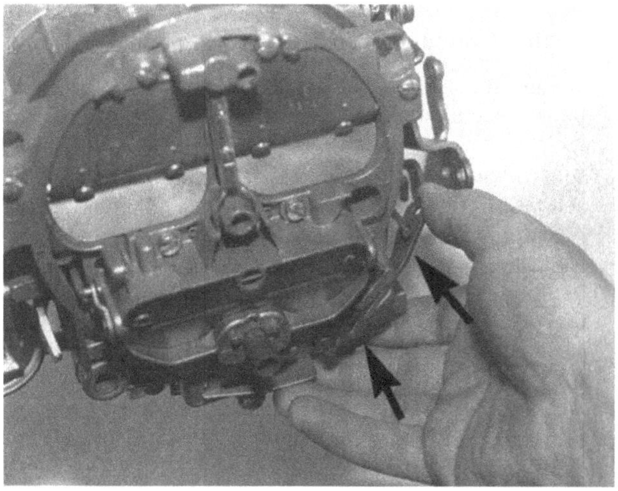

Fig. 16-13. Accelerator pump plunger (arrows) offers two stroke length settings. For high altitude operation, you can easily re-position the accelerator pump rod to shorten stroke and prevent engine flooding.

The Right Jets

There are three types of Quadrajet primary main jets. Numbers at the top of each jet signify the diameter of the jet orifice in thousandths of an inch. (Example: 74 means 0.074".) Jet styles are the 90° straight shoulder (Group A), 60° short taper (Group B) or 60° long taper (Group C). Each design delivers a different fuel flow curve as the power piston lifts the metering rods.

Metering rods come with two basic tapers. Early (1965–67) single taper metering rods have two-digit numbers. 1968–up rods have double tapers, two digits and a letter. Numbers represent the diameter of the rod at its largest step (the first step below shank). (Example: 44B is a late style, double taper rod of 0.044" diameter at the top step.)

Combinations of jets, metering rods, and different tapers make Quadrajet tuning as precise as that for any other carburetor design. Performance tuners will find that time spent here can create near-perfect fuel flow from idle to peak rpm.

Running your truck at high altitudes for short periods should not demand rejetting. I built a 383 Chevrolet "stroker" V-8 for a hardcore off-pavement 4x4 and jetted the carburetor for sea level. The truck ran fine (albeit a little sooty around the tailpipe) at the 7000-foot reaches of the Sierra Nevada's Rubicon Trail. For a prolonged stay at higher elevations, you might need to adjust the accelerator pump stroke and idle mixture, and also advance the spark timing slightly to raise manifold vacuum.

Plenty Available

For a reliable multi-purpose carburetor, consider the GM/Rochester Quadrajet. Availability and sizing are no problem. Manifold patterns are common (although choke styles differ). Many aftermarket intake manifolds offer the Quadrajet spread-bore bolt pattern. An intake manifold designed for a spread bore will permit better fuel

Engine Tuning with an Oxygen Sensor

A number of aftermarket engine tuning devices use an exhaust-system-mounted oxygen sensor to indicate the air/fuel ratio or mixture. Sending a signal to LED display lights, such an instrument can provide an instant account of a carburetor or EFI system's air/fuel ratio delivery and jetting.

Deviations from the ideal 14.7:1 (stoichiometric for gasoline) air/fuel ratio are easy to detect. Tuning an aftermarket fuel injection system or jetting a carburetor is simple with such a device. As an experienced engine tuner, I find that road tuning with an exhaust stream (oxygen sensing) air/fuel ratio meter is much like using a wheel dynamometer. Equipped with this technology, you can quickly become a proficient engine tuner.

Few out-of-the-box aftermarket carburetors will produce exactly the right air/fuel ratios for your performance engine buildup. By using an air/fuel ratio meter, you can analyze the carburetor's performance over the entire span of fuel circuits—from idle to the full-on power cycle, from partial throttle response to cruising mixture.

The gains of tuning with an air/fuel ratio meter are better fuel economy, maximum performance and the assurance that the engine will not be over-fueled. Over-fueling of a newly rebuilt engine can damage the cylinder walls, prevent piston ring seating and radically shorten engine life by fuel diluting the lubricant in the crankcase.

0012674

J&S Electronics' combined anti-knock system and air/fuel ratio checker (shown here), K&N's A/F meter and a similar device from Edelbrock can each indicate approximate air/fuel ratios across the rich to lean scale. This is a tremendous tuning tool for carburetor jetting and trouble-shooting fuel and spark system problems. You can perform real-world exhaust analyzer simulations at a fraction of the cost of an infrared tester or dynamometer.

Threaded plugs are available for simple oxygen sensor installation into an exhaust pipe or header collector. If a muffler shop positions the plug to match the heat requirements of the oxygen sensor, the meter will offer concise and quick response.

distribution. OEM throttle linkage is common enough for improvising.

As a retrofit, avoid later closed-loop computer carburetors. These incorporate valves and switches for electronic fuel management. Although computer controlled versions have many useful advantages, retrofitting to an earlier engine requires a major amount of wiring, spark timing control changes, plus the use of a computer and a host of engine sensors.

Delco/Rochester and GM dealerships are the only source for new Quadrajet carburetors. These outlets need a model and application (tag) number to fill an order. Your shop manual or professional service and tune-up guidebook can provide help with these numbers.

I find that a stock Chevrolet V-8 spread-bore/Quadrajet intake manifold will work fine to 4500 rpm, offering strong low-end torque. Edelbrock's Performer manifold or similar aftermarket dual-plane designs offer good overall performance plus improved performance above 4000 rpm.

0012682

Fig. 16-14. OEM and aftermarket engine and transmission oil coolers make a good investment. Oil plays a crucial role in cooling your truck's engine and transmission. Cooling the oil can extend engine and transmission life.

Lubrication and Engine Oil Cooling

Internal combustion engines depend upon heat in the form of hot, expanding gases that move the pistons. However, thermal loss from the cylinders is tremendous, as heat dissipates throughout the engine. The cooling system must draw this excess heat away. A radiator, the engine fan and coolant play a key role here, yet there's far more to cooling an engine.

Oil, expected to lubricate and battle friction, is a major outlet for heat. On later truck engine designs, emission control and fuel economy standards lean the fuel mixes and advance the spark timing. As smaller engines do bigger jobs, upper cylinder temperatures increase.

The buildup of engine heat also increases the oxidation rate and acid content in the oil. Oxygen combines with oil hydrocarbons, producing easily recognizable sludge. This sludge may include varnishes, waxes, corrosive acids and the water of hydration compounds. According to Hayden, a respected manufacturer of engine and transmission oil coolers, each 20° F of excess oil temperature doubles the oil oxidation rate and bearing wear.

Launching a Second Front against Heat

Traditionally, water/coolant circulation and dissipation of heat through a fan assisted radiator have provided reasonable cooling for trucks. Porsche and Volkswagen, however, proved the effectiveness of direct oil-to-air cooling. Porsche, VW, and GM Corvair air-cooled engines have survived in desert dune buggies and Baja racers, illustrating that enough air, moving through the right oil cooler, can offer sufficient engine cooling.

Skeptics of air cooled engines need only look at their own water cooled truck engine. Outside the block's water jackets and cylinder head coolant ports, your entire engine is oil cooled. The valves and valvetrain, including the camshaft and timing chain or gear mechanisms, the connecting rods, pistons, rings, all bearings and even the crankshaft rely on the oil's ability to continuously carry heat away.

For many years, truck and industrial users have recognized the effectiveness of engine oil coolers. Newer trucks have optional OEM engine oil coolers, an obvious choice for the aware buyer. Mini-cooler/radiators also appear on other automotive systems, including the power steering unit of many trucks.

Aftermarket automatic transmission coolers, offered since the 1960s, have drastically extended transmission life. Despite OEM radiator cooling, in-line automatic transmission fluid coolers and engine oil coolers are a must for trailer pulling and other heavy duty uses.

Subjected to loads, hills and towing, oil heat rises rapidly. The best radiator and fan can only address coolant temperature, while oil temperature continues to increase. An add-on, external oil-to-air cooling system could prove vital to your truck's engine. If hot climate driving, off-pavement four-wheeling or travel trailer pulling fit your plans, OEM and aftermarket engine and transmission oil coolers add practical protection.

Engine Oil Cooler Installation Tips

Like any other accessory, an engine oil cooler requires careful fitup. Mounted improperly, the cooler may actually inhibit air flow through the radiator. Most oil cooler kits provide detailed instructions. Necessary hardware should include quality hose and fittings, designed for exposure to high temperature oil under pressure. Usually, an oil filter spacer/adapter provides the attachment point for both pressurized oil and the return flow.

Many aftermarket kits include quality coolers and adapters, but they fall short with attaching hardware. For simple installation, manufacturers have resorted to through-the-radiator plastic ties to secure the cooler. For off-pavement use and situations where vehicles jar, vibrate and twist, plastic ties lead to trouble.

I agree with radiator experts who suggest fabricating a lightweight metal framework for the oil cooler. The cooler may still mount in front of the radiator, isolated from the expensive fins and tubes of the radiator core. Also route hoses carefully, and consider potential road hazard damage or any risk of hose chafing on the body or chassis edges.

Supercharging

Aftermarket retrofit superchargers now fit a wide range of popular engines. By the late 1990s, in step with demands for greater fuel economy and performance, most domestic and import trucks will offer models with OEM supercharging.

Acceleration, mid-range power, and volumetric efficiency improve drastically with supercharging, yet a sensibly staged blower or turbocharger usually has no impact on engine start-up, idle quality or off-idle tip-in performance. As rpm rises, the blower boosts both manifold and cylinder pressures. The higher the speed, the greater the performance and efficiency.

Blower Basics

Mechanical superchargers or blowers receive power directly from the engine via a belt- or gear-drive mechanism. Altering the blower shaft speed regulates air displacement. There are five popular mechanical blower designs: Roots-type, sliding-vane, spiral, centrifugal and rotary piston.

GM's Detroit diesels popularized the Roots-type blower. Plentiful and relatively inexpensive, the 6-71 and 4-71 blowers have served the racing community for over three decades. Fitted to a gasoline engine, a blower increases torque, mid-range and top-end power.

The Roots-type blower, like other positive-displacement superchargers, provides smooth volumetric flow rates and high pressures—even at relatively low blower speeds. Although some pressure loss occurs through backflow, Roots-type superchargers provide useful boost over a wide speed range.

In the Roots-type blower, two rotors spin in a blower housing/cavity. (These twin rotors never touch each other or the housing.) The close tolerance fitup between the rotors and housing create high boost pressures.

Other mechanical superchargers share a common theme: Timed phases first draw air then squeeze, forcing air into the plenum. (Centrifugal superchargers compress air within the blower rather than in the intake plenum.) On OEM diesels, injectors spray pressurized fuel into each combustion or pre-combustion chamber as compression peaks.

When retrofitting Roots-type blowers to gasoline engines with carburetion or Throttle Body Injection (TBI), fuel passes through the compressor chamber. For Tuned Port Injection (TPI), the high speed, close tolerance centrifugal blower has become popular, as fuel does not pass through the compressor. Centrifugal blowers work well for late GM passenger car engines equipped with TPI.

Exhaust Turbocharging

Turbochargers receive their power from the exhaust gas exiting the engine. The exhaust spins a turbine mounted on a shaft. On the other end of the shaft, in the intake, is a vaned wheel. As the vane turns, it compresses the intake air flow. The result is an energy gain, as boost occurs when engine rpm (i.e., exhaust pressure/turbine speed) reaches a suitable level.

Turbochargers are usually of single-flow turbine design, and deliver a slight excess of boost. Excess boost bypasses through a wastegate system. The wastegate prevents cylin-

Fig. 16-15. Supercharger kits fit a wide range of GM truck engines—from the faithful Stovebolt and Jimmy inline sixes to the modern 350 and 454 V-8s and Vortec V-6s. Kits come with drive pulleys, accessory adapters, installation hardware and instructions. When shopping for a blower or exhaust turbocharger kit, consider the whole package.

der overcharging and minimizes the energy spent spinning the turbine/compressor.

> NOTE —
> High intake manifold vacuum reduces exhaust pressure and also the demand for boost. Reciprocally, low manifold vacuum (heavy loads) increases exhaust pressure and creates turbo boost. The adjustable wastegate sets a ceiling on boost pressure.

Intercoolers provide a major breakthrough for turbocharging. Compressed air generates heat. This heat expands the air/fuel mix and absorbs vital space. Cooling the air between the turbo unit and the intake plenum provides a denser air/fuel mass (and more power) for each cylinder.

Aftermarket Blowers

B&M Products: B&M has put years of product development into a complete line of blowers and an extensive blower accessory line. B&M now focuses on both 50-State street-legal and off-highway applications, ranging from streetable boost to the highly acclaimed and popular MegaBlower, a 6-71 size unit made completely from new

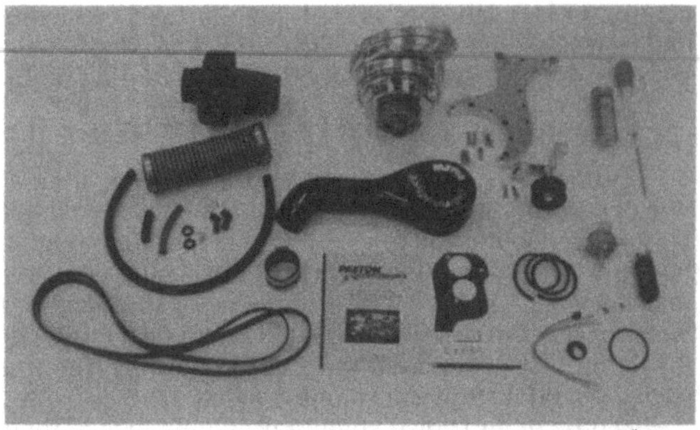

Fig. 16-16. Paxton has built automotive blower assemblies since 1951. The 50-State legal centrifugal blower kit for late GM truck V-8s is a quick way to make major horsepower gains and additional torque. Paxton blower kits come complete with all mounting hardware and instructions for a tidy installation.

materials. A small-block V-8 with 7.5:1 compression ratio and a Mega Blower is claimed to produce 540 horsepower at 6500 rpm. Torque peaks near 520 ft/lbs at 4500 rpm. Maximum boost for such a dual 750 CFM Holley carbureted system is 12 psi at 6500 rpm.

B&M also offers superchargers for milder engine applications. Kits permit use of stock factory accessories, which can be a real savings in cost and time. B&M has developed an impressive line of 144 and 162 cubic inch blower kits for GM V-6 engines—or individual parts for building that custom inline six blower system.

Camden Superchargers: John Camden began supercharging the very first 265 and 283 Chevrolet small-block V-8s. Camden's Road Warrior blowers pioneered several design features, including a highly efficient pressurized lubrication system with insert-type rotor shaft bearings.

Low profile for underhood clearance, the Camden street unit claims a 30% horsepower increase for engine compression ratios up to 8.5:1. Six-pound maximum boost helps assure engine longevity for stock, low compression engine applications. Camden offers kits for Chevrolet V-8s and some sixes.

Paxton: GM light truck V-8 owners rejoice! 50-State street-legal supercharger systems are available for many GM truck engine applications. Gains for these applications are notably high, as much as a 48% increase in horsepower with a massive boost in torque. Belt-driven, the unique and reliable Paxton planetary ball drive supercharger package has lead the industry with its street-legal V-8 blowers.

Vortech Engineering: Vortech has also developed 50-State legal centrifugal blower kits for GM V-8 engines. The Gearcharger blower is a high rpm design that provides the mild boost needed for maximum power and engine life. Vortech has focused on late model truck needs with these blower kits. Like Paxton, the Vortech kits offer all hardware necessary for a quick blower installation. GM truck owners with TBI V-8 engines can enjoy the benefits of a Vortech system.

Supercharging Compression Ratios, Camshafts and Air Filtration

Supercharging a gasoline engine requires compression ratios of 7:1 to 9:1 on engines with good cylinder sealing (10% maximum leakdown). Blower drive ratios determine the boost levels. Forged aluminum pistons, quality stainless steel exhaust valves, and hard steel exhaust valve seats are minimal requirements for higher boost pressures.

Weiand, a highly reputable manufacturer of automotive, marine, racing and pro-street type blowers, has found that high performance camshaft grinds for blower use feature 112° to 114° lobe centers, 0.450" to 0.500" lift and 220° to 234° valve opening duration at 0.050" lift (272° to 288° gross duration). (Logically, the exhaust valve must remain closed while the intake valve is open to prevent pressurized air/fuel charges from racing out the exhaust port.)

True blower grinds also have slightly longer duration on the exhaust side to totally clean out cylinders during the exhaust cycle. For mild or street-legal supercharging, a stock or RV camshaft grind works fine.

Air/fuel ratios are critical with blowers, so carburetor jetting and adequate air flow are essential. K & N Filtration and similar filtration systems provide the protection needed for expensive, close-tolerance blower systems. Although carburetor flow or cfm requirements may rise above stock demands, many OEM air cleaner assemblies still provide ample flow capacity when used with a K & N-type element.

Engine Modifications for Supercharging

Before considering a blower installation, assess the condition of your engine. Weiand, with extensive experience in this area, offers some general recommendations. To begin, the optimal engine compression ratio for a street blower installation is 8.5-to-1. This works nicely for 1971–up smog engines, but inhibits blower usage on 1960s and early 1970s muscle engines that sport 9.5:1 and higher compression ratios.

If pistons are of cast design, the boost limit should range from four to seven psi, with an engine rpm ceiling in the 4500 to 5000 range. Regardless of piston type, detonation should be avoided. Lower boost levels, a milder spark timing curve and/or a boost in fuel octane will help offset detonation.

CAUTION —
Detonation is the number one cause of damage in a supercharged engine.

Fuel leanout or starvation, an additional cause of detonation, can be avoided through use of larger fuel supply lines and a higher volume fuel pump. Attention to detonation cannot be overstated, as broken pistons, burned valves and crankshaft damage result from sustained periods of detonation.

An engine overhaul should be performed if excess wear exists on an engine intended for supercharging. Forged pistons, moly rings, close attention to tolerances and a general blueprinting philosophy should prevail. The blown engine produces far more cylinder pressure, and valve and gasket sealing become critical.

Although the Weiand and other blower kits will work with a street engine in good condition, any effort to improve engine stamina and longevity will also enhance performance. Select block and valvetrain parts with a known ability to last longer than standard OEM pieces.

Weiand has emphatic suggestions about carburetion and jetting, recommending that primaries be opened 5 to 10% and that secondaries provide 10 to 20% extra flow. For those contemplating a carburetor switch, the stock size carburetor works adequately with Weiand's Pro-Street Supercharger kits or a similar mild boost (street) system.

For the typical V-8 street blower installation, a 600 to 750 cfm flow rate with vacuum secondaries seems appropriate. A Holley "double pumper" may be needed for a more modified engine. Weiand's massive 6-71 Supercharger works best with a pair of 600 cfm vacuum secondary carburetors on a small-block V-8 engine, while a big-block may require a pair of 750 cfm carburetors.

Aside from a healthy cooling system, increased fuel supply network, and tight sealing air cleaner to prevent debris from ruining the rotors and blower housing, the ignition spark timing is critical. Initial, static spark timing should fall within six to ten crankshaft degrees advance, with the curve swinging to a combined static and mechanical maximum spark advance of 32 crankshaft degrees by 3400 rpm. Weiand notes that no more than 38 total crankshaft degrees of spark timing advance should be attempted under any circumstance.

The late model electronic spark control and closed-loop carburetor/EFI engines may create an obstacle. If such a computer-operated system prevents accurate control of spark or air/fuel ratios with a blower installed, Weiand recommends replacement with a conventional electronic ignition and carburetor.

NOTE —
Removal of any emission control components or the electronic fuel and spark management system is for off-highway/racing use only and violates Federal/EPA, state and local laws for vehicles driven on public roads.

When installing a blower, large tubing headers provide the best exhaust flow. Turbo-type or other low restriction mufflers also enhance performance. Proper tuning, including use of the correct spark plugs, will assure desired results.

Supercharging the 6.2L/6.5L GM V-8

The GM 6.2L and 6.5L V-8 diesels found in 1982 and newer GM trucks respond well to exhaust turbocharging. These are both rugged engine designs, fully capable of withstanding reasonable boost levels found in several aftermarket supercharger systems. The latest L65 6.5L factory Borg-Warner turbocharged GM V-8 is a prime competitor for popular 7.3L Navistar and 5.9L Cummins turbocharged diesels.

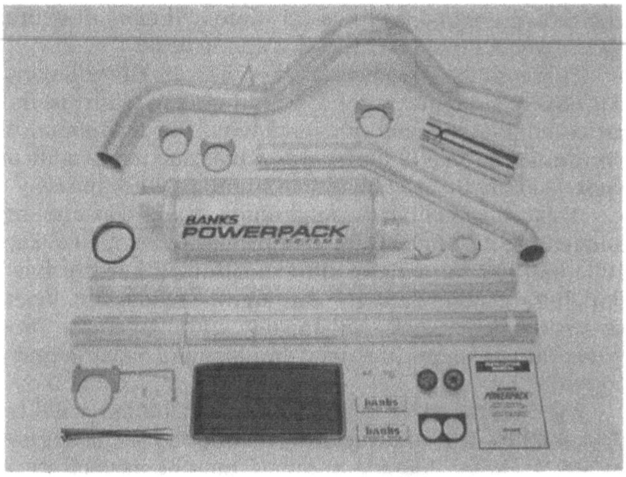

0014357

Fig. 16-17. Gale Banks has done considerable work with the GM 6.2L and 6.5L V-8 diesels. Banks Engineering offers a variety of retrofit turbocharging systems—complete kits that make installation a straightforward job. Banks Engineering also offers the "Powerpack" kit for 6.5L turbo diesels. Kit claims a whopping gain of 26 horsepower at the rear wheels.

Many retrofit turbo-diesel owners have discovered that both performance and engine longevity improve with the installation of a properly calibrated exhaust turbocharger. Having operated heavy equipment with Detroit, Caterpillar and Cummins engines, I would agree with these findings. A diesel engine labors far less with supercharging or turbocharging, and substantial gains in fuel economy (especially under load) indicate that the engine enjoys more efficiency under boost.

The appeal of OEM and aftermarket turbo systems has encouraged GM to offer the factory Borg-Warner electronically managed turbocharger and injection system, a first in the industry. This is a major breakthrough, and the engine burns cleaner, runs stronger and delivers good fuel economy.

For owners of non-turbocharged GM 6.5L and 6.2L diesel V-8s, the aftermarket offers several kits for turbocharging your engine. I am familiar with the kits offered by Banks Engineering, Hypermax, and ATS, and would use any one of them. Each has unique features and particular performance/fuel economy claims.

3. SIX-CYLINDER PERFORMANCE

Beginning with the very first Stovebolt and Jimmy inline OHV truck sixes, GM trucks have offered strong and reliable performance. The 1937–53 216 Chevrolet and original 228 GMC sixes each established a marque for light truck durability. These powerplant designs accommodated a full generation of users.

For the 1939–62 Chevrolet or 1939–59 GMC light truck owner who wishes to maintain traditional inline OHV six-cylinder power while grabbing a bit of attention, there are several vintage engine types that can provide substantial performance when built properly. Nearly three decades ago, I met a Bay Area youth who proved this point succinctly with a 1931 Chevrolet that sported a built 302 GMC inline OHV six.

Roy's flyweight coupe made a lasting impression, as the radically modified 302, closely akin to a 228, 248 or 270 GMC engine, gave Muscle Era pony cars a fit. The torque of that long stroke (under-square) engine was phenomenal, especially when competing with more modern high-compression over-square (larger cylinder bore diameter than the stroke length) performance engines.

The 270 and 302 GMC sixes have always been my favorite early inline OHV sixes, and many GMC truck owners are more than happy to keep these engines. Chevrolet's closest equivalent is the 1954–62 235 (late version) or 261 truck engine, another durable and easy to upgrade engine.

From a performance standpoint, I personally have little use for the 216 or early (pre-1954 non-Powerglide type) 235 Chevrolet OHV inline sixes with "dip-and-splash" oiling. The later 235/261 design or a GMC 228 to 302 inline OHV six, with its full direct-pressure lubrication system, holds much better potential. All pre-1963 inline GM sixes have only four main bearings; however, those with full oil pressure to insert type rod bearings offer better bearing life and more stable oil delivery.

If you have a fascination, or restoration need, around these early engines, Jack Clifford of Clifford Performance fame (see appendix) shares your interest. Jack once led me on a tour of his facility, a veritable shopping center for inline six-cylinder performance parts. From performance camshafts, valvetrain components, pistons and manifolds to exotic carburetor or retrofit EFI systems, lightweight flywheels and ignition upgrades, Jack Clifford can supply the goods for upgrading and extracting performance from an early Stovebolt or Jimmy inline OHV six.

Likewise, Jack Clifford can furnish the necessary pieces and suggestions for building up a 1963 or newer seven main bearing inline OHV six. These later engines have extremely rugged yet lightweight components, resembling the indomitable 283 cubic inch small-block V-8 in both cylinder dimensions and lightweight valvetrain design. The seven main bearing OHV inline sixes and the V-8s share many components.

Of the seven main bearing sixes, I favor the 250 or 292, and would suggest sticking with the 292 for heavy duty or 4x4 applications. These engines make a smart looking swap into an early truck chassis, and they offer the common bellhousing pattern of small- and big-block Chevrolet V-8s. This makes swaps and transmission alternatives much easier, and the 250 or 292 can serve in a variety of applications—from an all-out drag racing engine in a light chassis to a stump pulling, 4x4 rock crawler.

I am most familiar with the rock-crawling buildups, and here are some of my basic conclusions: 1) Use a high lift, short duration camshaft; 2) balance the reciprocating engine parts along with a large (168-tooth) factory steel flywheel and 11- to 12-inch Centerforce clutch assembly; and 3) use a compression ratio between 8.5:1 to 9.0:1.

Add cylinder head porting, a three-angle valve grind, Clifford's four-barrel intake manifold and headers. Blueprint an appropriate GM/Rochester Quadrajet four-barrel carburetor (refer to tuning section in this chapter) and re-curve a GM/Delco-Remy HEI distributor. This will provide ample muscle for a lighter weight off-highway vehicle.

0014304

Fig. 16-18. When Jim Homer wanted to maintain the stock look and original feel of his 1955 First Series show winning truck, he chose a 261 Chevrolet truck engine. Geared ultra low, the NAPCO 4x4 conversion 3600-Series model boasts an Offenhauser dual carburetor retrofit manifold. (Note the dual OEM-type carburetors and oil bath air cleaners.)A Fenton split exhaust manifold feeds dual exhausts. This is a pristine reproduction of a pre-V-8 era engine "hop-up."

For fuel saving power, the 250 is my engine of choice, as a 292 will often use more fuel than a comparably built 350 small-block Chevrolet V-8.

Again, for performance buildups, Clifford Performance provides a one-stop shopping outlet. The 230/250/292 family of Chevrolet inline OHV truck sixes prove inexpensive to operate and work best in trucks below 3500 pounds curb weight. In regard to performance goals, I would build a 350 cubic inch or larger V-8 for any GM truck over 3500 pounds curb weight—or if the truck pulls a weighty trailer.

Were I to consider swapping a more modern engine into a 1939–54 GM light truck model, my choice would be the OHV inline (seven main bearing) 250 or 292 six rather than the 262/4.3L V-6. The 4.3L has a wider 90° design—much like the small-block V-8 from a swap standpoint. Following the early chassis' narrow inline six engine bay design, I would opt for a 250 or 292 six.

As for other GM sixes, the 1960s 305 GMC V-6 engine is a notable torque monster. However, its extreme weight and the limited availability of high performance pieces makes this a poor engine for a buildup. In stock form, though, this is a highly rugged, long-lasting engine.

I have found that the later 305 V-6 OEM camshaft improves the fuel economy of early 305 engines. Also, the later two-barrel intake manifold and Stromberg carburetor provide better induction flow and additional fuel savings over the earlier one-barrel design

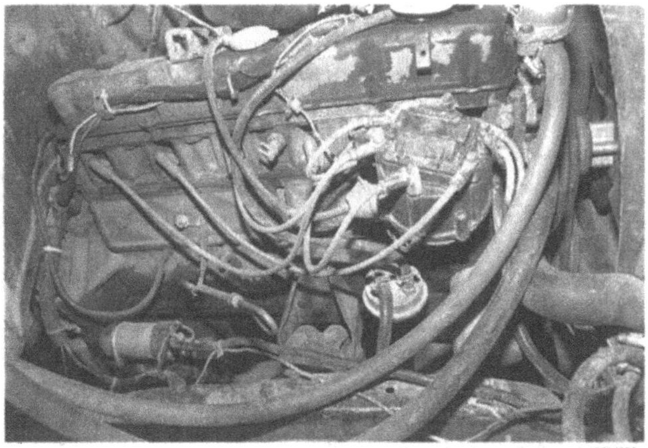

0014306

Fig. 16-19. Chevrolet's inline OHV seven main bearing sixes have exceptional durability and good performance buildup potential. Available from 1963–87 in various forms, these engines share many small-block V-8 features and components. I prefer the 250 and 292 for all-out performance buildups, and these engines would make nice swap material for a 1939 to First Series 1955 Chevrolet or GMC light truck.

0014307

Fig. 16-20. Although the GMC 305 V-6 has attracted very little performance interest, this is a highly rugged, roguish torque design. If you have a 1960s GMC truck with this engine, the two-barrel manifold, Stromberg carburetor and later OEM camshaft design will provide much needed fuel economy—without sacrificing noteworthy torque.

4.3L V-6

The late 4.3L Vortec V-6 is also an engine noted for its rugged design. Fuel efficient in stock form, this powerplant shares 350 V-8 features. Although numerous aftermarket performance pieces have made this engine an attention grabber, I would still regard this as an engine better suited for the S/T-Series trucks than a full-size C/K model.

If you want maximum economy and reasonable performance in a truck under 3,500 pounds curb weight, the 4.3L/262 V-6 might suffice. As load and performance expectations increase, consider the larger 350/5.7L V-8.

Since this book deals with the full-size and C/K models, I will avoid in-depth discussion of the 4.3L V-6 engine. This engine is too small to be considered a wise buildup choice for a high performance C/K truck. One exception would be a 2WD short wheelbase model built strictly for street performance, and even here, money spent on the V-6 buildup could provide far better results if applied to a 350 V-8 buildup.

If you find the 4.3L V-6 of further interest, I highly recommend the *Chevrolet Power* book, available through your local Chevrolet dealer. If, for whatever reason, your plans include the buildup of a 4.3L V-6, the design is very durable and efficient. Engineering benefits from the success of Chevrolet's 350 small-block V-8, a proven and highly respected powerplant.

I am partial to the later 4.3L L35 and R8Y V-6 engineering with CPI (Central Point Injection). These versions employ a balance shaft to overcome the inherent imbalance of any 90° V-6 engine. The CPI engine's balance shaft delivers smoother and more efficient performance than those 1985 and newer 4.3L engines that do not offer a balance shaft.

0014308 / 0014309

Fig. 16-21. CPI/EFI, found in late L35 and R8Y 4.3L V-6 engines, promises great fuel economy with a higher horsepower output. The balance shaft in these versions of the 4.3L engine delivers the smoothest performance possible from a 90° V-6 engine.

Chevrolet and GMC S- and T-Series trucks have successfully used the L35 and R8Y CPI/balance shaft engines. My guess is that the low emission, fuel efficient Central Point Injection design will replace TBI on all V-type gasoline truck engines. CPI's innovative electronically activated (variable flow) plenum vane contributes to better fuel economy, improved torque and added horsepower.

NOTE —
As of the 1994 model year, no C/K model has offered a 4.3L CPI engine option. Since 1985, all C/K models equipped with the 4.3L V-6 have used a conventional (non-balance shaft) block and either carburetion (1985–86) or TBI (1987–up).

4. ULTIMATE V-8 PERFORMANCE: 454 TURBO-JET POWER

When Chevrolet dropped the 348/409 engine design and switched to the big-block 396 and 427 engines in 1965 and 1966 (respectively), American consumers were ready for the change. Chevrolet had earned only marginal success with the high performance 348 passenger car engine, a design that better served as a medium duty truck powerplant from 1958 to the mid-1960s.

The 409, however, had offered impressive performance and a durable record in both NASCAR and NHRA competition. While many over-revved 348s had succumbed to broken camshafts and crankshaft/connecting rod assembly failures in 1958–61 high performance Chevrolet cars, the 409 soundly overcame this poor image and proved to be a more rugged design.

396/427 engineering, campaigned and tested on the tortuous NASCAR tracks before public release of the 396 in mid-1965, gleaned much from the 409's improved block and crankshaft design. As Muscle Era competitors, the 396 and 427 Chevrolet engines quickly built legends.

By the late 1960s, in the heyday of Chevelle, Nova and Camaro high performance, the big-block engine had won its share of victories. With horsepower a dominant theme in the sales arena, Chevrolet introduced a still more powerful big-block contender, the 454 Turbo-Jet V-8.

While the 396, 402 (which is actually a 0.030-inch overbored 396) and 427 share a 3.76-inch stroke length, the 454 has a 4-inch stroke and a huge 4.250-inch bore diameter. The 427 passenger car type engine also offers the 4.250-inch bore diameter, while the 396 has an odd 4.094-inch bore, and the 402 has a 4.125-inch bore.

Like the small-block V-8, Chevrolet has offered the big-blocks in a wide range of displacements, including all-out racing aluminum block types with cast iron (dry) cylinder liners, to 510 cubic inches. There is also a full line of medium duty truck engines built around the basic big-block engineering, which includes the rugged 366 and tall-block 427, which differs from the passenger car design.

Of all the passenger car, production variety Chevrolet high performance big-blocks, I like the 427 best. The rod angle and severely over-square bore/stroke ratio is better suited for high rpm operation. Beyond question, if I were building an engine for sustained high rpm usage, this would be my choice. For an all-out *heavy* trailer puller or a monstrously strong torque engine, I would opt for the popular 454. In racing environments, the late Generation V (Gen-V) aftermarket GM/Chevrolet marine and automotive high performance (H.O.) engine deserves attention.

The iron block Gen-V marine/off-highway automotive engine is offered in crated H.O. long-block (complete engine with cylinder heads) form and displaces 502 cubic inches (4.466" bore diameter; 4.00" stroke length). In racing dress, this engine can easily produce 500-plus horsepower. Middle cylinders are siamesed like the 400 small-block, raising concerns about cooling in highway use. For a trailer puller or utility truck, I prefer a milder 454 or the 383 small-block stroker V-8 with a modest compression

0014310

Fig. 16-22. For the street or race truck, an LS6 or LS7 454 V-8 serves as a model for high performance build-ups.

ratio, short valve opening duration and strong lift. (See 383 tow engine section in this chapter.)

Light trucks were not exempt from the Muscle Era horsepower wars, and 275 and 310 horsepower 396 V-8 options came on line in 1968. These were somewhat de-tuned, lower compression versions of the same basic engine design that had rated 425 horsepower in its 1965 high performance passenger car debut—with a staggering 11:1 compression ratio.

The 454 truck V-8 would wait, however, until U.S. EPA smog requirements severely drove down the horsepower ratings. For 1972, a low compression ratio 454 light truck engine became the remaining heavy hauler option of the Chevrolet/GMC light truck fleet.

By 1972, the famous 327 small-block was already several model years into history, while its even stronger successor, the 350 V-8, was substantially de-tuned to meet emission requirements. More cubic inches became the only means for offsetting the heavy constraints of emission controls.

LS6 and LS7: Pure Muscle Prototype

A muscle-era LS6 or LS7 Chevrolet engine looks no different than a Genuine Goodwrench replacement engine for your light truck. With massive iron cylinder heads and block, the LS6 certainly *feels* like a weighty 454 truck powerplant.

Officially regarded as a replacement engine for a 1970 Chevrolet high performance muscle car or Corvette, this is definitely not your standard truck engine—nor does it resemble the low-compression standard replacement for a lunched 454 fifth wheel puller. Until the emergence of the H.O. 502 Gen-V engine, Chevrolet offered a streetable

continued on third page following

GM Motorsports and the Chevrolet Raceshop Program

Scores of authors have dealt with the subject of high performance Chevrolet engine buildups. As a feature writer, technical editor and columnist for Argus Publishers' *Popular Hot Rodding, Guide to Muscle Cars, OFF-ROAD, Super Street Truck,* and other automotive publications, I've had ample opportunity to share my sense for Chevrolet and GMC truck engines.

There is likely more in-depth data and technical information written about Chevrolet high performance engine buildups than any other engine design in automotive history. For a dozen years, GMC and Chevrolet truck owners have spent hard earned money on engine modifications and tuning procedures that I suggested.

Recognizing the importance of that responsibility, I have built a significant resource library. Within my stacks of books and research materials, I find that the genuine *Chevrolet Power* series, bearing GM's official "Mr. Goodwrench" logo, provides the most thorough, detailed and accurate account of high performance Chevrolet engine buildups.

Of the series, the 5th and 6th Editions remain my prime resources, the kind of information that a professional racer, automotive engineer, master machinist or responsible journalist demands. The latest 7th Edition takes a slightly different slant, providing a friendly consumer guide for the vast array of quality Genuine Chevrolet, Chevrolet Raceshop and GM Motorsports high performance products.

Having read my book to this point, you realize that I respect factory engineering and a more conservative approach to modifications. For this reason, I prefer modifications and engine changes that offer the kind of engineering integrity found in OEM product. You, too, will find that this approach can provide a greater degree of reliability and more satisfying results.

See Your Local Chevrolet or GMC Truck Dealer

GM Motorsports and the Chevrolet Raceshop programs provide quality components for building your performance engine. The painstaking, relevant research found in the *Chevrolet Power* books is also available in Chevrolet Raceshop bulletins and genuine General Motors high performance engine parts.

Through your local GM dealership's parts department, you can secure parts ranging from the proven Z-28 small-block intake manifold and camshaft kit to a complete H.O. 502 cubic inch V-8 engine assembly. The Chevrolet Raceshop and GM Motorsports supply the products described within the *Chevrolet Power* book.

Perhaps you need a stronger camshaft for trailering, something like the classic 300 horsepower 327 V-8 hydraulic grind. Or maybe you want a complete restoration engine, a replacement for the awesome LS-6 or LS-7 Muscle Era 454 found in high performance Corvettes. (These engines rated 450 and 460 horsepower, respectively.) Your local Chevrolet dealership can provide such OEM level products.

Current products have evolved from original Muscle Era engines like the original 350 LT-1 and 454 LS-7. These designs, enhanced by nearly twenty-five years of additional research, upgrades and improvements, can offer severe service for the serious performance buff.

If your plans include maximum performance and the need for high quality, compatible components, see your local Chevrolet dealership and secure a copy of *Chevrolet Power*. (Photos courtesy of High Performance Communications/Chevrolet Raceshop.)

> **NOTE —**
> Always check your state's emission requirements before considering an engine change or modification.

0014439

GM's #10185085 H.O. 502 V-8 is 8.2L of massive torque and horsepower. Tested with a 750 cfm Holley four-barrel and 2-inch by 30-inch primary headers, this fully assembled 8.75:1 compression ratio crate engine pulled 440 horsepower at a reasonable 5250 rpm. A torque peak of 515 lb/ft at 3500 rpm attests to the potential of Chevrolet's big-block family of engines. (See comments on the Gen V engine design in this chapter.) This rugged marine-block engine uses #14096801 cylinder heads and a #14096209 camshaft. Siamesed cylinder jackets may not work in all applications. For sustained high temperature operation, like desert racing, consider the original (GM #10069285) production-type High Performance 427/454 short deck block with non-siamesed cylinders.

0014440

For high performance use over the long haul, it's impossible to beat a 300 horsepower 350 V-8 engine. Called GM's "Special Performance Assembly #12355345," this is an emissions-legal replacement engine for 1968 and older V-8 trucks, at a somewhat modest 9.1:1 compression, with four-bolt mains.

0014441

Producing 345 horsepower, the H.O. 350 is similar to Muscle Era engines. Modern advantages are the full-circumference rear main seal (also on the #12355245 300 hp engine), a hydraulic roller lifter camshaft, an HEI distributor, the latest #10185063 dual-plane intake manifold, plus hypereutectic pistons. Note the high performance centrifugal and vacuum advance HEI distributor, a new water pump assembly and crankshaft damper.

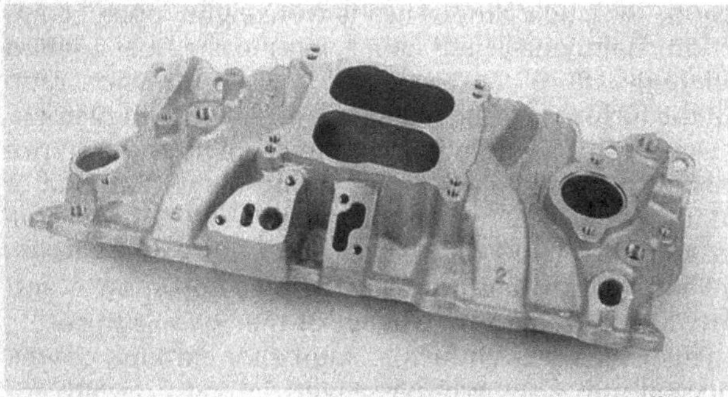

0014442

ZZ3 aluminum intake manifold, #10185063, offers a low profile and advantages of a dual-plane design. This intake rivals the flow of legendary high-rise manifolds, yet it accepts an EGR valve, hot air choke and either a Holley square-flange or GM Quadrajet carburetor. Such a manifold works well with H.O. 350's #10185071 roller/hydraulic camshaft grind, for strong mid-range to high rpm performance, without sacrificing a large amount of low-end pulling torque.

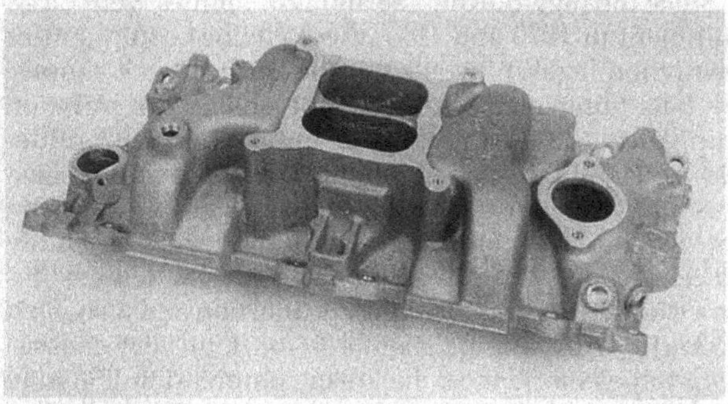

0014443

#10185024 ZZ2 intake for small-blocks has roots to the original Z-28/LT-1 Muscle Era engines. Notably, this updated manifold also fits later engines with raised rocker cover rails. Oil fill tube and choke stove mounting holes have been deleted. Like 1967–71 High-Rise manifolds, this dual plane design accepts square-flange Holley carburetors. Built for engines like the current 300 and 345 horsepower 350 V-8, this manifold contributes to the supremacy of Bow-Tie power.

LS6 replacement engine. Lurking within the pair of innocuous looking cylinder heads were eight "open" combustion chambers. These larger volume chambers netted a tolerable, more conservative 10.2:1 compression ratio with the factory "closed chamber" design forged pistons.

Deeper in the engine, a mechanical high performance camshaft provided a 0.500-inch lift profile with a total of 316° intake and 302° exhaust duration. With milder valve overlap than factory racing camshafts, this GM #3863143 camshaft still produced a wild 450-plus horsepower and nearly 500 ft/lbs of torque in out-of-the-box LS6 trim.

This was a proven factory source for extreme power. Squeezed into Chevrolet passenger car and Corvette engine bays during the twilight years of the Muscle Era, the LS6 and its counterpart, the even more potent LS7, serve well as strictly "off-highway" hardware.

The LS6 engine buildup includes a factory hi-riser high performance aluminum intake manifold. The LS7-type engines, with open chamber heads and open chamber design pistons, boast a 12:1 compression ratio. Sound interesting? Well, the only practical application is an out-and-out drag strip, mud bog, pull competition or sand drag racing truck—or a "pro-street" and show truck.

Since the high output LS6 and LS7 engines were OEM equipment in 1970 and 1971, these engines could suffice as emission legal if installed in the correct truck chassis. (See beginning of this chapter for details on emission compliance.) At the present, using California's guidelines, you could fit such an engine to a 1971 or older chassis as long as you use all of the OEM LS6 or LS7 emission controls, an OEM carburetor, OEM air cleaner assembly and related parts. You would need a special Referee Station visual inspection for smog certification and also need to comply with tailpipe standards for your year chassis. For tailpipe compliance, the lower compression LS6 may possibly comply; however, the more radical camshaft in the LS7 would likely fail the tailpipe emission output test. Before foregoing the expense of such an engine, make sure that such a swap will meet your state, local and US/EPA emission regulations. Keep in mind that rules are subject to change.

454 Final Buildup Details

The LS6 came with the "tall" iron water pump, GM #14085852, but an aluminum #19058915 pump may be used. Matching pulleys for the original LS6 water pump are the GM #3899660 crankshaft pulley (6-inch type) and #3995647 water pump pulley.

Pulleys and accessory brackets are available through Chevrolet, and a patient parts counterperson can assist here. The alternator, power steering pump mount and use of air conditioning will dictate the correct pulleys or water pump required. Big-block water pumps come in two standing heights. Be certain, by part number, which pieces you're using. Misaligned pulleys and belts lead to major problems and lack of reliability.

Bellhousing, flywheel, and starter motor selection is important. The LS6 used a nodular iron, 14" flywheel with 168-tooth starter ring and 8" crankshaft balancer (GM #3963530). Although the 168-tooth flywheel design seems common to truck owners, 454 engines, like the 400 small-block, have external balancing. *Always be certain to use a designated 454 flywheel or flexplate, whether using the 168-tooth or 153-tooth type.*

0014312

***Fig. 16-23.** The LS6 engine buildups should include a 14", 168-tooth starter ring flywheel. Externally balanced 454 engines require a special flywheel or flexplate. Truck V-8 bellhousing can accommodate a 454 truck-type 168-tooth flywheel that accepts a large diameter clutch.*

A smaller, lightweight nodular iron flywheel is available for the 454, accommodating a maximum clutch size of 10-1/2 inches. When using a smaller flywheel, the correct starter motor must be found. Select your Chevrolet starter motor by the starter ring tooth count, engine block mounting bolt pattern, and nose end length.

> **NOTE —**
> For 1973–up big-block trucks, use the 168-tooth flywheel or flexplate and GM/Delco-Remy's heavy duty starter unit #1108400, which uses the #1984098 iron nose section. Always use the #354353 starter motor brace in heavy duty V-8 applications, plus GM's #1409728 and #1409729 starter bolts.

I find that GM high performance truck engines do well with the iron 1972 and earlier OEM truck bellhousings, available with two transmission indexing hole diameters. Trucks from 1968–up with the four-speed 465 Muncie and NP435 truck transmissions use a 5.125-inch index hole. Many GM truck manual transmission models use the familiar GM light-duty three-speed index bore of 4.686 inches. This index bore diameter is found in all GM light truck transmission applications prior to 1968.

NOTE —
All 1960–62 and the 1963 K-model GM trucks use a right-side clutch release lever with hydraulic clutch linkage. This bellhousing has been popular in some swaps where there is limited clearance at the left side of the engine and transmission. The transmission index bore is 4.686-inches on these bellhousings and can be carefully machined to 5.125-inch for use with the later Muncie 465 or NP435 four-speeds.

The iron bellhousing incorporates a starter motor mount for a common and durable iron nosed starter. The attaching bolts lay on a horizontal plane, unlike the passenger car and later truck starters that have long bolts running vertically into the block casting.

Iron starter noses and iron bellhousings are more durable than the later aluminum types. Since most cast iron truck bellhousings accept the larger 168-tooth flywheel, you also have the choice of a larger clutch assembly.

As for final installation details, always use molded radiator hoses, available through OEM and aftermarket sources. If the parts counterperson draws a blank stare, ask for 396 or 454 truck components. Should this fail, make a mock-up of your needed hose shapes with a piece of welding rod, make friends with the parts manager, then wade through the OEM replacement hoses in the back of the parts store until you find appropriate shapes and inlet/outlet sizes—record these part numbers for future reference.

As for carburetion, some racers, and respected tuners like Jack O'Donnell (owner of Precision Carburetion at San Diego, California), prefer the annular discharge 9380 Holley square flange unit, which produces better torque in the 3600 to 5000 rpm range.

Chevrolet has also used Holley square flange carburetors on factory high performance 454 engines. Holley symmetrically jetted square flange carburetors, 830 cfm or bigger, seem the best place to begin. Some of the GM/OEM square flange 4150-Series Holley carburetor applications that served LS6 and LS7 non-California emissions engines were the List numbers R-4557-A, R-4492-A and R-4559-A.

The ignition system, often restricted by limited firewall clearance on many GM light truck applications, could call for a Mallory, Accel, MSD or a small diameter (breaker point type or transistor) OEM GM distributor. Breaker point GM distributors can be converted to breakerless ignition with a Crane/Allison electronic kit.

Spark timing will be dictated by camshaft, fuel and other factors. A stock LS6, however, with Holley R-4557-A carburetion, called for 17 (crankshaft) degrees of advance @ 2000 rpm and maximum 24 to 28 degrees (crankshaft) at 3800 rpm. (Add to these figures an initial factory spark advance of four crankshaft degrees.) A vacuum canister adds an additional 12.8 crankshaft degrees (maximum reached at 12 inch-height of vacuum) spark advance for improved street driveability and low speed response.

CAUTION —
Do not drive under street loads or at low speeds with the spark timing fully advanced. Damage to the engine will likely occur.

NOTE —
Overriding the factory engine timing is in direct violation of US EPA and state emissions law for public road use.

454 V-8 Engine Conversion

The 454 LS6 or LS7 engine will fit engine bays of Second Series 1955 and newer full-size Chevrolet and GMC trucks. Although engineered to accept the small-block V-8, these bays are large, and the common Chevrolet bellhousing and engine mount designs make the swap a natural for those who need—and can safely handle—this excessive kind of horsepower and torque.

WARNING —
These two ultra-high-performance engine designs can be dangerous when installed in older trucks. Older light truck models were engineered for one-third this amount of horsepower. Chassis dynamics, suspension design, four-wheel drum braking and limited steering response may not be a match for this power. Make sure the steering, brakes and overall roadworthiness of your truck can handle this kind of horsepower.

As for installation, the 454 LS6, LS7 or any other "rat motor" (big-block Chevrolet V-8) can physically fit into a 1955 Second Series or newer light truck. For 1967–up trucks, the parts prototype is the 1968 and newer truck chassis that uses the big-block 396, 402 or 454 V-8 engine. Earlier models with front-of-the-block, four-point engine and bellhousing mounting require a different approach.

Once you determine which type of installation your truck requires, appropriate front or side motor mounts can either be formed from OEM V-8 pieces or fabricated to accommodate your type of chassis.

Prior to 1973 models, a common engine mounting method for Chevrolet trucks was to locate motor mounts at each side of the clutch bellhousing. This V-8 configuration began with the 1955–59 models and carried over from the OHV six-cylinder inline era. In the first GM light truck V-8 models, the front motor mounts attach to L-shaped brackets at the front face of the engine block casting, forming a four-point engine and transmission mounting system.

The big-block Chevrolet powerplant is longer than a small-block V-8, and this affects its installation in Second Series 1955 and newer models that have no provision on the frame for side engine mounts. Such an installation will require some finesse and innovative fabrication work, either to emulate the stock front engine mounts or to fabricate side frame rail brackets that will allow use of the later side-type engine mounts.

0014166

Fig. 16-24. The big-block motor mounts set further forward. This requires proper frame brackets, motor mounts or fabrication work. Try to use OEM parts, if possible, before resorting to cutting and welding new frame brackets. By keeping the bellhousing in the stock location, you can maintain the original location of the clutch linkage, the transmission and driveshaft.

Since many conversions also involve use of later Turbo-Hydramatic transmissions like the TH350 or TH400, some fabricators prefer the three-point (two engine block side mounts and one rear transmission mount) approach. For manual transmission swaps, however, I have a bias here.

If the truck had four-point (two front and two bellhousing) mounts as the OEM design, I attempt to emulate the OEM system if possible. The paired bellhousing and front mounts provide very stable support. In the case of big-blocks into an early chassis, this does involve fabricating a front engine saddle mount to accommodate these two front engine mounts.

Again, you also need to appropriately place the early style biscuit and pin front engine mounts. I use the stock bellhousing location as the reference point to begin engine alignment. With the bellhousing mounts attached, the front mounts can then be positioned.

At the back of the block, simply use the OEM Chevrolet V-8 bellhousing, and place the big-block engine securely in the early V-8 truck chassis. All Chevrolet V-8s, the seven main bearing inline OHV sixes and the Vortec V-6 use a common bellhousing pattern. Flywheels differ, however, with the 1986–up V-6s and V-8s using a smaller diameter flywheel/flexplate bolt pattern to facilitate the late, and improved, one-piece style rear main seal.

Select the correct flywheel and clutch assembly, use an appropriate throwout bearing to match your clutch linkage and transmission type, and the installation job is nearly done. Headers will usually aid a big-block installation, although the factory iron manifolds will work in most cases.

For the 1967–up chassis, the big-block is a natural fit. In 1968, the use of the 396 engine option in 2WD models proves this point succinctly, although the big-block into a 4x4 K-10/1500 or K-20/2500 often creates some difficulty. The K-model chassis is different than the 2WD models, and the older (pre-Sierra) 1/2-ton and 3/4-ton 4WD models do not offer a big-block engine option.

The 1976–up K-30/3500 models, however, do offer a 454 option. This includes use of the Turbo 400 automatic, a genuine improvement over the lighter K-models and their use of the TH350. The TH350, although a durable transmission in mild horsepower applications, is a poor choice for the high horsepower user.

Like the high output muscle cars, the trucks with a 454 engine hold up far better with either the TH400 automatic, the late 4L80E overdriving automatic, the 465 Muncie truck four-speed or the latest 4500 Series New Venture five-speed overdrive manual unit.

Longer than a 350 or other small-block V-8 engines, the 396-454 block casting measures 23.63 inches from front machined face to rear machined face. Wider, too, the 454 does, however, fit squarely into most 1955 (Second Series) and newer GM light truck engine bays. In some cases, tubular exhaust headers must be aligned carefully while the engine is lowered into the chassis.

The TH400 main body housing is longer than the TH350, and this is where fitup can also become problematic—especially on 4x4 models. Other than these issues, engine and transmission length should present no problem for Second Series 1955 and newer GM trucks. Chevrolet and GMC's use of inline sixes through 1987, plus the 1988–up Sierra chassis' accommodation of the 454, make big-block V-8 swaps possible over all of these years.

As with any other V-8 changeover, the appropriate radiator and fan shroud are essential. On 1967–up models with cross-flow radiators, most swaps involve replacement of the original radiator core with an aftermarket four-row core, commonly available through a local radiator shop.

For these 1967–up light trucks, the big-block conversion using OEM parts calls for a frame bracket change. (Use the 1968 or later 396, 402 or 454 type brackets that apply for your year chassis.) Brackets are available from Chevrolet dealers, in some instances, or from recycling sources. The same issue applies with motor mounts, and here you need to see your Chevrolet/GMC Truck dealer or local parts outlet.

5. THE 383 STROKER V-8 ALTERNATIVE

454, LS6, LS7 or H.O. 502 power is certainly not for everyone. For the real world of everyday driving, in terms of fuel economy and in the interest of occasional trailer pulling, I find that the best overall engine buildup for most Chevrolet and GMC light truck users is the 383 V-8 "stroker" motor.

A 383 consists of parts from both the 350 V-8 and the 400 (small-block) engines. The Chevrolet 350 has a good record and was first offered in 1968 passenger cars and 1969 light trucks. 350s share the same 4.00" bore as the legendary 327 small-block. A longer stroke of 3.48" and a durable big journal crankshaft contribute to this engine's stamina and reliability.

Small-block Background

During the early production years of the 350 V-8, gasoline octane ratings averaged 6 to 10 points higher than today. Emission requirements were more lenient, allowing richer air/fuel ratios to offset detonation (ping) on engines that ranged from 8.5:1 to 11.5:1 compression ratio.

As emission control requirements stiffened in the 1970s, compression ratios dropped drastically and air/fuel ratios became leaner. High output Chevrolet small-block V-8s, which by design benefit from over-square features (bigger cylinder bore/shorter stroke lengths like the legendary 4.00" x 3.00" 302 Camaro Z-28 V-8), require high compression ratios to develop peak performance.

The 283, 302, 327 and 350 put out their best performance with large valves, a 10:1 or higher compression ratio, a healthy fuel supply and 100-plus octane fuel. (The potent 327, last used in 1969 trucks, totally loses its effectiveness when compression drops below a 9:1 ratio.) The 350 V-8, due to its longer stroke design, can still pull impressively with an 8.5:1 compression ratio.

When stiffer emission control guidelines reduced the effectiveness of truck engines by 1972, Chevrolet/GMC turned to the 454 big-block as a trailer hauling solution. The four-barrel 350 remained the largest engine option for 1/2- and 3/4-ton four-wheel drive trucks until 1976, when GM introduced the small-block based 400 V-8 to the K-models.

Although the 400 small-block offers a substantial stroke increase at 3.75", this engine's cooling suffers from the siamesed middle cylinders. The 400's bore, increased to 4.125", maintains the same bore centers as other small-block engines. The 400, a response to heavy emission control demands, suffers from its marginal cooling design, especially under heavy loads. By 1981, GM retired the 400 V-8 truck/van engine, opting for the less troublesome 305 and 350 small-blocks and big-block 454 V-8.

Role Model: The 305 V-8

Chevrolet's 305 small-block V-8 is a strong running, small displacement engine, using the 350's 3.48" stroke and a small 3.75" bore that more closely approaches the square point. The 3.75" bore also has significance as the same bore dimension found in the original 265 cubic inch small-block Chevrolet V-8.

Like an industrial or medium duty gasoline truck engine, the 305 develops substantial low-speed torque. This helps meet emission and fuel economy demands, which require higher (lower numerical) axle gear ratios.

The formula has proven a success. 305 engines generate nearly as much usable torque and pulling power as their larger 350 brethren, albeit with less total horsepower at higher rpm. Flexibility also makes the long stroke 305 okay for low GVWR light trucks and later High Output passenger cars like the Camaro/Firebird Cross-Fire EFI engines (circa 1982–83) and the 1985–up IROC 305 Tuned Port EFI engine.

The 305 V-8 achieved the goal that Chevrolet's 400 small-block had narrowly missed. Both engines proved that a closer to square bore/stroke ratio better serves in a low compression, low octane, leaner burning world. With better block cooling, the 400 may well have survived. Instead, these facts led to the aftermarket phenomena of the 383 stroker engine.

Basis for the 383

Although the 400 itself has faded like the 307 and 262 designs, its unique torque, produced by its long 3.75-inch stroke, has given the 400's crankshaft a key role in the racing and performance arenas.

The horsepower and torque losses resulting from stringent emission standards and the demands of low octane fuels can be offset by increasing the stroke length. Perhaps from observing the success of the 305 V-8, or maybe by mere curiosity, high performance engine builders mated a 3.75" stroke 400 crankshaft to the 4.00" bore 350 V-8 block. The result is phenomenal.

A stock 400 crankshaft has 0.200" larger diameter main bearing journals than the 350. The 400 cast crankshaft can easily part with this excess metal, and the machining takes only a bit more effort than a standard crankshaft grinding and polishing job. Severe duty testing and the rigors of racing environments have proven that a properly undersized 400 crankshaft is both strong and reliable.

NOTE —
The popularity of the 383 engine has opened a market for new crankshafts, specially built in the aftermarket for this application. As cores of original 400 crankshafts run short, there will likely be sources for these aftermarket 350/stroker crankshafts.

A remachined 400 crankshaft with 400 connecting rods and short skirt forged aluminum pistons easily fits the 350 V-8 block. An alternative is use of stock 350 rods with special pistons that compensate for the longer stroke by relocating the piston pin hole. Either way, substantial low-rpm torque and a major horsepower increase at the mid- and upper-rpm ranges will result.

The term "383" actually addresses two factors. Use of a 400 crankshaft provides a 0.270" longer stroke, while the standard cleanup rebore of a recycled 350 engine block is 0.030" oversize. Since most hybrid 383 engines begin with a used four-bolt main 350 block, 0.030" oversize has become a standard for the 383 buildup.

383 Torque Goals

Torque is a measurement of the twisting force available at the crankshaft. In automotive uses, torque overcomes inertial loads and allows an engine to perform work. There is a distinct relationship between torque and horsepower, and in basic terms, automotive engines cannot develop peak horsepower before exceeding their maximum torque output.

An engine's torque rating, often overlooked when choosing a trailer pulling or camper hauling truck package, is the singlemost important measurement of strength and efficiency. Torque and gearsets provide the means for moving weight. The ideal utility truck engine provides high torque at the lowest possible rpm.

The current 454/7.4L TBI big-block, with its 4.251" bore and long 4.00" stroke, has a 7.9:1 compression ratio and develops maximum torque of 385 lb/ft at an impressively low 1600 rpm. It reaches 230 peak horsepower at only 3600 rpm. The LS6 and LS7 454 produced 450 to 460 horsepower around 5600 rpm and delivered an impressive 490 lb/ft of torque at 3000 rpm. But with their high compression ratios and fuel octane requirements, the LS6 or LS7 is clearly of a bygone era.

The goal for a trailer pulling 383 engine is strong low speed torque with maximum horsepower by 4000 to 4500 rpm. Engine builders acknowledge that this is the maximum operational rpm for a tow vehicle under load.

383 Stroker: Truck V-8 for the Times

A prime example of a 383 prospect is a truck owned by my friend, Arden Rogers, of Oakridge, Oregon. His GM truck is a 1976 Chevrolet K-20 3/4-ton four-wheel drive pickup that came from the factory with a 350 V-8, THM350 automatic transmission (M40 option), 4.10 axle gearing and a full array of options, which includes power steering and air conditioning. The OEM tire size was 7.50x16 (currently LT235/85R16).

The truck's 350 engine ran well, despite 109,000 miles of hard work. Equipped with a permanent fifth wheel mount and hefty tool box, the truck weighs 6,450 pounds with two men aboard. The truck also pulls a 4,100-plus pound Alpenlite 24-foot fifth wheel trailer on trips and treks to Yuma, Arizona.

Switching to Mobil 1 oil at high mileage virtually halted engine wear, and oil consumption of one quart in 2,000 miles of trailer pulling gave every indication that the 350 was still operational. Arden noted that performance of the engine had not dropped much, although when I ran a compression check and cylinder leakdown test, the cumulative effect of moving large gross combination weights, rates as high as six tons, showed up.

When new, this four-barrel carbureted 8.5:1 compression Federal (49-State) emission engine produced 265 lb/ft torque at 2400 rpm and 160 horsepower at 4000 rpm. Normal cylinder cranking pressure of 150 psi was long past when I ran the tests, however, with a lowest reading of 123 psi in number six cylinder. Closer inspection with a leak down test revealed 18% leakage at that cylinder.

Arden had considered either trading his truck for a later 454-powered one-ton K-30 4x4 or installing a 454 in the 1976 model. The geartrain, chassis and body were in good operating condition and had been well maintained. When we discussed the 383 small-block stroker V-8 alternative, Arden opted for the 350/383 buildup.

0014313

Fig. 16-25. Arden Rogers tows a 24-foot Alpenlite fifth wheel trailer behind his 1976 Chevrolet K-20 pickup. The truck without trailer weighs 6,450 pounds with driver, one passenger, a stowage box and fuel.

Proving a Point

I had built a highly successful 383 stroker engine and knew what worked well for both four-wheeling and trailer pulling. In addition to this, I consulted Jimmy Dorris at Racing Head Service (RHS), the respected engine builders at Memphis, Tennessee.

We decided that RHS would build the engine assembly, and we would keep close tabs on Before and After performance data. In an effort to create a fair comparison to the completely stock 350 engine, we rigidly limited the engine's peripheral equipment to the original manifolds, the old exhaust system, ignition, carburetor, emission controls and all engine accessories.

A mild compression ratio of 8.7:1 would permit use of regular grade fuel yet still develop high manifold vacuum. Usable torque and horsepower, along with improved fuel economy, were clear goals. According to RHS's dynamometer tests of similar 383 engines, we knew that a properly built 383 could exceed the output of a new 454 TBI engine while still delivering lower tailpipe emissions than the original 350 V-8.

Although emission standards for a 1976 Federal (49-State) 3/4-ton 4x4 truck were very mild, our aim was cleaner air. Ultimately, the RHS 383 at 8.7:1 compression with mild RV/torque camshaft profile and original HEI spark timing curve tested well below pollutant limits set for this truck. Idle carbon monoxide held steady at a 2.25% reading. Slight adjustment of the idle mixture screws dropped hydrocarbons to 120 ppm, with smoothest engine operation around 140 ppm. These figures reflect less than one half the carbon monoxide output and 70% of hydrocarbon pollutants found with this truck's original 350 engine—using the same, untouched OEM carburetor.

While any competent machine shop can construct a 383 stroker engine from a 350 block and 400 crankshaft, RHS has focused on the concerns of trailer pullers. The RHS Tow Torque Special engine results from gruelling dynamometer and real world tests to assure longevity, consistent power output and cooler operation under extreme loads.

RHS's 383 Tow Torque Special buildup reuses a thoroughly cleaned and remachined 350 four-bolt main bearing block, custom machined 400 crankshaft and 5.7" (350 type) connecting rods. All other parts, including the cylinder head assemblies and engine bolts, are new.

For cylinder heads, RHS chooses the 76cc combustion chamber World Products design, which feature thick walled bronze valve guides, special hardened exhaust valve seats, stainless steel 1.5" diameter exhaust and 1.94" diameter intake valves, new valve springs and chrome moly spring retainers.

Arden Rogers' 383 engine buildup boasts Silv-O-Lite/Keith Black hypereutectic D cup pistons, Speed Pro plasma moly piston rings, Vandervell engine bearings, heavy duty ARP rod bolts and main studs, a complete Competition Cams heavy duty valve train with 1.5:1 (stock) ratio roller tip rocker arms, and a new GM harmonic balancer and transmission flexplate for proper external balance of the 400 crankshaft.

RHS evaluated the higher altitudes at which the truck works and selected a CompCams CS 252H-10 grind camshaft designed for RV use. Valve opening duration of this

383 Superflow Dynamometer Tests

As a special service, RHS took Arden Rogers' 383 Tow Torque Special engine through extensive testing. Off the assembly line, preliminary checks included the compression (which ranged from 215 to 220 psi at test stand speeds), bearing oil flow and oil pressure (68 psi with a new high volume pump). The engine then went on the dynamometer for eleven full test sequences.

Equipment used for running the engine on the dynamometer included an Edelbrock Performer (dual plane) manifold, 600 cfm Edelbrock carburetor and a set of 1-5/8" Hedman headers. (On Arden Rogers' 1976 K-20 chassis installation, we reused the factory iron intake and exhaust manifolds and the original, unmodified Quadrajet carburetor.)

Figures for the test sequence reflect Unocal regular grade gasoline, a standard correction factor to 29.92 in/hg atmosphere, 60° F air temperature and, notably, a dry air environment:

RPM	Lb./Ft. Torque	Horsepower	Volumetric Efficiency
2000	384.7*	146.5	92.6%
2500	410.6	198.3	94.2%
3000	411.4	235.0	96.1%
3500	414.6**	276.3	96.9%**
4000	402.7	306.7	95.3%
4500	361.7	309.9**	90.1%
5000	306.5	291.8	83.7%

* 2000 rpm is lowest point for accurate readings on dyno. Here, 383 engine has already matched the *maximum* torque of a late 454 TBI engine.

** Peak performance for Arden Rogers' engine.

0014315

Fig. 16-26. RHS Tow Torque Special 383 engine accepts all OEM 350 hardware. Here, manifolding has been installed. (These impressive chrome valve covers required replacement with OEM items to comply with emission control needs.) Installed properly, 383 engine is indistinguishable from original 350 assembly.

0014316

Fig. 16-27. World Product SR cylinder heads accept 1976 engine brackets for air conditioning, power steering and alternator. Stock intake manifold and Quadrajet carburetor provide a bonafide comparison of 350 versus 383 engine designs. Likewise, end dump factory exhaust manifolds, although notably restrictive in flow, were also reused.

0014317

Fig. 16-28. 400 crankshaft is externally balanced. RHS includes a new factory 400 harmonic balancer and flexplate with these engines. (A 350 flywheel or flexplate will fit the 400 engine but will not provide proper balance.) RHS also matchweights and balances other reciprocating pieces.

torque camshaft is a mild 252° (intake and exhaust) measured from 0.006" tappet lift. Single pattern lobe centerlines of 106° with a healthy 0.431" intake/exhaust lift provide very stable manifold vacuum at all engine speeds plus a rapid torque rise to get a heavy load rolling.

Variations on the Theme

Some design variations for a 383 engine include use of shorter 400 connecting rods, higher compression ratios and camshafts ranging from original equipment grinds to all-out racing profiles. The RHS towing formula, however,

383 Real-World Driving Performance

We translated the impressive dynamometer figures to real world driving conditions, subjecting both the original 350 V-8 and new RHS 383 engine assemblies to the same tests, using regular pump gas and stock base timing advance of 8° BTDC. The altitude at our test site is 1400 feet above sea level. Air temperatures during both tests ranged from 86 to 92° F. We conducted tests with the automatic transmission's shifter in Drive mode and allowed automatic upshifts of the stock Turbo 350 transmission*:

Test Criteria	Original 350	New 383
0–60 mph without trailer (weight of truck was 6,450 pounds.)	17.85 seconds	10.27 seconds
40–60 mph Run without trailer	9.10 seconds	4.97 seconds
O–60 mph with 4,100 pound trailer	37.82 seconds	24.16 seconds
40–60 mph with trailer	21.83 seconds	9.53 seconds(!)
Combined fuel economy w/o trailer	10 mpg	11.2 mpg
Fuel economy with trailer	8 mpg	11 mpg

* Truck has original NP203 full-time 4x4 system. We reinstalled the original torque converter.
Tests conducted when engine had three dyno hours and less than 800 miles clocked on the odometer. (Expect slight gains after full break-in.)

0014318

Fig. 16-29. *Arden Rogers has added stock valve covers, a new water pump, belts, hoses, fuel pump, filters, ignition rotor, spark plugs, cables, distributor cap, thermostat and coolant. New 383 is ready for work. Despite tremendous performance gains, engine assumes same outward appearance as stock 350. Cool running 350 block and new World Products' cylinder heads serve well for trailer towing.*

Manifold Vacuum: Test of Fuel and Energy Efficiency

A simple manifold vacuum test says a lot. After adjusting the spark timing and idle mixture on the original 350 V-8, Arden and I conducted several vacuum tests. We repeated the same tests with the new engine.

Stationary and not under load, the 700, 1000, 1500 and 2000 rpm readings for the original 350 engine were 20, 20.5, 22 and 23 in/hg manifold vacuum, respectively. The same rpm tests on the new 383 produced 20, 21, 23 and 24 in/hg vacuum, respectively. This indicates a practical matchup of the camshaft, compression ratio and overall design.

Despite these very healthy readings for the new 383, the most impressive figure was a stall/load test that I conducted. With each engine, we placed the transmission in drive, holding one foot firmly on the brake. Bringing the engine to precisely 1250 rpm, I took manifold vacuum readings.

The original 350 engine yielded 10 in/hg of vacuum under this loaded condition. 383 tests produced a whopping 14.5 in/hg vacuum at the same load and speed. Manifold vacuum equates directly to energy efficiency and power, and this test illustrates a major low rpm gain from both the 400 crankshaft and CompCams CS252-H10 camshaft grind.

0014314

Manifold vacuum is an excellent test of engine condition and energy efficiency. Readings of both original 350 and new 383 reveal similar low speed (unloaded) vacuum patterns, with 383 running slightly higher. Under stall load at 1250 rpm, however, 383 pulls 14.5 in/hg vacuum versus weaker 10 in/hg of Arden's stock 350.

is an ideal model for trailer pulling with a heavy truck chassis.

Facing low octane fuels and the heat buildup of trailer pulling engines, we avoided a higher compression ratio. Although a stock profile 350 or 400 camshaft could easily work with a mild compression 383 stroker engine, the RHS RV/torque grind gave us a quicker torque rise.

As for shorter 400 rods versus 5.7" length 350 type connecting rods, I explored further, comparing the two rod lengths on Alan Lockheed's Engine Expert software, a sophisticated engine design program. The 5.7" center-to-center rod length used by RHS requires a specially located piston pin (nearer the piston crown), while 400 rods of 5.56" length will work with *short*-skirted forged aluminum 350 replacement pistons.

0014319

Fig. 16-30. Air cleaner assembly and all other emission package components went back in place. Stock ignition and carburetor help assure acceptable emission levels. Here, GM decal notes "September 1975" build date of original 350 engine and Federal (EPA) compliance guidelines. Truck is a non-catalyst model due to GVWR, and has no fuel restrictor, EGR valve or unleaded fuel requirement. Closed crankcase (PCV), thermal air cleaner and evaporative system remain operational.

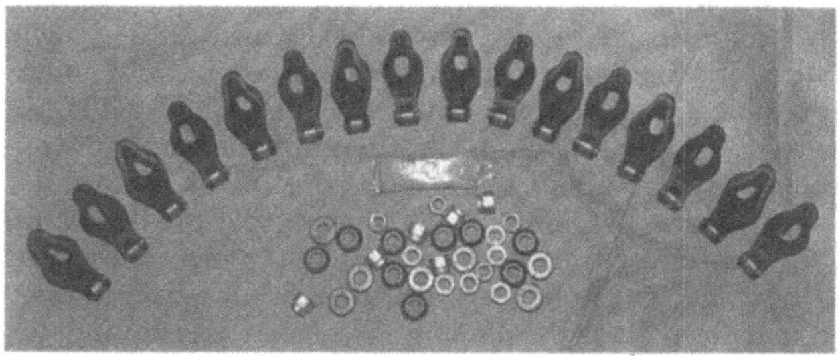

0014323

Fig. 16-31. RHS 383 Tow Torque Special engine uses Competition Cams' valvetrain pieces, including these roller tip replacement rocker arms. RHS choice for Arden Rogers' 383 is stock rocker arm ratio of 1.5:1. Smoother operation and improved performance result from less friction plus accurate valve lift and duration.

Our focus was durability, and Engine Expert revealed that a 383's critical tension (failure point) is at 7839 rpm with 5.7" 350 rods and 7814 rpm with the 5.56" 400 rods. Maximum horsepower for the trailer puller 383 is at 4500 rpm. Both rod lengths will work effectively here, with pistons readily available to accommodate either approach.

After three hours and eleven sequences of Superflow dynamometer testing and break-in, RHS shipped Arden Rogers' 383 engine. When we installed the engine, I stayed with totally stock tuning specifications. Arden drove his 1976 K-20 for seven-hundred and fifty miles of break-in before we subjected the new 383 tow engine to any road or trailer towing tests.

Arden and I drove back to the original test site, and with Arden at the wheel, we repeated the maneuvers of our pre-tests with the stock 350 V-8. Our carefully timed real-world runs, including pulls with the 24-foot Alpenlite trailer in tow, corroborated the RHS dyno results. The performance increase was dramatic, as indicated on the test charts, and Arden is very glad that he kept his 1976 Chevrolet truck.

6. 1955–59 GMC TRUCKS: POTENT PONTIAC V-8 MUSCLE

1955 was a milestone year for GM light trucks. Chevrolet's small-block 265 V-8 quickly dominated the high performance automotive scene. Simultaneously, Pontiac Motor Division launched its own assault with a new and potent overhead valve (commonly known as a valve-in-head or OHV) V-8. Unfortunately, the Pontiac car line shared archaic chassis and geartrain designs with heavyweight Buick and Oldsmobile models, a stigma that overshadowed one of the hottest V-8 engine designs in General Motors' history.

Even with these liabilities and a relatively small 287 cubic inch displacement 1955 powerplant, the Pontiacs displayed their prowess and won respect on NASCAR and drag racing circuits. The new OHV V-8 design, which replaced the sluggish Pontiac L-head straight eights of the postwar era, came with a radical block, bearing and crankshaft design, plus a stamped steel rocker arm set, similar to the Chevrolet 265 V-8's innovative design.

The early Pontiac/GMC V-8 proved an ideal truck engine. A 288, 316, 336 or 347 GMC truck V-8 develops massive torque while offering high reliability, two ingredients that vintage GMC trucks have always provided.

Best of all, like the Chevrolet V-8s, Pontiac's earliest 287 shares much of its design with the later Pontiac 389 and larger engines. Using the correct motor mounts and timing cover, a Pontiac 389 or bigger engine can easily replace a stock Second-Series 1955–59 GMC truck V-8. For the GMC truck restorer or street truck builder who wants an original looking yet more powerful V-8 engine, consider the later 389 to 455 cubic inch Pontiac engines.

Evolution of a Roguish V-8 Engine

The 287 Pontiac V-8 (called the 288 in 2nd-Series 1955 GMC light trucks) grew to 317 cubic inches (called the 316 in GMC trucks) in 1956. This engine provided much better performance, and by 1957, as Chevrolet introduced the 283, Pontiac/GMC again bumped displacement—this time to 347 cubic inches. In 1958, while Pontiac passenger car versions crept to 370 cubic inches, GMC light trucks offered a slightly hybridized 336 cubic inch Pontiac V-8 design.

The rare 1957 and 1958 Pontiac Bonneville models, which borrowed Rochester's Corvette fuel injection system, were the peak of early Pontiac V-8 performance. During these years, Tri-Power (triple two-barrel carburetion) systems also raised horsepower. 347 and 370 engines, ranging from two-barrel and four-barrel versions to Tri-Power and FI, displayed the flexibility of Pontiac's rugged V-8s.

Pontiac displacement was again bumped in 1959, with the advent of the first 389 V-8. Smokey Yunick's engines dominated the NASCAR circuit. Mickey Thompson's daring land speed record was set with four Pontiac V-8 engines. These and other racing laurels put Pontiac at the forefront of performance respectability.

GMC light trucks used the Pontiac 347 V-8 in 1957 and the hybrid 336 V-8 in 1958–59. The larger 389 Pontiac engine never saw service in GM light trucks. In 1960, GMC switched to its new and somewhat staid 305 V-6 power-

0014324 / 0014325

Fig. 16-32. 347 Pontiac/GMC V-8 (bottom) in 1957 half-ton pickup is akin to 335 horsepower 1970 455 HO Pontiac Trans Am engine (top).

train, and when GMC again optioned V-8 engines, the choices were the Chevrolet small-block and, later, big-block V-8s.

Pontiac 389 and Larger V-8s

Potent 389 engines placed Pontiac squarely in competition with the Ford 390, Mopar 383 and Chevrolet 348 engines. It took the 1962 Ford 406, Chevrolet 409 and Mopar 413 engines to outrun the Pontiac 389. Pontiac quickly solved that problem.

For 1963, as horsepower became synonymous with car sales, Pontiac submitted its bid. The 421, all 370 conservative horsepower, made history. As with earlier displacement increases, the 421 Pontiac V-8 again increased main bearing journal size, jumping a full 0.250" over the already durable 389 design.

The Muscle Car Era was well underway, and Pontiac V-8 engines vied heavily for high performance successes over the next decade. By 1967, the new 400 Ram Air engines came on line. Right off the showroom floor, a 3250 pound Firebird with Ram Air could trip the drag strip lights in the 14 second range at 105 mph.

Toward the end of the Muscle Car Era, the 428 replaced the awesome 421, and Pontiac launched the 455 HO engines. In direct competition with Chevrolet's 454 and other big-block engines, the new Pontiac LS-5 option 455 HO suffered severely from the General Motors' new corporate directive to limit compression ratios to a maximum of 8.5:1. This measure coincided with pending changes in the tailpipe emission regulations.

So powerful is the 455 Pontiac V-8, however, that in detuned 8.4:1 compression form the 1971 engine still delivers 335 gross horsepower. Considering today's low octane fuels, the 455 HO engine's compression ratio is an excellent level for a classic Second-Series 1955–59 GMC street truck buildup.

> **NOTE —**
> Net power ratings, an effort to de-emphasize the horsepower race, still peg the 455 HO Pontiac engine at 305 horsepower. Pontiac buffs emphasize that both the net and gross horsepower figures understate the thunderous torque and throttle response of a 455 engine.

From the 1955 287 V-8 until the last 455 built in 1976, Pontiac turned a fundamental engine design into each year's potent performer. The 455 V-8, born in 1970, was history after the 1976 model run, the loss of a reliable, high horsepower engine.

Building a Pontiac V-8

Potential lurks in an array of H.O. Pontiac V-8s. Each will fit a Second-Series 1955–59 GMC truck, although you will need to use the correct V-8 motor mounts and, where possible, the early style Pontiac V-8 timing cover. 400, 428 and 455 engines abound, but the most desirable powerplants are those H.O. blocks with four-bolt main caps.

A number of Pontiac V-8 engine blocks are drilled for the four-bolt main caps but fitted with two-bolt types. These blocks afford easy use of new or reconditioned four-bolt main caps following "line bore" machining. Recycler sources indicate a strong supply of 1959–76 Pontiac V-8 engines—at inexpensive prices.

Follow-up parts, like high performance factory or aftermarket exhaust manifolds and a heavy duty radiator buildup, will round out the swap.

Muscle in the 300 to 425 horsepower range is easily available by mildly blueprinting a factory powerplant. The hotter, yet streetable, 5000 to 6000 rpm range thunder of a Pontiac V-8 equipped with a McKellar-grind hydraulic camshaft would clearly top the choices.

For reliability, seek out a circa 1973 or 1974 Super Duty 455 from a Trans Am. Although low on compression (with 8.25:1 pistons), these engines have race breeding. Coded LS-2, they rate a conservative 310 net brake horsepower (later lowered to 290 bhp for political reasons) at a very low 4000 rpm.

For racing goals, the SD-455/LS-2 is probably the last real muscle engine built for a US production car. Its 4-bolt main bearing caps nestle beneath reinforced iron block bulkheads. Aluminum pistons (0.030" larger in diameter than the standard 400 pistons) and forged steel rods spin a nitrided crankshaft with a 0.460" longer stroke than the 400 engine. Oil pan baffling, some serious factory cylinder head port work, and header-type exhaust manifolds complete the tale. This last Trans Am engine was obviously on the drawing board long before the curtain fell on high performance.

7. ENGINE REBUILDING

As your truck engine reaches the upper end of its service life, you have two options: an in-the-chassis ring-and-valve job (overhaul) or a complete, out-of-chassis engine rebuild.

An in-chassis overhaul is relatively easy with many truck engines. Following your factory-level service guide, you'll remove the cylinder head(s), oil pan and timing cover; ream the cylinder ridges before removing the rods and pistons; fit new rod and main bearings, along with new piston rings, a timing chain/sprocket set and a new or reconditioned oil pump.

Most likely, you will send the cylinder head(s) to a machine shop for reconditioning, then carefully hone the cylinder bores (protecting the crankshaft bearing journals from any debris or abrasive materials and restoring cleanliness throughout the engine). A new or reground camshaft and lifters and a new oil pump round out the job.

Overhauls work on mildly worn engines and those having hard, durable cylinder walls. An overhaul buys extra miles of driving yet falls short of a complete rebuild. Restricted by the chassis and body, many rebuilding steps are neglected during an in-the-frame overhaul. By contrast, a complete, professional engine rebuild involves replacement or precision machining of every moving part in the engine.

The "Real" Engine Rebuild

Emission control hardware and a maze of carburetor plumbing overwhelm most 1972–86 GM light truck engines. The basic long-block engine assembly, however, remains relatively unchanged. Once out of the chassis (see your GM truck shop manual for removal procedures), your six-cylinder or V-8 engine can undergo a thorough rebuild.

A quality rebuild will virtually remanufacture your engine. Caustic block and head cleaning, replacing hard-to-reach freeze plugs and installing camshaft bearings are just a few of the procedures.

Unless run on a high grade synthetic oil from day one, the typical 120,000-plus mile GM truck engine will have 0.006" or more cylinder taper. (A simple ring-and-valve job overhaul would serve little purpose here, as rings cannot seal properly against a tapered cylinder wall.) Here, restoration to OEM tolerances will take place during a machine shop remanufacture of your engine.

Some Engine Assembly Survival Tips

Sometimes it is easier to have the machine shop completely assemble your long block (cylinder head[s] and block parts). If, however, you plan to assemble your newly machined engine parts, you will need to follow some important guidelines. Although your GM truck shop manual can help with step-by-step procedures, there are some fundamental concerns that I will share.

For example, never fill hydraulic lifters with oil. Hydraulically pumped-up lifters can cause valve-to-piston interference during initial cranking of the engine. (You should, however, coat the lifter bases and bores with engine assembly lube.) After the engine is completely assembled and the valves are adjusted to specification, you can prime the engine's lubrication system before start-up.

Fortunately, most GM truck engines have what I consider reasonably low compression ratios and can tolerate today's lower fuel octane ratings. For the purpose of rebuilding your engine, a compression ratio of 8.0:1 to 8.7:1 works very well on a carbureted V-8 or six. I've found that longer stroke engines, like the carbureted 292 inline six or a 454 V-8, can survive nicely on 8.7:1 compression.

Usually, spark timing changes (like a mild initial spark advance and limited spark curve) will permit use of a higher compression ratio. Some 1960s' engines had 9:1 or higher compression, and surviving with such a ratio may be possible by simply retarding the spark timing slightly to prevent detonation. The yardstick that I use for truck purposes is to be able to run 87 to 88 octane fuel without detonating, damaging pistons or pitting valve faces.

On an older GM engine with a 9:1 compression ratio or higher, one means of lowering the compression is to replace the factory shim-type or thinner head gasket with a thicker (Detroit or similar make) composition type gasket. Apply sealant and install the gasket according to the manufacturer's guidelines. Use Permatex's Teflon Thread Compound on head bolt threads that enter water jackets.

During an engine overhaul or rebuild, you can upgrade performance with high-quality aftermarket parts. Speed-Pro Performance recognizes the potent GM truck engines and offers race-quality Plasma Moly file-fit gap piston rings. For the less stressed engine, another approach is TRW or Sealed Power high grade or Premium OEM replacement rings.

After refinishing and measuring each cylinder wall, wash your bores thoroughly and coat them with clean oil. Many shops recommend Speed-Pro/Sealed Power rings, fitted to the stock or OEM type cast alloy pistons, to help provide greater durability. Likewise, a full set of Speed-Pro or equivalent valves (stainless steel exhaust valves especially) and a three-angle valve seat grind will assure consistent cylinder sealing and longevity.

Knowing When to Rebuild Your Engine

An engine rebuild is necessary when oil loss increases and fixing the leaks doesn't help. A noticeable decrease in oil pressure is also a bad sign, or when a subtle, deep in the engine knock develops. Another portent of trouble is a power decrease to the point that your torquey V-8 or six feels like a mini-truck's four-cylinder engine, even after a thorough tune-up—or when a steady miss is neither fuel system nor spark related.

The story can only worsen, and if ignored, a connecting rod might well wave, "Good-bye!"—just as some minor off-highway hill places a load on the engine. Assuming the rest of the truck still stands tall, the engine wear can easily be remedied by a proper rebuild of the long block. By catching the damage in time, your old engine can serve as a thoroughly useful and rebuildable core.

As for the merits of a seasoned cylinder block, many racers insist that these blocks are far better than new ones. Heat and stress have likely distorted and twisted the castings to their final form, and assuming that magnafluxing or sonic testing of cylinders has shown no casting flaws or cracks, the remachined older block may actually hold closer tolerances under severe service.

I have found that engine parts often wear at uneven rates. Timing chain and valve/carbon problems usually have a head start on other parts. Sometimes, in fact, a valve job and timing chain replacement can buy tens of thousands of miles before a major rebuild is necessary.

Piston ring wear, however, will follow. (In off-pavement use, air filtration is critical, or rings will fail even sooner than normal.) Cylinder walls generally taper toward the top (compression end) of their bores, and ring replacement usually calls for re-boring and refitting with new, oversized pistons. Sometimes, especially in the case of high nickel/chrome content in an engine block, the cylinders can simply be power honed, with new rings fitted to the original pistons.

Any need to replace rings will warrant a valve grind and new engine bearings. Since carbon and sludge find their way into most engine assemblies, a complete teardown will afford hot tanking the engine parts to remove all traces of grime and deposits. Once piston ring, crankshaft, or block work becomes necessary, the best cure is removal of the engine from the chassis and either a complete teardown and rebuild or an exchange of the core for another long block.

Engine Diagnosis Leading to a Rebuild

Before jerking your engine from the chassis and floating a short-term loan at the credit union, be certain the engine *needs* a rebuild. Start with a standard compression test, isolating the lowest cylinder readings. Follow up with a leakdown test to distinguish valve from piston ring wear. I am so sold on the superior accuracy of a leakdown test that I only use a conventional compression gauge to pinpoint the lowest cylinder readings. At that point, I use my portable Snap-On or Sun scope's leakdown tester to isolate wear and specific defects.

I hold to a maximum compression variance of 10% between the highest and lowest cylinder readings on any engine that calls for a normal compression reading under 160 psi. Although OEM guidelines may allow more latitude than this, especially on high cylinder pressure engines, an engine with 15 to 25% or more compression variance definitely has ring or valve wear.

Using my 10% standard, a cylinder with a normal reading of 150 psi on a compression gauge test will tolerate *no less than* 135 psi pressure on its lowest cylinder. Ideally, even this imbalance should be eliminated if possible. If valve or carbon troubles are not suspected, follow up with a leakdown test to confirm whether there is piston ring trouble.

A properly performed leakdown test should yield 8 to 12% cylinder leakage in a good engine. (10% leak is the maximum allowed for retrofitting a turbocharger.) By 20% leak, the engine definitely requires attention. Should ring wear be noted, I would remove and tear down the engine for rebuilding.

In all cases, if any crankshaft bearing has failed or a loss of oil pressure related to bearing wear has occurred, the engine must be torn down for complete rebuilding. The failure of bearings will contaminate the lubrication system, leaving metal particles to tear up new bearings. Complete disassembly and hot tank cleaning of parts is necessary to assure that the engine is clean.

When camshaft lobes grind away, I would also advise a major engine teardown. Hard metal has circulated through the engine, and the oil filter is not always able to catch all of the metal that has worn away. This is especially true of earlier engines with by-pass oil filtration systems.

Long Block Versus Short Block Replacement

When faced with the choice to rebuild an engine, two alternatives exist: 1) rebuilding the short block (fitted engine block without the cylinder heads) or 2) rebuilding the entire long block.

If your choice is to have an automotive machine shop assemble the engine, a long block will come with the head gaskets, heads, and all valve train parts installed. The valve lifters, pushrods, rocker arms, and related parts will be assembled, and valve clearances will likely be set. Your job would be the installation of the manifolds, the water pump and engine accessories.

The second alternative, the short block, consists of an engine block assembled with the crankshaft, rods, pistons/rings, bearings, camshaft, timing chain/sprockets, and possibly the oil pump and pan. Your cylinder head(s) could be rebuilt separately, and you would install the head(s) plus all related parts.

The final alternative would be sending out only the machine shop work. If your skills include the ability to completely disassemble and reassemble an engine, you can save money.

Rebuilding a V-8 Short Block

Once you've decided to rebuild and remachine your engine, the machine shop is the next stop. Find a machine shop with a good reputation. (AERA or PERA membership is a good sign.)

For some insight into engine rebuilding, I will share one of my own rebuild jobs on a small-block V-8. The basic simplicity of these engines makes this a good example, as the principles involved apply to any Chevrolet or GMC light truck engine.

> ***CAUTION —***
> *Startup of a newly rebuilt engine is the most critical moment in its life. Cleanliness during assembly is a must. Use engine assembly lube on all bearings, the lifter bases and bores and the valve stems.*

The job begins with a complete teardown for cleaning. To enable proper cleanup of the block, all oil artery plugs, freeze plugs, engine bearings and seals must be removed. The crankshaft, rods/pistons, camshaft and camshaft bearings, plus any loose gasket material, are also separated from the block.

CAUTION —
Main crankshaft bearing caps cannot be mixed, switched, turned around, or borrowed from another engine. Every block has matched and fitted main caps. If you find a damaged main cap on teardown, a new or used cap can only be used after line boring. (Line boring aligns the bores of the main bearings.) Truing a distorted or retrofit main bearing cap usually consists of slight milling of the main cap's block mating surface; then a boring bar is run through the block/main cap centerline to reestablish a concentric and properly sized crankshaft main bearing centerline(s).

Then, stripped to its basic casting, the block is placed in a highly caustic hot tank solution and, literally, boiled until there is nothing left but bare casting metal and badly etched camshaft bearings. As for other ferrous metal parts, including the oil pan, cylinder heads, crankshaft, and connecting rods, these may also be dipped in the caustic.

After thoroughly scouring all debris, carbon and sludge from the block, a thorough wash, rinse and brush cleaning of oil galleries and other passages takes place. Once clean, the block will later be carefully refurbished with new Teflon tape wrapped artery plugs and sealant coated brass type freeze plugs. Now, however, cylinder boring and piston fitting will take place.

Boring cylinders is precise work. Tolerances run to the *ten-thousandths* of an inch, and machining tools must be deadly accurate. Depending upon engine use and the machinist's preference, torque plates may be mounted to the block deck before boring. These plates, thick steel and attached to the cylinder head bolt holes, simulate the mounted cylinder head with its attendant torque stress on the block deck.

Regardless of whether torque plates are used, the boring is critical. Pistons come in standard oversizes ranging 0.010", 0.020", 0.030", 0.040" and 0.060". (Metric oversizes are typically .25mm, .50mm, .75mm, 1.00mm, 1.25mm and 1.50mm.)

Piston-to-cylinder-wall clearances must be on tolerance for the piston / ring design and / or the OEM engine standards. Too close, and piston seizure could occur. Excessive, and oil consumption or piston damage will be likely.

For a quiet and long running Chevrolet small-block, I will see that a Sunnen CK-10 or equivalent properly cross-hatched hone job takes place to assure very true cylinder walls. (The CK-10 can counter out-of-round and distortion caused by hard spots in the cylinder walls.) Under these conditions, I will run 0.0015" (fifteen ten-thousandths of an inch) piston-to-wall clearance with cast, OEM type replacement pistons and cast / moly rings. For forged type replacement pistons, 0.0025" to 0.003" is optimal for a somewhat quiet and trouble-free engine.

Some forged alloy racing piston designs demand 0.005" to 0.0075" piston-to-wall clearance, far more than I find suited to a highway driven engine. For anything less than an all-out racing effort, I avoid these piston types, as their cold start-up noise level and increased oil consumption can be troublesome. High-clearance pistons typically serve racing applications and use zero-gap piston rings.

0014396

Fig. 16-33. *Gary Sweetwood begins his post-boring finish work. The block benefits from Sunnen's CK-10 machine, which precisely trues the bore while leaving a perfect cross hatch pattern. Gary works within ten-thousandths of an inch (.0001") standard to assure proper fitup of the pistons to cylinder walls. Clearances established here will increase engine life.*

0014397

Fig. 16-34. *Coarseness of cutting versus finishing stones can be seen on these two walls. The depth of stone cuts helps control oil consumption and regulates piston ring wear and break-in.*

Once the cylinder wear has determined the correct oversize required, boring begins with setup of the engine block. Clamped securely in position, with the crankshaft centerline absolutely perpendicular to the boring bar, each cylinder is centered carefully and bored. Constant measurements are taken by the machinist to assure that results conform to his or her plan for the engine.

For a GM light truck engine subjected to heavy loads, I prefer a maximum rebore of 0.030" over standard. 0.040" oversize is tolerated by many GM engines, but 0.060" or more presses the limits of engine cooling and wanders into the realm of core shift concerns. If I were to build up a 400 small-block V-8 (which is highly unlikely since the 383 stroker hybrid is a much more sensible approach), I would limit the bore oversize to a maximum of 0.020" to protect the siamesed middle cylinders from overheating.

Once bored to near finished size, enough material is left in each bore to allow finish honing. The goal is a true, perfectly finished cylinder wall with the correct, predetermined angle in the cross-hatch pattern. This is decided by the piston ring and piston design, with each ring type demanding a specific finish. An incorrect cross-hatch pattern angle or improper wall coarseness can ruin piston rings and/or cause oil consumption problems.

By now, you can see the dramatic difference between precision machining versus in-the-chassis ring jobs with a glaze buster. Remanufacturers or machine shop rebuilders actually restore seasoned engine blocks, rods, crankshafts, and cylinder heads to OE standards of performance.

The Rebuild Continues

While the block is being prepared, the machinist refurbishes the crankshaft and connecting rods. Crankshafts can be reground to 0.010", 0.020", and 0.030" undersizes (0.25mm, 0.50mm, and 0.75mm metric).

When the rod journal with the worst wear or out-of-round condition has been determined, all rod journals will be turned to that size. Likewise, main bearing journals will be undersized uniformly. This follows the same logic as boring and honing all cylinders to the same oversize for uniform performance.

0014400

Fig. 16-35. *Super tough, heavy duty steel Chevrolet 1182 crankshaft is being machined here. Cast crankshafts, like the one the 400 uses, can give substantial service, too, especially when machined to tolerance and balanced.*

0014401

Fig. 16-36. *Franco puts the finishing touch on crankshaft journals that have been ground. His polishing technique and chamfering of oil holes will give better than new service to this crankshaft.*

If a rod or main journal has been severely damaged, it can often be safely repaired by a special welding process. Once welded, a lighter undersize or even standard size bearings can be utilized after machining. Ideally, the least amount of undersizing (.010" by US standard or 0.25mm on a metric engine) is desirable. This leaves ample material and adheres closer to the original engine balance.

Like cylinder boring, crankshaft grinding is an art. The crankshaft must be on dead center, as the main bearings and rod journals, or throws, are machined on an offset. For proper bearing clearance, the crankshaft machinist must decide whether high or low sided tolerances will work best on a given engine.

Bearing clearances also control the oil pressure. The type of oil pump volume employed will also affect the grinder's decision. Excessive clearance with a lower volume pump may not provide the necessary bearing protection, and failure of bearings could result.

In addition to a proper radius of the journals, the grinder may chamfer the oil feed holes and, finally, polish the surface of each journal to enhance service life and increase the refinement of the tolerances.

> NOTE —
> The crankshaft plays a critical role within the engine, and this is a good place to invest in precision finishing work and balancing. (See engine balance section within this chapter.)

After the crankshaft is ground and finished, a thorough cleanout of all passages takes place. Brush, solvent and air pressure cleaning is not overkill, since *any* debris within a newly machined crankshaft can cause immediate and irreparable damage to rod or main bearings. Remember, debris in crank passages will immediately hit the bearings.

With a clean block and crankshaft, cam bearings can be carefully fitted. Installed with special driving tools and a heavy hammer by most shops, the cam bearings must be true and centered perfectly to align oil passages. Oil

0014398

Fig. 16-37. Rod shanks are decked before big end of the rod is honed. The roundness of the rod bores determines bearing clearance and correct fitup of parts.

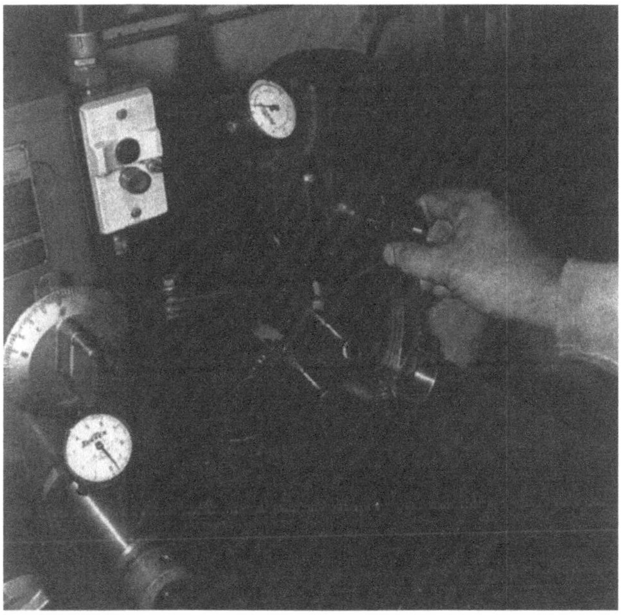

0014420

Fig. 16-38. Honing and sizing of the connecting rods can increase engine life considerably. In conjunction with rod alignment, true piston travel can be assured.

pressure control can often be affected by misaligned cam bearings, and even slight misfitting can cause serious engine damage.

With cam bearings installed, a new rear cam plug and new Teflon or sealant coated artery plugs, the block is ready for parts reassembly. The new pistons have by now been fitted to the refurbished connecting rods. The small and big end bores of the rods are machined and honed to assure concentricity, and rod alignment is checked after the pistons have been pin-fitted. (Modern shops use a special piston warmer to allow easy installation of the wrist pins.)

Once the ring end gaps have been verified in their cylinder bores, piston rings are carefully installed on the pistons. The piston and rod assemblies are then ready for assembly.

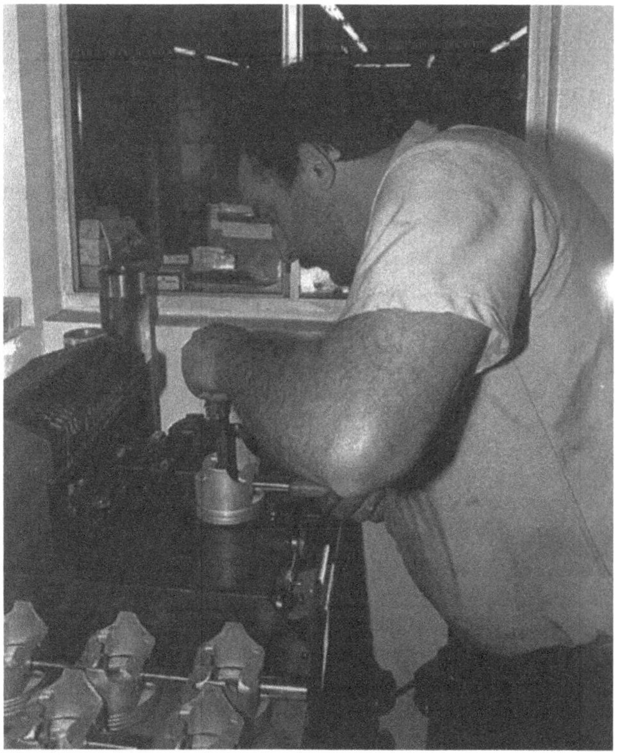

0014402

Fig. 16-39. Using heat, Nick Bongiorno precisely fits new pistons to the remachined connecting rods. The last step is check for rod and piston alignment. With the block bores now perfectly perpendicular to the crankshaft centerline, these straight parts will run friction free.

Assembling the Short Block

If you have the right tools and can keep a work area super clean, assembly is not very difficult. With all new machining, and parts ready for installation, a careful job can be performed in a few hours.

Most builders like to install the crankshaft first. "Laying" the crank involves carefully placing the main bearings in their saddles and coating them with assembly lube or oil. Keeping the rear main seal area dry, sealant is properly applied to the seal's outer surface and the joining point (on two-piece seals) before installation.

I use a thin film of Permatex's Ultra-Blue silicone sealant and prefer this type to any other product currently available. Avoid rear main seal leaks.

With the main seal installed, the *clean* crankshaft is carefully centered over the upside down block. With the block in this position, the crankshaft can be lowered directly onto the bearing half-shells. Once in position, the main bearing caps will center easily.

Bearing halves centered and seated, with all clearances correct, the main cap bolts can be installed finger tight. As dry threads create friction and poor torque readings, engine oil or graphite thread dressing is often recommended to help assure torque uniformity.

> **CAUTION —**
> *When tightening critical engine bolts and nuts, note the torque specifications in your truck's shop manual and whether these figures are with oiled or dry threads.*

With bolts installed and main caps setting flush, the torque sequence begins. Follow OEM shop manual guidelines for proper torque, starting with a lower measurement, then increasing tension on the entire set uniformly. Three or four steps, over the entire bolt set, will provide good results.

Once the final tightening tension has been reached at every bolt, I let them set for a few minutes, then check each one again. Thread friction can cause one or two bolts to be *slightly* loose. After the threads cool and bolts stabilize, slight torque gains can sometimes be made.

Major Gains from Balancing Your Engine

Precision balancing of engine parts provides a major benefit. Take, for instance, the fact that a quarter-ounce of imbalance just 4" from the center of the crankshaft becomes a seven-pound force at 2000 rpm and 120-pound force at 8000 rpm. Claims of *doubling* the life of production engines are not far fetched, since balancing can come within *tenths of a gram* accuracy.

General Motors light truck engines benefit tremendously from balancing the crankshaft and reciprocating parts. Since the popular 383 buildup involves 350 and 400 small-block components, balance is even more critical. The 350 and other small-blocks are internally balanced, while the 400 small-block and 454 big-block have external balancing.

For long and smooth engine life, I always balance the damper, crankshaft, flywheel/flexplate and manual clutch assembly. Match weighting the rods, pistons, rings and other reciprocating parts is also paramount to top engine performance and longevity. Here is a pictorial look at a 383 Chevrolet V-8 hybrid engine that I had balanced by Cliff Priest at Santee, California.

Cliff uses Stewart-Warner Model 2000D balancing equipment for crankshafts, flywheels, and clutch covers. Cliff begins an engine balancing job with boxed pistons and separate connecting rods. He cuts each piston to the exact gram weight of the lightest in the set, and follows by matching the rods. Then, with exact measurements of the reciprocating versus the rotating weights, balancing begins.

Cliff determines reciprocating weight on a V-8 engine by adding one piston, piston pin, piston pin lock set (when utilized), the ring set weight for the one piston and the estimated weight of oil. Rotating weight for a V-8, with two rods sharing each crankpin, would be the weight of two rod big ends, their insert bearings, nuts and locking hardware, and oil weight.

Once these calculations are made, bobweights can be attached to the crankshaft. The bobweights strive for a simulated 100% of rotating weight and 50% of reciprocal weight on V-8 engine balancing jobs.

As the crankshaft spins on the balancer, Cliff adjusts for its front and rear weightiness and imbalance. On my 383 Chevy stroker crankshaft balancing job, the flywheel was easily drilled to correct imbalance, and the clutch pressure plate got a similar treatment.

When I assembled this engine, the results were dramatic. Compared to the typical small-block Chevrolet production V-8, this precisely weight matched engine, even with less than 100 miles wear-in time, sung happily from a s-m-o-o-t-h 650 rpm idle to an impressive and heavy throttled 5000 rpm.

A precisely balanced engine just loves to spin. Very regular, even power strokes distinguish these engines, and the results of balancing can be heard in the exhaust note and felt in the extra miles between gas stops.

0014491

Connecting rod weight is precisely determined.

0014492

Bobweights simulate the reciprocating and rotating mass of the rods, pistons/pins, rings, bearings, and even motor oil.

0014403

Fig. 16-40. Once the main bearings and crankshaft have been "laid," piston ring installation, with care and proper alignment of the rings, readies the rod/piston assemblies for placement in the block. Follow piston ring installation instructions carefully.

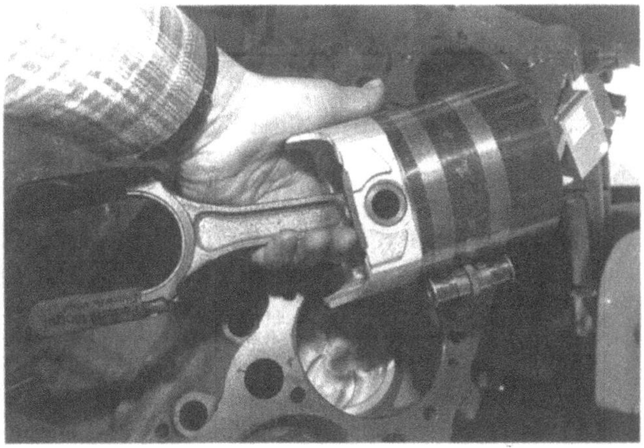

0014404

Fig. 16-41. Conventional ring compressors work well. Lightly oiled and square, the tool allows for an easy hammer handle tap to insert pistons into their cylinders. Note the plastic caps over rod bolts to protect the fresh and precisely polished crankshaft from accidental nicks.

CAUTION —
The crankshaft should rotate smoothly as you torque the bolts in sequence. Floating in oil or assembly lube, no part should resist rotation in a fresh engine.

There's no such thing as a "tight" engine. In fact, a properly machined engine, with correct clearances at critical points, should turn as easily during assembly as when the rings have seated after break-in. No part should create friction severe enough to prevent rotation. Ring drag on the cylinder walls, valve spring tension, and the general mass of moving parts will provide whatever resistance a new engine has. Of course, rotation gets tougher after the spark plugs have been installed.

With the crankshaft installed, the rod/piston/ring assemblies can be fitted. If OEM rods from the original engine are being used, the rods are each numbered for their respective cylinders. Pistons generally have arrows or similar marks on their crowns designating the front of the engine. In many GM light truck engines, the goal is to install each rod and piston with the rod's oil squirt hole facing correctly in the block. This consideration is critical to engine survival. Check with the machinist or your factory-level shop manual if any question arises over the location of the rod oil holes.

Plastic boots are placed on the rod bolts to protect the crankshaft during assembly. The rod's crankpin is rotated as far away from the top of the block as possible, and the rings are staged or staggered according to the manufacturer's recommendation. With the rings in their proper alignment, the ring compressor is oiled and installed.

Holding the piston squarely in the cylinder bore, I use a soft hammer handle to *gently* tap the rings through the compressor and into the bore. Watch the rod to be certain that it drops easily and free of any parts. Guide the centered rod, carefully, toward the crankpin.

Some mechanics have already installed the rod bearing shells before installing the piston/rod assembly, while others insert the bearings just before attaching the rod. Either way, the bearing shells must be in place, oiled or coated with assembly lube before the rod reaches the crankpin.

0014405

Fig. 16-42. With crankshaft rotated to place rod journals at the bottom of their arc, pistons are carefully installed. Cleanliness and light handling of these parts will pay big dividends in extra miles of service.

With the rod gently drawn squarely to the crankpin journal, the rod cap can be installed. The cap should only be installed *one way*, generally marked or numbered to match the rod. Care must be used here, as the rod bearing saddles have been trued, and only the correct installation direction will provide a perfectly round bearing bore.

When each rod has been fitted to the crankshaft, the nuts can be firmly and evenly secured. Stay below the actual torque setting for the rod until a pair of rods (in the case of V-type engines that share rod throws) have been attached. Final torque can then be met. In the case of six-cylinder engines that do not have rods that share journals, the final torque can be set during initial fitup.

Be certain that nuts are tightened sequentially and in stages, and always rotate the crankshaft after setting torque to be certain the parts are free of friction. Re-check torque at each rod after turning the crankshaft to be certain torque settings have held.

With Chevrolet V-8s and other GM light truck engines, the oil pump drive shaft and its snap-lock sleeve must be installed prior to installing the oil pump. (Otherwise, the oil pan and oil pump must be removed again!) When all of the rods have been secured, install the oil pump and torque the oil pump mounting bolt(s) carefully. Install and adjust the new oil pickup screen. The oil pan can now be carefully installed with the engine still upside down on the stand.

> ***CAUTION —***
> *Oil pump pickup screen height is critical to proper engine oiling. You must follow the guidelines in your GM truck shop manual when setting screen height.*

Once the timing cover is securely in place, the oil pan can be fitted. Follow oil pan installation instructions, carefully using Ultra-Blue or its equivalent at the junction corners where the seals meet the side rail gaskets. Tighten pan bolts lightly and evenly from one end toward the other in cross, or adhere to the OEM installation tightening sequence. Check all bolts several times, taking care not to overtighten.

Whether the timing cover needs installation before the oil pan or not, the camshaft must be carefully installed. The camshaft is a valve train component and requires careful installation to assure proper break-in.

Camshaft Installation and Indexing

Camshaft and hydraulic lifter installation should follow the manufacturer's instructions. Use of lifter lube is vital. Apply a liberal coating to the lifter bases and lifter bores to assure a safe initial start-up for the new engine. With its bearing journals well lubed, the camshaft can be carefully aligned with the front cam bearing.

0014414

Fig. 16-43. *Here, camshaft of choice is Rhoads' VVT-211. The camshaft comes complete with Rhoads lifters and special lubricant. Care in installation assures top performance and longevity of parts.*

0014415

Fig. 16-44. *Camshaft timing sprocket bolts are new and installed with Loctite 242. Use of a double roller chain and sprockets will lengthen service life and deliver more accurate valve timing.*

> ***CAUTION —***
> *Never fill hydraulic lifters with oil by compressing their plungers in an oil bath. New lifters take many crankshaft revolutions to bleed down, and if the camshaft profile has a high degree of valve overlap, the normal pre-load setting may cause valves to interfere with the piston crowns upon cranking. Before installing lifters, apply lifter lube to the block's lifter bores and the base of each lifter.*

Installing a camshaft can be tricky. Some blocks permit hand access to the cam through the center of the lifter valley, while others do not. Chevrolet V-8s offer very little top access to the camshaft. To make a safe installation, without galling the new cam bearings, the camshaft must be supported from its front end and *carefully* fed through each cam bearing.

Crossing areas where the cam does not have bearing support is most critical, as the sharp edged lobes could nick or otherwise damage the cam bearings. Here, you must grasp the camshaft from within the block or use a long rod, threaded into the front end of the camshaft, to lend support. Once the camshaft is in place, with the rear block plug coated with sealant and carefully installed, the camshaft sprocket and timing chain can be installed.

Valve timing is critical. There's no room for "maybe" as you carefully align the two timing sprockets. Follow the manufacturer's marks and method. Align the camshaft sprocket with a straight-edge, then bolt into place. Apply Loctite 242 or its equivalent to any camshaft sprocket bolts that do not have locking hardware.

The ideal method of setting and checking valve timing is with a degree wheel and dial indicator. Attached to the crankshaft or camshaft, the wheel can detect minute chain or sprocket deviations from straight up (zero-indexed) valve timing. The use of a dial indicator on a magnetic stand can help locate the exact TDC (top-dead-center) point for the #1 cylinder's piston.

0014406

Fig. 16-45. Final touch in verifying the piston heights and accuracy of machining and fitup is the use of a dial indicator. I find TDC by this method before installing the camshaft and indexing the valve timing. This tool can assure proper valve timing and help set the timing cover tab for accurate ignition timing.

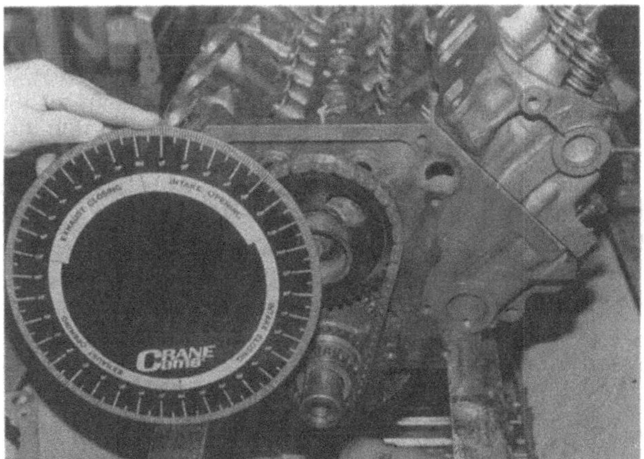

0012704

Fig. 16-46. Valve timing is a critical part of engine performance. When you install a new camshaft, sprockets, and chain (or gears), set the valve timing accurately and according to the camshaft grinder's specifications.

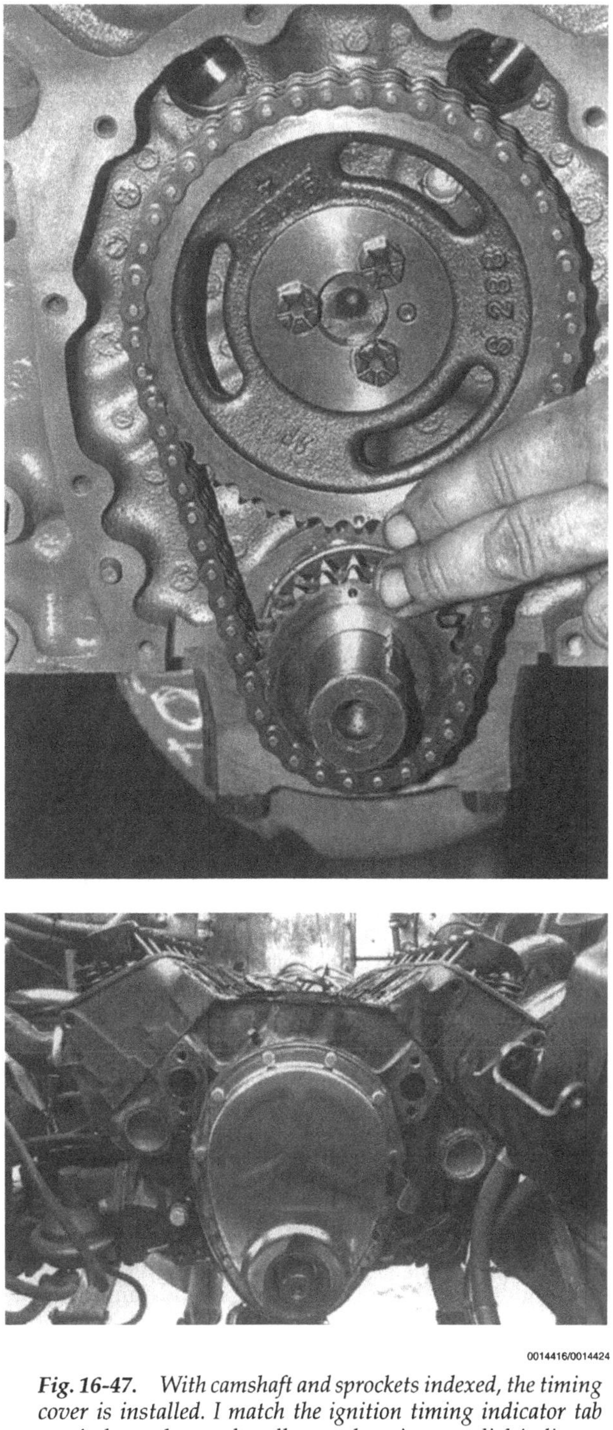

0014416/0014424

Fig. 16-47. With camshaft and sprockets indexed, the timing cover is installed. I match the ignition timing indicator tab precisely to the crank pulley mark, using my dial indicator above #1 piston crown to find absolute TDC.

With the #1 piston at exact TDC, align the degree wheel precisely to zero. Then rotate the crankshaft carefully, while the dial indicator checks the movement of the valve lifters. Valve timing may be calibrated within 0.0010" of piston location, resulting in substantial performance gains. Error is nearly impossible when you use a dial indicator for your camshaft installation and degreeing.

On many engines, the engine's timing cover has an ignition timing pointer or advance degree plate to indicate exact TDC or precise degrees of advance for the #1 piston when timing the engine. On some engines, and the Chevrolet V-8s fall into this category, the timing cover and index tab may be inaccurate.

To avoid ignition timing error, install the timing cover and crankshaft pulley/damper before the cylinder heads. Using the dial indicator at the #1 piston, find TDC for that piston. Observe the location of the pulley's timing mark on the timing cover tab, looking from approximately the same angle that a timing light would be shined. Depending on the timing indicator's design, if marks don't align, bend the tin tab or pointer slightly, or scribe a new mark.

Aftermarket timing covers with an adjustable tab are available for Chevrolet V-8 engines. Also, you can get an aftermarket degree tape to wrap around the damper. This enables a look at spark timing at higher engine speeds.

Upper Engine Rebuilding

Machining now done, the block fitted with the crankshaft, pistons, rings, rods, bearings and camshaft, you can address the rest of the valve train and cylinder head work.

Cylinder head machine work and the type of valve train parts will determine the performance character of an engine. Once the compression level has been decided, and the correct pistons fitted to achieve that ratio, the rest of the performance story will be told through the camshaft grind, valve and cylinder head work, and finally, "tune" related components like the rocker arms, manifolds, fuel system and ignition.

Cylinder head choices should follow an engine's intended use. The intake and exhaust valve sizes, port shapes, and combustion chamber design might be entirely different for two engines of identical size and type. For off-pavement crawling, low- to mid-range horsepower may dictate smaller intake valves than a mud bog, tractor pull, or NASCAR engine would require—these engines will run for maximum horsepower and be geared to operate well over 4000 rpm at all times.

Combustion chamber area and shape will determine both compression ratio (by the volume of space into which air/fuel is compressed) and spark or flame characteristics. Again, the rpm operating range of the engine and loads placed on the engine at various speeds will dictate flow and the combustion flame-front angles. Compression ratios vary according to fuel octane availability, horsepower expectations, camshaft demands and the nature of the load the engine will sustain.

When building a workhorse or reliable utility engine, I shy away from high horsepower expectations. My goal is an engine with lots of torque, good mid-range performance, and a reasonable rpm redline of 5000. Variations on this engine can suit your individual requirements, but for highway and back country use, *utility* should still be your principal goal.

For the small-block Chevrolet 350 V-8, I begin with a pair of common smog era head castings that have 1.94" diameter intake valves and 1.50" exhaust valve diameters (typically casting numbers like 336, 441, 487, 882, 493, or 997), with larger 76cc combustion chamber volumes.

Why? Because these heads will work with light *truck* engines. While 2.02" intake/1.60" exhaust size valves will fit 350 small-blocks, truck needs and lower engine speeds call for smaller diameter valves. These 1.94" intake/1.50" exhaust heads also serve lower compression ratios; they have all the accessory bolt holes needed for modern equipment; and such castings are available in every automotive machine shop's core bin.

0014417

***Fig. 16-48.** Depending upon space and tools available, many home mechanics prefer working with a "short engine," placing the block assembly in the chassis. The heads, remaining valvetrain components, and intake/exhaust systems must then be installed over the fenders. To assure cleanliness, you may prefer building the "long" engine (shown here minus pushrods and rocker arms) on your engine stand, then install the engine in more complete form.*

Whichever engine you choose to build for your Chevrolet or GMC light truck, understand that selecting heads is as important as choosing the right carburetor or ignition spark advance curve.

Remachining Your Cylinder Heads

Head service has become a specialty. Years ago, when engines were lower in compression, the proverbial ring-and-valve job or carbon-and-valve job was performed by a general service garage. Although many contemporary garages can perform quality head service, the AERA- or PERA-member full-service automotive machine shop has become the central source for consistently high quality work.

Machine shops can either rework your heads or furnish heads on an exchange basis. Regardless, cylinder head rebuilding begins with an initial cleanup. Carbon, burnt oil, and deposits disappear as caustic tanking or heat oven cleaning scours castings to a like-new appearance. Once clean, the machinist examines the head(s) closely. The focus is casting integrity, valve guide wear, the condition and depth of the valve seats and the overall condition of the valves, springs and related hardware.

Valves often can be reused, as long as their stems and faces are straight and not excessively worn. Valve faces must be free of cracks, with enough material still available for safe regrinding. If any question of excess wear or distortion exists, or if heat has damaged the valve stem or head (crystallization), the valve(s) should be discarded.

Valve springs can also be inspected for heat damage, as well as their free standing height and tension. If height or tension is slightly erratic, many shops install shims beneath the springs. Any questionable spring should be tossed out, as a broken valve spring can cause a valve to interfere with the piston or cause other serious damage.

0014410

Fig. 16-49. Surfacing the cylinder head will true the deck, making cylinder head surface precisely parallel with the top of the block.

Loose valve guides are trouble. Excess valve stem clearance in the guide allows oil to be sucked past the guide on the intake stroke. Worn guides also impair proper valve seating and reduce the compression seal. Manifold vacuum suffers, as does compression, and the engine's performance falters.

A good deal of controversy exists over the various alternatives for valve guide service, but the traditional method of knurling worn guides has generally fallen from practice. Most machinists and I would agree that knurling of old guides simply buys a little time. I would place their lifespan at anywhere from one-tenth to one-half that of the OEM valve guide—even when installation service is performed properly.

Current service technology favors complete replacement of worn guides. Various methods for both service and replacement of guides exist, including installation of bronze valve guide sleeves or the complete replacement of the guides with either new cast iron or bronze types.

Bronze works well with stainless (racing or ultra high performance) steel valve stems, while cast iron replacement guides better suit the softer OEM type non-stainless steel valve stems.

Bronze, copper, and silicone bronze guide liner sleeves have also become popular with the engine remanufacturing industry, due largely to a sleeves' quick and inexpensive ability to salvage even badly worn guide bores. Service life of sleeves exceeds that of knurling but does not match the replacement of the entire guide. Cost often dictates the use of liners or sleeves, however.

With guide service performed, valve seat grinding can start. Inspection reveals whether the existing valve seats are free of cracks and of ample thickness. Cracked valve seats, especially those that do not involve a water jacket, can be repaired or replaced with ultra hard steel inserts. These replacement seats far exceed the quality of the original casting material.

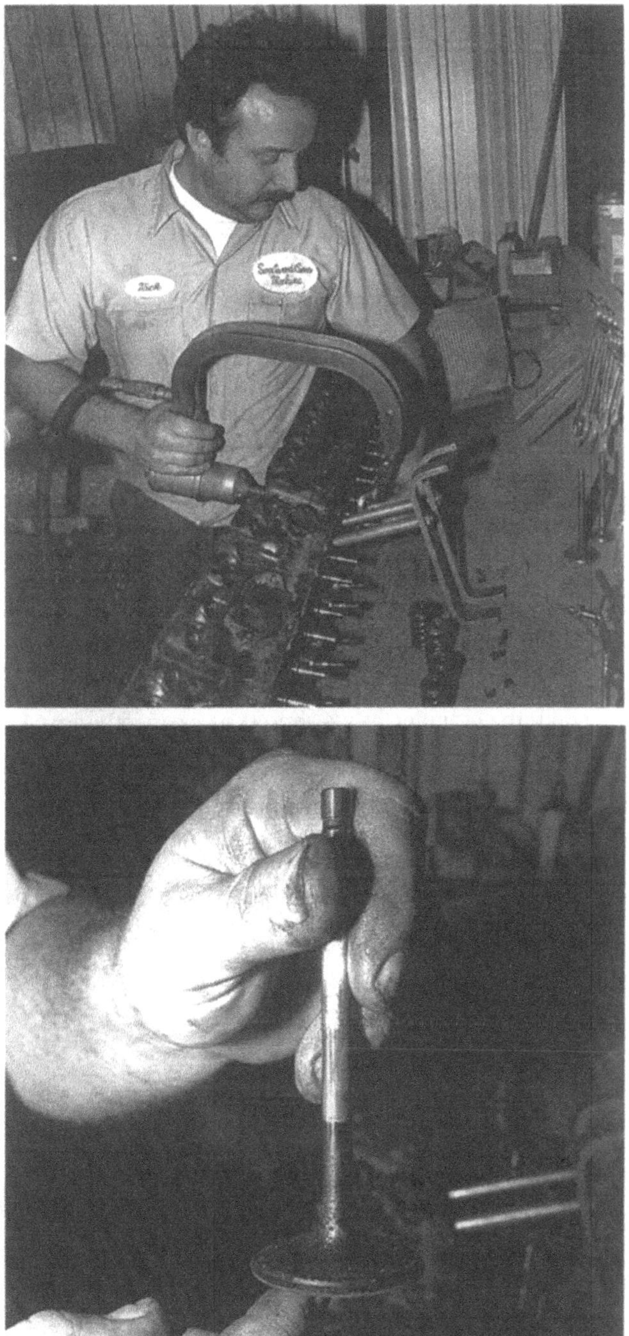

0014407 / 0014423

Fig. 16-50. Valve seat grinding at three angles will be necessary to restore these heads. Stones need continual sharpening to produce quality results. Careful grinding is repeated at each seat. If valve faces show excess wear, replace the valves.

Today, engines are more apt to generate valve seat cracks, especially at exhaust valves. Heat kills valve seats. Properly installed nickel/stellite seats are often recommended as an aid for improving engine reliability, even when the original seats show no evidence of cracking. Once valve seats have been restored, grinding can begin.

NOTE —
Beginning with unleaded fuel engines of the mid-1970s, GM cylinder heads have induction hardened exhaust valve seats. If your engine is older than this, I strongly advise the installation of hard steel exhaust valve seats and stainless exhaust valves to prevent valve seat recession and wear from the use of unleaded fuel.

Valve seat grinding follows some general rules: Seats should be concentric, not too narrow or wide, and centered on the face of the refinished valve. Normal wear will widen the original seat considerably. Grinding will widen it further yet, so reshaping of the seat becomes necessary. The usual procedure calls for precise, *three-angle* seat cuts. This requires three sharpened stones or hard steel cutters.

If the normal seat angle is 45°, one cutter will be 45°. To lower the top portion of the widened seat, a 30° cutter might be utilized, while the port or inside edge of the seat can be *raised* with the use of a 60° cutting stone. This process requires critically sharp and properly angled stones or cutting tools, enabling the seat width to finish on specification and be centered.

Once all intake and exhaust seats have been cut and finished, the cylinder heads should be cleaned again. As with every process of engine assembly, cleanliness translates to longevity and quality service.

Reusable valves can be ground on the valve refacing machine. I bathe the valve in oil during grinding, and generally set my valve face angle to 44-1/2° (on a specified 45° valve). My machine shop mentor taught that this slight variance, 1/2° flatter, assures a slight crush force to assure proper cleaning of carbon and correct seating as the valve wears in.

NOTE —
If the head-to-block mating surface requires machining to correct warp or assure head gasket seal, such work should take place before the valve grind to assure thorough cleanup of any casting debris before the valve work begins.

0014408

Fig. 16-51. *Finished seats show three angles: 30, 45 and 60°. On most general use Chevrolet V-8 truck engines, the goal is a seat width of 3/64" to 1/16" on intake valves and 1/16" to 3/32" on exhaust valves. (See the shop manual for specifics on your engine.) Seat angles are 45°, and the fresh seat must be concentric and center on the valve face.*

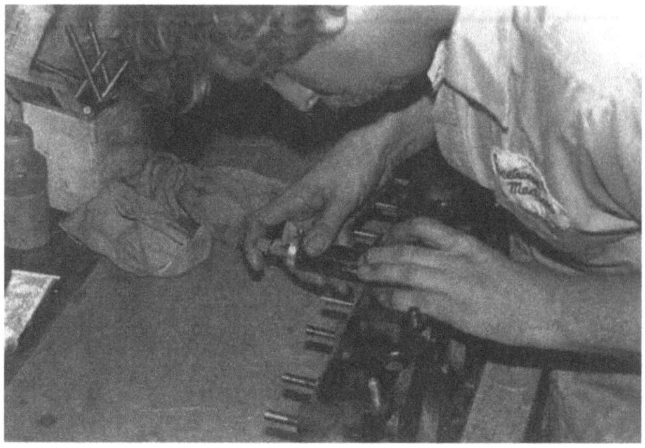

0014409

Fig. 16-52. *Valve stems and valve guides are carefully fitted. Guides often require sizing to fit.*

After grinding the valves, traditional lapping may be useful. (Smoothly dressed grinding stones usually eliminate the need for such work.) The use of lapping compound and blue dye, however, does enable a machinist to see whether the valve face and seat have mated properly. As an alternative, some shops employ a vacuum check to test a valve's sealing ability, and this can detect unwanted seepage at the seats or valve guides.

In assembling the valves, new guide seals will be installed. A variety of seal types exist, including the common GM O-ring types. Additionally, several aftermarket seals, like the original Perfect Circle (PC) nylon wiper type, improve sealing quality by better fit at the stems and tighter sealing around the valve guide boss.

Valve springs must be installed correctly, noting whether the spring is progressively wound (more tightly wound on one end than the other). Tight winds fit against the head boss, and improper installation can cause poor spring action or worse: valve and/or piston damage.

Valve stem keepers or locks must also receive close attention. Many mechanics and machinists rap the end of the valve stem lightly with a plastic hammer head after assembly to be certain that the lock and spring retainer have seated.

At this stage the heads are ready for new brass freeze plugs; then the head is ready for installation on the block assembly.

Valvetrain And Cylinder Head Installation

Cylinder head installation begins with careful placement of the head gasket(s). Often, the gasket should fit only one way, requiring proper assembly to assure good sealing. Look for notations like "This Side Up," "Top" or "Front."

Place the head *evenly* and *gently* on the head gasket. In most cases, the head gasket will not require sealant. (Fel-pro, Victor and others offer "one torque" materials with impregnated sealant, usually including silicones or Teflon.) Clean, straight head installation will prevent problems later. Be careful not to dent or nick the new gaskets.

Head bolts should be coated with sealant. I use Snap-On's Never-Seez compound or Permatex/Loctite's Teflon Sealant on those bolts that enter water jackets. On some

0014418

Fig. 16-53. Here, both heads and most valve train pieces have been installed. Adjusting the valves still remains. Note that rocker arm adjusting nuts are very loose. If adjusters are too tight, the valves will interfere with the piston crowns when you rotate the engine. This could ruin your entire rebuilding effort.

engines, head bolts reach the coolant, so rusted threads, corrosion, and bolt seizure develop over time. After long operation, bolts coated with Never-Seez will readily unfasten, leaving the block threads clear and undamaged.

I like to lightly install all bolts and follow the torque tightening sequence, beginning with a 30 ft/lbs setting. This will seat the parts evenly and compress the head gasket flatly. Start the tightening sequence again, this time splitting the difference between 30 ft/lbs and the final torque required. Finally, follow through with the actual torque required, and then allow the engine to set for several minutes before repeating the sequence at the final torque specification once more.

On engines using one torque gaskets, the head bolts will require no more attention. Older gasket styles may dictate re-torquing after initial engine warm-up, but with the use of modern sealant impregnated gaskets, that method is now rare.

With the heads installed, the lifter bases and bores lubed, the lifters fitted, pushrods inserted, and rocker arms in position, you can now install the rocker pivot balls and start the adjusting nuts. (On GM engines with rocker shaft assemblies, like the Stovebolt and Jimmy inline OHV sixes and the GMC 305 V-6, the rocker shaft and arms [with adjuster nuts backed way off] can be installed once the lifters and pushrods are in position.)

On engines with stamped steel rocker arms, like the 1963 and later OHV seven main bearing inline sixes and all Chevrolet OHV V-8s and V-6s, install one pair of rocker arms at a time. Make sure that both camshaft lobes are at the lowest point (heel) of their profiles.

With the camshaft in this position and both valves closed completely, you can turn the adjusting nut slowly. These engines with stamped rocker arms have hydraulic valve lifters, so hold two fingers on the pushrod tube, and tighten the adjuster until the play *has just been removed.* At this point, you have reached zero lash.

Once at zero lash, the lifter's plunger is still fully extended. Further tightening of the adjuster nut will compress the lifter. That compression distance, referred to as lifter pre-load, varies with different camshaft designs and manufacturer's specifications. (Rhoads lifters call for 1/2 turn past zero lash on each adjuster nut. Some references call for 3/4 turn.) Carefully set the pre-load to specification before moving to the next rocker arm.

Zero lash and the pre-load setting is easier with the intake manifold removed, as the pushrod and lifter relationship can be easily viewed. Note the point where the lifter plunger begins to move below its snap ring—This begins the preload setting.

Prepping the Long Block for a Successful Start-up

Valves adjusted, at least for preliminary run-in, the intake manifold can be installed. The manifold gaskets should be coated with sealant in accord with the manufacturer's specifications, giving special consideration to corners and gasket junctions. Torquing and tightening a manifold should follow the recommended sequence of three torque steps to the final setting.

Once the intake manifold has been properly secured, you can prime the engine's lubrication system. Make a dummy distributor from an old distributor housing and shaft. Remove the drive gear and modify the top end of the drive shaft to accept a large drill motor chuck.

Install your dummy distributor housing and engage its drive shaft with the oil pump. Attach the drill motor to the top end of the shaft, and with fresh oil at the FULL line of the crankcase dipstick, apply pressure downward (to prevent damage to the oil pump drive), and spin the shaft. Engaged with the oil pump drive key, the dummy shaft will rotate the oil pump. Use a high torque, low speed drill motor, and allow the pump to spin for a couple of minutes in the direction that the distributor normally rotates to charge all oil galleries with fresh oil. (To avoid an oil bath, place the valve covers on those GM engines that oil the rocker arms through the pushrods.)

By charging the lubrication system thoroughly, your engine will crank over in a pre-primed state, and bearing scoring from dry cranking will not occur. Priming prevents oil starvation, aeration and cavitation.

Once the oil system has been primed, the engine can be installed in the chassis. With mounts secured and exhaust manifolds attached, the ignition distributor and plug wire installation can proceed. Many engine builders successfully complete all phases of the long block assembly, only to mess up the ignition timing.

In Chapter 8, Engine Tune-up and Emission Controls, you will find my methods for static timing the engine. Follow these procedures closely, and your new engine will be correctly timed before you ever touch the starter. Make sure the number one piston is at the top of its *compression stroke* before static timing the engine.

Later, upon start up, you can verify the timing with a timing light. Although static timing may require some practice, it will place your engine within two crankshaft degrees of exact timing, a very safe range for starting even the most exotic engine.

Now the engine is ready to run. Install all accessories, cooling system components, and the fuel system pieces. Make preliminary adjustments on the carburetor, if necessary, and get ready. Your fresh engine will soon burst into life. Assuming that spark and fuel needs are properly met, the engine should start immediately. Try it, and appreciate your effort.

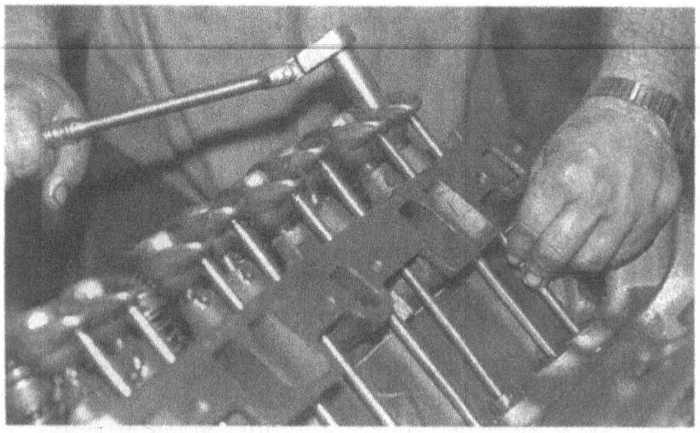

0014413

Fig. 16-54. *Final step is machinist's reassembly of new or reconditioned parts. Quality cylinder head work provides long service and maximum performance. Here, rocker arm and lifter pre-load adjustment prepares engine for start-up.*

NOTE —
See the engine run-in recommendations in the Appendix of this book. A new engine must be cycled properly during its initial start-up and first hours of running.

Adjuncts to an Engine Rebuild

Your newly rebuilt engine will produce more horsepower and greater torque. The engine now needs proper break-in and care. This requires adequate cooling, good water pump circulation and a working fan. A marginal OEM radiator, erratic fan clutch or worn water pump becomes a glaring problem when new found horsepower places higher demands on the cooling system.

Protect your newly rebuilt engine, with its hot tanked, scale-free block and cylinder head. Have the radiator hot tanked, rodded and pressure checked to assure clean and adequate coolant flow.

0014419

Fig. 16-55. *With care and a methodical approach, the end result is an engine that runs. These steps or exchanging your old engine for a completely assembled, ready-to-run long block could be just what your truck needs.*

Plugged, soldered and damaged radiator cores, or a radiator filled with rust and scale, will prevent your new engine from cooling adequately. Engine break-in heavily taxes the cooling system. If in good shape, your truck's cooling system helps the engine meet the variety of challenges that the vehicle will face.

In addition to installing a new water pump and reconditioning the radiator, pay attention to all hoses, clamps, the thermostat and drive belts. New parts here are cheap insurance. Test the fan clutch and replace if necessary.

Any transmission or clutch parts that were sub-standard before the overhaul now need attention. The new engine will place a higher load on worn geartrain parts, especially when you drive in the off-pavement environment. Replace the clutch assembly (if necessary, re-surface the flywheel), service the transmission, and be certain that the gear assemblies work well before installing the fresh engine.

Chapter 17

Geartrain Modifications

NINETEEN THIRTY-NINE TO PRESENT GM truck transmissions and axles span several engineering epochs. The earliest light truck transmissions had either three forward speeds with synchromesh on second and third gears only or the archaic spur gear four-speed with no synchromesh on any of the four forward speeds or reverse.

Axle designs include the more primitive torque-tube types used on the lighter half-ton models through 1955 (First Series). Heavier duty 1939–55 First Series models and all trucks built since Second Series 1955 have open drivelines and either a drop-in carrier or an integral housing type axle. These GM light truck axles offer ample stamina for their weight/load ratings.

The original and popular cone-and-drum type synchromesh three-speed Muncie transmission design began in the 1930s and survives until the late 1960s. In 1965, GM light trucks began offering the all-synchromesh Saginaw three-speeds, durable designs that offer more versatility than earlier types. (An optional overdrive became available with 1955 Second Series trucks, and three-speeds with overdrive survive as a light truck option through the 1970 model year.)

Well into the 1960s, GMC Truck Division sought many of its three-speed transmission offerings from outside the GM parts pool. Heavy Duty three speeds from Borg-Warner were common on Pontiac/GMC V-8 powered models. Chevrolet and GMC trucks with higher GVWRs often offer heavier duty three-speeds or a truck four-speed option.

0014482

Fig. 17-1. Torque tube rear axle on this 1941 Chevrolet truck chassis is common to all Chevrolet and GMC half-ton models through 1955 First Series.

For sheer ruggedness, the 1947 Advance Design truck's Muncie SM420 four-speed option was a milestone. This heavy duty gearbox offered synchromesh on second, third and fourth gears, a first for GM light trucks—and several years ahead of Ford and other American truck builders.

The rugged SM420 has served nobly in many 1947–67 GM light trucks. In 1968, GM replaced the SM420 with an even beefier Muncie 465 four-speed unit, again relying on an iron case and heavy duty gearsets that could easily serve in a two-ton capacity truck.

GM's 465 Muncie and the comparatively strong New Process 435 four-speed have built an excellent service record in Chevrolet and GMC trucks since the late 1960s. The last light truck use of the 465 Muncie was in pre-Sierra pickups and the conventional Blazer/Jimmy, Suburban and Crew Cab (C/K-30/3500) models through 1991.

As for durability, I believe that Muncie's SM420 and 465 designs, plus the New Process NP435 manual four-speed gearbox, exceed all other GM light truck transmission offerings of their epoch. Only in the newest heavy-duty NV4500 Series five-speed overdrive units do we find the kind of durability characterized by these earlier iron-cased four-speed transmissions.

In 1955 Second Series models, the GMC light trucks turned to Spicer axles for stamina, while Chevrolet remained committed to GM Corporate offerings. The Spicer Model 45 (similar to the popular 44) became a GMC half-ton mainstay, lasting until GM introduced the tough Saginaw 12-bolt axle to Chevrolet and GMC half-tons during the mid- to late-1960s.

Likewise, while Chevrolet used Corporate axles in most 3/4-ton and one-ton applications, GMC frequently opted for the common Spicer/Dana full-floating 60, 60HD and 70 type units. Until the 1980s, all 3/4-ton and one-ton truck rear axles were full-floating types. Since the early 1980s, only the heavier duty models use full-floating type rear axle assemblies. (See earlier chapters for model descriptions and equipment options.)

All Spicer axles are integral designs, with the differential carrier bearing saddles built into the axle housing assembly. Unlike the early GM/Corporate and other GM removable carrier housing types, overhaul of an integral axle is usually done in the chassis. GM's own Saginaw 10-bolt, 12-bolt and 14-bolt integral axles replaced the drop-in carrier type axle designs found in earlier GM light trucks.

0012742

Fig. 17-2. I took this photo to make a graphic statement about truck transmission stamina. Massive unit at left is GM's 465 Muncie box, which dwarfs a compact truck T-5 overdrive. Three-speed Borg-Warner T-14 and T-90 (with V-8 adapter attached) set in middle, while T-18 Ford truck box rests to right. In foreground is an early (pre-1968) GM Muncie SM420 truck four-speed. GM's 420 and 465 Muncie iron units clearly offer superior stamina.

0012744

Fig. 17-3. Transmission countergears show the relationship between a real truck four-speed and lighter duty OEM offerings. Left to right, the T-18, T-90, T-14, and T-5 gears stand next to GM's impressive 465 Muncie countergear.

0014358

Fig. 17-4. As a truck fleet mechanic, I could remove, completely rebuild and reinstall these popular Chevrolet light truck three speeds in less than two hours. 1955–66 model light GM trucks were the easiest to service, with the clutch/bellhousing supported on rear motor mounts. You can remove this 1955–59 type transmission in twenty minutes.

1. PERFORMANCE TRANSMISSION CHOICES

In addition to the virtually indestructible nature of a cast iron four-speed gearbox, these units feature extremely low ratios in compound low (first gear). The most common first gear ratio for a New Process 435 is 6.69:1. One version of the GM/Muncie SM420 has an even lower 7.05:1 first gear ratio!

For 4x4 trucks with a two-speed transfer case and relatively low (like 4.10 or 4.56:1) axle ratio, the overall reduction ratio is enhanced further. Final drive crawl ratios of 70:1 or even lower in first gear/low range are attainable. Taller, more economical axle gearing (3.40 to 3.73:1) can still yield a compound low, low range final driving ratio of over 60:1 when coupled to a transfer case that offers a very low gear ratio in low range.

Some GM 4x4 transfer cases have less low range gear reduction than others. Here a truck-type four-speed, or the latest NV4500-Series five-speed overdrive unit, provides enough gear reduction in first gear to handle the most challenging off-pavement and heavy pulling situations.

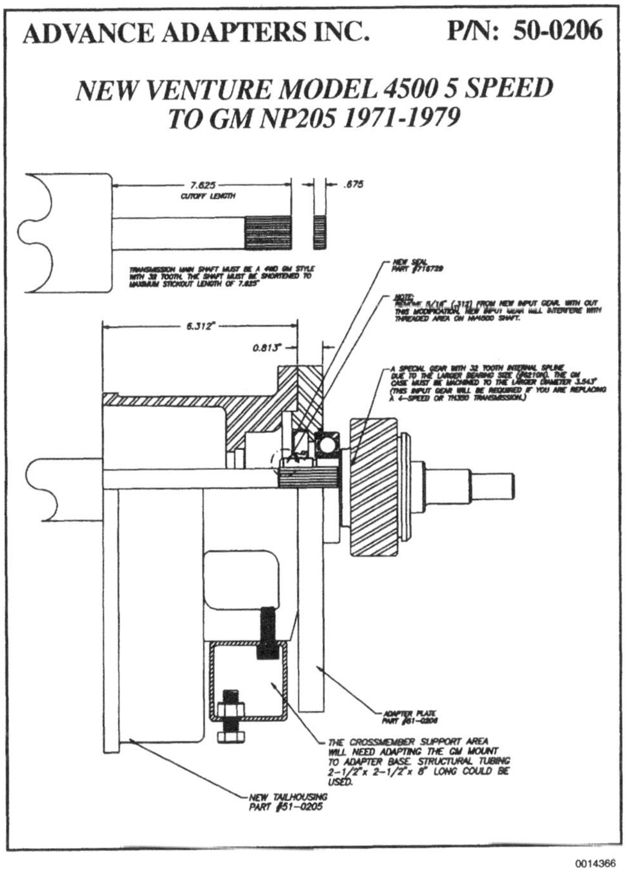

Fig. 17-5. GM's truck-type four-speed or the latest NV4500 provides enough gear reduction for any situation. Many hardcore 4x4 users find that Advance Adapters' NV4500 transmission retrofit kit (shown) is the best means for attaining maximum gear reduction for off-pavement chores plus the benefit of overdrive for optimal highway economy.

Compound low gear gives a 4x4 truck both crawling and pulling advantages. Such low gearing can save your chassis and powertrain. In hardcore rock-crawling, your truck can inch its way through the roughest terrain, with light use of the brakes, less tire spin and less skidding.

Stalled on a precarious slope, you can engage the clutch with the transmission in compound first gear and the transfer case in low range four-wheel drive. The 12-volt starter motor can pull the truck up a steep incline while firing the engine.

Unless your truck has a load, little starter drag will occur. The low-low gearing will afford a smooth chug forward as the engine catches (providing you have your foot very lightly on the throttle).

> *WARNING —*
> *Know how your truck will respond to a start-up in gear. Practice this technique before traveling dangerous terrain. Be aware that you cannot start your truck with the clutch engaged if the truck's starter wiring includes a neutral or clutch pedal safety switch.*

Installing a four-speed or NV4500 five-speed truck transmission eliminates chassis abuse in rough terrain. Tall geared trucks bend springs and twist their frames as they bash and skid their way through rockpiles. Your GM 4x4 truck with a two-speed transfer case and very low first gear (compound low) ratio will perform far better, as ultra-low gearing yields great dividends in extending chassis parts life, vehicle safety and driver/passenger comfort.

High output engines have great difficulty breaking an iron truck gearbox or late NV4500 unit in good condition. A GM SM420 or Muncie 465, or the New Process 435 truck four-speed, can easily handle 300-plus horsepower in a light truck. A truck four-speed's second gear has a lower ratio than the first gear of most three-speed transmissions. On such a four-speed with synchromesh down to second gear, three-speed driving is the norm until you need heavy crawling power. A truck equipped with correct axle gearing only uses compound low gear under heavy loading.

Truck-type Manual Four-speed Changeover

If you own a GM light truck equipped with a lighter duty three-speed or five-speed overdrive transmission, you may prefer a four-speed truck-type gearbox. For all GM trucks, such a changeover is possible using factory/OEM parts. Begin by finding a truck similar to your chassis that has a four-speed unit, and note all of the components that your truck currently lacks. If you select the right circa parts for your truck's chassis, a stock truck bellhousing can mate the upgrade gearbox to any of the GM truck engines.

Consider the cost of either recycled or new components that will complete such a conversion. At the same time, you might evaluate whether it's better to sell your truck at fair market value and replace the vehicle with a four-speed or later NV4500 five-speed-equipped truck.

If the changeover is cost effective, consider the labor involved and look closely at the factory shop manual for mechanical procedures. An accepted industry flat-rate labor estimating guide can help determine a reasonable time frame for performing the job and any sublet labor costs if someone else does the work.

Example: Although the pre-Advance Design era light trucks offer a less desirable non-synchromesh four-speed, the late-1947 models were available with the SM420 synchromesh transmission. You could use 1947 or newer parts to couple your 1939 Stovebolt 216 inline OHV six to an SM420 four-speed. The SM420, in various forms, was available from 1947–67.

A basic fitup difference between the SM420 and 465 Muncie is the index bore of the bellhousing. The 465 requires a larger 5.125-inch bore. Previous GM truck three- and four-speed transmissions share a common 4.686-inch diameter.

If replacing a three-speed transmission, determine which four-speed transmission options were available when your truck was built. Seek out a recycling yard truck with those components. This is your easiest route.

> **NOTE —**
> A recycling yard has interchange manuals that can determine year, make and model sources for transmissions, axles and related parts.

Some street truck builders opt for passenger car four-speed transmissions like the all synchromesh Borg-Warner T-10, GM/Muncie or GM/Saginaw units from the Muscle Car era. These gearboxes can handle horsepower but not severe loads. For hauling, towing or carrying a cabover camper, I would stick with a truck-type four-speed gearbox that offers a compound low gear. The passenger car four-speed might better serve in a lightweight street truck project like a classic 1939–59 half-ton model.

A transmission changeover sometimes will require use of a larger diameter flywheel, different bellhousing and starter change. Truck four-speeds have high torque ratings and usually come with a larger diameter clutch assembly. You will want this added stamina when you make a four-speed transmission changeover.

> ***CAUTION —***
> *Use the correct flywheel for your engine. GM truck crankshafts have either internal or external balancing, and crankshaft and flywheel types differ. Be sure your flywheel selection matches the engine's balance method.*

I encourage the use of a cast iron bellhousing if available and suitable for your application. Four-speed truck transmissions are very heavy and hang a massive amount of weight off the rear of the bellhousing. Later model trucks use aluminum alloy housings, and the stress to bolt threads and the casting can become an issue. In some applications, there is a cast iron clutch housing from an earlier or medium duty truck that will work with your later chassis, clutch linkage and clutch type.

> ***CAUTION —***
> *When selecting a bellhousing, be certain the index hole that centers the transmission is of the correct diameter to accept the four-speed's front bearing retainer collar. This bore helps keep the transmission in alignment and also centers the input shaft with the crankshaft pilot bearing. The fit should be nearly snug, and the housing bore must index on center.*

> **NOTE —**
> Aftermarket formed steel racing bellhousings are available, often with universal bolt patterns and detailed instructions for custom fit machining.

Extra Considerations

When planning a transmission swap, determine the driveline length required. You may need to find a driveshaft of the correct length or U-joint type. An alternative is to have a driveline constructed. (See earlier chapters for driveline details.)

> **NOTE —**
> On earlier GM half-ton truck models with a torque tube rear axle, a transmission conversion may require changing the entire rear end or torque tube assembly. It is often easier to convert to a later open driveline and Hotchkiss type rear axle.

The new four-speed transmission may come with a speedometer gear assembly that served different axle gearing or tire diameters. Check your speedometer error, and secure the correct drive gear from your local GM dealer or another recycled transmission. If you have difficulty with this detail, consult a speedometer shop. They can install a speedometer speed correction kit if necessary. For a four-speed upgrade, you must also account for the transmission input shaft length. This is the distance from the crankshaft pilot bearing to the front face of the transmission.

Clutch linkage may also differ between transmission types. Release fork or throwout bearing designs for heavy duty transmissions may be different than those parts used with lighter duty transmissions. When securing parts, make sure to include all four-speed pieces, and note their assembly order. Use the correct clutch release arm, linkage and return spring(s)—and attach them properly.

Why Not an Overdrive Five-speed Conversion?

Light truck five-speed (overdrive type) transmissions reduce fuel consumption and engine wear. Many late GM trucks have five-speed manual transmissions, and earlier truck owners often consider retrofitting such a unit.

Until recently, I was not an advocate of manual overdrive transmission conversions for several reasons: 1) These transmissions fit only a limited number of engine types; 2) they use hydraulic clutch linkage and have other features that could make a retrofit complicated; 3) the service record of aluminum housed transmissions was

0012746

Fig. 17-6. Advance Adapters offers the two-speed underdrive or overdrive Torque Splitter gear unit. Mounted between the clutch/bellhousing and transmission, this auxiliary transmission provides a durable synchromesh shift mechanism and an extra range of forward and reverse gears. I tested such a unit behind a 280-horsepower engine, pulling heavy loads and a travel trailer. If you want a rugged overdrive for your four-speed equipped truck, here is one option.

questionable; 4) repair parts for overdrive transmissions are very costly, with special tools required for disassembly and fitup work; and 5) recycled earlier aluminum case five-speed overdrive transmissions, although increasingly more available, are often defective or in need of an overhaul.

GM's latest NV4500 Series five-speed overdrive, however, has changed my thinking. This aluminum-cased unit, easily identified by its *two* PTO outlets, was designed for use in heavy duty light truck applications. Its durability is comparable to traditional four-speed gearboxes. If overdrive is your choice, the NV4500 conversion may be right for your truck.

There are other economy and overdrive alternatives that I would consider. These include: 1) the use of tall (numerically low) axle gear ratios with a compound low four-speed transmission; or 2) the installation of an add-on aftermarket overdrive unit, like Advance Adapters' Torque Splitter.

Enhancing the 700R-4 Automatic's Reliability

The 1980s were turbulent years for automotive technology. As the decade began, CAFE and EPA mandates demanded even greater fuel economy and further decreases in tailpipe emissions. General Motors, unwilling to give up more engine performance, turned to electronic fuel and spark management systems and the use of overdrive transmissions.

In 1982, the Turbo-Hydramatic 700R-4 automatic overdrive transmission came on line. Despite mandatory tall (numerically low) axle ratios, the 700R-4 achieved both highway mileage and better performance. The strong feature of the 700R-4 was its lower first gear ratio. Engineered with reasonably spaced second through fourth gear ratios and aided by a 3-element torque converter with a lock-up clutch, the 700R-4 showed great promise.

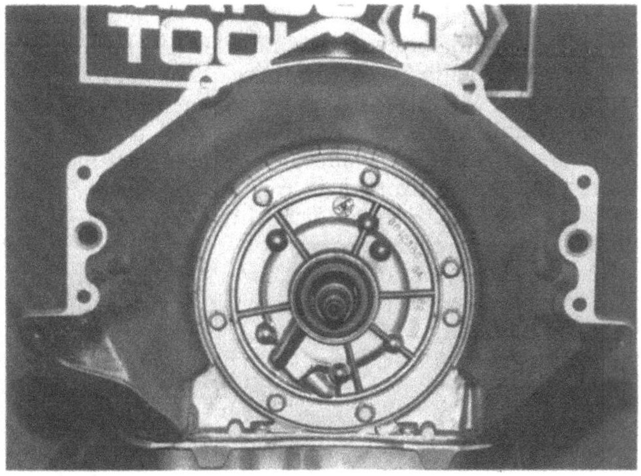

0014436

Fig. 17-7. A familiar front view of Chevrolet V-8 housing pattern looks similar to THM 350 or 400. 700R-4 has a much improved track record from 1986-onward.

The 700R-4 overdrive provides exceptional fuel economy, with highway cruising below 2000 rpm. Detented downshifts to third easily tap into the truck's muscle. Aware of the quality found in THM350 and THM400 transmissions, buyers easily accepted the new 700R-4 automatic. Many 1980s GM light trucks and passenger cars have this transmission.

By design, the 700R-4 is much like other late model overdrive automatics. Two planetary gear sets, seven clutches (two roller and five multiple-disc) and a second/fourth gear band account for the four forward speeds and reverse. A valve body-directed hydraulic system coordinates the various gear changes, while a vane front pump creates pressure for the hydraulic system.

The torque converter provides customary power coupling between the engine and transmission, with hydraulic torque multiplication available at breakaway loads. At speed, the lock-up clutch provides zero slippage within the torque converter for maximum fuel economy.

700R-4 in the Real World

GM's 700R-4 automatic, like other innovations of its era, was a victim of rapid design and hasty production. In a rush to meet marketing and EPA/CAFE mandated demands, the 700R-4 transmission would require improvements and parts upgrades for several model years.

The original 700R-4 engineering appeared fundamental enough. Clutch units resemble GM's other THM transmissions, with spring assemblies, pistons, drive and driven clutch plates and snap ring retainers. A roller and a sprag clutch work much like other one-way clutching assemblies, while Torrington-type bearings and plastic spacer washers protect the thrust surfaces of the 700R-4.

Conspicuously obvious in the 700R-4, however, are weight saving materials. These include aluminum drums and housing members and extensive use of stamped steel components. Manufacturers have frequently found that stamped and lightened components lead to reliability problems. Despite metallurgical tricks, strategically placed welds and exotic heat treating measures, lighter components sometimes fail in real world service—especially under high torque loads.

Such was the situation with early 700R-4 automatics. The overall integrity of the transmission was often less than the traditional THM 350/400 designs delivered. Under high performance demands and heavy hauling, many owners found their overdrive transmissions failed.

Weak Points in the Early 700R-4

As overhaul and service data accumulated, the early 700R-4 showed several shortcomings. The rear planetary ring gear fractured under load, with the planetary gears often failing in the process. Front pump troubles surfaced, while sprag clutch weaknesses led to the loss of third gear.

Throttle valve problems affected upshifts and downshifts. Cracking of the turbine (input) shaft caused a fluid pressure drop and failure of the third/fourth gear clutch. Front pump seal leaks plagued many transmissions. Broken housings, clutch and planetary components, plus the contamination of the entire hydraulic system with metal debris, could accompany a major parts failure.

General Motors, recognizing the design flaws, upgraded key components to increase reliability. These changes incorporated retrofit parts for the repair of failed transmissions in the field. A number of upgraded, superceded factory components became the backbone for a reliable transmission overhaul.

Despite a genuine effort to remedy the 700R-4 problems, GM took from 1982 until 1986 to implement the wide range of production changes needed. For GM light truck owners, this means at least four model years with potentially weak transmissions.

When transmission troubles occur in a pre-1986 700R-4 overdrive automatic, you can rebuild the unit to enhance its reliability. Although the alternative of swapping a Turbo 350 or 400 transmission has appealed to many light truck owners, the emission controls, engine management system and motor vehicle laws limit this option. Tall axle gearing also enters the equation, as trucks equipped with the 700R-4 transmission typically have numerically low axle ratios.

Furthermore, owners accustomed to a lower first gear ratio's acceleration rate, plus the slow engine rpm in overdrive at highway cruise speeds, find a conventional three-speed automatic inhibiting. Although owners and transmission specialists agree that overdrive is strictly for highway use, the feature has real value.

NOTE —
Constant banging in and out of overdrive, as in city traffic, creates unnecessary and damaging stress to the 700R-4. I find that the best way to protect a 700R-4 from damage is to keep the selector in the first to third gear range for all driving conditions except flat, highway/interstate cruising at light throttle loads.

Signs of Impending Doom

The 700R-4 usually serves notice before failing. Common symptoms include racheting, buzzing or whining sounds, which signify a front pump defect, unless the sound disappears on the upshift to second gear. If this occurs, planetary ring gear trouble has likely developed.

When third gear fails, the sprag clutch has likely broken or worn to excess. Third-gear failure can also relate to turbine shaft cracking. Front seal failure is a regular problem on early 700R-4 transmissions. According to transmission repair specialists, this defect diminishes after 1985 models. A service remedy for front seal leaks is available, and most shops implement the upgrade during overhaul.

As with other automatic designs, service guidelines exist for some of the simpler, in-truck repairs. The throttle valve cable adjustment is one such procedure. These cables are theoretically self-adjusting, but binding or other problems can create trouble.

You will find procedures for simpler fixes, like the valve body, filter, torque converter and such, in the factory-level shop manual for your truck. Your local Chevrolet or GMC Truck dealership or a quality transmission shop can help determine whether your truck is a candidate for a simple remedy. Simpler repairs should be attempted first, as a major overhaul of the 700R-4 transmission can put a hefty dent in your wallet.

Some Overhaul Guidelines

For a deeper understanding of your 700R-4 overhaul needs, I consulted Sparky's Transmissions in Santee, California. Shop owner Michael Nowlin has addressed the repair and overhaul of these transmissions for many years. Working with master technician Rudy Vargas, I discovered the best methods of overhaul, with the focus on upgrading components for a long transmission life.

After a careful, complete transmission teardown, parts cleaning affords close inspection for wear and damage. (Since many pieces are aluminum, magnafluxing may not be practical, as aluminum is nonferrous.) Thorough washing and very detailed inspection discloses hairline cracks in shafts, the case or any other parts intended for reuse.

Rudy focused attention on the front pump assembly. The front pump is always rebuilt to improved, later standards. This involves an upgrade rotor to replace the early 7-vane unit. A better pressure regulating spring, steel ring and plastic thrust washer replace the earlier types.

Fig. 17-8. *Enlarging this pressure relief hole prevents oil pressure from dislodging the front pump seal. A thorough upgrade overhaul will involve safeguards such as this.*

Fig. 17-9. *An aftermarket steel ring and a stouter slide spring improve front pump reliability.*

CAUTION —

Since the oil pump housing is aluminum, a new bushing must be fitted with Loctite, as aluminum tends to distort slightly during the removal of the old bushing.

On the front of the 700R-4 oil pump, a pressure relief hole removes excess pressure from the area of the seal. With early 700R-4 units, this hole is too small, and fluid pressure can actually force the front seal loose. This causes a major loss of fluid—quickly.

Like the pump bushing, the new seal requires use of Loctite during installation. Additionally, GM provides an upgrade service part (a spring retainer) to cage the seal and prevent it from dislodging.

Fig. 17-10. *Oil pump on this early 700R-4 shows housing wear. Experienced shops replace this steel ring with an upgrade design from the aftermarket.*

Fig. 17-11. *Front pump bushing (top) and seal outer edge (bottom) receive coat of Loctite before installation. The caged spring retainer is a GM retrofit part to prevent the seal from dislodging.*

0014432

Fig. 17-12. At Sparky's Transmissions in Santee, California, Rudy Vargas points out this factory mark on replacement rear planetary ring gear. This upgrade piece should always *replace the weaker original gear.*

0014433

Fig. 17-13. Sprag (roller one-way) clutch is another weak point in the 700R-4. Inspect this assembly closely, and replace if any wear exists.

During an overhaul, Rudy installs a spring beneath the throttle valve, a measure that prevents the valve from sticking. For the rear planetary ring gear, there is an upgraded, heavy duty replacement part that you should always include in an overhaul. As with any automatic transmission rebuild, reassembly includes high quality replacement clutch friction plates, seals, thrust washers and spacers.

As a final step, Rudy pressure checks all clutch drums and the front pump. Sealing rings on the turbine shaft are another area of 700R-4 trouble, and the pressure in this area must also be tested. There's nothing more frustrating to automatic transmission technicians than an internal oil pressure leak. Make sure that the turbine shaft passes close inspection before reusing it.

0014434

Fig. 17-14. Look closely at the turbine shaft. Cracking occurs near this oil feed hole, causing a loss of oil pressure. Expect a third- and fourth-gear clutch failure if this were to happen.

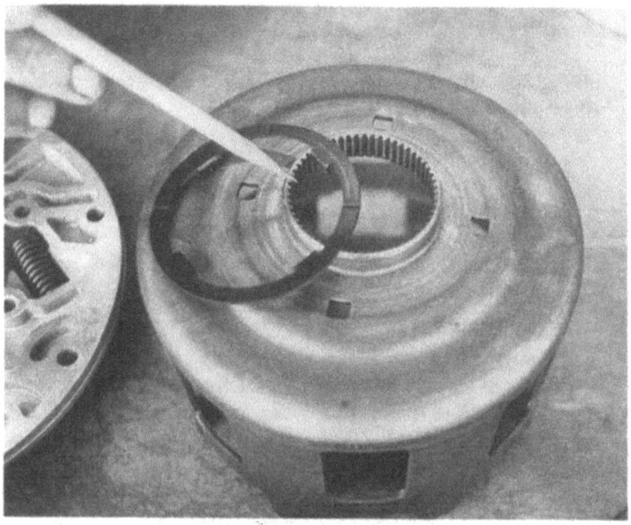

0014435

Fig. 17-15. Use of plastic/nylon thrust spacers leads to trouble. A disintegrated spacer will allow the drum to rock, usually breaking the tiny reaction gear teeth. An upgraded aftermarket thrust spacer is available to transmission shops.

0014437

Fig. 17-16. Input housing holds a series of clutching members. Housing is aluminum, requiring close inspection for hairline cracks. Non-ferrous material prevents magnafluxing.

Prognosis for the Long Haul

When overhauled properly, the 700R-4 can offer quality service. Factory computer and mechanical refinements, especially the later 4L60E light truck version of this transmission, offer smoother upshifts and less abuse to the overdrive unit. The lockup converter has also become more integrated in the computer shifting program.

Art Carr, of racing transmission fame, has told me repeatedly that a properly built 700R-4 will sustain the torque of a very high horsepower racing engine. Art strongly supports the use of this transmission in upgraded, high performance form.

Unfortunately, progress came too late for many. Dissatisfied original owners of 1982–84 GM light trucks abandoned their trucks long ago. These vehicles often resell at a very reasonable fare, due largely to the reputation of the 700R-4. This can help the buyer of such a used model. An upgrade overhaul of the 700R-4 transmission can make such a truck perform well and deliver quality service.

0014368

Fig. 17-17. By the early 1990s, GM began controlling the shifts of automatic transmission electronically. The 4L60E is basically a 700R-4 with electronically controlled shifts. A larger heavy duty design, the THM400-based 4L80E four-speed overdrive automatic, offers greater stamina for trucks equipped with diesel engines and higher GVW ratings.

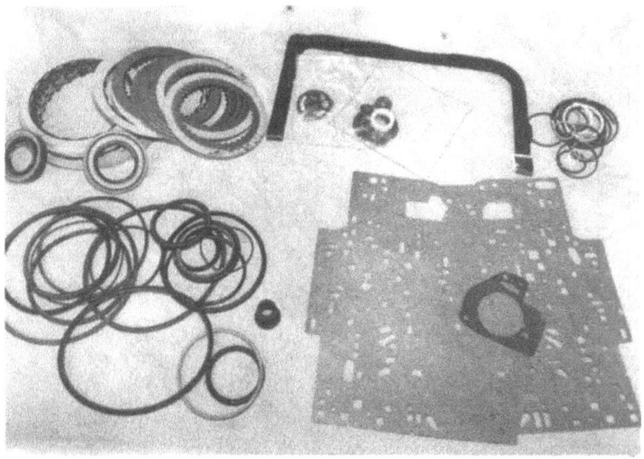

0014438

Fig. 17-18. A complete 700R-4 overhaul kit includes clutch components and all necessary seals. High quality, upgraded "hard parts" are available from local Chevrolet/GMC dealerships. Independent shops rely on the automatic transmission aftermarket suppliers for additional pieces.

2. CLUTCH UPGRADES

Eventually, your truck's clutch will fatigue and fail. When it does, the aftermarket clutch industry offers a variety of rebuilt and new clutch units to restore or improve performance. You can select a clutch that will handle your engine's torque and horsepower demands.

Traditionally, a high performance clutch was a non-diaphragm design. Two varieties include a centrifugal arm / fulcrum arrangement (Long) and a high spring rate type.

Centrifugally weighted clutch fingers allow two distinct clutch behaviors. To ease take-off and reduce shock loads to the transmission, transfer case or axle, the initial squeeze or clamp pressure is lower. As engine rpm increases in each gear, the centrifugal weights move outward. At speed, the fingers' fulcrum leverage applies increasingly more pressure to the clutch disc.

The complaint with older centrifugal clutch designs is high pedal pressure at higher rpm. In racing and high performance activities, applying the clutch pedal at high revs with hydraulic clutch linkage can actually blow out the slave and clutch master cylinder seals. Under these same circumstances, mechanical linkage will place an overwhelming load on the driver's clutch foot! Reciprocally, relatively low apply pressure often allows damaging clutch slippage.

Borg & Beck Type Clutch

An alternative design, the non-centrifugal, three-finger clutch popularized by Borg & Beck, eliminates guesswork about apply pressure at any given rpm. Spring pressure clutches apply the entire force of the pressure plate at one time. This means that the spring rate built into the clutch cover unit is exactly the rate sandwiching the clutch disc against the flywheel face.

Accurate clutch pressures can be set for vehicle weight, engine power output and the vehicle's usage. In heavy duty towing and 4x4 applications intended for

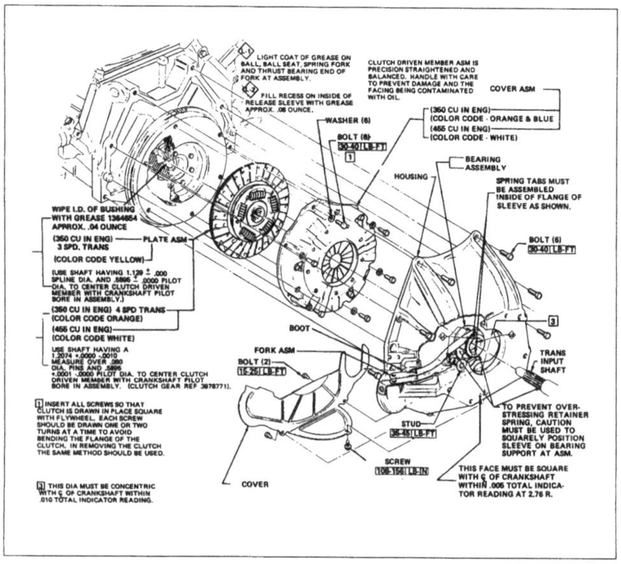

0012778

Fig. 17-19. OEM service guidelines prevent trouble. Note critical measurements and proper tightening techniques to prevent warpage of a new clutch cover. (See your GM truck shop manual for specifications that apply to your model.) Apply high temp grease sparingly to clutch lever release stud and crankshaft pilot bearing bore (if bronze bushing type). Diaphragm type clutch affords smooth engagement and immediate application of full spring pressure. (Courtesy of General Motors.)

brute work, the clutch apply pressure (static) is 2,200 pounds or better. Users generally choose a non-centrifugal clutch of 2,200-2,400 pounds clamping force for heavy hauling or a large increase in horsepower.

In a lighter duty vehicle, say an earlier Stovebolt six powered model or a later GM C/K model with a 305 V-8 or 4.3L V-6 engine, the maximum pressure demands would seldom require more than 2,000 static pounds. While adding static pressure will decrease the chance of slippage, it also increases the shock to vital geartrain parts during initial clutch engagement.

Diaphragm Clutch

The third common clutch design is the multi-fingered diaphragm type. General Motors popularized the use of diaphragm clutches many years ago, and early high performance enthusiasts discarded these types of clutches regularly in favor of Borg & Beck and Long type clutches.

Traditionally, diaphragm clutches were unable to handle high performance demands, as they offered few means for increasing apply pressures. Worse yet, clutch overheat quickly damages the flat diaphragm clutch springs.

A diaphragm clutch has two advantages, however. The pedal pressure to disengage the diaphragm clutch is minimal, as sixteen fingers apply leverage instead of three. The long spring fingers allow relatively high apply pressures with minimal pressure at the clutch pedal. Pedal take-up distance is relatively short with a diaphragm design, and clutch engagement occurs very smoothly.

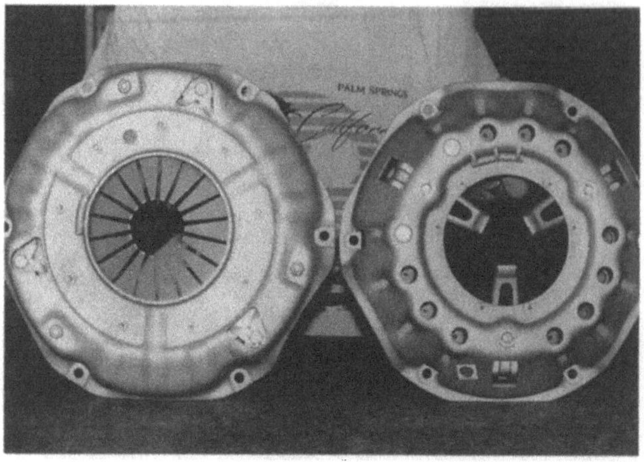

0012748

Fig. 17-20. OEM-type diaphragm clutch (left) shows multiple spring/lever design. Spring tension alone squeezes the disc between the pressure plate and flywheel. At right is a common Borg & Beck style OEM replacement clutch.

Aftermarket Clutches

Thanks largely to aftermarket innovation, several performance clutch designs are available for your truck. One of the more exciting options is Midway's Centerforce clutch. A diaphragm clutch with unique centrifugal weights, the Centerforce unit uses the best features of each popular clutch design.

Borrowing from the diaphragm unit, the Centerforce clutches have low release pressure, short pedal effort and smooth take-up. Drawing on centrifugal principles, the Centerforce clutch cover design incorporates an ingenious weighting of the diaphragm fingers to allow higher apply pressure as clutch rpm rises. Centerforce claims increased disc and pressure plate life, and weights can be designed to accommodate a variety of user needs.

Although many clutch manufacturers build healthy aftermarket replacement clutches, Midway's Centerforce II and Dual Friction designs have a wide reputation for

0012749

Fig. 17-21. Midway's Centerforce unit is a firm clamping diaphragm design with the advantage of centrifugal weights for high clamp pressures as rpm increases. Centrifugal weights apply tremendous pressure at higher rpm.

their rugged performance, reliability and light pedal apply pressure. For multi-purpose truck usage, I prefer the Centerforce centrifugal weight clutch assembly over all other designs.

Clutch Linkage

GM light truck models can develop clutch linkage trouble. If you have plans to upgrade your powertrain, don't overlook the clutch linkage.

The more troublesome GM linkage systems are 1967 to mid-1980s mechanical linkage types. Here, the engine mounting system changed to a single rear mount under the transmission and two engine side mounts. Engine movement with this layout contributes to linkage wear, and loose mounts can cause rough clutch engagement.

Often, a mechanic suspects clutch wear when the real trouble is loose motor mounts, a worn transmission mount or fatigued clutch linkage and bushings. The 1939-59 and 1963–66 GM light trucks, despite their mechanical linkage, are less likely to develop clutch linkage trouble. 1939–59 models feature a chassis mounted clutch pedal, while all of these models offer rear engine mounts at each side of the bellhousing. This drastically reduces unwanted movement of the clutch linkage.

Ironically, the often cursed 1960–62 (1960-63 on 4x4s) adjustable type hydraulic linkage is one of the best designs around. When this hydraulic system is in good working order and adjusted to OEM shop manual specifications, the linkage works fine. Later model GM trucks with hydraulic clutch linkage are also reliable, although I prefer the durability of the older systems and their cast steel cylinders.

> ***CAUTION —***
> *Late GM truck hydraulic clutch cylinders have aluminum housings. The bores of such cylinders can easily become damaged if abrasive contaminants enter the system. Use care and cleanliness when inspecting clutch fluid or servicing the system.*

Inspect all mechanical linkage parts when changing or upgrading the clutch. As interior bellhousing parts are

0014367

Fig. 17-22. Factory hydraulic clutch linkage on 1960–62 GM light trucks (through 1963 on 4x4s) works well, offering less pedal pressure and smooth clutch engagement.

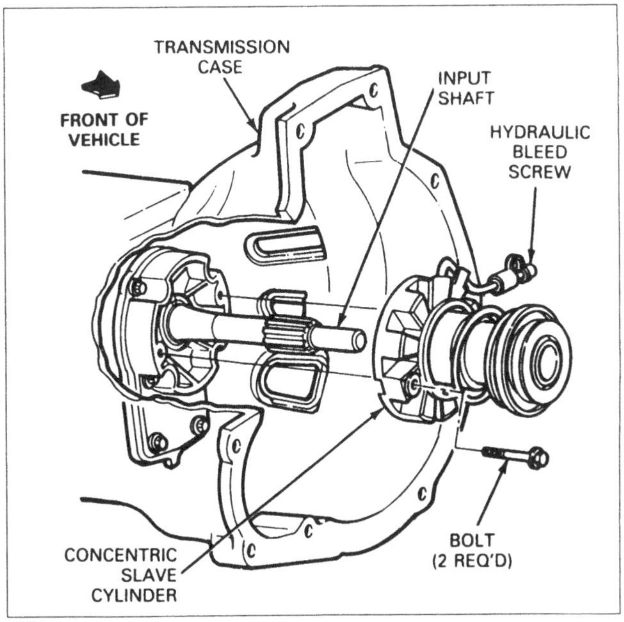

0012751

Fig. 17-23. When fabricating a clutch linkage system, I avoid use of hydraulically actuated clutch release bearings. Although this design eliminates mechanical clutch linkage, a release bearing hydraulic leak could ruin the clutch disc and require a major amount of labor to repair—especially on a 4x4 model.

difficult to reach, I highly recommend the use of a new, high quality throwout bearing. Install the best pilot bearing type available, and make sure it fits the crankshaft and transmission input gear properly. Look closely for any release arm / fork and pivot stud wear.

Aftermarket hydraulic throwout / release bearings are available, and some OEMs have turned to this design. I avoid such systems, especially on 4x4 models. This is a poor concept, as the simplest leak repair or seal replacement might require removal of two driveshafts, the transfer case, the transmission and other parts.

3. AXLES AND TRACTION

4x4 GM trucks prove their worth battling climate extremes, stretching over rocks, clawing at mud in fast flowing streams and pulling through deep snow on barren winter paths. Four-wheelers, seasoned by unruly trails, argue that there's no such thing as too much traction.

For GM light trucks, engine power flows through the clutch or torque converter, transmission, transfer case (4WD models) and driveline(s). The driveshaft rotates the axle's pinion gear. At the differential, power changes direction. The differential also determines the amount of power (torque) that flows to each wheel.

Conventional differential action has a severe limitation: When the truck encounters a loose traction surface, the differential mechanism directs power to the wheel with the least resistance.

This inherent weakness in open differentials has a major impact on a truck's traction. In loose terrain, it's easy to spot the truck with a conventional or open differential because one wheel spins furiously while the opposite wheel, on a better traction surface, stands still.

Traction Differentials: Controlling Wheelspin

A factory/OEM positive-traction or limited-slip differential helps deliver traction yet still provides vital differential speed between the axle shafts. Traction axles have used a variety of trade names, including Posi-Traction, Power-Lok and NoSPIN (Detroit). A number of aftermarket performance systems, well suited for severe on- and off-pavement traction demands, are also available.

The typical GM truck posi-traction or limited-slip unit features a clutching mechanism within the differential. Loss of traction at one wheel reads as no resistance in the differential unit. Most clutching devices apply torque to the axle shaft with more resistance, which is the same as delivering power to the wheel with better traction.

One variation of this design is the later GM governor type locking differential. These systems rely on a fly-weighted governor to telegraph wheelspin and initiate the process of applying torque to the opposite wheel. Such a system strives to match or balance the rotational speed at each wheel of the axle.

Most OEM limited-slip units incorporate a multi-plate spring loaded clutch assembly with a standard spider and side gear arrangement. Under normal driving conditions, these differentials flow power through the spider and side gears in the conventional manner. They can also direct power from the differential case directly to the side gears when the clutches apply.

When one tire loses traction and spins, the clutches within the differential provide power to the other wheel by directly driving its side gear. The spider gears, driving through beveled teeth, want to separate or spread the side gears. As the side gears move apart, they exert force on the clutch plates. When the load increases, so does the side gear pressure against the clutch plates. This directs more power to the wheel with traction.

Fig. 17-24. *This spool, shown for a 9-inch Ford axle application, is the ultimate traction device. Axle shafts fit directly into spool splines, eliminating the differential completely. Spools serve strictly for sand drags, pulls and other forms of all-out racing.*

Fig. 17-25. *The Dana Trac-Lok is a limited-slip aftermarket differential engineered for various applications. Dana 44 and 60 front axle units have been popular in GM 4x4 light truck front ends. Users find that OEM style limited-slip units deliver high traction without the risks of severe shock loads.*

While part of the load on the clutches comes from springs in the differential assembly, the majority of the force is from spreading the side gears. Torque load acting as the decisive factor, this explains why slight application of the brakes will cause a limited-slip differential to direct more power to the wheel with good footing.

The clutch type limited-slip unit, which retains the standard spider gears and side gears, still allows wheel speed to vary on corners. Varied wheel speed under normal load causes the clutches to slip, which allows the spider gears to perform their function. Applying heavy power in a turn, however, can load the clutches enough to lock the side gears against the differential case. This will cause both wheels to turn at the same speed.

Although various clutch styles exist, the principle remains the same: Provide a direct flow of power from the differential case to each of the side gears and wheels rather than only to the wheel with the least traction. Although their method of delivery is entirely different, aftermarket lockers also accommodate this need.

Which Differential?

Your highway driving environment or off-pavement tastes dictate which traction differential to buy. Yes, there is such thing as too much traction, and driver caution is a must with any traction differential. A truck with a limited-slip or locking differential can go sideways when both wheels lose traction at the same time.

> *WARNING —*
> *On ice or slick off-camber pavement, torque application at both ends of an axle assembly can create unwanted trouble. If your truck has a traction differential(s) and you're traveling on ice, be very careful. The truck could easily slip sideways if both wheels spin at the same time and the road camber is steep.*

As an expert on differentials, Tom Reider, president of Reider Racing Enterprises, notes, "While differential choices vary enough to satisfy most everyone's needs, the differential that satisfies everyone's wants still hasn't been invented. For most highway situations, an open differential is all that most people need and is, therefore, found in 90% of all vehicles. Its ability to move the vehicle, however, is limited by the minimum traction available to any of the driving wheels. When operated in slippery conditions or with minimum weight on any of the drive wheels, it often causes the vehicle to become a land-locked barge.

"The alternatives available to us are to install limited slip or locking type differentials which will then provide the type of power flow to the ground that we expect out of our vehicle. Benefits and drawbacks exist for both types of differentials."

While manual and automatic lockers have the advantage of providing 100% traction to the opposite wheel when an axle shaft breaks, if you break a semi-floating axle shaft, or if you snap a 4x4's front axle shaft anywhere near the steering knuckle, you cannot drive safely.

Full-floating rear axles, like those commonly found on all older 3/4-ton and one-ton class trucks and the current C/K2500 and -3500 trucks equipped for higher GVW ratings, will continue to operate with a broken axle shaft if the differential has limited-slip or a locker unit. If possible, remove the broken axle section to protect other parts. Reinstall the outer flange to keep debris out and prevent gear oil loss. You can make it home for repairs. Firewood haulers might find this reassuring.

0012754

Fig. 17-27. Multiplate OEM style differential provides power to the wheel and axle with traction. The spider gears press the side gears against the clutches to deliver more torque to the wheel with traction.

0014503

Fig. 17-26. Safety tire chains are a primary traction device. Meeting needs of over-the-road truckers for nearly half a century, Burns Bros., Inc., also owns Security Chain Company, the largest safety chain plant in the United States. Innovative Z-Chain cable design works well with latest ABS braking systems and is officially rated as a high speed safety chain. Easy to install in a blizzard, Z-Chain devices complement a limited slip differential.

Traction Guide

A variety of aftermarket and OE-type traction differentials are available for your truck. The need for these devices depends upon your driving environment and the importance of delivering maximum torque or traction at each wheel. (On some 4x4 applications, this could mean a traction device at both the front and rear differentials.) Several manufacturers offer traction differential kits for improving your truck's axle(s).

Detroit Locker/NoSPIN: A highly respected differential unit that has stood the test of time is the Detroit Locker or NoSPIN unit, built by Tractech, Inc., a subsidiary of Dyneer Corporation. The NoSPIN was an OEM and dealer installed option years ago.

Speed sensitive, the NoSPIN allows your truck to maneuver corners and operate over irregular terrain. The unique design offers the equivalent of a completely locked differential (similar to a spool) during straight ahead driving conditions.

For differential action, the NoSPIN has a central spider assembly with dog teeth on both sides, two driven clutches (one for each axle shaft) with dog teeth to engage the spiders and a pair of side gears. This spider assembly fits in the middle of the differential case. The case drives the spider assembly, while the driven clutch assemblies ride on splines machined on the outside of the side gears. Coil springs keep the clutches engaged with the spider assembly. This directs power from the spider to the side gears.

As the truck corners and the outside wheel speeds up, cam ramps on the inside edges of the spider unit cause the clutch assembly for that wheel to disengage from the spider. The wheel now coasts freely. As with conventional or factory limited slip differentials, NoSPIN also prevents axle binding on turns. The method differs, however, as NoSPIN completely disconnects the power flow to the outer wheel as the vehicle makes a turn.

0012756

Fig. 17-28. *The Detroit Locker/NoSPIN has a loyal following. The Detroit Locker features positive engagement to the wheel with greater traction. Cutaway display model shows high quality and simplicity of mechanism. Display model has survived years of customer abuse on this parts counter.*

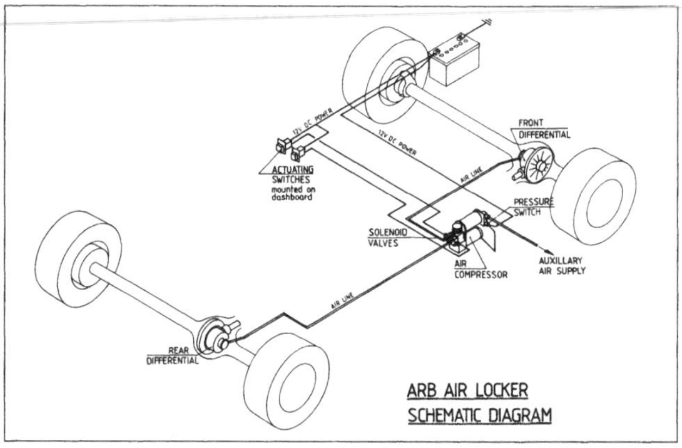

0012757

Fig. 17-29. *ARB's Air Locker leaves the traction to the driver. With the push of a switch, the differential locks up and both axle shafts rotate in unison, much like a spool. When disengaged, Air Locker provides the smooth highway operation of a conventional axle.*

When wheel speeds are again equal, the free-wheeling clutch engages with the spider. Power now flows evenly to both wheels. The unique factor with this differential is that power flow is either equal at both wheels or going to the wheel with the greater amount of traction.

If one wheel hangs in the air, the NoSPIN unit stays locked, providing as much power to the wheel on the ground as traction will allow. If you spin the inside wheel on a turn, once the inner wheel's speed reaches that of the outside wheel, the unit will return to a locked position.

ARB Air Locker: After seven years of severe use in Australia, the ARB Air Locker hit the U.S. market by storm several years ago. This differential locking system now has a loyal following among those who prefer manual control of the differential(s). Winner of the coveted 1989 SEMA Best Product Award, the ARB Air Locker is a popular item with hard-core off-pavement users.

The Air Locker provides conventional open differential operation for normal driving conditions. When your truck needs power to both wheels, Air Locker pneumatically locks the spider gears and side gears within the differential.

Inside the differential case, the Air Locker has a slider shift mechanism, much like sliders found in manual transmissions or a transfer case. The outside of the slider has splines. They engage and slide inside the differential case.

The slider also attaches to a hollow piston which surrounds the spider and side gears. Actuated by pressurized air, the piston moves the slider. Teeth on the inside of the slider match a set of teeth on the outside of one side gear. When the piston moves the slider over the outer teeth of the side gear, the side gear, slider and differential case lock up as a single unit. The locked side gears and spiders rotate both axle shafts at the same speed as the differential case.

An ARB Air Locker can engage solid power flow to each wheel, much like a racing spool. This is unsurpassed tractability; however, the driver now bears full responsibility for locking and unlocking the unit.

For durability, most ARB Air Locker applications have four spider gears, compared to the two spiders found in most OEM conventional axle designs. An Air Locker fitup requires electrical wiring and the installation of an air compressor and air lines to the differential(s). Although installation is more involved than other traction devices, each kit includes instructions and all necessary parts.

I have installed and tested the ARB Air Locker. The differential installation was much like changing a ring-and-pinion gear set and requires use of a dial indicator for setting up the ring and pinion gears plus blue dye to perform tooth contact tests. It takes time to fit and route air hoses carefully and mount the compressor. Wiring, which features nicely made harnesses, also requires effort to assure a neat and reliable installation. From my experience with a common truck axle, the task should take the reasonably equipped home mechanic from 10-16 hours to perform. Despite the time involved, I was very pleased with the results and unique advantages of this system.

Auburn Gear: For truck owners looking for a high-quality limited-slip differential, Auburn Gear provides a smart alternative. Although Auburn focuses mainly on the high-performance automobile market, its heavy duty limited-slip design has applications for popular light truck axle.

Like OEM limited-slip designs, Auburn Gear delivers power to both wheels through a clutching mechanism. However, instead of using clutch plates with high frictional loads, Auburn Gear uses a cone type clutch system. (A cone attaches to the back side of a side gear and nests inside a matching machined surface in the differential case.) When loaded by either the differential springs or the spider gears, the side gear wedges itself within the differential case.

By design, much less force is necessary to lock the side gear to the differential case. Since there is direct steel-to-steel contact without clutch plates to wear out, peak performance can last much longer than with other units. Auburn traction differentials also boast large spider and side gears that deliver exceptional strength and durability for a limited-slip type differential.

Torque delivery to the wheel with traction is superior with this design. If I were to consider a limited-slip traction device, the latest Auburn design would be my choice.

0012758

Fig. 17-30. Auburn Gear's SureGrip is a rugged, heavy duty limited-slip unit.

LA Locker/LOCK-RIGHT: LA Locker's differential functions much like the NoSPIN/Detroit Locker. Originally designed for military Dodge trucks and larger W300 civilian Power Wagons, this design has gone widely civilian since 1986. In addition to larger truck axles, LA Lockers fit the popular Spicer 44 unit and many other OEM axle applications.

The dramatic difference between LA Locker and other traction devices, including the NoSPIN, is its quiet operation during clutch lockup. Like the popular NoSPIN, LA Locker delivers 100% of the available power to the traction wheel(s) at all times. This design offers a very simple cam action and lockup, shifting smoothly enough for use at rear or front (4x4 model) axles.

> *WARNING —*
> *Although many four-wheelers use an LA Locker at both the rear and front axles, this design exaggerates the usual understeer associated with running a four-wheel drive truck on a hard surface with the front hubs engaged. Unlock your front hubs as you normally would for driving in 2WD mode on hard pavement. Always follow the traction device manufacturer's operating guidelines for using two- or four-wheel drive.*

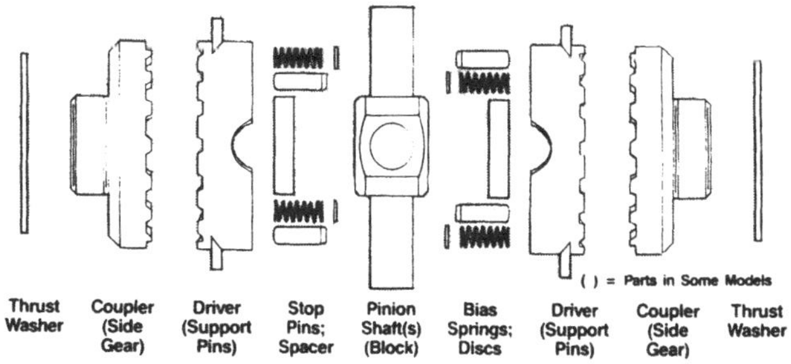

0012759

Fig. 17-31. LA Locker diagram shows components of the differential. Cam teeth on each coupler allow overrun and disengagement when the axles rotate at uneven speeds.

The LA Locker installs in the existing differential case, which saves considerable cost. During installation, there's no demand to remove differential bearings, so resetting ring gear backlash is often unnecessary. The LA Locker/LOCK-RIGHT is a tough, military-proven design. If you're attracted to the no-nonsense traction of a Detroit Locker/NoSPIN or ARB Air Locker, this quiet and rugged automatic locker deserves a look.

Spicer and Other OEM Limited Slips: Many trucks have factory-installed limited-slip differentials. GM and Spicer have supplied OEM traction differentials since the 1950s, and satisfied users often restore their worn differentials with OEM/GM or Spicer replacement parts.

Spicer traction units also work as retrofits for conventional Spicer/Dana axles. Since many GM 4x4 light trucks have used Spicer/Dana axles in the front (many earlier models use them at the rear, too), a Spicer limited-slip (Trac-Lok) unit is a retrofit option.

> NOTE —
> Users who prefer a milder application of power and subtler traction at the front axle choose a factory-type limited-slip or positive traction differential. An OEM type limited slip in front and Detroit or LA Locker at the rear is a popular combination for four-wheelers seeking maximum off-pavement traction.

Rating Differential Traction Devices*

Differential style	Smoothness of operation	Tractability	Adverse effect on tires/driveline	Cost	Used for
Conventional (open)	Excellent	Poor	None	Lowest	Highway
OEM Limited slip	Very good	Good	Very little	Modest	Modest off-road
Aftermarket limited-slip	Good	Very good	Modest	Moderate	Modest off-road
Automatic lockers (LA and Detroit)	Good to poor	Extremely good	Modest	Higher	Heavy off-road
Manual locker (ARB)	Good to excellent	Excellent (locked) Poor (unlocked)	Poor (locked) None (unlocked)	Highest	Heavy off-road
Spool/welded diff.	Poor	Excellent	Poor	Modest	Racing

*Source: Tom Reider, Reider Racing Enterprises

Traction Differential Footnotes

Installing a differential carrier assembly involves close tolerances. Ring gear backlash settings require a dial indicator and patience. Before buying a traction differential, read the installation instructions carefully. Decide whether to sublet the job to a capable shop or tackle the work yourself.

Give the broader traction issue some thought, too. Consider tires, traction bars and shock absorbers. Added traction to the wheels means a greater challenge keeping traction on the ground. Expect more wheel hop and spring wrap up, especially with large tires.

There is such a thing as too much traction, especially when driving on icy, off-camber pavement. I like an open differential (non-locking/non-limited slip unit) in this kind of environment, as it allows for better vehicle control and straighter, more stable steering.

Conversion Axles

A variety of axle designs have met GM light truck needs. Spicer/Dana has played a large role in domestic truck axle development, and many GM 4x4 light trucks have featured Spicer or Dana live front axles. Some GM truck rear axles have also been Spicer/Dana designs, although GM's own Corporate and Saginaw units have served the majority of light truck rear axle applications.

Although Spicer/Dana is one of the most respected names in the automotive industry, the use of a Dana/Spicer axle is no pat assurance that your truck's axle is bulletproof. The size (capacity rating) or application of the axle determines its stamina.

One example of how this works is that many GM half-ton and three-quarter-ton conventional (solid front axle) 4x4 models use the same Dana 44 front axle. The difference is in the parts used from the steering knuckle outboard through the wheel hubs.

Strength of these assemblies rests with their load rating although, clearly, the larger one-ton model's front axle, a Dana 60 unit, would offer greater differential and axle shaft stamina. Especially when carrying a weighty cabover camper, I would seek out a conventional K-30/3500 4WD chassis rather than the K-20/2500 4WD type. (See comments in early chapters on selecting a used truck.)

0014484

Fig. 17-32. This large carrier-type axle is a full-floating design common to pre-1973 3/4- and one-ton capacity GM trucks. "Corporate" integral-type axles serve current models.

GM light truck rear axles, with the exception of the early torque tube types found in half-ton models, are reasonably durable and practical designs. (Even a torque tube type is durable, although there is no way to upgrade such a unit.)

When considering an upgrade or retrofit rear axle for an open driveshaft 1/2-ton GM truck, however, my first choice is GM's own 12-bolt (twelve differential cover screws) Saginaw integral-type. The later 10-bolt (ten differential cover screws) integral rear axle design, although adequate for most C/K-10/1500 chores, has not earned the respect of GM's previous 12-bolt light truck axle.

For the earlier (1939–64) half-ton GM trucks, some builders install a 12-bolt rear axle in place of the original GM axle. (GMC trucks with the Spicer 45 type rear axle offer reasonably good service with the OEM unit.) If you plan a 12-bolt axle swap, make sure you match brake sizing, match the track width and install the correct length driveline. (See Chapter 10, Tranfer Case, Driveshafts, Axles and Hubs.)

Three-quarter-ton GM trucks have benefitted from the Spicer/Dana 60 series axles and GM's own Corporate 14-bolt full-floating rear axles. I would again emphasize that the full-floating, heavy duty axle design is superior to the later semi-floating versions of these axle types.

All GM one-ton rated trucks equipped with a full-floating rear axle have ample stamina. Pre-1973 models of 3/4-ton and one-ton trucks often use Eaton or Corporate rear axles with a drop-in type center member. For these axles, new parts have become increasingly more difficult to secure—and expensive. Reasonable swap material would be a Corporate 14-bolt integral/full-floating axle design or a full-floating Spicer/Dana 60, 60HD (heavy duty) or 70 rear axle. Use an axle with the correct GVW load rating for your chassis and hauling plans.

If you have an early 1980s or newer C/K-20/2500 pickup with a semi-floating rear axle, and you want to carry a gooseneck trailer with 1,500 pounds resting on a bed-mounted fifth wheel, consider retrofitting a full-floating axle unit. Find an application compatible with your truck's chassis. Make sure of the new axle's braking capacity and be certain your axle choice will interface safely with OEM ABS or any other braking devices. Match U-joint requirements and be certain the driveline length is correct. Axle retrofits usually require some fabrication work.

> ***CAUTION —***
> *Compatibility with a later model's ABS braking system is a concern. With any axle swap, you will likely need to perform fabrication work (such as spring perch relocation, a perch design change, brake line fitup or an emergency brake control adaptation).*

Full-floating Rear Axle Upgrade

Until 1980, GM, Dodge, Ford and several other manufacturers offered the added stamina and safety of a full-floater type rear axle in 3/4-ton models. In 1980, Ford initiated the switch to semi-floating rear axles on F250 models, a move soon followed by GM 3/4-ton trucks and the Suburbans.

Loss of full-floating wheel hub support is not the only drawback with the later semi-floating GM axles. While GM's Corporate 14-bolt full-floaters feature a huge 10-1/2" diameter ring gear, the newer semi-floating 14-bolt axles have a smaller 9-1/2" diameter ring gear. A 9-1/2" ring gear is still very tough, but the 10-1/2" diameter ring gear places a GM 3/4-ton or one-ton capacity rear axle in the more brutish Spicer 70 class.

Characterizing a Full-floating Rear Axle

A full-floating axle is easy to spot, as its hub flange protrudes through the rear wheel centers. The outside flange of a floating axle shaft bolts to the outer face of the wheel hub. You can safely remove a full-floating axle shaft with the truck's wheels attached and on the ground.

For large trucks that carry a heavy load, the full-floatingfull-floating axle has a distinct advantage. An inner and outer bearing set supports the load, much like the wheel bearings of a 4x4's full-floating front axle. These bearings ride on spindles that extend outward past the brake shoe set. The hefty spindles of a Corporate 14-bolt axle are an integral part of the axle housing.

By design, the full-floating axle shaft simply connects the differential's side gear with the wheel hub. If the axleshaft breaks, the wheel remains in place, safely supported by the hub's inner and outer bearings.

In later semi-floating axles like the 9-1/2" Corporate unit, the inner end of the axle shaft also engages the side gear at the differential. This keeps the axle aligned and the wheel flange straight.

By contrast to a full-floater, however, the vehicle load presses directly against the outboard section of the axle shaft. A roller type bearing uses the axle shaft for its inner race. When the axle shaft or bearing wear, the shaft can become scrap and must be replaced at great expense. Also, although GM has substantially increased the size and strength of these semi-floating axle shafts, shaft breakage could allow the hub, brake drum and wheel/tire assembly to separate from the vehicle.

0014359

Fig. 17-33. *Massive brake drum on 1986 Suburban looks much like a king-size passenger car application. Brake shoe size of 13" x 2-1/2" demands huge drum castings. Like passenger car design, the wheel sandwiches drum against axle flange.*

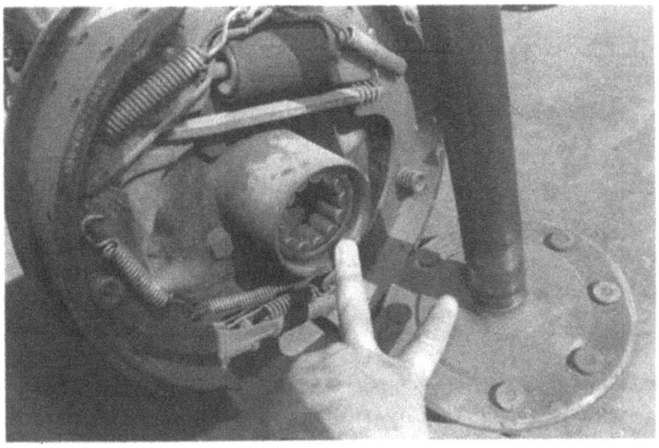

0014360

Fig. 17-34. *Semi-floating axle shaft serves as wheel bearing inner race. Vehicle load and weight bear directly on outer section of axle shaft. If shaft breaks, the flange, brake drum, wheel and tire could separate from truck.*

0014361

Fig. 17-35. *Semi-floating axle shaft (left) is much heavier than full-floater; however, it is not necessarily stronger. Semi-floating axle shaft must bear loads and weight of vehicle and is more heavily stressed. Full-floater shaft simply acts as power link between the differential side gear and outer flange of the full-floating hub.*

0014362

Fig. 17-36. *Here is spindle section of full-floating axle housing. Wheel hub rides on inner and outer bearing sets, with an adjusting nut/lock nut holding the hub in place. If axle shaft breaks, hub still rides safely on bearing sets.*

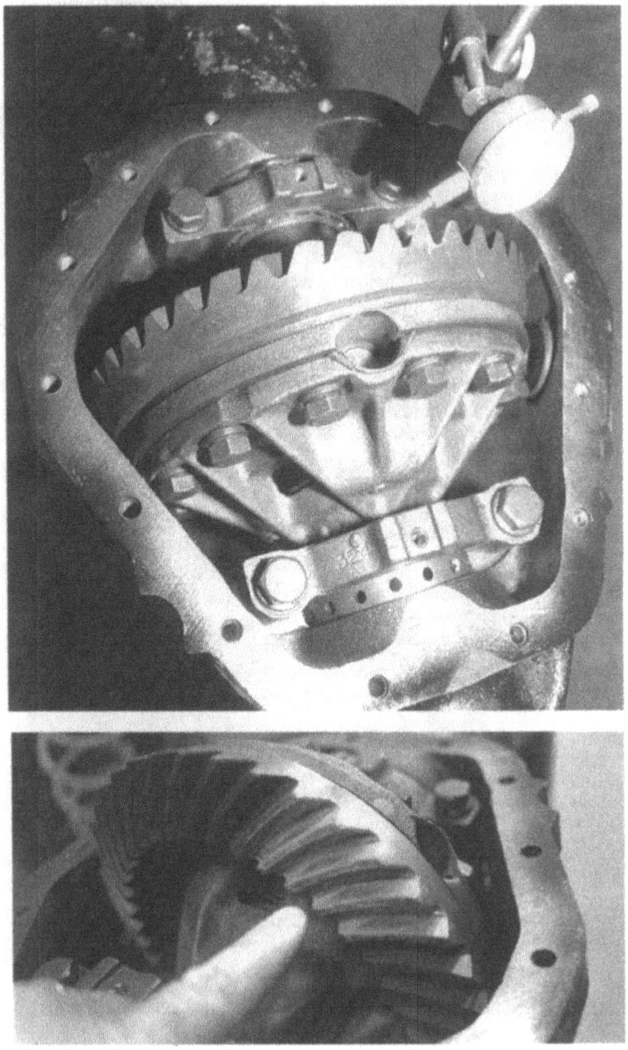

0014507 / 0014364

Fig. 17-37. *Close inspection of tooth contact pattern on new ring and pinion gear reveals correct pinion depth and ring gear backlash. Jeff Sugg's two decades of gear system rebuilding experience assure component longevity.*

0014097

Fig. 17-38. *After packing and adjusting wheel bearings to specification like with full-floating front wheel bearings, Jeff installs axle shaft reusing 1986 brake backing plates with new shoes and wheel cylinders. Measure and match brake shoe size and also the wheel cylinder bore dimensions when changing over parts. In this case, the 1986 brake backing plates fit the earlier full-floating axle housing perfectly, allowing use of the OEM emergency brake cables and other brake hardware.*

A full-floating Corporate 14-bolt axle is stronger and better equipped to handle heavy working loads. If your truck demands ultimate stamina, a 1981–84 full-floater will easily retrofit to an early 1980s or newer conventional (non-Sierra chassis) 3/4-ton 4x4 pickup or Suburban. A number of 1973–80 assemblies will also fit. Match drum/brake shoe size and hardware when selecting an axle. Do not tamper with or modify the later rear anti-lock braking system.

My 1986 trailer-pulling GMC Suburban K-2500 4x4 had the factory 9-1/2" semi-floating rear axle. When the

0014365

Fig. 17-39. *Full-floating axle accepts original shocks, wheels and hubcaps. Jeff installed a longer driveshaft tube (being balanced here) to match the shorter pinion shaft length found on the 10-1/2" Corporate axle. Other modifications, like slightly re-sizing the bracket holes when mounting the Suburban's OEM rear brake proportioning valve lever, took only minutes.*

expensive factory governor-type limited slip began to show wear, the truck was otherwise still in excellent condition. This model proved an excellent candidate for a bolt-for-bolt full-floating rear axle changeover.

Jeff Sugg at M.I.T. in El Cajon, California refurbished a full-floating Corporate axle, installing a new ring and pinion gearset, all new bearings, plus new brake lining and wheel cylinders.

The reconditioned axle assembly will likely outlast this very well built and rugged Suburban K-2500. Jeff Sugg and Andy Thomas made the full-floater conversion look easy, using OEM pieces and a new driveshaft.

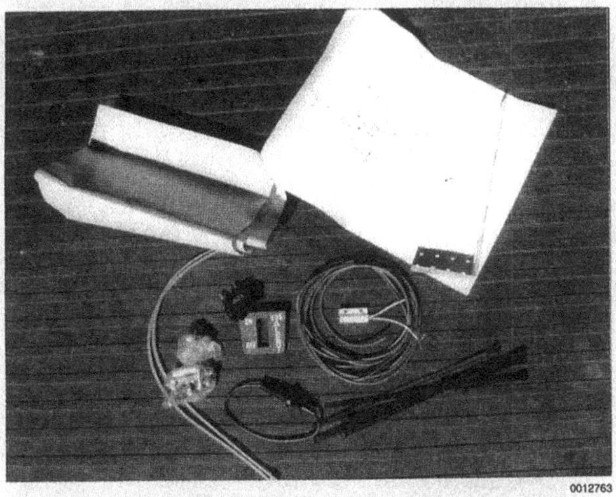

0012763

Hub-A-Lert: Watchdog for 4x4 Front Hubs

Knowing whether your truck's hubs have engaged or disengaged depends on more than the 4-Wheel Drive light on the console or dashboard. In many applications, the OEM 4x4 indicator lamp signal originates at the transfer case and simply indicates that the shifter/fork has moved to 4-High or 4-Low.

This means that power is flowing to the front axle, but if the hubs are not completely engaged, torque cannot rotate the front wheels. Similarly, with automatic locking hubs, simply backing the truck up is no guarantee that the automatic hubs have disengaged. Dash lights cannot see inside the front hub mechanisms.

There's a better way to monitor front axle activity. Hub-A-Lert, an easy-to-install device built by 4x4 Specialty Products, can read front driveshaft rotation. The device sends a signal to an LED dash lamp and takes the guesswork out of hub disengagement.

During normal two-wheel drive operation, no shaft rotation (other than the minor lubricant spin common to some geardrive transfer cases) will display on the LED lamp. If a defective hub begins to drag, however, the front driveshaft will spin and flash a signal on the dashboard.

Simple and designed by a savvy victim of several automatic hub and consequent transfer case failures, Hub-A-Lert is automatic hub insurance—at a fraction of the cost for a damaged front axle, transfer case or wheel hub assembly.

4. Driveshaft Upgrades

The common U-joint size used on many light GM trucks with open drivelines is sufficient for most engine types. If your truck is a hardcore off-pavement runner, low driveshaft speeds and twisty, constantly changing driveshaft angles require stronger tubing sizes and a heftier rear coupler/splined shaft. A competent driveline shop can build a shaft with an increased tube diameter and wall thickness.

> NOTE —
> Your driveshaft(s) must be straight, within close tolerances and in balance. The driveshaft built to a high degree of straightness requires very little, if any, balancing.

When driveshaft parts must handle more than 300 horsepower, you need heavy duty 3/4-ton or one-ton truck size U-joints. This is also necessary for a custom street truck that runs a high output powertrain, a pickup pulling a massive trailer, or the 4x4 desert race truck.

For a radical 4x4 chassis lift, double Cardan type CV-joints will help reduce vibration caused by steep driveshaft angles.

A complete U-joint conversion can include heavier driveshaft tubing and larger U-joint flanges. For many GM light truck owners, the 1350-series Spicer joint (or its equivalent size in another design) can handle severe loads. Dana/Spicer 44, 45 and 60 axle units can easily be fitted with 1350 size replacement flanges. These larger yokes are also available for popular GM axles, transfer case inputs and outputs, and the live front axles on 4x4 models.

Steep driveshaft angles reduce the load capacity and safety of driveline assemblies. Speed also determines safe driveline angles. Modified trucks often violate both of these considerations with steep driveshaft slopes and lower (higher numerically) axle gear ratios. (See chapter on driveshafts for more information.)

> *CAUTION —*
> *Be certain to use OEM replacement U-joints at the open front steering knuckles. These permanently sealed joints have no grease fitting and offer more strength than a U-joint with a cross yoke drilled for a grease fitting.*

> NOTE —
> In four-wheel drive, the torque splits between front and rear axles, reducing overall load on each U joint. Two-wheel drive mode is actually much harder on U-joints than running a truck in four-wheel drive.

Chapter 18

Suspension, Wheel and Tire Upgrades

MOST STATES NOW HAVE MANDATES setting limits on vehicle chassis height and body modifications. Motor vehicle safety administrators, law enforcement agencies and a wary citizenry have targeted unsafely customized street trucks and poorly modified off-pavement prototype pre-runner and 4x4 trucks registered for public road use.

Evidence of sensational accidents and senseless traffic deaths supports this sentiment. The more reputable aftermarket suspension manufacturers share many views with the state legislators. Increasing a truck's height, for example, raises issues like correct safety engineering versus a homespun botch job to achieve a particular look.

Teams of factory engineers work endlessly at improving the ride, handling, steering and brakes of Chevrolet and GMC light trucks. These mechanical engineers, versed in chassis dynamics and equipped with elaborate computer and laboratory equipment, build trucks to comply with known standards of handling and braking.

WARNING —
Any suspension modification will affect the handling characteristics of your truck. Poor braking, risk of a rollover, loss of vehicle control, chronic failure of driveline parts and marginal braking each can result from improper modifications. Before you consider any modification to your truck's chassis or body height, make safety a priority. Take extreme care when modifying the suspension. When in doubt, always follow OEM standards or the information furnished by a reputable aftermarket equipment manufacturer.

1. Chassis Modifications

Chassis and suspension engineering provide a challenge with any multipurpose truck. Highway driving, trailer

0014369

Fig. 18-1. *Custom fabrication work on a Nelson & Nelson built pre-runner truck reveals serious engineering and ultra-heavy duty components. A homespun look-alike cannot duplicate the stamina and materials displayed here. For high performance driving, safety must be your ultimate consideration.*

Fig. 18-2. No nonsense in the suspension department on this Chevrolet Class 8 off-road racer. For racing purposes, custom independent front suspension provides 20-plus inches of wheel travel. Fabrication work reveals serious engineering and ultra-heavy duty components characteristic of competitive desert race truck systems. A homespun look-alike cannot duplicate the stamina and materials displayed here.

pulling, trail running and hardcore desert racing each call for different chassis dynamics.

Visualize your truck sweeping through corners, fighting a crosswind with a trailer in tow, braking hard, bracing against a loose traction surface or negotiating a precarious, off-camber sidehill. The interaction of the springs, shocks, stabilizers, brakes and tire / wheel mass is a blur. An automotive engineer or race truck fabricator must address each of these conditions.

On the test course or skidpad, a safe truck meets many criteria. Along with center of gravity, terms like Ackerman steering angles, lateral acceleration, roll axis, roll center, roll couple distribution, roll steer and toe change, roll stiffness, shock damping, spring / wheel rate, and vertical load transfer each apply to handling. The frame, suspension and axle design (Hotchkiss, solid hypoid, twin A-arm, rear coil-and-link, coil spring or torsion bar IFS, live IFS or mono-beam) also enter the equation.

At speed, aerodynamics and road load add to the burden. Braking is critically dependent upon load distribution and the anti-dive / anti-lift characteristics of the overall chassis design. Tire slip angle also becomes a factor, and the safest truck chassis balances each of these demands into a reasonably compliant package.

Modifying Your GM Truck's Chassis

Changes in front end geometry, roll center, center of gravity, unsprung weight and tire design each have an effect on your truck's handling. GM truck engineers generally set up a chassis for good ride, steering control and manageable braking. Aftermarket components often meet the additional needs of special terrain, extra loads and exceptionally harsh driving conditions.

The better engineered aftermarket spring and shock absorber kits offer substantial improvements for your truck. Additional clearance for specialty tires, improved spring rates, massive shock absorbers and a stouter steering damper shock can make our vehicles far better suited for off-highway perils. Many of these parts enhance the truck's handling and control under a variety of driving conditions.

For some GM light truck owners, trends and fads also motivate chassis modifications. Achieving a certain status may even override safety concerns. Poor braking, risk of a rollover, loss of vehicle control, chronic failure of driveline parts and marginal braking characterize the worst modifications.

The Culprits

Unfortunately, some truck owners go far beyond the OEM and aftermarket parts sources, seeking to establish their own records for the highest, biggest, fastest and fattest truck. Without the benefit of engineering credentials or a sense for chassis dynamics, builders of homespun, radically lifted trucks have encouraged the wrath of motor vehicle and public safety administrators.

A large number of improperly modified trucks sport crude and unsafe spacer block lifts, disfigured springs, bound up steering linkage, stretched brake hoses and pipes, overheight bumpers and ridiculous headlamp angles that glare menacingly into the eyes of oncoming drivers.

These same trucks, with massively oversize tires creating an unsprung weight imbalance, have overtaxed brake systems that prevent controlled stops. Radically sloped steering linkage and drag link angles, common to

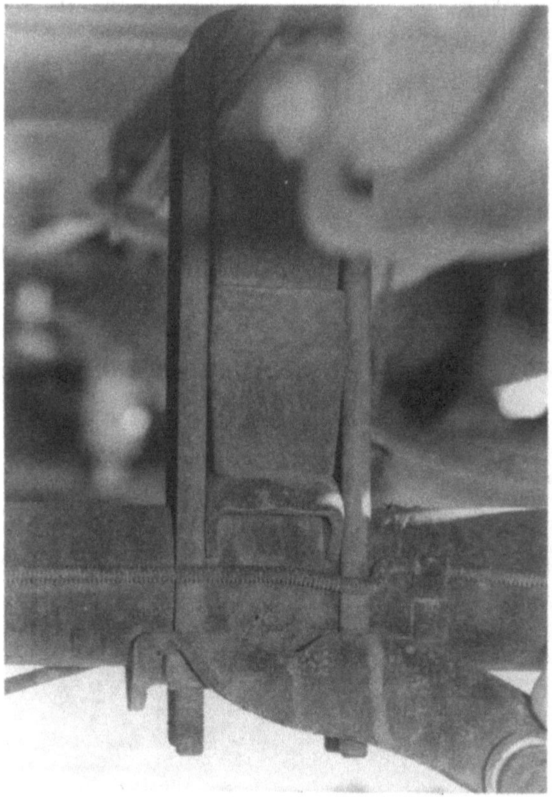

Fig. 18-3. Here's an illegal setup by many state standards. Two sets of stacked spacer blocks make up this rear lift. Shifting of blocks and failure under load are possible. Never stack rear spacer blocks. Never install spacer blocks at the front springs.

0012268

Fig. 18-4. The ride height may look hot, but this front end geometry is unsafe. Note the radical slope angle on the draglink. As springs compress and the solid axle rises, bump steer shifts the wheels to the right.

poorly constructed chassis lifts, create bump steer. The slightest blip in the road can cause the truck to veer uncontrollably.

Many law enforcement officers are also light truck owners and recreationalists, yet most have a profound bias against radically lifted trucks. Each state's motor vehicle safety office has files on highway mayhem caused by poorly crafted, radically lifted 4x4 trucks. Horror stories of homespun junk run the gamut, including cases of monstrous 4x4 trucks rear ending other vehicles—with the lower edge of the front bumper overrunning the entire trunk of the car!

Equally appalling, some of the homemade street truck chassis systems include hastily slammed or lowered suspension and marginal steering hardware. Personal expression is a fundamental human right; highway safety, however, is a collective responsibility.

State Lift Laws and Accountability

Although a few states have no current laws directly regulating chassis lift or excessively oversize tires, a trend is clear. Federal safety laws, interstate highway funding, and the issues of public liability make each state accountable to the same issues.

The aftermarket suspension and body lift manufacturers have similar accountability. For a reputable company to survive, product liability insurance is essential. The cost of this insurance can become prohibitive. Here, the incentive is a safely engineered kit. A good safety record can effectively reduce product liability and operating overhead.

OEM standards remain the best baseline. General Motors Corporation and other new vehicle manufacturers must comply with U.S. Department of Transportation (DOT), Society of Automotive Engineers (SAE) and other professional engineering guidelines when constructing their vehicles.

Vehicle lift results from changes in tire size, suspension modifications and installation of body mount spacers. Before investing time and money either raising your truck's chassis/body or mounting a set of expensive oversize tires, review the laws for your state.

NOTE —
If you've heard rumors of a height limit change, consult your nearest state police or highway patrol office for the new rulings. These agencies will prove very helpful. Their primary concerns are public safety and compliance with motor vehicle regulations.

Choosing a Quality Lift Kit

There are many aftermarket lift kits available for GM light 4x4 trucks. When selecting a kit, consider these features:

- Make sure the kit uses new replacement leaf spring sets at the front for a solid axle model. Avoid shackle extensions and front add-a-leafs.
- If the lift is substantial, make sure that longer brake hoses, dropped sway bar brackets, bump stop drop kits, longer shock absorbers, a raised steering arm or

Massachusetts' Suspension Modification Formula

Here's an example of a current lift law as it applies to 4x4 (and other) vehicles' safety. Massachusetts devised a formula for allowable mechanical (body and suspension) lift that accounts for both vehicle stability and safe handling: Wheel base multiplied by Wheel Track (the tire tread center-to-center measurement at the wider axle) divided by a factor of 2200. The wheel track width may be increased up to four inches—by way of rim offset only; no wheel spacers are allowed.

The test is relatively easy. Suppose your GM truck has a 117-inch wheelbase and wide rims that provide a 68-inch tread centerline width (four-inch increase over OEM tread width of 64 inches). 117 x 68 = 7956, divided by 2200 = 3.6" lift. Under Massachusetts' Sections 6.04 and 6.05, the tire diameter (based on the largest size available as an OEM option) may also be increased the same amount as the mechanical lift.

Simply put, this GM truck could have tires up to 3.51" larger diameter than stock plus a 3.51" mechanical lift by way of chassis and/or a body lift kit. Accordingly, the body/door sill height could set a total of 5.26" over stock with installation of these wide rims, oversized tires and the mechanical (chassis or body) lift.

Example: If the OEM maximum tire diameter was 31", you could install 34-1/2" diameter tires on a wide offset rim size (two inch wider track/wheel centerline measurement per wheel) and add a 3-1/2" chassis lift kit for tire clearance. Within the Massachusetts formula, the added track width restores the center of gravity when you increase suspension height and tire diameter.

All parts must be equal to or better than OEM standards, and the vehicle safety cannot be compromised. Massachusetts has addressed OEM vehicle design, roll center, center of gravity and all other handling concerns with this statute. Other equipment on the truck must comply with general safety standards. This is a sound approach, allowing reasonable lifts for both off-pavement and highway usage.

Fig. 18-5. Rancho Suspension makes this quality lift kit for the late model Chevrolet/GMC IFS Sierra 4WD chassis. If you must lift your 4x4 truck and install oversized tires, look to a major aftermarket vendor like Rancho Suspension, Warn/Black Diamond, Trailmaster or SuperLift for a complete and thorough kit.

dropped Pitman arm (whichever is applicable) and other parts will compensate for the longer distance between the frame and axles.

- On later IFS 4WD systems or a 2WD IFS model, make sure that the lift kit includes new steering knuckle/arm assemblies that will allow for adequate wheel travel. Avoid kits that simply jack up the torsion bars (or provide longer coil springs).
- Quality kits attempt to restore the OEM wheel travel, steering arcs and sway control. Consult a high performance/4WD frame and alignment shop that does this kind of installation before selecting a kit for your chassis.
- Driveline slope, driveshaft length and axle pinion angles are of real concern. Make sure that the kit addresses these needs. A stretched driveshaft or bad U-joint angles make trouble. (See driveline section in an earlier chapter.)
- Consider CV-joint and boot/seal angles on later IFS models, and make sure the chassis lift kit does not compromise these angles or cause stress to these parts.
- Always have a frame and alignment shop check out your kit's installation and fine-tune the caster, camber and toe-in settings.
- Go with a known product, as its research and development budget is more apt to produce quality results.
- Make sure that the lift is necessary. Lifts and the attendant work to fine-tune a chassis can get expensive and prove very time consuming. Do you really need big tires? Is this where your money is best spent?
- Consider the degree of change that your truck will undergo. Will this enhance its value? Can you restore the truck to stock if necessary? Will legal rulings ban your truck from the public road soon? Think this through before spending hard earned money on a lift, big wheels and oversized tires.

2. OFF-PAVEMENT SUSPENSION TUNING

Suspension tuning can enhance off-pavement performance. An upgraded spring and shock absorber package transforms a multipurpose 4x4 into a highly versatile trail machine. The right handling, suspension travel and shock damping provide better vehicle control, stability and greater utility.

Several factors determine the need for spring rate and chassis changes. Conversion to a heavier engine, the addition of a hefty front mounted winch or installing a protective front bumper/brush guard each place a load on the front springs. An oversize fuel tank, heavy duty truck-type manual or automatic transmission, a trailer towing package, a camper shell/cap, a utility or tool box and heavy fuel and water containers can weight the rear springs.

When your fatigued OEM shocks and sagging springs need replacement, an upgrade spring and shock absorber package can improve your truck's performance. Sagging coil or leaf springs allow the axle housing(s) to rest close to the rubber bump stops. Weak front coil springs create more bounce, sagging and loss of steering precision.

Loss of suspension travel means that your truck will have difficulty negotiating twisty terrain. Traction off-pavement becomes poor, with body roll and steering control problems. If the springs and shock absorbers now show these symptoms on your truck, or if modestly oversize tires create tire-to-body interference, consider an aftermarket suspension package.

Aftermarket Suspension Improvements

Your goal should be a reasonably firm spring rate and solid traction—without unduly harsh rebound and overly stiff leaf stacks. Spring rebound damping and deflection control remain vital to maximum traction, yet timid shocks lose effectiveness in just a few miles of trail pounding. The best all around kits have easy ride springs and quality shock absorbers.

From my experience, a mild lift/soft-ride suspension package provides several benefits. Once installed, these kits maintain a legal frame/front bumper height when used in conjunction with 31- to 33-inch diameter tires. The truck now has greater tire-to-body clearance, a much improved spring rate and better handling, both on- and off-pavement.

WARNING —
Use extreme caution when installing a lift kit or otherwise working under your truck. Always support the truck's frame on jackstands rated for the load. Do not rest the vehicle only on a jack, on cinder blocks or on pieces of wood.

WARNING —
Limit your truck's lift to just that amount necessary for tire installation and a full range of suspension travel. Select your tire size with care. Follow practical and safe tire and chassis guidelines, and make certain the wheel rim size is correct for your tires.

NOTE —
Before considering a suspension lift kit, consult your state's lift laws on height and track width limits. Select your chassis lift and tire size accordingly.

Shock Absorbers

Single shocks, dual shocks, gas shocks and more...The market is ripe with shock absorbers. What does your GM light truck need? Which shock works best? Is there a formula for choosing the right shock absorbers? You bet!

Shock absorbers wear out. For some light trucks, the shock absorbers fail fast. Why? Shocks deteriorate from high heat, excess friction and overload—symptoms common to driving on washboard roads and off-pavement poundings.

Most truck shock absorbers look similar, and despite different designs, they each meet the same goals: damping the springs' oscillating motion, limiting the effects of uneven loads transferring to each wheel, and keeping the wheels on the ground when the suspension moves violently. This translates as better steering control and an easier seat-of-the-pants ride.

Off-pavement, your truck's suspension travels constantly, with full extension and pounding compression. Damping such forces, the shock absorbers pay severely, often succumbing to leakage or ineffective performance. Driver discomfort and unnecessary chassis or body rattles will usually follow.

The Right Features

When buying replacement shock absorbers for your GM light truck, consider a twin-tube type, preferably gas-cell type. Piston head size, rod diameter, seal types and valving design determine the strength, reliability and performance of a shock absorber.

Most OEM telescoping shocks offer meager 1" to 1-1/8" piston diameters. Replacement shocks should have pistons of 1-5/16" or larger size. Popular for many years, the 1-3/8" piston head has satisfied all but the most brutal off-pavement maulers and heavyweight haulers.

Severe Duty Shocks

For heavy duty use, look to a nitrogen gas pressurized shock with a 1-5/8" piston diameter. These brute shocks hover around 200 psi, demanding tremendous piston/rod strength. Where a 9/16" or 14mm chrome-hardened rod will do just fine under most driving conditions, shocks like Rancho's RS7000 and others call for a 17.3mm rod, serious enough for real punishment. Complementing this feature, the RS7000 and similar shocks offer superior sealing ability, which also contributes to the shock's life expectancy.

Pistons should be O-ring sealed, cylinders double walled and tough. Larger fluid reservoirs provide better cooling and greater resistance to fading. Lastly, precise valving gives the shock absorber its real advantage. The valve's ability to sense terrain and load demands will determine the shock absorber's worth. Damping properly,

Axle Trusses

Pounding off-pavement can bend or break axle housings. Often, 4x4 owners add stiff spring rates and hefty shock absorbers without concern for the axles. If serious trail running or high performance driving is your truck's lot, consider axle trusses as part of your suspension buildup.

0012771

Bill Broyes at Autofab in Santee, California has built a show winning GM 4x4 truck. Bill likes Rhino's combination rear axle truss/skid plate, which doubles as a shock mount. Rhino clamps provide a simple installation. Although some axle tube support results from this design, its stronger point is skid plate protection.

0012809

0012810

Dana 44 open-knuckle front axle (top right) receives Rhino truss and skid plate combination. Open-knuckle support at axle housing end generally holds up without bracing. This truss design focuses on tube bracing.

Here is a combination skid plate/truss on a 4x4's rear axle. Low running clearance benefits from protection.

Rancho Suspension's RS9000 Shock Absorbers

The term "adjustable shock absorber" has a variety of meanings. Non-air adjustable shocks mean crawling under your truck, removing the units from the chassis and rotating their housings a number of clicks. Adjusting these kinds of shocks is such a hassle that most users wind up using only one setting.

Rancho Suspension has eliminated these obstacles with its RS9000 shock absorber system. The five-position adjustable shocks offer an easily accessible manual valve for setting the compression and rebound damping. An air-compressor actuated option is also available for cab control of the settings while you drive.

0014371

Rancho RS9000 adjustable shocks offer an optional air-actuated cab control system. Standard valving allows quick five-position adjustment at each shock absorber. Air-actuated adjustment kit allows even faster driver adjustment from the dashboard.

Position 1 provides a good highway ride; 2 makes for slightly firmer control; 3, programmed much like the classic RS5000 shock, offers versatile on- and off-road performance; position 4 addresses light to moderate off-roading; and position 5 provides the heavy off-pavement pounding or trailer lugging mode.

A pin-and-slider design, the adjustable valve enhances a proven cellular gas shock design that features 15-stage valving and an advanced tri-tube, mono-flow design.

I have tested the RS9000 shock absorbers and optional air-actuated adjusting system, exceeding the point where a standard shock absorber would fade completely—challenges like running a truck repeatedly through desert dry washes, whoops and a modest simulation of an off-road course. This is my top choice for multi-purpose use.

the shock absorbers are a basic element in your truck's suspension system.

Shock mounting grommets and eyes must hold up. A loose shock absorber is useless, and a weak set of grommets permits wasted movement and undamped travel. Proper shock absorber angles (a crucial engineering decision) also contribute to handling.

Single Versus Multi-shock Installations

Show trucks, street trucks, lifted trucks and even some OEM suspensions feature multiple shock absorbers. On factory dual-shock installations, the mounting angle and position of the additional shock is vital to the truck's handling. The shocks must counter jarring, chassis/spring oscillation and friction forces along critical paths of frame motion and suspension travel.

Many homespun, multi-shock assemblies defy logic. Few hobbyists have the engineering expertise to properly reposition shock absorbers. Unless looks override every other consideration, do your homework. If your GM 4x4 truck operates off-pavement, begin your suspension buildup around a healthy set of aftermarket replacement shocks.

Urethane Bushings

Polyurethane, a product of mid-1930s German pharmaceutical technology, meets a wide range of automotive chores. Urethane is used in dashboards, arm rests, paints, door panels, foam seats and suspension components.

Urethane suspension and roll cage bushings provide the chassis tuning and durability that many desert racers demand. Recreational four-wheelers and street truck builders also benefit from urethane suspension pieces.

Why is urethane desirable? First, unlike rubber products, urethane resists road salt, ozone, gasoline and automotive oils. Precise hardness control provides a variety of stiffnesses for suspension uses. More importantly, urethane offers high resistance to abrasion, yet engineers can factor elasticity into the product during the molding process. Manufacturers of urethane suspension bushings have a large measure of control over the finished product.

The Right Mix for Your Truck's Chassis

Don Bunker, founder of Energy Suspensions in San Clemente, California, comments on the differences in urethane materials. "Obviously," Don notes, "bump stops have to be somewhat soft to perform their duties, where high performance control arm bushings are generally of a firmer durometer hardness for maximum control. Urethane can be as soft as the Slime toys that kids buy or as hard as a bowling ball!"

Poor ratio mixes create low quality finished products. Noting the disparity between good and poor product, Don Bunker states flatly, "All urethane is not created equal!" He cites the bitter experience of early urethane users who broke eyelets loose from their shock absorbers. Although owners often condemned the shocks, the real problem was the bushings. When excessively hard, the urethane acts as rigid as metal. Shock eyes, which actually travel in an arc, can bind up if the bushings are too hard. Eyelets break from the force.

If you upgrade your truck's chassis with urethane suspension bushings, squeak is not uncommon, especially in twisting situations. Several manufacturers have addressed this problem. Some have graphite-impregnated bushings to counter noise and friction.

0014372

Fig. 18-6. Greg Williams' highly modified K-10 Chevrolet prerunner, a support truck for Nelson & Nelson Racing, features rollbar bracket and suspension bushings made of urethane. Urethane comes in a variety of colors. The correct hardness of finished bushings, however, is far more important than color considerations.

Urethane Parts under Construction

There are two methods of urethane bushing production: injection molding and liquid cold pour casting. Injection molding provides the more precise results. Liquid cold pour castings serve in parts that require less critical tolerances.

Aftermarket urethane producers invest substantially in each bushing mold. Molds determine the fitup and ultimate reliability of the parts. Intricate machining is necessary to produce a quality mold. Correct mixture ratios complete the process, while colorful finishes are merely an aesthetic consideration.

NOTE —
When looking for quality in a urethane sleeved bushing, seek out a product with seamless sleeves.

Where Does Urethane Work Best?

Urethane suspension arm, radius rod and stabilizer bushings are popular. Front and rear stabilizers benefit from polyurethane bushings, which allow greater application of force (unlike the loose action of factory rubber bushings).

Polyurethane mounts offer a major gain over factory rubber cab and body mounts. Unlike aftermarket aluminum spacers, which deliver a rigid and harsh ride, urethane can provide firm yet functional suspension while maintaining the alignment of body panels.

Leaf spring bushings, mounting pin kits and most lift kits offer urethane bushings. The trick is to select the right bushings for your particular driving style. Before grabbing the most colorful set off the shelf, consider options like graphite-impregnated products.

If your truck demands more stamina and a finely tuned suspension system, consider the urethane bushing option. The right bushings can drastically improve your truck's steering control and responsiveness.

SEMA: Growth of the Truck Parts Aftermarket

The truck aftermarket has come of age. The future is bright for quality, well-engineered and safe suspension and body lift products. SEMA and the suspension/body lift kit manufacturers strive hard to protect consumer interests, making every effort to rid the highways of unsafe equipment, while lobbying to preserve truck owners' rights to reasonable tire, chassis and body modifications.

When selecting aftermarket components for your GM light truck, you will find that SEMA supports the quality manufacturers within the industry. Look for the SEMA label on products and in advertising literature.

3. STEERING GEAR CONVERSIONS

The earliest GM light trucks offer the less efficient worm-and-sector steering gears. By the early 1940s, GM's much improved and innovative Saginaw recirculating ball-and-nut steering gear came on line.

Twenty-five years later, GM introduced Saginaw integral power steering, using the same recirculating ball principle found in the early 1940s' gears. These manual and power steering gear assemblies have become the most respected designs in automotive history, used by scores of manufacturers around the globe.

> NOTE —
> The primitive worm-and-sector type manual steering gears are high in friction and offer much shorter service lives than recirculating ball-and-nut or ball-and-power rack/piston gears. Fortunately, with the exception of only the first few model years covered by this book, GM trucks have largely benefitted from the use of smooth and durable recirculating-ball-type steering gears.

Just prior to World War II, GM introduced recirculating ball-and-nut steering gears to light trucks. Postwar models and all trucks built from the Advance Design era forward feature Saginaw-type recirculating ball-and-nut steering. Beginning in the 1950s, these manual gears also served with factory optioned or dealer installed (add-on) linkage power assist.

In 1968, 2WD models switched to the more advanced Saginaw integral-type power steering gears, followed by 4x4s in 1969 and 1970. This change became a highly desirable option, enhancing both driver comfort and overall handling. Having owned and thoroughly tested trucks equipped with GM's Saginaw integral power steering, I would not be without it.

Linkage type power assist steering with a conventional manual steering gear is a less desirable means for adding power steering. The clumsy hoses, low hanging hydraulic ram, and an exposed control valve are each vulnerable to damage from trail obstacles and road debris. Also, service and replacement parts for linkage power steering have become more difficult to locate. If you have this kind of system or manual steering, consider a conversion to Saginaw integral power steering. Use OEM parts and engineering methods. (Some frame adaptation and fabrication may be necessary.)

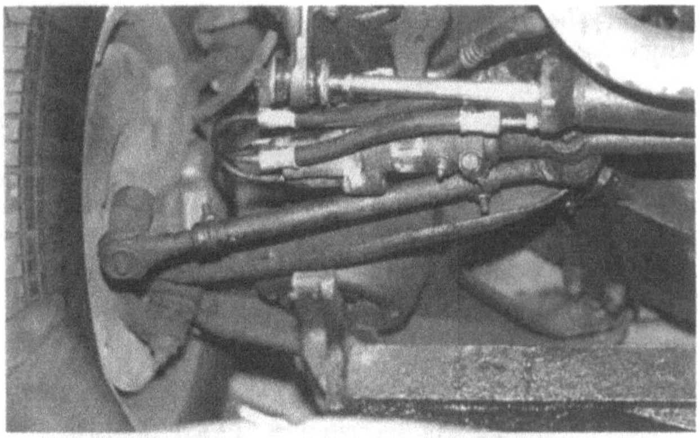

0014485

Fig. 18-7. *Linkage-type power steering is both complex and vulnerable to damage. Trail debris can tear at exposed hoses and parts. Integral power steering was a major improvement.*

0014373

Fig. 18-8. *Advance Adapters makes universal brackets for adapting popular Saginaw integral power steering gear units to vintage vehicles. If your earlier GM truck needs a power steering conversion, you may find this weld-on frame adapter useful. Wide use of Saginaw integral power steering can provide a range of OEM components to complete your installation.*

> *WARNING —*
> *When converting to modern power steering, do not weld, cut, bend or modify steering linkage or other steering components. Find the mix of OEM pieces that will enable a simple and factory-level installation.*

> NOTE —
> Advance Adapters (see appendix) offers a universal plate for mating Saginaw integral power and manual steering gears to the frame.

Your model and year of GM truck will determine which integral power steering gear unit to use. In addition to the steering gear assembly, proper power steering hoses and a matching pump unit with engine brackets and drive pulleys will be needed.

Retrofitting an integral power steering gear unit may involve welding, fabricating and engineering. If you have limited expertise in this area, do not attempt such a changeover. Seek out a professional shop with experience at this type of conversion, and be sure that they have a working knowledge of the task at hand. Some of the credentials needed for a safe installation include a history of building similar systems on GM trucks and also certification as a professional welder. Do not take shortcuts on this kind of work. Controlled and predictable steering is a fundamental requirement for your truck.

Choosing the Right Steering Gear

If you make a power or manual steering gear conversion with later OEM steering parts, you must consider the steering gear ratio and related engineering. The quicker (approximately three turns lock-to-lock) gears are entirely too fast for a light truck, and they make a short wheelbase model steer like a sprint race car. Avoid these ultra-quick steering ratios. Follow the ratios offered for a later model GM truck with a similar size chassis.

Length of the Pitman arm or the steering arms also contributes to the final steering ratio. If you have a choice, select a Pitman arm or steering arms that provide good road feel and still offer correct travel of the steering linkage.

> *CAUTION —*
> *Make sure steering linkage moves freely and on OEM proscribed arcs. Assess how the linkage will react as the wheels turn and as the suspension moves.*

When setting up a retrofit steering gear and linkage on a solid front axle 2WD or 4x4 truck, keep the steering drag link on its level, OEM plane. This will prevent bump steer. Check linkage alignment with the truck setting on flat ground and loaded normally.

> NOTE —
> Many 4x4 lift kits contain a raised or dropped Pitman arm (depending on the arm's location and its relationship to the chassis). This can help align the linkage and prevent bump steer.

Make certain that the steering gear does not reach its full range of movement before the knuckles reach their stops. Hyper-extending the steering gear can severely damage the ball races, nut or power rack. Always make sure that the steering gear is on its center with the front wheels and tires in the straight-ahead position.

> *CAUTION —*
> - *Power steering systems require careful engineering. The force of an integral power unit is sufficient to rip a gear loose from the frame. When setting up a power gear and Pitman arm, care must be taken to prevent excess pressure build-up when the knuckles turn against their stops.*
> - *Consult factory service manuals for pump and gear pressure specifications. Test your system for correct travel and pressure in all positions.*

4. TIRES

Preparing your truck for a special environment always includes tires. For rock crawling in rough terrain or scaling a wagon road to an abandoned silver mine, you need the right rubber. Ground clearance, superior traction and resistance to rock abrasions each depend on your tire choices.

Wider wheels and oversize tires will affect the handling characteristics of your truck. Take extreme care when selecting your truck's wheels. When in doubt, always follow the recommendations of the manufacturer.

> *WARNING —*
> *Wider wheels and oversize tires usually require other changes to your truck. Larger tires and wheels may place excessive stress on suspension components, including bearings, hubs, and brakes.*

There are mildly and wildly oversize wheels and tires. Oversize tires run anywhere from one or two sizes larger than your stock GM truck's rubber to monstrous tires. Concerned with safety and liability issues, the majority of light truck tire manufacturers limit their maximum tire sizes to 35" diameter.

For highly specialized uses, 36" to 44" tires are available from a small number of producers. An even smaller number of wheel manufacturers cater to the safety standards necessary for handling specialty rubber.

Why is 35" the usual limit? When it comes to mounting massive rubber on a light truck, major tire manufacturers don't have time to conduct safety schools. Product abuse and consumer negligence occur regularly in this realm.

Where Do Monster Tires Serve Best?

Lifted show trucks and boulevard cruisers have monster tires. Are these tires simply an artistic expression? Not always. The 35" to 44" tire is also a workhorse. At

UU14376

Fig. 18-9. *Wider wheels are necessary with most oversize tires. This 33x12.50x15 tire mounts on Golden Wheel Corporation's Enkei 89-series one piece alloy rim. Rim bead width is ten inches. Tires were fitted to a 1991 Blazer 4WD. A Rugged Trail/Black Diamond chassis lift was necessary to ensure adequate tire clearance.*

0014375

Fig. 18-10. In the back country, oversize tires have utility value. Here, traction on muddy and rutted roads benefits from large tires, which actually reduce environmental impact when the driver keeps wheel spin under control.

0014377

Fig. 18-11. Handling big rubber means serious chassis and powertrain modifications. Full-floating 3/4-ton truck rear axles are common on show trucks, and a very large tire size demands the advantages of a full-floater.

highly specialized jobsites, such as logging and mining operations, heavy loads and deep mud packs make a rubber-tire loader cringe. A heavy duty 3/4- or one-ton rated GM truck, given the unceremonious task of lugging supplies and equipment over miles of primitive road, can benefit from jumbo tires.

Warren Guidry of Interco Tire Corporation comments on the merits of monster tires. "For 4WD vehicles to obtain their full potential, bigger tires need to be used. Nothing will raise the axles except the tires, which in turn gives greater ground clearance, and this is very important to off-road use."

Obviously, there's a limit to monster tire use. These tires, which mount on specially built rims, fit a radically lifted truck. Huge tires require an elaborate spring and body lift for clearance, plus many other modifications to the engine, chassis, geartrain, steering and brakes.

Way Up Has Its Downside

There's a limit to everything. Mounting huge 100 pound tires on a half-ton rated 1959 3100-Series Chevrolet/NAPCO 4WD pickup or a 1965 GMC 1500-Series 4x4 overrides all safety considerations. On some light trucks, even a 32" diameter tire can create a precariously high center of gravity and brake overload.

Using 36" to 44" tires, with their mass and unsprung weight, involves radically altering the track width, brakes, powertrain, steering and suspension. Neither GM nor any other 1/2- or 3/4-ton capacity light truck builder offers an OEM brake system capable of handling the rolling mass of four 44" diameter, 130-pound tire and wheel assemblies.

Furthermore, manufacturers match gearing to their trucks' OE tire diameter. If your GM light truck has 30" diameter OE tires and a 3.50:1 axle gear ratio, a switch to 44" tires (if you could ever find a way to fit such a size!) would require an axle ratio around 5.13:1 to restore the engine's original operating rpm.

Radically lifted 4x4 show trucks have extensive frame, suspension, geartrain and engine upgrades to handle the taller vehicle profile and huge rubber. If you're serious about duplicating this look, don't stop with wheels, tires and a spring lift.

Safety First

"The truth is," Warren Guidry notes, "if a vehicle is professionally modified to accommodate larger tires, and if the larger tires are not just taller but also wider, the vehicle can be more stable than when it was stock."

Guidry concludes, "The wider tire and wheel combination increases the track of the vehicle and adds a tremendous amount of stability. The bigger, wider tires can carry more load with the same air pressure, and because of the greater volume of air are not under the load stresses that the smaller tires have to bear."

There's a clear relationship between track width and center of gravity. The savvy state laws, those that aim at restoring a stable center of gravity, suggest the use of a wider track width whenever height changes have been made to a vehicle.

As Warren Guidry suggests, the professional modification of a vehicle takes safety factors into account. If you're unsure of the safety requirements for your truck, consult a race or show truck fabricator who has built his credential around truck safety.

In general, larger tires represent more unsprung weight, which immediately suggests stouter springs, hefty gangs of shock absorbers, added steering stabilization, traction bars or torsion arms and a whole arsenal of heavy duty wheel and brake parts. Oversize brake rotors,

Tire Glossary

Bias (Diagonal) Ply: Before radial tires, all trucks rode on bias ply tires. Bias plies run in a diagonal direction to the tire centerline. Plies cross in an X pattern, making a very strong but stiff tire. Today's truck owners demand the better ride and handling of radial ply designs.

Load Carrying Capacity: All highway-legal tires have load capacity ratings (A, B, C, etc.). Inflation pressure, however, affects a tire's load capacity. Ratings apply to each tire size and design. Lower pressures decrease load carrying capacity.

Maximum Inflation: This is a tire's air pressure limit, which influences load carrying capacity. A tire with a load range C and a maximum inflation pressure of 36 PSI may have a 3,000 pound rating. This means that the tire can support 3,000 pounds at 36 PSI inflation. As pressure drops, so does the tire's carrying capacity. Beware.

Ply Rating: Plies are supporting layers of synthetic cord and/or steel built into a tire casing. These layers or belts mold within the tire's rubber. Ply ratings for big radial tires can get confusing. Load range C tires qualify for a traditional 6-ply rating. A closer look, however, may reveal a 4-ply tread and 2-ply sidewall. Plies also vary in thickness and strength, so evaluate a tire by its load rating, the ply materials and overall construction.

PSI: Pounds per Square Inch refers to the air pressure in your tires. Adding air increases PSI, while airing down reduces pressure. Always maintain your tires at recommended inflation levels. If you drop pressure too low, your tubeless tire may unseat from the rim. Excess air pressure can damage the plies or destroy a bead.

Radial Ply: Belts, whether steel or synthetic cord, circle the tire at a perpendicular angle to its tread centerline. Radial belts flex, allowing the sidewalls to cushion the ride. Tread conforms to the road, providing a better grip. Most new tires, including 36" to 44" monster tires, are radials.

Rim Offset: Wheel rim offset determines track width and frame/tire clearance. Rarely is a wheel's mounting flange aligned with the centerline of the tire. OEM rims offset toward the brake assembly. Aftermarket wheels must take OEM engineering into account, including back-spacing and negative (outboard) or positive (inboard) rim offset from the wheel mounting flange. Otherwise, stress to wheel bearings, spindles, axle shafts and steering components can occur. Steering geometry, tire wear, and handling are all affected by rim offset.

0014486

Rim Width: Rim width is the space between the outer faces of the tire beads. This measurement is crucial, and every tire has a rim width requirement. Sidewall and tread shape, the bead angle and even the vehicle's handling depend on rims that correctly match the tires.

Speed Rating: Although most trucks with big tires stay within posted speed limits, speed ratings also indicate a tire's margin of safety. Symbols represent maximum speed: S to 112 mph; T to 118 mph; H to 130 mph; V to 149 mph; and Z over 149 mph. Take heed.

pads, rear brake shoes and drums—even heavier drive axles—may be necessary.

> NOTE —
> Most custom 4x4 trucks that run 39" and larger diameter tires have full-floating rear axles. The full-floater adds stamina plus better wheel and axle bearing support.

Shock loads transfer back through the entire geartrain to the engine. U-joint upgrades, increased driveshaft wall thickness and/or diameter and other precautions help assure parts survival. Also, by changing axle gearing to restore the original engine speeds, you'll give the manual clutch or automatic transmission a chance to survive. Even so, consider upgrading the clutch or torque converter to handle the extra inertial loads of big tires.

0012799

Fig. 18-12. *The B.F. Goodrich Baja T/A tire (right), developed through actual desert racing tests, is an excellent off-pavement performer. Hard compound makes a harsher ride, but sidewall stamina is outstanding in rocky terrain.*

A Tried Trail Running Formula

I've never installed tires larger than 33" diameter on any of my 4x4 trucks, including the 3/4-ton models. I firmly believe that driving skill and a decent tire will handle even the most challenging off-pavement environments. Beyond a mud-bog racer, logging rig or swampland runner, successful traction for your truck is as close as a good tread pattern on a set of moderately oversized tires.

Specifically, I believe that a 31x10.50x15 tire is adequate for a relatively stock 1/2-ton rated 4x4. This size tire should not require modifying the body or chassis height. These tires are very popular for this chassis type.

Wider and bigger tires, like a 33x12.50x15 will also work on some 1/2-ton pickups, the Blazer/Jimmy and Suburban 4x4 models, although body clearance (primarily at front wheel well openings) does become an issue—especially on 1973 and newer GM trucks. If the load range is appropriate, 33" diameter tires will work well on most K-20/2500 or K-30/3500 4x4s.

The only drawback to a very wide tire on a lightweight truck is the high floatation effect of the wide tire print. Such tires work great on sand, but a narrower tire tends to provide more traction on ice and snow.

The popular 6.50x16 size tires and narrow wheel rims on early GM half-ton models and 7.50x16s on 3/4-ton trucks teach a good lesson. These trucks, at curb weights of around 3,800-5,500 pounds, get exceptional traction in rock and snow. The narrower tire tread places more weight on each tire print.

Tread design advantages provide a more realistic indicator of tractability, which often has little to do with the tire size. The newer 16-inch diameter (narrower) OE wheels will work fine if you select an appropriate tread pattern for your driving environment.

You can choose from a host of tire tread patterns. Fifty years of off-pavement testing, complemented by three decades of desert racing, have produced specialized and multipurpose tread patterns for a wide range of light truck uses.

An extra set of tires, mounted and balanced on spare rims, make a good investment for your truck. Consider a specialized tread pattern that aims at your driving terrain and habits, tires that you can install when you're ready to tackle the rough stuff.

Tire Inflation and Other Concerns

Despite nail holes, rock punctures and other natural hazards of four-wheeling or back country driving, the number one cause of tire blowout is under-inflation. Low tire pressure places tremendous stress on sidewalls and generates unsafe heat levels.

Interco Tire, manufacturer of Super Swamper tires, notes, "Do not allow the air pressure to get below 20 PSI regardless of how light the vehicle may be. Pressures below 20 PSI may let the bead of the tire become unseated, especially from lateral forces. An exception would be while running in soft sand, where you may wish to reduce air pressure below 20 PSI. This should be an emergency procedure only. As soon as possible, pressure must be brought back up. Remember, overloading and/or under-inflation causes excessive heat buildup which can cause separation of the tire body."

0012800

Fig. 18-13. Interco's Swamper series tires make a big impression! The tire has a strong following among 4x4 competition, recreational and show truck users. Traction gains are obvious.

Like all other tire manufacturers, Interco recommends that you maintain correct air pressure, checking each tire cold at least once a month. (Cold means the truck has parked out of direct sunlight at least three hours.)

Match pressure to the weight of your truck and its current load. Remember, maximum load capacity is at the maximum pressure rating for the tire. If you lower the pressure to improve the ride, or for any other reason, load capacity also decreases. Deceptively, big tires stand up easily, so give them more than a glance.

> **NOTE —**
> Invest in a quality tire pressure gauge; cheap gauges seldom read the same pressure twice.

Tire wear depends on proper wheel alignment, inflation pressures, balancing and rotation. Interco recommends tire rotation at 2,500 to 4,000 miles. The traditional pattern of rotation for radial tires has been front-to-rear and rear-to-front. Some manufacturers now recommend a modified cross-rotation method. Consult your tire manufacturer for proper tire rotation procedures.

Many oversize tires benefit from balancing on the truck. When you have your tires balanced with a floor balancer (wheels mounted on the truck), tire rotation involves one more step: Your tires will require rebalancing. Once rotated, or even repositioned on the wheel hub, tire balance changes. Beware!

Installing Your Wheels on the Truck

Your new tires, correctly mounted to the correct rim, may be ready to install—but are the OE lug studs and nuts ready? Grossly oversize wheel and tire packages have a lot of mass. Even if your new wheels fit the axle hub flange properly, there's still the matter of stamina. The inertial load may place excess stress on your truck's OE lug studs.

Fig. 18-14. Rim width measures between edges where tire beads seat. Rim offset (negative or positive) created by wide wheels is equally important.

> *WARNING —*
> *Some aftermarket wheel flanges are much thicker than a stock-length OEM lug stud can handle. If lug nuts do not fit securely onto the studs, you should install longer lug studs or select another wheel type.*

GM light trucks have used 7/16", 1/2", 9/16", 5/8" and some metric size wheel studs. For many years, the 2WD and 4x4 GM half-ton rated trucks used six bolts with a 7/16" stud size. The later five-lug 1/2-ton truck size is 1/2", which is common to many lighter GVWR domestic trucks and passenger cars. Eight-lug 3/4-ton and one-ton trucks most commonly use 9/16", 5/8" or larger thread wheel studs.

> NOTE —
> Before mounting a set of monster size alloy wheels and big tires, consider the OEM wheel lug size. Consult your wheel and tire manufacturers for their recommendations. Your tires and wheels may demand an upgrade in either stud diameter or length.

Be sure to tighten the lug nuts securely. Use a torque wrench to prevent under- or overtightening. Overtorquing is a common cause of wheel damage and stud breakage, especially on models that use 7/16" studs. GM and aftermarket wheel manufacturers recommend specific torque settings. (Consult your GM truck shop manual or owner's glovebox handbook for tightening specifications.)

Factory torque settings take load, braking, vehicle weight and stud diameter into account. Use a torque wrench whenever possible to verify the torque setting. Always tighten lug nuts gradually and in cross. This prevents distortion of the rim and damage to nut seats.

Choosing Wheels

Big tires increase unsprung mass, raise load capacities and present special mounting concerns. Many OE and aftermarket wheels cannot match the big tire loads. Mickey Thompson/Alcoa and Clement Composite wheels address big tire requirements.

Other wheel suppliers, including Golden Wheel Corporation, Ultra Wheel and American Racing Equipment, satisfy a broad cross-section of user needs. Before selecting wheels, make sure that the load rating and warranty will satisfy your big tire demands.

Sources for Big Specialty Tires

For most four-wheel drive uses, tires built by major tire companies like B.F. Goodrich, Goodyear, General Tire, Michelin, Yokahama or Bridgestone provide excellent selection and tread patterns for back country and multi-purpose use. When your plans lean toward the extraordinary, however, several specialty manufacturers produce 36" to 44" monster tires.

Fig. 18-15. 33x12.50x15 Bridgestone Desert Dueler tires on 10" wide, one-piece Enkei 89-Series alloy wheels provide a stunning look on a 4WD GM truck.

When shopping for your truck's tires, look closely at construction, ply ratings and the load capacity, not just diameter and price.

Interco's Swamper Tires: The original 78-series Swamper tire has been around for over a quarter century. Originally a 6- or 8-ply bias ply tire, Swamper offers a popular tread pattern. Interco also builds grossly oversize tires, including the Super Swamper TSL 36x12.50-15LT through 18.5/44-15 sizes and an 18.5/44-16.5 tire. These heavy duty bias ply tires with massive lugs and self-cleaning ability meet on- and off-pavement demands for the 4x4 GM truck with an ultra stout, highly modified chassis and appetite for massive rubber.

Super Swamper Radial/TSL tires come in LT315/85R15, 38x15.50R15 and 38x15.50R16.5LT sizes. These are smooth riding, low noise level biggies with a 6-ply rating. If noise, handling and ride are top priorities, consider these tires. For severely rugged and rocky terrain, Super Swamper's TSL/SX comes in 36x12.50-15 and 16.5 sizes and rates six plies with a nylon bias body and steel belt reinforcement under the tread. Sidewall lugs protect and add extra traction in ruts and rocks.

Gateway Buckshot and Gumbo Mudders: Campfire talk has the Buckshot Radial Mudder pegged as the hot setup for tall, narrow traction. The QR78-15LT and QR78-16 varieties fit the 36" big tire category, yet they still fit a 7JJx15 or 6.5Hx16 rim. These are tubeless, 6-ply rated tires with a polyester and steel belt cord. Stiff bead areas and provision for studs make the Buckshot a versatile choice, without the need for exotic wheels.

Also available from Gateway are the Buckshot Wide Mudder, Buckshot Metric Radial Mudder and the famed Gumbo Monster Mudders. Gumbo Monster series tires fit the big tire category with ease. These tires begin at 36-inch diameter and grow to 43.6" giants for 15" or 16.5" rims. Tread widths for the 6-ply rated tires range from 10.4" to 14.1", which requires wide rims. For the radial user, the Gumbo Monster Radial Mudder is available in 36" to 38" sizes with a width of 10.4" to 10.7" (cross-sections 14.2" to 15.2"). These radials require 10x15 and 9.75x16.5 rims.

Mickey Thompson Tires/Alcoa Wheels: Mickey Thompson and off-road desert racing go back to the beginning. Mickey Thompson's Baja-Belted polyester and fiberglass belt tires offer an aggressive tread pattern with a soft ride, long wear and Sidebiters for extra traction. The Tall Baja-Belted tire line offers several big tire sizes, including 15/39 and 18/39 for 15" and 16.5" rims.

Mickey Thompson has joined with Alcoa Aluminum to produce the M/T Alcoa Aluminum Wheel. Most wheel manufacturers void their warranties when you mount really big tires. Alcoa has engineered these wheels of one-piece forged aircraft aluminum, with a non-porous and leak proof surface. Polished and machined for a 0.020" maximum runout, these wheels have a 2,600 or 3,000 pound load rating, depending upon application. Available in 15" x 10", 12" or 14" width (3,000 pound rated) and 8" width (2,600 pound rated), these wheels are available in popular 5- and 6-lug truck patterns.

Dick Cepek Tires: Dick Cepek is a household name among four-wheeling recreationalists. A full line of vehicle and outdoor equipment makes Cepek a one-stop shopping center for four-wheelers. When buyers want tires, Dick Cepek has a full line to match every need.

0012801

Fig. 18-16. Buckshot Radial Mudder provides a high traction option for users who want a narrower wheel width.

0012802

Fig. 18-17. M/T Alcoa aluminum wheels carry a rating for big tires. Load capacity to 3,000 pounds in 8", 10", 12" or 14" widths.

Radial F-C/Fun Country tires aim at mileage. As a steel belted flotation tire, these tires run quietly, yet the tread design offers self-cleaning. These are legitimate mud and snow tires, much like the popular Fun Country nylon bias-ply design. Dick Cepek's Mud Country I tires can be used for snow plowing or logging trails, while Mud Country II boasts better flotation characteristics.

0012803

Fig. 18-18. The Dick Cepek Radial F-C offers the ride and handling benefits of a radial tire. Radial tires satisfy users who do most of their driving on the highway but still need superior traction off-pavement.

Cepek has also introduced a Super Wide Radial F-C tire available to 38" diameter. These tires concentrate on width, providing all around performance in mud, snow, sand, rock and on the highway. Quietness, an aggressive tread design, steel belts (for a 50,000 mile limited warranty) and tread at least 4" wider than competitors' tires distinguish the Super Wide Radial F-C.

Goodyear—One Big Wrangler RT: Goodyear Tire and Rubber Company is the only major tire producer to offer a tire in the really big category. The Wrangler RT-GC0530 provides a rugged, multipurpose tread design and is available in 36-12.50-16.5 size only. Hummer drivers would recognize this design, as Goodyear developed the tire for military use on this vehicle.

Although Goodyear offers a complete line of Wrangler light truck radial tires, the RT is its only entry in the 36" or larger market. If you're looking for big tires, these load range C biggies may meet your needs. (Order under Goodyear's product code No. 309-552-321.)

Denman Tires Ground Hawg: Denman's line of big tires has a huge following with the 4x4 show truck crowd. The roguish Ground Hawg is a beefy tire, hell-bent on maximum traction. For a flexible tread and superior traction, Denman delivers radial benefits with a deep, self-cleaning tread design. The biggest Ground Hawg tire is 18.5/44x16.5 inches.

5. BRAKE SYSTEM UPGRADES

Years ago, one cure for undersize truck brakes was to retrofit an in-line Bendix Hydrovac booster (common to older medium duty trucks with hydraulic brakes). This fix applies more pressure to the hydraulic cylinders and brake shoes, which also raises the likelihood of either hazardous brake fade or rupture of a fluid seal. This is not the fix for a weak brake system!

Fortunately, even the early GM light trucks covered in this book have sufficient brake shoe and drum sizing for their era. In good condition, with the hydraulic system functioning properly and the brake shoe and drum surfaces in top shape, an early GM truck can stop reasonably well.

Before the advent of disc front brakes, a GM light truck with four-wheel drum brakes could match the braking performance of any other light truck in its class. No GM truck with drum brakes, however, can match the performance of a comparable later model with a disc front/drum rear braking system—or better yet, a truck equipped with four-wheel disc brakes.

Hydraulic Brake System Improvements

Before 1967, most brake system manufacturers recommended annual flushing and rebuilding of all hydraulic brake cylinders. Although some vehicles tolerate years of neglect without a brake system flush or rubber cup/seal replacement, 4x4s and other off-pavement use trucks are far more susceptible to fluid contamination and parts failure.

0014290

Fig. 18-19. Rear anti-lock braking system has become popular. Beware of the negative effect that oversized tires or a lift kit might have on anti-lock (ABS) braking or a rear axle mounted proportioning valve. Consult your GM truck dealership before attempting a lift on a late model truck with ABS.

0014378

Fig. 18-20. A 2-1/2" Rugged Trail lift package was necessary for tire clearance, and this was barely enough for the 1991 Blazer V-5 model. (Tires rubbed slightly at the rear of the front fender wells on tight, bouncy turns.) Factory front dual shock brackets readily accepted Rugged Trail's NitroCell shocks. Rugged Trail has become the Black Diamond Division of Warn Industries.

Most 1967-up truck tandem master cylinders have air bellows in the master cylinder cap gasket. A bellows gasket completely seals the system and eliminates the need for a master cylinder vent to atmosphere. Problems like moisture, debris, dust and corrosive contamination occur far less often with 1967 and newer GM truck brake systems.

One cure for the earlier GM truck brake problems is to custom fit a 1967 or newer tandem master cylinder system, including necessary pedal linkage and hydraulic hardware. Such a retrofit could also include a hydraulic clutch master cylinder (if you mount both cylinders on the firewall), a hydraulic clutch slave cylinder and mounting bracket, appropriate clutch linkage and a set of suspended brake and clutch pedals. A modern vacuum brake booster could complete the package.

0014388

Fig. 18-21. SuperLift makes this Vehicle Speed Sensor (VSS) Kit for late GM trucks that have ABS. When increasing the diameter of tires, the powertrain management and ABS computers become confused. SuperLift offers this kit to offset such problems.

WARNING —
On any hydraulic system modification, make certain that the master cylinder bore and brake pipe sizing can move enough fluid to operate the brakes at factory engineered levels.

Upgrading or modernizing the wheel brake system of any truck may require special hydraulic system components to meet the demands of a disc brake rotor/caliper conversion or the retrofitting of bigger brake shoes, drums, wheel hubs and wheel cylinders. For baseline engineering, begin with a prototype OEM braking system that will meet your braking demands. Select wheel brake parts and hydraulic components that make up this prototype system. Try to duplicate the complete OEM package to assure a proper match of wheel brake components and hydraulic system parts.

WARNING —
Find a safe place to perform braking tests. Determine whether front-to-rear brake system balance (proportioning) is correct. If required, a variety of OEM or adjustable aftermarket proportioning valves are available.

6. A Pragmatic GM Truck Buildup

In 1991, I was assigned a four-wheel drive photojournalist's dream: a project buildup of a spanking new 1991 Blazer V-5 for Argus' *OFF-ROAD* Magazine. This was an opportunity to conceptualize, then implement, the kinds of modifications that many owners of conventional (solid front axle) 4x4s might want.

1991 was the last year for the conventional chassis Blazer. The model's origins went back to 1969, with only a few changes since 1973. A true blend of classic and contemporary styling, the 1991 Blazer V-5 4WD can benefit from a wide array of factory options and aftermarket accessories. Additionally, Chevrolet's full-size Blazer offered traditional truck stamina and utility, plus something we always appreciate: great performance.

0014380

Fig. 18-22. Rear lift and Rugged Trail dual shock conversion balance out the suspension.

0014381

Fig. 18-23. *Large tie-rod ends on later solid axle K-trucks require a major offset of the wheels. Enkei has engineered plenty of offset. Steep OEM caster angle limits the tire clearance, however, so guard against tire rub at the rear of front fender wells.*

When it came to chassis changes, I took my usual conservative tack. While some owners opt for very large tires and a radical chassis lift, this project benefitted from a popular 2-1/2" chassis lift offered by Rugged Trail. The spring rates were carefully selected to firm up the ride and provide necessary clearance for 33x12.50x15 Bridgestone Desert Dueler tires mounted on stunning 10"-wide, one-piece alloy 89-Series Enkei wheels.

Even with a 2-1/2" lift, 33x12.50x15 tires barely cleared the front fenders on full turns. Some users find it easier to reshape the fender. I chose to leave the body intact. A 4-inch chassis lift, an aftermarket raised steering arm, longer OEM-type brake hoses, and sway bar drop brackets would have proven wiser in this application.

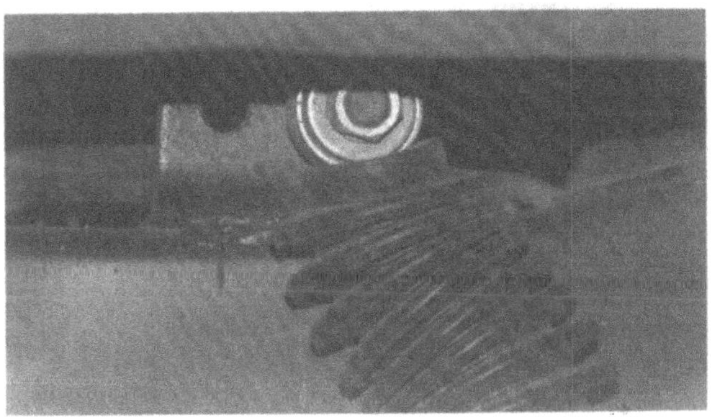

0014383

Fig. 18-24. *Barry Carlson at Archer Brothers in Eugene, Oregon installed the Rugged Trail suspension package. He improved the extra rear shock mount by installing this bracket on the frame rail. Barry's approach keeps the shock sets at matching angles and provides uniform mounting locations. The NitroCell shocks provided excellent damping.*

0014047

Fig. 18-25. *Rugged Trail suspension package is complete with all hardware. Note the multiple leaf spring stacks. Rate and ride work well for Warn's 12,000-pound winch and an Enforcer bumper. NitroCell steering damper shock replaced OEM unit.*

Rugged Trail's package came complete with a pair of precisely rated, stacked leaf front springs and dual NitroCell shocks. The rear lift, accomplished with a pair of spacer blocks, provided a double shock conversion kit to enhance spring damping. Complete with brightly finished installation hardware, the overall package created just the right spring rate for Warn's 12,000-pound capacity winch, the Warn Enforcer front bumper and some occasional towing.

Head-turning Tow Package

I had the opportunity to order the new 1991 Blazer test truck, which included options like the last 465 Muncie iron-cased heavy duty four-speed manual transmission. The package came only with a 3.42:1 axle ratio, slightly taller than I wanted, and, unfortunately, a factory trailering package was not available with the 465 Muncie four-speed that year.

This puzzling twist sent me scrambling for a platform/frame mount hitch to pull a trailer. I wanted a 5,000-pound rated (Class III) hitch that would tow a 3,000-plus-pound load, and my choice was a Quality S hitch, a very rugged unit made of rectangular tubing and flat plate that bolts neatly to the truck's frame with minimal drilling.

One test exercise was to tow a fully equipped CJ-5 Jeep for 2,000-plus miles. Since the Blazer had 3.42:1 gearing and 33" diameter tires, the effect in fourth gear was much like overdrive. This required compound low startups to prevent excess load on the clutch and other powertrain and geartrain components.

Since the EFI 350 V-8 could handle the tall axle gearing and bigger tires, the truck achieved a maximum of 14 mpg (highway) fuel economy under flatland towing conditions. At higher altitudes (towing over 8,000 foot elevation), performance remained steady—despite the need to gear down when under load. The closely spaced third/fourth gear ratios on these Muncie four-speeds easily accomodate this demand.

0014385

Fig. 18-26. Quality S bolt-on platform hitch is a Class III rated frame mount receiver unit. Construction is very strong, installation relatively easy. Accurate instructions, complete hardware and minimal drilling make Quality S hitches popular with many installers and users.

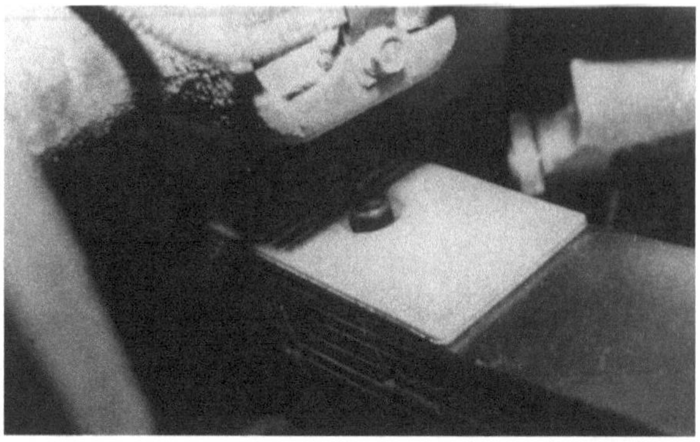

0012770

Fig. 18-27. In some suspension kits, wedge-shaped caster shims for the front or rear leaf springs can restore pinion, driveshaft or caster angles. These wedges are sometimes made of aluminum alloy. Steel wedges serve better and are available from NAPA and wheel alignment shops.

Actually, a switch to 4.10:1 gearsets would have offset the increased tire diameter, and such a choice is practical if you intend to increase tire size in a similar way. During a late spring outing with the local 4x4 club, where the group encountered slushy snow drifts across a graded gravel road, only pure horsepower prevailed, as the axle gearing once again proved taller than desirable.

For continuous off-pavement use or towing, increasing tire size may require a switch to 4.10, 4.27 or even 4.56 gearing, depending upon how you plan to use your truck, its curb weight and the loads you plan to haul.

Anatomy of a Dual-purpose 4WD Chassis

Equipped with oversize tires and a quality suspension package, the project truck met a variety of needs. Off-pavement, K/V-5 Blazers have always benefitted from hefty weight over the front axle. With a widened track width and an appropriate spring rate, such a truck can also offer a very stable ride.

The addition of a strong winch and heavy front bumper helped even further—except in deep Cascade Range snow drifts, where the front heavy Blazer sank like a rock. Here, some TREAD LIGHTLY! tools (Warn's Tree Saver Strap and a 12,000 pound single line pull winch) got a good workout.

A Truck for All Seasons

Rugged Saginaw power steering, power disc front brakes, rear wheel anti-lock in 2WD mode, heavy duty shocks, a massive front stabilizer, a stainless steel exhaust system, front tow hooks, a heavy duty battery, the 31 gallon fuel tank and a long list of convenience items rounded out the 1991 Blazer's standard equipment. The option list ran for an additional page. (See earlier chapter for how to order a new truck.)

The Blazer's odometer logged over 3,500 miles during its first month and a half of road testing while delivering ample performance, precise handling, and comfort. Designed as a shorter version of the 1973-87 K-10/1500 1/2-ton truck chassis, the V-5 felt like a much bigger truck.

During the one-year test sequence, just over 18,000 miles accrued. Despite some minor warranty work, performed quickly and conveniently at the local Chevrolet dealership, the truck offered exceptionally reliable service. The engine and powertrain performed flawlessly, requiring nothing more than simple, routine maintenance. Ease of serviceability and access to service points reached their high mark with the 1991 Blazer, and this model reflects a strong willingness to perform.

Chevrolet's TBI version of the 5.7L/350 V-8, available since 1987, was a nice fit for the classic Blazer chassis and styling. GM's TBI/EFI readily accommodates different driving environments, altitudes, slope angles and load conditions, proving a welcome advancement for light trucks.

The 1991 Blazer V-5 4WD merged classic GM truck looks with advanced and useful technology. Like other GM truck milestones, the '91 Blazer V-5 left a lasting impression.

MANUALS AND RECOMMENDED BOOKS

The General Motors factory workshop manuals for the GMC Truck and Chevrolet light truck models provide official, first-hand information. Highly detailed, with all specifications, the factory workshop manual is your assurance of a professional level, quality repair.

You will find that new shop manuals are available for more recent year models. Aftermarket specialty suppliers (especially those that cater to truck restorers) can provide authentic reprints of original manuals for the older Chevrolet and GMC trucks.

Most manuals cover all truck body types, powertrains, geartrains and chassis for a given model year or series of years. Some later factory manuals often require sets, consisting of "Powertrain/Geartrain" and "Body, Chassis, Electrical" books. Models covered in a later factory shop manual typically include the C/K1500, C/K2500, C/K3500, full-size Blazer/Yukon/Tahoe and the Suburban chassis.

See your local GM truck dealership's parts department for availability of a shop manual. For an older model, you may need to consult a new or used book source that specializes in automotive literature. (Several advertise in *Hemmings Motor News*.) Seek out original GM shop manuals if you want the most accurate and model-specific data. Equipped with such a manual, you could confidently rebuild or restore your early GMC or Chevrolet truck.

Catalogs from Advance Adapters (engine and transmission conversion parts for trucks, including GM models) serve as useful reference guides for geartrain interchangeability and component applications. Similarly, catalogs from 4-Wheel Parts, Dick Cepek and others offer valuable reference information.

If you want accurate information about engine and other powertrain castings, consider Alan L. Colvin's *Chevrolet by the Numbers*, a painstakingly thorough guide to engine and geartrain pieces found in V-8 era Chevrolet automobiles. (Although aimed specifically at passenger car and Corvette restoration, this information also applies to some light truck components.) The series is available through Robert Bentley, Publishers. Detailed text and many useful illustrations will help determine which parts you have on hand----or which ones you will need----for your truck's high performance buildup or OEM restoration.

For the Chevrolet light truck history buff or the detail oriented restorer, John Gunnell's *Chevrolet Pickups, 1946-72* is an exceptional chronicle of the styling, chassis and powertrain/geartrain changes of that era. You will find Gunnell's book, and its sequel, *Chevrolet Pickup Red Book* by Peter C. Sessler, indispensable resources for selecting the right model for restoration----or determining which parts of your older truck are actually original. Both books strongly serve the restorer and collector of GM light trucks from this period.

Maps And Travel Guides

A variety of map sources and atlas guides serve back country travelers. My favorite references are U.S. Forest Service and B.L.M. topographical maps and the popular state- by-state atlas guides built around these types of maps.

Specialty map sources include the series by Sidekick, which produces a range of maps on California and Baja California four-wheel drive trails. A Sidekick Map details each region, including highlights of local sites, the area's history, minesites, ghost towns, directions from major highways, access costs, camping facilities and public agency offices in the area. Sidekick map/pamphlets are printed on high quality paper stock and include color pictures.

Sidekick
12475 Central Avenue, Suite 352
Chino, CA 91710
714-628-7227

Appendix 1: Sources

Parts

Your GM truck is a popular vehicle, and parts availability seldom presents a problem. The local Chevrolet or GMC Truck dealer can provide pieces for most 1970s and newer models and, recently, dealerships have begun offering a line of 'Genuine Chevrolet' restoration parts for popular older truck models. Owners of early (pre-1970) GM light trucks will find a wide variety of parts sources throughout the United States.

In addition to the GM dealership, retail auto parts outlets can supply tune-up, powertrain and even chassis/steering parts. NAPA provides excellent parts coverage for GM trucks. Quality filters and oil products are available from NAPA and other outlets.

For GM truck geartrain parts sources, your local GM truck dealership or Border Parts at Spring Valley, California can supply gear parts for many models, including the earliest SM420 gearbox and others. 4-Wheel Parts, 4WD Hardware, Inc., Dick Cepek, Inc., and Reider Racing Enterprises also offer geartrain and axle pieces. Each of these outlets can provide OEM-type replacement parts or aftermarket performance components.

GM truck engine parts are readily available. From the earliest 216.5 cubic inch 'Stovebolt' inline OHV six to the latest TBI V-type powerplants, GM replacement engine parts abound. Popular aftermarket suppliers include TRW, Sealed Power, Dana Corporation, Perfect Circle, Wolverine and Badger.

Axle, Transfer Case and Transmission Service

M.I.T.
1112 Pioneer Way
El Cajon, California 92020
619-579-7727

Holbrook Specialties/4 Wheel Drive Center
115 E. Arlington
Gladstone, Oregon 97027
503-655-4747

Engine/Transmission Conversion Kits

Advance Adapters
P.O. Box 247
Paso Robles, CA 93447
805-238-7000

Engine/High Performance

Camden Superchargers
401M E. Braker Lane
Austin, TX 78753
512-339-4772

The Carburetor Shop
1457 E. Philadelphia, Ste. #24
Ontario, California 91761
714-947-7744

Clifford Performance Products
2330 Pomona-Rincon Road
Corona, CA 91720
714-734-3310
Inline six-cylinder specialists

Dyers Machine Service, Inc.
7665 W. 63rd Street
Summit, IL 60501
312-496-8100
Superchargers

Edelbrock
2700 California St.
Torrance, CA 90509
213-781-2222
Manifolds, camshafts, carburetors

Flex-A-Lite Fans
P.O. Box 9037
Tacoma, WA 98409
206-475-5772
Engine and transmission cooling

General Motors Corporation (Chevrolet/GMC and other Divisions)
"The Race Shop" and "Motorsports" Programs of various GM Divisions.
A line of high quality off-highway oriented high performance components, partial engine and complete engine assemblies available through your local Chevrolet, Pontiac or GMC Truck dealership. Also available is the guidebook, *Chevrolet Power.* (Look for the official "Goodwrench" logo on this book.)

J&S Engineering (Electronics)
Box 2199
Garden Grove, CA 92642-2199
714-534-6975
Electronic spark retard system

Jacobs Electronics
500 N. Baird St.
Midland, TX 79701
800-626-8800
Ignition specialty items

K&N Engineering
P.O. Box 1329
Riverside, CA 92502
714-684-9762
Filtration products

MSD/Autotronic Controls Corp.
1490 Henry Brennan Drive
El Paso, TX 79936
915-857-5200
Ignitions

Paxton Superchargers
1260 Calle Suarte
Camarillo, CA 93012
310-450-4800

Racing Head Service/RHS
3410 Democrat Road
Memphis, TN 38118
901-794-283
Custom engines and buildup kits

Speed-Pro Performance/Sealed Power
100 Terrace Plaza
Muskegon, MI 49443
616-724-5688
OEM/high performance components

Exterior Trim, Tops, Light Bars, Roll Cages, Seat Harnesses, Misc.

Beachwood Canvas Works
39 Lake Ave.
Island Heights, NJ 08732
908-929-3168
Restoration canvas and upholstery

Bell Auto Racing
Route 136 East
Rantoul, IL 61866
217-893-9300
Harnesses/safety equipment

Bushwhacker
9200 N. Decatur
Portland, OR 97203
503-283-4335
Fender flares, protective trim items

Filler Products
9017 San Fernando Rd.
Sun Valley, CA 91352
818-768-7770
Racing safety equipment

Grizzly/Mercury Tube
1802 Santo Domingo Ave.
Duarte, CA 91010
818-301-0226
Steel tubing bumpers; utility products

Hobrecht
15632 Commerce Lane
Huntington Beach, CA 92649
714-893-8561
Roll cages/steel tubing products/running boards

Keiper/Recaro
905 W. Maple Rd.
Ste. 100, Clawson, MI 48017
313-288-6800
Seating

Schroth
(See your local performance parts outlet)
Safety harnesses/rally belts

Smittybilt
2090 California Ave.
Corona, CA 91719
714-272-3176
(Roll cages/steel tubing products)

SNUGTOP
1711 Harbor Avenue
Long Beach, CA 90801
310-432-5454
Pickup tops

TRW

(See your local performance parts outlet)
Safety harnesses/equipment

Free-wheeling Front Hubs, Winches

HUB-A-LERT
4x4 Specialty Products
P.O. Box 813
Highland, CA 92346

Ramsey Winch Company
1600 N. Garnett
Tulsa, OK 74116
918-438-2760

Warn Industries
13270 S.E. Pheasant Court
Milwaukie, OR 97222
503-786-4462.

Superwinch
Winch Drive
Putnam, CT 06260
203-928-1143

Rare, OEM and Restoration Parts

Note: A long list of restoration parts sources and specialty services is available in both *Hemmings Motor News* and the appendix of John Gunnell's book, *Chevrolet Pickup, 1946-72.* If you plan to authentically restore a vintage GM truck model, either of these resource guides can provide useful information on parts sourcing and restoration services.

Automotive Obsolete
1023 E. 4th Street
Santa Ana, CA 92701

Autofab
10996 N. Woodside
Santee, CA 92071
619-562-1740
Body, fiberglass

Archer Brothers
19745 Meekland Ave.
Hayward, CA 94541
415-537-9587
4WD and surplus truck components

Border Parts
3875 Bancroft Drive
Spring Valley, CA 92077
619-461-0171
Geartrain pieces

Charley's Off-Road Center
14190 E. Firestone Boulevard
Santa Fe Springs, CA 90670
1-800-922-4111
Body panels and more

Chevy Parts
Box 936
Greensburg, KS 67054
NOS classic truck parts

Dick Cepek, Inc.
17000 Kingsview Ave.
Carson, CA 90746

Golden State Pickup Parts
618 E. Gutierrez Street
Santa Barbara, CA 93103
Caters to restorers of classic GM trucks

Grumpy's Truck Parts
Box 4721
Phoenix, AZ 85029
Restoration parts for older GM trucks

LMC Truck
P.O. Box 14991
Lenexa, KS 66285-4991
1-800-222-5664
Restoration parts for Chevy pickups

Obsolete Chevrolet Parts Co.
P.O. Box 68
Nashville, GA 31639

Old Chevy Trucks
3014 Dedman
Pasadena, TX 77503

Vintage Ford and Chevrolet Parts
3427 E. McDowell Road
Phoenix, AZ 85008
602-275-7990

Restoration and Specialty Tools

Eastwood Company Tools
Box 296
Malvern, PA 19355
1-800-345-1178

Easco/K.D. Tools
(Contact Eastwood Company or your local tool supplier)

Rinda Technologies
5112 N. Elston Ave.
Chicago, IL 60630
312-736-6633
Diacom diagnostic software

Suspension/Chassis

Air Lift Company
P.O. Box 80167
Lansing, MI 48908-0167
517-322-2144
Air suspension kits

Energy Suspension Systems
960 Calle Amanecer
San Clemente, CA 92672
714-361-3935
Urethane bushings

Heckethorn Off Road
P.O. Box 526
Dyersburg, TN 38024
901-285-9000
Shocks/steering stabilizers

JT Industries
8157 Wing Avenue
El Cajon, CA 92020
619-562-3390
Urethane bushings

Rancho Suspension (USA)
6925 Atlantic Ave.
Long Beach, CA 90805
213-630-0700
Complete suspension packages

Rugged Trail/Black Diamond
A Division of Warn Industries
(See your local Warn products dealer)
Suspension kits

Skyjacker
P.O. Box 1878
West Monroe, LA 71291-1878
318-388-0816
Suspension kits

Superlift
211 Horn Lane
West Monroe, LA 71292
318-322-3458
Suspension kits, traction bars and Vehicle Speed Sensor kits for late GM trucks with ABS and electronic powertrain functions.

Trail Master
649 E. Chicago Road
Coldwater, MN 49036
517-278-4011
Suspension kits

Tires

Bridgestone Tire
See your local dealer

Dunlap & Kyle Co.
P.O. Box 720
Batesville, MS 38606
601-563-7601

Dick Cepek, Inc.
17000 Kingsview Avenue
Carson, CA 90746

Denman Tire Corporation
216-898-5256

The Goodyear Tire & Rubber Company
See your local dealer

B.F. Goodrich T/A
See your local dealer

Interco Tire Corporation
P.O. Box 486
Rayne, LA 70578
318-334-3814

Mickey Thompson Performance Tires
P.O. Box 227
Cuyahoga Falls, OH 44222
216-928-9092

Manual Clutch and Automatic Transmission

Art Carr Transmissions
10575 Belcher River Ave.
Fountain Valley, CA 92708
714-962-6655
Automatic transmission specialists

B&M Automotive
9152 Independence Ave.
Chatsworth, CA 91311
818-882-6422
Automatic transmission specialists

Centerforce Clutches
7171 Patterson Drive
Garden Grove, CA 92641
714-898-4477
Manual clutch and flywheel

REGIONAL FOUR-WHEEL DRIVE ASSOCIATIONS

Arizona State Association Of 4-Wheel Drive Clubs
P.O. Box 23904
Tempe, AZ 58282
602-258-4BY4

California Association Of 4-Wheel Drive Clubs
2856 Arden Way, #231
Sacramento, CA 95825
916-974-3984

Colorado Association Of 4-Wheel Drive Clubs
P.O. Box 1413
Wheat Ridge, CO 80034
303-321-1266

East Coast 4-Wheel Drive Association, Inc.
101 South Miami Avenue
Cleves, OH 45002
513-941-1450

4-Wheel Drive Association Of British Columbia
Box 284 Surrey, B.C. V3T 4W8
604-590-1502

Great Lakes 4-Wheel Drive Association
13911 Townline Road
St. Charles, MI 48655
517-865-6983

Indiana 4-Wheel Drive Association
2203 Osman Lane
Greenfield, IN 46140
317-326-2329

Midwest 4-Wheel Drive Association
W 762 State Rd. 23 and 49
Green Lake, WI 54941
920-748-7852

Montana 4x4 Association, Inc.
516 N. 4th
Bozeman, MT 59715
406-587-8307

Pacific Northwest 4-Wheel Drive Association
948 18th
Longview, WA 98632
800-537-7845

Southern 4-Wheel Drive Association
Box 3473 Oak Ridge, TN 37831
815-482-6912

Utah 4-Wheel Drive Association, Inc.
P. O. Box 20310
Salt Lake City, UT 84120
801-250-1302

Virginia 4-Wheel Drive Association
P.O. Box 722
Mechanicsville, VA 23111
804-883-6115

Wisconsin 4-Wheel Drive Association
203 Greunwald Ave.
Neenah, WI 54956
414-722-3777

United Four-Wheel Drive Associations
For information about UFWDA or regional associations, phone
1-800-44-UFWDA

TRAILSIDE TOOLBOX AND SPARE PARTS KIT

Your properly maintained GM truck might never break down in the back country. Yet for long trips, like the Alaska Highway, Baja California or the Far North, bringing along a full set of tools and spare parts can safeguard your adventure and provide a reasonable level of self-reliance.

> *CAUTION —*
> *Store your tools and spare parts safely and securely. Take into account the worst case scenario, the possibility that your truck could break in desolate country. Under such conditions, you would need quick access to your winching accessories or tools.*

On-board Tools for Remote Trailside Fixes

1. A complete socket set
2. A full set of common hand tools
3. Oil filter wrench
4. Compact volt-ohmmeter
5. Induction ammeter and starter current meter
6. Flare nut wrench set
7. Plumber's small chain wrench
8. Snap ring plier set
9. Front wheel bearing spindle nut wrench
10. Pry bar
11. Vacuum gauge
12. Compact timing light
13. Wire repair kit and crimping pliers
14. Tubing flare tool and repair kit
15. Grease gun with chassis lube
16. Enough tools to break down and repair a tubeless tire
17. Air compressor
18. On-board welder
19. Jacks for tire repairs and transmission/axle work
20. A 'Hi-Lift' jack and 'Pull-Pal' anchor
21. A quality winch and winch accessory kit

Spare Parts for the Long Trail

1. Fuses, light bulbs and at least one headlamp
2. 25-foot rolls of 12-, 14- and 16-gauge automotive wire
3. Two rolls of electrical tape
4. Solderless crimp connectors and terminals
5. Roll of duct tape
6. Package of radiator and gas tank repair putty
7. Fuel hose and spare clamps
8. Spare drive belt(s)
9. Upper and lower radiator hoses
10. Thermostat and housing gasket
11. Tubes of silicon gasket sealant
12. Tube of metal mender (Permatex's LocWeld or equivalent)
13. Exhaust system patch kit
14. Thread locker
15. Teflon tape
16. Clean brake fluid
17. A fuel pump and pump gasket
18. Roll of mechanic's wire
19. Spare tire valve stems
20. Patch kit for repairing tubeless (radial or bias ply) tires
21. Spare universal joints
22. Front wheel grease seals (full-floating axles and wheel hubs)
23. At least one oil filter and enough oil for a crankcase refill
24. An oversized and self-tapping oil pan drain plug
25. Two squeeze bottle quarts of gear lubricant
26. Wheel bearing grease
27. Clean rags or shop towels
28. Fuel filter(s)
29. Air cleaner element
30. Spare fuel and potable water (minimum 5 gallons of each), ignition distributor cap, rotor, points or module
31. Ignition spark plug wire set
32. Carburetor float and air horn gasket
33. Water pump and gasket
34. Suitable fire extinguisher(s)
35. Axe, bucket, shovel
36. Backup C.B. radio

> *CAUTION —*
> *Always carry a quality first aid kit and safety flares. Stow a ground cloth, shelter materials and rope for setting up an emergency habitat. Freeze dried or canned rations will provide a means for survival in the event that your truck becomes stranded.*

Appendix 3: Engine Break-In

New or Rebuilt Engine Break-in Procedure

There is little information available on the proper break-in of a new or freshly rebuilt engine. Your truck engine's performance and longevity depend upon correct break-in. The following procedures are those recommended by Sealed Power Corporation, a major supplier of parts to the engine remanufacturing industry.

> ***CAUTION —***
> *These run-in schedules are good basic procedures to follow for engine break-in. They are recommended as a practical guide for engine rebuilders who are not advised of specific factory run-in schedules. If available, follow OEM guidelines for engine break-in.*

Engine Run-in Procedure (engine in vehicle)

Before starting the engine: Make preliminary adjustments to the carburetor or diesel injection system where applicable, adjust tappets and set ignition timing. Always install new oil and air filters. Prime the engine lubrication system before attempting to start the engine. Clean crankcase ventilation components—breathers, road draft tubes or positive crankcase ventilation system. Carefully check coolant and crankcase oil levels.

> ***CAUTION —***
> *When an engine is started for the first time, the most common cause of bearing scuff and seizure is a dry start. This can happen in the short length of time before the oil, under pressure, is delivered to bearings and other vital parts. Pre-priming the oil system can be accomplished with a pressure tank or pre-lubricator attached to the system or by mechanically driving the oil pump to supply the necessary oil throughout all oil passages.*

Initial Starting Steps (before run-in schedule)

1) Start engine and establish throttle setting at a fast idle (1000 to 1500 RPM) and watch oil pressure gauge. If oil pressure is not observed immediately, shut engine down and check back on assembly of oil pump and lubricating system. When engine running is resumed, continue at the fast idle until coolant reaches normal operating temperature.

2) Stop engine and recheck oil and water levels.

3) Make necessary adjustments to carburetor (or injectors), ignition timing, tappets, fan belt tightness, etc.

4) Retorque cylinder heads following engine manufacturer's recommendations.

5) Check for oil and coolant leaks, making corrections where necessary.

Run-in Schedule for Light and Medium Duty Trucks

Set engine at a fast idle. Put vehicle under a moderate load and accelerate to 50 miles per hour with alternate deceleration. Continue this intermittent cycling under this load for at least 50 miles. Additional time is desirable.

Note: Harmful Practices

(A) Avoid lugging under any load condition. Lugging exists when the vehicle does not readily respond as the accelerator is depressed. The engine speed being too low, does not allow the engine to develop sufficient horsepower to pull the load. (Keep rpm up.)

(B) Avoid long periods of idling. Excessive idling will drop engine temperature and can result in incomplete burning of fuel. Unburned fuel washes lubricating oil off cylinder walls and results in diluted crankcase oil and restricted (poor) lubrication to all moving parts. The relatively dry cylinder walls depend upon oil throw-off to lubricate them and a speed above a slow idle is necessary for this. Long idling periods produce glazing of cylinder walls, detrimental to ring and cylinder wall seating.

(C) Avoid stopping engine too quickly. When an engine has completed the test run-in schedule or at any time it becomes heavily worked, it is a good policy to disengage the load from the engine and decelerate gradually. Allow it to idle a few minutes before turning the ignition to the off position.

The few minutes of idling will allow the engine to cool gradually and promote a desirable dissipation of heat from any localized area of concentrated temperature. Such good practice avoids the rapid cooling that can cause valve and seat warpage, block distortion, etc.

Engine Run-in procedure (engine on dynamometer)

(See chart on next page.)

Engine Run-in procedure (engine on dynamometer)

NOTE —
Note: Follow necessary preliminary procedures outlined for engine in vehicle.

Gasoline Engines: Light Truck and Passenger Car

Stage of test	Complete test cycle of dynamometer break-in						
	1st	2nd	3rd	4th	5th	6th	7th
RPM	800—1200	1500	2000	2500	3000	3000	800
Manifold vacuum in inches of mercury	No load	15 in.	10 in.	10 in.	6 in.	Full load	No load
Time limit	Warm-up 10 min.	10 min.	15 min.	15 min.	15 min.	5 min.	3 min.

Appendix 4: 4X4 Trials

Rules and Regulations for 4X4 Vehicle Trials

Revisiting the Rubicon in the summer of 1988, I saw many four-wheelers place unnecessary stress on both their machines and the environment. It was clear that these drivers believed a heavy throttle and plenty of power were the only ways to overcome this brutal trail. Believing very strongly that the opposite is true, I sought a useful way to illustrate my point.

In the ensuing months, I carefully drafted a guideline for 4x4 Trials, a competitive event that discredits a driver for displaying wheelspin, misusing power or failing to maintain smooth progress in rough terrain. As the concept unfolded, California Association of 4WD Clubs' Central District (CA4WDC) endorsed the idea of a pilot competition at the 1989 Molina Ghost Run.

I worked with Bruce Swanson and other Central District members at constructing a special course, and we officially established our first 4x4 trials event. The participant drivers and crowd showed real enthusiasm for the project, and we realized that the program could work.

At the 1990 Molina Ghost Run, Bruce Swanson set up an outstanding course. (The low environmental impact of trials competition permits quick course construction, a factor that makes 4x4 trials well suited to clubs with limited space and resources. A large lot and some imagination can produce an event!) Bruce's course was tight and twisty, laced with rocks, and steeper than our first effort.

As Sunday morning's sunlight pierced the deep ravine, each competitor got a first glimpse of the 1990 trials course. The 1989 winners, brothers Harry Hetzer and Alvin Hetzer, Sr., looked over the steep starting bank and shook their heads. "Boy," Harry exclaimed, "my truck's wheelbase is plenty long for this course!"

Minutes before the start, Bruce walked the attentive drivers through the course. For the next hour and a half, seven hardcore four-wheelers battled against the stopwatches as they squeezed through a ravine, inched over two rockpiles, straddled a nasty trench and crept up and down two steep slopes.

These veteran four-wheelers caught on quickly. Few points were lost to tire spin, and high torque again joined forces with driving skill to produce a winning score.

The "Brothers Hetzer," as we now called them, pulled an upset. Alvin, who placed a solid second in the 1989 event, had shown up with a 101" wheelbase '59 Jeep CJ-6. A transplant Chevrolet V-8 with a high carburetor float level (which caused flooding and rough idle) quickly troubled his score.

Harry Hetzer, the 1989 first-place winner with a 103" wheelbase Jeep Scrambler (CJ-8), triumphed once again over nimbler CJ-5s and others. Despite wide skepticism about the longer CJ-8 wheelbase, Harry proved once more that 4x4 trials is a driver's sport.

Creeping and crawling his retrofit T-18 truck four speed and AMC inline 258 six (bone stock with OE carburetion and a maze of California smog hardware!), Harry Hetzer ran to a tight tie with highly skilled Mark Booker from Fresno. Mark and his CJ-5 outperformed everyone except Harry, who racked up another *zero tirespin* score with his CJ-8. In a hair splitting run-off, Harry edged out Mark for first place.

CA4WDC/Central District trophies went to Mark Booker for 2nd Place, and Harry Hetzer took another 1st Place home to Daly City, California. 4x4 trials became a reality at Molina, and these crawl masters now know what it takes to win.

When the course got tougher, the driver skills just came on stronger. Bruce Swanson even hinted about trying a log teeter-totter at a future 4x4 Trials event. Winching skills may also enter into the competition.

I encourage all 4x4 clubs and individuals with a competitive spirit to pick up the trials challenge. A trials course is very easy to construct, and you can spend a fun afternoon competing for trophies or other prizes. 4x4 Trials promotes better driving skills, heightens awareness of the environment and provides a chance to work your four-wheel drive truck through its low-range paces with minimal engine and geartrain stress.

Use these rules and regulations to foster friendly competition—and always remember to TREAD LIGHTLY!

Official Rules and Regulations For 4x4 Trials

In the interest of safe and environmentally sound off- pavement recreation, the following rules and regulations have been established. The sole intent of 4x4 Vehicle Trials is to promote, within a friendly, competitive atmosphere, those driving techniques and skills that minimize vehicle impact upon terrain and natural habitat.

4x4 trials will enhance the off-pavement driving skills of both new and experienced four-wheel drive vehicle operators. The goals set forth for 4x4 trials competition provide a far-reaching model for all off-pavement driving. Safety and preservation of the natural environment underlie these standards, rules, regulations and amendments for conducting trials events.

I. Vehicle Requirements—Any street-legal, four-wheel drive truck or sport/utility model may compete. Engine size, wheelbase and wheel/tire size are optional, providing that 1) the vehicle complies with local, state, and federal regulations for safe use on public highways, 2) tires are of conventional, highway legal "mud and snow" or "highway" tread design, recognized as commercially available, and 3) no aspect of the vehicle has been modified in a manner that would increase impact on the trials road course, terrain or local habitat.

Safety equipment should include, but not be limited to, a Red Cross approved First Aid Kit, a charged and "tagged" fire extinquisher, a four-point (or better) padded roll cage, a properly mounted and operational winch*, minimally of 6000 lbs. (single line) capacity, and an approved "tree saver" strap. Vehicle inspection for operationally safe hydraulic and emergency brakes, lights and brake lamps, and assurances of reasonable operating condition will take place before each event.

(*Events may test operator skills at safely utilizing a winch, with due consideration for trees, fauna and local habitat.)

II. Driver Requirements—Drivers must possess a valid state vehicle operator's license or legally recognized international driver's license. Learner's permits will not be acceptable, and proof of license is a requirement. A valid driver's license with notable restrictions shall not disqualify any driver, unless such restrictions either 1) prevent driving the vehicle during hours in which the trials event has been scheduled or 2) place the driver, passenger/occupants, other drivers/vehicles or spectators at unusual risk.

The driver must be in good physical condition. Use of illegal drugs, alcohol* or medical prescriptions and over-the-counter drugs that impair driving skills shall be cause for disqualification. Reckless, erratic or aberrant driving displays shall be cause for immediate disqualification and removal from the event. In all instances, the officials and judges of the event shall make the final decision regarding qualification and disqualification of drivers.

(*Alcohol at legally acceptable levels for safe vehicle operation on public highways shall be the maximum allowable under any circumstances. Additionally, any driver believed to be adversely influenced or impaired by the use of alcohol must prove his or her ability to compete safely. In each instance, use of alcohol by competitors shall be discouraged. No competitor is to carry alcoholic beverages in or about the vehicle.)

III. The Course—For each 4x4 trials event, the selection of a designated course shall meet with appropriate local, state and federal regulations. Public use permits and use of the 4x4 trials course shall comply with applicable land use regulations. Every reasonable effort shall be made to meet land use regulations. Officials of the 4x4 trials event shall provide participants and spectators with a list of rules, regulations and land use standards for the area assigned for the event. Whenever possible, land use agencies shall be encouraged to assist or participate in the establishment and layout of the trials course. Impact to the local environment will be minimized, and trials event damage to terrain, fauna or local waterways shall be reasonably alleviated by the 4x4 trials organizers or their assignees.

III. Scoring—An ideal score shall be zero ("0"). During the event, each participant will be penalized points according to the methods set forth in Section IV. OBJECTIVES. Penalty points shall be added to the starting score of zero, winners to be the driver(s) with the lowest number of penalty points. Each event's obstacles shall be clearly indicated, and officials will monitor times between course markers in 1/100ths of a second. Penalty points accrue as both the drivers' time errors and technique infractions.

IV. Objectives—There is only one 4x4 Trials winning criterion: TRAVEL THE COURSE IN THE DESIGNATED TIME OR SLOWER, WITHOUT STOPPING AND WITHOUT TIRE SPIN. Trials is not a speed contest, and any exhibition of speed shall be cause for points deduction or disqualification. Points shall also be deducted for running off course or excess abuse of terrain, as determined by the offical(s). Damage to the vehicle or "high centering" on chassis, body or powertrain components shall also be cause for points deductions. The overall winner is a highly competent driver, in full control of his or her vehicle at all times. Such a competitor leaves the least impact upon the course, the environment, his or her vehicle and passengers.

A. Designated Time: Well marked Start and Stop points shall be noted throughout the course. Upon starting from a given marker, the competitor/driver has a specific, minimum time to reach the next stop point. The driver must keep the vehicle moving without leaving the course or spinning tires. (As an option, a co- driver or passenger may assist by keeping time with a conventional stopwatch.)

B. Tire Spin: Each tire of competitors' vehicles shall be marked with one (1) swath of white, washable paint. Paint shall be applied with a 3-inch wide brush, from the wheel center outward to the tread area of each tire. Officials will watch the rotation of tires over the varied course terrain. Points shall be deducted for any occurrence of tire/wheel spin. Spin shall be defined as 1) the rotation of any tire without forward movement of the vehicle or 2) any moment in which one tire/wheel rotates faster than the other three tires/wheels, the one exception being a required, safe maneuver in which a wheel temporarily becomes suspended above the ground. One (1) point shall be deducted for each instance of tire/wheel spin observed.

C. High Center: For the purpose of 4x4 Trials competition, "high centering" shall be defined as interference or contact of vehicle undercarriage components with the course terrain. Such interference refers to, but is not limited to, chassis, suspension, powertrain and body components. Specific course requirements may involve the application of washable paint to undercarriage components. In such instances, officials will judge and penalize drivers for each indication of paint removed by undercarriage interference/contact with terrain. Such a course shall afford sufficient opportunity to avoid high centering.

Water crossings, log climbs, and other obstacles may be designed into any 4x4 trials course. In events with such special obstacles, additional rules and scoring methods shall be thoroughly discussed with all drivers at the "DRIVER'S PRELIMINARY MEETING." To qualify for competition, each driver must attend any and all such meetings. Special obstacles will be clearly marked on course maps and en route.

V. Entry Fees—Organizers of 4x4 Trials events may assign vehicle / driver entry fees for each eligible competitor. These fees shall be clearly designated and posted for the benefit of interested participants. Entry fees must be paid as stated, before each scheduled event. Any eligible competitor who becomes disabled or is unable to participate in an event must notify a designated official one (1) hour before the scheduled start of his or her event. A refund of entry fees or a portion thereof, according to posted and established guidelines, may then be afforded. Any competitor disqualified from competition for any rule or regulation infraction shall forfeit his or her paid entry fees.

VI. Rules Philosophy—4x4 Trials competition is a thorough test of driving skill. Skillful off-pavement driving requires total vehicle control and an awareness of road hazards and obstacles. When driving on off-pavement trails, respect for the natural environment is equally important. 4x4 Trials, conducted over a specified course, simulates the trying situations encountered in serious four-wheeling. Under the watchful eyes of officials and spectators, 4x4 operators can develop and display greater off-pavement / trail driving ability. "RULES AND REGULATIONS FOR 4X4 VEHICLE TRIALS" is for the sole purpose of achieving these goals. Such rules may be changed, amended, or modified to improve this competitive sport. Any changes must promote safety and driving habits that protect our public lands.

Index

> *WARNING —*
> - *Automotive service, repair, and modification is serious business. You must be alert, use common sense, and exercise good judgement to prevent personal injury.*
> - *Before using this book or beginning any work on your vehicle, thoroughly read the Warning on the copyright page, and any Warnings and Cautions listed on the inside front cover.*
> - *Always read a complete procedure before you begin the work. Pay special attention to any Warnings and Cautions, or any other information, that accompanies that procedure.*

A

B

C

WARNING —

- *Automotive service, repair, and modification is serious business. You must be alert, use common sense, and exercise good judgement to prevent personal injury.*
- *Before using this book or beginning any work on your vehicle, thoroughly read the Warning on the copyright page, and any Warnings and Cautions listed on the inside front cover.*
- *Always read a complete procedure before you begin the work. Pay special attention to any Warnings and Cautions, or any other information, that accompanies that procedure.*

Selected Books and Repair Information From Bentley Publishers

Also by Moses Ludel

Jeep Owner's Bible - Third Edition
Moses Ludel
ISBN 978-0-8376-1117-4

Jeep® CJ Rebuilder's Manual:1972 to 1986
Moses Ludel
ISBN 978-0-8376-0875-4

Jeep® CJ Rebuilder's Manual:1946 to 1971
Moses Ludel
ISBN 978-0-8376-1037-5

Harley-Davidson Evolution V-Twin Owner's Bible
Moses Ludel
ISBN 978-0-8376-0146-5

Ford F-Series Pickup Owner's Bible
Moses Ludel
ISBN 978-0-8376-0152-6

Toyota Truck and Land Cruiser Owner's Bible
Moses Ludel
ISBN 978-0-8376-0159-5

Motorsports

Alex Zanardi: My Sweetest Victory
Alex Zanardi and Gianluca Gasparini
ISBN 978-0-8376-1249-2

The Unfair Advantage
Mark Donohue and Paul van Valkenburgh
ISBN 978-0-8376-0069-7

A French Kiss with Death: Steve McQueen and the Making of Le Mans
Michael Keyser
ISBN 978-0-8376-0234-9

Equations of Motion - Adventure, Risk and Innovation
William F. Milliken
ISBN 978-0-8376-1570-7

Engineering

Maximum Boost: Designing, Testing, and Installing Turbocharger Systems
Corky Bell
ISBN 978-0-8376-0160-1

Supercharged! Design, Testing and Installation of Supercharger Systems
Corky Bell
ISBN 978-0-8376-0168-7

Scientific Design of Exhaust and Intake Systems
Phillip H. Smith & John C. Morrison
ISBN 978-0-8376-0309-4

Bosch Automotive Handbook
Updated 9th Edition
Robert Bosch GmbH
ISBN 978-0-8376-1732-9

Physics for Gearheads
Randy Beikmann
ISBN 978-0-8376-1615-5

BMW

Memoirs of a Hack Mechanic
Rob Siegel
ISBN 978-0-8376-1720-6

BMW X5 (E53) Service Manual: 2000-2006
Bentley Publishers
ISBN 978-0-8376-1643-8

BMW 3 Series (E46) Service Manual: 1999-2005
Bentley Publishers
ISBN 978-0-8376-1657-5

BMW 3 Series (E90, E91, E92, E93) Service Manual: 2006-2011
Bentley Publishers
ISBN 978-0-8376-1723-7

BMW Z3 (E36/7)Service Manual: 1996-2002
Bentley Publishers
ISBN 978-0-8376-1617-9

Ford

Ford Fuel Injection and Electronic Engine Control: 1988-1993 Charles O. Probst, SAE ISBN 978-0-8376-0301-8

Ford Fuel Injection and Electronic Engine Control: 1980-1987 Charles O. Probst, SAE ISBN 978-0-8376-0302-5

The Official Ford Mustang 5.0 Technical Reference & Performance Handbook: 1979-1983 Al Kirchenbaum ISBN 978-0-8376-0210-3

Porsche

Porsche 911 (996) Service Manual: 1999-2005
Bentley Publishers
ISBN 978-0-8376-1710-7

Porsche Boxster Service Manual: 1997-2004
Bentley Publishers
ISBN 978-0-8376-1645-2

Porsche 911 SC Service Manual: 1987-1983
Bentley Publishers
ISBN 978-0-8376-0290-5

Porsche: Excellence Was Expected
Karl Ludvigsen
ISBN 978-0-8376-0235-6

Volkswagen

Volkswagen Jetta Service Manual: 2005-2008 *Bentley Publishers*
ISBN 978-0-8376-1558-5

Volkswagen Jetta, Golf, GTI Service Manual: 1999-2005
Bentley Publishers
ISBN 978-0-8376-1251-5

Volkswagen Passat Service Manual: 1998-2005
Bentley Publishers
ISBN 978-0-8376-1483-0

Volkswagen Rabbit, GTI Service Manual: 2006-2009
Bentley Publishers
ISBN 978-0-8376-1560-8

Volkswagen Jetta, Golf, GTI: 1993-1999, Cabrio: 1995-2002 Service Manual
Bentley Publishers
ISBN 978-0-8376-0366-7

Toyota

Toyota Pruis Repair and Maintenace Manual: 2004-2008 *Bentley Publishers*
ISBN 978-08376-1553-0

BentleyPublishers®
Automotive Reference

Automotive Reference

Bentley Publishers has published service manuals and automobile books since 1950. For more information, please contact Bentley Publishers at 1734 Massachusetts Avenue, Cambridge, MA 02138, visit our web site at **www.BentleyPublishers.com** or call 1-800-423-4595 for a free copy of our complete catalog.

Please read these Warnings and Cautions before proceeding with maintenance and repair work.

WARNING—

• Do not reuse self-locking nuts or any other fasteners that are fatigued or deformed in normal use. They are designed to be used only once, and become unreliable and may fail when used a second time. This includes, but is not limited to, bolts, washers, self-locking nuts, circlips and cotter pins that secure the subframe, control arms, stabilizer bar, ball joints and other suspension, steering and brake components. Always replace these fasteners with new parts where indicated, and any other time it is deemed necessary.

• Never work under a lifted vehicle unless it is solidly supported on stands designed for the purpose. Do not support a vehicle on cinder blocks, hollow tiles, or other props that may crumble under continuous load. Do not work under a vehicle that is supported solely by a jack.

• If you are going to work under a vehicle on the ground, make sure the ground is level. Block the wheels to keep the vehicle from rolling. Never work under the vehicle while the engine is running. Disconnect the battery ground strap to prevent others from starting the vehicle while you are under it.

• Never run the engine unless the work area is well ventilated. Carbon monoxide kills.

• Friction materials such as brake or clutch discs may contain asbestos fibers. Do not create dust by grinding, sanding, or by cleaning with compressed air. Avoid breathing asbestos fibers and asbestos dust. Breathing asbestos can cause serious diseases such as asbestosis or cancer, and may result in death.

• Tie long hair behind your head. Do not wear a necktie, a scarf, loose clothing, or a necklace when you work near machine tools or running engines. If your hair, clothing, or jewelry were to get caught in the machinery, severe injury could result.

• Disconnect the battery ground strap whenever you work on the fuel system or the electrical system. When you work around fuel, do not smoke or work near heaters or other fire hazards. Keep an approved fire extinguisher handy.

• Finger rings should be removed so that they cannot cause electrical shorts, get caught in running machinery, or be crushed by heavy parts.

• Keep sparks, lighted matches, and open flames away from the top of the battery. If hydrogen gas escaping from the cap vents is ignited, it will ignite gas trapped in the cells and cause the battery to explode.

• Catch draining fuel, oil, or brake fluid in suitable containers. Do not use food or beverage containers that might mislead someone into drinking from them. Store flammable fluids away from fire hazards. Wipe up spills at once, but do not store the oily rags, which can ignite and burn spontaneously.

• Always observe good workshop practices. Wear goggles when you operate machine tools or work with battery acid. Gloves or other protective clothing should be worn whenever the job requires it.

• Some aerosol tire inflators are highly flammable. Use extreme care when repairing a tire that may have been inflated using an aerosol tire inflator. Keep sparks, open flame or other sources of ignition away from the tire repair area. Inflate and deflate the tire at least four times before breaking the bead from the rim. Completely remove the tire from the rim before attempting any repair.

• Do not attempt to work on your vehicle if you do not feel well. You can increase the danger of injury to yourself and others if you are tired, upset or have taken medicine or any other substance that may impair you from being fully alert.

Please read the Safety Notice and disclaimer on the Copyright page.

• Illuminate your work area adequately but safely. A fluorescent worklight is preferable to an incandescent worklight. Use a portable safety light for working inside or under the vehicle. Make sure the bulb is enclosed by a wire cage. The hot filament of an accidentally broken bulb can ignite spilled fuel or oil.

• Greases, lubricants and other automotive chemicals contain toxic substances, many of which are absorbed directly through the skin. Read manufacturer's instructions and warnings carefully. Use hand and eye protection. Avoid direct skin contact.

• Some of the vehicles covered by this manual are equipped with a Supplemental Restraint System (SRS) that automatically deploys an airbag in the event of a frontal impact. The airbag unit is an explosive device. Handled improperly or without adequate safeguards, the system can be very dangerous. The SRS system should be serviced only through an authorized Chevrolet or GMC dealer.

• SRS airbags that have been activated during an accident must always be replaced. Only trained personnel should work on or replace the airbag. Improper installation may result in inadvertent activation or rendering the system useless. The Chevrolet or GMC authorized dealer has training, instructions and tools to perform SRS service and repair.

• When driving or riding in an airbag-equipped vehicle never hold test equipment in your hands or lap while the vehicle is in motion. Objects between you and the airbag can increase the risk of injury in an accident.

CAUTION—

• If you lack the skills, tools and equipment, or a suitable workshop for any procedure described in this book, we suggest you leave such repairs to an authorized Chevrolet or GMC dealer or other qualified shop. We especially urge you to consult an authorized Chevrolet or GMC dealer before beginning repairs on any vehicle that may still be covered wholly or in part by any of the extensive warranties issued by Chevrolet or GMC.

• Chevrolet or GMC is constantly improving its vehicles and sometimes these changes, both in parts and specifications, are made applicable to earlier models. Always check with your authorized Chevrolet or GMC dealer for the latest parts and service information.

• Before starting a job, make certain that you have all the necessary tools and parts on hand. Read all the instructions thoroughly, do not attempt shortcuts. Use tools appropriate to the work and use only replacement parts meeting Chevrolet or GMC specifications. Makeshift tools, parts, and procedures will not make good repairs.

• Use pneumatic and electric tools only to loosen threaded parts and fasteners. Never use these tools to tighten fasteners, especially on light alloy parts.

• Be mindful of the environment and ecology. Before you drain the crankcase, find out the proper way to dispose of the oil. Do not pour oil onto the ground, down a drain, or into a stream, pond, or lake. Consult local ordinances that govern the handling and disposal of chemicals and wastes.

• Before doing any electrical welding on vehicles equipped with the Antilock Braking System (ABS), disconnect the ABS control unit connector.

• Do not quick-charge the battery (for boost starting) for longer than one minute, and do not exceed 15.0 volts at the battery with the boosting cables attached. Wait at least one minute before boosting the battery a second time.

• Chevrolet and GMC offer extensive warranties, especially on components of the fuel delivery and emissions control systems. Therefore, before deciding to repair a Chevrolet or GMC that may still be covered wholly or in part by any warranties issued by Chevrolet or GMC, consult your authorized Chevrolet or GMC dealer.

202401R001

9 780837 601571